Managerial Economics and Business Strategy

THE IRWIN SERIES IN ECONOMICS

Appleyard and Field
International Economics
Second Edition

Appleyard and Field
International Economics: Trade Theory and Policy
Second Edition

Appleyard and Field
International Economics: Payments, Exchange Rates, and Macro Policy
Second Edition

Aslanbeigui and Naples
Rethinking Economic Principles: Critical Essays on Introductory Textbooks

Baily and Friedman
Macroeconomics, Financial Markets, and the International Sector
Second Edition

Barron and Lynch
Economics
Third Edition

Baye
Managerial Economics and Business Strategy
Second Edition

Bornstein
Comparative Economics Systems: Models and Cases
Seventh Edition

Brickley, Smith and Zimmerman
Organizational Architecture: A Managerial Economics Approach

Brown and Moore
Readings, Issues, and Problems in Public Finance
Fourth Edition

Callon and Thomas
Environmental Economics and Management: Theory, Policy, and Applications

Colander
Economics
Second Edition

Colander
Microeconomics
Second Edition

Colander
Macroeconomics
Second Edition

Fisher
State and Local Public Finance
Second Edition

Hadjimichalakis and Hadjimichalakis
Contemporary Money, Banking, and Financial Markets

Hyman
Economics
Fourth Edition

Hyman
Microeconomics
Fourth Edition

Hyman
Macroeconomics
Fourth Edition

Hyman
Modern Microeconomics Analysis and Applications
Third Edition

Katz and Rosen
Microeconomics
Second Edition

Lehmann
Real World Economic Applications: *The Wall Street Journal* Workbook
Fifth Edition

Lindert and Pugel
International Economics
Tenth Edition

Maurice and Thomas
Managerial Economics: Applied

Microeconomics for Decision Making
Fifth Edition

O'Sullivan
Urban Economics
Third Edition

O'Sullivan
Essentials of Urban Economics

Roger and Daniel
Principles of Economics Software Simulation

Rosen
Public Finance
Fourth Edition

Schwarz and Van Dyken
Manager: Managerial Economics Software

Rosser and Rosser
Comparative Economics in a Transforming World Economy

Santerre and Neun
Health Economics: Theories, Insights and Industry Studies

Sharp, Register, and Grimes
Economics of Social Issues
Twelfth Edition

Slavin
Economics
Fourth Edition

Slavin
Microeconomics
Fourth Edition

Slavin
Macroeconomics
Fourth Edition

Walton and Wykoff
Understanding Economics Today
Fifth Edition

SECOND EDITION

Managerial Economics and Business Strategy

Michael R. Baye
Pennsylvania State University

Irwin
McGraw-Hill

Boston, Massachusetts   Burr Ridge, Illinois   Dubuque, Iowa
Madison, Wisconsin   New York, New York   San Francisco, California   St. Louis, Missouri

Irwin/McGraw-Hill

A Division of The **McGraw·Hill** *Companies*

Irwin Book Team

Publisher: *Michael W. Junior*
Senior sponsoring editor: *Gary Nelson*
Developmental editor: *Ellen Cleary*
Marketing manager: *Katie Rose*
Project editor: *Mary Conzachi*
Production supervisor: *Dina L. Genovese*
Senior designer: *Heidi J. Baughman*
Prepress buyer: *Charlene R. Perez*
Compositor: *Weimer Graphics, Inc., Division of Shepard Poorman Communications Corp.*
Typeface: *$10^{1}/_{2}/12$ Times Roman*
Printer: *R.R. Donnelley & Sons Company*

Libary of Congress Cataloging-in-Publication Data

Baye, Michael R., 1958-
    Managerial economics and business strategy -- 2nd ed. / Michael
Baye.
       p.   cm.
    Includes index.
    ISBN 0-256-17955-7
    1. Managerial economics. 2. Strategic planning.   I. Title.
HD30.22.B38   1997
338.5′024658—dc20   96–17337

Printed in the United States of America
5 6 7 8 9 0 DO 3 2 1 0 9 8

To Natalie, with love.

About the Author

Michael Baye is a Professor of Economics at The Pennsylvania State University. He received his B.S. from Texas A&M University in 1980, where he won both the University Senior Honors Thesis Prize for best undergraduate thesis and the Alfred Chalk Award for outstanding senior in the economics department. He earned a Ph.D. three years later from Purdue University.

Baye has taught managerial economics, industrial organization, and microeconomics at Purdue University, the University of Kentucky, Texas A&M University, and Penn State University, and has won two outstanding teaching awards. A prolific researcher, Baye's research on game theory, industrial organization and consumer behavior has been published in leading journals such as the *American Economic Review, Journal of Political Economy, Econometrica,* and the *Review of Economic Studies.* He has also co-authored two other books.

Baye has held visiting appointments at Erasmus University Rotterdam, Tilburg University, and the New Economic School in Moscow, Russia. He has served on numerous advisory boards and is the editor of *Advances in Applied Microeconomics.*

Preface

Thank you for making the first edition of Managerial Economics and Business Strategy such a success. I introduced that text to the marketplace because I believed that a modern managerial economics course must blend tools from intermediate microeconomics, industrial organization, and game theory. Happily, I am not alone in that position. Users praised the first edition both for its balanced coverage of topics and for its flexibility. Feedback from other managerial economics instructors encouraged me to stay the course.

As in the first edition, this second edition includes modern topics that have not traditionally been covered in managerial economics textbooks—contracts, vertical integration, bargaining, principal-agent problems, oligopoly, multistage and repeated games, auctions, and search, to name just a few. I am gratified by the positive response to my treatment of the organization of the firm (Chapter 6), oligopoly (Chapter 9), game theory (Chapter 10), pricing strategies (Chapter 11), and the economics of information (Chapter 12). But *Managerial Economics and Business Strategy* also covers traditional topics such as present value analysis, supply and demand, elasticities, regression analysis, indifference curve analysis, production theory and costs, and the basic models of perfect competition, monopoly, and monopolistic competition, which makes it appropriate for a wide variety of managerial economics classrooms.

In preparing for this revision, my editors at Irwin and I gathered a lot of information about the managerial economics market in general (through a series of surveys and manuscript reviews) and about the first edition of my book. The results of this market research were very interesting indeed. First, there is a significant amount of change going on in managerial economics classrooms and, as a result, these instructors have genuinely heterogeneous needs when it comes to textbooks. Users of the first edition of this text assured us that they could easily exclude material or even entire chapters without losing continuity. The second edition preserves this flexibility, so that instructors are free to choose the topics they deem most important. Clearly this depth of flexibility is key in a time of such great change.

New to the Second Edition

Based on extensive feedback from reviewers and users of the first edition, the book has been improved in several areas. While the basic layout and structure remains the same, the writing style has been smoothed out and, where needed, explanations have been sharpened. Several new topics have been included in the second edition, including transfer pricing and more detailed treatments of moral hazard, adverse selection, and price discrimination. To accommodate the needs of instructors who teach regression techniques, the coverage of regression analysis in Chapter 3 has been substantially expanded. An important addition, according to the reviewers, is the material that shows students how to perform and interpret regressions from standard spreadsheet programs like *Excel* or *Quattro Pro* that are readily accessible to students and managers.

Here is a partial list of changes in the second edition:

· Updated and expanded "Headlines"
· Expanded coverage of regression analysis
· New and revised end-of-chapter problems
· Spreadsheet-based data diskette
· Expanded coverage of elasticities
· Expanded treatment of price discrimination
· Transfer pricing
· Updated "Selected Readings"
· Extensive list of "Additional Readings"

Key Features

Headlines

As in the first edition, each chapter begins with a Headline that is based on a real-world economic problem—a problem that students should be able to address after completing the chapter. The headlines have been thoroughly revised and expanded, and reveal the types of practical issues that can be addressed after completing a chapter. Each headline is answered at the end of the relevant chapter—when the student is better prepared to deal with the complications of real-world problems. Adopters of the first edition liked the headlines not only because they motivated students to learn the material in the chapter, but because the answers at the end of each chapter taught students how to think like an economist.

Demonstration Problems

I firmly believe that the best way to learn economics is to work problems. So, in addition to the problems contained in the Headlines to each chapter, many Demonstration Problems are sprinkled throughout the narrative. Detailed answers to the problems are given in the main text. Users of the first edition found this feature not only provides students with a low-cost way of verifying that they have mastered the material, but they also reduce the cost to students and instructors of having to meet during office hours to discuss answers to problems.

Inside Business Applications

The second edition contains updated boxed material (called Inside Business applications) that illustrate real-world applications of the theory developed in the text. As in the first edition, I have tried to strike a balance between applications drawn from the current economic literature and the popular press.

Calculus and Non-Calculus Alternatives

Users of the first edition remarked how easy it was to include or exclude the calculus-based material without losing content or continuity. That's because the basic principles and formulae needed to solve a particular class of economic problems (e.g., $MR = MC$) are first stated without appealing to the notation of calculus. Immediately following each principle or formula is a clearly marked Calculus Alternative. Each of these calculus alternatives states the preceding principle or formula in calculus notation, and explains the relation between the calculus- and non-calculus-based formula. Thus, the book is designed for use by professors who want to integrate calculus into managerial economics, and by those who do not require students to use calculus.

Key Terms and Concepts

Each chapter ends with a list of key terms and concepts. These provide an easy way for professors to glean material covered in each chapter and for students to check their mastery of terminology.

End-of-Chapter Problems

Reviewers and survey respondents both commented on the importance of breadth and depth in the end-of-chapter problem material in managerial economics textbooks. When I looked critically at my first edition, I realized that I had not adequately met this important need. I needed to write more of them and I needed to provide a greater variety of problems for you, the instructors, to choose from. While some of the first edition material was revised and retained, I have added more than 100 end-of-chapter problems to this edition. As in the first edition, answers to selected problems are presented in an appendix at the end of the book and a complete set of answers is available to instructors in the instructor's manual.

Suggested Readings/Additional Readings

At the end of each chapter, you will find an updated list of suggested readings. In addition, I've included an end-of-book appendix that contains an extensive list of additional readings for each chapter. These readings will be very useful for professors who wish to assign course papers, projects, or who use the mini-cases also included in the instructor's manual.

Supplements

Instructor's Manual

Richard Beil and I prepared a revised instructor's manual that provides (1) a summary of each chapter, (2) a teaching outline for each chapter, (3) a set of open-ended mini-cases compiled by Darrell Parker, (4) complete answers to all end-of-chapter questions, (5) a hard-copy of the questions contained in the computerized test bank, and (6) transparency masters for key figures in the text.

Computerized Test Bank

The exam questions provided in the instructor's manual are also available in a computerized test bank. There is a WordPerfect 5.1 computerized testbank as well as Irwin's Windows-based Computest to serve the needs of all adopters.

Data Disk

By popular demand, I have written a data diskette that contains the raw data for 100 regression problems. A copy of this spreadsheet (e.g., Excel or Quattro Pro)-based data disk accompanies each student book. Regression output for each of these problems is contained on a separate data diskette that accompanies the instructor's manual.

Student Workbook

In addition to the numerous problems and answers contained in the textbook, a thoroughly revised study guide prepared by yours truly rounds out the assortment of ancillaries for the second edition of Managerial Economics and Business Strategy.

ACKNOWLEDGMENTS

I am grateful to all of the instructors and students who provided feedback to improve the quality of this book. I owe a special debt to Richard Beil at Auburn University, who helped make the first edition a success. I thank my friend and colleague, Keith Crocker, for his help in organizing Chapter 6. Numerous individuals provided feedback at various stages of production of the first and second editions, and I particularly thank Dan Black, Lynn Gillette, Karen Hallows, and Darrell Parker for using early versions in their classes at the University of Kentucky, Texas A&M University, The University of Missouri, and Winthrop University, respectively. I owe a substantial debt to Sue Bryant for her patience and excellent assistance, and to my managerial economics and intermediate microeconomics students at Texas A&M and Penn State for inspiring me to write this book.

I also thank reviewers of the first and second edition for thoughtful comments and constructive criticisms. These included Dean Baim (Pepperdine University), Barbara C. Beliveau (University of Connecticut), Dan Black (University of Kentucky), Robert L. Chapman (Florida Metropolitan University), Ian Cromb (University of Western Ontario), Audrey B. Davidson (University of Louisville), Martine Duchatelet (Barry University), Kevin C. Duncan (University of Southern Colorado), David Ely (San Diego State University), Lynn G. Gillette (Northeast Missouri State University), Andrea Mays Griffith (California State University/Long Beach), Gail Heyne Hafer (Lindenwood College), Karen Hallows (University of Missouri), Mehdi Harian (Bloomsburg University), Lowell R. Jacobsen (William Jewell College), Jaswant R. Jindia (Southern University), W. J. Lane (University of New Orleans), Dwight Porter (College of St. Thomas), Craig Schulman (University of Arkansas), Peter Schwartz (University of North Carolina at Charlotte), Edward Shinnick (University College, Cook Ireland), Dean Showalter (Southwest Texas State University), Mark Stegeman (University of North Carolina), Barbara M. Suleski (Cardinal Stritch College), Roger Tutterow (Kennesaw State College), Leonard White (University of Arkansas), Mike Williams (Bethune Cookman College/Daytona Beach Community College), and Richard Winkelman (Arizona State University).

In addition I'd like to recognize and thank the more than 300 managerial economics instructors who responded to the detailed market survey and, as a result of their thoughtful suggestions, helped shape the revision plan for this book. I wish I had space to thank you each individually. As planning for the third edition will begin all too soon, I'd welcome your feedback to this revision. Visit my webpage at http://packrat.la.psu.edu/~mbaye/bayehom.htm or write to me directly at my internet address: baye@psu.edu.

Finally, I thank my family at home—M'Lissa, Natalie, and Mitchell—as well as my family at Irwin—Gary Nelson and Ellen Cleary—for their patience, support, and encouragement throughout this project.

Michael R. Baye
University Park
March 1996

Contents

11   Pricing Strategies for Firms with Market Power   404

CHAPTER

1

The Fundamentals of Managerial Economics

Headline

Amcott Loses $3.5 Million; Manager Fired

On Tuesday software giant Amcott posted a year-end 1996 operating loss of $3.5 million. Reportedly, $1.7 million of the loss stemmed from its foreign language division.

With short-term interest rates at 7 percent, Amcott decided to use $20 million of its 1992 retained earnings to purchase the rights to Magicword, a software package that converts generic word processor files saved as French text into English. Sales revenue from the software was $7 million in 1993 and rose to $7.1 million in 1994, when sales were halted pending a copyright infringement suit filed by Foreign, Inc. Amcott lost the suit in 1995 and paid damages of $1.7 million to Foreign, Inc., in December 1996. Industry insiders say that the copyright violation pertained to "a very small component of Magicword."

Ralph Barnes, the Amcott manager who was fired over the incident, was quoted as saying, "I'm a scapegoat for the attorneys [at Amcott] who didn't do their homework before buying the rights to Magicword. I projected annual sales of $7 million per year for three years. My sales forecasts for 1993 were right on target. Actual 1994 sales actually exceeded my forecasts, and would have been even higher if the suit hadn't publicized my sales forecasts and plans to release the next generation of Magicword software in late 1995."

Do you know why Ralph Barnes was fired?

Introduction

Many students taking managerial economics ask, "Why should I study economics? Will it tell me what the stock market will do tomorrow? Will it tell me where to invest my money or how to get rich?" Unfortunately, managerial economics by itself is unlikely to provide definitive answers to such questions. Obtaining the answers would require an accurate crystal ball. Nevertheless, managerial economics is a valuable tool for analyzing business situations such as the ones raised in the headlines that open each chapter of this book.[1]

In fact, if you surf the Internet, browse a business publication such as the *Wall Street Journal, Forbes,* or *Fortune,* or read a trade publication like *Restaurant News* or *Supermarket Business,* you will find a host of stories that involve managerial economics (a recent search generated the following ones):

"OPEC Members are Likely to Reduce Output in Wake of Cut by Venezuela"
"Coke's Plan to Pump Up the Volume"
"Airlines to Raise Domestic Fares"
"Sizzler Mocks Fast Food with $3.99 Lunch Tactic"
"Wal-Mart's Way: No. 1 Retailer Relies on Word-of-Mouth, Not Ads"
"Great News: A Recession"

Knowledge of managerial economics not only allows you to decipher the stories behind each of these headlines, but enables you to make effective managerial decisions.

After completing this course, you will know when it is optimal to cut output, as OPEC did, and when to expand output, as did Coca-Cola. You will know how to sell more of a given product, such as meat, without the need for expensive advertising campaigns. You will know when it is best to cut prices, as Sizzler did, and when it pays to raise prices, like the airlines. Managerial economics even explains why recessions are not bad for all firms and why restaurants find it profitable to charge $1.00 for a glass of soda that costs the firm $.20 while offering a steak, potato, and salad that costs $4.00 for the bargain price of $3.99.

Managerial economics is not only valuable to managers of Fortune 500 companies; it is also valuable to managers of not-for-profit organizations. It is useful to the manager of a food bank who must decide the best means for distributing food to the needy. It is valuable to the coordinator of a shelter for the homeless whose goal is to help the largest possible number of homeless, given a very tight budget. In fact, managerial economics provides use-

[1]Each chapter concludes with the solution to that chapter's opening headline. After you read each chapter, you should attempt to solve the opening headline on your own and then compare your solution to that contained at the end of the chapter.

ful insights into every facet of the business and nonbusiness world in which we live—including household decision making.

Why is managerial economics so valuable to such a diverse group of decision makers? The answer to this question lies in the meaning of the term *managerial economics.*

The Manager

manager
A person who directs resources to achieve a stated goal.

A *manager* is a person who directs resources to achieve a stated goal. This definition includes all individuals who (1) direct the efforts of others, including those who delegate tasks within an organization such as a firm, a family, or a club; (2) purchase inputs to be used in the production of goods and services such as the output of a firm, food for the needy, or shelter for the homeless; or (3) are in charge of making other decisions, such as product price or quality.

A manager generally has responsibility for his or her own actions as well as for the actions of individuals, machines, and other inputs under the manager's control. This control may involve responsibilities for the resources of a multinational corporation or for those of a single household. In each instance, however, a manager must direct resources and the behavior of individuals for the purpose of accomplishing some task. While much of this book assumes the manager's task is to maximize the profits of the firm that employs the manager, the underlying principles are valid for virtually any decision process.

Economics

economics
The science of making decisions in the presence of scarce resources.

The primary focus of this book is on the second word in *managerial economics. Economics* is the science of making decisions in the presence of scarce resources. *Resources* are simply anything used to produce a good or service or, more generally, to achieve a goal. Decisions are important because scarcity implies that by making one choice, you give up another. A computer firm that spends more resources on advertising has fewer resources to invest in research and development. A food bank that spends more on soup has less to spend on fruit. Economic decisions thus involve the allocation of scarce resources, and a manager's task is to allocate resources so as to best meet the manager's goals.

One of the best ways to comprehend the pervasive nature of scarcity is to imagine that a genie has appeared and offered to grant you three wishes. If resources were not scarce, you would tell the genie you have absolutely nothing to wish for; you already have everything you want. Surely, as you begin this course, you recognize that time is one of the scarcest resources of all. Your primary decision problem is to allocate a scarce resource—time—to achieve a goal—presumably earning an A in this course.

Managerial Economics Defined

managerial economics
The study of how to direct scarce resources in the way that most efficiently achieves a managerial goal.

✳*Managerial economics,* therefore, is the study of how to direct scarce resources in the way that most efficiently achieves a managerial goal. It is a very broad discipline in that it describes methods useful for directing everything from the resources of a household to maximize household welfare to the resources of a firm to maximize profits.

To understand the nature of decisions that confront managers of firms, imagine that you are the manager of a Fortune 500 company that makes computers. You must make a host of decisions to succeed as a manager: Should you purchase components such as disk drives and chips from other manufacturers or produce them within your own firm? Should you specialize in making one type of computer or produce several different types? How many computers should you produce, and at what price should you sell them? How many employees should you hire, and how should you compensate them? How can you ensure that employees work hard and produce quality products? How will the actions of rival computer firms affect your decisions?

The key to making sound decisions is to know what information is needed to make an informed decision and then to collect and process the data. If you work for a large firm, your legal department can provide data about the legal ramifications of alternative decisions; your accounting department can provide tax advice and basic cost data; your marketing department can provide you with data on the characteristics of the market for your product; and your firm's financial analysts can provide summary data for alternative methods of obtaining financial capital. Ultimately, however, the manager must integrate all of this information, process it, and arrive at a decision. The remainder of this book will show you how to perform this important managerial function by using six principles that comprise effective management.

The Economics of Effective Management

The nature of sound managerial decisions varies depending on the underlying goals of the manager. Since this course is designed primarily for managers of firms, this book focuses on managerial decisions as they relate to maximizing profits or, more generally, the value of the firm. Before embarking on this special use of managerial economics, we provide an overview of the basic principles that comprise effective management. In particular, an effective manager must (1) identify goals and constraints; (2) recognize the nature and importance of profits; (3) understand incentives; (4) understand markets; (5) recognize the time value of money; and (6) use marginal analysis.

An effective manager must:

Identify Goals and Constraints

The first step in making sound decisions is to have well-defined *goals* because achieving different goals entails making different decisions. If your goal is to maximize your grade in this course rather than maximize your overall grade-point average, your study habits will differ accordingly. Similarly, if the goal of a food bank is to distribute food to needy people in rural areas, its decisions and optimal distribution network will differ from those it would use to distribute food to needy inner-city residents. Notice that in both instances, the decision maker faces *constraints* that affect the ability to achieve a goal. The 24-hour day affects your ability to earn an A in this course; a budget affects the ability of the food bank to distribute food to the needy. Constraints are an artifact of scarcity.

Different units within a firm may be given different goals; those in a firm's marketing department might be instructed to use their resources to maximize sales or market share, while those in the firm's financial group might focus on earnings growth or risk-reduction strategies. Later in this book we will see how the firm's overall goal—maximizing profits—can be achieved by giving each unit within the firm an incentive to achieve potentially different goals.

Unfortunately, constraints make it difficult for managers to achieve goals such as maximizing profits or increasing market share. These constraints include such things as the available technology and the prices of inputs used in production. The goal of maximizing profits requires the manager to decide the optimal price to charge for a product, how much to produce, which technology to use, how much of each input to use, how to react to decisions made by competitors, and so on. This book provides tools for answering these types of questions.

Recognize the Nature and Importance of Profits

The overall goal of most firms is to maximize profits or the firm's value, and the remainder of this book will detail strategies managers can use to achieve this goal. Before we provide these details, let us examine the nature and importance of profits in a free-market economy.

Economic versus Accounting Profits

When most people hear the word *profit,* they think of accounting profits. *Accounting profits* are the difference between the total amount of money taken in from sales (total revenue, or price times quantity sold) minus the dollar cost of producing goods or services. Accounting profits are what show up on the firm's income statement, and are typically reported to the manager by the firm's accounting department.

A more general way to define profits is in terms of what economists refer to as economic profits. *Economic profits* are the difference between the total revenue and the total opportunity cost of producing the firm's goods or services. The *opportunity cost* of using a resource includes both the *explicit cost* of the resource and the *implicit cost* of giving up the next-best alternative use of the resource. The opportunity cost of producing a good or service generally is higher than accounting costs because it includes both the dollar value of costs (explicit, or accounting costs) and any implicit costs.

Implicit costs are very hard to measure and therefore are often overlooked by managers. Effective managers, however, continually seek out data from other sources to identify and quantify implicit costs. Managers of large firms can use sources within the company, including the firm's finance, marketing, and/or legal departments, to obtain data about the implicit costs of decisions. In other instances managers must collect data on their own. For example, what does it cost you to read this book? The price you paid the bookstore for this book is the explicit (or accounting) cost, while the implicit cost is the value of what you are giving up by reading the book. You could be studying some other subject or watching TV, and each of these alternatives has some value to you. The "best" of these alternatives is your implicit cost of reading this book; you are giving up this alternative to read the book. Similarly, the opportunity cost of going to school is much higher than the cost of tuition and books; it also includes the amount of money you would earn had you decided to work rather than go to school.

In the business world, the opportunity cost of opening a restaurant is the next best alternative use of the resources used to establish the restaurant—say, opening a hairstyling salon. Again, these resources include not only the explicit financial resources needed to open the business but any implicit costs as well. Suppose you own a building in New York that you use to run a small pizzeria. At the end of the year, you add up the costs of supplies (the costs entered in your accountant's books) and conclude that your costs were $20,000. If your revenues were $100,000, your accounting profits would be $80,000.

However, these accounting profits overstate your economic profits, because the costs include only accounting costs. First, the costs do not include the time you spent running the business. Had you not run the business you could have worked for someone else, and this fact reflects an economic cost not accounted for in accounting profits. To be concrete, suppose you could have worked for someone else for $30,000. Your opportunity cost of time would have been $30,000 for the year. Thus, $30,000 of your accounting profits are not profits at all but one of the implicit costs of running the pizzeria.

Second, accounting costs do not account for the fact that, had you not run the pizzeria, you could have rented the building to someone else. If the

economic profits
The difference between total revenue and total opportunity cost.

opportunity cost
The cost of the explicit and implicit resources that are forgone when a decision is made.

What Are the Goals of Firms?

One of the best ways to identify the goals of firms and managers is to ask large investors and stockholders what they want to see managers do, and what are the consequences of a manager's failure to achieve the desired goals. Clifton R. Wharton, former CEO of Teachers Insurance and Annuity Association–College Retirement Equities Fund (TIAA–CREF), a pension fund that has approximately $100 billion invested in financial instruments, explains how his firm signals managers.

According to Wharton, managers must resist a narrow focus that looks only at short-term profits. The goal of TIAA–CREF's management team is to attempt to consistently improve the long-term health of the corporation. Wharton explains, "[If] our analysis shows that management of a given company . . . is underperforming due to its own shortcomings, our strategy will call for CREF to cast its proxy ballot so as to withhold its vote on an entire management slate of directors." Given the size of an investor like TIAA–CREF, this action effectively signals to the board and other investors that the present management team is in danger of being replaced. The purpose "is not to tell management how to run their business, but rather to say that we do not believe that the board and management are living up to their potential."

A similar view is held by Lord Hanson, CEO of Hanson PLC, who says that the goal of his firm is to maximize the company's wealth. According to Hanson, "A truly responsible company must be aware of its duty to society. Service to its customers, quality of its goods and services, effective research and development, a positive attitude about the environment, combined with the welfare of its employees and pensioners are critical. But these must be aligned with management's primary responsibility to increase shareholders' value."

Ultimately, the goal of a continuing company must be to maximize the value of the firm. This goal often is achieved by trying to hit intermediate targets, such as minimizing costs, improving the production process, decreasing the time it takes management to make decisions, and improving product quality. If a firm does not maximize its value over time, it will be in danger of either going out of business, being taken over by other owners (as in a leveraged buyout), or having its stockholders elect to replace management. You can reduce the likelihood of being replaced in your role as a firm manager by learning how to use the tools of managerial economics to maximize the value of your firm.

Sources: Clifton R. Wharton, "Just Vote No," *Harvard Business Review* 69 (November–December 1991), p. 139; Lord Hanson, "Shareholder Value: Touchstones of Managerial Capitalism," *Harvard Business Review* 69 (November–December 1991), p. 142.

---

rental value of the building is $100,000 per year, you gave up this amount to run your own business. Thus, the costs of running the pizzeria include not only the costs of supplies ($20,000) but the $30,000 you could have earned in some other business *and* the $100,000 you could have earned in renting the building. The economic cost of running the pizzeria is $150,000—the amount you gave up to run your business. Considering the revenue of $100,000, you actually lost $50,000 by running the pizzeria.

Throughout this book, when we speak of costs we always mean economic costs. Economic costs include not only the accounting costs but also the opportunity costs of the resources used in production.

The Role of Profits

A common misconception is that the firm's goal of maximizing profits is necessarily bad for society. Individuals who want to maximize profits often are considered self-interested, a quality that many people view as undesirable. However, consider Adam Smith's classic line from *The Wealth of Nations:* "It is not out of the benevolence of the butcher, the brewer, or the baker, that we expect our dinner, but from their regard to their own interest."[2]

Smith is saying that by pursuing its self-interest—the goal of maximizing profits—a firm ultimately meets the needs of society. If you cannot make a living as a rock singer, it is probably because society does not appreciate your singing; society would more highly value your talents in some other employment. If you break five dishes each time you clean up after dinner, your talents are perhaps better suited for balancing the checkbook or mowing the lawn. Similarly, the profits of businesses signal where society's scarce resources are best allocated. When firms in a given industry earn economic profits, the opportunity cost to resource holders outside the industry increases as they recognize that by continuing to use their resources as those resources are being utilized, they are giving up profits. This induces new firms to enter the markets in which economic profits are available. As more firms enter the industry, the market price falls, and economic profits decline.

Thus, profits signal the owners of resources where the resources are most highly valued by society. By moving scarce resources toward the production of goods most valued by society, the total welfare of society is improved. As Adam Smith first noted, this phenomenon is due not to benevolence on the part of the firms' managers but to the self-interested goal of maximizing the firms' profits.

Principle

Profits Are a Signal
Profits signal resource holders where resources are most highly valued by society.

Understand Incentives

In our discussion of the role of profits, we emphasized that profits signal the holders of resources when to enter and exit particular industries. In effect, changes in profits provide an incentive to resource holders to alter their use of resources. Within a firm, *incentives* affect how resources are used and how hard workers work. To succeed as a manager, you must have a clear grasp of the role of incentives within an organization such as a firm and how to construct incentives to induce maximal effort from those you manage.

---

[2]Adam Smith, *An Inquiry into the Causes of The Wealth of Nations,* ed. Edwin Cannan (Chicago: University of Chicago Press, 1976).

Inside Business 1–2

Profits and the Computer Industry

The computer industry was one of the most dynamic industries in the world during the early 1990s and probably will continue to be a vital industry for some time to come. During the 1980s the computer industry underwent many changes. Many new firms entered the industry, and less efficient firms left. The role of profits in the computer industry is to guide the use of resources used in manufacturing computers.

When profits in a given industry are higher than in other industries, we would expect more firms to enter that industry. When losses are recorded, some firms will likely leave the industry.

In the early 1980s small, medium-size, and large firms in the computer industry earned positive profits. According to economic theory, we would expect to see new firms enter the market to reap some of those profits. This is precisely what happened: From the end of 1983 to the end of 1986, the number of firms in the computer industry increased from 835 to 1,186. Interestingly, most of those new firms were smaller firms. As a result of new entry by smaller firms, the overall profitability of small firms declined.

Thus, profits are a motivating factor in moving resources in and out of an industry. If we look at the advances in computer technology during the last decade, we see enormous improvement. In that short span of time, the speed of computers more than tripled, and storage capacity grew by more than a factor of 4. Profits therefore signaled productive resources into and out of the computer industry and helped generate great advances in technology. The ultimate result was better products at lower prices.

Chapter 6 is devoted entirely to this special aspect of managerial decision making, but it is useful here to provide a synopsis of how to construct proper incentives.

The first step in constructing incentives within a firm is to distinguish between the world, or the business place, as it is and the way you wish it were. Many professionals and owners of small establishments have difficulties because they do not fully comprehend the importance of the role incentives play in guiding the decisions of others.

A friend of mine—Mr. O—opened a restaurant and hired a manager to run the business so he could spend time doing the things he enjoys. Recently, I asked him how his business was doing, and he reported that he had been losing money ever since the restaurant opened. When asked whether he thought the manager was doing a good job, he said, "For the $75,000 salary I pay the manager each year, the manager *should* be doing a good job."

Mr. O believes the manager "should be doing a good job." This is the way he wishes the world was. But in the real world, individuals often are motivated by self-interest. This is not to say that people never act out of kindness or charity, but rather that human nature is such that people naturally tend to look after their self-interest. Had Mr. O taken a managerial economics course, he would know how to provide the manager with an incentive to do what is in Mr. O's best interest. The key is to design a mechanism such that if the manager does what is in *his* own interest, he will indirectly do what is best for Mr. O.

Since Mr. O is not physically present at the restaurant to watch over the manager, he has no way of knowing what the manager is up to. Indeed, his unwillingness to spend time at the restaurant is what induced him to hire the manager in the first place. What type of incentive has he created by paying the manager $75,000 per year? The manager receives $75,000 per year regardless of whether he puts in 12-hour or 2-hour days. The manager receives no reward for working hard and incurs no penalty if he fails to make sound managerial decisions. The manager receives the same $75,000 regardless of the restaurant's profitability.

Fortunately, most business owners understand the problem just described. The owners of large corporations are shareholders, and most never set foot on company ground. How do they provide incentives for chief executive officers (CEOs) to be effective managers? Very simply, they provide them with "incentive plans" in the form of bonuses. These bonuses are in direct proportion to the firm's profitability. If the firm does well, the CEO receives a large bonus. If the firm does poorly, the CEO receives no bonus and risks being fired by the stockholders. These types of incentives are also present at lower levels within firms. Some individuals earn commissions based on the revenue they generate for the firm's owner. If they put forth little effort, they receive little pay; if they put forth much effort and hence generate many sales, they receive a generous commission.

The thrust of managerial economics is to provide you with a broad array of skills that will enable you to make sound economic decisions and to structure appropriate incentives within your organization. We will begin under the assumption that everyone with whom you come into contact is greedy, that is, interested only in his or her own self-interest. In such a case, understanding incentives is a must. Of course, this is a worst-case scenario; more likely, some of your business contacts will not be only selfishly inclined. If you are so lucky, your job will be all the easier.

Understand Markets

In studying microeconomics in general, and managerial economics in particular, it is important to bear in mind that there are two sides to every transaction in a market: For every buyer of a good there is a corresponding seller. The final outcome of the market process, then, depends on the relative power of buyers and sellers in the marketplace. The power, or bargaining position, of consumers and producers in the market is limited by three sources of rivalry that exist in economic transactions: consumer–producer rivalry, consumer–consumer rivalry, and producer–producer rivalry. Each form of rivalry serves as a disciplining device to guide the market process, and each affects different markets to a different extent. Thus, your ability as

Bargaining Position limited by 3 sources of rivalry

a manager to meet performance objectives will depend on the extent to which your product is affected by these sources of rivalry.

Consumer–Producer Rivalry

Consumer–producer rivalry occurs because of the competing interests of consumers and producers. Consumers attempt to negotiate or locate low prices, while producers attempt to negotiate high prices. In a very loose sense, consumers attempt to "rip off" producers, and producers attempt to "rip off" consumers. Of course, there are limits to the ability of these parties to achieve their goals. If a consumer offers a price that is too low, the producer will refuse to sell the product to the consumer. Similarly, if the producer asks a price that exceeds the consumer's valuation of a good, the consumer will refuse to purchase the good. These two forces provide a natural check and balance on the market process even in markets in which the product is offered by a single firm (a monopolist).

A classic example of consumer—producer rivalry is the transaction between the buyer of a new automobile and an automobile dealer. The consumer comes to the dealership with an idea of how much she is willing and able to pay for a new car. Of course, she wants to pay as little as possible, but she knows the dealer will not give her a car for free. If the highest price the consumer is willing and able to pay is less than the minimum price the dealer is willing and able to accept, no trade will take place. A car sale will result only when there is an overlap between the two prices.

In the case of the car dealership, the first offer usually is made by the car dealer in the form of a sticker price. Since the dealer wants to get as much money from the customer as possible, this first offer will be relatively high, but not so high as to scare off the customer. The customer, in turn, makes an initial offer for the car that is less than the amount she is actually willing and able to pay, but the offered price will not be so low that it scares off the dealer. After the initial offers have been made, the competition begins. Since neither party knows the most or the least the other is willing and able to pay, the parties never know how close they got in the final transaction. However, one thing is certain: The buyer will try to get the lowest price possible, and the seller will try to get the highest price possible.

Consumer–Consumer Rivalry

A second source of rivalry that guides the market process occurs among consumers. *Consumer–consumer rivalry* reduces the negotiating power of consumers in the marketplace. It arises because of the economic doctrine of scarcity. When limited quantities of goods are available, consumers will compete with one another for the right to purchase the available goods. Consumers who are willing to pay the highest prices for the scarce goods will outbid other consumers for the right to consume the goods. Once again, this source of rivalry is present even in markets in which a single firm is selling a product.

A good example of consumer–consumer rivalry is an auction, a topic we will examine in detail in Chapter 12. The seller of the good attempts to get as many people as possible to bid on the item to initiate consumer–consumer rivalry. In the United States most auctions are ascending in nature. The auctioneer asks for a bid and, after receiving an opening bid, asks for someone to improve on that bid. Each potential consumer wants to buy the product for sale at the lowest possible price. However, each knows that if she or he offers some price that is lower than what others are willing and able to pay for the good, someone else will offer a higher price. At the end of the auction, the person who is willing and able to pay the highest price will get the item. But no matter what that price is, you can rest assured the actual buyer would have preferred to pay a lower price.

Producer–Producer Rivalry

A third source of rivalry in the marketplace is *producer–producer rivalry.* Unlike the other forms of rivalry, this disciplining device functions only when multiple sellers of a product compete in the marketplace. Given that customers are scarce, producers compete with one another for the right to service the customers available. Those firms that offer the best-quality product at the lowest price earn the right to serve the customers.

Pizza restaurants provide an excellent example of producer–producer rivalry. Each producer of pizza would prefer to be the only seller in a town and be able to sell pizzas at a much higher price. But because there are many producers, the price of a pizza is relatively low. If only one store existed, the price of a pizza might be $20 or more. In fact, the first pizza parlors charged very high prices. Since there were economic profits to be made in the market for pizza, more companies opened restaurants. To attract customers, they offered a product similar to the pizza the existing restaurants offered, but at a lower price. The competition among producers of pizza is so strong that in most towns, two pizzas can be purchased for under $10. With producer–producer rivalry, each firm wants to sell its product for as much as possible, but the intense competition among sellers results in a much lower price.

Government and the Market

When agents on either side of the market find themselves disadvantaged in the market process, they frequently attempt to induce government to intervene on their behalf. For example, the market for electricity in most towns is characterized by a sole local supplier of electricity, and thus there is no producer–producer rivalry. Consumer groups may initiate action by a public utility commission to limit the power of utilities in setting prices. Similarly, producers may lobby for government assistance to place them in a better bargaining position relative to consumers and foreign producers. Thus, in modern economies government also plays a role in disciplining the market process. Chapter 13 explores how government affects managerial decisions.

Recognize the Time Value of Money

The timing of many decisions involves a gap between the time when the costs of a project are borne, and the time when the benefits of the project are received. In these instances it is important to recognize that $1 today is worth more than $1 received in the future. The reason is simple: The opportunity cost of receiving the $1 in the future is the forgone interest that could be earned were $1 received today. This opportunity cost reflects the *time value of money.* To properly account for the timing of receipts and expenditures, the manager must understand present value analysis.

Present Value Analysis

The *present value (PV)* of an amount received in the future is the amount that would have to be invested today at the prevailing interest rate to generate the given future value. For example, suppose someone offered you $1.10 one year from today. What is the value today (the present value) of $1.10 to be received one year from today? Notice that if you could invest $1.00 today at a guaranteed interest rate of 10 percent, one year from now $1.00 would be worth $1.00 \times 1.1 = $1.10. In other words, over the course of one year, your $1.00 would earn $.10 in interest. Thus, when the interest rate is 10 percent, the present value of receiving $1.10 one year in the future is $1.00.

A more general formula follows:

Formula (Present Value).   The present value *(PV)* of a future value *(FV)* received *n* years in the future is

$$PV = \frac{FV}{(1 + i)^n},\qquad\qquad (1\text{--}1)$$

where *i* is the guaranteed (risk-free) rate of interest.

For example, the present value of $100.00 in 10 years if it could be invested at 7 percent is $50.76, since

$$PV = \frac{\$100}{(1 + .07)^{10}} = \frac{\$100}{1.97} = \$50.76.$$

This essentially means that if you invested $50.76 today at a 7 percent interest rate, in 10 years your investment would be worth $100.

Notice that the interest rate appears in the denominator of the expression in Equation 1–1. This means that the higher the interest rate, the lower the present value of a future amount, and conversely. The present value of a future payment reflects the difference between the *future value (FV)* and the *opportunity cost of waiting (OCW): PV = FV − OCW.* Intuitively, the higher the interest rate, the higher the opportunity cost of waiting to receive a future amount and thus the lower the present value of the future amount. For example, if the interest rate is zero, the opportunity cost of waiting is zero, and the present value and the future value coincide. This is consistent with Equation 1–1, since the righthand side becomes $FV/(1 + 0)^n = FV$ when the interest rate is zero.

The basic idea of the present value of a future amount can be extended to a series of future payments. For example, if you are promised FV_1 one year in the future, FV_2 two years in the future, and so on for n years, the present value of this sum of future payments is

$$PV = \frac{FV_1}{(1 + i)^1} + \frac{FV_2}{(1 + i)^2} + \frac{FV_3}{(1 + i)^3} + \cdots + \frac{FV_n}{(1 + i)^n}.$$

Formula (Present Value of a Stream).   When the interest rate is i, the present value of a stream of payments of $FV_1, FV_2, \ldots FV_n$ is

$$PV = \sum_{t=1}^{n} \frac{FV_t}{(1 + i)^t}.$$

Given the present value of the income stream that arises from a project, one can easily compute the net present value of the project. The *net present value (NPV)* of a project is simply the present value *(PV)* of the income stream generated by the project minus the current cost (C_0) of the project: $NPV = PV - C_0$. If the net present value of a project is positive, then the project is profitable because the present value of the earnings from the project exceed the current cost of the project. On the other hand, a manager should reject a project that has a negative net present value, since the cost of such a project exceeds the present value of the income stream that project generates.

Formula (Net Present Value).   Suppose that by sinking C_0 dollars into a project today, a firm will generate income of FV_1 one year in the future, FV_2 two years in the future, and so on for n years. If the interest rate is i, the net present value of the project is

$$NPV = \frac{FV_1}{(1 + i)^1} + \frac{FV_2}{(1 + i)^2} + \frac{FV_3}{(1 + i)^3} + \cdots + \frac{FV_n}{(1 + i)^n} - C_0.$$

DEMONSTRATION PROBLEM 1–1

The manager of Automated Products is contemplating the purchase of a new machine that will cost $300,000 and has a useful life of five years. The machine will yield (year-end) cost reductions to Automated Products of $50,000 in year 1, $60,000 in year 2, $75,000 in the year 3, and $90,000 in years 4 and 5. What is the present value of the cost savings of the machine if the interest rate is 8 percent? Should the manager purchase the machine?

Answer

By spending \$300,000 today on a new machine, the firm will reduce costs by \$365,000 over five years. However, the present value of the cost savings is only

$$PV = \frac{50,000}{1.08} + \frac{60,000}{1.08^2} + \frac{75,000}{1.08^3} + \frac{90,000}{1.08^4} + \frac{90,000}{1.08^5} = \$284,503.$$

Consequently, the net present value of the new machine is

$$NPV = PV - C_0 = \$284,503 - \$300,000 = -\$15,497.$$

Since the net present value of the machine is negative, the manager should not purchase the machine. In other words, the manager could earn more by investing the \$300,000 at 8 percent than by spending the money on the cost-saving technology.

Inside Business 1–3

Joining the Jet Set

A few years ago an advertisement from the USAir System Timetable offered a one-year membership in the USAir Club for \$125. Alternatively, one could purchase a three-year membership for \$300. Many managers and executives join air clubs because they offer a quiet place to work or relax while on the road; thus, productivity is enhanced.

Let's assume you wish to join the club for three years. Should you pay the up-front \$300 fee for a three-year membership or pay \$125 per year for three years for total payments of \$375? For simplicity, let's suppose USAir will not change the annual fee of \$125 over the next three years.

On the surface it appears that you save \$75 by paying for three years in advance. But this approach ignores the time-value of money. Is paying for all three years in advance profitable when you take the time value of money into account?

The present value of the cost of membership if you pay for three years in advance is \$300,

since all of that money is paid today. If you pay annually, you pay \$125 today, \$125 one year from today, and \$125 two years from today. Given an interest rate of 5 percent, the present value of these payments is

$$PV = \$125 + \frac{\$125}{1.05} + \frac{\$125}{(1.05)^2},$$

or

$$PV = 125 + 119.05 + 113.38$$
$$= \$357.43.$$

Thus, in present value terms, you save \$57.43 if you pay for three years in advance. If you wish to join for three years and expect annual fees to either remain constant or rise over the next three years, it is better to pay in advance. Given the current interest rate, USAir is offering a good deal, but the present value of the savings is \$57.43, not \$75.00.

The Value of the Firm

Present value analysis is also useful in determining the value of a firm. The *value of a firm* is the present value of all future profits of the firm. For example, if the interest rate is i, π_0 represents current profits, π_1 the profits one year from today, π_2 the profits two years from today, and so on, the value of a firm that will be in business for T years is

$$PV_{firm} = \pi_0 + \frac{\pi_1}{(1+i)} + \frac{\pi_2}{(1+i)^2} + \cdots + \frac{\pi_T}{(1+i)^T} = \sum_{t=0}^{T} \frac{\pi_t}{(1+i)^t}.$$

In other words, the value of the firm today is the present value of all of its future profits. Notice that this notion of the value of a firm takes into account the long-term impact of decisions on profits. When economists say that the goal of a firm is to maximize profits, it should be understood to mean that the firm's goal is to maximize its value, which is the present value of all future profits.

Principle

Profit Maximization

Maximizing profits means maximizing the value of the firm, which is the present value of all future profits.

With a few assumptions and a little algebra, we may obtain a very simple formula for the value of a firm. This methodology is frequently used by long-term planners within a firm, as well as by securities analysts whose job is to determine whether a company's stock is under- or overvalued. Suppose the firm's profits grow each year at a rate of g percent. Thus, if π_0 represents the current level of profits, profits one year from today are $\pi_1 = (1 + g)\pi_0$, profits two years from today are $\pi_2 = (1 + g)^2\pi_0$, and so on. If the life of the firm is extremely long (technically, infinitely long) and the interest rate is i, the value of the firm is

$$PV_{firm} = \sum_{t=0}^{\infty} \frac{\pi_t}{(1+i)^t}. \tag{1–2}$$

Substituting $\pi_t = (1 + g)^t\pi_0$ into Equation 1–2 yields

$$PV_{firm} = \sum_{t=0}^{\infty} \left(\frac{(1+g)^t\pi_0}{(1+i)^t}\right) = \pi_0\left[\sum_{t=0}^{\infty}\left(\frac{1+g}{1+i}\right)^t\right]. \tag{1–3}$$

If the growth rate of profits is less than the rate of interest ($g < i$), then $(1 + g)/(1 + i)$ is less than 1. Furthermore, under our assumption that the growth rate of profits and the interest rate are constant, $(1 + g)/(1 + i)$ is a constant less than 1. A well-known mathematical property of an infinite series is

$$\sum_{t=0}^{\infty} \delta^t = \frac{1}{1-\delta} \qquad (1\text{--}4)$$

whenever $|\delta| < 1$. Notice that in Equation 1–3, $(1 + g)/(1 + i)$ plays the same role as δ in Equation 1–4. Thus,

$$\sum_{t=0}^{\infty} \left(\frac{(1+g)}{(1+i)}\right)^t = \frac{1}{1 - \frac{(1+g)}{(1+i)}} = \frac{1+i}{i-g}.$$

The value of the firm when profits grow at a constant rate, $g < i$, may thus be simplified to

$$PV_{firm} = \pi_0 \left(\frac{1+i}{i-g}\right), \qquad (1\text{--}5)$$

where π_0 is the current level of profits. Notice that for a given interest rate and growth rate of the firm, maximizing the lifetime value of the firm (long-term profits) is equivalent to maximizing the firm's current profits (short-term profits).

Principle

Maximizing Short-Term Profits May Maximize Long-Term Profits
If the growth rate in profits is less than the interest rate and both are constant, maximizing the present value of all future profits is the same as maximizing current profits.

DEMONSTRATION PROBLEM 1–2

Suppose the interest rate is 10 percent and the firm is expected to grow at an annual rate of 5 percent for the foreseeable future. If the current profits of the firm are $100 million, what is the value of the firm (the present value of all present and future earnings)?

Answer

Using the formula in Equation 1–5, we see that

$$PV_{firm} = \left(\frac{1 + .1}{.1 - .05}\right) 100 = (22)100 = \$2,200 \text{ million.}$$

While the notion of the present value of a firm is very general, the simplified formula in Equation 1–5 is based on the assumption that the growth rate of the firm's profits is constant. In reality, however, the investment and marketing strategies of the firm will affect its growth rate. Moreover, the strategies used by competitors generally will affect the growth rate of the firm. In such instances, there is no substitute for using the general formula given in Equation 1–2 and understanding the concepts developed in later chapters in this book.

Use Marginal Analysis

Marginal analysis is one of the most important managerial tools—a tool we will use repeatedly throughout this text in alternative contexts. Simply put, *marginal analysis* states that optimal managerial decisions involve comparing the marginal (or incremental) benefits of a decision with the marginal (or incremental) costs. For example, the optimal amount of studying for this course is determined by comparing (1) the improvement in your grade that will result from an additional hour of studying and (2) the additional costs of studying an additional hour. So long as the benefits of studying an additional hour exceed the costs of studying an additional hour, it is profitable to continue to study. However, once an additional hour of studying adds more to costs than it does to benefits, you should stop studying.

More generally, let $B(Q)$ denote the total benefits derived from Q units of some variable that is within the manager's control. This is a very general idea: $B(Q)$ may be the revenue a firm generates from producing Q units of output; it may be the benefits associated with distributing Q units of food to the needy; or, in the context of our previous example, it may represent the benefits derived by studying Q hours for an exam. Let $C(Q)$ represent the total costs of the corresponding level of Q. Depending on the nature of the decision problem, $C(Q)$ may be the total cost to a firm of producing Q units of output, the total cost to a food bank of providing Q units of food to the needy, or the total cost to you of studying Q hours for an exam.

Discrete Decisions

We first consider the situation where the managerial control variable is discrete. In this instance, the manager faces a situation like that summarized in columns 1 through 3 in Table 1–1. Notice that the manager cannot use fractional units of Q; only integer values are possible. This reflects the discrete nature of the problem. In the context of a production decision, Q may be the number of gallons of soft drink produced. The manager must decide how many gallons of soft drink to produce (0, 1, 2, and so on), but cannot choose to produce fractional units (for example, one pint). Column 2 of Table 1–1 provides hypothetical data for total benefits; column 3 gives hypothetical data for total costs.

TABLE 1–1   Determining the Optimal Level of a Control Variable: The Discrete Case

(1) Control Variable Q	(2) Total Benefits B(Q)	(3) Total Costs C(Q)	(4) Net Benefits N(Q)	(5) Marginal Benefit MB(Q)	(6) Marginal Cost MC(Q)	(7) Marginal Net Benefit MNB(Q)
Given	Given	Given	(2) − (3)	Δ(2)	Δ(3)	Δ(4) or (5) − (6)
0	0	0	0	—	—	—
1	90	10	80	90	10	80
2	170	30	140	80	20	60
3	240	60	180	70	30	40
4	300	100	200	60	40	20
5	350	150	200	50	50	0
6	390	210	180	40	60	−20
7	420	280	140	30	70	−40
8	440	360	80	20	80	−60
9	450	450	0	10	90	−80
10	450	550	−100	0	100	−100

Suppose the objective of the manager is to maximize the net benefits

$$N(Q) = B(Q) - C(Q),$$

which represent the premium of total benefits over total costs of using Q units of the managerial control variable, Q. The net benefits—$N(Q)$—for our hypothetical example are given in column 4 of Table 1–1. Notice that the net benefits in column 4 are maximized when net benefits equal 200, which occurs when 5 units of Q are chosen by the manager.[3]

To illustrate the importance of marginal analysis in maximizing net benefits, it is useful to define a few terms. *Marginal benefit* refers to the additional benefits that arise by using an additional unit of the managerial control variable. For example, the marginal benefit of the first unit of Q is 90, since the first unit of Q increases total benefits from 0 to 90. The marginal benefit of the second unit of Q is 80, since increasing Q from 1 to 2 increases total benefits from 90 to 170. The marginal benefit of each unit of Q—$MB(Q)$—is presented in column 5 of Table 1–1.

marginal benefit
The change in total benefits arising from a change in the managerial control variable, Q.

---

[3]Actually, net benefits are equal to 200 for either 4 or 5 units of Q. This is due to the discrete nature of the data in the table, which restricts Q to be selected in one-unit increments. In the next section, we show that when Q can be selected in arbitrarily small increments (for example, when the firm can produce fractional gallons of soft drink), net benefits are maximized at a single level of Q. At this level of Q, marginal net benefits are equal to zero, which corresponds to 5 units of Q in Table 1–1.

marginal cost
The change in total costs arising from a change in the managerial control variable, *Q*.

Marginal cost, on the other hand, is the additional cost incurred by using an additional unit of the managerial control variable. Marginal costs—*MC(Q)*—are given in column 6 of Table 1–1. For example, the marginal cost of the first unit of *Q* is 10, since the first unit of *Q* increases total costs from 0 to 10. Similarly, the marginal cost of the second unit of *Q* is 20, since increasing *Q* from 1 to 2 increases total costs by 20 (costs rise from 10 to 30).

Finally, the *marginal net benefits* of *Q—MNB(Q)*—are the change in net benefits that arise from a one-unit change in *Q*. For example, by increasing *Q* from 0 to 1, net benefits rise from 0 to 80 in column 4 of Table 1–1 and thus the marginal net benefit of the first unit of *Q* is 80. By increasing *Q* from 1 to 2, net benefits increase from 80 to 140, so the marginal net benefits due to the second unit of *Q* is 60. Column 7 of Table 1–1 presents marginal net benefits for our hypothetical example. Notice that marginal net benefits may also be obtained as the difference between marginal benefits and marginal costs:

$$MNB(Q) = MB(Q) - MC(Q).$$

Inspection of Table 1–1 reveals a remarkable pattern in the columns. Notice that by using 5 units of *Q*, the manager ensures that net benefits are maximized. At the net-benefit-maximizing level of *Q* (5 units), the marginal net benefits of *Q* are zero. Furthermore, at the net-benefit-maximizing level of *Q* (5 units), marginal benefits equal marginal costs (both are equal to 50 in this example). There is an important reason why *MB* = *MC* at the level of *Q* that maximizes net benefits: So long as marginal benefits exceed marginal costs, an increase in *Q* adds more to total benefits than it does to total costs. In this instance, it is profitable for the manager to increase the use of the managerial control variable. Expressed differently, when marginal benefits exceed marginal costs, the net benefits of increasing the use of *Q* are positive; by using more *Q*, net benefits increase. For example, consider the use of 1 unit of *Q* in Table 1–1. By increasing *Q* to 2 units, total benefits increase by 80 and total costs increase by only 20. Increasing the use of *Q* from 1 to 2 units is profitable, because it adds more to total benefits than it does to total costs.

Principle

***

Marginal Principle
To maximize net benefits, the manager should increase the managerial control variable to the point where marginal benefits equal marginal costs. This level of the managerial control variable corresponds to the level at which marginal net benefits are zero; nothing more can be gained by further changes in that variable.

***

Notice in Table 1–1 that while 5 units of *Q* maximizes net benefits, it does not maximize total benefits. In fact, total benefits are maximized at 10 units of *Q*, where marginal benefits are zero. The reason the net-benefit-maximizing level of Q is less than the level of Q that maximizes total benefits is that there are costs associated with achieving more total benefits. The goal of maximizing net benefits takes costs into account, while the goal of maximizing total benefits does not. In the context of a firm, maximizing total benefits is equivalent to maximizing revenues without regard for costs. In the context of studying for an exam, maximizing total benefits requires studying until you maximize your grade, regardless of how much it costs you to spend that much time studying.

Continuous Decisions

The basic principles for making decisions when the control variable is discrete also apply to the case of a continuous control variable. The basic relationships in Table 1–1 are depicted graphically in Figure 1–1. The top panel of the figure presents the total benefits and total costs of using different levels of Q under the assumption that Q is infinitely divisible (instead of allowing the firm to produce soft drinks only in one-gallon containers as in Table 1–1, it can now produce fractional units). The middle panel presents the net benefits, $B(Q) - C(Q)$, and represent the vertical difference between B and C in the top panel. Notice that net benefits are maximized at the point where the difference between $B(Q)$ and $C(Q)$ is the greatest in the top panel. Furthermore, the slope of $B(Q)$ is $\Delta B/\Delta Q$, or marginal benefit, and the slope of $C(Q)$ is $\Delta C/\Delta Q$, or marginal cost. The slopes of the total benefits curve and total cost curves are equal when net benefits are maximized. This is just another way of saying that when net benefits are maximized, $MB = MC$.

Principle

Marginal Value Curves Are the Slopes of Total Value Curves

When the control variable is infinitely divisible, the slope of a total value curve at a given point is the marginal value at that point. In particular, the slope of the total benefit curve at a given Q is the marginal benefit of that level of Q. The slope of the total cost curve at a given Q is the marginal cost of that level of Q. The slope of the net benefit curve at a given Q is the marginal net benefit of that level of Q.

A Calculus Alternative

Since the slope of a function is the derivative of that function, the preceding principle means that the derivative of a given function is the marginal value of that function. For example,

$$MB = \frac{dB(Q)}{dQ}$$

$$MC = \frac{dC(Q)}{dQ}$$

$$MNB = \frac{dN(Q)}{dQ}.$$

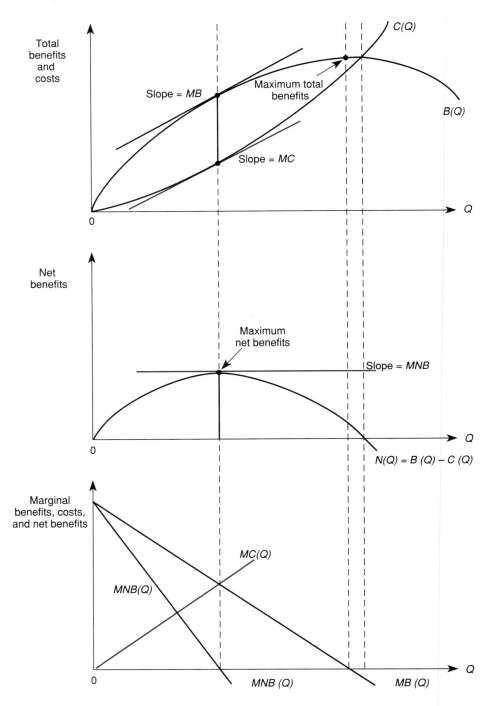

The bottom panel of Figure 1–1 depicts the marginal benefits, marginal costs, and marginal net benefits. At the level of Q where the marginal benefit curve intersects the marginal cost curve, marginal net benefits are zero. That level of Q maximizes net benefits.

DEMONSTRATION PROBLEM 1–3

An engineering firm recently conducted a study to determine its benefit and cost structure. The results of the study are as follows:

$$B(Y) = 300\,Y - 6Y^2 \qquad\qquad (1\text{–}6)$$

$$C(Y) = 4Y^2, \qquad\qquad (1\text{–}7)$$

so that $MB = 300 - 12Y$ and $MC = 8Y$.[4] The manager has been asked to determine the maximum level of net benefits and the level of Y that will yield that result.

Answer

Equating MB and MC yields $300 - 12Y = 8Y$. Solving this equation for Y reveals that the optimal level of Y is $Y^* = 15$. Plugging $Y^* = 15$ into the net benefit relation yields the maximum level of net benefits:

$$NB = 300(15) - (6)(15^2) - (4)(15^2) = 2{,}250.$$

Learning Managerial Economics

Before we continue our analysis of managerial economics, it is useful to provide some hints about how to study economics. Becoming proficient in economics is like learning to play music or ride a bicycle: The best way to learn economics is to practice, practice, and practice some more. Practicing managerial economics means practicing making decisions, and the best way to do this is to work and rework the problems presented in the text and at the end of each chapter. Before you can be effective at practicing, however, you must understand the language of economics.

The terminology in economics has two purposes. First, the definitions and formulas economists use are needed for precision. Economics deals with very complex issues, and much confusion can be avoided by using the

---

[4]If you know calculus, you should be able to derive MB and MC from Equations 1–6 and 1–7.

language economists have designed to break down complex issues into manageable components. Second, precise terminology helps practitioners of economics communicate more efficiently. It would be impossible to communicate if, like Humpty Dumpty, each of us made words mean whatever we wanted them to mean. However, the terminology is not an end in itself but simply a tool that makes it easier to communicate and analyze different economic situations.

Understanding the definitions used in economics is like knowing the difference between a whole note and a quarter note in music. Without such an understanding, it would be very difficult for anyone other than an extremely gifted musician to learn to play an instrument or to communicate to another musician how to play a new song. Given an understanding of the language of music, anyone who is willing to take the time to practice can make beautiful music. The same is true of economics: Anyone who is willing to learn the language of economics and take the time to practice making decisions can learn to be an effective manager.

Answering the Headline

Why was Ralph Barnes fired from his managerial post at Amcott? As the manager of the foreign language division, he probably relied on his marketing department for sales forecasts and on his legal department for advice on contract and copyright law. The information he obtained about future sales was indeed accurate, but apparently his legal department did not fully anticipate all of the legal ramifications of distributing Magicword. Sometimes, managers are given misinformation.

The real problem in this case, however, is that Ralph did not properly act on the information that was given to him. Ralph's plan was to generate $7 million per year in sales by sinking $20 million into Magicword. Assuming there were no other costs associated with the project, the projected net present value to Amcott of purchasing Magicword was

$$NPV = \frac{\$7,000,000}{(1 + .07)^1} + \frac{\$7,000,000}{(1 + .07)^2} + \frac{\$7,000,000}{(1 + .07)^3} - \$20,000,000$$

$$= -\$1,629,788,$$

which means that Ralph should have expected Amcott to lose over $1.6 million by purchasing Magicword.

Ralph Barnes was probably not fired because of the mistakes of his legal department but was fired for his managerial ineptness. The lawsuit publicized to Amcott's shareholders, among others, that Ralph Barnes was not properly processing information given to him: He did not recognize the time value of money.

Key Terms and Concepts

accounting cost
accounting profits
constraints
consumer–producer rivalry
economic profits
economics
explicit cost
future value (FV)
goals
implicit cost
manager

managerial economics
marginal cost
marginal benefit
marginal net benefit
net present value (NPV)
opportunity cost
present value (PV)
producer–producer rivalry
time value of money
value of a firm

Problems

1. You are the manager of a Fortune 500 hotel chain and must decide where to locate a new hotel. Based on tax considerations, your accounting department suggests that Atlantic City is the best choice, followed closely by Las Vegas. In particular, your current year tax savings from locating in Atlantic City are $4 million but only $3 million in Las Vegas. Your marketing department, on the other hand, has provided you sales estimates that suggest that the present value of the gross (of tax) operating profits from locating in Atlantic City are only $10 million but are $14 million for Las Vegas. It will cost $14 million to build the hotel in either location. Ignoring all other considerations, where should you build the hotel? What are your firm's economic profits if you locate the hotel in Atlantic City?

2. You are the manager of a firm that plans to expand the human resource base of its operations by hiring additional business school graduates over the next few years. You recently read an article in *The Wall Street Journal* that reports that enrollments in business schools have declined, as students are moving into the "hard sciences." That same article reports that the shakeup of upper-management is over at U.S. firms, and that over the next decade there will be a nationwide surge in the demand for MBA's. How will these events affect your firm's ability to expand its own base of MBA's?

3. You have just been hired as a consultant to help a firm to decide which of three options to take to maximize the value of the firm over the next three years. The following table shows year-end profits for each option. Interest rates are expected to be stable at 8 percent over the next three years.

Option	Profits in Year 1	Profits in Year 2	Profits in Year 3
A	$70,000	$ 80,000	$ 90,000
B	$50,000	$ 90,000	$100,000
C	$30,000	$100,000	$115,000

    a. Discuss the differences in the profits associated with each option. Provide an example of real-world options that might generate such profit streams.

    b. Which option has the greatest present value?

4. A potential entrepreneur is trying to decide whether to open a new health spa. She presently makes $35,000 per year as an aerobics instructor and will have to give up this job if she opens the new spa. If she chooses to open the spa, it will cost her $200,000 per year in rent and other operating expenses.

    a. What are her accounting costs?

    b. What are her opportunity costs?

    c. How much would she need to make in revenues to earn positive accounting profits? Positive economic profits?

5. You are the manager of a firm that specializes in selling exotic animals to zoos around the world. Your goal is to determine the number of baby zebras (Z) that must be born on your firm's farm each month in order to maximize profits. The total benefits (revenues) and costs to your firm of producing various quantities of zebras is given in the first three columns of the table below. Based on this scenario, complete the table and answer the accompanying questions:

(1) Control Variable Z	(2) Total Benefits $B(Z)$	(3) Total Costs $C(Z)$	(4) Net Benefits $N(Z)$	(5) Marginal Benefit $MB(Z)$	(6) Marginal Cost $MC(Z)$	(7) Marginal Net Benefit $MNB(Z)$
0	0	0		—	—	—
1	200	10				
2	380	30				
3	540	60				
4	680	100				
5	800	150				
6	900	210				
7	980	280				
8	1,040	360				
9	1,080	450				
10	1,100	550				

    a. What level of zebra births maximizes net benefits?

    b. What is the relation between marginal benefit and marginal cost at this level of *Z*?

    c. Graph the total cost and total benefit curves.

    d. On another graph, plot the points for the marginal cost, marginal benefit, and marginal net benefit.

    e. Show how the two graphs relate to each other.

6. A recent survey of new graduates in High Tech Cauldron Coalescence (HTCC) revealed that every graduate had at least two job offers and the average offer was $100,000 per year. With the release of this information, what do you expect to see happen to the number of HTCC majors? What do you expect to happen to salaries in the HTCC field in 10 years? Why?

7. A new manager recently was given an assignment to create two possible wage schemes for a design firm. The manager came up with the following packages: (1) Each employee will start at $15 per hour and will work eight hours per day; (2) each employee will receive $8 per hour and one-tenth of 1 percent of profits (expected profits are $80,000 per day if everyone puts out maximum effort). Which program will motivate the employees more? Which program would you choose? Why?

8. Your firm's research department has estimated your total revenues to be $R(Q) = 3,000Q - 8Q^2$ and your total costs to be $C(Q) = 100 + 2Q^2$.[5] (If you do not know calculus, you may peek at footnote 5 to get the expression for *MB* and *MC*. Given the *MB* and *MC* relations, you should be able to work this problem.)

    a. What level of *Q* maximizes net benefits?

    b. What is marginal benefit at this level of *Q*?

    c. What is marginal cost at this level of *Q*?

    d. What is the maximum level of net benefits?

    e. What is another word for *net benefits* in this example?

9. A major U.S. Airline offers a one-year membership in its Air Club for $125, a three-year membership for $300, and a lifetime membership for $1,250.

    a. Assuming the interest rate is 5 percent, how long would you have to live for the lifetime membership to be a good deal?

    b. If you expect to live forever, what would the interest rate have to be for the lifetime membership to be a good buy? (Hint: Use Equation 1–4 on page 17.)

10. Suppose that in Problem 9, the interest rate is 5 percent but you expect the airline to *decrease* annual membership fees by 10 percent per year. Does it pay to buy a three-year membership for $300, or should you wait and pay your dues annually?

---

[5]$MB = 3,000 - 16Q$ and $MC = 4Q$.

11. Delta Software earned $10 million this year. Suppose the growth rate of Delta's profits and the interest rate are both constant and Delta will be in business forever. Determine the value of Delta Software when
    a. The interest rate is 10 percent and profits grow by 4 percent per year.
    b. The interest rate is 10 percent and profits grow by 0 percent per year.
    c. The interest rate is 10 percent and profits decline by 4 percent per year.
    d. The interest rate is 10 percent and profits grow by 12 percent per year. (This part of the question is tricky.)

12. AMS recently instituted an in-house recycling program. The benefits of this program include not only the benefits to the environment of recycling but also the goodwill generated by AMS's leadership in this area. The costs of recycling include all of the energy, labor, and space required to do the recycling. Suppose these benefits and costs are given by $B(Q) = 100\,Q - 2Q^2$ and $C(Q) = 2Q$.[6] (If you do not know calculus, you may peek at footnote 6 to get the expression for *MB* and *MC*. Given the *MB* and *MC* relations, you should be able to work this problem.)
    a. What level of Q maximizes the total benefits of recycling?
    b. What level of Q minimizes the total costs of recycling?
    c. What level of Q maximizes the net benefits of recycling?
    d. What level of recycling is optimal? Why?

13. You are a strong advocate for a one-year investment project that would cost your firm $10,000 today, but generate virtually certain earnings of $15,000 at year-end. Those in your firm's financial group concur that the investment is virtually risk-free, but nonetheless your boss is concerned about the firm's cash flow problems. In fact, the problems are so severe that the firm's bank currently charges it 20 percent on one-year loans. Convince your boss to undertake the project.

14. Individuals who choose to attend school have made a decision to invest in human capital. Use the terminology of net present value analysis to explain why you are attending school.

15. In 1995 a $50 million major renovation project of the 19-year-old Seattle Kingdome was completed nearly $18 million over the initial budget. Several million dollars in other expenses were incurred during the renovation phase, including payments to the Seattle Seahawks football team and the Mariners baseball team for revenue they lost by not being able to play in the Kingdome. If you were on the city council, what information would you have needed to determine whether the renovation project was a sound investment?

---

[6]$MB = 100 - 4Q$, and $MC = 2$.

Selected Readings

Anders, Gary C., Ohta, Hiroshi, and Sailors, Joel, "A Note on the Marginal Efficiency of Investment and Related Concepts." *Journal of Economic Studies* 17(2), 1990, pp. 50–57.

Clark, Gregory, "Factory Discipline." *Journal of Economic History* 54(1), March 1994, pp. 128–63.

Fizel, John L. and Nunnikhoven, Thomas S., "Technical Efficiency of For-profit and Non-profit Nursing Homes." *Managerial and Decision Economics* 13(5), Sept. Oct. 1992, pp. 429–39.

Gifford, Sharon, "Allocation of Entrepreneurial Attention." *Journal of Economic Behavior and Organization* 19(3), December 1992, pp. 265–84.

McNamara, John R., "The Economics of Decision Making in the New Manufacturing Firm." *Managerial and Decision Economics* 13(4), July Aug. 1992, pp. 287–93.

Mercuro, Nicholas, Sourbis, Haralambos, and Whitney, Gerald, "Ownership Structure, Value of the Firm, and the Bargaining Power of the Manager." *Southern Economic Journal* 59(2), October 1992, pp. 273–83.

Parsons, George R. and Wu, Yangru, "The Opportunity Cost of Coastal Land-Use Controls: An Empirical Analysis." *Land Economics* 67, Aug. 1991, pp. 308–16.

Phillips, Owen R., Battalio, Raymond C., and Kogut, Carl A., "Sunk Costs and Opportunity Costs in Valuation and Bidding." *Southern Economic Journal* 58, July 1991, pp. 112–28.

Pindyck, Robert S., "Irreversibility, Uncertainty, and Investment." *The Journal of Economic Literature* 29, Sept. 1991, pp. 1110–48.

APPENDIX
THE CALCULUS OF MAXIMIZING NET BENEFITS

This appendix provides a calculus-based derivation of the important rule that to maximize net benefits, a manager must equate marginal benefits and marginal costs.

Let $B(Q)$ denote the benefits of using Q units of the managerial control variable, and let $C(Q)$ denote the corresponding costs. The net benefits are $N(Q) = B(Q) - C(Q)$. The objective is to choose Q so as to maximize

$$N(Q) = B(Q) - C(Q).$$

The first-order condition for a maximum is

$$\frac{dN}{dQ} = \frac{dB}{dQ} - \frac{dC}{dQ} = 0.$$

But

$$\frac{dB}{dQ} = MB$$

is nothing more than marginal benefits, while

$$\frac{dC}{dQ} = MC$$

is simply marginal costs. Thus, the first-order condition for a maximum implies that

$$\frac{dB}{dQ} = \frac{dC}{dQ},$$

or $MB = MC$.

The second-order condition requires that the function $N(Q)$ be concave in Q or, in mathematical terms, that the second derivative of the net benefit function be negative:

$$\frac{d^2N}{dQ^2} = \frac{d^2B}{dQ^2} - \frac{d^2C}{dQ^2} < 0.$$

Notice that $d^2B/dQ^2 = d(MB)/dQ$, while $d^2C/dQ^2 = d(MC)/dQ$. Thus, the second-order condition may be rewritten as

$$\frac{d^2N}{dQ^2} = \frac{d(MB)}{dQ} - \frac{d(MC)}{dQ} < 0.$$

In other words, the slope of the marginal benefit curve must be less than the slope of the marginal cost curve.

DEMONSTRATION PROBLEM 1–4

Suppose $B(Q) = 10Q - 2Q^2$ and $C(Q) = 2 + Q^2$. What value of the managerial control variable, Q, maximizes net benefits?

Answer

Net benefits are

$$N(Q) = B(Q) - C(Q) = 10Q - 2Q^2 - 2 - Q^2.$$

Taking the derivative of $N(Q)$ and setting it equal to zero gives

$$\frac{dN}{dQ} = 10 - 4Q - 2Q = 0$$

Solving for Q gives $Q = 10/6$. To verify that this is indeed a maximum, we must check that the second derivative of $N(Q)$ is negative. But

$$\frac{d^2N}{dQ^2} = -4 - 2 = -6 < 0.$$

Therefore, $Q = 10/6$ is indeed a maximum.

Market Forces: Demand and Supply

President Proposes Hike in Minimum Wage

John Noble, owner and CEO of Employment Enterprises, arrives at the office and glances at the headline of the *Wall Street Journal* waiting on his desk. He recalls that the President vowed to raise the minimum wage in his State of the Union Address last month, and begins reading the article for the latest details:

> Today, the President proposed raising the minimum wage by 90 cents, from $4.25 to 5.15 per hour . . .

Employment Enterprises is a mid-sized job placement firm located in San Antonio. For a flat fee, Employment Enterprises provides unemployed workers with job training and then guarantees placement at businesses needing semiskilled workers. Currently, 97 percent of Employment Enterprises' revenues stem from those accepting jobs in the San Antonio area. The average worker receives $5.25 an hour, which is the national average for semiskilled workers. Due to the low unemployment rate in the area, however, it has experienced stagnant earnings growth over the past three years.

After reading the article, John grins. He picks up the phone and calls an old college classmate who is the owner of a packing firm in Chicago that relies heavily on semiskilled workers: "George, it looks like I'll be springing for our Super Bowl tickets next year!" Why?

Introduction

The purpose of this chapter is to enable managers to analyze scenarios such as the one posed in the opening headline. The chapter describes supply and

TABLE 2–1   The Demand Schedule for Jeans

Price of Jeans	Quantity of Jeans Sold	Average Consumer Income	Advertising Expenditure	Average Price of Shirts
$ 0	80,000	$25,000	$50,000	$20
5	70,000	25,000	50,000	20
10	60,000	25,000	50,000	20
15	50,000	25,000	50,000	20
20	40,000	25,000	50,000	20
25	30,000	25,000	50,000	20
30	20,000	25,000	50,000	20
35	10,000	25,000	50,000	20
40	0	25,000	50,000	20

demand, which are the driving forces behind a market economy such as that in the United States.

The model of supply and demand constitutes one of the most important managerial tools because it assists the manager in predicting changes in product and input prices. For those who have taken a principles-level course in economics, some parts of this chapter will be a review. However, make sure you have complete mastery of the tools of supply and demand. The rest of this book will assume you have a thorough working knowledge of the material in this chapter.

Demand

Suppose Levi Strauss desires information about the impact of its pricing decisions on the demand for its jeans. To obtain this information, it might engage in market research to determine how many pairs of jeans consumers would purchase each year at alternative prices. The numbers from such a market survey would look something like those in Table 2–1. The market research reveals that if jeans were priced at $10 per pair, 60,000 pairs of jeans would be sold per year; at $30 per pair, 20,000 pairs of jeans would be sold annually.

Notice that the only difference among the rows in Table 2–1 is the change in the price of jeans and in the quantity of jeans sold. Everything else that might influence buyer decisions, such as consumer income, advertising, and the prices of other goods such as shirts, is held constant. In effect, the market survey does not ask consumers how much they would buy at alternative levels of income or advertising; it simply seeks to determine how much would be purchased at alternative prices. The market research reveals that, holding all other things constant, the quantity of jeans

FIGURE 2–1

The demand curve

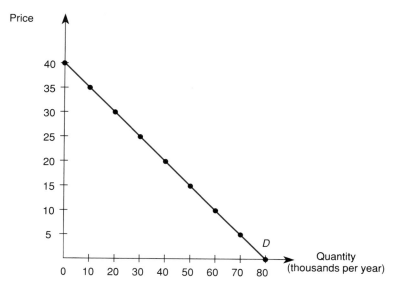

market demand curve
A curve indicating the total quantity of a good all consumers are willing and able to purchase at each possible price, holding the prices of related goods, income, advertising, and other variables constant.

change in quantity demanded
Changes in the price of a good lead to a change in the quantity demanded of that good. This corresponds to a movement along a given demand curve.

change in demand
Changes in variables other than the price of a good, such as income or the price of another good, lead to a change in demand. This corresponds to a shift of the entire demand curve.

consumers are willing and able to purchase goes down as the price rises. This fundamental economic principle is known as the *law of demand:* price and quantity demanded are inversely related. That is, as the price of a good rises (falls) and all other things remain constant, the quantity demanded of the good falls (rises).

Figure 2–1 plots the data in Table 2–1. The straight line, called the *market demand curve,* interpolates the quantities consumers would be willing and able to purchase at prices not explicitly dealt with in the market research. Notice that the line is downward sloping, which reflects the law of demand, and that all other factors that influence demand are held constant at each point on the line.

Demand Shifters

Economists recognize that variables other than the price of a good influence demand. For example, the number of pairs of jeans individuals are willing and financially able to buy also depends on the prices of other goods, such as shirts, consumer income, advertising expenditures, and so on. Variables other than the price of a good that influence demand are known as *demand shifters.*

When we graph the demand curve for good *X,* we hold everything but the price of *X* constant. A representative demand curve is given by D^0 in Figure 2–2. The movement along a demand curve, such as the movement from *A* to *B,* is called a *change in quantity demanded.* Whenever advertising, income, or the price of related goods change, it leads to a *change in demand;* the position of the entire demand curve shifts. A rightward shift

FIGURE 2–2

Changes in demand

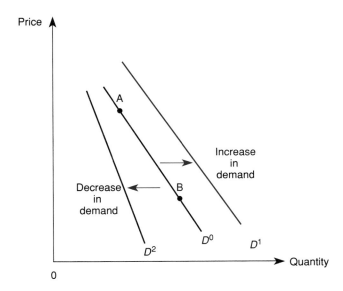

in the demand curve is called an *increase in demand,* since more of the good is demanded at each price. A leftward shift in the demand curve is called a *decrease in demand.*

Now that we understand the general distinction between a shift in a demand curve and a movement along a demand curve, it is useful to explain how five demand shifters—consumer income, prices of related goods, advertising and consumer tastes, population, and consumer expectations—affect demand.

Income

Because income affects the ability of consumers to purchase a good, changes in income affect how much consumers will buy at any price. In graphical terms, a change in income shifts the entire demand curve. Whether an increase in income shifts the demand curve to the right or to the left depends on the nature of consumer consumption patterns. Accordingly, economists distinguish between two types of goods: normal and inferior goods.

A good whose demand increases (shifts to the right) when consumer incomes rise is called a *normal good.* Normal goods may include goods such as steak, airline travel, and designer jeans: As income goes up, consumers typically buy more of these goods at any given price. Conversely, when consumers suffer a decline in income, the demand for a normal good will decrease (shift to the left).

In some instances, an increase in income reduces the demand for a good. Economists refer to such a good as an *inferior good.* Bologna, bus travel, and "generic" jeans are possible examples of inferior goods. As in-

normal good
A good for which an increase (decrease) in income leads to an increase (decrease) in the demand for that good.

inferior good
A good for which an increase (decrease) in income leads to a decrease (increase) in the demand for that good.

Inside Business 2–1

Wal-Mart and Recessions

In late 1989 and early 1990, most retailers in the United States were having severe problems because of falling incomes during the recession. But not Wal-Mart. Read the following excerpt from *Forbes* and see if you can figure out why.

If ever there was a recession-proof retailer, Wal-Mart Stores, Inc., is it. Good times or bad, it grows rapidly.

Built by folksy billionaire Sam Walton, Wal-Mart has seen its sales mushroom at a compound annual rate of better than 36% in each of the past ten years. Last year sales approached $26 billion. Wal-Mart often gains market share during recessions, its executives claim, because it wins customers who defect from more expensive department and specialty stores.

"There's far more opportunity ahead of us than behind us," says David Glass, Wal-Mart's president and chief executive officer. "This company is geared to grow."

What's the Wal-Mart edge? Nothing more than hard work and clear thinking. Top executives work six and seven days a week, spending more than half their time visiting stores. Important decisions, such as what items to display in desirable spots, are often delegated to employees closest to the customer, the clerks on the sales floor. The network of 1,355 Wal-Mart stores (plus 120 Sam's Wholesale Club warehouse outlets and 3 giant Hyper-Mart USA food

and discount stores) is held together by the industry's best computer and communications systems.

Thus, the company's selling, general, and administrative costs, at just 16% of sales, are 10 percentage points or more below those of most competitors. That allows it to offer prices that are often far lower than competing discounters'. And Wal-Mart works harder to keep its old stores fresher than any other retailer, doing major remodeling at 70 stores a year. That's why sales gains at Wal-Mart stores open at least a year, recently around 10%, are usually nearly double the industry same store average.

Early in this article, we find that Wal-Mart experienced tremendous growth during 1989–1990. Part of the growth is due to greater consumer awareness of Wal-Mart, which shifts demand to the right. Interestingly, Wal-Mart does especially well during recessions. How can this be?

Its image makes Wal-Mart an inferior good to a large segment of the market. This does not mean that Wal-Mart sells poor-quality products or provides inferior service. It simply means that when income declines due to a recession, the demand for Wal-Mart increases.

Source: Forbes, January 8, 1990, p. 194. Reprinted by permission of FORBES magazine. © Forbes Inc., 1990.

come goes up, consumers typically consume less of these goods at each price. It is important to point out that by calling such goods *inferior,* we do not imply that they are of poor quality; we use this term simply to define products that consumers purchase less of when their incomes rise, and purchase more of when their incomes fall.

Prices of Related Goods
Changes in the prices of related goods generally shift the demand curve for a good. For example, if the price of a Coke increases, most consumers will begin to substitute Pepsi, because the relative price of Coke is higher than

before. As more and more consumers substitute Pepsi for Coke, the quantity of Pepsi demanded at each price will tend to increase. In effect, an increase in the price of Coke increases the demand for Pepsi. This is illustrated by a shift in the demand for Pepsi to the right. Goods that interact in this way are known as *substitutes*.

substitutes
Goods for which an increase (decrease) in the price of one good leads to an increase (decrease) in the demand for the other good.

Many pairs of goods readily come to mind when we think of substitutes: chicken and beef, cars and trucks, raincoats and umbrellas. Such pairs of goods are substitutes for most consumers. However, substitutes need not serve the same function; for example, automobiles and housing could be substitutes. Goods are substitutes when an increase in the price of one good increases the demand for the other good.

complements
Goods for which an increase (decrease) in the price of one good leads to a decrease (increase) in the demand for the other good.

Not all goods are substitutes; in fact, an increase in the price of a good such as computer software may lead consumers to purchase fewer computers at each price. Goods that interact in this manner are called *complements*. Beer and pretzels are another example of complementary goods. If the price of beer increased, most beer drinkers would decrease their consumption of pretzels. Notice that when good X is a complement to good Y, a reduction in the price of Y actually increases (shifts to the right) the demand for good X. More of good X is purchased at each price due to the reduction in the price of the complement, good Y.

Advertising and Consumer Tastes

Another variable that is held constant when drawing a given demand curve is the level of advertising. An increase in advertising shifts the demand curve to the right, from D^1 to D^2, as in Figure 2–3. Notice that the impact

FIGURE 2–3

Advertising and the demand for clothing

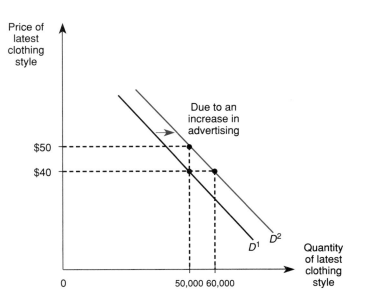

of advertising on demand can be interpreted in two ways. Under the initial demand curve, D^1, consumers would buy 50,000 units of high-style clothing per month when the price is $40. After the advertising, consumers would buy 60,000 units of the good when the price is $40. Alternatively, when demand is D^1, consumers will pay a price of $40 when 50,000 units are available. Advertising shifts the demand curve to D^2, so consumers will pay a higher price—$50—for 50,000 units.

Why does advertising shift demand to the right? Advertising often provides consumers with information about the existence or quality of a product, which in turn induces more consumers to buy the product. These types of advertising messages are known as *informative advertising.*

Advertising can also influence demand by altering the underlying tastes of consumers. For example, advertising that promotes the latest fad in clothing may increase the demand for a specific fashion item by making consumers perceive it as "the" thing to buy. These types of advertising messages are known as *persuasive advertising.*

Population
The market demand for a product is also influenced by changes in the size and composition of the population. Generally, as the population rises, more and more individuals wish to buy a given product, and this has the effect of shifting the demand curve to the right. Over the twentieth century, the demand curve for food products has shifted to the right considerably with the increasing population.

It is important to note that changes in the composition of the population can also affect the demand for a product. To the extent that middle-aged consumers desire different types of products than retirees, an increase in the number of consumers in the 30- to 40-year-old age bracket will increase the demand for products like real estate. Similarly, as a greater proportion of the population ages, the demand for medical services will tend to increase.

Consumer Expectations
Consumer expectations also can influence the position of the demand curve for a product. For example, if consumers expect the price of automobiles to be significantly higher next year, the demand for automobiles today will increase. In effect, buying a car today is a substitute for buying a car next year. If consumers expect future prices to be higher, they will substitute current purchases for future purchases. This type of consumer behavior often is referred to as *stockpiling* and generally occurs when products are durable in nature. The current demand for a perishable product such as bananas generally is not affected by expectations of higher future prices.

Other Factors
In concluding our list of demand shifters, we simply note that any variable that affects the willingness or ability of consumers to purchase a particular

good is a potential demand shifter. Health scares affect the demand for cigarettes. The birth of a baby affects the demand for diapers.

The Demand Function

By now you should understand the factors that affect demand and how to use graphs to illustrate those influences. The final step in our analysis of the demand side of the market is to show that all the factors that influence demand may be summarized in what economists refer to as a *demand function*.

demand function
A function that describes how much of a good will be purchased at alternative prices of that good and related goods, alternative income levels, and alternative values of other variables affecting demand.

The demand function for good X describes how much X will be purchased at alternative prices of X and related goods, alternative levels of income, and alternative values of other variables that affect demand. Formally, let Q_x^d represent the quantity consumed of good X, P_x the price of good X, P_y the price of a related good, M income, and H the value of any other variable that affects demand, such as the level of advertising, the size of the population, or consumer expectations. Then the demand function for good X may be written as

$$Q_x^d = f(P_x, P_y, M, H).$$

Thus, the demand function explicitly recognizes that the quantity of a good consumed depends on its price and on demand shifters. Different products will have demand functions of different forms. One very simple but useful form is the linear representation of the demand function: Demand is *linear* if Q_x^d is a linear function of prices, income, and other variables that influence demand. The following equation is an example of a linear demand function:

linear demand function
A representation of the demand function in which the demand for a given good is a linear function of prices, income levels, and other variables influencing demand.

$$Q_x^d = \alpha_0 + \alpha_x P_x + \alpha_y P_y + \alpha_M M + \alpha_H H.$$

The α_is are fixed numbers that are typically provided to the manager by the firm's research department or an economic consultant. (Chapter 3 provides an overview of the statistical techniques used to obtain these numbers.)

By the law of demand, an increase in P_x leads to a decrease in the quantity demanded of good X. This means that $\alpha_x < 0$. The sign of α_y will be positive or negative depending on whether goods X and Y are substitutes or complements. If α_y is a positive number, an increase in the price of good Y will lead to an increase in the consumption of good X; therefore, good X is a substitute for good Y. If α_y is a negative number, an increase in the price of good Y will lead to a decrease in the consumption of good X; hence, good X is a complement to good Y. The sign of α_M also can be positive or negative depending on whether X is a normal or an inferior good. If α_M is a positive number, an increase in income (M) will lead to an increase in the consumption of good X, and good X is a normal good. If α_M is a negative number, an increase in income will lead to a decrease in the consumption of good X, and good X is an inferior good.

DEMONSTRATION PROBLEM 2–1

An economic consultant for X Corp. recently provided the firm's marketing manager with this estimate of the demand function for the firm's product:

$$Q_x^d = 12,000 - 3P_x + 4P_y - 1M + 2A_x,$$

where Q_x^d represents the amount consumed of good X, P_x is the price of good X, P_y is the price of good Y, M is income, and A_x represents the amount of advertising spent on good X. Suppose good X sells for $200 per unit, good Y sells for $15 per unit, the company utilizes 2,000 units of advertising, and consumer income is $10,000. How much of good X do consumers purchase? Are goods X and Y substitutes or complements? Is good X a normal or an inferior good?

Answer

To find out how much of good X consumers will purchase, we substitute the given values of prices, income, and advertising into the demand equation to get

$$Q_x^d = 12,000 - 3(200) + 4(15) - 1(10,000) + 2(2,000).$$

Adding up the numbers, we find that the total consumption of X is 5,460 units. Since the coefficient of P_y in the demand equation is $4 > 0$, we know that a $1 increase in the price of good Y will increase the consumption of good X by 4 units. Thus, goods X and Y are substitutes. Since the coefficient of M in the demand equation is $-1 < 0$, we know that a $1 increase in income will decrease the consumption of good X by 1 unit. Thus, good X *is* an inferior good.

The information summarized in a demand function can be used to graph a demand curve. Since a demand curve is the relation between price and quantity, a representative demand curve holds everything but price constant. This means one may obtain the formula for a demand curve by inserting given values of the demand shifters into the demand function, but leaving P_x in the equation to allow for various values. If we do this for the demand function in Demonstration Problem 2–1 (where $P_y = \$15$, $M = \$10,000$, and $A_x = 2,000$), we get

$$Q_x^d = 12,000 - 3P_x + 4(15) - 1(10,000) + 2(2,000).$$

which simplifies to

$$Q_x^d = 6,060 - 3P_x. \qquad (2-1)$$

Because we usually graph this relation with the price of the good on the vertical axis, it is useful to represent Equation 2–1 with price on the left-

FIGURE 2–4

Graphing the inverse demand function

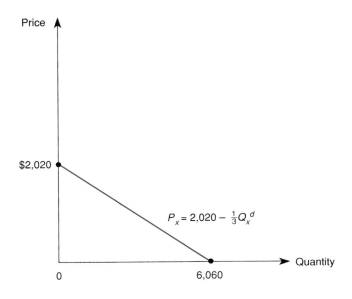

hand side and everything else on the right-hand side. This relation is called an *inverse demand function*. For this example, the inverse demand function is

$$P_x = 2,020 - (1/3)Q_x^d.$$

It reveals how much consumers are willing and able to pay for each additional unit of good *X*. This demand curve is graphed in Figure 2–4.

Consumer Surplus

The demand curve reveals the amount of a product consumers will buy at a given price. Alternatively, the demand curve indicates the price a consumer (or, in the case of a market demand curve, a group of consumers) would be willing to pay for each additional unit of a good. For example, the demand curve in Figure 2–5(a) indicates that a total amount of 4 units will be purchased when the price is $1. Alternatively, if 4 units are available, consumers will pay $1 for another unit of the good.

Notice that the amount a consumer is willing to pay for an additional unit of a good falls as more of the good is consumed. For instance, in Figure 2–5(a) the consumer is willing to pay $4 for the first unit of *X*, $3 for the second unit, $2 for the third unit, and $1 for the fourth unit.

The fact that the amount a consumer is willing to pay for additional units of a good declines as more is purchased can be easily explained. Imagine you are in the desert and are extremely thirsty. You would pay handsomely for a liter of water. Your thirst partially quenched, you would be

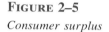

FIGURE 2–5

Consumer surplus

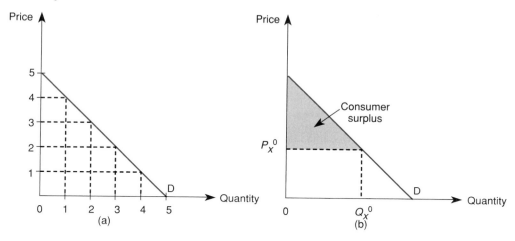

willing to pay less for a second liter and even less for a third. You value each additional unit of the good—water—less than you do the previous units.

With this in mind, suppose a consumer with the demand function in Figure 2–5(a) is charged a price of $1 for good X. The consumer's quantity demanded at this price is 4 units, so she would spend $1 \times 4 = \$4$ for the 4 units. She gets to buy each unit at a price of $1, even though she values each unit much more than $1. (The first unit is worth $4 to her, the second $3, and so on.) Effectively, by buying 4 units of the good at a price of $1 each, the consumer receives more in value than she is required to pay for the goods. This "extra" value is known as *consumer surplus*—the value consumers get from a good but do not have to pay for. This concept is important to managers because it tells how much extra money consumers would be willing to pay for a given amount of a purchased product.

consumer surplus
The value consumers get from a good but do not have to pay for.

Geometrically, consumer surplus is the area above the price paid for a good but below the demand curve. For instance, the shaded triangle in Figure 2–5(b) illustrates the consumer surplus of a consumer who buys Q_x^0 units at a price of P_x^0. To see why, recall that each point on the demand curve indicates the value to the consumer of another unit of the good. The difference between each price on the demand curve and the price P_x^0 paid represents surplus (the value the consumer receives but does not have to pay for). When we add up the "surpluses" received for each unit between 0 and Q_x^0 (this sum equals the shaded region), we obtain the consumer surplus associated with purchasing Q_x^0 units at a price of P_x^0 each.

The notion of consumer surplus can be used by managers to determine the total amount consumers would be willing to pay for a bundle of goods.

While this will be discussed in detail in Chapter 11 where we examine pricing strategies, we illustrate the basic idea in the following problem.

DEMONSTRATION PROBLEM 2–2

Grapes Undergarments produces underwear and faces a demand curve for its product like that in Figure 2–5(a). The company's manager is considering selling its product in packages of three. What is the most a typical consumer would pay for a package of three undergarments?

Answer

If the firm prices the underwear at $2, it will sell 3 units and earn revenue of $6. But then consumers will receive a positive consumer surplus. Since the area of the consumer surplus triangle is 1/2 (base × height), we see the consumer surplus is 1/2 (3 × 3) = $4.50. Thus, if the firm charges $10.50 for a package of 3 undergarments, consumer surplus will be zero and the firm will extract all of the consumer surplus associated with 3 units of underwear.

Supply

market supply curve
A curve indicating the total quantity of a good that all producers in a competitive market would produce at each price, holding input prices, technology, and other variables affecting supply constant.

In the previous section we focused on the demand side of the market which represents half of the forces that determine price in a market. The other determinant is market supply. In a competitive market there are many producers, each producing a similar product. The *market supply curve* summarizes the total quantity all producers are willing and able to produce at alternative prices holding other factors that affect supply constant.

While the market supply of a good generally depends on many things, when we graph a supply curve we hold everything but the price of the good constant. The movement along a supply curve, such as the one from A to B in Figure 2–6, is called a *change in quantity supplied*. The fact that the market supply curve slopes upward reflects the *law of supply:* As the price of a good rises (falls) and other things remain constant, the quantity supplied of the good rises (falls). Producers are willing to produce more output when the price is high than when it is low.

change in quantity supplied
Changes in the price of a good lead to a change in the quantity supplied of that good. This corresponds to a movement along a given supply curve.

Supply Shifters

Variables that affect the position of the supply curve are called *supply shifters*, and include the prices of inputs, the level of technology, the number of firms in the market, taxes, and producer expectations. Whenever one or

FIGURE 2–6

Changes in supply

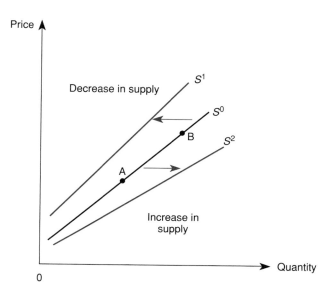

change in supply
Changes in variables
other than the price
of a good, such as
input prices or
technological
advances, lead to a
change in supply.
This corresponds to
a shift of the entire
supply curve.

more of these variables changes, the position of the entire supply curve shifts. Such a shift is known as a *change in supply*. The shift from S^0 to S^2 in Figure 2–6 is called an *increase in supply* since producers sell more output at each given price. The shift from S^0 to S^1 in Figure 2–6 represents a *decrease in supply* since producers sell less of the product at each price.

Input Prices
The supply curve reveals how much producers are willing to produce at alternative prices. As production costs change, the willingness of producers to produce output at a given price changes. In particular, as the price of an input rises, producers are willing to produce less output at each given price. This decrease in supply is depicted as a leftward shift in the supply curve.

Technology or Government Regulations
Technological changes and changes in government regulations also can affect the position of the supply curve. Changes that make it possible to produce a given output at a lower cost, such as the ones highlighted in Inside Business 2–2, have the effect of increasing supply. Conversely, natural disasters that destroy existing technology and government regulations such as emissions standards that have an adverse affect on businesses shift the supply curve to the left.

Number of Firms
The number of firms in an industry affects the position of the supply curve. As additional firms enter an industry, more and more output is available at

Inside Business 2–2

NAFTA and the Supply Curve

On January 1, 1994, an historic trade agreement between the United States, Canada, and Mexico went into force. This agreement, called the North American Free Trade Agreement (NAFTA), has provisions that are designed to reduce the cost of producing goods both at home and abroad, and thus increase the North American supply of goods and services. Key provisions of NAFTA are highlighted below:

- Phaseout of most tariffs and nontariff barriers in industrial products over 10 years, including textiles and apparel that have substantial regional content.
- Phaseout of tariffs and most nontariff barriers in agricultural products over 15 years.

- Investment rules ensuring national treatment, eliminating most performance requirements in all sectors, and reduced barriers to investment in the Mexican petrochemicals and financial services sectors.
- Liberalization of financial, land transportation, and telecommunications services markets.
- A dispute resolution mechanism.
- Protection of intellectual property rights.
- Funds for environmental cleanup and community adjustment along the border.

Source: *Economic Report of the President,* Washington, D.C.: U.S. Government Printing Office, February 1995, Pages 220–221.

each given price. This is reflected by a rightward shift in the supply curve. Similarly, as firms leave an industry, fewer units are sold at each price, and the supply decreases (shifts to the left).

Substitutes in Production

Many firms have technologies that are readily adaptable to several different products. For example, General Motors can convert a truck assembly plant into a car assembly plant by altering its production facilities. When the price of cars rises, General Motors can convert some of its truck assembly lines to car assembly lines to increase the quantity of cars supplied. This has the effect of shifting the truck supply curve to the left.

Taxes

The position of the supply curve is also affected by taxes. An *excise tax* is a tax on each unit of output sold, where the tax revenue is collected from the supplier. For example, suppose the government levies a tax of $.20 per gallon on gasoline. Since each supplier must now pay the government $.20 for each gallon of gasoline sold, each must receive an additional $.20 per gallon to be willing to supply the same quantity of gasoline as before the tax. An excise tax shifts the supply curve up by the amount of the tax, as in

FIGURE 2–7

A per unit (excise) tax

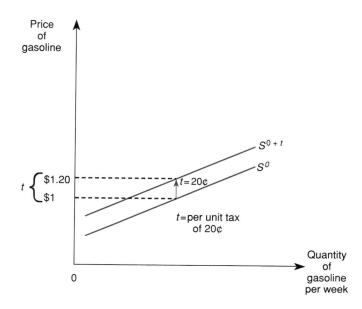

Figure 2–7. Note that at any given price, producers are willing to sell less gasoline after the tax than before. Thus, an excise tax has the effect of decreasing the supply of a good.

Another form of tax often used by a government agency is an ad valorem tax. *Ad valorem* literally means "according to the value." An *ad valorem tax* is a percentage tax; the sales tax is a well-known example. If the price of a good is $1 and a 10 percent ad valorem tax is attached to that good, the price after the tax is $1.10. Because an ad valorem tax is a percentage tax, it will be higher for high-priced items than for low-priced ones.

In Figure 2–8, S^0 represents the supply curve for backpacks before the inception of a 20 percent ad valorem tax. Notice that 1,100 backpacks are offered for sale when the price of a backpack is $10 and 2,450 backpacks are offered when the price is $20. Once the 20 percent tax is implemented, the price required to produce each unit goes up by 20 percent at any output level. Therefore, price will go up by $2 at a quantity of 1,100 and by $4 at a quantity of 2,450. An ad valorem tax will rotate the supply curve counterclockwise, and the new curve will shift farther away from the original curve as the price increases. This explains why S^1 is steeper than S^0 in Figure 2–8.

Producer Expectations

Producer expectations about future prices also affect the position of the supply curve. In effect, selling a unit of output today and selling a unit of output tomorrow are substitutes in production. If firms expect prices to be

FIGURE 2–8

An ad valorem tax

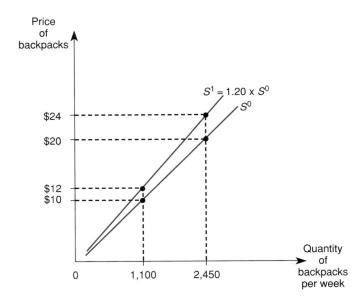

higher in the future and the product is not perishable, producers can hold back output today and sell it later at a higher price. This has the effect of shifting the current supply curve to the left.

The Supply Function

You should now understand the difference between supply and quantity supplied and recognize the factors that influence the position of the supply curve. The final step in our analysis of supply is to show that all of the factors that influence the supply of a good can be summarized in a supply function.

supply function
A function that describes how much of a good will be produced at alternative prices of that good, alternative input prices, and alternative values of other variables affecting supply.

The *supply function* of a good describes how much of the good will be produced at alternative prices of the good, alternative prices of inputs, and alternative values of other variables that affect supply. Formally, let Q_x^s represent the quantity supplied of a good, P_x the price of the good, W the price of an input (such as the wage rate on labor), P_r the price of technologically related goods, and H the value of some other variable that affects supply, such as the existing technology, the number of firms in the market, taxes, or producer expectations. Then the supply function for good X may be written as

$$Q_x^s = f(P_x, P_r, W, H).$$

Thus, the supply function explicitly recognizes that the quantity produced in a market depends not only on the price of the good but also on all of the factors that are potential supply shifters. While there are many different functional forms for different types of products, a particularly useful

linear supply function
A representation of the supply function in which the supply of a given good is a linear function of input prices and other variables affecting supply.

representation of a supply function is the linear relationship. Supply is *linear* if Q_x^s is a linear function of the variables that influence supply. The following equation is representative of a linear supply function:

$$Q_x^s = \beta_0 + \beta_x P_x + \beta_r P_r + \beta_w W + \beta_H H.$$

The coefficients (the β_is) represent given numbers that have been estimated by the firm's research department or an economic consultant.

DEMONSTRATION PROBLEM 2–3

Your research department estimates that the supply function for television sets is given by

$$Q_x^s = 2,000 + 3P_x - 4P_r - P_w,$$

where P_x is the price of TV sets, P_r represents the price of a computer monitor and P_w is the price of an input used to make televisions. Suppose TVs are sold for \$400 per unit, computer monitors are sold for \$100 per unit, and the price of an input is \$2,000. How many television sets are produced?

Answer

To find out how many television sets are produced, we insert the given values of prices into the supply equation to get

$$Q_x^s = 2,000 + 3(400) - 4(100) - 1(2,000).$$

Adding up the numbers, we find that the total quantity of television sets produced is 800.

The information summarized in a supply function can be used to graph a supply curve. Since a supply curve is the relationship between price and quantity, a representative supply curve holds everything but price constant. This means one may obtain the formula for a supply curve by inserting given values of the supply shifters into the supply function, but leaving P_x in the equation to allow for various values. If we do this for the supply function in Demonstration Problem 2–3 (where $P_r = \$100$ and $P_w = 2,000$), we get

$$Q_x^s = 2,000 + 3P_x - 4(100) - 1(2,000),$$

which simplifies to

$$Q_x^s = 3P_x - 400. \tag{2–2}$$

FIGURE 2–9

Producer surplus

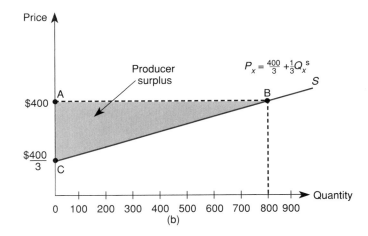

Since we usually graph this relation with the price of the good on the vertical axis, it is useful to represent Equation 2–2 with price on the left-hand side and everything else on the right-hand side. This is known as an *inverse supply function*. For this example, the inverse supply function is

$$P_x = 400/3 + (1/3)\, Q_x^s,$$

which is the equation for the supply curve graphed in Figure 2–9. This curve reveals how much producers must receive to be willing to produce each additional unit of good *X*.

Producer Surplus

Just as consumers want price to be as low as possible, producers want price to be as high as possible. The supply curve reveals the amount producers will be willing to produce at a given price. Alternatively, it indicates the price firms would have to receive to be willing to produce an additional unit of a good. For example, the supply curve in Figure 2–9 indicates that a total of 800 units will be produced when the price is $400. Alternatively, if 800 units are produced, producers will have to receive $400 to be induced to produce another unit of the good.

producer surplus
The amount producers receive in excess of the amount necessary to induce them to produce the good.

Producer surplus is the producer analog to consumer surplus. It is the amount of money producers receive in excess of the amount necessary to induce them to produce the good. More specifically, note that producers are willing to sell each unit of output below 800 units at a price of less than $400. But if the price is $400, producers receive an amount equal to $400 for each unit of output below 800, even though they would be willing to sell those individual units for a lower price.

Geometrically, producer surplus is the area above the supply curve but below the market price of the good. Thus, the shaded area in Figure 2–9 represents the surplus producers receive by selling 800 units at a price of $400—an amount above what would be required to produce each unit of the good. The shaded area, ABC, is the producer surplus when the price is $400. Mathematically, this area is one-half of 800 times $266.67, or $106,668.

Producer surplus can be a powerful tool for managers. For instance, suppose the manager of a major fast-food restaurant currently purchases 10,000 pounds of hamburger meat each week from a supplier at a price of $1.25 per pound. The producer surplus the meat supplier earns by selling 10,000 pounds of hamburger at $1.25 per pound tells the restaurant manager the dollar amount that the supplier is receiving over and above what it would be willing to accept for meat. In other words, the meat supplier's producer surplus is the maximum amount the restaurant could save in meat costs by bargaining with the supplier over a package deal for 10,000 pounds of meat. Chapters 6 and 10 will provide details about how managers can negotiate such a bargain.

Market Equilibrium

As we mentioned in the introduction to this chapter, price in a competitive market is determined by the interactions of all buyers and sellers in the market. The concepts of market supply and market demand make this notion of interaction more precise: The price of a good in a competitive market is determined by the interaction of market supply and market demand for the good.

Since we will focus on the market for a single good, it is convenient to drop subscripts at this point and let P denote the price of this good and Q the quantity of the good. Figure 2–10 depicts the market supply and demand curves for such a good. To see how the competitive price is determined, let the price of the good be P^L. This price corresponds to point B on the market demand curve; consumers wish to purchase Q^1 units of the good. Similarly, the price of P^L corresponds to point A on the market supply curve; producers are willing to produce only Q^0 units at this price. Thus, when the price is P^L, there is a *shortage* of the good, that is, there is not enough of the good to satisfy all consumers willing to purchase it at that price.

In situations where a shortage exists, there is a natural tendency for the price to rise. As the price rises from P^L to P^e in Figure 2–10, producers have an incentive to expand output from Q^0 to Q^e. Similarly, as the price rises, consumers are willing to purchase less of the good. When the price rises to P^e, the quantity demanded is Q^e. At this price, just enough of the good is produced to satisfy all consumers willing and able to purchase at that price; quantity demanded equals quantity supplied.

Suppose the price is at a higher level—say, P^H. This price corresponds to point F on the market demand curve, indicating that consumers wish to purchase Q^0 units of the good. The price P^H corresponds to point G on the

FIGURE 2–10

Market equilibrium

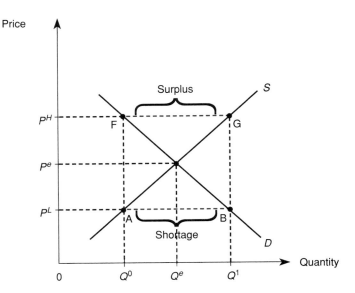

market supply curve; producers are willing to produce Q^1 units at this price. Thus, when the price is P^H, there is a *surplus* of the good; firms are producing more than they can sell at a price of P^H.

Whenever a surplus exists, there is a natural tendency for the price to fall to equate quantity supplied with quantity demanded. As the price falls from P^H to P^e, producers have an incentive to reduce quantity supplied to Q^e. Similarly, as the price falls, consumers are willing to purchase more of the good. When the price falls to P^e, the quantity demanded is Q^e; quantity demanded equals quantity supplied.

Thus, the interaction of supply and demand ultimately determines a competitive price, P^e, such that there is neither a shortage nor a surplus of the good. This price is called the *equilibrium price* and the corresponding quantity, Q^e, is called the *equilibrium quantity* for the competitive market. Once this price and quantity are realized, the market forces of supply and demand are balanced; there is no tendency for prices either to rise or fall.

Principle

Competitive Market Equilibrium

Equilibrium in a competitive market is determined by the intersection of the market demand and supply curves. The equilibrium price is the price that equates quantity demanded with quantity supplied. Mathematically, if $Q^d(P)$ and $Q^s(P)$ represent the quantity demanded and supplied when the price is P, the equilibrium price, P^e, is the price such that

$$Q^d(P^e) = Q^s(P^e).$$

The equilibrium quantity is simply $Q^d(P^e)$ or, equivalently, $Q^s(P^e)$.

DEMONSTRATION PROBLEM 2–4

Imagine that you are an aide to a Senator on the Foreign Relations Committee of the U.S. Senate. The Russian government plans to privatize an industry, and you have been asked to help the Committee determine the market price and quantity that would prevail in the Russian market if competitive forces were allowed to equilibrate the market. The best estimates of the market demand and supply for the Russian good (in U.S. dollar equivalent prices) are given by $Q^d = 10 - 2P$ and $Q^s = 2 + 2P$, respectively. Determine the competitive equilibrium price and quantity.

Answer

Competitive equilibrium is determined by the intersection of the market demand and supply curves. Mathematically, this simply means that $Q^d = Q^s$. Equating demand and supply yields

$$10 - 2P = 2 + 2P,$$

or

$$8 = 4P.$$

Solving this equation for P yields the equilibrium price, $P^e = 2$. To determine the equilibrium quantity, we simply plug this price into either the demand or the supply function (since, in equilibrium, quantity supplied equals quantity demanded). For example, using the supply function, we find that

$$Q^e = 2 + 2(2) = 6.$$

Price Restrictions and Market Equilibrium

The previous section showed how prices and quantities are determined in a free market. In some instances, government places limits on how much prices are allowed to rise or fall, and this restriction can affect the market equilibrium. In this section, we examine the impact of price ceilings and price floors on market allocations.

Price Ceilings

One basic implication of the economic doctrine of scarcity is that there are not enough goods to satisfy the desires of all consumers at a price of zero. As a consequence, some method must be used to determine who gets to consume goods and who does not. People who do not get to consume goods are essentially discriminated against. One way to determine who gets a good and who does not is to allocate the goods based on hair color: If you have red hair, you get the good; if you don't have red hair, you don't get the good.

The price system uses price to determine who gets a good and who does not. The price system allocates goods to consumers who are willing and able to pay the most for the goods. If the competitive equilibrium price of a pair of jeans is $20, consumers willing and able to pay $20 will purchase the good; consumers unwilling or unable to pay that much for a pair of jeans will not buy the good.

It is important to keep in mind that it is not the price system that is "unfair" if one cannot afford to pay the market price for a good; rather, it is unfair that we live in a world of scarcity. Any method of allocating goods will seem unfair to someone, because there are not enough resources to satisfy everyone's wants. For example, if jeans were allocated to people on the basis of hair color instead of the price system, you would think this allocation rule was unfair unless you were born with the "right" hair color.

Often individuals who are discriminated against by the price system attempt to persuade the government to intervene in the market by requiring producers to sell the good at a lower price. This is only natural, for if we were unable to own a house because we had the wrong hair color, we most certainly would attempt to get the government to pass a law allowing people with our hair color to own a house. But then there would be too few houses to go around, and some other means would have to be used to allocate houses to people.

Suppose that, for whatever reason, the government views the equilibrium price of P^e in Figure 2–11 as "too high" and passes a law prohibiting firms from charging prices above P^c. Such a price is called a *price ceiling*.

price ceiling
The maximum legal price that can be charged in a market.

Do not be confused by the fact that the price ceiling is below the initial equilibrium price; the term *ceiling* refers to that price being the highest permissible price in the market. It does not refer to a price set above the equilibrium price. In fact, if a ceiling were imposed above the equilibrium price, it would be ineffective and have no effect; the equilibrium price would be below the maximum legal price.

Given the regulated price of P^c, quantity demanded exceeds quantity supplied by the distance from A to B in Figure 2–11; there is a shortage of $Q^d - Q^s$ units. The reason for the shortage is twofold. First, producers are willing to produce less at the lower price, so the available quantity is reduced from Q^e to Q^s. Second, consumers wish to purchase more at the lower price; thus, quantity demanded increases from Q^e to Q^d. The result is that there is not enough of the good to satisfy all consumers willing and able to purchase it at the price ceiling.

How, then, are the goods to be allocated now that it is no longer legal to ration them on the basis of price? In most instances, goods are rationed on the basis of "first come, first served." As a consequence, price ceilings typically result in long lines such as those created in the 1970s due to price ceilings on gasoline. Thus, price ceilings discriminate against people who

FIGURE 2–11

A price ceiling

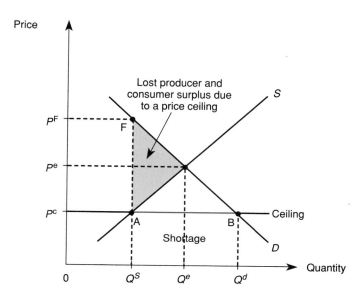

have a high opportunity cost of time and do not like to wait in lines. If a consumer has to wait in line two hours to buy 10 gallons of gasoline and his or her time is worth $5 per hour, it costs the consumer $2 \times \$5 = \$10$ to wait in line. Since 10 gallons of gasoline are purchased, this amounts to $1 per gallon spent in line waiting to purchase the good.

This basic idea can be depicted graphically. Under the price ceiling of P^c, only Q^s units of the good are available. Since this quantity corresponds to point F on the demand curve in Figure 2–11, we see that consumers are willing to pay P^F for another unit of the good. By law, however, they cannot pay the firm more than P^c. The difference, $P^F - P^c$, reflects the price per unit consumers are willing to pay by waiting in line. The *full economic price* paid by a consumer (P^F) is thus the amount paid to the firm (P^c), plus the implicit amount paid by waiting in line ($P^F - P^c$). The latter price is paid not in dollars but through opportunity cost and thus is termed the *nonpecuniary price*.

full economic price
The dollar amount paid to a firm under a price ceiling, plus the nonpecuniary price.

$$P^F \quad = \quad P^c \quad + \quad (P^F - P^c).$$

| Full Economic Price | Dollar Price | Nonpecuniary Price |

As Figure 2–11 shows, P^F is greater than the initial equilibrium price, P^e. When opportunity costs are taken into account, the full economic price paid for a good is actually higher after the ceiling is imposed. The shaded area in Figure 2–11 reflects the producer and consumer surplus that is lost when output is reduced to Q^s.

DEMONSTRATION PROBLEM 2–5

Based on your answer to the Senate Foreign Relations Committee (Demonstration Problem 2–4), one of the senators raises a concern that the free market price might be too high for the typical Russian citizen to pay. Accordingly, she asks you to explain what would happen if the Russian government privatized the market, but then set a ceiling price at the Russian equivalent of $1. How do you answer? Assume that the market demand and supply curves (in U.S. dollar equivalent prices) are still given by

$$Q^d = 10 - 2P \text{ and } Q^s = 2 + 2P.$$

Answer

Since the price ceiling is below the equilibrium price of $2, a shortage will result. More specifically, when the price ceiling is $1, quantity demanded is

$$Q^d = 10 - 2(1) = 8$$

and quantity supplied is

$$Q^s = 2 + 2(1) = 4.$$

Thus, there is a shortage of $8 - 4 = 4$ units.

To determine the full economic price, we simply determine the maximum price consumers are willing to pay for the four units produced. To do this, we first set quantity equal to 4 in the demand formula:

$$4 = 10 - 2P^F,$$

or

$$2P^F = 6.$$

Next, we solve this equation for P^F to obtain the full economic price, $P^F = 3$. Thus, consumers pay a full economic price of $3 per unit; $1 of this price is in money, and $2 represents the nonpecuniary price of the good.

Based on the preceding analysis, one may wonder why the government would ever impose price ceilings. One answer might be that politicians do not understand the basics of supply and demand. This probably is not the answer, however.

The answer lies in who benefits from and who is harmed by ceilings. When lines develop due to a shortage caused by a price ceiling, people with high opportunity costs are hurt, while people with low opportunity costs may actually benefit. For example, if you have nothing better to do than wait in line, you will benefit from the lower dollar price; your nonpecuniary price is close to zero. On the other hand, if you have a high opportunity cost of time because your time is valuable to you, you are made worse off by the ceiling. If a particular politician's constituents tend to have a lower than average opportunity cost, that politician naturally will attempt to invoke a price ceiling.

In some shortages created by a ceiling, goods are not allocated on the basis of lines. Producers may discriminate against consumers on the basis of other factors, including whether or not consumers are regular customers. During the gasoline shortage of the 1970s, many gas stations sold gas only to customers who regularly used the stations. In other situations, such as ceilings on interest rates, firms allocate goods to consumers who are relatively well-to-do.

The key point is that in the presence of a shortage created by a ceiling, managers must use some method other than price to allocate the goods. Depending on which method is used, some consumers will benefit and others will be worse off.

Price Floors

price floor
The minimum legal price that can be charged in a market.

In contrast to the case of a price ceiling, sometimes the equilibrium competitive price may be considered too low for producers. In these instances, individuals may lobby for the government to legislate a minimum legal price for a good. Such a price is called a *price floor*. Perhaps the best-known price floor is the minimum wage, the lowest legal wage that can be paid to workers.

If the equilibrium price is above the price floor, the price floor has no effect on the market. But if the price floor is set above the competitive equilibrium level, such as P^f in Figure 2–12, there is an effect. Specifically, when the price floor is set at P^f, quantity supplied is Q^s and quantity demanded is Q^d. In this instance, more is produced than consumers are willing to purchase at that price, and a surplus develops. In the context of the labor market, there are more people looking for work than there are jobs to go around at that wage, and unemployment results. In the context of a product market, the surplus translates into unsold inventories. In a free market, price would fall to alleviate the unemployment or excess inventories, but the price floor prevents this mechanism from working. Consumers end up paying a higher price and purchasing fewer units.

What happens to the unsold inventories? Sometimes the government agrees to purchase the surplus. This is the case with price floors on many agricultural products, such as cheese. Under a price floor, the quantity of unsold product is given by the distance from G to F in Figure 2–12, or $Q^s - Q^d$. If the government purchases this surplus at the price floor, the total cost to the government is $P^f(Q^s - Q^d)$. Since the area of a rectangle is its base times its height, the cost to the government of buying the surplus is given by the shaded area FGQ^sQ^d in Figure 2–12.

FIGURE 2–12

A price floor

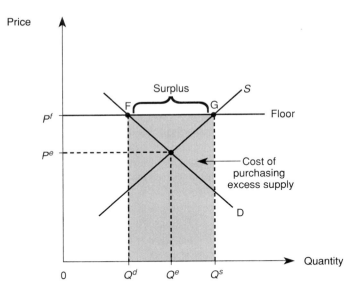

DEMONSTRATION PROBLEM 2–6

One of the members of the Senate Foreign Relations Committee has studied your analysis of Russian privatization (Demonstration Problems 2–4 and 2–5), but is worried that the free market price might be too low to enable producers to earn a fair rate of return on their investment. He asks you to explain what would happen if the Russian government privatized the market, but agreed to purchase the good from suppliers at a floor price of $4. What do you tell the Senator? Assume that the market demand and supply curves (in U.S. dollar equivalent prices) are still given by

$$Q^d = 10 - 2P \text{ and } Q^s = 2 + 2P.$$

Answer

Since the price floor is above the equilibrium price of $2, the floor results in a surplus. More specifically, when the price is $4, quantity demanded is

$$Q^d = 10 - 2(4) = 2$$

and quantity supplied is

$$Q^s = 2 + 2(4) = 10.$$

Thus, there is a surplus of $10 - 2 = 8$ units. Consumers pay a higher price ($4), and producers have unsold inventories of 8 units. However, the Russian government must purchase the amount consumers are unwilling to purchase at the price of $4. Thus, the cost to the Russian government of buying the surplus of 8 units is $4 $\times$ 8 = $32.

Comparative Statics

You now understand how equilibrium is determined in a competitive market and how government policies such as price ceilings and price floors affect the market. Next, we show how managers can use supply and demand to analyze the impact of changes in market conditions on the competitive equilibrium price and quantity. The study of the movement from one equilibrium to another is known as *comparative static analysis*. Throughout this analysis, we assume that no legal restraints, such as price ceilings or floors, are in effect and that the price system is free to work to allocate goods among consumers.

Changes in Demand

The Wall Street Journal recently reported that consumer incomes are expected to rise by about 2.5 percent over the next year, and the number of individuals over 16 years of age will reach an all-time high by the end of the year. We can use our supply and demand apparatus to examine how these changes in market conditions will affect car rental agencies like Avis, Hertz, and Budget. It seems reasonable to presume that rental cars are normal goods: a rise in consumer incomes will most likely increase the demand for rental cars. The increased number of consumers aged 16 and older will also increase demand, since those who rent cars must be at least 16 years old.

    We illustrate the ultimate effect of this increase in the demand for rental cars in Figure 2–13. The initial equilibrium in the market for rental cars is at point A, where demand curve D^0 intersects the market supply curve, S. The changes reported in *The Wall Street Journal* suggest that the demand

FIGURE 2–13

Effect of a change in demand for rental cars

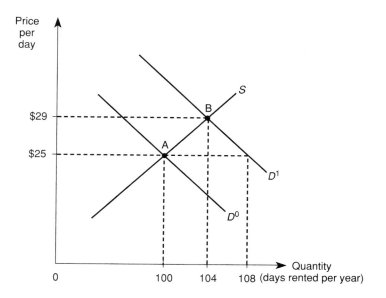

for rental cars will increase over the next year, from D^0 to some curve like D^1. The equilibrium moves to point B, where car rental companies rent more cars and charge a higher price than before the demand increase.

The reason for the rise in rental car prices is as follows. The growing number of consumers aged 16 or older, coupled with the rise in consumer incomes, increases the demand for rental cars. At the old price of $25 per day, there are only 100 cars available for rental on the lot. This is not enough to satisfy the 108 customers willing to rent cars at that price. Car rental companies thus find it in their interest to raise their prices and to increase their quantity supplied of rental cars until ultimately enough cars are available at the new equilibrium price of $29 to exactly equal the quantity demanded at this higher price.

DEMONSTRATION PROBLEM 2–7

The manager of a fleet of cars currently rents them out at the market price of $29 per day, with renters paying for their own gasoline and oil. In a front-page newspaper article, the manager learns that economists expect gasoline prices to rise dramatically over the next year, due to increased tensions in the Middle East. What should she expect to happen to the price of rental cars, and to the number of cars her company rents?

Answer

Since gasoline and rental cars are complements, the increase in gasoline prices will decrease the demand for rental cars. To see the impact on the market price and quantity of rental cars, let D^1 in Figure 2–13 represent the initial demand for rental cars, so that the initial equilibrium is at point B. An increase in the price of gasoline will shift the demand curve for rental cars to left (to D^0), resulting in a new equilibrium at point A. Thus, she should expect the price of rental cars to fall and to rent out fewer cars over the next year.

Changes in Supply

We can also use our supply and demand framework to predict how changes in one or more supply shifters will affect the equilibrium price and quantity of goods or services. For instance, consider a bill before Congress that would require all employers, small and large alike, to provide healthcare to their workers. How would this bill affect the prices charged for goods at retailing outlets?

Changes in Japanese Tastes and Incomes: The Market for Mayonnaise

Japanese consumers dramatically changed their consumption patterns during the late 1980s. According to an article by O. Abe in *Business Japan,* the Japanese moved away from consuming animal fats and salad oils during the late 1980s. This change in behavior, caused by increasingly health-conscious Japanese consumers, has dramatically affected the market for mayonnaise in Japan. Figure 2–14 demonstrates this market change.

In 1988 we start out with an equilibrium level of mayonnaise consumption at point A. However, as Japanese consumers became more health conscious, the demand for mayonnaise shifted to the left to D^{1989}. The new equilibrium for 1989 is at point B, which corresponds to a lower equilibrium price and a lower equilibrium quantity.

Between 1989 and 1995, however, Japanese incomes increased. Since mayonnaise is a normal good, the result has been to shift the demand for mayonnaise rightward to D^{1995}, and a new equilibrium at point C. As you can see from the graph, the decline in demand due to changes in Japanese tastes was much larger than the more recent increase in demand due to rising Japanese incomes. Consequently, the price was still lower in 1995 than in 1988.

Source: O. Abe, "Health-Conscious Consumers Change Demand of Oils and Fats Industry," *Business Japan* (February 1989).

FIGURE 2–14

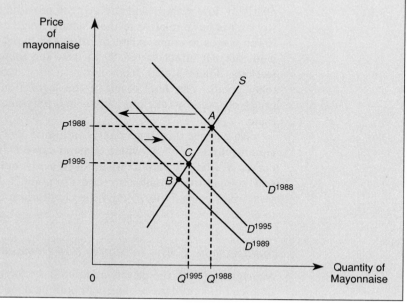

FIGURE 2–15

Effect of a change in supply

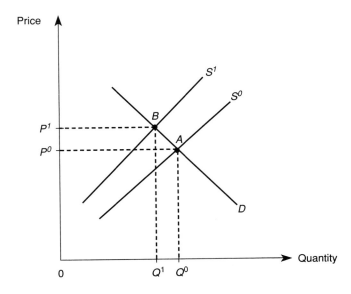

This type of mandate would increase the cost to retailers and other firms of hiring workers. Many retailers rely on semiskilled workers who earn relatively low wages, and the cost of providing health insurance to these workers is large relative to their annual wage earnings. While firms might lower wages to some extent to offset the mandated health insurance costs paid, the net effect would be to raise the total cost to the firm of hiring workers. These higher labor costs, in turn, would decrease the supply of retail goods. The final result of the legislation would be to increase the prices charged by retailing outlets, and to reduce the quantity of goods sold there.

We can see this more clearly in Figure 2–15. The market is initially in equilibrium at point A, where demand curve D intersects the market supply curve, S^0. Higher input prices decrease supply from S^0 to S^1, and the new competitive equilibrium moves to point B. In this instance, the market price rises from P^0 to P^1, and the equilibrium quantity decreases from Q^0 to Q^1.

Simultaneous Shifts in Supply and Demand

Managers in both the private and public sector sometimes encounter events that lead to simultaneous shifts in both demand and supply. A tragic example occurred in 1995 when an earthquake hit Kobe, Japan. The earthquake did considerable damage to Japan's sake wine industry, and the nation's supply of sake wine decreased as a result. Unfortunately, the stress caused by the earthquake led many to increase their demand for sake and other

FIGURE 2–16

*A simultaneous
increase in demand
and decrease in
supply raises the
equilibrium price*

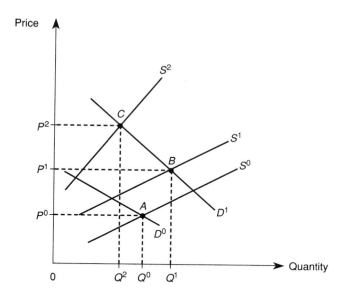

alcoholic beverages. We can use the tools of this chapter to examine how these simultaneous changes in supply and demand affected the equilibrium price and quantity consumed of sake in Japan.

In Figure 2–16, the market is initially in equilibrium at point A, where demand curve D^0 intersects market supply curve S^0. Since the earthquake led to a simultaneous decrease in supply and increase in demand for sake, suppose supply decreases from S^0 to S^1 and demand increases from D^0 to D^1. In this instance, a new competitive equilibrium occurs at point B: the price of sake increases from P^0 to P^1, and the quantity consumed increases from Q^0 to Q^1.

As the curves are drawn in Figure 2–16, the effect of the decrease in supply and increase in demand was to increase both the price and the quantity. But what if instead of shifting from S^0 to S^1, the supply curve shifted much farther to the left to S^2 so that it intersected the new demand curve at point C instead of B? In this instance, price would still be higher than the initial equilibrium price, P^0. But the resulting quantity would be lower than the initial equilibrium (point C implies a lower quantity than point A). Thus, we have seen that when demand increases and supply decreases, the market price rises, but the market quantity may rise or fall depending on the relative magnitude of the shifts.

In general, other simultaneous changes in demand and supply also will lead to some ambiguity regarding whether the equilibrium price or quantity rises or falls. When using supply and demand analysis to predict the effects of simultaneous changes in demand and supply, you must be careful that the predictions are not artifacts of how far you have shifted the curves.

DEMONSTRATION PROBLEM 2–8

Suppose you are the manager of a chain of computer stores. For obvious reasons you have been closely following developments in the computer industry, and have just learned that Congress has passed a two-prong program designed to further enhance the U.S. computer industry's position in the global economy. The legislation provides increased funding for computer education in primary and secondary schools, as well as tax breaks for firms that develop computer software. As a result of this legislation, what do you predict will happen to the equilibrium price and quantity of software?

Answer

The equilibrium quantity certainly will increase, but the market price may rise, remain the same, or fall depending on the relative changes in demand and supply. To see this, note that the funding for computer education at primary and secondary schools will lead to an increase in the demand for computer software, since it is a normal good. The reduction in taxes on software manufacturers will lead to an increase in the supply of software. To examine the impact of these simultaneous changes, suppose the initial equilibrium is at point A in Figure 2–17, where demand curve D^0 and supply curve S^0 intersect. Suppose demand increases to D^1. If supply increases a small amount to S^1, the resulting equilibrium (point C) implies a higher price and quantity. If supply increases by the same amount as demand to S^2, the resulting equilibrium (point E) implies no change in price but a higher quantity. If supply increases by much more than the increase in demand to S^3, the resulting

FIGURE 2–17

A simultaneous increase in demand and supply raises the equilibrium quantity

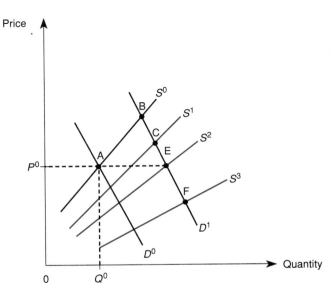

equilibrium (point F) implies a lower price and greater quantity. In all cases, the equilibrium quantity increases. But the effect on the market price depends on the relative magnitudes of the increases in demand and supply.

Answering the Headline

Now that we have developed a formal apparatus for understanding how markets work, we will return to the story that opened this chapter.

If the administration is successful in raising the minimum wage from $4.25 per hour to $5.15 an hour, John stands to gain and his former college classmate stands to lose. Let's first consider why the owner and CEO of Employment Enterprises will benefit if the minimum wage hike is passed. Figure 2–18(a) shows the San Antonio market for unskilled labor, where the minimum wage is currently $4.25. Notice that if the minimum wage increases to $5.15 an hour, more unskilled workers look for jobs but fewer are hired, and the result is an increase in the number of unemployed workers in the area. Employment Enterprises specializes in training unskilled workers and placing them in semiskilled jobs in San Antonio. Since there will be more unemployed unskilled workers in San Antonio if the minimum wage increase passes, John reasonably expects additional unskilled workers

FIGURE 2–18

The effect of a minimum wage hike

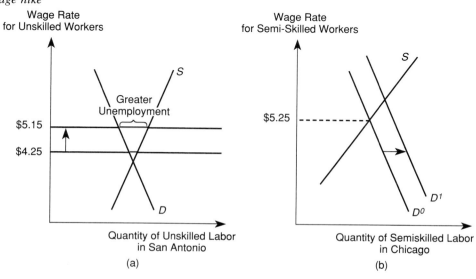

(a)

(b)

to use the services of Employment Enterprises. As the owner of the firm, he stands to earn higher profits.

George's firm, on the other hand, relies heavily on semiskilled workers in the Chicago labor market, and John reasons they are paid the national average of $5.25 an hour. If the minimum wage increases to $5.15 an hour, firms in Chicago that currently use cheaper unskilled labor will likely be willing to pay the extra 10 cents per hour to hire semiskilled labor, and thus will substitute towards semiskilled labor. This increase in the demand for semiskilled labor in the Chicago area shifts the demand for semiskilled workers to the right in Figure 2–18(b), and thus increases the wage paid to semiskilled workers in Chicago. George's firm will see an increase in costs and reduction in profits if the minimum wage legislation is passed.

Summary

This chapter provided an overview of supply and demand and the interaction of these forces. We covered applications of demand, supply, price ceilings, price floors, and comparative statics. By reading this chapter and working through the demonstration problems presented, you should have a basic understanding of how to analyze the workings of a competitive market.

The model of supply and demand is just a starting point for this book. Throughout the remainder of the book, we assume you have a thorough understanding of the concepts presented in this chapter. In the next chapter, we will present the concepts of elasticity and show how to use them in making managerial decisions. We will also present some additional quantitative tools to help managers make better decisions.

Key Terms and Concepts

ad valorem tax	law of demand
change in demand	law of supply
change in quantity demanded	nonpecuniary price
change in quantity supplied	normal good
change in supply	price ceiling
comparative statics	price floor
consumer surplus	producer surplus
demand	shortage
demand function	substitutes
excise tax	supply
full economic price	supply function
inferior good	surplus

Problems

1. When Iraq invaded Kuwait, the market price of crude petroleum jumped from $21.54 per barrel to $30.50 per barrel—an increase of almost 42 percent. Your boss is puzzled, because the price increase actually occurred before there was a physical reduction in the current amount of oil available for sale.

   a. Explain why the price of oil increased so rapidly.

   b. One year after the Iraq invasion, the price of oil fell to $21.32 per barrel, its prewar level. Explain why.

2. Caviar and champagne are complements. Recently pollution has been a problem in the Volga River, where much of the world's caviar comes from. The sturgeon that live in these waters are laying fewer eggs than before. Show graphically and explain the effects on the market for caviar and the market for champagne.

3. A recent breakthrough in the production of laser disk technology has decreased the cost of laser disks. These disks supposedly will increase the quality of music recordings tenfold over that available from CDs. What will happen to the price and quantity of CDs sold? Of laser disks sold?

4. A proposal is before Congress to raise the minimum wage to $6.25 per hour. Using only supply and demand analysis, determine and explain how this increase in the minimum wage will affect the following;

   a. Unemployment

   b. Union wages

   c. Small retailers

   d. Large firms like GM and IBM

   e. New high school graduates

   f. New college graduates

   g. Homelessness

   h. You

5. Apples and oranges are substitutes. A freeze in Florida destroys most of the orange crop. What would you expect to happen to the market for the following;

   a. Oranges?

   b. Apples?

   c. Orange juice?

6. In 1987 a 386 PC sold at a price of $6,995. Five years later, you could purchase essentially the same computer for $1,495. Today, you can purchase a faster Pentium for a fraction of the initial price of a slower 386 PC.

   a. Why have computer prices fallen so dramatically?

   b. What impact, if any, do you think the growing use of the Internet, Prodigy, and CompuServe will have on the price of computers?

7. American Tennishoe, Inc., is concerned because Congress has proposed an excise tax of $1 on each pair of tennis shoes sold in the United States. They are lobbying against the tax through an advertising campaign that says the tax will raise the price of tennis shoes by $1. Use supply and demand graphs to show how much of the tax will actually be passed on to consumers.

8. RB, Inc., is a wholesaler specializing in dry foods, such as rice and dry beans. Its manager is troubled by a recent article in *The Wall Street Journal* that says a recession is imminent and that income will fall by 3 percent over the next year. What do you think is likely to happen to the price of the products RB, Inc., sells? Why?

9. Consider the market for two goods that are substitutes, such as pens and pencils. If a technological breakthrough reduced the cost of producing pens;
   a. What would happen to the supply of pens?
   b. What would happen to the price of pens and the quantity exchanged?
   c. What effect would this change in the price of pens have on the market for pencils?

10. In early 1995 Russian state television imposed a temporary ban on all TV commercials. Your firm specializes in exports to Russia. In 1994 90 percent of its sales were consumer goods shipped to Russia. Your supervisor wants to know the likely impact of the Russian ban on your firm's 1995 operations. What do you tell her?

11. The federal government recently decided to raise the excise tax on hard liquor.
   a. Graphically illustrate the effects of this tax increase on the market for hard liquor.
   b. Would a $1 increase in the excise tax on liquor increase the equilibrium price of liquor by $1? Explain.
   c. How would the excise tax on hard liquor affect a beer distributor?

12. The Clinton Administration estimated that the North American Free Trade Agreement (NAFTA) will ultimately result in tariff cuts averaging 38 percent globally. Assuming these estimates are correct, would you expect the price of the average imported good to fall by 38 percent? Explain.

13. The government decides that a specific scarce good should be provided for everyone who wants it at a price of zero and passes a law making it illegal to buy or sell the good. However, people can give the good away. This good is highly desirable for some of the population. What effect will this law have on the market? What would happen in this market if the law were removed?

14. You are the manager of a car dealership that sells luxury automobiles, which are normal goods. Although a recession is expected next year,

you expect your clients' incomes to increase over the coming year. What will you do about ordering cars for next year as compared to last year? Why?

15. You are the manager of Fast & Easy Donuts. Almost all of your donut sales are derived from the drive-through window. You know from experience that coffee is a complement for your donuts. The morning newspaper says that a major storm has just destroyed 50 percent of this year's coffee bean crop. Will this affect how much flour you order? Will it affect how many employees you schedule? What will happen to prices?

16. You are an economic adviser to the Treasurer of the United States. Congress is considering increasing the sales tax on gasoline by $.03 per gallon. Last year motorists purchased 10 million gallons of gas per month. The demand curve is such that every $.01 increase in price decreases sales by 100,000 gallons per month. You also know that for every $.01 increase in price, producers are willing to provide 50,000 more gallons of gasoline to the market. The legislature has stated that the $.03 tax will increase government revenues by $300,000 per month and raise the price of gasoline by $.03 per gallon. Is this correct?

17. Suppose you are an aide to a U.S. Senator who is concerned about the impact of a recently proposed excise tax on the welfare of her constituents. You explained to the Senator that one way of measuring the impact on her constituents is to determine how the tax change affects the level of consumer surplus enjoyed by the constituents. Based on your arguments, you are given the go-ahead to conduct a formal analysis, and obtain the following estimates of demand and supply: $Q^d = 500 - 5P$ and $Q^s = 2P - 60$.
    a. Graph the supply and demand curves.
    b. What are the equilibrium quantity and equilibrium price?
    c. How much consumer surplus exists in this market?
    d. If a $2 excise tax is levied on this good, what will happen to the equilibrium price and quantity?
    e. What will the consumer surplus be after the tax?

18. The demand for your product has been estimated to be $Q_x^d = 7,880 - 4P_x - 2P_y + P_z - .1M$. The relevant price and income data are as follows: $P_x = 10$, $P_y = 15$, $P_z = 50$, $M = 40,000$.
    a. Which goods are substitutes for X? Which are complements?
    b. Is X an inferior or a normal good?
    c. How much X will be purchased?
    d. Graph the demand curve for X given the above information.
    e. How will the demand curve change if M falls to 35,000?

19. Suppose the supply curve for a product is given by $Q_x^d = -300 + 4P_x + 2P_z$ and $P_x = 30$, $P_z = 40$.
    a. How much X is produced?

  b. What is the inverse supply curve for X given the above information?

  c. Graph this supply curve.

  d. Show what happens to this supply curve if the price of Z goes up by $10.

20. Consider the following demand and supply curves: $Q^d = 5{,}800 - 6P$ and $Q^s = 4P - 120$.

  a. Graph the supply and demand curves.

  b. What are the equilibrium quantity and equilibrium price?

  c. How much consumer surplus exists in this market?

  d. What happens in this market if a price floor of $600 is placed on this good?

  e. What happens to consumer surplus in part *d?*

  f. If a price ceiling of $500 instead of a price floor were placed on this good, how would the market be affected?

  g. What is the full economic price after the implementation of the price ceiling in part *f?*

Selected Readings

Ault, Richard W., Jackson, John D., and Saba, Richard P., "The Effect of Long Term Rent Control on Tenant Mobility." *Journal of Urban Economics* 35(2), March 1994, pp. 140–58.

Espana, Juan R., "Impact of the North American Free Trade Agreement (NAFTA) on U.S. Mexican Trade and Investment Flows." *Business Economics* 28(3), July 1993, pp. 41–47.

Friedman Milton, *Capitalism and Freedom*. Chicago: University of Chicago Press 1962.

Katz, Lawrence F. and Murphy, Kevin M., "Changes in Relative Wages, 1963–1987: Supply and Demand Factors." *Quarterly Journal of Economics* 107(1), February 1992, pp. 35–78.

Olson, Josephine E. and Frieze, Irene Hanson, "Job Interruptions and Part Time Work: Their Effect on MBAs' Income." *Industrial Relations* 28(3), Fall 1989, pp. 373–86.

O'Neill, June and Polachek, Solomon, "Why the Gender Gap in Wages Narrowed in the 1980s." *Journal of Labor Economics* 11(1), January 1993, pp. 205–28.

Simon, Herbert A., "Organizations and Markets." *Journal of Economic Perspectives* 5(2), Spring 1991, pp. 25–44.

Smith, Vernon L., "An Experimental Study of Competitive Market Behavior." *Journal of Political Economy* 70(2), April 1962, pp. 111–39.

Williamson, Oliver, *The Economic Institutions of Capitalism*. New York: Free Press, 1985.

Quantitative Demand Analysis

Winners of Wireless Auction to Pay $7 Billion

The CEO of a regional telephone company picked up the March 14, 1995 *New York Times* and began reading on page D1:

> The Federal Government completed the biggest auction in history today, selling off part of the nation's airwaves for $7 billion to a handful of giant companies that plan to blanket the nation with new wireless communications networks for telephones and computers . . .

The CEO read the article with interest because his firm is scrambling to secure loans to purchase one of the licenses the FCC plans to auction off in his region next year. The region serviced by the firm has a population that is 7 percent greater than the average where licenses have been sold before, yet the FCC plans to auction the same number of licenses. This troubled the CEO, since in the most recent auction 99 bidders coughed up a total of $7 billion—an average of $7.07 million for a single license.

Fortunately for the CEO, the *New York Times* article contained a table summarizing the price paid per license in 10 different regions, as well as the number of licenses sold and the population of each region. The CEO quickly entered this data into his spreadsheet, clicked the regression tool button, and found the following relation between the price of a license, the quantity of licenses available, and regional population size (price and population figures are expressed in millions of dollars and people, respectively):

$$\log P = 2.23 - 1.2 \log Q + 1.25 \log \text{Pop}.$$

Based on the CEO's analysis, how much money does he expect his company will need to buy a license? How much confidence do you place in this estimate?

Introduction

In Chapter 2 we saw that the demand for a firm's product (Q_x^d) depends on its price (P_x), the prices of substitutes or complements (P_y), consumer incomes (M), and other variables (H) such as advertising, the size of the population, or consumer expectations:

$$Q_x^d = f(P_x, P_y, M, H).$$

Up until now, our analysis of the impact of changes in prices and income on consumer demand has been qualitative rather than quantitative; that is, we have indicated only the directions of the changes and said little about their magnitude. The first half of this chapter remedies this by showing how a manager can use elasticities of demand to quantify the impact of changing market conditions on the firm's sales.

The second half of the chapter describes regression analysis, which is the technique economists use to estimate the parameters of demand functions. The primary focus is on how a manager can use managerial economics to evaluate information available in the library or provided by the firm's research department. Accordingly, we will explain how to interpret regression results and how managers can use regression tools contained in spreadsheet programs like Excel or Lotus to actually estimate simple demand relationships.

Elasticities of Demand

Suppose some variable, such as the price of a product, increased by 10 percent. What would happen to the quantity demanded of the good? Based on the analysis in Chapter 2 and the law of demand, we know that the quantity demanded would fall. It would be useful for a manager to know whether the quantity demanded would fall by 5 percent, 10 percent, or some other amount.

The primary tool used to determine the magnitude of such a change is elasticity analysis. Indeed, the most important concept introduced in this chapter is elasticity. Elasticity is a very general concept. An *elasticity* measures the responsiveness of one variable to changes in another variable. For example, the elasticity of your grade with respect to studying, denoted $E_{G,S}$, is the percentage change in your grade (%ΔG) that will result from a given percentage change in the time you spend studying (%ΔS). In other words,

elasticity
A measure of the responsiveness of one variable to changes in another variable; the percentage change in one variable that arises due to a given percentage change in another variable.

$$E_{G,S} = \frac{\%\Delta G}{\%\Delta S} = \left(\frac{\Delta G}{\Delta S}\right)\left(\frac{S}{G}\right)$$

Key
G = Grade
S = Time Studied

Since $\%\Delta G = \Delta G/G$ and $\%\Delta S = \Delta S/S$, we may also write this as $E_{G,S} = (\Delta G/\Delta S)(S/G)$. Notice that $\Delta G/\Delta S$ represents the slope of the functional relation between G and S; it tells the change in G that results from a given change in S. By multiplying this by S/G, we convert each of these changes into percentages, which means that the elasticity measure does not depend on the units in which we measure the variables G and S.

A Calculus Alternative

If the variable G depends on S according to the functional relationship $G = f(S)$, the elasticity of G with respect to S may be found using calculus:

$$E_{G,S} = \frac{dG}{dS}\frac{S}{G}.$$

If eks. is +
↑S ⇒ ↑G

if eks is −
↑S ⇒ ↓G

if |e| > 1 then
small % ΔS leads to
by % ΔG

if |e| < 1 then
small % ΔS leads to
small % ΔG

Two aspects of an elasticity are important: (1) whether it is positive or negative and (2) whether it is greater than 1 or less than 1 in absolute value. The sign of the elasticity determines the relationship between G and S. If the elasticity is positive, an increase in S leads to an increase in G. If the elasticity is negative, an increase in S leads to a decrease in G.

Whether the absolute value of the elasticity is greater or less than one determines how responsive G is to changes in S. If the absolute value of the elasticity is greater than 1, the numerator is larger than the denominator in the elasticity formula, and we know that a small percentage change in S will lead to a relatively large change in G. If the absolute value of the elasticity is less than one, the numerator is smaller than the denominator in the elasticity formula. In this instance, a given percentage change in S will lead to a relatively small change in G. It is useful to keep these points in mind as we define some specific elasticities.

Own Price Elasticity

own price elasticity
A measure of the responsiveness of the quantity demanded of a good to a change in the price of that good; the percentage change in quantity demanded divided by the percentage change in the price of the good.

We begin with a very important elasticity concept: the *own price elasticity* of demand, which measures the responsiveness of quantity demanded to a change in price. Later in this section we will see that this measure can be used by managers to determine the quantitative impact of price hikes or cuts on the firm's sales and revenues. The own price elasticity of demand for good X, denoted E_{Q_x, P_x}, is defined as

$$E_{Q_x, P_x} = \frac{\%\Delta Q_x^d}{\%\Delta P_x}.$$

⇒ Price ekstisityof demand

If the own price elasticity of demand for a product is -2, for instance, we know that a 10 percent increase in the product's price leads to 20 percent decline in the quantity demanded of the good, since $-20\%/10\% = -2$.

A Calculus Alternative

The own price elasticity of demand for a good with a demand function $Q_x^d = f(P_x, P_y, M, H)$ may be found using calculus:

$$E_{Q_x, P_x} = \frac{\partial Q_x^d}{\partial P_x} \frac{P_x}{Q_x}.$$

Recall that two aspects of an elasticity are important: (1) its sign and (2) whether it is greater or less than 1 in absolute value. By the law of demand, there is an inverse relation between price and quantity demanded; thus, the own price elasticity of demand is a negative number. The absolute value of the own price elasticity of demand can be greater or less than 1 depending on several factors that we will discuss next. However, it is useful to introduce some terminology to aid in this discussion.

elastic demand
Demand is elastic if the absolute value of the own price elasticity is greater than 1.

First, demand is said to be *elastic* if the absolute value of the own price elasticity is greater than 1:

$$|E_{Q_x, P_x}| > 1.$$

inelastic demand
Demand is inelastic if the absolute value of the own price elasticity is less than 1.

Second, demand is said to be *inelastic* if the absolute value of the own price elasticity is less than 1:

$$|E_{Q_x, P_x}| < 1.$$

unitary elastic demand
Demand is unitary elastic if the absolute value of the own price elasticity is equal to 1.

Finally, demand is said to be *unitary elastic* if the absolute value of the own price elasticity is equal to 1:

$$|E_{Q_x, P_x}| = 1.$$

Conceptually, the quantity consumed of a good is relatively responsive to a change in the price of the good when demand is elastic and relatively unresponsive to changes in price when demand is inelastic. This means that price increases will reduce consumption very little when demand is inelastic. However, when demand is elastic, a price increase will reduce consumption considerably.

Elasticity and Total Revenue

Table 3–1 shows the hypothetical prices and quantities demanded of software, the own price elasticity, and the total revenue ($TR = P_x Q_x$) for the linear demand function, $Q_x^d = 80 - 2P_x$. Notice that the absolute value of the own price elasticity gets larger as price increases. In particular, the slope of this linear demand curve is constant ($\Delta Q_x^d / \Delta P_x = -2$), which implies that $E_{Q_x, P_x} = (\Delta Q_x^d / \Delta P_x)(P_x / Q_x)$ increases in absolute value as P_x increases. Thus, the own price elasticity of demand varies along a linear demand curve.

When the absolute value of the own price elasticity is less than 1 (points A through D in Table 3–1), an increase in price increases total revenue. For

TABLE 3–1   **Total Revenue and Elasticity ($Q_x^d = 80 - 2P_x$)**

	Price of Software (P_x)	Quantity of Software Sold (Q_x)	Own Price Elasticity (E_{Q_x, P_x})	Total Revenue ($P_x Q_x$)
A	0	80	0.00	0
B	5	70	−0.14	350
C	10	60	−0.33	600
D	15	50	−0.60	750
E	20	40	−1.00	800
F	25	30	−1.66	750
G	30	20	−3.00	600
H	35	10	−7.00	350
I	40	0	−∞	0

example, an increase in price from $5 to $10 per unit increases total revenue in Table 3–1 by $250. Notice that for these two prices, the corresponding elasticity of demand is less than 1 in absolute value.

When the absolute value of own price elasticity is greater than 1 (points F through I in Table 3–1), an increase in price leads to a reduction in total revenue. For example, when price increases from $25 (where the own price elasticity is −1.66) to $30 (where the own price elasticity is −3), we see that total revenue decreases by $150. The price-quantity combination that maximizes total revenue in Table 3–1 is at point E, where the own price elasticity equals −1.

The demand curve corresponding to the data in Table 3–1 is presented in the top panel of Figure 3–1, while the total revenue associated with each price-quantity combination on the demand curve is graphed in the lower panel. As we move up the demand curve from point A to point I, demand becomes increasingly elastic. At point E, where demand is unitary elastic, total revenue is maximized. At points to the northwest of E, demand is elastic and total revenue decreases as price increases. At points to the southeast of E, demand is inelastic and total revenue increases when price increases. This relationship among the changes in price, elasticity, and total revenue is called the *total revenue test.*

Principle

Total Revenue Test

If demand is elastic, an increase (decrease) in price will lead to a decrease (increase) in total revenue. If demand is inelastic, an increase (decrease) in price will lead to an increase (decrease) in total revenue. Finally, total revenue is maximized at the point where demand is unitary elastic.

Managers who decide to "cut price and make it up in volume" are, in effect, using the total revenue test. To see this, suppose the research

FIGURE 3–1:

Demand, elasticity, and total revenue

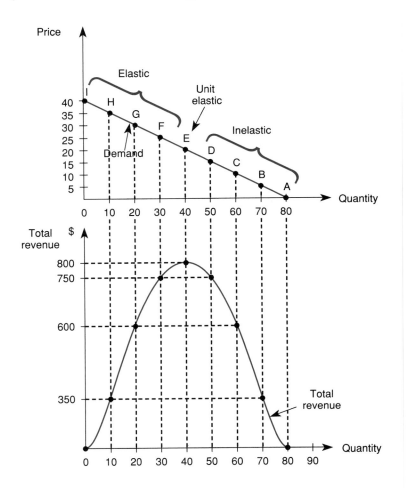

department of a chain of discount stores estimates that the own price elasticity of demand for products sold at its outlets is −1.7. If the company cuts prices by 5 percent, will sales increase enough to increase revenues due to the increased sales volume? We can answer this question by setting −1.7 = E_{Q_x, P_x} and −5% = %ΔP_x in the formula for the own price elasticity of demand:

$$-1.7 = \frac{\%\Delta Q_x^d}{-5\%}.$$

Solving this equation for %ΔQ_x^d yields %ΔQ_x^d = 8.5%. In other words, the quantity of goods sold will rise by 8.5 percent if store prices are reduced by 5 percent. Since the percentage increase in quantity demanded is greater than the percentage decline in prices ($|E_{Q_x, P_x}| > 1$), the price cut will actually raise the firm's sales revenues. Expressed differently, since demand is elastic,

FIGURE 3–2:

Perfectly elastic and inelastic demand

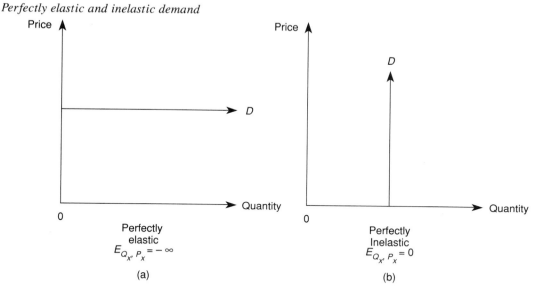

(a)

(b)

a price cut results in a greater than proportional increase in sales, and thus increases the firm's total revenues.

In extreme cases the demand for a good may be perfectly elastic or perfectly inelastic. Demand is *perfectly elastic* if the own price elasticity of demand is infinite in absolute value. Demand is *perfectly inelastic* if the own price elasticity of demand is zero.

When demand is perfectly elastic, a manager who raises price even slightly will find that none of the good is purchased. In this instance the demand curve is horizontal, as illustrated in Figure 3–2(a). In contrast when demand is perfectly inelastic, consumers do not respond at all to changes in price. In this case the demand curve is vertical, as shown in Figure 3–2(b).

Usually, however, demand is neither perfectly elastic nor perfectly inelastic. In these instances knowledge of the particular value of an elasticity can be useful for a manager. Large firms, the government, and universities commonly hire economists or statisticians to estimate the demand for products. The manager's job is to know how to interpret and use such estimates.

perfectly elastic demand
Demand is perfectly elastic if the own price elasticity is infinite in absolute value. In this case the demand curve is horizontal.

perfectly inelastic demand
Demand is perfectly inelastic if the own price elasticity is zero. In this case the demand curve is vertical.

Factors Affecting the Own Price Elasticity

Now that you understand what the own price elasticity is and how it can be used to assess the impact of price changes on sales volume and revenues, we will discuss three factors that affect the magnitude of the own price elasticity of a good: available substitutes, time, and expenditure share.

Inside Business 3–1:

Calculating and Using the Arc Elasticity: An Application to the Housing Market

The text shows how managers can use the own price elasticity of demand to analyze the impact of a price change on a good's sales volume. While in many instances managers can obtain estimates of elasticities from the library or the firm's research staff, sometimes managers are confronted with situations where elasticity estimates are not readily available. Fortunately, all is not lost in these instances thanks to a concept called the arc elasticity of demand.

To be specific, suppose a manager has data that shows when the price of some good is P_1, consumers purchased Q_1 units of the good, and when the price changed to P_2, Q_2 units were purchased. Other things equal, these data can be used to approximate the own price elasticity of demand for the good by using the arc elasticity formula:

$$E_{Q_x, P_x}^{Arc} = \frac{\Delta Q_x^d}{\Delta P_x} \times \frac{Average\ P}{Average\ Q}.$$

In the formula the average Q is $(Q_1 + Q_2)/2$ and the average P is $(P_1 + P_2)/2$.

In order to see that this formula can be used to compute an elasticity from real-world data, consider the table from *The Wall Street Journal* that is reprinted below. This table reports data on housing price changes and existing home sales that is updated monthly in *The Wall Street Journal*. According to the second column of the Housing Price Changes section, the median sales price of existing single-family homes in the U.S. was $108,100 in November of 1994. The corresponding entry in the Existing-Home Sales section of the table reports that, at this price, 3,820,000 homes were sold. Thus, $P_1 = $108,100$ and $Q_1 = 3,820,000$ represent one point on the demand curve—the price and quantity of existing single-family homes in November 1994.

Similarly, $P_2 = $107,700$ and $Q_2 = 3,890,000$ represent the price and quantity of existing single-family homes one month later, in December 1994. Elsewhere in this issue of *The Wall Street Journal* we learn that interest rates and income—the two primary determinants of the demand for housing, were roughly constant between November and December of 1994. Thus, it is reasonable to assume that demand was stable (did not shift) over this one-month period, and that this price-quantity pair represents another point on the demand curve for single family homes in the U.S.

Based on these two points on the demand curve, we may approximate the own price elasticity of demand for existing single-family homes in the U.S. by using the arc elasticity formula:

$$
\begin{aligned}
E_{Q_x, P_x}^{Arc} &= \frac{(Q_1 - Q_2)}{(P_1 - P_2)} \frac{(P_1 + P_2)/2}{(Q_1 + Q_2)/2} \\[6pt]
&= \frac{(3,820,000 - 3,890,000)}{(108,100 - 107,700)} \\[6pt]
&\quad \times \frac{(108,100 + 107,700)/2}{(3,820,000 + 3,890,000)/2} \\[6pt]
&= -4.9.
\end{aligned}
$$

The own price elasticity of demand is greater than one in absolute value, so by the total revenue test we know that the decline in housing prices over the period resulted in greater total expenditures on housing. We might also speculate that the incomes of real estate agents increased over this period, due to the greater real estate commissions generated by these higher expenditures on housing.

It is important to point out that the arc elasticity technique described here only approximates

Inside Business 3–1 continued

Inside Business 3–1 concluded

the true elasticity of demand for housing. The accuracy of the approximation depends crucially on the assumption that the demand curve did not shift between November and December of 1994. If the demand for single family housing in the U.S. shifted to the right over the period, due to unusually good house-hunting weather, for instance, then the true elasticity of demand will be lower in absolute value than our approximation.

Housing Price Changes
Median sales price of existing
single-family homes

	DEC-94	NOV-94
U.S.	$107,700	$108,100

Source: National Association of Realtors

Existing-Home Sales
Seasonally adjusted annual sales rate of
existing single-family homes

	DEC-94	NOV-94
U.S.	3,890,000	3,820,000

Source: National Association of Realtors
Source: *The Wall Street Journal,* March 10, 1995.

Available Substitutes

One key determinant of the elasticity of demand for a good is the number of close substitutes for that good. Intuitively, the more substitutes available for the good, the more elastic the demand for it. In these circumstances, a price increase leads consumers to substitute toward another product, thus reducing considerably the quantity demanded of the good. When there are few close substitutes for a good, demand tends to be relatively inelastic. This is because consumers cannot readily switch to a close substitute when the price increases.

A key implication of the effect of the number of close substitutes on the elasticity of demand is that the demand for broadly defined commodities tends to be more inelastic than the demand for specific commodities. For example, the demand for food (a broad commodity) is more inelastic than the demand for beef. Short of starvation, there are no close substitutes for food, and thus the quantity demanded of food is much less sensitive to price changes than is a particular type of food, such as beef. When the price of beef increases, consumers can substitute toward other types of food, including chicken, pork, and fish. Thus, the demand for beef is more elastic than the demand for food.

Table 3–2 shows some own price elasticities from market studies in the United States. These studies reveal that broader categories of goods indeed

TABLE 3–2   **Selected Own Price Elasticities**

Market	Own Price Elasticity
Transportation	−0.6
Motor vehicles	−1.4
Motorcycles and bicycles	−2.3
Food	−0.7
Cereal	−1.5
Clothing	−0.9
Women's clothing	−1.2

Sources: M. R. Baye, D. W. Jansen, and J. W. Lee, "Advertising Effects in Complete Demand Systems," *Applied Economics* 24 (1992), pp. 1087–96; W. S. Commanor and T. A. Wilson, *Advertising and Market Power* (Cambridge, Mass.: Harvard University Press, 1974).

have more inelastic demand than more specifically defined categories. The own price elasticity of food is slightly inelastic, whereas the elasticity of cereal, a more specific type of food, is elastic. We would expect this outcome because there are many substitutes for cereal, but no substitutes exist for food. Table 3–2 also reveals that the demand for women's clothing is more elastic than the demand for clothing in general (a broader category).

Finally, consider the reported estimates of the own price elasticities for motorcycles and bicycles, motor vehicles, and transportation. Transportation is the most broadly defined group, followed by motor vehicles and then motorcycles and bicycles. Therefore, we would expect the demand for motorcycles and bicycles to be more elastic than the demand for motor vehicles and the demand for motor vehicles to be more elastic than the demand for transportation. The numbers in Table 3–2 are consistent with these expectations; market studies support the statement that demand is more elastic when there are more close substitutes for a product.

Time
Demand tends to be more inelastic in the short term than in the long term. The more time consumers have to react to a price change, the more elastic the demand for the good. Conceptually, time allows the consumer to seek out available substitutes. For example, if a consumer has 30 minutes to catch a flight, he or she is much less sensitive to the price charged for a taxi ride to the airport than would be the case if the flight were several hours later. Given enough time, the consumer can seek alternative modes of transportation such as a bus, a friend's car, or even on foot. But in the short term, the consumer does not have time to seek out the available substitutes, and demand for taxi rides is more inelastic.

Table 3–3 presents short-term and long-term own price elasticities for transportation, food, alcohol and tobacco, recreation, and clothing. Notice

---

Inside Business 3–2

GM's Pricing Strategy for the Saturn

In the fall of 1990, General Motors set the base price for its new Saturn sedan at $7,995. This bargain basement price was about $1,000 less than most analysts had expected. The reason for the low price was to penetrate the economy car market. Was this the right strategy for this product?

The first step in evaluating the price of a new product involves estimating the demand for that product. How many units will be bought at what prices in a given market during a given period of time? GM thought the Saturn would be in the elastic portion of its demand at this base price.

Therefore, GM's strategy of setting the price lower than expected would result in greater revenue to the firm than would a price $1,000 higher, because the lower price would be more than offset by the increase in the number of cars sold. Market data show that economy cars are both normal goods and relatively elastic in this price range. The penetration strategy GM chose therefore increased the volume of sales by more than enough to offset the lower price.

Source: G. Leaming, "Saturn Strategy: On Solid Ground or Up in the Stars?" *Marketing News,* November 26, 1990.

TABLE 3–3   Selected Short- and Long-Term Own Price Elasticities

Market	Short-Term Own Price Elasticity	Long-Term Own Price Elasticity
Transportation	−0.6	−1.9
Food	−0.7	−2.3
Alcohol and tobacco	−0.3	−0.9
Recreation	−1.1	−3.5
Clothing	−0.9	−2.9

Source: M. R. Baye, D. W. Jansen, and J. W. Lee, "Advertising Effects in Complete Demand Systems," *Applied Economics* 24 (1992), pp. 1087–96.

that all the short-term elasticities are less (in absolute value) than the corresponding long-term elasticities. In the short term, all the own price elasticities are less than 1 in absolute value, with the exception of the own price elasticity for recreation. The absolute values of the long-term own price elasticities are all greater than 1, except for alcohol and tobacco.

Expenditure Share

Goods that comprise a relatively small share of consumers' budgets tend to be more inelastic than goods for which consumers spend a sizable portion of their incomes. In the extreme case, where a consumer spends her or his entire budget on a good, the consumer must decrease consumption when the price rises. In essence, there is nothing to give up but the good itself. When a good comprises only a small portion of the budget, the consumer can reduce the consumption of other goods when the price of the good increases. For example, most consumers spend very little on salt; a small increase in the price of salt would reduce quantity demanded very little, since salt constitutes a small fraction of consumers' total budgets.

Would you expect the own price elasticity of demand for food to be more or less elastic than that for transportation? Since food is a much greater necessity than transportation (after all, you could always walk), you might expect the demand for food to be more inelastic than the demand for transportation. However, Table 3–3 reveals that the demand for transportation is more inelastic (in both the short and long term) than the demand for food. How can this be true?

The answer lies in the percentage of income Americans spend on food and transportation. *The Economic Report of the President* reports that in 1994, U.S. consumers spent 15 percent of their incomes on food and only 3.2 percent on transportation. The average consumer therefore spent almost five times as much on food as on transportation, indicating that the average consumer is more sensitive to price changes for food. Even though food is more "important" in a biological sense than transportation, it tends to be more elastic because a much larger proportion of people's budgets is spent on food.

Marginal Revenue and the Own Price Elasticity of Demand

We learned in Chapter 1 that *marginal revenue (MR)* is the change in total revenue due to a one unit change in output, and that to maximize profits a firm should produce where marginal revenue equals marginal cost. We will explore profit-maximizing output and pricing decisions in detail later in this book, but it is useful at this point to show how a firm's marginal revenue is linked to the own price elasticity of demand for the firm's product.

The line labeled MR in Figure 3–3 is the marginal revenue associated with each price-output pair on the demand curve. Notice that for a linear demand curve, the marginal revenue schedule lies exactly halfway between the demand curve and the vertical axis. Furthermore, marginal revenue is less than the price for each unit sold.

Why is marginal revenue less than the price charged for the good? To induce consumers to purchase more of a good, a firm must lower its price. When the firm charges the same price for each unit sold, this lower price is received not only on the last unit sold, but also on those units that could have been sold at higher prices had firms not lowered prices. To be concrete, suppose consumers purchase 1 unit of output at a price of $5 per unit, for total expenditures (revenues to producers) of $5 \times 1 = \$5$. Consumers will purchase an additional unit of the good only if the price falls, say from $5

FIGURE 3–3:

Demand and marginal revenue

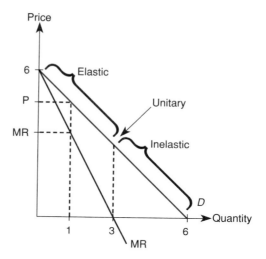

to $4 per unit. Now the firm receives $4 on the first unit sold, and $4 on the second unit sold. In effect, the firm loses $1 in revenue because the first unit now brings $4 instead of $5. Total revenue rises from $5 to $8 as output is increased by one unit, so marginal revenue is $8 − $5 = $3, which is less than price.

Notice in our example that by decreasing price from $5 to $4, quantity demanded increased from 1 unit to 2 units, and total revenues increased from $5 to $8. By the total revenue test, this means that demand is elastic over this range. In contrast, had the price reduction increased quantity demanded but decreased total revenues, demand would be inelastic over the range and marginal revenue would be negative. In fact, the more inelastic the demand for a product, the greater the decline in revenue that results from the increased quantity demanded brought on by a price cut.

This intuition leads to the following general relationship between marginal revenue and the elasticity of demand:

$$MR = P \left[\frac{1 + E}{E} \right]$$

This formula, which is formally derived in Chapter 8, simplifies notation by dropping subscripts: P is the price of the good and E is the own price elasticity of demand for the good. Notice that when $E < -1$, demand is elastic, and the formula implies that MR is positive. When $E = -1$, demand is unitary elastic, and marginal revenue is zero. As we learned in Chapter 1, the point where marginal revenue is zero corresponds to the output at which total revenue is maximized. Finally, when $-1 < E$, demand is inelastic, and marginal revenue is negative. These general results are consistent with what you saw earlier in Table 3–1 for the case of linear demand.

Cross-Price Elasticity

cross-price elasticity
A measure of the responsiveness of the demand for a good to changes in the price of a related good; the percentage change in the quantity demanded of one good divided by the percentage change in the price of a related good.

Another important elasticity is the *cross-price elasticity* of demand, which reveals the responsiveness of the demand for a good to changes in the price of a related good. This elasticity helps managers ascertain how much its demand will rise or fall due to a change in the price of another firm's product. The cross-price elasticity of demand between goods X and Y, denoted E_{Q_x, P_y}, is mathematically defined as

$$E_{Q_x, P_y} = \frac{\%\Delta Q_x^d}{\%\Delta P_y}.$$

For instance, if the cross-price elasticity of demand between WordPerfect and Wordstar word processing software is 3, a 10 percent hike in the price of Wordstar will increase the demand for WordPerfect by 30 percent, since $30\%/10\% = 3$. This increase in demand for WordPerfect occurs because consumers substitute away from Wordstar and towards WordPerfect, due to the price increase.

A Calculus Alternative

When the demand function is $X^d = f(P_x, P_y, M, H)$, the cross-price elasticity of demand between goods X and Y may be found using calculus:

$$E_{Q_x, P_y} = \frac{\partial Q_x^d}{\partial P_y}\frac{P_y}{Q_x}.$$

More generally, whenever goods X and Y are substitutes, an increase in the price of Y leads to an increase in the consumption of X. Thus, $E_{Q_x, P_y} > 0$ whenever goods X and Y are substitutes. When goods X and Y are complements, an increase in the price of Y leads to a decrease in the consumption of X. Thus, $E_{Q_x, P_y} < 0$ whenever goods X and Y are complements.

Table 3–4 provides some representative cross-price elasticities. For example, clothing and food have a cross-price elasticity of -0.18. This means that if the price of food increases by 10 percent, the demand for clothing

TABLE 3–4   Selected Cross-Price Elasticities

	Cross Price Elasticity
Transportation and recreation	−0.05
Food and recreation	0.15
Clothing and food	−0.18

Source: M. R. Baye, D. W. Jansen, and J. W. Lee, "Advertising Effects in Complete Demand Systems," *Applied Economics* 24 (1992), pp. 1087–96.

Inside Business 3–3

Using Cross-Price Elasticities to Improve New-Car Sales in the Wake of Increasing Gasoline Prices

The increases in the price of gasoline during the 1970s and 1980s led to decreases in demand for products that are complements for gasoline, such as automobiles. The reason was that higher gasoline prices moved consumers to substitute toward public transportation, bicycling, and walking. A recent econometric study by Patrick McCarthy provides quantitative information about the impact of fuel costs on the demand for automobiles. One of the more important determinants of the demand for automobiles is the fuel operating cost, defined as the cost of fuel per mile driven. The study reveals that for each 1 percent increase in fuel costs, the demand for automobiles will decrease by .214 percent. A 10 percent increase in the price of gasoline increases the cost of fuel per mile driven by 10 percent and thus reduces the demand for a given car by 2.14 percent.

What did automakers do during this period to mitigate the negative impact of rising gasoline prices on the demand for new automobiles? They made cars more fuel efficient. The results just summarized imply that for every 10 percent increase in fuel efficiency (measured by the increase in miles per gallon), the demand for automobiles increases by 2.14 percent. Auto manufacturers could completely offset the negative impact of higher gasoline prices by increasing the fuel efficiency of new cars by the same percentage as the increase in gasoline prices. In fact, by increasing fuel efficiency by a greater percentage than the increase in gasoline prices, they would actually *increase* the demand for new automobiles.

Source: Patrick S. McCarthy, "Consumer Demand for Vehicle Safety: An Empirical Study," *Economic Inquiry* 28 (July 1990), pp. 530–43.

will decrease by 1.8 percent; food and clothing are complements. More important, these data provide a quantitative measure of the impact of a change in the price of food on the consumption of clothing.

Based on the data summarized in Table 3–4, are food and recreation complements or substitutes? If the price of recreation increased by 15 percent, what would happen to the demand for food? These questions are imbedded in the following problem.

DEMONSTRATION PROBLEM 3–1

You have just opened a new grocery store. Every item you carry is generic (generic beer, generic bread, generic chicken, etc.). You recently read an article in *The Wall Street Journal* reporting that the price of recreation is expected to increase by 15 percent. How will this affect your store's sales of generic food products?

Answer

Table 3–4 reveals that the cross-price elasticity of demand for food and recreation is 0.15. If we insert the given information into the formula for the cross-price elasticity, we get

$$0.15 = \frac{\%\Delta Q_x^d}{15\%}.$$

Solving this equation for $\%\Delta Q_x^d$, we get

$$\%\Delta Q_x^d = 2.25.$$

Thus, food and recreation are substitutes. If the price of recreation increases by 15 percent, you can expect the demand for generic food products to increase by 2.25 percent.

---

income elasticity
A measure of the responsiveness of the demand for a good to changes in consumer income; the percentage change in quantity demanded divided by the percentage change in income.

Income Elasticity

Income elasticity is a measure of the responsiveness of consumer demand to changes in income. Mathematically, the income elasticity of demand, denoted $E_{Q_x, M}$, is defined as

$$E_{Q_x, M} = \frac{\%\Delta Q_x^d}{\%\Delta M}.$$

A Calculus Alternative

The income elasticity for a good with a demand function $Q_x^d = f(P_x, P_y, M, H)$ may be found using calculus:

$$E_{Q_x, M} = \frac{\partial Q_x^d}{\partial M} \frac{M}{Q_x}.$$

When good X is a normal good, an increase in income leads to an increase in the consumption of X. Thus, $E_{Q_x, M} > 0$ when X is a normal good. When X is an inferior good, an increase in income leads to a decrease in the consumption of X. Thus, $E_{Q_x, M} < 0$ when X is an inferior good.

Table 3–5 presents some recent estimates of income elasticities for various products. Consider, for example, the income elasticity for transportation, 1.8. This number gives us two important pieces of information about the relationship between income and the demand for transportation. First, since the income elasticity is positive, we know that consumers increase the amount they spend on transportation when their incomes rise. Transporta-

TABLE 3–5   Selected Income Elasticities

	Income Elasticity
Transportation	1.80
Food	0.80
Ground beef, nonfed	−1.94

Sources: M. R. Baye, D. W. Jansen, and J. W. Lee,
"Advertising Effects in Complete Demand Systems," *Applied Economics* 24 (1992), pp. 1087—96. G. W. Brester and M. K. Wohlsenant, "Estimating Interrelated Demands for Meats Using New Measures for Ground and Table Cut Beef," *American Journal of Agricultural Economics* 73 (November 1991), p. 21.

tion thus is a normal good. Second, since the income elasticity for transportation is greater than 1, we know that expenditures on transportation grow more rapidly than income.

The second row of Table 3–5 reveals that food also is a normal good, since the income elasticity of food is 0.8. Since the income elasticity is less than 1, when income increases expenditures on food increase by a lower percentage than the percentage increase in income. When income declines, expenditures on food decrease less rapidly than income.

The third row of Table 3–5 presents the income elasticity for nonfed ground beef. Nonfed beef comes from cattle that have not been fed a special diet. Most cattle are fed corn for 90 to 120 days before going to market and thus produce more tender beef than nonfed cattle. The income elasticity for nonfed ground beef is negative; hence, we know that nonfed ground beef is an inferior good. The consumption of nonfed ground beef will decrease by 1.94 percent for every 1 percent rise in consumer income. Therefore, managers of grocery stores should decrease their orders of nonfed ground beef during economic booms and increase their orders during recessions.

DEMONSTRATION PROBLEM 3–2

Your firm's research department has estimated the income elasticity of demand for nonfed ground beef to be −1.94. You have just read in the *Wall Street Journal* that due to an upturn in the economy, consumer incomes are expected to rise by 10 percent over the next three years. As a manager of a meat-processing plant, how will this forecast affect your purchases of nonfed cattle?

Answer

Set $-1.94 = E_{Q_x, M}$ and $10\% = \Delta M\%$ in the formula for the income elasticity of demand to obtain

$$-1.94 = \frac{\%\Delta Q_x^d}{10\%}.$$

Solving this equation for $\%\Delta Q_x^d$ yields -19.4 percent. Since nonfed ground beef has an income elasticity of -1.94 and consumer income is expected to rise by 10 percent, you can expect to sell 19.4 percent less nonfed ground beef over the next three years. Therefore, you should decrease your purchases of range cattle by 19.4 percent, unless something else changes.

Other Elasticities

Given the general notion of an elasticity, it is not difficult to conceptualize how the impact of changes in other variables, such as advertising, may be analyzed in elasticity terms. For example, the *own advertising elasticity* of demand for good X defines the percentage change in the consumption of X that results from a given percentage change in advertising spent on X. The *cross-advertising elasticity* between goods X and Y would measure the percentage change in the consumption of X that results from a given percentage change in advertising directed toward Y.

Table 3–6 shows estimates of the advertising elasticities for clothing and recreation. Both elasticities are positive and less than 1. The fact that they are positive reveals, as you might expect, that increases in advertising lead to an increase in the demand for the products; that is, if clothing manufacturers increase their advertising, they can expect to sell more clothing at any given price. However, the fact that the advertising elasticity of clothing is 0.04 means that a 10 percent increase in advertising will increase the demand for clothing by only .4 percent. As a broad category, clothing is not very advertising elastic.

TABLE 3–6   Selected Long-Term Advertising Elasticities

	Advertising Elasticity
Clothing	0.04
Recreation	0.25

Source: M. R. Baye, D. W. Jansen, and J. W. Lee, "Advertising Effects in Complete Demand Systems," *Applied Economics* 24 (1992), pp. 1087–96.

To illustrate how estimates such as these can be used by managers, imagine that you have just been hired by the U.S. Department of Commerce to help direct the tourist trade in the United States. Your boss knows you recently took a course in managerial economics and asks you how much she should increase advertising to increase the demand for recreation in the United States by 15 percent.

From Table 3–6, we know that $E_{Q_x, A_x} = 0.25$. Plugging this and $\%\Delta Q_x^d = 15\%$ into the general formula for the elasticity of Q_x^d with respect to A yields

$$0.25 = \frac{\%\Delta Q_x^d}{\%\Delta A_x} = \frac{15\%}{\%\Delta A_x}.$$

Solving this equation for the percentage change in advertising shows that advertising must increase by a hefty 60 percent to increase the demand for recreation by 15 percent.

Obtaining Elasticities from Demand Functions

Now that you understand what elasticities are and how to use them to make managerial decisions, we will examine how to calculate elasticities from demand functions. First, we will consider elasticities based on linear demand functions. Then we will see how to calculate elasticities from particular nonlinear demand functions.

Elasticities for Linear Demand Functions

Given an estimate of a linear demand function, it is quite easy to calculate the various elasticities of demand.

Formula: Elasticities for Linear Demand. If the demand function is linear and given by

$$Q_x^d = \alpha_0 + \alpha_x P_x + \alpha_y P_y + \alpha_M M + \alpha_H H,$$

the elasticities are:

own price elasticity: $\quad E_{Q_x, P_x} = \alpha_x \dfrac{P_x}{Q_x}$,

cross-price elasticity: $\quad E_{Q_x, P_y} = \alpha_y \dfrac{P_y}{Q_x}$,

income elasticity: $\quad E_{Q_x, M} = \alpha_M \dfrac{M}{Q_x}$.

A Calculus Alternative

The elasticities for a linear demand curve may be found using calculus. Specifically,

$$E_{Q_x, P_x} = \frac{\partial Q_x^d}{\partial P_x} \frac{P_x}{Q_x} = \alpha_x \frac{P_x}{Q_x},$$

and similarly for the cross-price and income elasticities.

Thus, for a linear demand curve, the elasticity of demand with respect to a given variable is simply the coefficient of the variable multiplied by the ratio of the variable to the quantity demanded. For instance, the own price elasticity of demand is simply the coefficient of P_x (which is α_x in the demand equation) multiplied by the ratio of the price of X to the quantity consumed of X.

For a linear demand curve, the value of an elasticity depends on the particular price and quantity at which it is calculated. This means that the own price elasticity is not the same as the slope of the demand curve. In fact, for a linear demand function, demand is elastic at high prices and inelastic at lower prices. To see this, note that when $P_x = 0$, $|E_{Q_x, P_x}| = \left| \alpha_x \frac{0}{Q_x} \right| = 0 < 1$. In other words, for prices near zero, demand is inelastic. On the other hand, when prices rise, Q_x decreases and the absolute value of the elasticity increases.

DEMONSTRATION PROBLEM 3–3

The daily demand for Invigorated PED shoes is estimated to be

$$Q_x^d = 100 - 3P_x + 4P_y - .01M + 2A_x,$$

where A_x represents the amount of advertising spent on shoes (X), P_x is the price of good X, P_y is the price of good Y, and M is average income. Suppose good X sells at $25 a pair, good Y sells at $35, the company utilizes 50 units of advertising, and average consumer income is $20,000. Calculate and interpret the own price, cross price, and income elasticity of demand.

Answer

To calculate the own price elasticity for linear demand, we use the formula

$$E_{Q_x, P_x} = \alpha_x \frac{P_x}{Q_x}.$$

Here $\alpha_x = -3$, and $P_x = 25$. The only other information we need to calculate the elasticity is the quantity consumed of X. To find Q_x we substitute the given values of prices, income, and advertising into the demand equation to get

$$Q_x = 100 - 3(25) + 4(35) - .01(20{,}000) + 2(50) = 65 \text{ units.}$$

Hence the own price elasticity of demand is given by

$$E_{Q_x, P_x} = -3\left(\frac{25}{65}\right) = -1.15.$$

If Invigorated PED raises shoe prices, the percentage decline in the quantity demanded of its shoes will be greater in absolute value than the percentage rise in price. Consequently, demand is elastic: total revenues will fall if it raises shoe prices.

Similarly, the cross price elasticity of demand is

$$E_{Q_x, P_y} = 4\left(\frac{35}{65}\right) = 2.15.$$

Since this is positive, good Y is a substitute for Invigorated PED's shoes. The income elasticity of demand for Invigorated PED's shoes is

$$E_{Q_x, M} = -0.01\left(\frac{20{,}000}{65}\right) = -3.08.$$

Invigorated PED's shoes are inferior goods, since this is a negative number.

Elasticities for Nonlinear Demand Functions

Managers frequently encounter situations where a product's demand is not a linear function of prices, income, advertising, and other demand shifters. In this section we demonstrate that the tools we developed can easily be adapted to these more complex environments.

Suppose the demand function is not a linear function but instead is given by

$$Q_x^d = cP_x^{\beta_x}P_y^{\beta_y}M^{\beta_M}H^{\beta_H},$$

where c is a constant. In this case, the quantity demanded of good X is not a linear function of prices and income but a nonlinear function. If we take the logarithm of this equation, we obtain an expression that is linear in the logarithms of the variables:

$$\log Q_x^d = \beta_0 + \beta_x \log P_x + \beta_y \log P_y + \beta_M \log M + \beta_H \log H,$$

log-linear demand
Demand is log-linear if the logarithm of demand is a linear function of the logarithms of prices, income, and other variables.

where $\beta_0 = \log(c)$ and the β_i's are arbitrary real numbers. This relation is called a *log-linear demand* function.

As in the case of linear demand, the sign of the coefficient of P_y determines whether goods X and Y are substitutes or complements, whereas the sign of the coefficient of M determines whether X is a normal or an inferior good. For example, if β_y is a positive number, an increase in the price of good Y will lead to an increase in the consumption of good X; in this instance, X and Y are substitutes. If β_y is a negative number, an increase in the price of good Y will lead to a decrease in the consumption of good X; in this instance, goods X and Y are complements.

Similarly, if β_M is a positive number, an increase in income leads to an increase in the consumption of good X, and X is a normal good. If β_M is a negative number, an increase in income leads to a decrease in the consumption of good X, and X is an inferior good.

Formula: Elasticities for Log-Linear Demand.   When the demand function for good X is log-linear and given by

$$\log Q_x^d = \beta_0 + \beta_x \log P_x + \beta_x \log P_y + \beta_M \log M + \beta_H \log H,$$

the elasticities are:

$$\text{own price elasticity:} \quad E_{Q_x, P_x} = \alpha_x,$$

$$\text{cross-price elasticity:} \quad E_{Q_x, P_y} = \alpha_y,$$

$$\text{income elasticity:} \quad E_{Q_x, M} = \alpha_M.$$

A Calculus Alternative

The above result may also be derived using calculus. Taking the antilogarithm of the equation for log-linear demand gives

$$Q_x^d = c P_x^{\beta_x} P_y^{\beta_y} M^{\beta_M} H^{\beta_H},$$

where c is a constant. Using the calculus formula for an elasticity yields

$$E_{Q_x, P_x} = \frac{\partial Q_x^d}{\partial P_x}\left(\frac{P_x}{Q_x}\right) = \beta_x c P_x^{\beta_x - 1} P_y^{\beta_y} M^{\beta_M} H^{\beta_H}\left(\frac{P_x}{c P_x^{\beta_x} P_y^{\beta_y} M^{\beta_M} H^{\beta_H}}\right) = \beta_x$$

and similarly for the cross-price and income elasticities.

Notice that when demand is log-linear, the elasticity with respect to a given variable is simply the coefficient of the corresponding logarithm. The own price elasticity of demand is the coefficient of $\log(P_x)$, and in fact, the coefficient of *any* other logarithm on the right-hand side of the log-linear demand relation tells us the elasticity of demand with respect to that demand shifter. Since all of these coefficients are constants, none of the elasticities depend on the value of variables like prices, income, or advertising.

Table 3–7 shows the results of a statistical study that found the demand for breakfast cereal to be log-linear. Since this is a log-linear demand relation, we know that the coefficients may be interpreted as elasticities.

The study summarized in Table 3–7 focused primarily on the effect of advertising on the demand for breakfast cereal. Other factors affecting the demand for cereal include its price and the average (per capita) income of

TABLE 3–7   The Log-Linear Demand for Breakfast Cereal

$Q_C = -7.256 - 1.647 \log (P_C) + 1.071 \log (M) + 0.146 \log (A)$
Q_C = per capita consumption of breakfast cereal
P_C = price of cereal
M = per capita income
A = a measure of advertising by the top four cereal firms

Source: Adapted from Michael R. Baye, *The Economic Effects of Proposed Regulation of TV Advertising Directed at Children: A Theoretical and Empirical Analysis,* senior honors thesis, Texas A&M University, 1980.

consumers. Surprisingly, the study found that the price of milk was not an important determinant of the demand for breakfast cereal.

In Table 3–7, the coefficient of the logarithm of price is -1.647. This shows that the demand for cereal is elastic and downward sloping. Furthermore, a decrease of 10 percent in the price of cereal will increase the quantity of cereal demanded by 16.47 percent, and therefore raise the sales revenues of cereal manufacturers. The coefficient of the logarithm of income is $+1.071$, indicating that cereal is a normal good. A 10 percent increase in consumers' per capita income would result in a 10.7 percent increase in cereal demand. The coefficient of the logarithm of advertising is positive, indicating that an increase in cereal advertising will increase cereal demand. However, notice that the advertising elasticity is relatively small. A 10 percent increase in cereal advertising increases the demand for cereal by only 1.46 percent. Apparently, cereal advertising does not induce consumers to eat cereal for lunch and dinner.

As a final check of your ability to utilize elasticities, try to work the following problem.

DEMONSTRATION PROBLEM 3–4

An analyst for a major apparel company estimates that the demand for its raincoats is given by

$$\log Q_x^d = 10 - 1.2 \log P_x + 3 \log R - 2 \log A_y,$$

where R denotes the daily amount of rainfall and A_y represents the level of advertising on good Y. What would be the impact on demand of a 10 percent increase in the daily amount of rainfall? What would be the impact of a 10 percent reduction in the amount of advertising directed toward good Y? Can you think of an example of a good that might be good Y in this example?

Answer

We know that for log-linear demand functions, the coefficient of the logarithm of a variable gives the elasticity of demand with respect to that variable. Thus, the elasticity of demand for raincoats with respect to rainfall is

$$E_{Q_x, R} = \beta_R = 3.$$

Furthermore,

$$E_{Q_x, R} = \frac{\%\Delta Q_x^d}{\%\Delta R}.$$

Hence,

$$3 = \frac{\%\Delta Q_x^d}{10\%}.$$

Solving this equation yields $\%\Delta Q_x^d = 30$. In other words, the 10 percent increase in rainfall will lead to a 30 percent increase in the demand for raincoats.

To examine the impact on the demand for raincoats of a 10 percent reduction in advertising spent on good Y, again note that for log-linear demand functions, each coefficient gives the elasticity of demand with respect to that variable. Thus, the elasticity of demand for raincoats with respect to advertising directed toward good Y is

$$E_{Q_x, A_y} = \beta_{A_y} = -2.$$

Furthermore,

$$E_{Q_x, A_y} = \beta_{A_y} = \frac{\%\Delta Q_x^d}{\%\Delta A_y}.$$

Hence,

$$-2 = \frac{\%\Delta Q_x^d}{-10\%}.$$

Solving this equation yields $\%\Delta Q_x^d = 20\%$. In other words, the 10 percent reduction in advertising directed toward good Y leads to a 20 percent increase in the demand for raincoats. Perhaps good Y is umbrellas, for one would expect the demand for raincoats to increase whenever fewer umbrella advertisements are made.

Regression Analysis

The preceding analysis assumes the manager knows the demand for the firm's product. We pointed out several studies that provide explicit estimates of demand elasticities and functional forms for demand functions. As a manager, you may obtain estimates of demand and elasticity from published studies available in the library or from a consultant hired to estimate the demand function based on the specifics of your product. Or, you might enter data into a spreadsheet program and click the regression toolbar to obtain an estimated demand function, along with some regression diagnostics. Regardless of how the manager obtains the estimates, it is useful to have a general understanding of how demand functions are estimated and what the various diagnostic statistics that accompany the reported output mean. This entails knowledge of a branch of economics called *econometrics*.

Econometrics is simply the statistical analysis of economic phenomena. It is far beyond the scope of this book to teach you how to estimate demand functions, but it is possible to convey the basic ideas econometricians use to obtain such information. Your primary job as a manager is to use the information to make decisions similar to the examples provided in previous sections of this chapter.

Let us briefly examine the basic ideas underlying the estimation of the demand for a product. Suppose there is some underlying data on the relation between a dependent variable, Y, and some explanatory variable, X. Suppose that when the values of X and Y are plotted, they appear as points A, B, C, D, E, and F in Figure 3–4. Clearly, the points do not lie on a straight line, or even a smooth curve (try alternative ways of connecting the dots if you are not convinced).

The job of the econometrician is to find a smooth curve or line that does a "good" job of approximating the points. For example, suppose the econometrician believes that, on average, there is a linear relation between Y and X, but there is also some random variation in the relationship. Mathematically, this would imply that the true relationship between Y and X is

$$Y = a + bX + e,$$

FIGURE 3–4:

The regression line

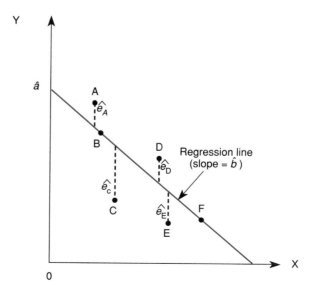

where a and b are unknown parameters and e is a random variable (an error term) that has a zero mean. Because the parameters that determine the expected relation between Y and X are unknown, the econometrician must find out the values of the parameters a and b.

Note that for any line drawn through the points, there will be some discrepancy between the actual points and the line. For example, consider the line in Figure 3–4, which does a reasonable job of fitting the data. If a manager used the line to approximate the true relation, there would be some discrepancy between the actual data and the line. For example, points A and D actually lie above the line, while points C and E lie below it. The deviations between the actual points and the line are given by the distance of the dashed lines in Figure 3–4, namely $\hat{e}_A$, $\hat{e}_C$, $\hat{e}_D$, and $\hat{e}_E$. Since the line represents the expected, or average, relation between Y and X, these deviations are analogous to the deviations from the mean used to calculate the variance of a random variable.

The econometrician uses a regression software package to find the values of a and b that minimize the sum of the squared deviations between the actual points and the line. In essence, the *regression line* is the line that minimizes the squared deviations between the line (the expected relation) and the actual data points. These values of a and b, which frequently are denoted $\hat{a}$ and $\hat{b}$, are called *parameter estimates*, and the corresponding line is called the *least squares regression*.

least squares regression
The line that minimizes the sum of squared deviations between the line and the actual data points.

The least squares regression line for the equation

$$Y = a + bX + e$$

is given by

$$Y = \hat{a} + \hat{b}X.$$

The parameter estimates, $\hat{a}$ and $\hat{b}$, represent the values of a and b that result in the smallest *sum of squared errors* between a line and the actual data.

Spreadsheet software packages, such as Excel or Lotus, make it easy to use regression analysis to estimate demand functions. To illustrate, suppose a television manufacturer has data on the price and quantity of TVs sold last month at 10 outlets in Pittsburgh. Here we use price and quantity as our explanatory and dependent variables, respectively. When the data are entered into a spreadsheet, it looks like the first 11 rows in Table 3–8. A few clicks of the mouse, and the spreadsheet calculates the average price and quantity reported in row 12. Furthermore, by clicking the regression toolbar, the regression output reported in rows 16 through 33 is produced. Cell 32-B shows that the intercept of the estimated demand function for TVs is 1631.47, and cell 33-B shows that the estimated coefficient of price is -2.60. Thus, the linear demand function for TVs that minimizes the sum of squared errors between the actual data points and the line through the points is

$$Q = 1631.47 - 2.60\,P.$$

TABLE 3–8:   Using a Spreadsheet to Perform a Regression

	A	B	C	D	E	F	G
1	Observation	Quantity	Price				
2	1	180	475				
3	2	590	400				
4	3	430	450				
5	4	250	550				
6	5	275	575				
7	6	720	375				
8	7	660	375				
9	8	490	450				
10	9	700	400				
11	10	210	500				
12	Average	477.22	450.00				
13							
14							
15							
16	*Regression Statistics*						
17							
18	Multiple R	0.87					
19	R-Square	0.75					
20	Adjusted R-Square	0.72					
21	Standard Error	112.22					
22	Observations	10.00					
23							
24	*Analysis of Variance*						
25		*df*	*Sum of Squares*	*Mean Square*	*F*	*Significance F*	
26	Regression	1.00	301470.89	301470.89	23.94	0.0012	
27	Residual	8.00	100751.61	12593.95			
28	Total	9.00	402222.50				
29							
30		*Coefficients*	*Standard Error*	*t-Statistic*	*P-value*	*Lower 95%*	*Upper 95%*
31							
32	Intercept	1631.47	243.97	6.69	0.0001	1068.87	2194.07
33	Price	−2.60	0.53	−4.89	0.0009	−3.82	−1.37

Notice that the spreadsheet program also produces detailed information about the regression and the estimated coefficients as a byproduct of the regression. As discussed below, these statistics enable the manager to test for the statistical significance of the estimated coefficients and to assess the performance of the overall regression.

Evaluating the Statistical Significance of Estimated Coefficients

Rows 30 through 33 of the regression output in Table 3–8 provide information about the precision with which the parameters of the demand function are estimated. The coefficients reported in cells 32-B and 33-B are merely the parameter estimates—estimates of the true, unknown coefficients. Given different data generated from the same true demand relation, different estimates of the true coefficients would be obtained. The *standard error* of each estimated coefficient is a measure of how much each estimated coefficient would vary in regressions based on the same underlying true demand relation, but with different observations. The smaller the standard error of an estimated coefficient, the smaller the variation in the estimate given data from different outlets (different samples of data).

The least squares parameter estimates are unbiased estimators of the true demand parameters whenever the errors (the e_i's) in the true demand relation have a zero mean. If, in addition, the e_i's are independently and identically distributed normal random variables (in short, *iid normal* random variables), the reported standard errors of the estimated coefficients can be used to construct confidence intervals and to perform significance tests. These techniques are discussed below.

Confidence Intervals

Given a parameter estimate, its standard error, and the iid normal assumption, the firm manager can construct upper and lower bounds on the true value of the estimated coefficient by constructing a 95 percent confidence interval. A useful rule of thumb is presented in the principle below, but fortunately regression packages compute precise confidence intervals for each coefficient estimated in a regression. For instance, the last two cells of Table 3–8 indicate that the upper and lower bounds of the 95 percent confidence interval for the coefficient of price is -3.82 and -1.37. The parameter estimate for the price coefficient, -2.60, lies in the middle of these bounds. Thus, we know that the best estimate of the price coefficient is -2.60, and that we are 95 percent confident that the true value lies between -3.82 and -1.37.

Principle

Rule of Thumb for a 95 Percent Confidence Interval
If the parameter estimates of a regression equation are $\hat{a}$ and $\hat{b}$, the 95 percent confidence intervals for the true values of a and b can be approximated by

$$\hat{a} \pm 2\sigma_{\hat{a}}$$

and

$$\hat{b} \pm 2\sigma_{\hat{b}},$$

where $\sigma_{\hat{b}}$ and $\sigma_{\hat{b}}$ are the standard errors of $\hat{a}$ and $\hat{b}$, respectively.

The *t*-Statistic

t-statistic
The ratio of the value of a parameter estimate to the standard error of the parameter estimate.

The *t*-statistic of a parameter estimate is the ratio of the value of the parameter estimate to its standard error. For example, if the parameter estimates are $\hat{a}$ and $\hat{b}$ and the corresponding standard errors are $\sigma_{\hat{a}}$ and $\sigma_{\hat{b}}$, the *t*-statistic for $\hat{a}$ is

$$t_{\hat{a}} = \frac{\hat{a}}{\sigma_{\hat{b}}}$$

and the *t*-statistic for $\hat{b}$ is

$$t_{\hat{b}} = \frac{\hat{b}}{\sigma_{\hat{b}}}.$$

big *t*:
$\bar{x} \approx \mu$

When the *t*-statistic for a parameter estimate is large in absolute value, then you can be confident that the parameter estimate is close to the true value. The reason for this is that, when the absolute value of the *t*-statistic is large, the standard error of the parameter estimate is small relative to the absolute value of the parameter estimate. Thus, one can be more confident that, given a different sample of data drawn from the true model, the new parameter estimate will be in the same ballpark.

$t \geq 2$ - statistically different from 0

A useful rule of thumb is that if the absolute value of a *t*-statistic is greater than or equal to 2, then the corresponding parameter estimate is statistically different from zero. Regression packages report *P*-values, which are a much more precise measure of statistical significance. For instance, in cell 33-E of Table 3–8 we see that the *P*-value for the estimated coefficient of price is .0009. This means that there is only a 9 in 10,000 chance that the true coefficient of price is actually 0. Notice that the lower the *P*-value for an estimated coefficient, the more confident you are in the estimate.

Usually, *P*-values of .05 or below are considered low enough for a researcher to be confident that the estimated coefficient is statistically significant. If the *P*-value is .05, we say that the estimated coefficient is statistically significant at the 5 percent level. Notice that the *P*-value reported in Table 3–8 for the coefficient of price implies that it is statistically significant at the .09 percent level: the estimated coefficient is highly significant. It is important to note that, like confidence intervals, reported *P*-values presume that the errors in the true regression equation are iid normal.

Principle

A Rule of Thumb for Using *t*-Statistics
When the absolute value of the *t*-statistic is greater than 2, the manager can be 95 percent confident that the true value of the underlying parameter in the regression is not zero.

Evaluating the Overall Fit of the Regression Line

In addition to evaluating the statistical significance of one or more coefficients, one can also measure the precision with which the overall regression line fits the data. Two yardsticks frequently used to measure the overall fit of the regression line—the *R*-square and the *F* statistic—are discussed next.

The *R*-Square

Rows 18 through 20 of Table 3–8 provide diagnostics that indicate how well the regression line explains the sample of observations of the dependent variable (in the example, quantity is the dependent variable, and price is the explanatory variable). *The R-square* (also called the *coefficient of determination*) tells the fraction of the total variation in the dependent variable that is explained by the regression. It is computed as the ratio of the sum of squared errors from the regression ($SS_{Regression}$) to the total sum of squared errors (SS_{Total}):

$$R^2 = \frac{Explained\ Variation}{Total\ Variation} = \frac{SS_{Regression}}{SS_{Total}}.$$

For instance, in cell 26-C of Table 3–8 we see that the sum of squared errors from the regression is 301470.89, while cell 28-C reveals that the total sum of squared errors is 402222.50. Thus, the *R*-square is .75 (=301470.89/402222.50). This means that the estimated demand equation (the regression line) explains 75 percent of the total variation in TV sales across the sample of 10 outlets. Most spreadsheet regression packages automatically calculate the *R*-square, as seen in cell 19-B of Table 3–8.[1]

The value of an *R*-square ranges from 0 and 1:

$$0 \leq R^2 \leq 1.$$

The closer the *R*-square is to 1, the "better" the overall fit of the estimated regression equation to the actual data. Unfortunately, there is no simple cut-off that can be used to determine whether an *R*-square is close enough to 1 to indicate a "good" fit. With time series data, *R*-squares are often in excess of .9; with cross sectional data, .5 might be considered a reasonably good fit. Thus, a major drawback of the *R*-square is that it is a subjective measure of goodness of fit.

Another problem with the *R*-square is that it cannot decrease when additional explanatory variables are included in the regression. Thus, if we included income, advertising, and other explanatory variables in our regression, but held other things constant, we would almost surely get a higher *R*-square. Eventually, when the number of estimated coefficients increased to the number of observations, we would end up with an *R*-square of 1.

---

[1]The square root of the *R*-square, called the Multiple *R*, is also reported by most spreadsheet regression programs. It is given in cell 18-B of Table 3–8.

Sometimes, the *R*-square is very close to 1 merely because the number of observations is small relative to the number of estimated parameters. This situation is undesirable from a statistical viewpoint, because it can provide a very misleading indicator of the goodness of fit of the regression line. For this reason, many researchers use the adjusted *R*-square reported in cell 20-B of Table 3–8 as a measure of goodness of fit.

The *adjusted* R-*square* is given by

$$\overline{R^2} = 1 - (1 - R^2)\frac{(n - 1)}{(n - k)}$$

where *n* is the total number of observations and *k* is the number of estimated coefficients. In performing a regression, the number of parameters to be estimated cannot exceed the number of observations. The difference, $n - k$, represents the *residual degrees of freedom* after conducting the regression. Notice that the adjusted *R*-square "penalizes" the researcher for performing a regression with only a few degrees of freedom (that is, estimating numerous coefficients from relatively few observations). In fact, the penalty can be so high that, in some instances, the adjusted R-square is actually negative.

In our example, cell 22-B in Table 3–8 shows us that $n = 10$. Cells 32-B and 33-B indicate that we estimated 2 parameters, so $k = 2$. With 8 residual degrees of freedom, the adjusted *R*-square of our regression is $1 - (1 - .75)(9/8) = .72$. This number is reported in cell 20-B. There is little difference between the *R*-square and the adjusted *R*-square, so it does not appear that the "high" *R*-square is a result of an excessive number of estimated coefficients relative to the sample size.

The *F*-Statistic

While the *R*-square and adjusted *R*-square of a regression both provide a gauge of the overall fit of a regression, we noted that there is no universal rule for determining how "high" they must be to indicate a good fit. An alternative measure of goodness of fit, called the F-*statistic*, does not suffer from this shortcoming. The *F*-statistic provides a measure of the total variation explained by the regression relative to the total unexplained variation. The greater the *F*-statistic, the better the overall fit of the regression line through the actual data. In our example, the *F*-statistic is reported as 23.94 in cell 26-E of Table 3–8.

The primary advantage of the *F*-statistic stems from the fact that its statistical properties are known. Thus, one can objectively determine the statistical significance of any reported *F* value. The significance value for our regression, .0012, is reported in cell 26-F of Table 3–8. This low number means that there is only .12 percent chance that the estimated regression model fit the data purely by accident.

As with *P*-values, the lower the significance value of the *F*-statistic, the more confident you can be of the overall fit of the regression equation.

[Handwritten margin note: R^2 & adj. R^2 then coefficients relative to sample size is fine]

Regressions that have *F*-statistics with significance values of 5 percent or less are generally considered significant. Based on the significance value reported in cell 26-F of Table 3–8, our regression is significant at the .12 percent level. The regression is therefore highly significant.

Nonlinear and Multiple Regressions

The techniques described above to estimate a linear demand function with a single explanatory variable can also be used to estimate nonlinear demand functions. These same tools can be used to estimate demand functions in which the quantity demanded depends on several explanatory variables, such as prices, income, advertising, and so on. These issues are discussed below.

Nonlinear Regressions

Sometimes, a plot of the data will reveal nonlinearities in the data, as seen in Figure 3–5. Here, it appears that price and quantity are not linearly related: the demand function is a curve. The log-linear demand curve we examined earlier in this chapter has such a curved shape.

To estimate a log-linear demand function, the econometrician takes the logarithm of prices and quantities before executing the regression routine that minimizes the sum of squared errors (*e*):

$$\log Q = \beta_0 + \beta_P \log P + e.$$

In other words, by using a spreadsheet to compute $Q' = \log Q$ and $P' =$

FIGURE 3–5:

Log-linear regression line

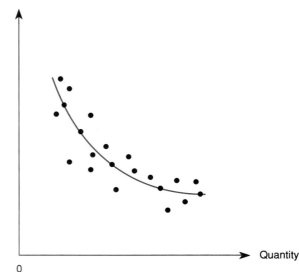

$\log Q = Q'$
$\log P = P'$

log P, this demand specification can be viewed equivalently as

$$Q' = \beta_0 + \beta_P \, P' + e,$$

which is linear in Q' and P'. Therefore, one can use procedures identical to those described earlier and regress the transformed Q' on P' to obtain parameter estimates. Recall that the resulting parameter estimate for β_P in this case is the own price elasticity of demand, since this is a log-linear demand function.

Multiple Regression

In general, the demand for a good will depend not only on the good's price, but also on demand shifters. Regression techniques can also be used to perform multiple regressions—regressions of a dependent variable on multiple explanatory variables. For the case of a linear demand relation, one might specify the demand function as

$$Q_x^d = \alpha_0 + \alpha_x P_x + \alpha_y P_y + \alpha_M M + \alpha_H H + e,$$

where the α's are the parameters to be estimated, P_y, M, and H are demand shifters, and e is the random error term that has a zero mean. Alternatively, a log-linear specification might be appropriate if the quantity demanded is not linearly related to the explanatory variables:

$$\log Q_x^d = \beta_0 + \beta_x \log P_x + \beta_y \log P_y + \beta_M \log M + \beta_H \log H + e.$$

Provided the number of observations is greater than the number of parameters to be estimated, one can use standard regression packages included in spreadsheet programs to find the values of the parameters that minimize the sum of squared errors of the regression. The R-square, F-statistic, t-statistics, and confidence intervals for multiple regressions have the same use and interpretations described earlier for the case of a simple regression with one explanatory variable. The following demonstration problem illustrates this fact.

DEMONSTRATION PROBLEM 3–5:

FCI owns 10 apartment buildings in a college town, which it rents exclusively to students. Each apartment building contains 100 rental units, but the owner is having cash flow problems due to an average vacancy rate of nearly 50 percent. The apartments in each building have comparable floor plans, but some buildings are closer to campus than others. The owner of FCI has data from last year on the number of apartments rented, the rental price (in dollars), and the amount spent on advertising (in hundreds of dollars) at each of the 10 apartments. This data, along with the distance (in miles) from each apartment building to campus is presented in rows

TABLE 3–9:   Input and Output from a Multiple Regression

	A	B	C	D	E	F	G
1	**Observation**	**Quantity**	**Price**	**Advertising**	**Distance**		
2	1	28	250	11	12		
3	2	69	400	24	6		
4	3	43	450	15	5		
5	4	32	550	31	7		
6	5	42	575	34	4		
7	6	72	375	22	2		
8	7	66	375	12	5		
9	8	49	450	24	7		
10	9	70	400	22	4		
11	10	60	375	10	5		
12	**Average**	52.33	425.00	21.67	5.78		
13							
14							
15							
16	*Regression Statistics*						
17							
18	Multiple *R*	0.89					
19	*R*-Square	0.79					
20	Adjusted *R*-Square	0.69					
21	Standard Error	9.18					
22	Observations	10.00					
23							
24	*Analysis of Variance*						
25		*df*	*Sum of Squares*	*Mean Square*	*F*	*Significance F*	
26	Regression	3.00	1920.99	640.33	7.59	0.0182	
27	Residual	6.00	505.91	84.32			
28	Total	9.00	2426.90				
29							
30		*Coefficients*	*Standard Error*	*t-Statistic*	*P-value*	*Lower 95%*	*Upper 95%*
31							
32	Intercept	135.15	20.65	6.54	0.0001	84.61	185.68
33	Price	−0.14	0.06	−2.41	0.0393	−0.29	0.00
34	Advertising	0.54	0.64	0.85	0.4191	−1.02	2.09
35	Distance	−5.78	1.26	−4.61	0.0013	−8.86	−2.71

1 through 12 of Table 3–9. The owner regressed the quantity demanded of apartments on price, advertising, and distance. The results of the regression are reported in rows 16 through 35 of Table 3–9. What is the estimated demand function for FCI's rental units? If FCI raised rents at one complex by $100, what would you expect to happen to the number of units rented? If FCI raised rents at an average

apartment building, what would happen to FCI's total revenues? What inferences should be drawn from this analysis?

Answer:

Letting P, A, and D represent price, advertising, and distance from campus, the estimated coefficients imply the following demand for rental units at an apartment building:

$$Q_x^d = 135.15 - 0.14\,P + 0.54\,A - 5.78\,D.$$

Since the coefficient of price is -0.14, a \$100 increase in price reduces the quantity demanded at an apartment building by 14 units. The own price elasticity of demand for FCI's rental units, calculated at the average price and quantity, is $(-.14)(425/52.33) = -1.14$. Since demand is elastic, raising the rent at an average apartment building would decrease not only the number of units rented, but total revenues as well.

The R-square of .79 indicates that the regression explains 79 percent of the variation in the quantity of apartments rented across the 10 buildings. The F-statistic suggests that the regression is significant at the 1.82 percent level, so the manager can be reasonably confident that the good fit of the equation is not due to chance. Notice that all of the estimated parameters are statistically significant at the 5 percent level, except for the coefficient of advertising. Thus, it does not appear that advertising has a statistically significant effect on the demand for his rental units.

Distance from campus appears to be a very significant determinant of the demand for apartments. The t-value for this coefficient is in excess of 4 in absolute value, and the P-value is .13 percent. Based on the lower and upper bound of its confidence interval, the owner can be 95 percent confident that for every mile an apartment is away from campus, FCI loses between 2.71 and 8.86 renters.

Since FCI can't relocate its apartments closer to campus, and advertising does not have a statistically significant impact on units rented, it would appear that all FCI can do to reduce its cash flow problems is to lower rents at those apartment buildings where demand is elastic.

Answering the Headline

At the beginning of the chapter we asked how much money the CEO of a regional telephone company would need to win a new license in an FCC auction. Based on the provided regression, the expected price paid for a license is negatively related to the number of licenses available, and positively related to the size of the population in the region:

$$\log P = 2.23 - 1.2 \log Q + 1.25 \log \text{Pop}.$$

Since this is a log-linear regression, the coefficients are elasticities. In particular, the coefficient of log Pop (1.25) tells us the percentage change in price resulting from a given percentage change in population. Since the population in the relevant region is 7 percent higher than the average, this means $1.25 = \%\Delta P/7\%$, or $\%\Delta P = 8.75\%$. In other words, the price the CEO expects to pay in his region is 8.75 percent higher than the average price paid in the March 14th auction. Since that price was $7.07 million, the expected price needed to win the auction in his region is, other things equal, $7.69 million. The CEO's model predicts that the demand for licenses will be greater in his region, due to the greater size of the market ultimately serviced by the holders of the licenses.

The CEO should exercise caution in using this estimate, however. The regression does not include information about regional income and the number of bidders—two pieces of information that might be useful for predicting the price. One would expect the average income of a region to have a positive effect on the price firms are willing to pay, since ultimately higher incomes in a region will translate into higher prices for wireless communication services. In addition, the greater the number of bidders for licenses, the greater the competition and thus the higher one would expect the price to be. If these two variables differ significantly across regions, then the CEO's regression estimates will be biased.

Subject to these caveats, however, the regression results summarized in Table 3–10 (based on the actual data reported in the *New York Times*)

TABLE 3–10: Regression Output Based on Actual Data from the *New York Times* on the FCC Auction

	A	B	C	D	E	F	G
1	*Regression Statistics*						
2							
3	Multiple R	0.92					
4	R-Square	0.85					
5	Adjusted R- Square	0.81					
6	Standard Error	0.32					
7	Observations	10.00					
8							
9	*Analysis of Variance*						
10		*df*	*Sum of Squares*	*Mean Square*	*F*	*Significance F*	
11	Regression	2.00	4.02	2.01	19.95	0.0013	
12	Residual	7.00	0.71	0.10			
13	Total	9.00	4.73				
14							
15		*Coefficients*	*Standard Error*	*t-Statistic*	*P-value*	*Lower 95%*	*Upper 95%*
16							
17	Intercept	2.23	0.43	5.24	0.0005	1.23	3.24
18	Log Pop	1.25	0.20	6.11	0.0002	0.77	1.73
19	Log Q	−1.20	0.20	−6.10	0.0002	−1.66	−0.73

suggest that the CEO's model does a good job of explaining the prices of licenses. The R-square of .85 indicates that 85 percent of the total variation in prices is explained by the model, and the F-statistic indicates that the regression is highly significant (at the .13 percent level). The t-statistics are all well in excess of 2, with P-values all below .05 percent. This suggests that the CEO can be reasonably confident that the true coefficients are different from zero, and in fact reasonably close to the estimated ones.

Nonetheless, the predictions based on this regression equation will not perfectly reveal the price the CEO's firm will have to pay next year to win a license. Since the upper bound of the 95 percent confidence interval for the coefficient of Log Pop is 1.73, the CEO can be 95 percent confident that $7.93 million will enough to win a license. This is because 1.73 = $\%\Delta P/7\%$, so $\%\Delta P = 12.11\%$. In other words, he will need 12.11 percent more than the $7.07 million paid for a license during the March 14th auction to be 95 percent confident. Given the magnitude of the amount involved, the CEO might want to get his research department or an economic consultant to perform a more detailed analysis of the situation.

Summary

In this chapter we covered quantitative aspects of demand analysis, including the own price elasticity, income elasticity, and cross-price elasticity of demand. We examined functional forms for demand functions, including linear and log-linear specifications, and discussed the regression procedures used to estimate demand relationships. Armed with these tools, a manager can predict not only the direction of changes in demand but how far demand will move when one of the determinants of demand changes. Knowing the concepts of elasticity and the use of t-statistics and confidence intervals is extremely important when making decisions about how much inventory to hold, how many employees to schedule, and how many units of a product to produce when different determinants of demand change.

In this chapter, we saw that increasing price does not always increase revenues. If the absolute value of own price elasticity is greater than 1, an increase in price will decrease total revenue. We also covered the magnitude of changes caused by a change in the price of a substitute or a complement.

Finally, we introduced the concepts of regression and confidence intervals. By utilizing the elasticities based on an estimated demand function and constructing a confidence interval, a manager can be 95 percent certain about the amount by which demand will move when a variable like income or advertising changes.

Key Terms and Concepts

adjusted *R*-square
confidence interval
cross-advertising elasticity
cross-price elasticity
econometrics
elastic demand
elasticity
F-statistic
iid normal assumption
income elasticity
inelastic demand
least squares regression
linear demand
log-linear demand

multiple regression
nonlinear regression
own advertising elasticity
own price elasticity of demand
P-value
perfectly elastic demand
perfectly inelastic demand
R-square
regression analysis
residual degrees of freedom
t-statistic
total revenue test
unitary elastic demand

Problems

1. Several years ago the National Association of Broadcasters imposed restrictions on the amount of nonprogram material (commercials) that could be aired during children's television shows, effectively reducing the quantity of advertising allowed during children's viewing hours by 33 percent. Within four months, the price of a minute of advertising on network television increased by roughly 14 percent. What impact do you think this had on the revenues of the networks?

2. A study sponsored by the American Medical Association suggests that the absolute value of the own price elasticity for surgical procedures is smaller than that for the own price elasticity for office visits. Explain why this would be expected.

3. Suppose the monthly demand for soda by a consumer is given by $Q = 10 - 8P$.
   a. If the price of soda is $1 per can, how many sodas will the consumer purchase in a typical month?
   b. What is the elasticity of demand for soda?

4. The demand function for VCRs has been estimated to be

$$Q_v = 134 - 1.07P_t + 46P_m - 2.1P_v - 5M,$$

where Q_v is the quantity of VCRs, P_t is the price of a videocassette, P_m is the price of a movie, P_v is the price of a VCR, and M is income. Based on this information, answer the following questions.
   a. Are VCRs normal or inferior goods?

b. Are movies substitutes or complements for VCRs?

c. What additional information is needed to calculate the price elasticity of demand for VCRs?

5. When the price of butter was "low," consumers spent $5 billion annually on its consumption. When the price doubled, consumer expenditures increased to $7 billion. Recently you read that this means that the demand curve for butter is upward sloping. Do you agree? Explain.

6. The cross-price elasticity for textbooks and copies of old exams is −3.5. If the price of copies of old exams increases by 10 percent, what will happen to the quantity demanded of textbooks?

7. Which of the following goods would you expect to have the most inelastic demand? Why?

a. Swiss cheese

b. Cheese

c. Dairy products

8. The following estimates have been obtained for the market demand for cereal:

$$\log Q = 9.01 - 0.68 \log P + 0.75 \log A - 1.3 \log M,$$

where Q is the quantity of cereal, P is the price of cereal, A is the level of advertising, and M is income. Based on this information, determine the effect on the consumption of cereal of

a. A 5 percent reduction in the price of cereal.

b. A 4 percent increase in income.

c. A 20 percent reduction in cereal advertising.

9. Suppose you are the manager of a home-building company and the government is considering eliminating the tax deductibility of mortgage interest payments. A typical consumer's marginal tax rate is 25 percent, and the elasticity of demand for new homes is −1.5. Your boss wants to know the impact of the proposed government policy on your business. What do you tell him?

10. You work for an unemployment agency that distributes unemployment checks to unemployed workers in your state. Your boss recently learned that the President proposed a 21 percent increase in the minimum wage, and wants you to provide her with an estimate of the number of additional workers who will file for unemployment compensation claims next year if the bill passes. Based on library research at a nearby university, you learn that about 200,000 workers in your state earn at or below the current minimum wage. Further library research turns up a study that reports the own price elasticity of demand for minimum wage earners to be −0.30. Based on your findings, how many additional workers do you think will file unemployment claims in your state?

11. The income elasticity of demand for your firm's product is estimated to be 0.75. A recent report in *The Wall Street Journal* says that national income is expected to decline by 3 percent this year.
    a. What should you do with your stock of inventories?
    b. What do you expect to happen to your sales?
    c. How would you answer parts *a* and *b* if you expected a 5 percent increase in income instead of a decrease?

12. A consumer spends all of her income on only one good. What is the income elasticity of demand for this good? What is the own price elasticity of demand for this good?

13. As the manager of a local hotel chain, you have hired an econometrician to estimate the demand for one of your hotels (*H*). The estimation has resulted in the following demand function:

$$Q_H = 2{,}000 - P_H - 1.5\, P_C - 2.25 P_{SE} + 0.8 P_{OH} + .01\, M,$$

where P_H is the price of a room at your hotel, P_C is the price of concerts in your area, P_{SE} is the price of sporting events in your area, P_{OH} is the average room price at other hotels in your area, and *M* is the average income in the United States. What would be the impact on your firm of
    a. A $500 increase in income?
    b. A $10 reduction in the price charged by other hotels?
    c. A $7 increase in the price of tickets to local sporting events?
    d. A $5 increase in the price of concert tickets, accompanied by an $8 increase in income?

14. Your firm's research department has estimated the elasticity of demand for toys to be -0.7. As the manager of a local chain of toy stores, determine the impact of an 8 percent increase in toy prices on your total revenues.

15. The demand for Wanderlust Travel Services (*X*) is estimated to be

$$Q_x = 22{,}000 - 2.5 P_x + 4 P_y - 1M + 1.5 A_x,$$

where A_x represents the amount of advertising spent on *X* and the other variables have their usual interpretations. Suppose the price of good *X* is $450, good *Y* sells for $40, the company utilizes 3,000 units of advertising, and consumer income is $20,000.
    a. Calculate the own price elasticity of demand at these values of prices, income, and advertising.
    b. Is demand elastic, inelastic, or unitary elastic?
    c. How will your answers to parts *a* and *b* change if the price of *Y* increases to $50?

16. The demand for company *X*'s product is given by

$$Q_x = 12 - 3 P_x + 4 P_y.$$

Suppose good X sells for $3.00 per unit and good Y sells for $1.50 per unit.

a. Calculate the cross-price elasticity of demand between goods X and Y at the given prices.

b. Are goods X and Y substitutes or complements?

c. What is the own price elasticity of demand at these prices?

d. How would your answers to parts a and c change if the price of X dropped to $2.50 per unit?

17. Your firm's research department has estimated the income elasticity of demand for Art Deco lawn furniture to be -0.85. You have just learned that due to an upturn in the economy, consumer incomes are expected to rise by 5 percent next year. How will this event affect your ordering decision for PVC pipe, which is the main component in your furniture?

18. Suppose the demand for sunscreen (X) has been estimated to be

$$\log Q_x = 5 - 1.7 \log P_x + 3 \log S - 3 \log A_y,$$

where S denotes the average hours of sunshine per day and A_y represents the level of advertising for good Y.

a. What would be the impact on demand of a 5 percent increase in the daily amount of sunshine?

b. What would be the impact of a 10 percent reduction in the amount of advertising toward good Y?

c. What might be good Y in this example?

19. An econometrician has estimated the inverse demand relation $P = a + bQ + e$ and found that $\hat{a} = 400$, $\hat{b} = -2.75$, $\sigma_{\hat{a}} = 8$, and $\sigma_{\hat{b}} = 0.75$. Find the approximate 95 percent confidence interval for the true values of a and b.

20. A firm is considering raising its price by 9 percent and has hired an econometrician to estimate the elasticity of demand for its product. The econometrician estimates the parameters of a log-linear demand function and reports that the parameter estimate for the elasticity of demand is -1.5 and the standard error of the estimate is 0.3.

a. If the firm raises its price by 9 percent, what is the expected change in quantity demanded?

b. Approximate the upper and lower bounds on the 95 percent confidence interval for the change in quantity demanded.

21. The manager of a major health insurance company obtained data from 9 states on the number of individuals who purchase private health insurance. Based on this data, she used her spreadsheet to run a log-linear regression (the relevant output is presented in Table 3–11). Based on the estimated log-linear demand for health insurance:

a. Do the signs of the coefficients of the explanatory variables make economic sense? Explain.

b. Which regression coefficients are statistically significant at the 5 percent level?

c. The Federal government is considering raising the tax on cigarettes, which would raise the price of cigarettes by 22 percent. What impact would you expect this to have on the number of people who purchase health insurance? How confident are you in this prediction?

d. In New York consumer incomes are 10 percent higher than the average income of the 9 states included in the sample. Find a lower bound estimate of how much more or less insurance would be purchased in New York, other things being equal, presuming you want to be 95 percent confident in your prediction.

e. Evaluate the overall fit of the regression. Can you think of any important explanatory variables missing from the regression?

22. Baker Enterprises sells software in 50 states in the U.S. The firm's marketing department obtained data from 30 of the firm's outlets in each state. The data consists of the quantity and price of software sold at each outlet, as well as the average income (in thousands of dollars) of consumers who purchased the product at that outlet. The diskette

TABLE 3–11

	A	B	C	D	E	F	G
1	*Regression Statistics*						
2							
3	Multiple *R*	0.89					
4	*R*-Square	0.79					
5	Adjusted *R*-Square	0.66					
6	Standard Error	0.57					
7	Observations	9.00					
8							
9	*Analysis of Variance*						
10		*df*	*Sum of Squares*	*Mean Square*	*F*	*Significance F*	
11	Regression	3.00	6.02	2.01	6.26	0.0381	
12	Residual	5.00	1.60	0.32			
13	Total	8.00	7.63				
14							
15		*Coefficients*	*Standard Error*	*t-Statistic*	*P-value*	*Lower 95%*	*Upper 95%*
16							
17	Intercept	3.13	1.01	3.09	0.0150	0.52	5.73
18	Income	1.05	0.28	3.79	0.0053	0.34	1.77
19	Price of Health Ins.	−0.32	0.77	−0.41	0.6929	−2.30	1.67
20	Price of Cigarettes	−0.17	0.13	−1.31	0.2281	−0.51	0.17

that accompanies this textbook contains the data for each state in XLS (spreadsheet) format under the filename **22__ZIP.XLS,** where "zip" refers to the two-digit zip code of the state. For instance, the data for Texas is contained in the file named **22__TX.XLS.**

a. Import the data from your state into your spreadsheet, and print the data.

b. Assume that the underlying demand relation is a linear function of price and income. Use your spreadsheet program to obtain least-squares estimates of your state's demand for Baker software. (Note: Make sure you include a constant in your regression.) Print the regression output.

c. Provide the CEO of Baker Enterprises with an economic interpretation of the regression output.

23. A consultant recently collected data from a firm that placed advertisements through Advertising Inc. The data consists of the quantity sold of the firm's product at each of the firm's outlets, the average price at that outlet, the average income (in thousands of dollars) of consumers making purchases at that outlet, and the firm's level of advertising at that outlet. Advertising is measured in terms of deviations from the firm's average: an advertising measure of -20.5 at an outlet means that the firm advertised that outlet 20.5 minutes less than the average outlet. The data for each state are contained on the data disk that accompanies this textbook in XLS (spreadsheet) format under the filename **23__ZIP.XLS,** where "zip" refers to the two-digit zip code of the state. For instance, the data for Texas is contained in the file named **23__TX.XLS.**

a. Import the data from your state into your spreadsheet, and print the data.

b. Assume that the underlying demand relation is a linear function of price, income, and advertising. Use your spreadsheet program to obtain least-squares estimates of the demand parameters for your state. (Note: Make sure you include a constant in your regression.) Print the regression output.

c. Provide an economic interpretation of the regression output. Do advertisements placed through Advertising Inc. appear to have a statistically significant effect on demand in your state? Explain.

Selected Readings

Chiles, Ted W., Jr. and Sollars, David L., "Estimating Cigarette Tax Revenue." *Journal of Economics and Finance* 17(3), Fall 1993, pp. 1–15.

Crandall, R., "Import Quotas and the Automobile Industry: The Cost of Protectionism." *Brookings Review* 2(4), Summer 1984, pp. 8–16.

Houthakker, H. and Taylor, L., *Consumer Demand in the United States: Analyses and Projections,* 2nd ed. Cambridge: Harvard University Press, 1970.

Maxwell, Nan L. and Lopus, Jane S., "The Lake Wobegon Effect in Student Self Reported Data." *American Economic Review* 84(2), May 1994, pp. 201–5.

Pratt, Robert W., Jr., "Forecasting New Product Sales from Likelihood of Purchase Ratings: Commentary." *Marketing Science* 5(4), Fall 1986, pp. 387–88.

Sawtelle, Barbara A., "Income Elasticities of Household Expenditures: A U.S. Cross Section Perspective." *Applied Economics* 25(5), May 1993, pp. 635–44.

Stano, Miron and Hotelling, Harold, "Regression Analysis in Litigation: Some Overlooked Considerations." *Journal of Legal Economics* 1(3), December 1991, pp. 68–78.

Williams, Harold R. and Mount, Randall I., "OECD Gasoline Demand Elasticities: An Analysis of Consumer Behavior with Implications for U.S. Energy Policy." *Journal of Behavioral Economics* 16(1), Spring 1987, pp. 69–79.

CHAPTER

4 | The Theory of Individual Behavior

Headline

Packaging Firm Uses Overtime Pay to Overcome Labor Shortage

Boxes Ltd. produces corrugated paper containers at a small plant in Sunrise Beach, Texas. Sunrise Beach is a retirement community with an aging population, and over the past decade the size of its working population has shrunk. During the early 1990s this labor shortage hampered Boxes Ltd.'s ability to hire enough workers to meet its growing demand and production targets. This is despite the fact that it pays $10 per hour—almost twice the local average— to its workers.

Last year, Boxes Ltd. hired a new manager who instituted an overtime wage plan at the firm. Under her plan workers earn $10 per hour for the first eight hours worked each day, and $15.00 per hour for each hour worked in a day in excess of eight hours. This plan eliminated the firm's problems, as the firm's production levels and profits are up by 20 percent this year.

Why did the new manager institute the overtime plan instead of simply raising the wage rate in an attempt to attract more workers to the firm?

Introduction

This chapter develops tools that help a manager understand the behavior of individuals, such as consumers and workers, and the impact of alternative incentives on their decisions. This is not as easy as you might think. Human beings use complicated thought processes to make decisions, and the human brain is capable of processing vast quantities of information. At this very

113

moment your heart is pumping blood throughout your body, your lungs are providing oxygen and expelling carbon dioxide, and your eyes are scanning this page while your brain processes the information on it. The human brain can do what even supercomputers and sophisticated "artificial intelligence" technology are incapable of doing.

Despite the complexities of human thought processes, managers need a model that explains how individuals behave in the marketplace and in the work environment. Of course, attempts to model individual behavior cannot capture the full range of real-world behavior. Life would be simpler for managers of firms if the behavior of individuals were not so complicated. On the other hand, the rewards for being a manager of a firm would be much lower. If you achieve an understanding of individual behavior, you will gain a marketable skill that will help you to succeed in the business world.

Our model of behavior will necessarily be an abstraction of the way individuals really make decisions. Yet we must begin with a simple model that focuses on essentials instead of dwelling on behavioral features that would do little to enhance our understanding. Keep these thoughts in mind as we begin our study of an economic model of consumer behavior.

Consumer Behavior

Now that you recognize that any theory about individual behavior must be an abstraction of reality, we may begin to develop a model to help us understand how consumers will respond to the alternative choices that confront them. A *consumer* is an individual who purchases goods and services from firms for the purpose of consumption. As a manager of a firm, you are interested not only in who consumes the good but in who purchases it. A six-month-old baby consumes goods but is not responsible for purchase decisions. If you are employed by a manufacturer of baby food, it is the parent's behavior you must understand, not the baby's.

In characterizing consumer behavior, there are two important but distinct factors to consider: consumer opportunities and consumer preferences. *Consumer opportunities* represent the possible goods and services consumers can afford to consume. *Consumer preferences* determine which of these goods will be consumed. The distinction is very important: While I can afford (and thus have the opportunity to consume) one pound of beef liver each week, my preferences are such that I would be unlikely to choose to consume beef liver at all. Keeping this distinction in mind, let us begin by modeling consumer preferences.

In today's global economy literally millions of goods are offered for sale. However, to focus on the essential aspects of individual behavior and to keep things manageable, we will assume that only two goods exist in the economy. This assumption is made purely to simplify our analysis: all of the conclusions that we draw from this two-good setting remain valid when there are many goods. We will let X represent the quantity of one good and Y the quantity of the other good. By using this notation to represent the two goods, we have a very general model in the sense that X and Y can be any two goods rather than restricted to, say, beef and pork.

Assume a consumer is able to order his or her preferences for alternative bundles or combinations of goods from best to worst. We will let $>$ denote this ordering and write $A > B$ whenever the consumer prefers bundle A to bundle B. If the consumer views the two bundles as equally satisfying, we will say she or he is indifferent between bundles A and B and use $A \sim B$ as shorthand notation. If $A > B$, then, if given a choice between bundle A and bundle B, the consumer will choose bundle A. If $A \sim B$, the consumer, given a choice between bundle A and B, will not care which bundle he or she gets. The preference ordering is assumed to satisfy four basic properties: completeness, more is better, diminishing marginal rate of substitution, and transitivity. Let us examine these properties and their implications in more detail.

Property 4–1: Completeness.   For any two bundles—say, A and B—either $A > B$, $B > A$, or $A \sim B$.

By assuming that preferences are *complete*, we assume the consumer is capable of expressing a preference for, or indifference among, all bundles. If preferences were not complete, there might be cases where a consumer would claim not to know whether he or she preferred bundle A to B, preferred B to A, or was indifferent between the two bundles. If the consumer cannot express her or his own preference for or indifference among goods, the manager can hardly predict that individual's consumption patterns with reasonable accuracy.

Property 4–2: More Is Better.   If bundle A has at least as much of every good as bundle B and more of some good, bundle A is preferred to bundle B.

FIGURE 4–1

The indifference curve

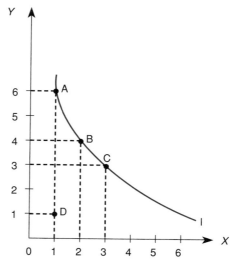

If *more is better,* the consumer views the products under consideration as "goods" instead of "bads." Graphically, this implies that as we move in the northeast direction in Figure 4–1, we move to bundles that the consumer views as being better than bundles to the southwest. For example, in Figure 4–1 bundle *A* is preferred to bundle *D* because it has the same amount of good *X* and more of good *Y.* Bundle *C* is also preferred to bundle *D,* because it has more of both goods. Similarly, bundle *B* is preferred to bundle *D.*

While the assumption that more is better provides important information about consumer preferences, it does not help us determine a consumer's preference for all possible bundles. For example, note in Figure 4–1 that the "more is better" property does not reveal whether bundle *B* is preferred to bundle *A* or bundle *A* is preferred to bundle *B.* To be able to make such comparisons, we will need to make some additional assumptions.

indifference curve
A curve that defines the combinations of two or more goods that give a consumer the same level of satisfaction.

An *indifference curve* defines the combinations of goods *X* and *Y* that give the consumer the same level of satisfaction; that is, the consumer is indifferent between any combination of goods along an indifference curve. A typical indifference curve is depicted in Figure 4–1. By definition, all combinations of *X* and *Y* located on the indifference curve provide the consumer with the same level of satisfaction. For example, if you asked the consumer, "Which would you prefer—bundle *A,* bundle *B,* or bundle *C?*" the consumer would reply, "I don't care," because bundles *A, B,* and *C* all lie on the same indifference curve. In other words, the consumer is indifferent among the three bundles.

The shape of the indifference curve depends on the consumer's preferences. Different consumers generally will have indifference curves of different shapes. One important way to summarize information about a consumer's preferences is in terms of the marginal rate of substitution. The *marginal rate of substitution (MRS)* is the absolute value of the slope of an indifference curve. The marginal rate of substitution between two goods is the rate at which a consumer is willing to substitute one good for the other and still maintain the same level of satisfaction.

marginal rate of substitution (MRS)
The rate at which a consumer is willing to substitute one good for another good and still maintain the same level of satisfaction.

The concept of the marginal rate of substitution is actually quite simple. In Figure 4–1, the consumer is indifferent between bundles *A* and *B.* In moving from *A* to B, the consumer gains 1 unit of good *X.* To remain on the same indifference curve, she or he gives up 2 units of good *Y.* Thus, in moving from point *A* to point *B,* the marginal rate of substitution between goods *X* and *Y* is 2.

The careful reader will note that the marginal rate of substitution associated with moving from A to B in Figure 4–1 differs from the rate at which the consumer is willing to substitute between the two goods in moving from B to C. In particular, in moving from B to C, the consumer gains 1 unit of good *X.* But now he or she is willing to give up only 1 unit of good *Y* to get the additional unit of *X.* The reason is that this indifference curve satisfies the property of *diminishing marginal rate of substitution.*

Property 4–3: Diminishing Marginal Rate of Substitution.   As a consumer obtains more of good *X*, the rate at which he or she is willing to substitute good *X* for good *Y* decreases.

This assumption implies that indifference curves are convex from the origin; that is, they look like the indifference curve in Figure 4–1. To see how the locations of various indifference curves can be used to illustrate different levels of consumer satisfaction, we must make an additional assumption: that preferences are *transitive*.

Property 4–4: Transitivity.   For any three bundles, *A, B,* and *C,* if $A > B$ and $B > C$, then $A > C$. Similarly, if $A \sim B$ and $B \sim C$, then $A \sim C$.

The assumption of transitive preferences, together with the more-is-better assumption, implies that indifference curves do not intersect one another. It also eliminates the possibility that the consumer is caught in a perpetual cycle in which she or he never makes a choice.

To see this, suppose Billy's preferences are such that he prefers jelly beans to licorice, licorice to chocolate, and chocolate to jelly beans. He asks the clerk to fill a bag with jelly beans, because he prefers jelly beans to licorice. When the clerk hands him a bagful of jelly beans, Billy tells her he likes chocolate even more than jelly beans. When the clerk hands him a bagful of chocolate, he tells her he likes licorice even more than chocolate. When the clerk hands him a bagful of licorice, Billy tells her he likes jelly beans even more than licorice. The clerk puts back the licorice and hands Billy a bagful of jelly beans. Now Billy is right back where he started! He is unable to choose the "best" kind of candy because his preferences for kinds of candy are not transitive.

The implications of our four assumptions are conveniently summarized in Figure 4–2, which depicts three indifference curves. Every bundle on

FIGURE 4–2

A family of indifference curves

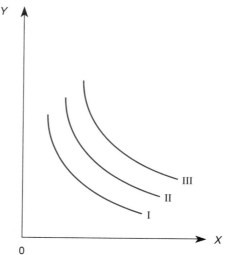

Inside Business 4–1

Indifference Curves and Risk Preferences

Have you ever wondered why some individuals choose to undertake risky prospects, such as skydiving and investing in risky financial assets, while others choose safer activities? Indifference curve analysis provides an answer to this question.

The accompanying table presents the five-year average annual returns and quality ratings of three investment options offered by T. Rowe Price, a major no-load mutual fund. A mutual fund is an investment company that invests in a portfolio of financial assets (the assets listed in the table are portfolios of municipal bonds, which are debt obligations issued by municipal governments). *No-load* simply means that investors do not pay a fee to purchase or sell shares in the fund.

Selected 5-Year Average Annual Returns and Quality Ratings of Three T. Rowe Price Mutual Funds

Fund Name	5-Year Average Annual Return	Quality[a]
A Tax-Exempt Money Fund	4.90%	2.0
B Tax-Free Income Fund	6.02%	2.6
C Tax-Free High-Yield Fund	8.06%	3.8

[a] The T. Rowe Price quality scale ranges from 1 for "highest" to 10 for "lowest."
Source: T. Rowe Price, November 30, 1991, and December 31, 1991.

The three options are tax-free investments with varying degrees of risk. With tax-free investments, the interest income received is exempt from federal income taxes. This makes these investments attractive to individuals in high tax brackets.

The quality scale used by T. Rowe Price assigns the safer funds a lower number than more risky funds; a 1 is assigned to the least risky and a 10 to the most risky fund. Thus, fund A is the safest investment, but it offers the lowest reward; fund B is of medium safety, with a moderate reward; and fund C is the least safe, but it carries the highest reward. Points A, B, and C in Figure 4–3 characterize these three investment options.

Investors view safety and the level of the return on an investment as "goods"; investments with higher returns and higher levels of safety are preferred to investments with lower returns and lower levels of safety. Investors are willing to substitute between the level of return and the level of safety. Given the three options, from an investor's viewpoint, there is a trade-off between a higher reward (return) and the level of safety of the investment.

The relatively steep indifference curves drawn on panel (*a*) of Figure 4–3 describe an investor who has a high marginal rate of substitution between return and safety; she or he must receive a large return to be induced to give up a small amount of safety. The relatively flat indifference curves drawn in panel (*b*) indicate an investor with a low marginal rate of substitution between return and safety. This individual is willing to give up a lot of safety to get a slightly higher return. An investor with indifference curves such as those in panel (*a*) finds investment option *A* most attractive, because it is associated with the highest indifference curve. In contrast, an investor with indifference curves such as those in panel (*b*) achieves the highest indifference curve with investment option *C*. Both types of investors are rational, but one investor is willing to give up some additional financial return for more safety, while the other is not.

Inside Business 4–1 continued

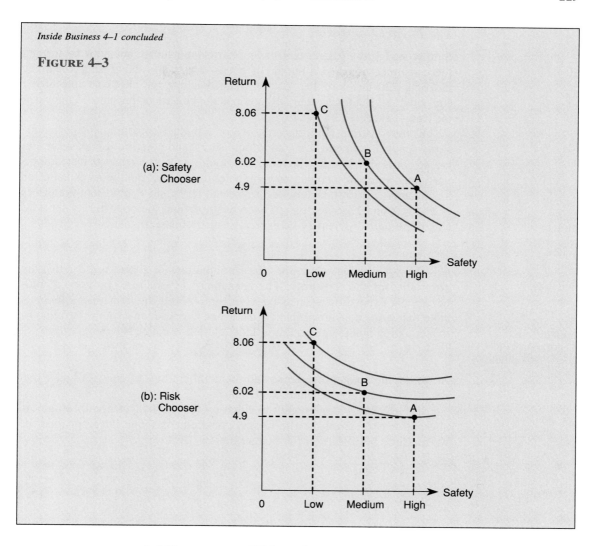

FIGURE 4–3

(a): Safety Chooser

(b): Risk Chooser

indifference curve III is preferred to those on curve II, and every bundle on indifference curve II is preferred to those on curve I. The three indifference curves are convex and do not cross. Curves farther from the origin imply higher levels of satisfaction than curves closer to the origin.

Constraints

In making decisions, individuals face *constraints*. There are legal constraints, time constraints, physical constraints, and, of course, budget constraints. To maintain our focus on the essentials of managerial economics without delving into issues beyond the scope of this course, we will examine the role prices and income play in constraining consumer behavior.

The Budget Constraint

Simply stated, the *budget constraint* restricts consumer behavior by forcing the consumer to select a bundle of goods that is affordable. If a consumer has only $30 in his or her pocket when reaching the checkout line in the supermarket, the total value of the goods the consumer presents to the cashier cannot exceed $30.

To demonstrate how the presence of a budget constraint restricts consumer choice, we need some additional shorthand notation. Let M represent the consumer's income, which can be any amount. By using M instead of a particular value of income, we gain generality in that the theory is valid for a consumer with any income level. We will let P_x and P_y represent the prices of goods X and Y, respectively. Given this notation, the opportunity set (also called the *budget set*) may be expressed mathematically as

$$P_x X + P_y Y \leq M.$$

budget set
The bundles of goods a consumer can afford.

In words, the budget set defines the combinations of goods X and Y that are affordable for the consumer: The consumer's expenditures on good X, plus her or his expenditures on good Y, do not exceed the consumer's income. Note that if the consumer spends his or her entire income on the two goods, this equation holds with equality. This relation is called the *budget line:*

budget line
The bundles of goods that exhaust a consumer's income.

$$P_x X + P_y Y = M.$$

In words, the budget line defines all the combinations of goods X and Y that exactly exhaust the consumer's income.

It is useful to manipulate the equation for the budget line to obtain an alternative expression for the budget constraint in slope-intercept form. If we multiply both sides of the budget line by $1/P_y$, we get

$$\frac{P_x}{P_y}X + Y = \frac{M}{P_y},$$

so that

$$Y = \frac{M}{P_y} - \frac{P_x}{P_y}X.$$

Y is a linear function of X with a vertical intercept of M/P_y and a slope of $-P_x/P_y$.

The consumer's budget constraint is graphed in Figure 4–4. The shaded area represents the consumer's budget set, or opportunity set. In particular, any combination of goods X and Y within the shaded area, such as point G, represents an affordable combination of X and Y. Any point above the shaded area, such as point H, represents a bundle of goods that is unaffordable.

The upper boundary of the budget set in Figure 4–4 is the budget line. If a consumer spent her or his entire income on good X, the expenditures

FIGURE 4–4

The budget set

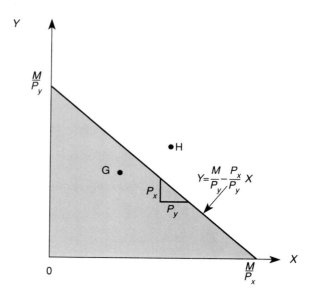

on good X would exactly equal the consumer's income:

$$P_x X = M.$$

By manipulating this equation, we see that the maximum affordable quantity of good X consumed is

$$X = \frac{M}{P_x}.$$

This is why the horizontal intercept of the budget line is

$$\frac{M}{P_x}$$

Similarly, if the consumer spent his or her entire income on good Y, expenditures on Y would exactly equal income:

$$P_y Y = M.$$

Consequently, the maximum quantity of good Y that is affordable is

$$Y = \frac{M}{P_y}.$$

The slope of the budget line is given by $-P_x/P_y$ and represents the *market rate of substitution* between goods X and Y. To obtain a better understanding of the market rate of substitution between goods X and Y, consider Figure 4–5, which presents a budget line for a consumer who has \$10 in

FIGURE 4–5

The budget line

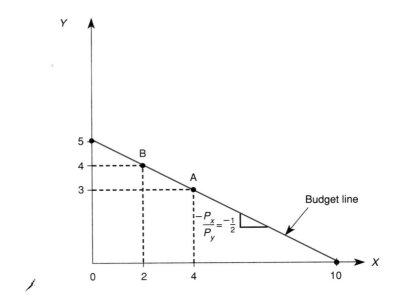

income and faces a price of \$1 for good X and a price of \$2 for good Y. If we substitute these values of P_x, P_y, and M into the formula for the budget line, we observe that the vertical intercept of the budget line (the maximum amount of good Y that is affordable) is $M/P_y = 10/2 = 5$. The horizontal intercept is $M/P_x = 10/1 = 10$ and represents the maximum amount of good X that can be purchased. The slope of the budget line is $-P_x/P_y = -(1/2)$.

The reason the slope of the budget line represents the market rate of substitution between the two goods is as follows. Suppose a consumer purchased bundle A in Figure 4–5, which represents the situation where the consumer purchases 3 units of good Y and 4 units of good X. If the consumer purchased bundle B instead of bundle A, she would gain one additional unit of good Y. But to afford this, she must give up 2 units ($4 - 2 = 2$) of good X. For every unit of good Y the consumer purchases, she must give up 2 units of good X in order to be able to afford the additional unit of good Y.

Changes in Income

The consumer's opportunity set depends on market prices and the consumer's income. As these parameters change, so will the consumer's opportunities. Let us now examine the effects on the opportunity set of changes in income by assuming prices remain constant.

Suppose the consumer's initial income in Figure 4–6 is M^0. What happens if M^0 increases to M^1 while prices remain unchanged? Recall that the slope of the budget line is given by $-P_x/P_y$. Under the assumption that prices

FIGURE 4–6

Changes in income shrink or expand opportunities.

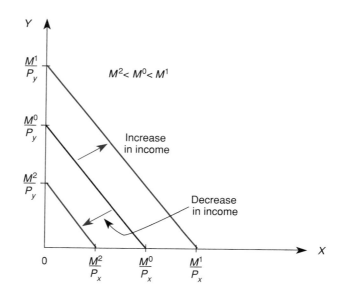

remain unchanged, the increase in income will not affect the slope of the budget line. However, the vertical and horizontal intercepts of the budget line both increase as the consumer's income increases, because more of each good can be purchased at the higher income. Thus, when income increases from M^0 to M^1, the budget line shifts to the right in a parallel fashion. This reflects an increase in the consumer's opportunity set, because more goods are affordable after the increase in income than before. Similarly, if income decreases to M^2 from M^0, the budget line shifts toward the origin and the slope of the budget line remains unchanged.

Changes in Prices

Now suppose the consumer's income remains fixed at M, but the price of good X decreases to $P_x^1 < P_x^0$. Furthermore, suppose the price of good Y remains unchanged. Since the slope of the budget line is given by $-P_x/P_y$, the reduction in the price of good X changes the slope, making it flatter than before. Since the maximum amount of good Y that can be purchased is M/P_y, a reduction in the price of good X does not change the Y intercept of the budget line. But the maximum amount of good X that can be purchased at the lower price (the X intercept of the budget line) is M/P_x^1, which is greater than M/P_x^0. Thus, the ultimate effect of a reduction in the price of good X is to rotate the budget line counterclockwise, as in Figure 4–7.

Similarly, an increase in the price of good X leads to a clockwise rotation of the budget line, as the next demonstration problem indicates.

FIGURE 4–7

A decrease in the price of good X

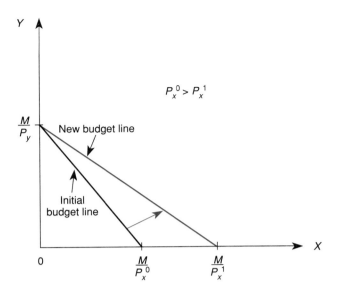

DEMONSTRATION PROBLEM 4–1

A consumer has initial income of $100 and faces prices of $P_x = 1$ and $P_y = 5$. Graph the budget line, and show how it changes when the price of good X increases to $P_x^1 = 5$.

Answer

Initially, if the consumer spends his entire income on good X, he can purchase $M/P_x = 100/1 = 100$ units of X. This is the horizontal intercept of the initial budget line in Figure 4–8. If the consumer spends his entire income on good Y, he can purchase $M/P_y = 100/5 = 20$ units of Y. This is the vertical intercept of the initial budget line. The slope of the initial budget line is $-P_x/P_y = -1/5$.

   When the price of good X increases to 5, the maximum amount of X the consumer can purchase is reduced to $M/P_x = 100/5 = 20$ units of X. This is the horizontal intercept of the new budget line in Figure 4–8. If the consumer spends his entire income on good Y, he can purchase $M/P_y = 100/5 = 20$ units of Y. Thus, the vertical intercept of the budget line remains unchanged; the slope changes to $-P_x^1/P_y = -5/5 = -1$.

FIGURE 4–8

An increase in the price of good X

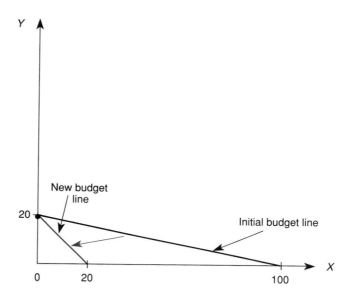

Consumer Equilibrium

The objective of the consumer is to choose the consumption bundle that maximizes his or her utility, or satisfaction. If there were no scarcity, the more-is-better assumption would imply that the consumer would want to consume bundles that contained infinite amounts of goods. However, one implication of scarcity is that the consumer must select a bundle that lies inside the budget set, that is, an affordable bundle. Let us combine our theory of consumer preferences with our analysis of constraints to see how the consumer goes about selecting the best affordable bundle.

Consider a bundle such as *A* in Figure 4–9. This combination of goods *X* and *Y* lies on the budget line, so the cost of bundle *A* completely exhausts the consumer's income. Given the income and prices corresponding to the budget line, can the consumer do better—that is, can the consumer achieve a higher indifference curve? Clearly, if the consumer consumed bundle *B* instead of bundle *A*, she or he would be better off since the indifference curve through *B* lies above the one through *A*. Moreover, bundle *B* lies on the budget line and thus is affordable. In short, it is inefficient for the consumer to consume bundle *A* because bundle *B* both is affordable and yields a higher level of well-being.

Is bundle *B* optimal? The answer is no. Bundle *B* exhausts the consumer's budget, but there is another affordable bundle that is even better: bundle *C*. Note that there are bundles, such as *D*, that the consumer prefers

FIGURE 4–9

Consumer equilibrium

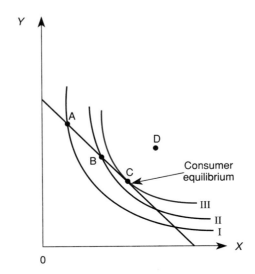

more than bundle *C*, but those bundles are not affordable. Thus, we say bundle *C* represents the consumer's *equilibrium choice*. The term *equilibrium* refers to the fact that the consumer has no incentive to change to a different affordable bundle once this point is reached.

An important property of consumer equilibrium is that at the equilibrium consumption bundle, the slope of the indifference curve is equal to the slope of the budget line. Recalling that the absolute value of the slope of the indifference curve is called the *marginal rate of substitution* and the slope of the budget line is given by $-P_x/P_y$, we see that at a point of consumer equilibrium,

$$MRS = \frac{P_x}{P_y}.$$

If this condition did not hold, the personal rate at which the consumer is willing to substitute between goods *X* and *Y* would differ from the market rate at which he or she is free to substitute between the goods. For example, at point A in Figure 4–9, the slope of the indifference curve is steeper than the slope of the budget line. This means the consumer is willing to give up more of good *Y* to get an additional unit of good *X* than she or he actually has to pay in the market. Consequently, it is in the consumer's interest to consume less of good *Y* and more of good *X*. This substitution continues until ultimately the consumer is at a point such as C in Figure 4–9, where the *MRS* is equal to the ratio of prices.

FIGURE 4–10

Change in consumer equilibrium due to a decrease in the price of good X. (Note that good Y is a substitute for X.)

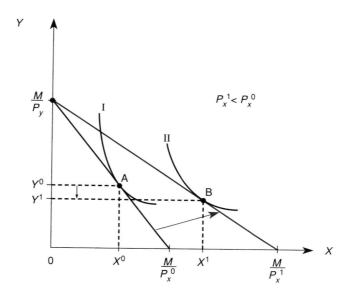

Comparative Statics

Price Changes and Consumer Behavior

A change in the price of a good will lead to a change in the equilibrium consumption bundle. To see this, recall that a reduction in the price of good X leads to a counterclockwise rotation of the budget line. Thus, if the consumer initially is at equilibrium at point A in Figure 4–10, when the price of good X falls to P_x^1, his or her opportunity set expands. Given this new opportunity set, the consumer can achieve a higher level of satisfaction. This is illustrated as a movement to the new equilibrium point, B, in Figure 4–10.

Precisely where the new equilibrium point lies along the new budget line after a price change depends on consumer preferences. Accordingly, it is useful to recall the definitions of substitutes and complements that were introduced in Chapter 2.

First, goods X and Y are called *substitutes* if an increase (decrease) in the price of X leads to an increase (decrease) in the consumption of Y. Most consumers would view Coke and Pepsi as substitutes. If the price of Pepsi increased, most people would tend to consume more Coke. If goods X and Y are substitutes, a reduction in the price of X would lead the consumer to move from point A in Figure 4–10 to a point such as B, where less of Y is consumed than at point A.

Second, goods X and Y are called *complements* if an increase (decrease) in the price of good X leads to a decrease (increase) in the consumption of

FIGURE 4–11

When the price of good X *falls, the consumption of complementary good* Y *rises.*

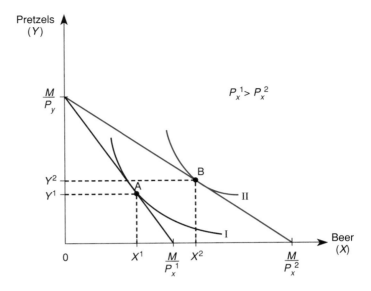

good Y. Beer and pretzels are an example of complementary goods. If the price of beer increased, most beer drinkers would decrease their consumption of pretzels. When goods X and Y are complements, a reduction in the price of X would lead the consumer to move from point A in Figure 4–11 to a point such as B, where more of Y is consumed than before.

From a managerial perspective, the key thing to note is that changes in prices affect the market rate at which a consumer can substitute among various goods, and therefore will change the behavior of consumers. Price changes might occur because of updated pricing strategies within your own firm. Or they might arise because of price changes made by rivals or firms in other industries. Ultimately, price changes alter consumer incentives to buy different goods, thereby changing the mix of goods they purchase in equilibrium. The primary advantage of indifference curve analysis is that it allows a manager to see how price changes affect the mix of goods that consumers purchase in equilibrium. As we will see below, indifference curve analysis also allows us to see how changes in *income* affect the mix of goods purchased by consumers.

Income Changes and Consumer Behavior

A change in income also will lead to a change in the consumption patterns of consumers. The reason is that changes in income either expand or contract the consumer's budget constraint, and the consumer therefore finds it optimal to choose a new equilibrium bundle. For example, assume the con-

Inside Business 4–2

Price Changes and Inventory Management for Multiproduct Firms

One of the more important decisions a manager must make is how much inventory to have on hand. Too little inventory means an insufficient quantity of products to meet the demand of consumers, in which case your customers may defect to another store. The opportunity cost of inventory is the forgone interest that could be earned on the money tied up in inventory. In performing inventory management, an effective manager recognizes the relationship that exists among products in the store and the impact of a change in the price of one product on the required inventories of other products. In the early 1990s, the price of personal computers declined dramatically. This not only increased the quantity demanded of computers but dramatically increased the demand for computer software, which is a complementary good. This result has obvious implications for inventory management.

A more subtle aspect of a reduction in the price of computers is its impact on the demand for and optimal inventories of substitute goods. If a store sells many products, and some of the products are substitutes for computers, a reduction in the price of computers will lead to a reduction in the sales of these other goods. When the price of computers is reduced, the consumption of computers increases as a direct consequence of the price reduction. However, note that the consumption of substitutes like calculators will decrease as a result of the reduction in the price of computers. If the manager does not understand the impact of a price reduction on the consumption of substitute goods, he or she will face a build-up of inventories of calculators when the price of computers decreases.

It is important to emphasize that we have not described the optimal pricing policy for firms that sell multiple products (we will do this in a later chapter). We have pointed out that managers of firms that sell multiple products must think carefully about all of the implications of a price change.

sumer initially is at equilibrium at point A in Figure 4–12. Now suppose the consumer's income increases to M^1 so that his or her budget line shifts out. Clearly the consumer can now achieve a higher level of satisfaction than before. This particular consumer finds it in her or his interest to choose bundle B in Figure 4–12, where the indifference curve through point B is tangent to the new budget line.

As in the case of a price change, the exact location of the new equilibrium point will depend on consumer preferences. Let us now review our definitions of normal and inferior goods.

Recall that good X is a *normal good* if an increase (decrease) in income leads to an increase (decrease) in the consumption of good X. Normal goods include goods such as steak, airline travel, and designer jeans. As income goes up, consumers typically buy more of these goods. Note in Figure 4–12 that the consumption of both goods X and Y increased due to the increase

FIGURE 4–12

*An increase in
income increases the
consumption of
normal goods*

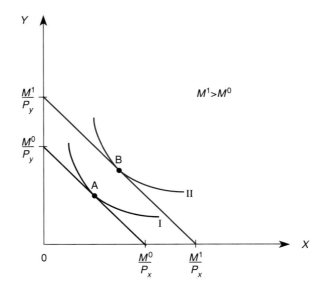

in consumer income. Thus, these preferences are for a consumer who views X and Y as normal goods.

Recall that good X is an *inferior good* if an increase (decrease) in income leads to a decrease (increase) in the consumption of good X. Bologna, bus travel, and generic jeans are examples of inferior goods. As income goes up, consumers typically consume less of these goods and services. It is important to repeat that by calling the goods *inferior*, we do not imply that they are of poor quality; it is simply a term used to define products consumers purchase less of when their incomes rise.

Figure 4–13 depicts the effect of an increase in income for the case when good X is an inferior good. When income increases, the consumer moves from point A to point B to maximize his or her satisfaction given the higher income. Since at point B the consumer consumes more Y than at point A, we know that good Y is a normal good. However, note that at point B less of good X is consumed than at point A, so we know this consumer views X as an inferior good.

Substitution and Income Effects

We can combine our analysis of price and income changes to gain a better understanding of the effect of a price change on consumer behavior. Suppose a consumer initially is in equilibrium at point A in Figure 4–14, along the budget line connecting points F and G. Suppose the price of good X increases so that the budget line rotates clockwise and becomes the budget line connecting points F and H. There are two things to notice about this change. First, since the budget set is smaller due to the price increase, the

FIGURE 4–13

*An increase in
income decreases the
equilibrium
consumption of good
X—an
inferior good.*

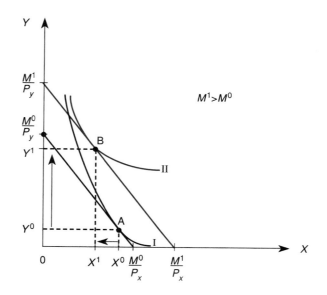

consumer will be worse off after the price increase. A lower "real income" will be achieved, as a lower indifference curve is all that can be reached after the price increase. Second, the increase in the price of good X leads to a budget line with a steeper slope, reflecting a higher market rate of substitution. These two factors lead the consumer to move from the initial consumer equilibrium (point A) to a new equilibrium (point C) in Figure 4–14.

It is useful to isolate the two effects of a price change to see how each effect individually alters consumer choice. In particular, ignore for the moment the fact that the price increase leads to a lower indifference curve. Suppose that after the price increase, the consumer is given enough income to achieve the budget line connecting points J and I in Figure 4–14. This budget line has the same slope as budget line FH, but it implies a higher income than budget line FH. Given this budget line, the consumer will achieve equilibrium at point B, where less of good X is consumed than in the initial situation, point A. The movement from A to B is called the *substitution effect;* it reflects how a consumer will react to a different market rate of substitution. The substitution effect is the difference $X^0 - X^m$ in Figure 4–14. Importantly, the movement from A to B leaves the consumer on the same indifference curve, so the reduction in the consumption of good X implied by that movement reflects the higher market rate of substitution, not the reduced "real income," of the consumer.

The consumer does not actually face budget line JI when the price increases but instead faces budget line FH. Let us now take back the income we gave to the consumer to compensate for the price increase. When this income is taken back, the budget line shifts from JI to FH. Importantly, this

Income Effects and the Business Cycle

An important consideration in running a firm is the impact of changes in prices on the demand for the firm's product. Suppose you are the manager of a firm that sells a product that is a normal good and are considering expanding your product line to include another good. There are several things you may wish to consider in making your decision. Since your product is a normal good, you will sell more of it when the economy is booming (consumer incomes are high) than when times are tough (incomes are low). Your product is a cyclical product, that is, sales vary directly with the economy. This information may be useful to you when considering alternative products to include in your store. If you expand your offerings to include more normal goods, you will continue to have an operation that sells more during an economic boom than during a recession. But if you include in your operation some inferior goods, the demand for these products will increase during bad economic times (when incomes are low) and perhaps offset the lost demand for normal goods. This is not to say that the optimal mix of products involves a 50-50 mix of normal and inferior goods; indeed, the optimal mix will depend on your own risk preference. The analysis does point out that running a gourmet food store will likely involve a higher level of risk than running a supermarket. In particular, gourmet shops sell almost exclusively normal goods, while supermarkets have a more "balanced portfolio" of normal and inferior goods. This explains why, during recessions, many gourmet shops go out of business while supermarkets do not.

It is also useful to know the magnitude of the income effect when designing a marketing campaign. If the product is a normal good, it is most likely in the firm's interest to target advertising campaigns toward individuals with higher incomes. These factors should be considered when determining which magazines and television shows are the best outlets for advertising messages.

shift in the budget line reflects only a reduction in income; the slope of budget lines JI and FH are identical. Thus, the movement from B to C is called the *income effect*. The income effect is the difference $X^m - X^1$ in Figure 4–14; it reflects the fact that when price increases, the consumer's "real income" falls. Since good X is a normal good in Figure 4–14, the reduction in income leads to a further reduction in the consumption of X.

The total effect of a price increase thus is composed of substitution and income effects. The substitution effect reflects a movement along an indifference curve, thus isolating the effect of a relative price change on consumption. The income effect results from a parallel shift in the budget line; thus, it isolates the effect of a reduced "real income" on consumption and is represented by the movement from B to C. The total effect of a price increase, which is what we observe in the marketplace, is the movement from A to C. The total effect of a change in consumer behavior results not only from the effect of a higher relative price of good X (the movement from

FIGURE 4–14

An increase in the price of good X *leads to a substitution effect (A to B) and an income effect (B to C).*

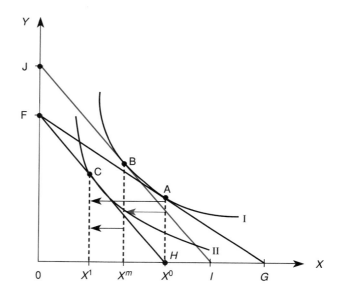

A to B) but also from the reduced real income of the consumer (the movement from B to C).

Applications of Indifference Curve Analysis

Choices by Consumers

Buy One, Get One Free

A very popular sales technique at pizza restaurants is to offer the following deal:

Buy one large pizza, get one large pizza free (limit one free pizza per customer).

It is tempting to conclude that this is simply a 50 percent reduction in the price of pizza so that the budget line rotates as it does for any price decrease. This conclusion is invalid, however. A price reduction decreases the price of each unit purchased. The type of deal summarized above reduces only the price of the second unit purchased (in fact, it reduces the price of the second large pizza to zero). The offer does not change the price of units below one pizza and above two pizzas.

The "buy one, get one free" marketing scheme is quite easy to analyze in our framework. In Figure 4–15, a consumer initially faces a budget line connecting points A and B and is in equilibrium at point C. Point C represents one-half of a large pizza (say, a small pizza), so the consumer decides it is best to buy a small pizza instead of a large one. Point D represents the

FIGURE 4–15

A buy-one, get-one-free pizza deal

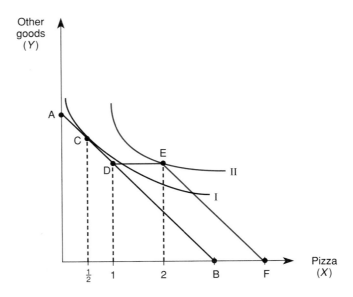

point at which she buys one large pizza, but, as we can see, the consumer prefers bundle C to bundle D, since it lies on a higher indifference curve.

When the consumer is offered the "buy one, get one free" deal, her budget line becomes ADEF. The reason is as follows. If she buys less than one large pizza, she gets no deal, and her budget line to the left of one pizza remains as it was, namely AD. But if she buys one large pizza, she gets a second one free. In this instance, the budget line becomes DE as soon as she buys one pizza. In other words, the price of pizza is zero for units between one and two large pizzas. This implies that the budget line for pizzas is horizontal between one and two units (recall that the slope of the budget line is $-(P_x/P_y)$, and for these units P_x is zero). If the consumer wants to consume more than two large pizzas, she must buy them at regular prices. But note that if she spent all of her income on pizza, she could buy one more than she could before (since one of the pizzas is free). Thus, for pizzas in excess of two units, the budget constraint is the line connecting points E and F. After the deal is offered, the opportunity set increases. In fact, bundle *E* is now an affordable bundle. Moreover, it is clear that bundle *E* is preferred to bundle *C*, and the consumer's optimal choice is to consume bundle *E*, as in Figure 4–15. The sales technique has induced the consumer to purchase more pizza than she would have otherwise.

Cash Gifts, In-Kind Gifts, and Gift Certificates

Along with death and taxes, lines in refund departments after Christmas appear to be an unpleasant but necessary aspect of life. To understand why, and to be able to pose a potential solution to the problem, consider the following story.

Figure 4–16

*A gift of one
fruitcake*

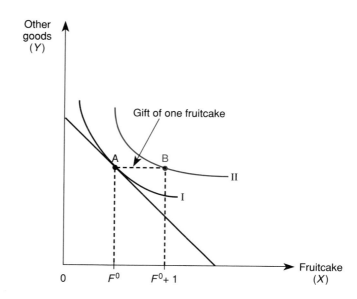

One Christmas morning, a consumer named Sam is in equilibrium, consuming bundle *A* as in Figure 4–16. He opens a package and, to his surprise, it contains a fruitcake. He fakes a smile and tells Aunt Sarah that he always wanted a fruitcake. Graphically, when Sam receives the gift his opportunity set expands to include point B in Figure 4–16. Note that bundle *B* is just like bundle *A* except that it has one more fruitcake than bundle *A*. Given this new opportunity set, Sam moves to the higher indifference curve through point B after receiving the gift.

While Sam is better off after receiving the gift than before, the gift is not what he would have purchased had Aunt Sarah given him the cash she spent on the fruitcake. For concreteness, suppose the cost of the fruitcake was $10. Had Sam been given $10 in cash, his budget line would have shifted out, parallel to the old budget line but through point B, as in Figure 4–17. To see why, note that when Sam gets additional income, prices are not changed, so the slope of the budget line is unchanged. Note also that if Sam used the money to buy one more fruitcake, he would exactly exhaust his income. Thus, the budget line after the cash gift must go through point B— and, given the cash gift, Sam would achieve a higher level of satisfaction at point C compared to the gift of a fruitcake (point B).

Thus, a cash gift generally is preferred to an in-kind gift of equal value, unless the in-kind gift is exactly what the consumer would have purchased personally. This explains why refund departments are so busy after the Christmas holidays; individuals exchange gifts for cash so that they can purchase bundles they prefer.

One way stores attempt to reduce the number of gifts returned is to sell gift certificates. To see why, suppose Sam received a gift certificate, good

FIGURE 4–17

*A cash gift yields
higher utility than
an in-kind gift.*

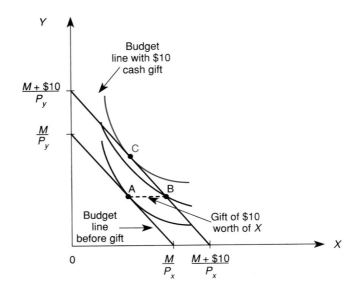

for $10 worth of merchandise at store X, which sells good *X*, instead of the
$10 fruitcake. Further, suppose the certificate is not good at store *Y*, which
sells good *Y*. By receiving a gift certificate, Sam cannot purchase any more
of good *Y* than he could before he received the certificate. But if he spends
all of his income on good *Y*, he can purchase $10 worth of good *X*, since he
has a certificate worth $10 at store X. And if he spends all of his income on
good *X*, he can purchase $10 more than he could before because of the gift
certificate. In effect, the gift certificate is like money that is good only at
store X.

Graphically, the effect of receiving a gift certificate at store X is depicted in Figure 4–18. The straight black line is the budget line before Sam
receives the gift certificate. When the $10 gift certificate is received, the
budget constraint becomes the blue one. In effect, the gift certificate allows
the consumer up to $10 worth of good *X* without spending a dime of his
own money.

The effect of gift certificates on consumer behavior depends, among
other things, on whether good *X* is a normal or inferior good. To examine
what happens to behavior when a consumer receives a gift certificate, let us
suppose a consumer initially is in equilibrium at point A in Figure 4–18,
spending $10 on good *X*. What happens if the consumer is given a $10 gift
certificate good only for items in store X? If both *X* and *Y* are normal goods,
the consumer will desire to spend more on both goods as income increases.
Thus, if both goods are normal goods, the consumer moves from A to C as
in Figure 4–18. In this instance, the consumer reacts to the gift certificate
just as she or he would have reacted to a cash gift of equal value.

FIGURE 4–18

A gift certificate valid at store X

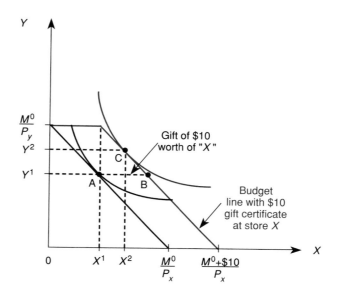

DEMONSTRATION PROBLEM 4–2

How would the analysis of gift certificates just presented change if good X were an inferior good? What does this imply about the benefits to a manager of selling gift certificates?

Answer

In this instance, a gift of $10 in cash would result in a movement from point A in Figure 4–19 to a point like D, since X is an inferior good. However, when a $10 gift certificate is received, bundle D is not affordable, and the best the consumer can do is consume bundle E. In other words, had the consumer been given cash, his or her budget line would have extended up along the dotted line, and point D would have been an affordable bundle. If given cash, the consumer would have purchased less of good X than she or he did with the gift certificate. Also, note that the consumer would have achieved a higher indifference curve with the cash than that achieved with the gift certificate. (An end-of-chapter problem asks you whether a gift certificate always leads to a lower indifference curve and higher sales than a cash gift when the good is inferior.)

This analysis reveals two important benefits to a firm of selling gift certificates. First, as a manager you can reduce the strain on your refund department by offering gift certificates to customers looking for gifts. This is

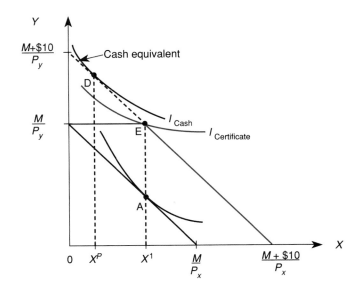

true for both normal and inferior goods. If you sell an inferior good, offering to sell gift certificates to those looking for gifts may result in a greater quantity sold than if customers resorted to giving cash gifts. (This assumes you do not permit individuals to redeem gift certificates for cash.)

Choices by Workers and Managers

Until now, our analysis of indifference curves has focused on the decisions of consumers of goods and services. Managers and workers also are individuals and therefore have preferences among the alternatives that confront them. In this section, we will see that the indifference curve analysis developed earlier for consumers can easily be modified to analyze the behavior of managers and other individuals employed by firms. In Chapter 6 we will show how these insights into the behavior of workers and managers can be used to construct efficient employment contracts.

A Simplified Model of Income-Leisure Choice

Most workers view both leisure and income as goods and substitute between them at a diminishing rate along an indifference curve. Thus, a typical worker's indifference curve has the usual shape in Figure 4–20, where we measure the quantity of leisure consumed by an employee on the horizontal axis and worker income on the vertical axis. Note that while workers enjoy leisure, they also enjoy income.

To induce workers to give up leisure, firms must compensate them. Suppose a firm offers to pay a worker $10 for each hour of leisure the worker gives up (i.e., spends working). In this instance, opportunities confronting

FIGURE 4–20

Labor–leisure choice

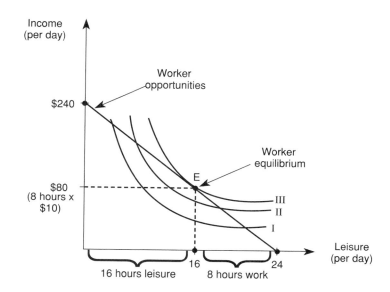

the worker or manager are given by the straight line in Figure 4–20. If the worker chooses to work 24-hour days, he or she consumes no leisure but earns $10 \times 24 = \$240$ per day, which is the vertical intercept of the line. If the worker chooses not to work, he or she consumes 24 hours of leisure but earns no income. This is the horizontal intercept of the line in Figure 4–20.

Worker behavior thus may be examined in much the same way we analyzed consumer behavior. The worker attempts to achieve a higher indifference curve until he or she achieves one that is tangent to the opportunity set at point E in Figure 4–20. In this instance, the worker consumes 16 hours of leisure and works 8 hours to earn a total of $80 per day.

DEMONSTRATION PROBLEM 4–3

Suppose a worker is offered a fixed wage of $5 per hour, plus a fixed payment of $40. What is the equation for the worker's opportunity set in a given 24-hour day? What are the maximum total earnings the worker can earn in a day? What are the minimum? What is the price to the worker of consuming an additional hour of leisure?

Answer

The total earnings (E) of a worker who consumes L hours of leisure in a 24-hour day is given by

$$E = \$40 + \$5(24 - L),$$

so the combinations of earnings (E) and leisure (L) satisfy

$$E = \$160 - \$5L.$$

The most a worker can earn in a 24-hour day thus is \$160 (by consuming no leisure); the least that can be earned is \$40 (by not working at all). The price of a unit of leisure is \$5, since the opportunity cost of an hour of leisure is one hour of work.

The Decisions of Managers

William Baumol[1] has argued that many managers derive satisfaction from the underlying output and profits of their firms. According to Baumol, higher profits and sales lead to a larger firm, and larger firms provide more "perks" like spacious offices, executive health clubs, corporate jets, and the like.

Suppose a manager's preferences are such that she or he views the "profits" and the "output" of the firm to be "goods" so that more of each is preferred to less. We are not suggesting that it is optimal for you, as a manger, to have these types of preferences, but there may be instances in which your preferences are so aligned. In many sales jobs, for example, individuals receive a bonus depending on the overall profitability of the firm. But the salesperson's ability to receive reimbursement for certain business-related expenses may depend on that individual's total output (e.g., number of cars sold). In this instance, the individual may value both output and profits. Alternatively, perks such as a company plane, car, and so forth may be allocated to individuals based on the firm's output. In that case, managerial preferences may depend on the firm's profits as well as output.

Panels a, b, and c of Figure 4–21 show the relation between profits and the output of a firm on the curve labeled "firm's profits." This curve goes from the origin through points C, A, and B, and represents the profits of the firm as a function of output. When the firm sells no output, profits are zero. As the firm expands output, profits increase, reach a maximum at Q_m, and then begin to decline until, at point Q_0, they are again zero.

Given this relationship between output and profits, a manager who views output and profits as "goods" (the Baumol hypothesis) has indifference curves like those in Figure 4–21(a). She attempts to achieve higher and higher indifference curves until she eventually reached equilibrium at point A. Note that this level of output, Q_u, is greater than the profit-maximizing level of output, Q_m. Thus, when the manager views both profits and output as "goods," she produces more than the profit-maximizing level of output.

---

[1] William J. Baumol, *Business Behavior, Value, and Growth*, rev. ed. (New York: Harcourt, Brace and World), 1967.

FIGURE 4–21

*A manager's
preferences might
depend on:*

*(a) profits
and
output*

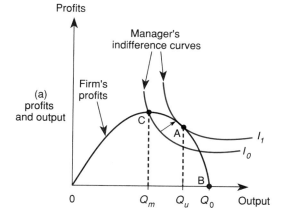

*(b) output
only*

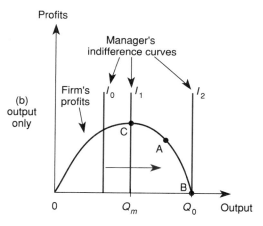

*(c) profits
only*

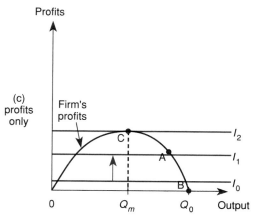

In contrast, when the manager's preferences depend solely on output, the indifference curves look like those in Figure 4–21(b), which are vertical straight lines. One example of this situation occurs when the owner of a car dealership pays the manager based solely on the number of cars sold (the manager gets nothing if the company goes bankrupt). Since the manager does not care about profits, his or her indifference curves are vertical lines, and satisfaction increases as the curves move farther to the right. A manager with such preferences will attempt to obtain the indifference curves farther and farther to the right until indifference curve I_2 is reached. Point B represents equilibrium for this manager, where Q_0 units of output are produced. Again, in this instance the manager produces more than the profit-maximizing level of output.

Finally, suppose the manager cares solely about the profits of the firm. In this instance, the manager's indifference curves are horizontal straight lines as shown in Figure 4–21(c). The manager maximizes satisfaction at point C, where the indifference curve I_2 is as high as possible given the opportunity set. In this instance, profits are greater and output is lower than in the other two cases.

An important issue for the firm's owners is to induce managers to care solely about profits so that the result is the maximization of the underlying value of the firm, as in Figure 4–21(c). We will examine this issue in more detail in Chapter 6.

The Relationship between Indifference Curve Analysis and Demand Curves

We have seen how the consumption patterns of an individual consumer depend on variables that include the prices of substitute goods, the prices of complementary goods, tastes (i.e., the shape of indifference curves), and income. The indifference curve approach developed in this chapter in fact is the basis for the demand functions we studied in Chapter 2. We conclude by examining the link between indifference curve analysis and demand curves.

Individual Demand

To see where the demand curve for a normal good comes from, consider Figure 4–22(a). The consumer initially is in equilibrium at point A, where income is fixed at M and prices are P_x^0 and P_y. But when the price of good X falls to the lower level, indicated by P_x^1, the opportunity set expands and the consumer reaches a new equilibrium at point B. The important thing to notice is that the only change that caused the consumer to move from A to B was a change in the price of good X; income and the price of good Y are

FIGURE 4–22

*Deriving an
individual's demand
curve*

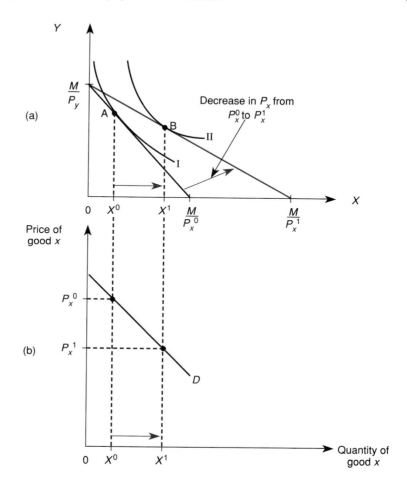

held constant in the diagram. When the price of good X is P_x^0, the consumer consumes X^0 units of good X; when the price falls to P_x^1, the consumption of X increases to X^1.

This relationship between the price of good X and the quantity consumed of good X is graphed in Figure 4–22(b) and is the individual consumer's demand curve for good X. This consumer's demand curve for good X indicates that, holding other things constant, when the price of good X is P_x^0, the consumer will purchase X^0 units of X; when the price of good X is P_x^1, the consumer will purchase X^1 units of X.

Market Demand

You will usually, in your role as a manager, be interested in determining the total demand by all consumers for your firm's product. This information is summarized in the market demand curve. The market demand curve is the

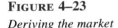

Figure 4-23

*Deriving the market
demand curve*

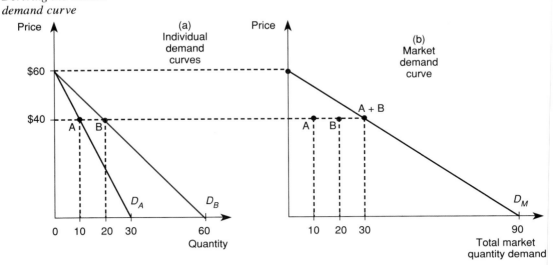

horizontal summation of individual demand curves and indicates the total quantity all consumers in the market would purchase at each possible price.

This concept is illustrated graphically in Figures 4–23(a) and 4–23(b). The curves D_A and D_B represent the individual demand curves of two hypothetical consumers, Ms. A and Mr. B, respectively. When the price is $60, Ms. A buys 0 units and Mr. B buys 0 units. Thus, at the market level, 0 units are sold when the price is $60, and this is one point on the market demand curve (labeled D_M in Figure 4–23(b)). When the price is $40, Ms. A buys 10 units (point A) and Mr. B buys 20 units (point B). Thus, at the market level (Figure 4–23(b)), 30 units are sold when the price is $40, and this is another point (point A + B) on the market demand curve. When the price of good X is zero, Ms. A buys 30 units and Mr. B buys 60 units; thus, at the market level, 90 units are sold when the price is 0. If we repeat the analysis for all prices between 0 and $60, we get the curve labeled D_M in Figure 4–23(b).

Thus, the demand curves we studied in Chapters 2 and 3 are implied by indifference curve analysis.

Answering the Headline

The question posed at the beginning of the chapter asked why Boxes Ltd. paid a higher overtime wage only on hours in excess of eight hours per day instead of offering workers a higher wage for every hour worked during a

FIGURE 4–24

An overtime wage increases hours worked.

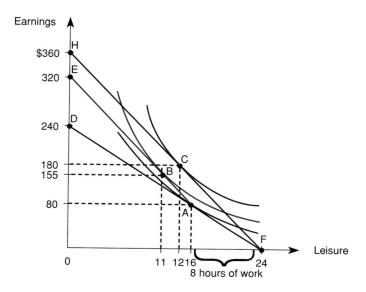

given day. Since Boxes Ltd. already pays twice the local market wage rate to workers, it is unlikely that increasing the wage would attract more workers to the firm. Thus, the key to expanding its output is to get its current workers to work more hours. We will show that the overtime wage plan is a more effective means of increasing worker hours than simply raising the wage.

Figure 4–24 presents the analysis of income-leisure choice for a hypothetical worker. When the wage is $10 per hour, the worker's opportunity set is given by line DF. If the worker consumed no leisure, his earnings would be $10 × 24 = $240. However, given a $10 wage, this worker maximizes satisfaction at point A, where he consumes 16 hours of leisure (works 8 hours per day) to earn $80 in wage income.

With overtime pay of $15 for each hour worked in excess of 8 hours, the opportunity set becomes EAF. The reason is simple. If the worker works 8 hours or less, he does not earn overtime pay, and this part of his budget line (AF) remains the same. But if he consumes less than 16 hours of leisure, he gets $15 instead of $10 for these hours worked, so the budget line is steeper (EA). When no leisure is consumed (point E), the first 8 hours given up generate $10 × 8 = $80 in earnings, while the last 16 hours of leisure given up generate $15 × 16 = $240 in earnings. Thus, point E on the overtime budget line corresponds to earnings of $80 + $240 = $320. Given the overtime option, this worker maximizes satisfaction at point B, where he works 13 hours to earn $155. Overtime pay increases the amount of work from 8 hours to 13 hours.

Why doesn't the firm simply increase the wage to $15 instead of initiating the more complicated overtime system? If this worker were paid a wage of $15 for every hour worked, his budget line would be HF. This worker would obtain a higher indifference curve at point C, where 12 hours of leisure are consumed (12 hours of work). When leisure is a normal good, the $15 wage yields fewer hours of work from each worker than does the overtime system.

To summarize, we have shown that the manager could get workers who view leisure as a normal good to work longer hours with overtime pay than she could by offering simply a higher wage on all hours worked.

Summary

In this chapter, we provided a basic model of individual behavior that enables the manager to understand the impact of various managerial decisions on the actions of consumers and workers.

After reading and working through the demonstration problems in this chapter, you should understand what a budget constraint is and how it changes when prices or income change. You should also understand that when there is a change in the price of a good, consumers change their behavior because there is a change in the ratio of prices (which leads to a substitution effect) and a change in real income (which leads to the income effect). The model of consumer behavior also articulates the assumptions underlying the demand curve.

In equilibrium, consumers adjust their purchasing behavior so that the ratio of prices they pay just equals their marginal rate of substitution. This information, along with observations of consumer behavior, helps a manager determine when to use a "buy one, get one free" pricing strategy instead of a half-price offer. During holiday seasons, the same manager will have a sound basis for determining whether offering gift certificates is a wise strategy.

Effective managers also use the theory of consumer behavior to direct the behavior of employees. In this chapter, we examined the benefits to the firm of paying overtime wages; additional issues will be discussed in Chapter 6.

In conclusion, remember that the models of individual behavior developed in this chapter are basic tools for analyzing the behavior of your customers and employees. By taking the time to become familiar with the models and working through the demonstration and end-of-chapter problems, you will be better able to make decisions that will maximize the value of your firm.

Key Terms and Concepts

budget set
"buy one, get one free"
  deals
completeness
consumer equilibrium
diminishing marginal rate of
  substitution
gift certificates
income effect

income-leisure choice
indifference curve
marginal rate of substitution
  (MRS)
market rate of substitution
more is better
substitution effect
transitivity

Problems

1. Airlines give away more than 10 million tickets each year through their frequent flyer programs, with the typical airline awarding a free ticket for each 25,000 miles flown on the airline. The average airline ticket costs $500 and is for a 2,500-mile round trip. Given this information, evaluate the following statement: Airlines could have the same effect on demand by eliminating their frequent flyer programs and simply lowering the average ticket price by 10 percent.

2. Natalie is always willing to give up 10 ounces of licorice for 1 ounce of chocolate. Mitchell, on the other hand, will always give up 10 ounces of chocolate for 1 ounce of licorice. Based on this information, answer the following questions:
   a. Do Natalie's preferences exhibit a diminishing marginal rate of substitution between chocolate and licorice? Why or why not?
   b. Assuming that Natalie and Mitchell have the same amount of money to spend on chocolate and licorice, who will purchase the most licorice? Why?

3. Suppose an individual's marginal rate of substitution is three slices of pizza for one beer at the present bundle of beer and pizza she is consuming. If the price of beer is $1.00 and the price of a slice of pizza is $1.50, is the consumer maximizing her welfare? If not, how should she change her consumption?

4. Clothing stores frequently run "sales" where they discount clothing prices by as much as 25 percent. What impact, if any, would you expect these "sales" to have on a store that specializes in selling shoes produced by Rockport?

5. A stockholder named Sue must cast a vote for chair of the board. Sue prefers Mr. Lee to Ms. Doe, Ms. Doe to Mr. James, and Mr. James to Mr. Lee.

    a. Are Sue's preferences consistent with our assumptions about consumer behavior? Explain.

    b. If all stockholders had the same preferences as Sue, who would win the appointment as chair of the board? Explain.

6. Over the past decade medical costs have increased more rapidly than other prices. In order to illustrate how rising medical costs have affected consumer alternatives, let X represent the quantity of medical services, and let Y represent the quantity of other goods. Furthermore, let income (M) be measured in hundreds of dollars, the price of medical services and other goods in terms of dollars per minute, with $M = 100$, $P_x = 4$, and $P_y = 5$.

    a. Graph the budget line, and determine the market rate of substitution.

    b. Illustrate the budget set.

    c. Show in your graph what happens to the budget constraint if P_x increases to \$10.

    d. What is the meaning of the slope of the two budget constraints?

7. At a very basic level, food and shelter constitute the two most important goods needed to sustain human life. Accordingly, assume that a poor person must allocate his income solely between food and shelter.

    a. Show that if shelter is an inferior good, food must be a normal good.

    b. If food is a normal good, is shelter necessarily an inferior good? Explain, and show your answer graphically.

8. Suppose you are the manager of a firm that produces Ultrasweet, a sugar substitute. Show graphically the effect of a reduction in the price of Sweet and Healthy, a competitor's product, on a typical consumer's consumption of Ultrasweet.

9. If shoes and socks are complements and both are normal goods, show graphically what would happen to the consumption of shoes and socks if (*a*) the price of shoes decreased and (*b*) consumer income increased.

10. Draw the opportunity set of a consumer with an income of \$200 who faces prices of $P_x = 5$ and $P_y = 10$. What is the market rate of substitution between the two goods?

11. Explain what would happen to the equilibrium consumption of two goods, X and Y, if (*a*) income doubled and all prices tripled, (*b*) all prices doubled and income tripled, and (*c*) all prices and income doubled. In each case, show the effects when both goods are normal goods and when one good is a normal good and the other an inferior good.

12. Joe consumes 10 units of food and 12 units of clothing. If food is an inferior good, will Joe be indifferent between receiving a \$12 gift

certificate at a clothing store and receiving $12 in cash? Explain and show graphically.

13. Suppose a consumer derives satisfaction from consuming two types of hamburgers, *X* and *Y*.
    a. Graph the budget line of the consumer under the assumption that he is offered a "buy two, get one free" deal for burger *X*.
    b. Graph the budget constraint under the assumption that the producer of burger *Y* also offers a "buy two, get one free" deal.
    c. Explain in words why each of the above budget constraints looks as it does.

14. A consumer has a choice of spending $13,000 on a Honda or $9,000 on a Saturn. She is observed buying the Saturn. Does this mean the consumer prefers the Saturn? Explain your answer.

15. Sally Consumer's indifference curve between cigarettes and hamburgers is upward sloping. Based on this information, can we conclude that Sally views cigarettes as "bads" and hamburgers as "goods"? Explain.

16. An economics professor went out to dinner one night and observed one of her students drinking heavily. The next day was a final exam. When the professor's companion found out the student was in her class, he said the student's behavior was irrational. The professor disagreed. Under what conditions is behavior irrational according to the properties of consumer behavior discussed in the chapter? What situations could make the student's behavior rational?

17. While at a discount shoe store, a customer asked a clerk, "I see that your shoes are 'buy one, get one free—limit one free pair per customer.' Will you sell me one pair for half-price?" The clerk answered, "I can't do that." When the customer started to leave the store, the clerk hastily offered, "However, I am authorized to give you a 40 percent discount on any pair in the store." Assuming the consumer has $200 to spend on shoes (*X*) or all other goods (*Y*), and that shoes cost $100 per pair, answer the following questions:
    a. Illustrate the consumer's opportunity set under the "buy one, get one free" deal and under a 40 percent discount.
    b. Why was the 40 percent discount offered only after the consumer rejected the "buy one, get one free" deal and started to leave the store?
    c. Why was the clerk willing to offer a "buy one, get one free" deal, but unwilling to sell a pair of shoes for half-price?

18. Use indifference curve and constraint analysis to analyze the behavior of employees who are paid
    a. An hourly wage rate of $4 per hour.
    b. A fixed hourly wage of $4 per hour, plus an overtime bonus of $4 for every hour worked in excess of eight hours.

    c. A fixed salary of $40 per day, plus $4 for each hour worked.

    d. Which of the above schemes would yield the largest number of hours worked? Explain.

19. In order to encourage energy conservation, many public utility companies charge consumers a higher rate on units of electricity consumed in excess of some threshold amount. In contrast, a common marketing ploy by other firms is to offer "quantity discounts" to consumers who purchase large quantities of a good. To illustrate how these pricing schemes alter the typical consumer's opportunity set, suppose income = $100, P_x = $2 if the consumer buys less than 40 units of *X*, P_x = $3 if the consumer buys more than 40 units of *X*, and P_y = $5. Draw the budget constraint. How would the budget constraint change if the price decreased to $1 after 40 units of *X* were consumed?

20. Suppose a worker is paid according to the following pay scheme: For every unit produced, the worker gets $8. Assume a worker can produce three units per hour.

    a. Express the worker's earnings as a function of hours worked.

    b. Graph the equation for earnings.

    c. Graphically depict equilibrium, and show the earnings and hours worked by the employee.

    d. Do you think that from the firm's point of view, this scheme is better, worse, or the same as paying the worker a wage of $24 per hour? Explain carefully.

21. In the answer to Demonstration Problem 4–2 in the text, we showed a situation where a gift certificate leads a consumer to purchase a greater quantity of an inferior good than he or she would if given a cash gift of equal value. Is this always the case? Explain.

Selected Readings

Baumol, William J., *Business Behavior, Value and Growth*. New York: Macmillan, 1959.

Battalio, Raymond C., Kagel, John H., and Kogut, Carl A., "Experimental Confirmation of the Existence of a Giffen Good." *American Economic Review* 81(4), September 1991, pp. 961–70.

Davis J., "Transitivity of Preferences." *Behavioral Science*, Fall 1958, pp. 26–33.

Evans, William N. and Viscusi, W. Kip, "Income Effects and the Value of Health." *Journal of Human Resources* 28(3), Summer 1993, pp. 497–518.

Gilad, Benjamin, Kaish, Stanley, and Loeb, Peter D., "Cognitive Dissonance and Utility Maximization: A General Framework." *Journal of Economic Behavior and Organization* 8(1), March 1987, pp. 61–73.

Lancaster, Kelvin, *Consumer Demand: A New Approach*. New York: Columbia University Press, 1971.

MacKrimmon, Kenneth and Toda, Maseo. "The Experimental Determination of Indifference Curves." *Review of Economic Studies* 37, October 1969, pp. 433–451.

Smart, Denise T. and Martin, Charles L., "Manufacturer Responsiveness to Consumer Correspondence: An Empirical Investigation of Consumer Perceptions." *Journal of Consumer Affairs* 26(1), Summer 1992, pp. 104–28.

APPENDIX
A CALCULUS APPROACH TO INDIVIDUAL BEHAVIOR

The Utility Function

Suppose the preferences of a consumer are represented by a utility function $U(X, Y)$. Let $A = (X^A, Y^A)$ be the bundle with X^A units of good X and Y^A units of good Y, and let $B = (X^B, Y^B)$ be a different bundle of the two goods. If bundle A is preferred to bundle B, then $U(A) > U(B)$; the consumer receives a higher utility level from bundle A than from bundle B. Similarly, if $U(B) > U(A)$, the consumer views bundle B as "better" than bundle A. Finally, if $U(A) = U(B)$, the consumer views the two bundles to be equally satisfying; she or he is indifferent between bundles A and B.

Utility Maximization

Given prices of P_x and P_y and a level of income M, the consumer attempts to maximize utility subject to the budget constraint. Formally, this problem can be solved by forming the Lagrangian:

$$\mathcal{L} \equiv U(X,Y) + \lambda(M - P_xX - P_yY),$$

where λ is the Lagrange multiplier. The first-order conditions for this problem are

$$\frac{\partial \mathcal{L}}{\partial X} = \frac{\partial U}{\partial X} - \lambda P_x = 0 \qquad\qquad (A1)$$

$$\frac{\partial \mathcal{L}}{\partial Y} = \frac{\partial U}{\partial Y} - \lambda P_y = 0 \qquad\qquad (A2)$$

$$\frac{\partial \mathcal{L}}{\partial \lambda} = M - P_xX - P_yY = 0$$

Equations (A1) and (A2) imply that

$$\frac{\partial U/\partial X}{\partial U/\partial Y} = \frac{P_x}{P_y}, \qquad\qquad (A3)$$

or in economic terms, the ratio of the marginal utilities equals the ratio of prices.

The Marginal Rate of Substitution

Along an indifference curve, utility is constant:

$$U(X,Y) = \text{constant}.$$

Taking the total derivative of this relation yields

$$\left(\frac{\partial U}{\partial X}\right)dX + \left(\frac{\partial U}{\partial Y}\right)dY = 0.$$

Solving for dY/dX along an indifference curve yields

$$\left.\frac{dY}{dX}\right|_{\text{utility constant}} = -\left(\frac{\partial U/\partial X}{\partial U/\partial Y}\right).$$

Thus, the slope of an indifference curve is

$$-\frac{\partial U/\partial X}{\partial U/\partial Y}$$

The absolute value of the slope of an indifference curve is the marginal rate of substitution (MRS). Thus,

$$MRS = \frac{\partial U/\partial X}{\partial U/\partial Y} \qquad (A4)$$

The $MRS = P_x/P_y$ Rule

Substitution of Equation (A4) into (A3) reveals that to maximize utility, a consumer equates

$$MRS = \frac{P_x}{P_y}.$$

The Production Process and Costs

Headline

Japan's Minister of Labor Calls American Workers "Lazy"

In the early 1990s the Minister of Labor of Japan accused the American work force of being lazy and unproductive. According to an article in *Fortune*, Honda could produce a Civic with 10.9 labor hours, while Ford used 16 hours of labor to produce one Escort.[1]

The accusation by Japan's Minister of Labor concerned stockholders at GM, Ford, and Chrysler. These firms experienced huge losses in the early 1990s, and shareholders feared that one reason was the explanation offered by the Minister of Labor. Management was able to calm stockholder concerns about inefficiencies within the U.S. automobile industry by pointing toward an article in *Automotive News* that documents that the average wage rate (including benefits) of American auto workers was approximately $16 per hour, whereas their Japanese counterparts earned an average of about $18 per hour.[2]

Why do these figures suggest that the Minister of Labor's assessment of the U.S. workforce is incorrect?

[1] See "A U.S.-Style Shakeup at Honda," *Fortune*, December 30, 1991, p. 115.
[2] See Mary Ann Maskery, "Japanese Workers Seek 8% Raise," *Automotive News*, Volume 11 (March 11, 1991), p. 11.

Introduction

In this chapter we will develop tools to help managers answer complex questions such as those posed in the opening headlines. Our analysis will show how managers can determine which inputs and how much of each input to use to produce output efficiently. The material in this chapter will serve as the foundation for later chapters, which describe in more detail pricing and output techniques for managers interested in maximizing profits.

The Production Function

We will begin by describing the technology available for producing output. Technology summarizes the feasible means of converting raw inputs, such as steel, labor, and machinery, into an output such as an automobile. The technology effectively summarizes engineering know-how. Managerial decisions, such as those concerning expenditures on research and development, can affect the available technology. In this chapter, we will see how a manager can exploit an existing technology to its greatest potential. In subsequent chapters, we will analyze the decision to improve a technology.

To begin our analysis, let us consider a production process that utilizes two inputs, *capital* and *labor,* to produce output. We will let K denote the quantity of capital, L the quantity of labor, and Q the level of output produced in the production process. Although we call the inputs *capital* and *labor,* the general ideas presented here are valid for any two inputs. However, most production processes involve machines of some sort (referred to by economists as *capital*) and people (*labor*), and this terminology will serve to solidify the basic ideas.

production function
A function that defines the maximum amount of output that can be produced with a given set of inputs.

The technology available for converting capital and labor into output is summarized in the production function. The *production function* is an engineering relation that defines the maximum amount of output that can be produced with a given set of inputs. Mathematically, the production function is denoted as

$$Q = F(K, L),$$

that is, the maximum amount of output that can be produced with K units of capital and L units of labor.

As a manager, your job is to use the available production function efficiently; this effectively means that you must determine how much of each input to use to produce output. In the short run, some factors of production are *fixed,* and this limits your choices in making input decisions. For example, it takes several years for Ford to build an assembly line. The level of capital generally is fixed in the short run. However, in the short run Ford can adjust its use of inputs such as labor and steel; such inputs are *variable* factors of production.

Where Does Technology Come From?

In this chapter, we simply assume that the manager knows the underlying technology available for producing goods. How do managers acquire information about technology? The answer varies considerably across firms. The accompanying table reports the results of a survey of 650 executives in 130 industries. They were asked to rate how they obtain technical knowledge of new technologies developed by competitors. The responses varied considerably among executives, and there were also systematic differences in responses depending on whether the technical knowledge pertained to a process innovation or a product innovation. A process innovation is simply a new method for producing a given good, while a product innovation is the creation of a new product.

Independent R&D. As the accompanying table shows, the most important means of acquiring product and process innovations is independent research and development (R&D). This essentially involves engineers employed by the firm to devise new production processes or products. Most large firms have a research and development department that is charged with engineering aspects of product and process innovations.

Licensing Technology. The firm that was originally responsible for developing the technology and thus owns the rights to the technology often sells the production function to another firm for a licensing fee. The fee may be fixed, in which case the cost of acquiring the technology is a fixed cost of production. The fee may involve payments based on how much output is produced. In this instance, the cost of the technology is a variable cost of production.

Publications or Technical Meetings. Trade publications and meetings provide a forum for

Methods of Acquiring Technology (Ranked from Most Important to Least Important)

	Rank	
Method of Acquisition	*Process Innovations*	*Product Innovations*
Independent R&D	1	1
Licensing	2	3
Publications/technical meetings	3	5
Reverse engineering	4	2
Hiring employees of innovating firms	5	4
Patent Disclosures	6	6
Conversations with employees of innovating firm	7	7

Source: Adapted from Richard C. Levin, "Appropriability, R&D Spending, and Technological Performance," *American Economic Review* 78 (May 1988), pp. 424–28.

the dissemination of information about production processes.

Reverse Engineering. As the term suggests, this involves working backward: taking a product produced by a competitor and devising a method of producing a similar product. The typical result is a product that differs slightly from the existing product and involves a slightly different production function from that used by the original developer.

Hiring Employees of Innovating Firms. Former employees of other firms often have information about the production process.

Inside Business 5–1 continued

Patent Disclosures.   A patent gives the holder the exclusive rights to an invention for a specified period of time—17 years in the United States and 20 years in most Western European countries. However, to obtain a patent an inventor must file detailed information about the invention, which becomes public information. Virtually anyone can look at the information filed, including competitors. In many instances, this information can enable a competitor to "clone" the product in a way that does not infringe on the patent. Interest-ingly, while a patent is pending, this information is not publicly available. For this reason, stretching out the time in which a patent is pending often provides more protection for an inventor than actually acquiring the patent.

Conversations with Employees of Innovating Firms.   Despite the obvious benefits of keeping trade secrets "secret," employees inadvertently relay information about the production process to competitors. This is especially common in industries where firms are concentrated in the same geographic region and employees from different firms intermingle in nonbusiness settings.

variable and fixed factors of production
Variable factors are the inputs a manager can adjust to alter production. Fixed factors are the inputs the manager cannot adjust.

The *short run* is defined as the time frame in which there are fixed factors of production. The *long run* is defined as the horizon over which the manager can adjust all factors of production. If it takes Ford three years to adjust the size of its physical plant, the long run for Ford's management is three years, and the short run is less than three years.

Short-Run Decisions

To illustrate the discretion a manager has in making short-run decisions, let us suppose the level of capital is fixed in the short run. Thus, for our simple two-input production process, the only short-run input decision to be made by a manager is how much labor to utilize. The short-run production function is essentially only a function of labor, since capital is fixed rather than variable. If K^* is the fixed level of capital, the short-run production function may be written as

$$Q = f(L) = F(K^*, L).$$

Columns 1, 2, and 4 of Table 5–1 give values of the components of the short-run production function. For example, 5 units of labor are needed to produce 1,100 units of output. Given the available technology and the fixed level of capital, if the manager wishes to produce 1,952 units of output, 8 units of labor must be utilized. In the short run, more labor is needed to produce more output, because increasing capital is not possible.

Measures of Productivity

An important component of managerial decision making is the determination of the productivity of inputs used in the production process. As we will see, these measures are useful for evaluating the effectiveness of a produc-

TABLE 5–1   The Production Function

(1) K* Fixed Input (Capital) [Given]	(2) L Variable Input (Labor) [Given]	(3) ΔL Change in Labor [$\Delta(2)$]	(4) Q Output [Given]	(5) $\frac{\Delta Q}{\Delta L} = MP_L$ Marginal Product of Labor [$\Delta(4)/\Delta(2)$]	(6) $\frac{Q}{L} = AP_L$ Average Product of Labor [(4)/(2)]
2	0	—	0	—	—
2	1	1	76	76	76
2	2	1	248	172	124
2	3	1	492	244	164
2	4	1	784	292	196
2	5	1	1,100	316	220
2	6	1	1,416	316	236
2	7	1	1,708	292	244
2	8	1	1,952	244	244
2	9	1	2,124	172	236
2	10	1	2,200	76	220
2	11	1	2,156	−44	196

tion process and for making input decisions that maximize profits. The three most important measures of productivity are total product, average product, and marginal product.

Total Product.   Total product (TP) is simply the maximum level of output that can be produced with given input usage. For example, the total product of the production process described in Table 5–1 when 5 units of labor are employed is 1,100. Since the production function defines the maximum amount of output that can be produced with a given level of inputs, this is the amount that would be produced if the 5 units of labor put forth maximal effort. Of course, if workers did not put forth maximal effort, output would be lower. Five workers who drink coffee all day cannot produce any output, at least given this production function.

Average Product.   In many instances, managerial decision makers are interested in the average productivity of an input. For example, a manager may wish to know, on average, how much each worker contributes to the total output of the firm. This information is summarized in the economic concept of average product. The *average product (AP)* of an input is defined as total product divided by the quantity used of the input. In particular, the average product of labor (AP_L) is

average product
A measure of the output produced per unit of input.

$$AP_L = \frac{Q}{L},$$

and the average product of capital (AP_K) is

$$AP_K = \frac{Q}{K}.$$

Thus, average product is a measure of the output produced per unit of input. In Table 5–1, for example, 5 workers can produce 1,100 units of output; this amounts to 220 units of output per worker.

marginal product
The change in total output attributable to the last unit of an input.

③ *Marginal Product.*   Another important economic concept that is useful in the analysis of inputs is marginal product. The *marginal product (MP)* of an input is the change in total output attributable to the last unit of an input. The marginal product of capital (MP_K) therefore is the change in total output divided by the change in capital:

$$MP_K = \frac{\Delta Q}{\Delta K}.$$

The marginal product of labor (MP_L) is the change in total output divided by the change in labor:

$$MP_L = \frac{\Delta Q}{\Delta L}.$$

For example, in Table 5–1 the second unit of labor increases output by 172 units, so the marginal product of the second unit of labor is 172.

Table 5–1 illustrates an important characteristic of the marginal product of an input. Notice that as the units of labor are increased from 0 to 5 in column 2, the marginal product of labor increases in column 5. This helps explain why assembly lines are used in so many production processes: By using several workers, each performing potentially different tasks, a manager can avoid inefficiencies associated with stopping one task and starting another. But note in Table 5–1 that after 5 units of labor, the marginal product of each additional unit of labor declines and eventually becomes negative. A negative marginal product means that the last unit of the input actually *reduced* the total product. This is consistent with common sense. If a manager continued to expand the number of workers on an assembly line, he or she would eventually reach a point where workers were packed like sardines along the line, getting in one another's way and resulting in less output than before.

Figure 5–1 shows graphically the relationship among total product, marginal product, and average product. The first thing to notice about the curves is that total product increases and its slope gets steeper as we move from point A to point E along the total product curve. As the use of labor increases between points A and E, the slope of the total product curve increases (becomes steeper); thus, marginal product increases as we move

FIGURE 5–1

Stages of production

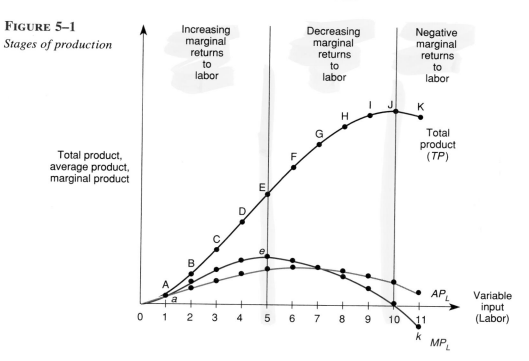

from point a to point e. The range over which marginal product increases is known as the range of *increasing marginal returns.*

In Figure 5–1, we see that marginal product reaches its maximum at point e, where 5 units of labor are employed. As the usage of labor increases from the 5th through the 10th unit, total output increases, but at a decreasing rate. This is why marginal product declines between 5 and 10 units of labor but is still positive. The range over which marginal product is positive but declining is known as the range of *decreasing* or *diminishing marginal returns* to the variable input.

In Figure 5–1, marginal product becomes negative when more than 10 units of labor are employed. The reason for this is simple. After a point, using additional units of input actually reduces total product, which is what it means for marginal product to be negative. The range over which marginal product is negative is known as the range of *negative marginal returns.*

The relationship between the marginal and average product curves in Figure 5–1 is important to note. As long as marginal product increases, marginal product is greater than average product. In fact, only after 7 units of labor—the point where average and marginal products are equal—does average product exceed marginal product.

Principle

Phases of Marginal Returns

As the usage of an input increases, marginal product initially increases (increasing marginal returns), then begins to decline (decreasing marginal returns), and eventually becomes negative (negative marginal returns).

In studying for an exam, you have very likely experienced various phases of marginal returns. The first few hours spent studying increase your grade much more than the last few hours. For example, suppose you will make a 0 if you do not study but will make a 75 if you study 10 hours. The marginal product of the first 10 hours thus is 75 points. If it takes 20 hours of studying to score 100 on the exam, the marginal product of the second 10 hours is only 25 points. Thus, the marginal improvement in your grade diminishes as you spend additional hours studying. If you have ever pulled an "all-nighter" and ended up sleeping through an exam or performing poorly due to a lack of sleep, you studied in the range of negative marginal returns. Clearly, neither students nor firms should ever employ resources in this range.

The Role of the Manager in the Production Process

The manager's role in guiding the production process described earlier is two-fold: (1) to ensure that the firm operates on the production function and (2) to ensure that the firm uses the correct level of inputs. These two aspects ensure that the firm operates at the right point on the production function. These two aspects of production efficiency are discussed next.

Produce on the Production Function

The first managerial role is relatively simple to explain, but it is one of the most difficult for a manager to perform. The production function describes the maximum possible output that can be produced with given inputs. For the case of labor, this means that workers must be putting forth maximal effort. To ensure that workers are in fact working at full potential, the manager must institute an incentive structure that induces them to put forth the desired level of effort. For example, the manager of a restaurant must institute an incentive scheme that ensures that food servers do a good job waiting on tables. Most restaurants pay workers low wages but allow them to collect tips, which effectively provides the workers with an incentive to perform on the job. More generally, many firms institute profit-sharing plans to provide workers with an incentive to produce on the production function. A more detailed discussion of this role of the manager is presented in Chapter 6.

Use the Right Level of Inputs

The second role of the manager is to ensure that the firm operates at the right point on the production function. For a restaurant manager, this means hiring the "correct" number of servers. To see how this may be accomplished, let us assume that the output produced by a firm can be sold in a market at a price of $3. Furthermore, assume each unit of labor costs $400. How many units of labor should the manager hire to maximize profits? To answer this question, we must first determine the benefit of hiring an additional worker. Each worker increases the firm's output by his or her marginal product, and this increase in output can be sold in the market at a price of $3. Thus, the benefit to the firm from each unit of labor is $3 \times MP_L$. This number is called the *value marginal product* of labor. The value marginal product of an input thus is the value of the output produced by the last unit of that input. For example, if each unit of output can be sold at a price of P, the value marginal product of labor is

value marginal product
The value of the output produced by the last unit of an input.

$$VMP_L = P(MP_L)$$

and the value marginal product of capital is

$$VMP_K = P(MP_K).$$

In our example, the cost to the firm of an additional unit of labor is $400. As Table 5–2 shows, the first unit of labor generates $VMP_L = \$228$ and the VMP_L of the second unit is $516. If the manager were to look only at the first unit of labor and its corresponding VMP_L, no labor would be hired. However, careful inspection of the table shows that the second worker will produce $116 in output above her or his cost. If the first worker is not hired, the second will not be hired.

In fact, each worker between 2 and 9 produces additional output whose value exceeds the cost of hiring the worker. It is profitable to hire units of labor so long as the VMP_L is greater than $400. Notice that the VMP_L of the 10th unit of labor is $228, which is less than the cost of the 10th unit of labor. It would not pay for the firm to hire this unit of labor, because the cost of hiring it would exceed the benefits. The same is true for additional units of labor. Thus, given the data in Table 5–2, the manager should hire 9 workers to maximize profits.

Principle

Profit-Maximizing Input Usage

To maximize profits, a manager should use inputs at levels at which the marginal benefit equals the marginal cost. More specifically, when the cost of each additional unit of labor is *w*, the manager should continue to employ labor up to the point where $VMP_L = w$ in the range of diminishing marginal product.

TABLE 5–2   The Value Marginal Product of Labor

(1) L Variable Input (Labor) [Given]	(2) P Price of Output [Given]	(3) $\frac{\Delta Q}{\Delta L} = MP_L$ Marginal Product of Labor [Column 5 of Table 5–1]	(4) $VMP_L = P(MP_L)$ Value Marginal Product of Labor [(2) × (3)]	(5) w Unit Cost of Labor [Given]
0	$3	—	—	$400
1	3	76	$228	400
2	3	172	516	400
3	3	244	732	400
4	3	292	876	400
5	3	316	948	400
6	3	316	948	400
7	3	292	876	400
8	3	244	732	400
9	3	172	516	400
10	3	76	228	400
11	3	−44	−132	400

The *profit-maximizing input usage* rule defines the demand for an input by a profit-maximizing firm. For example, in Figure 5–2 the value marginal product of labor is graphed as a function of the quantity of labor utilized. When the wage rate is w^0, the profit-maximizing quantity of labor is that quantity such that $VMP_L = w^0$, in the range of diminishing marginal returns. In the figure, we see that the profit-maximizing quantity of labor is L^0 units.

The downward-sloping portion of the VMP_L curve defines demand for labor by a profit-maximizing firm. Thus, an important property of the demand for an input is that it slopes downward because of the law of diminishing marginal returns. Since the marginal product of an input declines as more of an input is used, the value of the marginal product also declines as more of the input is used. Since the demand for an input is the value marginal product of the input in the range of diminishing marginal returns, the demand for an input slopes downward. In effect, each additional unit of an input adds less profits than the previous unit. Profit-maximizing firms thus are willing to pay less for each additional unit of an input.

Long-Run Decisions

In the long run, the manager is free to alter the quantities of all inputs to optimize the production process. This section provides a framework for extending the principles already set forth to these long-run instances. We begin

FIGURE 5–2

*The demand
for labor*

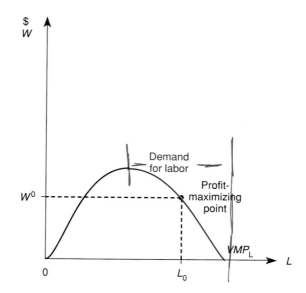

with algebraic examples of production functions that are functions of two variable inputs, K and L.

Algebraic Forms of Production Functions

Up until now, we have relied on tables and graphs to illustrate the concepts underlying production. The underlying notion of a production function can be expressed mathematically, and in fact it is possible to use statistical techniques to estimate a particular functional form for a production function. In this section, we highlight some more commonly encountered algebraic forms of production functions. We begin with the most simple production function: a linear function of the inputs.

**linear production
function**
A production
function that
assumes a perfect
linear relationship
between all inputs
and total output.

The *linear production function* is

$$Q = F(K, L) = aK + bL.$$

With a linear production function, there is a perfect linear relationship between all the inputs and total output. For instance, suppose it takes workers at a plant 4 hours to produce what a machine can make in 1 hour. In this case the production function is

$$Q = F(K, L) = 4K + L,$$

which is the mathematical way of stating that capital is always 4 times as productive as labor. Furthermore, since $F(5, 2) = 4(5) + 1(2) = 22$, we know that 5 units of capital and 2 units of labor will produce 22 units of Q.

Leontief production function
A production function that assumes that inputs are used in fixed proportions.

Another important technology is the Leontief production function. The *Leontief production function* is given by

$$Q = F(K, L) = \min\{bK, cL\}.$$

The Leontief production function is also called the *fixed-proportions production function,* because it implies that inputs are used in fixed proportions. To see this, suppose the production function for a word processing firm is Leontief, with $b = c = 1$; think of K as the number of keyboards and L as the number of keyboarders. The production function then implies that one keyboarder and one keyboard can produce one paper per hour, two keyboarders and two keyboards can produce two papers per hour, and so forth. But how many papers can one keyboarder and five keyboards produce per hour? The answer is only one paper. Additional keyboards are useful only to the extent that additional keyboarders are available to use them. In other words, keyboards and keyboarders must be used in the fixed proportion of one keyboarder for every one keyboard.

DEMONSTRATION PROBLEM 5–1

The engineers at Morris Industries obtained the following estimate of the firm's production function:

$$Q = F(K, L) = \min\{3K, 4L\}.$$

How much output is produced when 2 units of labor and 5 units of capital are employed?

Answer

We simply calculate $F(5, 2)$. But $F(5, 2) = \min\{3(5), 4(2)\} = \min\{15, 8\}$. Since the minimum of the numbers "15" and "8" is 8, we know that 5 units of capital and 2 units of labor produce 8 units of output.

Cobb-Douglas production function
A production function that assumes some degree of substitutability among inputs.

A production function that lies between the extremes of the linear production function and the Leontief production function is the Cobb-Douglas production function. The *Cobb-Douglas production function* is given by

$$Q = F(K, L) = K^a L^b.$$

Unlike in the case of the linear production function, the relationship between output and the inputs is not linear. Unlike in the Leontief production function, inputs need not be used in fixed proportions. The

Cobb-Douglas production function assumes some degree of substitutability between the inputs, albeit not perfect substitutability.

Algebraic Measures of Productivity

Given an algebraic form of a production function, we may calculate various measures of productivity. For example, we learned that the average product of an input is the output produced divided by the number of units used of the input. This concept can easily be extended to production processes that use more than one input.

To be concrete, suppose a consultant provides you with the following estimate of your firm's Cobb-Douglas production function:

$$Q = F(K, L) = K^{1/2}L^{1/2}.$$

What is the average product of labor when 4 units of labor and 9 units of capital are employed? Since $F(9, 4) = 9^{1/2}4^{1/2} = (3)(2) = 6$, we know that 9 units of capital and 4 units of labor produce 6 units of output. Thus, the average product of 4 units of labor is $AP_L = 6/4 = 1.5$ units.

Notice that when output is produced with both capital and labor, the average product of labor will depend not only on how many units of labor are used but also on how much capital is used. Since total output (Q) is affected by the levels of both inputs, the corresponding measure of average product depends on both capital and labor. Likewise, the average product of capital depends not only on the level of capital but also on the level of labor used to produce Q.

Recall that the marginal product of an input is the change in output that results from a given change in the input. When the production function is linear, the marginal product of an input has a very simple representation, as the following formula reveals.

linear

Formula: *Marginal Product for a Linear Production Function.* If the production function is linear and given by

$$Q = F(K, L) = aK + bL,$$

then

$$MP_K = a$$

and

$$MP_L = b.$$

A Calculus Alternative

The marginal product of an input is the derivative of the production function with respect to the input. Thus, the marginal product of labor is

$$MP_L = \frac{\partial Q}{\partial L}$$

and the marginal product of capital is

$$MP_K = \frac{\partial Q}{\partial K}.$$

For the case of the linear production function, $Q = aK + bL$, so

$$MP_K = \frac{\partial Q}{\partial K} = a$$

and

$$MP_L = \frac{\partial Q}{\partial L} = b.$$

Thus, for a linear production function, the marginal product of an input is simply the coefficient of the input in the production function. This implies that the marginal product of an input is independent of the quantity of the input used whenever the production function is linear; linear production functions do not obey the law of diminishing marginal product.

In contrast to the linear case, the marginal product of an input for a Cobb-Douglas production function does depend on the amount of the input used, as the following formula reveals.

Formula: Marginal Product for a Cobb-Douglas Production Function.   If the production function is Cobb-Douglas and given by

$$Q = F(K, L) = K^a L^b,$$

then

$$MP_L = bK^a L^{b-1},$$

and

$$MP_K = aK^{a-1} L^b.$$

A Calculus Alternative

The marginal product of an input is the derivative of the production function with respect to the input. Taking the derivative of the Cobb-Douglas production function yields

$$MP_K = \frac{\partial Q}{\partial K} = aK^{a-1} L^b$$

and

$$MP_L = \frac{\partial Q}{\partial L} = bK^a L^{b-1},$$

which correspond to the equations above.

Recall that the profit-maximizing use of an input occurs at the point where the value marginal product of an input equals the price of the input. As the next problem illustrates, we can apply the same principle to algebraic functional forms of production functions to attain the profit-maximizing use of an input.

DEMONSTRATION PROBLEM 5–2

A firm produces output that can be sold at a price of $10. The production function is given by

$$Q = F(K, L) = K^{1/2}L^{1/2}.$$

If capital is fixed at 1 unit in the short run, how much labor should the firm employ to maximize profits if the wage rate is $2?

Answer

We simply set the value marginal product of labor equal to the wage rate and solve for L. Since the production function is Cobb-Douglas, we know that $MP_L = bK^aL^{b-1}$. Here $a = 1/2$, $b = 1/2$, and $K = 1$. Hence, $MP_L = .5L^{1/2-1}$. Now, since $P = \$10$, we know that $VMP_L = P(MP_L) = 5L^{-1/2}$. Setting this equal to the wage, which is $2, we get $5L^{-1/2} = 2$. If we square both sides of this equation, we get $25/L = 4$. Thus the profit-maximizing quantity of labor is $L = 25/4 = 6.25$ units.

Isoquants

Our next task is to examine the optimal choice of capital and labor in the long run, when both inputs are free to vary. In the presence of multiple variables of production, there exist various combinations of inputs that enable the manager to produce the same level of output. For example, an automobile assembly line can produce 1,000 cars per hour by using 10 workers and 1 robot. It can also produce 1,000 cars by using only 2 workers and 3 robots. To minimize the costs of producing 1,000 cars, the manager must determine the efficient combination of inputs to use to produce them. The basic tool for understanding how alternative inputs can be used to produce output is an isoquant. An *isoquant* defines the combinations of inputs (K and L) that yield the producer the same level of output; that is, any combination of capital and labor along an isoquant produces the same level of output.

Figure 5–3 depicts a typical set of isoquants. Because input bundles A and B both lie on the same isoquant, each will produce the same level of

isoquant
Defines the combinations of inputs that yield the same level of output.

FIGURE 5–3

A family of isoquants

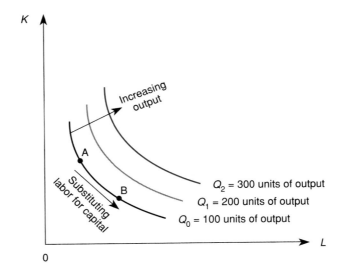

output, namely Q_0 units. Input mix *A* implies a more capital-intensive plant than does input mix *B*. As more of both inputs are used, a higher isoquant is obtained. Thus as we move in the northeast direction in the figure, each new isoquant is associated with higher and higher levels of output.

Notice that the isoquants in Figure 5–3 are convex. The reason isoquants are typically drawn with a convex shape is that inputs such as capital and labor are not perfectly substitutable. In Figure 5–3, for example, if we start at point A and begin substituting labor for capital, it takes increasing amounts of labor to replace each unit of capital that is taken away. The rate at which labor and capital can substitute for each other is called the *marginal rate of technical substitution (MRTS)*. The MRTS of capital and labor is the absolute value of the slope of the isoquant and is simply the ratio of the marginal products:

marginal rate of technical substitution (MRTS)
The rate at which a producer can substitute between two inputs and maintain the same level of output.

$$MRTS_{KL} = \frac{MP_L}{MP_K}.$$

Different production functions will imply different marginal rates of technical substitution. For example, the linear production function implies isoquants that are *linear,* as in Figure 5–4. This is because the inputs are perfect substitutes for each other and the rate at which the producer can substitute between the inputs is independent of the level of input usage. Specifically, for the linear production function $Q = aK + bL,$ the marginal rate of technical substitution is $b/a,$ since $MP_L = b$ and $MP_K = a.$ This is independent of the level of inputs utilized.

The Leontief production function, on the other hand, implies isoquants that are *L shaped,* as in Figure 5–5. In this case, inputs must be used in

FIGURE 5–4

Linear isoquants

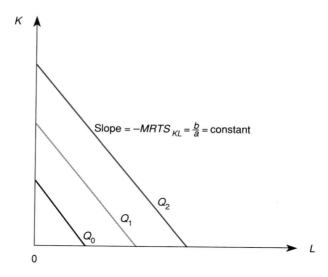

Slope $= -MRTS_{KL} = \frac{b}{a} =$ constant

FIGURE 5–5

Leontief isoquants

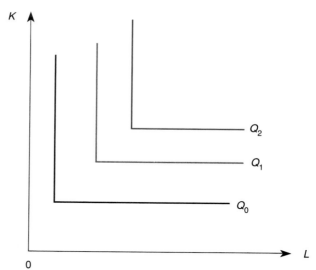

fixed proportions; the manager cannot substitute between capital and labor and maintain the same level of output. For the Leontief production function there is no MRTS, because there is no substitution among inputs along an isoquant.

For most production relations, the isoquants lie somewhere between the perfect-substitute and fixed-proportions cases. In these instances, the inputs are substitutable for one another, but not perfectly, and the rate at which a manager can substitute among inputs will change along an isoquant. For

A Cobb-Douglas Production Function for Water Desalination

One worldwide area of concern today is the availability of fresh water. Because of this issue, the production of fresh water through the process of desalination of salt water has become a viable area of research. The Middle East is a leader in this form of fresh-water extraction, but desalination is becoming a growing industry along the West Coast of the United States.

Recently three economists used statistical and econometric techniques to estimate the production function for a water desalination plant. The results of the study suggest that the production function is Cobb-Douglas and is given by

$$Q = F^{.6}H^{.4},$$

where Q is cubic meters of desalted water produced per day, F represents factors of production (an aggregation of evaporating pumps, maintenance of those pumps, and labor), and H is the per diem level of heat, which is used in the evaporation process. According to the authors of the study,

The technical inputs of water desalination can be classified into two groups: those for which the cost per unit of desalted water is increasing when the technical index of the number of effects is increas-

ing, and those for which this cost is decreasing under the same circumstances. This classification permits us to express production of desalted water as a function of two aggregates of inputs, corresponding to the above substitutional groups. Thus a production function is extracted for the general case of full-load annual operation of the desalination plant.

Since the estimated production function is Cobb-Douglas, we can apply our formulas for the marginal products of a Cobb-Douglas production function to obtain an algebraic expression for the marginal product of heat in the production of fresh water,

$$MP_H = .4F^{.6}H^{-.6},$$

and for the marginal product of other factors of production,

$$MP_F = .6F^{-.4}H^{.4}.$$

These equations reveal that the production of fresh water obeys the law of diminishing marginal product.

Source: N. Zagouras, Y. Caouris, and E. Kantsos, "Production and Cost Functions of Water Low-Temperature Solar Desalination," *Applied Economics* 21 (September 1989), pp. 1177–90.

law of diminishing marginal rate of technical substitution
A property of a production function stating that as less of one input is used, increasing amounts of another input must be employed to produce the same level of output.

instance, by moving from point A to point B in Figure 5–6, the manager substitutes 1 unit of capital for 1 unit of labor and still produces 100 units of output. But in moving from point C to point D, the manager would have to substitute 3 units of capital for 1 unit of labor to produce 100 units of output. Thus, the production function satisfies the *law of diminishing marginal rate of technical substitution* if, as a producer uses less of an input, increasingly more of the other input must be employed to produce the same level of output. It can be shown that the Cobb-Douglas production function implies isoquants that have a diminishing marginal rate of technical substitution. Whenever an isoquant exhibits a diminishing marginal rate of technical substitution, the corresponding isoquants are convex from the origin; that is, they look like the isoquants in Figure 5–6.

FIGURE 5–6

The marginal rate of technical substitution

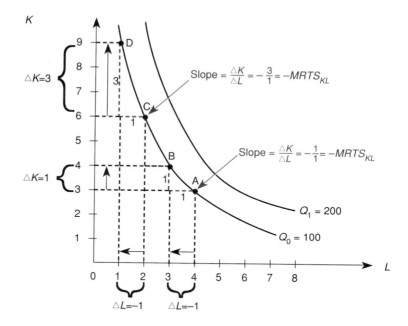

Isocosts

isocost
A line that represents the combinations of inputs that will cost the producer the same amount of money.

Isoquants describe the combinations of inputs that produce a given level of output. Notice that there exist different combinations of capital and labor that end up costing the firm the same amount. The combinations of inputs that will cost the firm the same amount comprise an *isocost line.*

The relation for an isocost line is graphed in Figure 5–7(a). To understand this concept, suppose the firm spends exactly $C on inputs. Then the cost of labor plus the cost of capital exactly equals $C:

$$wL + rK = C, \qquad (5\text{–}1)$$

where w is the wage rate (the price of labor) and r is the rental rate (the price of capital). This equation represents the formula for an isocost line.

We may obtain a more convenient expression for the slope and intercept of an isocost line as follows. We multiply both sides of Equation 5–1 by $1/r$ and get

$$\frac{w}{r}L + K = \frac{C}{r},$$

or

$$K = \frac{C}{r} - \frac{w}{r}L.$$

Thus, along an isocost line, K is a linear function of L with a vertical intercept of C/r and a slope of $-w/r$.

FIGURE 5–7

Isocosts

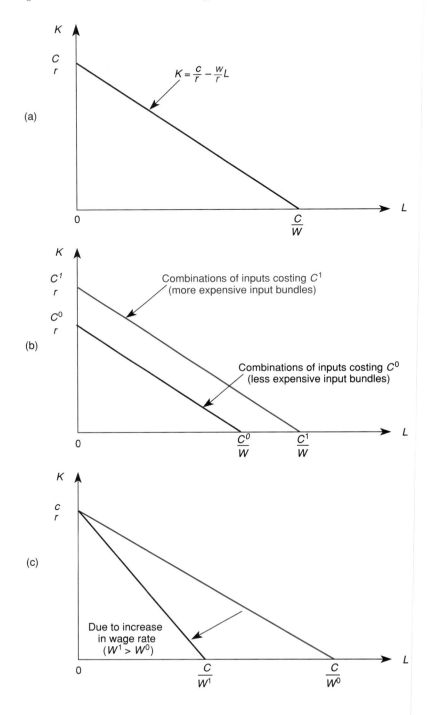

Note that if the producer wishes to use more of both inputs, more money must be spent. Thus, isocosts associated with higher costs lie above those with lower costs. When input prices are constant, the isocost lines will be parallel to one another. Figure 5–7(b) illustrates the isocost lines for cost levels C^0 and C^1, where $C^0 < C^1$.

Similarly, changes in input prices affect the position of the isocost line. An increase in the price of labor makes the isocost curve steeper, while an increase in the price of capital makes it flatter. For instance, Figure 5–7(c) reveals that the isocost line rotates clockwise when the wage rate increases from w^0 to w^1.

Principle

Changes in Isocosts

For given input prices, isocosts farther from the origin are associated with higher costs.
  Changes in input prices change the slopes of isocost lines.

Cost Minimization

The isocosts and isoquants just defined may be used to determine the input usage that minimizes production costs. If there were no scarcity, the producer would not care about production costs. But because scarcity is an economic reality, producers are interested in producing output at the lowest possible cost. After all, to maximize profits, the firm must first produce its output in the least-cost manner. Even not-for-profit organizations can achieve their objectives by providing a given level of service at the lowest possible cost. Let us piece together the theory developed thus far to see how to choose the optimal mix of capital and labor.

Consider an input bundle such as that at point A in Figure 5–8. This combination of L and K lies on the isoquant labeled Q_0 and thus produces Q_0 units of output. It also lies on the isocost line through point A. Thus, if the producer uses input mix A, he or she will produce Q_0 units of output at a total cost of C^1. Is this the cost-minimizing way to produce the given level of output? Clearly not, for by using input mix B instead of A, the producer could produce the same amount of output at a lower cost, namely C^2. In short, it is inefficient for the producer to use input mix A, because input mix B produces the same output and lies on a lower isocost line.

At the cost-minimizing input mix, the slope of the isoquant is equal to the slope of the isocost line. Recalling that the absolute value of the slope of the isoquant reflects the marginal rate of technical substitution and that the slope of the isocost line is given by $-w/r$, we see that at the cost-minimizing input mix,

$$MRTS = w/r.$$

FIGURE 5–8

Cost minimization

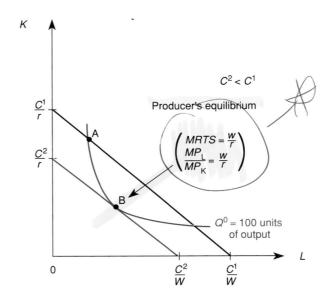

If this condition did not hold, the technical rate at which the producer could substitute between L and K would differ from the market rate at which she or he could substitute between the inputs. For example, at point A in Figure 5–8, the slope of the isoquant is steeper than the slope of the isocost line. Consequently, capital is "too expensive"; the producer finds it in his or her interest to use less capital and more labor to produce the given level of output. This substitution continues until ultimately the producer is at a point such as B, where the MRTS is equal to the ratio of input prices. The condition for the cost-minimizing use of inputs can also be stated in terms of marginal products.

Principle

Cost-Minimizing Input Rule

To minimize the cost of producing a given level of output, the marginal product per dollar spent should be equal for all inputs:

$$\frac{MP_L}{w} = \frac{MP_K}{r}.$$

Equivalently, to minimize the cost of production, a firm should employ inputs such that the marginal rate of technical substitution is equal to the ratio of input prices:

$$\frac{MP_L}{MP_K} = \frac{w}{r}.$$

To see why this condition must hold to be able to minimize the cost of producing a given level of output, suppose $MP_L/w > MP_K/r$. Then, on a last-dollar-spent basis, labor is a better deal than capital, and the firm should use less capital and more labor to minimize costs. In particular, if the firm reduced its expenditures on capital by $1, it could produce the same level of output if it increased its expenditures on labor by less than $1. Thus, by substituting away from capital and toward labor, the firm could reduce its costs while producing the same level of output. This substitution clearly would continue until the marginal product per dollar spent on capital exactly equaled the marginal product per dollar spent on labor.

DEMONSTRATION PROBLEM 5–3

Temporary Services uses 4 word processors and 2 typewriters to produce reports. The marginal product of a typewriter is 50 pages per day and the marginal product of a word processor is 500 pages per day. The rental price of a typewriter is $1 per day, whereas the rental price of a word processor is $50 per day. Is Temporary Services utilizing typewriters and word processors in the cost-minimizing manner?

Answer

Let MP_T be the marginal product of a typewriter and MP_W be the marginal product of a word processor. If we let P_W and P_T be the rental prices of a word processor and a typewriter, respectively, cost-minimization requires that

$$\frac{MP_T}{P_T} = \frac{MP_W}{P_W}.$$

Substituting in the appropriate values, we see that

$$\frac{50}{1} = \frac{MP_T}{P_T} > \frac{MP_W}{P_W} = \frac{500}{50}.$$

Thus, the marginal product per dollar spent on typewriters exceeds the marginal product per dollar spent on word processors. Word processors are 10 times more productive than typewriters, but 50 times more expensive. The firm clearly is not minimizing costs, and thus should use fewer word processors and more typewriters.

Optimal Input Substitution

A change in the price of an input will lead to a change in the cost-minimizing input bundle. To see this, suppose the initial isocost line in Figure 5–9 is FG and the producer is cost-minimizing at input mix *A,* producing Q_0 units of output. Suppose too that the wage rate increases so that if the firm spent the same amount on inputs, its isocost line would rotate clockwise to

FIGURE 5–9

*Substituting capital
for labor, due
to increase in the
wage rate*

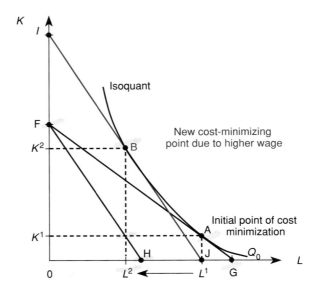

FH in Figure 5–9. Clearly, if the firm spends the amount it spent prior to the increase in the wage rate, it cannot produce the same level of output.

Given the new slope of the isocost line, which reflects a higher relative price of labor, the cost-minimizing way to maintain the output implied by the initial isoquant is at point B, where isocost line IJ is tangent to the isoquant. Due to the increase in the price of labor relative to capital, the producer substitutes away from labor and toward capital and adopts a more capital-intensive mode of production. This suggests the following important result:

Principle

Optimal Input Substitution

To minimize the cost of producing a given level of output, the firm should use less of an input and more of other inputs when that input's price rises.

Figure 5–10 shows the isocost line (AB) and isoquant for a firm that produces rugs using computers and labor. The initial point of cost minimization is at point M, where the manager has chosen to use 40 units of capital (computers) and 80 units of labor when the wage rate is $w = \$20$ and the rental rate of computers (capital) is $r^0 = \$20$. This implies that at point M, total costs are $C^0 = (\$20 \times 40) + (\$20 \times 80) = \$2,400$. Notice also at point M that the MRTS equals the ratio of the wage to the rental rate.

Now assume that due to a decrease in the supply of silicon chips, the rental rate of capital increases to $r^1 = \$40$. What will the manager do to

FIGURE 5–10

Substituting labor for computers, due to higher computer prices

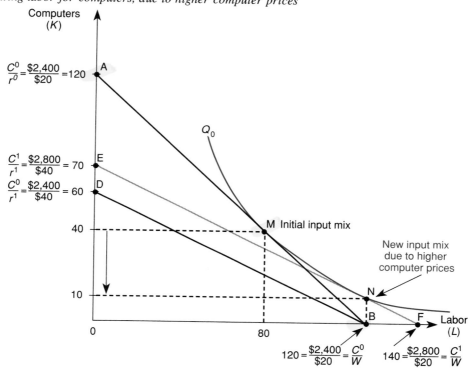

minimize costs? Since the price of capital has increased, the isocost line will rotate counterclockwise from AB to DB. To produce the same amount of output, the manager will have to spend more than $C^0 = \$2,400$. The additional expenditures will shift the isocost line out to EF in Figure 5–10. The new point of cost minimization is at point N, where the firm now employs more labor (120 units) and less capital (10 units) to minimize the production costs of rugs. Costs are now $C^1 = (\$40 \times 10) + (\$20 \times 120) = \$2,800$, which are higher than C^0.

The Cost Function

Now that we understand how a manager can use information about the production function to minimize the cost of producing a given level of output, it is useful to examine a very simple way to summarize the information contained in the production function. The idea behind such a summary is actually quite simple.

Inside Business 5–3

Fringe Benefits and Input Substitution

Government regulations often have unintended consequences. For instance, current federal tax law requires that firms provide fringe benefits in such a way as not to discriminate against lower-income workers. Presumably, the purpose of this regulation is to ensure that low-income workers will have access to health care, pension benefits, and other fringe benefits. Unfortunately, this policy often limits the employment opportunities of low-income workers.

To see why, consider a company that hires computer programmers and secretaries. Suppose the annual wage bill of a computer programmer is $30,000 and that of a secretary is $15,000. The company is considering offering a family health-care plan worth $3,600 annually to its employees. Ignoring the fringe-benefit bill, the relative price of a secretary to a computer programmer is $15,000/$30,000 = .5. But when the cost of the health-care plan is added in, the relative price of a secretary increases to a little over .55 of that of a computer programmer. Isoquant and isocost analysis suggests that firms should substitute away from the now higher-priced secretaries, to minimize costs.

Seem far-fetched? Recently economists Frank Scott, Mark Berger, and Dan Black examined the relationship between health-care costs and employment of low-wage workers. They found that industries that offered more generous health-care plans employed significantly fewer bookkeepers, keypunch operators, receptionists, secretaries, clerk-typists, janitors, and food service workers than did industries with lower health-care costs. Moreover, industries with higher levels of fringe benefits hired more part-time workers than did industries with lower fringe-benefit levels, since the IRS does not require firms to offer pension, health-care, and many other fringe benefits to part-time workers.

Source: Frank Scott, Mark Berger, and Dan Black, "Effects of Fringe Benefits on Labor Market Segmentation," *Industrial and Labor Relations Review* 42 (January 1989), pp. 216–29.

For given input prices, different isoquants will entail different production costs, even allowing for optimal substitution between capital and labor. Each isoquant corresponds to a different level of output, and the isocost line tangent to higher isoquants will imply higher costs of production, even assuming the firm uses the cost-minimizing input mix. Since the cost of production increases as higher isoquants are reached, it is useful to let $C(Q)$ denote the cost to the firm of producing isoquant Q in the cost-minimizing fashion. The function, C, is called the *cost function*.

The cost function is extremely valuable because, as we will see in later chapters, it provides essential information a manager needs to determine the profit-maximizing level of output. In addition, the cost function summarizes information about the production process. The cost function thus reduces the amount of information the manager has to process to make optimal output decisions.

Short-Run Costs

Recall that the short run is defined as the period over which the amounts of some inputs are fixed. In the short run, the manager is free to alter the use of variable inputs, but is "stuck" with existing levels of fixed inputs. Because inputs are costly whether fixed or variable, the total cost of producing output in the short run consists of (1) the cost of fixed inputs and (2) the cost of variable inputs. These two components of short-run total cost are called *fixed costs* and *variable costs,* respectively. *Fixed costs,* denoted *FC,* are costs that do not vary with output. Fixed costs include the costs of fixed inputs used in production. *Variable costs,* denoted *VC(Q),* are costs that change when output is changed. Variable costs include the costs of inputs that vary with output.

Since all costs fall into one or the other category, the sum of fixed and variable costs is the firm's short-run cost function. In the presence of fixed factors of production, the *short-run cost function* summarizes the minimum possible cost of producing each level of output when variable factors are being used in the cost-minimizing way.

Table 5–3 illustrates the costs of producing with the technology used in Table 5–1. Notice that the first three columns comprise a short-run production function, because they summarize the maximum amount of output that can be produced with two units of the fixed factor (capital) and alternative units of the variable factor (labor). Assuming capital costs $1,000 per unit and labor costs $400 per unit, we can calculate the fixed and variable costs of production, which are summarized in columns 4 and 5 of Table 5–3.

fixed costs
Costs that do not change with changes in output; include the costs of fixed inputs used in production.

variable costs
Costs that change with changes in output; include the costs of inputs that vary with output.

short-run cost function
A function that defines the minimum possible cost of producing each output level when variable factors are employed in the cost-minimizing fashion.

TABLE 5–3   The Cost Function

(1) K Fixed Input [Given]	(2) L Variable Input [Given]	(3) Q Output [Given]	(4) FC Fixed Cost [$1,000 × (1)]	(5) VC Variable Cost [$400 × (2)]	(6) TC Total Cost [(4) + (5)]
2	0	0	2,000	—	2,000
2	1	76	2,000	400	2,400
2	2	248	2,000	800	2,800
2	3	492	2,000	1,200	3,200
2	4	784	2,000	1,600	3,600
2	5	1,100	2,000	2,000	4,000
2	6	1,416	2,000	2,400	4,400
2	7	1,708	2,000	2,800	4,800
2	8	1,952	2,000	3,200	5,200
2	9	2,124	2,000	3,600	5,600
2	10	2,200	2,000	4,000	6,000
2	11	2,156	2,000	4,400	6,400

FIGURE 5–11

*The relationship
among costs*

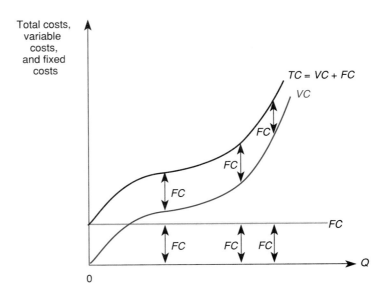

Notice that irrespective of the amount of output produced, the cost of the capital equipment is $1,000 \times 2 = \$2,000$. Thus, every entry in column 4 contains this number, illustrating the important principle that fixed costs do not vary with output.

To produce more output, more of the variable factor must be employed. For example, to produce 1,100 units of output, 5 units of labor are needed; to produce 1,708 units of output, 7 units of labor are required. Since labor is the only variable input in this simple example, the variable cost of producing 1,100 units of output is the cost of 5 units of labor, or $\$400 \times 5 = \$2,000$. Similarly, the variable cost of producing 1,708 units of output is $\$400 \times 7 = \$2,800$. Total costs, summarized in the last column of Table 5–3, are simply the sum of fixed costs (column 4) and variable costs (column 5) at each level of output.

Figure 5–11 illustrates graphically the relations among total costs *(TC),* variable costs *(VC),* and fixed costs *(FC).* Because fixed costs do not change with output, they are constant for all output levels and must be paid even if zero units of output are produced. Variable costs, on the other hand, are zero if no output is produced but increase as output increases above zero. Total cost is the sum of fixed costs and variable costs. Thus, the distance between the *TC* and *VC* curves in Figure 5–11 is simply fixed costs.

Average and Marginal Costs

One common misconception about costs is that large firms have lower costs than smaller firms because they produce larger quantities of output. One fundamental implication of scarcity is that to produce more output, more

TABLE 5–4   Derivation of Average Costs

(1) Q Output [Given]	(2) FC Fixed Cost [Given]	(3) VC Variable Cost [Given]	(4) TC Total Cost [(2) + (3)]	(5) AFC Average Fixed Cost [(2)/(1)]	(6) AVC Average Variable Cost [(3)/(1)]	(7) ATC Average Total Cost [(4)/(1)]
0	2,000	0	2,000	∞	—	∞
76	2,000	400	2,400	26.32	5.26	31.58
248	2,000	800	2,800	8.06	3.23	11.29
492	2,000	1,200	3,200	4.07	2.44	6.51
784	2,000	1,600	3,600	2.55	2.04	4.59
1,100	2,000	2,000	4,000	1.82	1.82	3.64
1,416	2,000	2,400	4,400	1.41	1.69	3.10
1,708	2,000	2,800	4,800	1.17	1.64	2.81
1,952	2,000	3,200	5,200	1.02	1.64	2.66
2,124	2,000	3,600	5,600	0.94	1.69	2.63
2,200	2,000	4,000	6,000	0.91	1.82	2.73

must be spent. What individuals most likely have in mind when they consider the advantages of producing large quantities of output is that the overhead is spread out over a larger level of output. This idea is intricately

average fixed cost
Fixed costs divided by the number of units of output.

related to the economic concept of average fixed cost. *Average fixed cost (AFC)* is defined as fixed costs *(FC)* divided by the number of units of output:

$$AFC = \frac{FC}{Q}.$$

Since fixed costs do not vary with output, as more and more output is produced, the fixed costs are allocated over a greater quantity of output. As a consequence, average fixed costs decline continuously as output is expanded. This principle is revealed in Column 5 of Table 5–4, where we see that average fixed costs decline as total output increases.

Average variable cost provides a measure of variable costs on a per-unit

average variable cost
Variable costs divided by the number of units of output.

basis. *Average variable cost (AVC)* is defined as variable costs *(VC)* divided by the number of units of output:

$$AVC = \frac{VC(Q)}{Q}.$$

Column 6 of Table 5–4 provides the average variable cost for the production function in our example. Notice that as output increases, average variable cost initially declines, reaches a minimum between 1,708 and 1,952 units of output, and then begins to increase.

TABLE 5–5   Derivation of Marginal Cost

(1) Q [Given]	(2) ΔQ [Δ(1)]	(3) VC [Given]	(4) ΔVC [Δ(3)]	(5) TC [Given]	(6) ΔTC [Δ5]	(7) MC [(6)/(2) or (4)/(2)]
0	—	0	—	2,000	—	—
76	76	400	400	2,400	400	400/ 76 = 5.26
248	172	800	400	2,800	400	400/172 = 2.33
492	244	1,200	400	3,200	400	400/244 = 1.64
784	292	1,600	400	3,600	400	400/292 = 1.37
1,100	316	2,000	400	4,000	400	400/316 = 1.27
1,416	316	2,400	400	4,400	400	400/316 = 1.27
1,708	292	2,800	400	4,800	400	400/292 = 1.37
1,952	244	3,200	400	5,200	400	400/244 = 1.64
2,124	172	3,600	400	5,600	400	400/172 = 2.33
2,200	76	4,000	400	6,000	400	400/ 76 = 5.26

Average total cost is analogous to average variable cost, except that it provides a measure of *total* costs on a per-unit basis. *Average total cost (ATC)* is defined as total cost *(TC)* divided by the number of units of output:

$$ATC = \frac{C(Q)}{Q}.$$

Column 7 of Table 5–4 provides the average total cost of various outputs in our example. Notice that average total cost declines as output expands to 2,124 units and then begins to rise. Furthermore, note that average total cost is the sum of average fixed costs and average variable costs (the sum of columns 5 and 6) in Table 5–4.

The most important cost concept is marginal (or incremental) cost. Conceptually, *marginal cost (MC)* is the cost of producing an additional unit of output, that is, the change in cost attributable to the last unit of output:

marginal (incremental) cost
The cost of producing an additional unit of output.

$$MC = \frac{\Delta C}{\Delta Q}.$$

To understand this important concept, consider Table 5–5, which summarizes the short-run cost function with which we have been working. Marginal cost, depicted in column 7, is calculated as the change in costs arising from a given change in output. For example, increasing output from 248 to 492 units ($\Delta Q = 244$) increases costs from 2,800 to 3,200 ($\Delta C = \$400$). Thus, the marginal cost of 492 units of output is $\Delta C/\Delta Q = 400/244 = \$1.64$.

When only one input is variable, the marginal cost is the price of that input divided by its marginal product. Remember that marginal product increases initially, reaches a maximum, and then decreases. Since mar-

FIGURE 5–12

*The relationship
among average and
marginal costs*

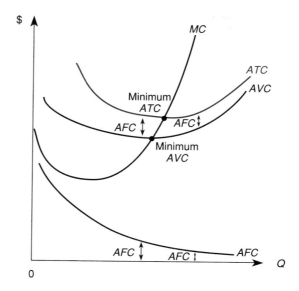

When MC < AC
AC↓

when MC > AC
AC↑

ginal cost is the reciprocal of marginal product times the input's price, it decreases as marginal product increases and increases when marginal product is decreasing.

Relations among Costs

Figure 5–12 graphically depicts average total, average variable, average fixed, and marginal costs under the assumption that output is infinitely divisible (the firm is not restricted to producing only the outputs listed in Tables 5–4 and 5–5 but can produce any outputs). The shapes of the curves indicate the relation between the marginal and average costs presented in those tables. These relations among the cost curves, also depicted in Figure 5–12, are very important. The first thing to notice is that the marginal cost curve intersects the ATC and AVC curves at their minimum points. This implies that when marginal cost is below an average cost curve, average cost is declining, and when marginal cost is above average cost, average cost is rising.

There is a simple explanation for this relationship among the various cost curves. Again consider your grade in this course. If your grade on an exam is below your average grade, the new grade lowers your average grade. If the grade you score on an exam is above your average grade, the new grade increases your average. In essence, the new grade is the marginal contribution to your total grade. When the marginal is above the average, the average increases; when the marginal is below the average, the average decreases. The same principle applies to marginal and average costs, and this is why the curves in Figure 5–12 look the way they do.

The second thing to notice in Figure 5–12 is that the ATC and AVC curves get closer together as output increases. This is because the only difference in ATC and AVC is AFC. To see why, note that total costs consist of variable costs and fixed costs:

$$C(Q) = VC(Q) + FC.$$

If we divide both sides of this equation by total output *(Q)*, we get

$$\frac{C(Q)}{Q} = \frac{VC(Q)}{Q} + \frac{FC}{Q}.$$

But *C(Q)/Q = ATC, VC(Q)/Q = AVC,* and *FC/Q = AFC.* Thus,

$$ATC = AVC + AFC.$$

The difference between average total costs and average variable costs is *ATC − AVC = AFC.* Since average fixed costs decline as output is expanded, as in Figure 5–12, this difference between average total and average variable costs diminishes as fixed costs are spread over increasing levels of output.

Fixed and Sunk Costs

We can make an important but subtle distinction concerning different types of fixed costs. As noted, in the short run some inputs are not free to vary, and the firm must pay for the inputs regardless of whether zero or 1 million units of output are produced. For example, if you buy a textbook that costs $50, then regardless of whether you read 300 pages or don't open the book at all, you are out the same amount of money. In the short run (i.e., for a given college degree plan), buying textbooks is a fixed cost of going to college.

Suppose, however, that at the end of the semester the bookstore will pay you $20 for your used book, which you purchased new for $50. Then, in effect, you really "sunk" only $30 into the textbook, since you recoup $20 when you sell back the used book. In economic terminology, the *sunk cost* of the textbook is $30—the cost that is forever lost after it has been paid.

sunk cost
A cost that is forever lost after it has been paid.

DEMONSTRATION PROBLEM 5–4

Flibynite Airlines is considering a purchase of 10 planes at a price of $2 million each. The company knows the resale market for the planes is not very good; it could resell one plane to a competitor for $1 million and the other nine planes to a scrap metal dealer for $50,000 each. What are the sunk costs to Flibynite Airlines if it buys 10 planes?

Answer

The sunk costs are the costs that cannot be recouped after they are paid. The total cost of the 10 planes is $20 million. After the purchase, the company can recoup some of its costs by selling one plane to a competitor and the other nine to the scrap metal dealer. The total recouped value is

$$9(\$50,000) + 1(\$1,000,000) = \$1,450,000.$$

Sunk costs are thus

$$\$20,000,000 - \$1,450,000 = \$18,550,000.$$

Algebraic Forms of Cost Functions

In practice cost functions may take many forms, but one form of the cost function is frequently encountered and closely approximates any cost function. The *cubic cost function* provides a reasonable approximation to virtually any cost function. The cubic cost function is given by

cubic cost function
Costs are a cubic function of output; provides a reasonable approximation to virtually any cost function.

$$C(Q) = f + aQ + bQ^2 + cQ^3,$$

where a, b, c, and f are real numbers.

Given an algebraic form of the cubic cost function, we may directly calculate the marginal cost function.

Formula: Marginal Cost for Cubic Costs.   For a cubic total cost function,

$$C(Q) = f + aQ + bQ^2 + cQ^3,$$

the marginal cost function is

$$MC(Q) = a + 2bQ + 3cQ^2.$$

A Calculus Alternative

Marginal cost is simply the derivative of the total cost function with respect to output:

$$MC(Q) = \frac{dC}{dQ}.$$

For example, the derivative of the cubic cost function with respect to Q is

$$\frac{dC}{dQ} = a + 2bQ + 3cQ^2,$$

which is the formula for marginal cost given above.

DEMONSTRATION PROBLEM 5–5

The cost function for Managerial Enterprises is given by $C(Q) = 20 + 3Q^2$. What are the marginal cost, average fixed cost, average variable cost, and average total cost of producing 10 units of output?

Answer

Using the formula for marginal cost (here $a = c = 0$), we know that $MC = 6Q$. Thus, the marginal cost of producing the 10th unit of output is $60.

To find the various average costs, we must first calculate total costs. The total cost of producing 10 units of output is

$$C(10) = 20 + 3(10)^2 = \$320.$$

Fixed costs are those costs that do not vary with output; thus fixed costs are $20. Variable costs are the costs that vary with output, namely $VC(Q) = 3Q^2$. Thus, $VC(10) = 3(10)^2 = \$300$. It follows that the average fixed cost of producing 10 units is $2, the average variable cost is $30, and the average total cost is $32.

Long-Run Costs

In the long run all costs are variable, because the manager is free to adjust the levels of all inputs. In Figure 5–13, short-run average cost curve ATC_0 is drawn under the assumption that there are some fixed factors of production. The average total cost of producing output level Q_0 given the fixed factors of production is $ATC_0(Q_0)$. In the short run, if the firm increases output to Q_1, it cannot adjust the fixed factors, and thus average costs rise to $ATC_0(Q_1)$. In the long run, however, the firm can adjust the fixed factors. Let ATC_1 be the average cost curve after the firm adjusts the fixed factor in the optimal manner. Now the firm can produce Q_1 with average cost curve ATC_1. If the firm produced Q_1 with average cost curve ATC_0, its average costs would be $ATC_0(Q_1)$. By adjusting the fixed factors in a way that optimizes the scale of operation, the firm economizes in production and can produce Q_1 units of output at a lower average cost, $ATC_1(Q_1)$. Notice that the curve labeled ATC_1 is itself a short-run average cost curve, based on the new levels of fixed inputs that have been selected to minimize the cost of producing Q_1. If the firm wishes to further expand output—say, to Q_2—it would follow curve ATC_1 in the short run to $ATC_1(Q_2)$ until it again changed its fixed factors to incur lower average costs of producing Q_2 units of output, namely $ATC_2(Q_2)$.

The *long-run average cost curve*, denoted $LRAC$ in Figure 5–13, defines the minimum average cost of producing alternative levels of output, allowing for optimal selection of all variables of production (both fixed and variable factors). The long-run average cost curve is the lower envelope of all the

long-run average cost curve
A curve that defines the minimum average cost of producing alternative levels of output, allowing for optimal selection of both fixed and variable factors of production.

FIGURE 5–13

Optimal plant size and long-run average cost

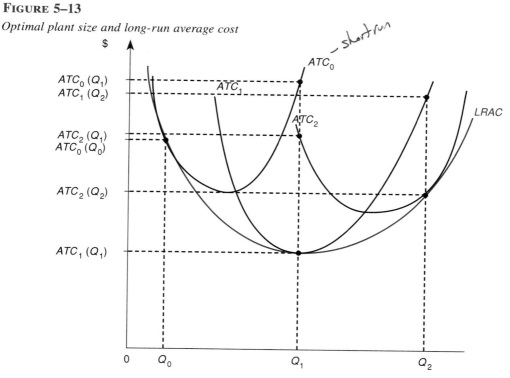

short-run average cost curves. This means that the long-run average cost curve lies below every point on the short-run average cost curves, except that it equals each short-run average cost curve at the points where the short-run curve uses fixed factors optimally. In essence, we may think of each short-run average cost curve in Figure 5–13 as the average cost of producing in a plant of fixed size. Different short-run average cost curves are associated with different plant sizes. In the long run, the firm's manager is free to choose the optimal plant size for producing the desired level of output, and this determines the long-run average cost of producing that output level.

DEMONSTRATION PROBLEM 5–6

Consider the three short-run average cost curves in Figure 5–14. Each curve is associated with a different size plant. Which plant can produce 5 units of output most efficiently? Which can produce 10 units most efficiently?

FIGURE 5–14

A medium-sized plant produces 5 units at lowest cost

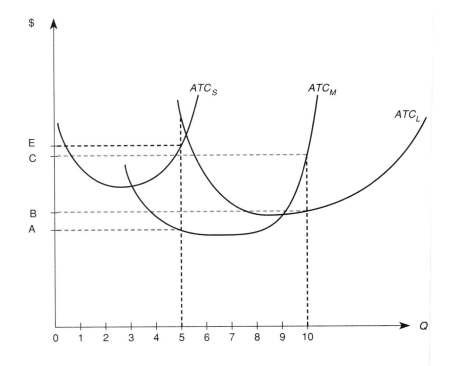

Answer

The smallest plant in Figure 5–14 is ATC_S, the largest plant is ATC_L, and the medium-size plant is ATC_M. If the firm wished to produce 5 units of output, it would choose the medium-size plant. The average cost would be at level A, which is the lowest possible cost for producing 5 units. If this company chose to produce 10 units, it would choose the largest plant.

---

economies of scale
Economies of scale exist whenever long-run average costs decline as output is increased. Diseconomies of scale exist when long-run average costs rise as output is increased. Constant returns to scale exist when long-run average costs remain constant as output is increased.

Economies of Scale

Notice that the long-run average cost curve in Figure 5–15(a) is U shaped. This implies that initially an expansion of output allows the firm to produce at lower long-run average cost, as is shown for outputs between 0 and Q^*. This condition is known as *economies of scale*. When there are economies of scale, increasing the size of the operation decreases the minimum average cost. After a point, such as Q^* in Figure 5–15(a), further increases in output lead to an increase in average costs. This condition is known as *diseconomies of scale*. Sometimes the technology in an industry allows a firm to produce different levels of output at the same minimum average cost, as in Figure 5–15(b). This condition is called *constant returns to scale*.

FIGURE 5–15

*Economies and
diseconomies of
scale*

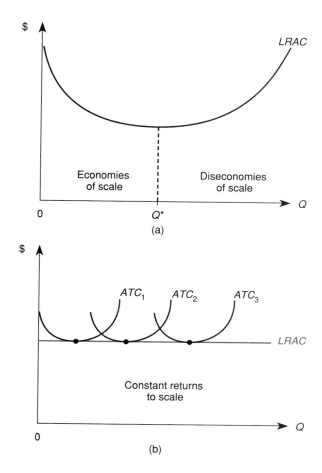

(a)

(b)

A Reminder: Economic Costs versus Accounting Costs

In concluding this section, it is important to recall the difference between economic costs and accounting costs. Accounting costs are the costs most often associated with the costs of producing. For example, accounting costs include direct payments to labor and capital to produce output. Accounting costs are the costs that appear on the income statements of firms.

These costs are not the only costs of producing a good, however. The firm could use the same resources to produce some other good. By choosing to produce one good, producers give up the opportunity for producing some other good. Thus, the costs of production include not only the accounting costs but also the opportunities forgone by producing a given product.

Multiple-Output Cost Functions

Up until now, our analysis of the production process has focused on situations where the firm produces a single output. There are also numerous examples of firms that produce multiple outputs. General Motors produces both cars and trucks (and many varieties of each); IBM produces many different types of computers and printers. While our analysis for the case of a firm that produces a single output also applies to multiproduct firms, the latter raise some additional issues. This section will highlight these concepts.

In this section, we will assume that the cost function for a multiproduct firm is given by $C(Q_1, Q_2)$, where Q_1 is the number of units produced of product 1 and Q_2 is the number of units produced of product 2. The *multiproduct cost function* thus defines the cost of producing Q_1 units of good 1 and Q_2 units of good 2 assuming all inputs are used efficiently.

multiproduct cost function
A function that defines the cost of producing given levels of two or more types of outputs assuming all inputs are used efficiently.

Notice that the multiproduct cost function has the same basic interpretation as a single-output cost function. Unlike with a single-product cost function, however, the costs of production depend on how much of each type of output is produced. This gives rise to what economists call *economies of scope* and *cost complementarities,* discussed next.

Economies of Scope

economies of scope
Exist when the total cost of producing two types of outputs together is less than the total cost of producing each type of output separately.

Economies of scope exist when the total cost of producing Q_1 and Q_2 together is less than the total cost of producing Q_1 and Q_2 separately, that is, when

$$C(Q_1, 0) + C(0, Q_2) > C(Q_1, Q_2).$$

In a restaurant, for example, to produce given quantities of steak and chicken dinners, it generally is cheaper to produce both products in the same restaurant than to have two restaurants, one that sells only chicken and one that sells only steak. The reason is, of course, that producing the dinners separately would require duplication of many common factors of production, such as ovens, refrigerators, tables, the building, and so forth.

Cost Complementarity

cost complementarity
Exists when the marginal cost of producing one type of output decreases when the output of another good is increased.

Cost complementarities exist in a multiproduct cost function when the marginal cost of producing one output is reduced when the output of another product is increased. Let $C(Q_1, Q_2)$ be the cost function for a multiproduct firm, and let $MC_1(Q_1, Q_2)$ be the marginal cost of producing the first output. The cost function exhibits cost complementarity if

$$\frac{\Delta MC_1(Q_1, Q_2)}{\Delta Q_2} < 0,$$

that is, if an increase in the output of product 2 decreases the marginal cost of producing output 1.

An example of cost complementarity is the production of doughnuts and doughnut holes. The firm can make these products separately or jointly. But the cost of making additional doughnut holes is lower when workers roll out the dough, punch the holes, and fry both the doughnuts and the holes instead of making the holes separately.

The concepts of economies of scope and cost complementarity can also be examined within the context of an algebraic functional form for a multiproduct cost function. For example, suppose the multiproduct cost function is quadratic:

$$C(Q_1, Q_2) = f + aQ_1Q_2 + (Q_1)^2 + (Q_2)^2.$$

For this cost function,

$$MC_1 = aQ_2 + 2Q_1.$$

Notice that when $a < 0$, an increase in Q_2 reduces the marginal cost of producing good 1. Thus, if $a < 0$, this cost function exhibits cost complementarity. If $a > 0$, there are no cost complementarities.

Formula: *Quadratic Multiproduct Cost Function.* The multiproduct cost function

$$C(Q_1, Q_2) = f + aQ_1Q_2 + (Q_1)^2 + (Q_2)^2$$

has corresponding marginal cost functions,

$$MC_1(Q_1, Q_2) = aQ_2 + 2Q_1$$

and

$$MC_2(Q_1, Q_2) = aQ_1 + 2Q_2.$$

To examine whether economies of scope exist for a quadratic multiproduct cost function, recall that there are economies of scope if

$$C(Q_1, 0) + C(0, Q_2) > C(Q_1, Q_2),$$

or, rearranging,

$$C(Q_1, 0) + C(0, Q_2) - C(Q_1, Q_2) > 0.$$

This condition may be rewritten as

$$f + (Q_1)^2 + f + (Q_2)^2 - [f + aQ_1Q_2 + (Q_1)^2 + (Q_2)^2] > 0,$$

which may be simplified to

$$f - aQ_1Q_2 > 0.$$

Thus, economies of scope are realized in producing output levels Q_1 and Q_2 if $f > aQ_1Q_2$.

Summary of the Properties of the Quadratic Multiproduct Cost Function

The multiproduct cost function $C(Q_1, Q_2) = f + aQ_1Q_2 + (Q_1)^2 + (Q_2)^2$

1. Exhibits cost complementarity whenever $a < 0$.
2. Exhibits economies of scope whenever $f - aQ_1Q_2 > 0$.

DEMONSTRATION PROBLEM 5–7

Suppose the cost function of firm A, which produces two products, is given by

$$C = 100 - .5Q_1Q_2 + (Q_1)^2 + (Q_2)^2.$$

The firm wishes to produce 5 units of good 1 and 4 units of good 2.
(1) Do cost complementarities exist? Do economies of scope exist?
(2) Firm A is considering selling the subsidiary that produces good 2 to firm B, in which case it will produce only good 1. What will happen to firm A's costs if it continues to produce 5 units of good 1?

Answer

(1) For this cost function, $a = -1/2 < 0$, so indeed there are cost complementarities. To check for economies of scope, we must determine whether $f - aQ_1Q_2 > 0$. This is clearly true, since $a < 0$ in this problem. Thus, economies of scope exist in producing 5 units of good 1 and 4 units of good 2.
(2) To determine what will happen to firm A's costs if it sells the subsidiary that produces good 2 to firm B, we must calculate costs under the alternative scenarios. By selling the subsidiary, firm A will reduce its production of good 2 from 4 to 0 units; since there are cost complementarities, this will increase the marginal cost of producing good 1. Notice that the total costs to firm A of producing the 5 units of good 1 fall from

$$C(5, 4) = 100 - 10 + 25 + 16 = 131$$

to

$$C(5, 0) = 100 + 25 = 125.$$

But the costs to firm B of producing 4 units of good 2 will be

$$C(0, 4) = 100 + 16 = 116.$$

Firm A's costs will fall by only $6 when it stops producing good 2, and the costs to firm B of producing 4 units of good 2 will be $116. The combined costs to the two firms of producing the output originally produced by a single firm will be $110 more than the cost of producing by a single firm.

The preceding problem illustrates some important aspects of mergers and sales of subsidiaries. First, when there are economies of scope, two firms producing distinct outputs could merge into a single firm and enjoy a reduction in costs. Second, selling off an unprofitable subsidiary could lead to only minor reductions in costs. In effect, when economies of scope exist, it is difficult to "allocate costs" across product lines.

Answering the Headline

Let us now address the issue of the productivity of American workers relative to their Japanese counterparts. The numbers reported in the headline that opened this chapter reveal that Honda produces one car with 10.9 hours of labor, whereas it takes Ford 16 hours of labor to produce one car. These numbers are derived by dividing the total number of hours worked by the total number of cars produced. You should now recognize that the measure of productivity cited in the headlines is nothing more than the reciprocal of the average product of Japanese and U.S. automobile workers. Thus, the average product of a Japanese autoworker is $AP_L^J = 1/10.9 = .09$, while the average product of an American autoworker is $AP_L^A = 1/16 = .06$. What would account for the higher average product of Japanese workers?

Assuming cars are produced with capital and labor, the average product of American autoworkers is

$$AP_L^A = \frac{F(K^A, L^A)}{L^A} = .06$$

and the average product of Japanese autoworkers is

$$AP_L^J = \frac{F(K^J, L^J)}{L^J} = .09.$$

The average wage rate (including benefits) of American autoworkers was approximately $16 per hour. Their Japanese counterparts earned an average of about $18 per hour. Assuming identical technologies and capital costs in the two countries, the higher labor costs in Japan induce Japanese firms to substitute capital for labor. Thus, to produce a given number of cars, U.S. automakers would produce at point A in Figure 5–16, while Japanese firms would produce at point B. In short, to produce on a given

FIGURE 5–16

FIGURE 5–16

*Differences in
capital–labor
ratios in the
U.S. and Japan*

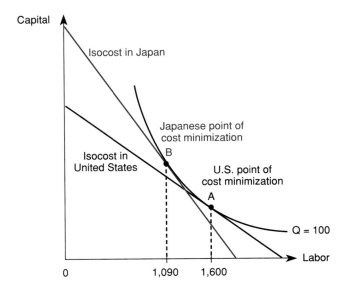

isoquant, Japanese automakers will use fewer workers than U.S. firms due
to the higher labor costs in Japan and use more capital than U.S. firms.
Japanese firms *choose* to use less labor than U.S. firms to produce automobiles. This increases the average product of autoworkers in Japan relative to
that of U.S. autoworkers. For example, suppose the isoquant corresponds
to 100 units of output and that, due to higher labor costs, Japanese automakers use 1,090 units of labor while U.S. automakers use 1,600 units of
labor. Then the average product of a Japanese autoworker is 100/1,090 =
.09, while that of an American autoworker is 100/1,600 = .06.

This analysis suggests a fun question for the Japanese Minister of Labor: Do Japanese firms use more capital-intensive technologies than American firms to minimize the use of "lazy" Japanese workers? You will get a
chance to answer this one in the problems at the end of the chapter.

Summary

In this chapter, we introduced the production and cost functions, which
summarize important information about converting inputs into outputs sold
by a firm. For firms that use several inputs to produce output, isocosts and
isoquants provide a convenient way to determine the optimal input mix.

We broke down the cost function into average total cost, average fixed
cost, average variable cost, and marginal cost. These concepts help build a

foundation for understanding the profit-maximizing input and output decisions that will be covered in greater detail in later chapters.

Given a desired level of output, isoquants and isocosts provide the information needed to determine the cost-minimizing level of inputs. The cost-minimizing level of inputs is determined by the point at which the ratio of input prices equals the ratio of marginal products for the various inputs.

Finally, we showed how economies of scale, economies of scope, and cost complementaries influence the level and mix of outputs produced by single and multiproduct firms. In the next chapter we will look at the acquisition of inputs. We will see how managers can use spot markets, contracts, or vertical integration to efficiently obtain the inputs needed to produce their desired mix of outputs.

Key Terms and Concepts

average fixed cost
average product
average total cost
average variable cost
Cobb-Douglas production
   function
cost function
cost minimization
decreasing (or diminishing)
   marginal returns
diminishing marginal rate of
   technical substitution
fixed costs
fixed factors of production
increasing marginal returns
isocost

isoquant
Leontief (or fixed proportions)
   production function
long run
marginal (incremental) cost
marginal product
optimal input substitution
production function
profit-maximizing input
   usage
short run
sunk costs
total cost
total product
value marginal product
variable costs

Problems

1. In 1995 Congress considered legislation that would have provided investment tax credits to businesses. Effectively, an investment tax credit reduces the cost to firms of using capital in production. Would you expect labor unions to lobby for or against such a bill? (Hint: What impact would such a plan have on the capital-to-labor ratio at the typical firm?)

2. You have been hired to replace the manager of a firm that uses only two inputs, capital and labor, to produce output. The firm can hire as much labor as it wants at a wage of $5 per hour and can rent as much capital as it wants at a price of $50 per hour. After you look at the company books, you learn that the company has been using capital and labor in amounts that imply a marginal product of labor of 50 and a marginal product of capital of 100. Do you know why the firm hired you? Explain.

3. The manager of a meat-packing plant can use either butchers (labor) or meat saws (capital) to prepare packages of sirloin steak. Based on estimates provided by an efficiency expert, the firm's production function for sirloin steak is given by

$$Q = K + L.$$

   a. Graph the isoquant corresponding to 5 units of output.
   b. What is the marginal product of capital and labor? Does the answer depend on how much labor and capital are used?
   c. If the price of labor is $2 per hour and the rental price of capital is $3 per hour, how much capital and labor should be used to minimize the cost of production?

4. The manager of a national retailing outlet recently hired an economist to estimate the firm's production function. Based on the economist's report, the manager now knows that the firm's production function is given by $Q = K^{1/2}L^{1/2}$ and that capital is fixed at 1 unit.
   a. Calculate the average product of labor when 9 units of labor are utilized.
   b. Calculate the marginal product of labor when 9 units of labor are utilized.
   c. Suppose the firm can hire labor at a wage of $10 per hour and output can be sold at a price of $100 per unit. Determine the profit-maximizing levels of labor and output.
   d. What is the maximum price of capital at which the firm will still make nonnegative profits?

5. An accountant for a car rental company was recently asked to report the firm's costs of producing various levels of output. The accountant knows that the most recent estimate available of the firm's cost function is $C(Q) = 100 + 10Q + Q^2$, where costs are measured in thousands of dollars and output is measured in thousands of hours rented.
   a. What is the average fixed cost of producing 2 units of output?
   b. What is the average variable cost of producing 2 units of output?
   c. What is the average total cost of producing 2 units of output?
   d. What is the marginal cost of producing 2 units of output?

e. What is the relation between the answers to (*a*), (*b*), and (*c*) above? Is this a general property of average cost curves?

6. There are over 5,000 banks in the United States—more than 10 times the number per person than in other industrialized countries. A recent study suggests that the long run average cost curve for an individual bank is relatively flat. If Congress took steps to consolidate banks, thereby reducing the total number to 2,500, what would you expect to happen to costs within the banking industry? Explain.

7. A production function exhibits constant returns to scale if a twofold (threefold, etc.) increase in all inputs leads to a twofold (threefold, etc.) increase in output. For example, by doubling the use of capital and labor, the firm would exactly double its output.
   a. What would the average and marginal cost curves look like under constant returns to scale? Explain.
   b. Give an example of a production process that exhibits constant returns to scale.

8. A production function exhibits decreasing returns to scale if a twofold (threefold, etc.) increase in all inputs increases output by less than twofold (less than threefold, etc.). For example, by doubling the use of capital and labor, the firm would less than double its output.
   a. What would the average and marginal cost curves look like under decreasing returns to scale? Explain.
   b. Give an example of a production process that exhibits decreasing returns to scale.

9. The total costs for Morris Industries are summarized in the following table. Based on this information, fill in the missing entries in the table for fixed cost, variable cost, average fixed cost, average variable cost, average total cost, and marginal cost.

(1) Q	(2) FC	(3) VC	(4) TC	(5) AFC	(6) AVC	(7) ATC	(8) MC
0			1,000				
10			2,000				
20			2,500				
30			4,000				
40			6,000				
50			10,000				
60			15,000				

10. The following table summarizes the short-run production function for your firm. Your product sells for $5 per unit, labor costs $5 per unit,

and the rental price of capital is $20 per unit. Complete the following table, and then answer the accompanying questions.

(1) K	(2) L	(3) Q	(4) MP_K	(5) AP_K	(6) AP_L	(7) VMP_K
0	5	0				
1	5	10				
2	5	30				
3	5	60				
4	5	80				
5	5	90				
6	5	95				
7	5	95				
8	5	90				
9	5	80				
10	5	60				
11	5	30				

a. Which inputs are the fixed inputs? Which are the variable inputs?
b. How much are your fixed costs?
c. What is the variable cost of producing 20 units of output?
d. How many units of the variable input should be used to maximize profits?
e. What are your maximum profits?
f. Over what range of variable input usage do increasing marginal returns exist?
g. Over what range of variable input usage do decreasing marginal returns exist?
h. Over what range of variable input usage do negative marginal returns exist?

11. Your firm produces two products, Q_1 and Q_2. An economic consulting firm has estimated your cost function to be $C(Q_1, Q_2) = 100 + Q_1 Q_2 + Q_1 + Q_2$.
a. Are there economies of scope?
b. Are there cost complementarities?
c. Your market for Q_1 is not very good, and an overseas firm has offered to buy the division of your company that produces Q_1. What will happen to your marginal cost of producing Q_2 if you sell the division?
d. You currently produce 2 units of Q_1 and 100 units of Q_2. If you sell the division that produces Q_1, what will happen to your average cost of producing Q_2 if you continue to produce 100 units of Q_2?

12. In the text, we showed that the multiproduct cost function

$$C(Q_1, Q_2) = f + aQ_1Q_2 + (Q_1)^2 + (Q_2)^2$$

exhibits cost complimentarity whenever $a < 0$ and exhibits economies of scope whenever $f - aQ_1Q_2 > 0$.
    a. Can cost complementarities exist without economies of scope?
    b. Can there be economies of scope when cost complementarities exist?

13. Here's the question we promised you in the concluding section of the chapter: Do Japanese firms use more capital-intensive technologies than American firms to minimize the use of "lazy" Japanese workers?

14. The analysis presented in the text of differences in the average products of automobile workers in the United States and Japan assumes that American and Japanese automobile firms have identical technologies, capital costs, and pools of potential workers. How would differences in any of these factors alter the analysis of differences in average products?

15. Suppose the production function for automobiles is given by $Q = K^{1/4}L^{3/4}$.
    a. Show that the marginal product of any given quantity of labor increases as capital is increased.
    b. Suppose Japanese and U.S. automakers produce on identical isoquants with this Cobb-Douglas production function and that labor costs are higher in Japan than in the United States. Do autoworkers in Japan have a higher marginal product than American autoworkers? Explain carefully.
    c. Now suppose Japanese automakers produce on a different isoquant from U.S. firms, but the prices of Japanese and American cars are identical. Do Japanese or American autoworkers have a higher marginal product? Why?

16. Show that the Cobb-Douglas production function $Q = K^{1/4}L^{3/4}$ exhibits the law of diminishing marginal rate of technical substitution.

17. You are the manager of a firm that sells output at a price of $40 per unit. You are interested in hiring a new worker who will increase your firm's output by 2,000 units per year. Several other firms also are interested in hiring this worker.
    a. What is the most you should be willing to pay this worker to come to your firm?
    b. What will determine whether or not you actually have to offer this much to the worker to induce him to join your firm?

18. To open a new business, a manager must obtain a license from the city for $2,000. The license is nontransferable and nonrefundable. Furthermore, a deposit of $20,000 must be paid to the owner of the building in which the new business will be located. Rent on the

building is $12,000 per month with the first payment due with the deposit. The owner of the building will refund the $20,000 deposit if the building is rented for at least 12 months; otherwise, the deposit will be forfeited.

a. How large are the fixed costs of opening the business?

b. How large are sunk costs?

19. The maker of Turbotax produces software that prepares Federal income tax returns. In addition, it produces software that prepares various state income tax returns. Why doesn't it pay for the firm to specialize in Federal software?

20. The management of Morris Industries is considering a plan to terminate a new employee. The action stemmed from documented evidence supplied by the firm's accounting department that this new employee did not add as much to the firm's overall output as did a worker hired two weeks earlier. Based on this evidence, do you agree that the latest worker hired should be fired? Explain.

21. In 1995 the U.S. Justice Department sued to block a merger between Microsoft and Intuit, the producer of the nation's best-selling business software. The Justice Department argued that the merger would lessen competition and raise prices of business software. Is there an economic argument that the merger might actually result in lower prices? Explain.

Selected Readings

Anderson, Evan E. and Chen, Yu Min, "Implicit Prices and Economies of Scale of Secondary Memory: The Case of Disk Drives." *Managerial and Decision Economics* 12(3), June 1991, pp. 241–48.

Carlsson, Bo, Audretsch, David B., and Acs, Zoltan J., "Flexible Technology and Plant Size: U.S. Manufacturing and Metalworking Industries." *International Journal of Industrial Organization* 12(3), 1994, pp. 359–72.

Eaton, C., "The Geometry of Supply, Demand, and Competitive Market Structure with Economies of Scope." *The American Economic Review* 81, Sept. 1991, pp. 901–11.

Ferrier, Gary D. and Lovell, C. A. Knox, "Measuring Cost Efficiency in Banking: Econometric and Linear Programming Evidence." *Journal of Econometrics* 46(12), Oct. Nov. 1990, pp. 229–45.

Gold, B., "Changing Perspectives on Size, Scale, and Returns: An Interpretive Survey." *Journal of Economic Literature* 19(1), March 1981, pp. 5–33.

Gropper, Daniel M., "An Empirical Investigation of Changes in Scale Economies for the Commercial Banking Firm, 1979–1986." *Journal of Money, Credit, and Banking* 23(4), November 1991, pp. 718–27.

Kohn, Robert E. and Levin, Stanford L., "Complementarity and Anticomplementarity with the Same Pair of Inputs." *Journal of Economic Education* 25(1), Winter 1994, pp. 67–73.

Mills, D., "Capacity Expansion and the Size of Plants." *The Rand Journal of Economics* 21, Winter 1990, pp. 555–66.

APPENDIX
THE CALCULUS OF PRODUCTION AND COSTS

The Profit-Maximizing Usage of Inputs

In this section we use calculus to show that the profit-maximizing level of an input is the level at which the value marginal product of the input equals the input's price. Let P denote the price of the output, Q, which is produced with the production function $F(K, L)$. The profits of the firm are

$$\pi = PQ - wL - rK.$$

PQ is the revenue of the firm and wL and rK are labor costs and capital costs, respectively. Since $Q = F(K, L)$, the objective of the manager is to choose K and L so as to maximize

$$\pi = PF(K, L) - wL - rK.$$

The first-order condition for maximizing this function requires that we set the first derivatives equal to zero:

$$\frac{\partial \pi}{\partial K} = P\left(\frac{\partial F(K, L)}{\partial K}\right) - r = 0$$

and

$$\frac{\partial \pi}{\partial L} = P\left(\frac{\partial F(K, L)}{\partial L}\right) - w = 0.$$

But since

$$\partial F(K, L)/\partial L = MP_L$$

and

$$\partial F(K, L)/\partial K = MP_K,$$

this implies that to maximize profits, $P(MP_L) = w$ and $P(MP_K) = r$; that is, each input must be used up to the point where its value marginal product equals its price.

The Slope of an Isoquant

In this section, we use calculus to show that the slope of an isoquant is the negative of the ratio of the marginal products of two inputs.

Let the production function be $Q = F(K, L)$. If we take the total derivative of this relation, we have

$$dQ = \left(\frac{\partial F(K, L)}{\partial K}\right)dK + \left(\frac{\partial F(K, L)}{\partial L}\right)dL.$$

Since output does not change along an isoquant, then $dQ = 0$. Thus,

$$0 = \left(\frac{\partial F(K, L)}{\partial K}\right)dK + \left(\frac{\partial F(K, L)}{\partial L}\right)dL.$$

Solving this relation for dK/dL yields

$$\frac{dK}{dL} = -\left(\frac{\partial F(K, L)/\partial L}{\partial F(K, L)/\partial K}\right).$$

Since

$$\partial F(K, L)/\partial L = MP_L$$

and

$$\partial F(K, L)/\partial K = MP_K,$$

we have shown that the slope of an isoquant *(dK/dL)* is

$$\frac{dK}{dL} = -\left(\frac{MP_L}{MP_K}\right).$$

The Optimal Mix of Inputs

In this section, we use calculus to show that to minimize the cost of production, the manager chooses inputs such that the slope of the isocost line equals the MRTS.

To choose K and L so as to minimize

$$wL + rK \text{ subject to } F(K, L) = Q,$$

we form the Lagrangian

$$H = wL + rK + \mu[Q - F(K, L)],$$

where μ is the Lagrange multiplier. The first-order conditions for a maximum are

$$\frac{\partial H}{\partial L} = w - \mu\left(\frac{\partial F(K, L)}{\partial L}\right) = 0, \qquad\qquad \text{(A–1)}$$

$$\frac{\partial H}{\partial K} = r - \mu\left(\frac{\partial F(K, L)}{\partial K}\right) = 0, \qquad\qquad \text{(A–2)}$$

and

$$\frac{\partial H}{\partial \mu} = Q - F(K, L) = 0.$$

Taking the ratio of Equations (A–1) and (A–2) gives us

$$\frac{w}{r} = \left(\frac{\partial F(K, L)/\partial L}{\partial F(K, L)/\partial K}\right),$$

which is

$$\frac{w}{r} = \left(\frac{MP_L}{MP_K}\right) = MRTS.$$

The Relation between Average and Marginal Costs

Finally, we will use calculus to show that the relation between average and marginal costs in the diagrams in this chapter is indeed correct. If $C(Q)$ is the cost function (the analysis that follows is valid for both variable and total costs, so we do not distinguish between them here), average cost is $AC(Q) = C(Q)/Q$. The change in average cost due to a change in output is simply the derivative of average cost with respect to output. Taking the derivative of $AC(Q)$ with respect to Q and using the quotient rule, we see that

$$\frac{dAC(Q)}{dQ} = \frac{Q\left(\frac{dC}{dQ}\right) - C(Q)}{Q^2} = \frac{1}{Q}[MC(Q) - AC(Q)],$$

since $dC(Q)/dQ = MC(Q)$. Thus, when $MC(Q) < AC(Q)$, average cost declines as output increases. When $MC(Q) > AC(Q)$, average cost rises as output increases. Finally, when $MC(Q) = AC(Q)$, average cost is at its minimum.

The Organization of the Firm

Headline

Mickey Mouse Incentives?

Walt Disney put Michael Eisner at the helm in 1984 in an attempt to boost Disney's performance. Eisner's compensation package included a base salary, plus stock options and bonuses tied to the firm's performance.

In late 1994 newspapers across the country reported that Eisner was among the highest paid CEOs in the country. Over the preceding three years, Eisner earned nearly $400 million, including unrealized gains on stock options. Many were understandably outraged by the reports, and members of Disney's board of directors were in the awkward position of having to justify Eisner's contract to the press.

Assuming you were on Disney's board of directors, how would you defend the contract?

Introduction

In Chapter 5 we saw how a manager can select the mix of inputs that minimizes the cost of production. However, the previous analysis in that chapter left unresolved two important questions. First, what is the optimal way to acquire this efficient mix of inputs? Second, how can the owners of a firm ensure that workers put forth the maximum effort consistent with their capabilities? In this chapter, we address these two issues.[1]

---

[1]Other questions that remain include how much output to produce and how to price the product. These important questions will be answered in the remaining chapters of this book.

FIGURE 6–1

*Producing at
minimum cost*

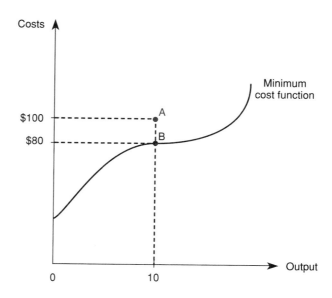

Figure 6–1 illustrates why it is important to resolve these two questions. The cost function defines the minimum possible cost of producing each level of output. Point A corresponds to the situation where a firm has costs in excess of the minimum costs necessary to produce a given level of output. At point A, 10 units of output are being produced for a total cost of $100. Notice that this cost is greater than $80, which is the minimum cost necessary to produce 10 units of output. Even if the firm has the right mix of inputs, if it did not obtain them efficiently, or if workers are not expending the maximum effort consistent with their capabilities, the firm's costs will be higher than the minimum possible costs.

In this chapter we consider techniques a firm can use to ensure that it is operating on the cost function (point B in Figure 6–1), and not above it (point A). We begin by discussing three methods managers can use to obtain inputs needed in production: spot exchange, contracts, and vertical integration. To minimize costs, a firm must not only use all inputs efficiently (the $MRTS_{KL} = w/r$ rule discussed in the previous chapter); it must use the least-cost method of obtaining the inputs. We will explain when it is optimal to acquire inputs (1) via spot exchange, (2) by writing contracts with input suppliers, or (3) by producing the inputs within the firm (vertical integration). Thus, the first part of this chapter provides managers with the information needed to acquire a given set of inputs in the optimal manner.

The second part of the chapter examines how a firm can ensure that labor inputs, including both managers and workers, put forth the maximum effort consistent with their capabilities. This is an important consideration, because conflicts of interest often arise among workers, managers, and the firm's owners. For example, the manager may wish to spend the firm's resources on plush office carpeting or corporate jets, while the owners prefer that the funds be invested to increase profits, which accrue to them by virtue of their status as owners. Or workers may wish to spend most of their day gossiping in the lunchroom instead of working. When employees and owners have conflicting interests, a *principal-agent* problem is said to exist. We will see how manager and worker compensation plans can be constructed to ensure that all employees put forth their highest levels of effort.

Methods of Procuring Inputs

A manager can use several approaches to obtain the inputs needed to produce a final product. Consider the manager of a car rental company. One input needed to produce output (rental cars) is automobile servicing (tune-ups, oil changes, lube jobs, and the like). The manager has three options: (1) simply take the cars to a firm that services automobiles and pay the market price for the services; (2) sign a contract with a firm that services automobiles and, when service is needed, pay the price negotiated in the contract for that particular service; or (3) create within the firm a division that services automobiles. Each of these methods of servicing automobiles generally will imply different cost functions for producing car rental services. The manager's job is to choose the method that minimizes costs. Before we examine how to determine the best method of acquiring a given type of input, it is useful to provide a broad overview of three methods of acquiring inputs.

Purchase the Inputs Using Spot Exchange

One method of acquiring inputs is to use spot exchange. *Spot exchange* occurs when the buyer and seller of an input meet, exchange, and then go their separate ways. If the manager of a car rental company simply takes a car to one of many firms that provide automobile servicing and pays for the services, the manager has used spot exchange to obtain automobile servicing. With spot exchange, buyers and sellers essentially are "anonymous"; the parties may make an exchange without even knowing each others' names, and there is no formal (legal) relationship between buyer and seller.

A key advantage of acquiring inputs with spot exchange is that the firm gets to specialize in doing what it does best: converting the inputs into output. The input manufacturer specializes in what it does best: producing inputs. Spot exchange often is used when inputs are "standardized." In that case, one simply purchases the desired input from one of many suppliers that sell the input.

Acquire Inputs under a Contract

A *contract* is a legal document that creates an extended relationship between a particular buyer and seller of an input. It specifies the terms under which they agree to exchange over a given time horizon, say, three years. For example, the manager of a car rental firm might choose to formalize her relationship with a particular firm that services automobiles by signing a contract. Such a contract specifies the range of services covered, the price of each service, and the hours during which the cars will be serviced. As long as the service requirements for the automobiles are understood beforehand, the parties can address all the important issues in the written contract. However, if the number of services needed during the term of the contract is very large, or if some types of unanticipated breakdowns occur, the contract may be incomplete. A contract is incomplete if, for example, a car needs a new transmission and the contract does not specify the price at which the servicing firm will provide this service. Of course, this opens the door to a dispute between the two parties regarding the price of the service needed but not spelled out in the contract.

By acquiring inputs with contracts, the purchasing firm enjoys the benefits of specializing in what it does best, because the other firm actually produces the inputs the purchasing firm needs. This method of obtaining inputs works well when it is relatively easy to write a contract that describes the characteristics of the inputs needed. One key disadvantage of contracts is that they are costly to write; it takes time, and often legal fees, to draw up a contract that specifies precisely the obligations of both parties. Also, it can be extremely difficult to cover all of the contingencies that could occur in the future. Thus, in complex contracting environments, contracts will necessarily be incomplete.

Produce the Inputs Internally

Finally, a manager may choose to produce the inputs needed for production within the firm. In this situation the manager of the car rental company dispenses with outside service firms entirely. She sets up a facility to service the automobile fleet with her own employees as service personnel. The firm thus bypasses the service market completely and does the work itself. When a firm shuns other suppliers and chooses to produce an input internally, it has engaged in *vertical integration.*

With vertical integration, however, a firm loses the gains in specialization it would realize were the inputs purchased from an independent supplier. Moreover, the firm now has to manage the production of inputs as well as the production of the final product produced with those inputs. This leads to the bureaucratic costs associated with a larger organization. On the other hand, by producing the inputs it needs internally, the firm no longer has to rely on other firms to provide the desired inputs.

DEMONSTRATION PROBLEM 6–1

Determine whether the following transactions involve spot exchange, a contract, or vertical integration:

1. Clone 1 PC is legally obligated to purchase 300 computer chips each year for the next three years from AMI. The price paid in the first year is $200 per chip, and the price rises during the second and third years by the same percentage by which the wholesale price index rises during those years.

2. Clone 2 PC purchased 300 computer chips from a firm that ran an advertisement in the back of a computer magazine.

3. Clone 3 PC manufactures its own motherboards and computer chips for its personal computers.

Answer

(1) Clone 1 PC is using a contract to purchase its computer chips.
(2) Clone 2 PC used spot exchange to acquire its chips.
(3) Clone 3 PC uses vertical integration to obtain its chips and motherboards.

Transaction Costs

transaction costs
Costs associated with acquiring an input that are in excess of the amount paid to the input supplier.

When a firm acquires an input, it may incur costs that are in excess of the actual amount paid to the input supplier. These costs are known as *transaction costs* and play a crucial role in the determination of optimal input procurement.

The transaction costs of acquiring an input are the costs of locating a seller of the input, negotiating a price at which the inputs will be purchased, and putting the input to use. Transaction costs include:

1. The cost of searching for a supplier willing to sell a given input.
2. The costs of negotiating a price at which the input will be purchased. These costs may be in terms of the opportunity cost of time, legal fees, and so forth.
3. Other investments and expenditures required to facilitate exchange.

Many transaction costs are obvious. For example, if an input supplier charges a price of $10 per unit but requires you to furnish your own trucks and drivers to pick up the input, the transaction costs to your firm include the cost of the trucks and the personnel needed to "deliver" the input to your plant. Clearly, the relevant price of the input to your firm includes not only the $10 per unit but also the transaction costs of getting the input to your plant.

Some more important transaction costs, however, are less obvious. To understand these "hidden" transaction costs, we must distinguish between transaction costs that are specific to a particular trading relationship and those that are general in nature. The key to this distinction is the notion of a specialized investment. A *specialized investment* is simply an investment in a particular exchange that cannot be recovered in another trading relationship. For example, suppose that to ascertain the quality of bolts, it is necessary to spend $100 on a machine that tests the bolts' strength. If the machine is useful only for testing a particular manufacturer's bolts and the investment in the machine is a sunk (and therefore nonrecoverable) cost, it is a specialized investment. In contrast, if the machine can be resold at its purchase price or used to test the quality of bolts produced by other firms, it does not represent a specialized investment.

When specialized investments are required to facilitate an exchange, the resulting relationship between the parties is known as *relationship-specific exchange.* The distinguishing feature of relationship-specific exchange is that the two parties are "tied together" because of the specific investments made to facilitate exchange between them. As we will see, this feature often creates transaction costs due to the sunk nature of the specific investments.

specialized investment
An expenditure that must be made to allow two parties to exchange but has little or no value in any alternative use.

relationship-specific exchange
A type of exchange that occurs when the parties to a transaction have made specialized investments.

Types of Specialized Investments

Before we examine how specialized investments affect transaction costs and the optimal method of acquiring inputs, it is important to recognize that specialized investments occur in many forms. Common examples of different types of specialized investments are provided next.

Site Specificity
Site specificity occurs when the buyer and the seller of an input must locate their plants close to each other to be able to engage in exchange. For example, electric power plants often locate close to a particular coal mine to minimize the transportation costs of obtaining coal; the output (electricity) is less expensive to ship than the input (coal). The cost of building the two plants close to each other represents a specialized investment that would have little value if the parties were not involved in exchange.

Physical-Asset Specificity
Physical-asset specificity refers to a situation where the capital equipment needed to produce an input is designed to meet the needs of a particular buyer and cannot be readily adapted to produce inputs needed by other buyers. For example, if producing a lawn mower engine requires a special machine that is useful only for producing engines for a particular buyer, the machine is a specific physical asset for producing the engines.

Dedicated Assets

Dedicated assets are general investments made by a firm that allow it to exchange with a particular buyer. For example, suppose a computer manufacturer opens a new assembly line to enable it to produce enough computers for a large government purchaser. If opening the new assembly line is profitable only if the government actually purchases the firm's computers, the investment represents a dedicated asset.

Human Capital

A fourth type of specialized investment is *human capital*. In many employment relationships, workers must learn specific skills to work for a particular firm. If these skills are not useful or transferable to other employers, they represent a specialized investment.

Implications of Specialized Investments

Now that you have a broad understanding of specialized investments and relationship-specific exchange, we will consider how the presence of specialized investments can affect the transaction costs of acquiring inputs. Specialized investments increase transaction costs because they lead to (1) costly bargaining, (2) underinvestment, and (3) opportunism.

Costly Bargaining

In situations where transaction costs are low and the desired input is of uniform quality and sold by many firms, the price of the input is determined by the forces of supply and demand. When specialized investments are not required to facilitate exchange, very little time is expended negotiating a price. The scenario differs, however, if specialized investments are required to obtain the input.

Specialized investments imply that only a few parties are prepared for a trading relationship. There is no other supplier capable of providing the desired input at a moment's notice; obtaining the input the buyer needs requires making a specialized investment before the input becomes available. Consequently, there generally is no "market price" for the input; the two parties in the relationship-specific exchange bargain with each other over a price at which the input will be bought and sold. The bargaining process generally is costly, as each side employs negotiators to obtain a more favorable price. The parties may also behave strategically to enhance their bargaining positions. For example, the buyer may refuse to accept delivery to force the seller to accept a lower price. Ultimatums may be given. The supplier may reduce the quality of the input and the buyer may complain about the input's quality through company attorneys. All of these factors generate transaction costs as the two firms negotiate a price for the input.

Underinvestment

When specialized investments are required to facilitate exchange, the level of the specialized investment often is lower than the optimal level. To see this, suppose the specialized investment is human capital. To work for a particular firm, a worker must first invest his own time in learning how to perform some task. If the worker perceives that he may not work at the firm for very long (due to being laid off or accepting another job), he will not invest as heavily in learning the task as he otherwise would. For example, if you plan to transfer to another university at the end of the semester, you will not invest very heavily in learning how to use the library facilities at your present university. The investment in learning about the library facilities is an investment in human capital specific to your present university and will have little value at another university with a completely different library setup.

Similar problems exist with other types of specialized investments. For example, if an input supplier must invest in a specific machine to produce an input used by a particular buyer (physical-asset specificity), the supplier may invest in a cheaper machine that produces an input of inferior quality. This is because the supplier recognizes that the machine will not be useful if the buyer decides to purchase from another firm, in which case the supplier will be "stuck" with an expensive machine it cannot use. Thus, specialized investments may be lower than optimal, resulting in higher transaction costs because the input produced is of inferior quality.

Opportunism and the "Hold-Up Problem"

When a specialized investment must be made to acquire an input, the buyer or seller may attempt to capitalize on the "sunk" nature of the investment by behaving opportunistically. To be concrete, suppose the buyer of an input must make a specific investment of $10—say, the cost of verifying the quality of a particular supplier's input. The manager knows there are many firms willing to sell the input at a price of $100, so she goes to one of them at random and spends $10 inspecting the input. Once she has paid this $10, the supplier attempts to take advantage of the specialized investment and behave in an opportunistic manner: it attempts to "hold up" the manager by asking for a price of $109—$9 more than the price charged by all other suppliers. Since the manager has already spent $10 inspecting this firm's input, she is better off paying the $109 than spending an additional $10 inspecting another supplier's input. After all, even if the other supplier did not engage in opportunistic behavior, it would cost the firm $10 + $100 = $110 to inspect and purchase another supplier's input. This is the "hold-up problem": Once a firm makes a specialized investment, the other party may attempt to "rob" it of its investment by taking advantage of the investment's sunk nature. This behavior, of course, would make firms reluctant to engage in relationship-specific investments in the first place unless they can structure contracts to mitigate the hold-up problem.

Inside Business 6–1

The Cost of Using an Inefficient Method of Procuring Inputs

A recent study by Scott Masten, James Meehan, and Edward Snyder not only quantifies the transaction costs of acquiring inputs but points out the high cost to managers of using an inappropriate method to acquire an input.

Based on the procurement decisions of a naval construction firm, the study reveals that transaction costs account for roughly 14 percent of the total costs of ship construction. Thus, transaction costs are an important component of costs; managers must consider them when they make decisions.

What is the cost of not carefully considering transaction costs when deciding which method to use to acquire an input? The authors of the study report that mistaken integration—that is, producing internally a component that should have been purchased from another firm—increased transaction costs by an average of 70 percent. Subcontracting work that would have been more efficiently performed within the firm, on the other hand, raised transaction costs by a factor of almost 3. The potential cost savings to a firm that chooses the best method of acquiring inputs are thus substantial.

Source: Scott Masten, James Meehan, and Edward Snyder, "The Costs of Organization," *Journal of Law, Economics and Organization* 7 (Spring 1991), pp. 1–25.

In many instances, both sides in a trading relationship are required to make specialized investments, in which case both parties may engage in opportunism. For example, suppose an automaker needs crankshafts as an input for making engines. The crankshafts are a specialized input designed for use by that particular automobile manufacturer and require an investment by the producer in highly specialized capital equipment to produce them. If the crankshaft manufacturer does not sell the crankshafts to the automaker, the automaker's investment in continuing production of the engine will be effectively worthless. Similarly, if the automobile manufacturer does not buy the crankshafts, the supplier's investment in the capital equipment is likely to be wasted as well, since the equipment is not designed to serve the needs of other automobile makers. The investments made by both parties have tied them together in relationship-specific exchange, giving each firm a potential incentive to engage in opportunistic behavior. Once the supplier has invested in the equipment to make crankshafts, the automaker may attempt to capitalize on the sunk nature of the investment by asking for a lower price. On the other hand, once the automaker reaches the stage of production where it must have crankshafts to finish the cars, the crankshaft supplier may ask for a higher price to capitalize on the sunk investment made by the automaker. The result is that the two parties spend considerable time negotiating over precisely how much will be paid for the crankshafts, thus increasing the transaction costs of acquiring the input.

Optimal Input Procurement

Now we will examine how the manager should acquire inputs in such a way as to minimize costs. The cost-minimizing method will depend on the extent to which there is relationship-specific exchange.

Spot Exchange

The most straightforward way for a firm to obtain inputs for a production process is to use spot exchange. If there are no transaction costs and there are many buyers and sellers in the input market, the market price (say, p^*) is determined by the intersection of the supply and demand curves for the input. The manager can easily obtain the input from a supplier chosen at random by paying a price of p^* per unit of input. If any supplier attempted to charge a price greater than p^*, the manager could simply decline and purchase the input from another supplier at a price of p^*.

Why, then, would a manager ever wish to bear the expense of drafting a contract or have the firm expend resources to integrate vertically and manufacture the inputs itself? The reason is that in the presence of specialized investments, spot exchange does not insulate a buyer from opportunism, and the parties may end up spending considerable time bargaining over the price and incur substantial cost if negotiations break down. These problems will occur each time the buyer attempts to obtain additional units of the input. Also, as we noted earlier, the input purchased may be of inferior quality due to underinvestment in specialized investments needed to facilitate the exchange.

DEMONSTRATION PROBLEM 6–2

Jiffyburger, a fast-food outlet, sells approximately 8,000 quarter-pound hamburgers in a given week. To meet that demand, Jiffyburger needs 2,000 pounds of ground beef delivered to its premises every Monday morning by 8:00 A.M. sharp.

(1) As the manager of a Jiffyburger franchise, what problems would you anticipate if you acquired ground beef using spot exchange?

(2) As the manager of a firm that sells ground beef, what problems would you anticipate if you were to supply meat to Jiffyburger through spot exchange?

Answer

(1) While ground beef for hamburgers is a relatively standardized product, the delivery of one ton of meat to a particular store involves specialized investments

(in the form of dedicated assets) on the part of both Jiffyburger and the supplier. In particular, Jiffyburger would face a hold-up problem if the supplier showed up at 8:00 A.M. and threatened not to unload the meat unless Jiffyburger paid it "ransom"; it would be difficult to find another supplier that could supply the desired quantity of meat on such short notice. The supplier may even attempt to unload meat of inferior quality. Thus, Jiffyburger is not protected from opportunism, bargaining, and underinvestment in quality when it uses spot exchange to acquire such a large quantity of ground beef.

(2) By showing up at Jiffyburger at 8:00 A.M. with one ton of meat, the supplier makes a specific investment in selling to Jiffyburger. Consequently, the supplier also is subject to a potential hold-up problem. Suppose Jiffyburger behaves opportunistically by asking 10 other suppliers to show up with a ton of meat at 8 A.M. too. Since each supplier would rather unload its meat at a low price than let it spoil, Jiffyburger can bargain with the suppliers to get a great deal on the meat. In this case, each supplier risks selling meat at a low price or not at all, since it is not protected from opportunism by using spot exchange.

When the acquisition of an input requires substantial specialized investments, spot exchange is likely to result in high transaction costs due to opportunism, bargaining costs, and underinvestment. Clearly, managers must consider alternatives to spot exchange when inputs require substantial specialized investments.

Contracts

Given the prospect of the hold-up problem and a need to bargain over price each time an input is to be purchased, an alternative strategy is to acquire an input from a particular supplier under an appropriately structured contract. While a contract often requires substantial upfront expenditures in terms of negotiations, attorneys' fees, and the like, it offers several advantages. First, a contract can specify prices of the input before the parties make specialized investments. This feature reduces the magnitude of costly opportunism down the road. For example, if the managers in Demonstration Problem 6–2 had written a contract that specified a price and a quantity of ground beef before the specialized investments were made, they would not have been subject to the hold-up problem. Both parties would have been legally obligated to honor the contracted price and quantity.

Second, by guaranteeing an acceptable price for both parties for an extended time horizon, a contract reduces the incentive for either the buyer or the seller to skimp on the specialized investments required for the exchange. For example, a worker who has a contract that guarantees employment with a particular firm for three years will have a greater incentive to invest in human capital specific to that firm. Similarly, if the firm knows the worker will be around for three years, it will be willing to invest in more training for the worker.

DEMONSTRATION PROBLEM 6–3

In the real world, virtually all purchases involve some type of specialized investment. For instance, by driving to a particular supermarket, you invest time (and gasoline) that is valuable to you only if you purchase groceries at that supermarket. Why, then, don't consumers sign contracts with supermarkets to prevent the supermarkets from engaging in opportunism once they are inside the store?

Answer

The cost of driving to another supermarket if you are "held up" is relatively low; the cashier may be able to extract an extra few cents on a can of beans, but not much more. Thus, when specialized investments involve only small sums of money, the potential cost of being held up is very low compared to the cost of writing a contract to protect against such opportunism. It doesn't make sense to pay an attorney $200 to write a contract that would potentially save you only a few cents. Moreover, when only a small gain can be realized by engaging in opportunistic behavior, the supermarket will likely not find it in its interest to hold up customers. If a supermarket attempts to take advantage of a customer's miniscule specialized investment, the customer can threaten to tell others not to ever shop at that store. In this instance, the extra few cents extracted from the customer would not be worth the lost future business. In essence, there is an implicit agreement between the two parties: not an agreement that is enforceable in a court of law but one that is enforceable by consumers' future actions. Thus, when the gains from opportunistic behavior are small compared to the costs of writing contracts, formal contracts will not emerge. However, when the gains from opportunism are sufficiently large, formal contracts are needed to prevent opportunistic behavior.

Once the decision is made to use a contract to acquire an input, how long should the contract last? The "optimal" contract length reflects a fundamental economic trade-off between the marginal costs and marginal benefits of extending the length of a contract. The marginal cost (MC) of extending contract length increases as contracts become longer, as illustrated in Figure 6–2. This is because as a contract gets longer, more time and money must be spent writing into the contract a larger number of increasingly hypothetical contingencies (for example, "If an Ice Age begins, the price will be . . ."). It may be easy to specify a mutually acceptable price

FIGURE 6–2

*Optimal contract
length*

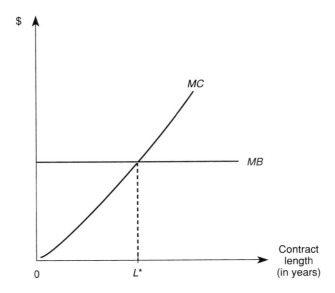

for a contract that is to be executed tomorrow, but with a 10-year agreement it is difficult (and expensive) to write clauses that include contingencies and prices for each year of the contract. Furthermore, the longer the contract, the more locked in the buyer is to a particular seller and the greater is the likelihood that some other supplier can provide the input at a lower cost in the future. In other words, the longer the contract, the less flexibility the firm has in choosing an input supplier. For these reasons, the marginal cost of contract length in Figure 6–2 is upward sloping.

The marginal benefit (MB) of extending a contract for another year is the avoided transaction costs of opportunism and bargaining. These benefits may vary with the length of the contract, but for simplicity we have drawn the curve in Figure 6–2 flat. The optimal contract length, L^*, is the point at which the marginal costs and marginal benefits of longer contracts are equal.

The optimal contract length will increase when the level of specialized investment required to facilitate an exchange increases. To see this, note that as specialized investments become more important, the parties face higher transaction costs once the contract expires. Since these costs can be avoided by writing longer contracts, higher levels of specialized investments increase the marginal benefit of writing longer contracts from MB^0 to MB^1 in Figure 6–3. The result is an increase in the length of the optimal contract from L_0 to L_1.

The optimal contract length also depends on factors that affect the marginal cost of writing longer contracts. As an input becomes more standard-

FIGURE 6–3

Specialized investments and contract length

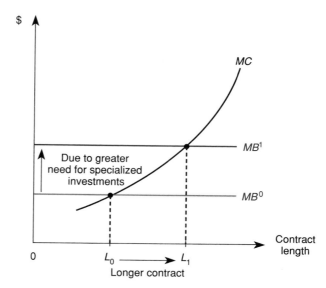

FIGURE 6–4

Contracting environment and contract length

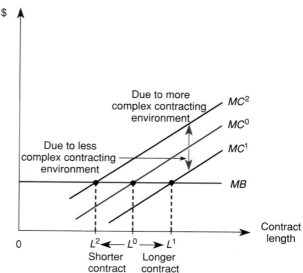

ized and the future economic environment becomes more certain, the marginal cost of writing longer contracts in Figure 6–4 decreases from MC^0 to MC^1. This decrease in the complexity of the contracting environment leads to longer optimal contracts (from L_0 to L_1). In contrast, as the input becomes more complex and the future economic environment becomes more uncertain, contracts must be made more detailed. This increase in the complexity of the contracting environment increases the marginal cost of

Factors Affecting the Length of Coal and Natural-Gas Contracts

Two studies have examined how specialized investments and the contracting environment affect the length of contracts. Paul Joskow studied the effect of specialized investments on the length of contracts between coal mines and electric utilities. As the importance of specialized investments increases, transaction costs due to opportunism and bargaining rise, and longer contracts are desirable. Joskow found that site specificity (the need for the utilities to locate close to the coal mine) increased the length of the contracts by an average of 12 years. Joskow also found that the degree of physical-asset specificity affected contract length. Since each generation facility uses equipment designed to burn a specific type of coal, plants designed to burn low-energy, low-sulfur western coal were tightly tied to their suppliers because there were few transportation alternatives. Plants designed to use high-energy, high-sulfur eastern coal, on the other hand, could purchase from numerous sources. Because physical-asset specificity is more pronounced in transactions involving western coal, the average contract for western coal was 11 years longer than contracts for eastern coal.

Keith Crocker and Scott Mastern examined how changes in the contracting environment affected the length of contracts between owners of natural-gas wells and owners of natural-gas pipelines. Historically, these contracts were long in duration due to the specialized investments involved in laying pipes and drilling wells. During the early 1970s, however, two factors affected the costs of writing contracts. First, price controls placed on natural-gas sales by the government induced pipelines to try to compensate well owners in nonprice terms of the contracts, such as agreeing to accept delivery of the gas when they preferred not to. These nonprice agreements made contracts less efficient and increased the costs of being bound by a contract. The result was that price controls reduced contract length by an average of 14 years. Second, the increased uncertainty in the natural-gas market caused by the Arab oil embargo raised the cost of writing contracts and reduced contract length by an additional three years.

Sources: Paul Joskow, "Contract Duration and Relationship-Specific Investments: Empirical Evidence from Coal Markets," *American Economic Review* 77 (March 1987), pp. 168–85; Keith Crocker and Scott Masten, "Mitigating Contractual Hazards: Unilateral Options and Contract Length," *Rand Journal of Economics* 19 (Autumn 1988), pp. 327–43.

writing longer contracts from MC^0 to MC^2 in Figure 6–4. Optimal contracts, in this case, will be shorter in duration.

As the contract length shortens due to the complexity of the contracting environment, firms must continually write new contracts as existing ones expire. Considerable sums are spent on attorneys' fees and bargaining over contract terms, and because of the complex contracting environment it is not efficient to write longer contracts to reduce these costs. Faced with such a prospect, a manager may wish to use yet another method to procure a necessary input: have the firm integrate vertically and make the input itself.

Vertical Integration

When specialized investments generate transaction costs (due to opportunism, bargaining costs, or underinvestment), and when the product being purchased is extremely complex or the economic environment is plagued by uncertainty, complete contracts will be extremely costly or even impossible to write. The only choice left is for the firm to set up a facility to produce the input internally. This process is referred to as *vertical integration* because it entails the firm moving farther up the production stream toward increasingly basic inputs. For example, most automobile manufacturers make their own fenders from sheet steel, having vertically integrated up the production stream from automobile assembly to the fabrication of body parts.

The advantage of vertical integration is that the firm "skips the middleman" by producing its own inputs. This reduces opportunism by uniting previously distinct firms into divisions of a single, integrated firm. While this strategy might seem desirable in general, because it mitigates transaction costs by eliminating the market, this approach has some disadvantages as well. Managers must replace the discipline of the market with an internal regulatory mechanism, a formidable task to anyone familiar with the failure of central planning often encountered in nonmarket economies. In addition, the firm must bear the cost of setting up production facilities for producing a product that at best may be tangentially related to the firm's main line of business; the firm no longer specializes in doing what it does best. Because of these difficulties, vertical integration often is viewed as a last resort, undertaken only when spot exchange or contracts have failed.

The Economic Trade-Off

The cost-minimizing method of acquiring an input depends on the characteristics of the input. Whether a manager chooses spot exchange or an alternative method such as a contract or vertical integration depends on the importance of the specialized investments that lead to relationship-specific exchange. The basic questions involved are illustrated in Figure 6–5.

When the desired input does not involve specialized investments, the firm can use spot exchange to obtain the input without concern for opportunism and bargaining costs. By purchasing the input from a supplier, the firm can specialize in doing what it does best and does not have to spend money writing contracts or engaging in vertical integration.

When substantial specialized investments are required to facilitate exchange, managers should think twice about using spot exchange to purchase inputs. Specialized investments lead to opportunism, bargaining costs, and underinvestment, and these transaction costs of using spot exchange often can be reduced by using some other method to acquire an input. When the contracting environment is simple and the cost of writing a contract is less

FIGURE 6–5

*Optimal
procurement of
inputs*

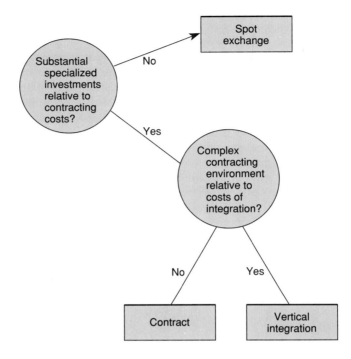

than the transaction costs associated with spot exchange, it is optimal to acquire the input through a contract. In this case, the optimal contract length is determined by the intersection of the marginal cost and marginal benefits of writing a longer contract, as we illustrated previously in Figure 6–2.

Finally, when substantial specialized investments are required and the desired input has complex characteristics that are difficult to specify in a contract, or when it is very costly to write into the contract all of the clauses needed to protect the parties from changes in future conditions, the manager should integrate vertically to minimize the cost of acquiring inputs needed for production—provided the costs of integration are not too high. In this instance, the firm produces the input internally. The firm no longer specializes in doing what it does best, but the elimination of opportunism, bargaining, and underinvestment more than make up for lack of specialization.

DEMONSTRATION PROBLEM 6–4

Big Bird Air is legally obligated to purchase 50 jet engines from ERUS at the end of two years at a price of $200,000 per engine. Confident that it is protected from opportunism with this contract, Big Bird begins making aircraft bodies designed to fit ERUS's engines. Due to unforeseen events in the aerospace industry, in the second year of the contract ERUS is on the brink of bankruptcy. It tells Big Bird that unless it increases the engine price to $300,000, it will go bankrupt.

(1) What should the manager of Big Bird Air do?

(2) How could this problem have been avoided?

(3) Did the manager of Big Bird Air use the wrong method of acquiring inputs?

Answer

(1) Big Bird is experiencing a hold-up problem because of an incomplete contract; the contract did not specify what would happen if ERUS went belly-up. ERUS claims it will go bankrupt if Big Bird does not pay $300,000 for the engines, in which case Big Bird will lose its specialized investment in aircraft bodies. The manager should verify that ERUS is indeed on the brink of bankruptcy. If not, Big Bird can take ERUS to court if ERUS does not honor the contract price. If ERUS is on the verge of bankruptcy, the manager should determine how much it would cost to obtain engines from another supplier versus making them within the firm. Once the manager knows the cost of each alternative, Big Bird may wish to bargain with ERUS over how much more it will pay for the engines. This could be risky, however; the lower the price negotiated, the greater the chance ERUS will go bankrupt. New clauses must be put into the contract to protect Big Bird against ERUS's bankruptcy. The manager should especially guard against attempts by ERUS to reduce the quality of the engines in an attempt to save money. In any event, Big Bird should not spend more money drawing up a new contract and paying for ERUS's engines than it would cost to obtain them from the best alternative source.

(2) This problem illustrates that when contracts are incomplete, unanticipated events can occur that lead to costly bargaining and opportunism. The problem could have been avoided had Big Bird written clauses into the contract that protected it against ERUS's going bankrupt. If this was not possible, it could have vertically integrated and produced its own engines.

(3) Big Bird's manager did not necessarily choose the wrong method of acquiring engines. If it was not possible (or would have been extremely costly) to write into the initial contract protection against ERUS's going bankrupt, and if the costs of vertically integrating would exceed the likely costs of opportunism due to an incomplete contract, the manager made the correct decision at the time. Sometimes bad things happen even when managers make good decisions. If this was not the case, either a more complete contract should have been written or Big Bird should have decided to make its own engines.

Managerial Compensation and the Principal-Agent Problem

You now know the principal factors in selecting the best method of acquiring inputs. Our remaining task in this chapter is to explain how to compensate labor inputs to ensure that they put forth their "best" effort. After

The Evolution of Input Decisions in the Automobile Industry

An interesting account of a firm moving from spot exchange to a long-term contractual relationship and finally to vertical integration is provided by the General Motors–Fisher Body relationship, which has been extensively documented by Benjamin Klein. In the early part of the century, car bodies were primarily open, wooden structures built by craftspeople with fairly general skills. Thus specialized investments were relatively unimportant, and General Motors bought the bodies for its cars using spot exchange.

As the automobile industry developed, it became apparent that closed metal bodies would be a superior method of manufacturing cars. This finding, however, introduced a high degree of physical-asset specificity because it required investment in very specialized machines to stamp out the body parts. To constrain opportunism, General Motors and Fisher Body signed a 10-year contract that set the price of the car bodies and obligated General Motors to purchase all of its closed metal car bodies from Fisher Body.

Initially this agreement worked well enough to permit the parties to make the necessary special-ized investments. But as time went on, it became clear that the original agreement was not nearly complete, leaving numerous opportunities for the parties to engage in opportunism. For example, the pricing formula contained in the contract permitted Fisher Body to receive a 17.6 percent profit on labor and transportation costs. This encouraged Fisher to produce with inefficient labor-intensive technologies in remotely located plants and pass on the costs of inefficiency to General Motors.

In retrospect, it appears that both General Motors and Fisher Body underestimated the difficulty of writing a contract to govern their relationship. Rather than spend time and money writing a more detailed contract, the problem was solved in 1926 when General Motors vertically integrated by purchasing Fisher Body.

Source: Benjamin Klein, "Vertical Integration as Organizational Ownership: The Fisher Body–General Motors Relationship Revisited," *Journal of Law, Economics and Organization* 4 (Spring 1988), pp. 199–213.

completing this section you will better understand why restaurants rely on tips to compensate employees, why secretaries usually are paid an hourly wage, and even why textbook authors are paid royalties. We will begin, however, by examining managerial compensation.

One characteristic of many large firms is the separation of ownership and control: The owners of the firm often are distantly located stockholders, and the firm is run on a day-to-day basis by a manager. The fact that the firm's owners are not physically present to monitor the manager creates a fundamental incentive problem. Suppose the owners pay the manager a salary of $50,000 per year to manage the firm. Since the owners cannot monitor the manager's effort, if the firm has lost $1 million by year's end, they will not know whether the fault lies with the manager or with bad luck. Uncertainty regarding whether low profits are due to low demand or to low effort by the manager makes it difficult for the owners to determine precisely why profits are low. Even if the fault lies with the manager—perhaps he or she never showed up at the plant but instead took an extended fishing trip—the manager can claim it was just a "bad year." The manager might say, "You should be very glad you hired me as your manager. Had I not worked 18-hour days, your company would have lost twice the amount it did. I was lucky to keep our loss to its current level, but I am confident things will improve next year when our new product line hits the market." Since the owners are not present at the firm, they will not know the true reason for the low profits.

By creating a firm, an owner enjoys the benefits of reduced transaction costs. But when ownership is separated from control, the *principal-agent problem emerges*: If the owner is not present to monitor the manager, how can she get the manager to do what is in her best interest?

The essence of the problem is that the manager likes to earn income, but he also likes to consume leisure. Clearly, if the manager spent every waking hour on the job, he would be unable to consume any leisure. But the less time he spends on the job, the more time he has for ballgames, fishing trips, and other activities that he values. The job description indicates that the manager is supposed to spend eight hours per day on the job. The important question, from the owner's point of view, is how much leisure (*shirking*) the manager will consume while on the job. Shirking may take the form of excessive coffee breaks, long lunch hours, leaving work early, or, in the extreme case, not showing up on the job at all. Note that while the manager enjoys shirking, the owner wants the manager to work hard to enhance profits.

When the manager is offered a fixed salary of $50,000, since the owner is not physically present at the workplace, he will receive the same $50,000 regardless of whether he works a full eight hours (hence, doesn't shirk) or spends the entire day at home (shirks eight hours). This situation is illustrated in Table 6–1. From the point of view of the owner, the fixed salary does not give the manager a strong incentive to monitor the other employees, and this has an adverse effect on the firm's profits. For example, as Table 6–1 shows, if the manager spends the entire day on the job monitoring the other employees (i.e., making sure that they put out maximum effort), shirking is zero and the firm's profits are $3 million. If the manager spends the entire day shirking, profits are zero. If the manager shirks two hours and thus works six hours, the firm's profits are $2.8 million. Since the fixed salary of $50,000 provides the manager with the same income regardless of his effort level, he has a strong incentive to shirk eight hours. In this case, the profits of the firm are zero but the manager still earns $50,000.

How can the owner of the firm get the manager to spend time monitoring the production process? You might think if she paid the manager a higher salary, the manager would work harder. But this will not work when the owner cannot observe the manager's effort; the employment contract is such that there is absolutely no cost to the manager of shirking. Many

TABLE 6–1   Managerial Earnings and Firm Profits under a Fixed Salary

Manager's Earnings	Hours Worked by Manager	Hours Shirked by Manager	Profits of Firm
$50,000	8	0	$3,000,000
50,000	7	1	2,950,000
50,000	6	2	2,800,000
50,000	5	3	2,500,000
50,000	4	4	2,000,000
50,000	3	5	1,800,000
50,000	2	6	1,300,000
50,000	1	7	700,000
50,000	0	8	0

TABLE 6–2   Managerial Earnings and Firm Profits with Profit Sharing

Hours Worked by Manager	Hours Shirked by Manager	Gross Profits for Firm (π)	Manager's Share of Profits ($.10 \times \pi$)
8	0	$3,000,000	$300,000
7	1	$2,950,000	$295,000
6	2	$2,800,000	$280,000
5	3	$2,500,000	$250,000
4	4	$2,000,000	$200,000
3	5	$1,800,000	$180,000
2	6	$1,300,000	$130,000
1	7	$ 700,000	$ 70,000
0	8	0	0

managers would prefer to earn money without having to work for it, and such a contract allows this manager to do just that.

Suppose the owner of the firm offers the manager the following *incentive contract*: The manager is to receive 10 percent of profits (gross of managerial compensation) earned by the firm. Table 6–2 summarizes the implications of such a contract. Note that if the manager spends eight hours shirking, profits are zero and the manager earns nothing. But if the manager does not shirk at all, the firm earns $3 million in gross profits and the manager gets compensation equal to 10 percent of those profits: $300,000.

Exactly what the manager does under the profit-sharing compensation scheme depends on his preferences for leisure and money. But one thing is clear: If the manager wants to earn income, he cannot shirk the entire day. The manager faces a trade-off: He can consume more leisure on the job, but at a cost of lower compensation. For example, suppose the manager has carefully evaluated the trade-off between leisure on the job and income in Table 6–2 and wishes to earn $250,000. He can achieve this by working five hours instead of shirking all day. What is the impact of the profit-sharing plan on the owner of the firm? The manager has decided to work five hours to earn $250,000 in compensation. The five hours of managerial effort generate $2.5 million in gross profits for the firm. Thus, by making managerial compensation dependent on performance, the gross profits for the owner rise from zero (under the fixed-salary arrangement) to $2.5 million. Note that even after deducting the manager's compensation, the owner ends up with a hefty $2,500,000 − $250,000 = $2.25 million in profits. The performance bonus has increased not only the manager's earnings, but the owner's net profits.

Forces That Discipline Managers

Incentive Contracts

Typically the chief executive officer of a corporation receives stock options and other bonuses directly related to profits. It may be tempting to argue that a CEO who earns over $1 million per year is receiving excessive compensation. What is important, however, is *how* the executive earns the $1 million. If the earnings are due largely to a performance bonus, it could be a big mistake to reduce the executive's compensation. This point is important, because the media often imply that it is unfair to heavily reward CEOs of major corporations. Remember, however, that performance-based rewards benefit stockholders as well as CEOs, and reducing such rewards may result in declining profits for the firm.

DEMONSTRATION PROBLEM 6–5

You are attending the annual stockholders' meeting of PIC Company. A fellow shareholder points out that the manager of PIC earned $100,000 last year, while the manager of a rival firm, CUP Enterprises, earned only $50,000. A motion is made to lower the salary of PIC's manager. Given only this information, what should you do?

Answer

There is not enough information to make an informed decision about the appropriate way to vote; you should ask for additional information. If none is forthcoming, you should move to table the motion until shareholders can obtain additional

Compensation in Fast-Food Restaurants

About 30 percent of firms in the fast-food industry are owned by the company, and 70 percent are franchised to owner-operators. The owner-operator's income is entirely derived from the profitability of the individual store. Typically the franchising parent requires the owner-operator to be in residence. The franchise owner receives profits, less a franchise fee, as remuneration.

In contrast, the manager of a company-owned store is usually paid a flat fee for managing a restaurant. This leads the manager to have less incentive to lower employee costs and other operating expenses. The manager whose income is not tied to profits also has less incentive to ensure high sales. Given that the income of a franchise manager is directly tied to profits whereas the income of the manager of the company-owned store is not, we would expect profits to be lower in company-owned stores. Company-owned stores also would face higher employee wages and less effective supervision of employees.

Alan B. Kruger provides some interesting insights into the relationship between employees and managers in the fast-food industry. As the accompanying table shows, employees subjectively rate managers in company-owned stores as less effective than those in franchisee-owned stores. Company-owned crew workers and franchise crew members earn roughly the same hourly wages; thus, the positive evaluations of franchise managers would not appear to be due to differentials in pay.

Historically, profitability is higher in franchised stores than in the company-owned stores. A 1967 survey showed that stores changing from franchise ownership to company ownership ex-

perienced a drop in profitability from 9.5 percent to 1.8 percent. It is clear why so many fast-food chains franchise their restaurants. Franchising mitigates the principal-agent problem by making managers' compensation dependent on profitability; thus, more profits are made than would otherwise be the case.

Employee Evaluation of Supervision in Company-Owned and Franchised Restaurants

Employee Evaluation of Manager	Proportion of Employees Agreeing (standard deviations in parentheses)	
	Company-Owned	Franchisee-Owned
Manager provides adequate supervision to workers	0.326 (0.010)	0.452 (0.014)
Assistant manager provides adequate supervision to workers	0.332 (0.010)	0.405 (0.013)
Supervisor provides adequate supervision to workers	0.360 (0.011)	0.468 (0.014)

Source: Data based on Alan B. Kruger, "Ownership, Agency, and Wages: An Examination of Franchising in the Fast-Food Industry," *Quarterly Journal of Economics* 106 (February 1991), pp. 75–102.

information about such things as the profits and sales of the two firms, how much of each manager's earnings is due to profit sharing and performance bonuses, and the like. Explain to the other shareholders that the optimal contract will reward the manager for high profits; if PIC's manager's high earnings are due to a huge performance bonus paid because of high profits, eliminating the bonus would not be prudent. On the other hand, if CUP's manager has generated larger profits for that firm than your manager has for PIC, you may wish to adjust your manager's contract to reflect incentives similar to those of the rival firm or even attempt to hire CUP's manager to work for PIC.

External Incentives

The preceding analysis focused on factors within the firm that provide the manager with an incentive to maximize profits. In addition, forces outside the firm often provide managers with an incentive to maximize profits.

Reputation

Managers have increased job mobility when they can demonstrate to other firms that they have the managerial skills needed to maximize profits. It is costly to be an effective manager; many hours must be spent supervising workers and planning production outlays. These costs represent an investment by the manager in a reputation for being an excellent manager. In the long run, this reputation can be sold at a premium in the market for managers, where other firms compete for the right to hire the best managers. Thus, even when the employment contract does not explicitly include a performance bonus, a manager may choose to do a good job of running the firm if he or she wishes to work for another firm at some future date.

Takeovers

Another external force that provides managers with an incentive to maximize profits is the threat of a takeover. If a manager is not operating the firm in a profit-maximizing manner, investors will attempt to buy the firm and replace management with new managers who will. By installing a better manager, the firm's profits will rise and the value of the firm's stock will increase. Thus, a cost to a manager of doing a poor job of running the firm is the increased likelihood of a takeover. To avoid paying this cost, managers will work harder than they otherwise would, even if they are paid only a fixed salary.

The Manager-Worker Principal-Agent Problem

When we introduced the principal-agent problem, the owner of the firm was viewed as having different objectives from the manager. There is nothing special about the owner-manager relationship that gives rise to the principal-agent problem; indeed, there is a similar problem between the manager and the employees she or he supervises.

Inside Business 6–5

What Are Profits Worth to CEOs?

A recent study by Marc Chopin provides interesting insights into the nature of the compensation of chief executive officers of major U.S. firms. The study provides a very detailed description of compensation contracts for specific CEOs in industries ranging from the automobile industry to retail department stores. Although the data span several decades, it is useful to present some general results reported for all U.S. industries in 1988.

To examine the impact of firms' performances on the compensation of CEOs, Chopin performed a least squares regression of total compensation (including bonuses) on two very broad measures of performance: profits and sales. The regression results for 1988 were

$$W = \$690,000 + 634\pi + 11.05S,$$
$$\quad\quad\quad\ (20.67)\quad (5.5)\quad\ (1.27)$$

where W is total CEO compensation (including salary and bonuses), π denotes profits (in millions of dollars), and S is sales (in millions of dollars). The t-statistics for the coefficients are reported in parentheses under the coefficient estimates.

The results of the regression reveal several interesting insights. First, note that the constant in the regression is the compensation that does not vary with firm performance. Thus, the constant—$690,000—represents the fixed component of the average Fortune 500 CEO's compensation in 1988—the amount that does not vary with the firm's performance. Indeed, it is profitable to climb to the top of the corporate ladder!

Second, note that the coefficient on π is 634. This means that for every $1 million the firm earns in profits, the average CEO receives a bonus of $634. This reward is quite sizable, particularly for firms earning millions or billions in profits. Furthermore, note that the t-statistic is 5.5, which reveals that profits are a very important determinant of CEOs' total compensation. By structuring contracts that reward CEOs based on profitability, shareholders can reduce to some extent the principal-agent problem.

Finally, notice that the coefficient on sales is 11.05. This means that for every $1 million in firm sales, the CEO receives $11.05. There is some incentive for CEOs to boost sales, although not nearly as strong as the incentive to improve profits. Furthermore, notice that the t-statistic associated with the coefficient on S is less than 2, suggesting that sales were not a statistically significant component of CEO incentive contracts.

In short, the empirical evidence suggests that shareholders indeed recognize the principal-agent problem and reward CEOs based largely on profits. On average, a Fortune 500 firm with sales of $2 billion and profits of $1 billion pays total compensation to the CEO of

$$W = \$690,000 + 634(1,000) + 11.05(2,000)$$
$$= \$690,000 + \$634,000 + \$22,100$$
$$= \$1,346,100.$$

On average, a CEO who earns $1,346,100 in a year receives almost half of her or his earnings from bonuses that are tied to the performance of the firm.

Source: Marc C. Chopin, *Market Structure, Compensation and Incentives: An Empirical Analysis of CEO Compensation.* Ph.D. dissertation, Texas A&M University, August 1991.

To see this, suppose the manager is being paid a fraction of profits and thus has an incentive to increase the firm's profits. The manager cannot be in several places at the same time and thus cannot monitor every worker even if he or she wanted to. The workers, on the other hand, would just as soon gossip and drink coffee as work. How can the manager (the principal) induce the workers (the agents) not to shirk?

Incentive-Based Contracts for School-Superintendents

Incentive-based contracts are becoming increasingly prevalent as school districts attempt to improve the quality of education through better management. As the accompanying table shows, both positive and negative rewards are used to provide school-superintendents a stronger incentive to meet specified goals.

Carrots and Sticks
Cities with incentive-based school-superintendent contracts

City	Goals	Incentives	
Philadelphia (1994–99)	Improve student achievement; increase parent and community participation; review all curricula for fair and appropriate 'multicultural inclusion'	**If met:**	Bonus of up to 10% ($16,000)
		If not:	Pay cut of up to 5% ($8,000)
Houston (1995–97)	Raise scores on state test; diversify district staff	**If met:**	15% pay increase ($15,000–$20,000)
		If not:	Can be bought out at any time; no grievance allowed if not renewed
Cincinnati (annual, as of 1995)	Raise test scores, graduation and passing rates; lower dropout rates	**If met:** **If not:**	Up to 4% annual merit raise No raise
Fairborn, Ohio (1989–)	Raise test scores and attendance rates	**If met:** **If not:**	1% merit raise No pay increase
Swanton, Ohio (1994–)	Raise test scores by 10%	**If met:** **If not:**	No increase Superintendent will resign
Minneapolis* (1994–95)	Improve test scores; zero growth in reading gap between white and minority students; reduce number of suspensions	**If met:** **If not:**	Up to $470,000 incentive pay No incentive pay

*Contract with private firm, Public Strategies Group Inc.

Source for Table: "Schools Tie Salaries to Pupil Performance," *The Wall Street Journal*, March 10, 1995, p. B1.

Solutions to the Manager-Worker Principal-Agent Problem

Profit Sharing
One mechanism the manager can use to enhance workers' efforts is to make the workers' compensation dependent on the underlying profitability of the firm. By offering workers compensation that is tied to underlying profitability, an incentive is provided for workers to put forth more effort.

Revenue Sharing

Another mechanism for inducing greater effort by workers is to link compensation with the underlying revenues of the firm. Examples of this type of incentive scheme include tips and sales commissions. Food servers usually receive a very low wage, plus tips. Tips are simply a commission paid by the person being served. If the server does a terrible job, the tip is low; if the server does an excellent job, the tip usually is higher. Similarly, car salespeople and insurance agents usually receive a percentage of the sales they generate. The idea behind all of these compensation schemes is that it is difficult, if not impossible, for the manager to monitor these people's effort, and there is uncertainty regarding what final sales will be. By making these workers' incomes dependent on their performance, the manager gives workers an incentive to work harder than they otherwise would. By working harder, they benefit both the firm and themselves.

Revenue sharing is particularly effective when worker productivity is related to revenues rather than costs. For example, a restaurant manager can design a contract whereby servers get some fraction of a tip; the tip is presumed to be an increasing function of the servers' quality (productivity). The manager of a sales firm can provide incentives to employees by paying them a percentage of the sales they generate.

One problem with revenue-based incentive schemes is that they do not provide an incentive for workers to minimize costs. For example, a food server may attempt to collect a big tip by offering a customer larger portions, free drinks, and the like, which will enhance the tip at the expense of the restaurant's costs.

Piece Rates

An alternative compensation method is to pay workers based on a piece rate rather than on a fixed hourly wage. For example, by paying a typist a fixed amount per page typed, the payment to the typist depends on the output produced. To earn more money, the typist must type more pages during a given time period.

A potential problem with paying workers based on a piece rate is that effort must be expended in quality control; otherwise, workers may attempt to produce quantity at the expense of quality. One advantage of revenue or profit sharing is that it reduces the incentive to produce low-quality products. Lower quality reduces sales, thus reducing compensation to those receiving revenue- or profit-sharing incentives.

DEMONSTRATION PROBLEM 6–6

Your boss, who just earned an MBA, finished reading Chapter 6 of a noted economics textbook. She asks you why the firm pays its secretaries an hourly wage instead of piece rates or a percentage of the firm's profits. How do you answer her?

Answer

Incentive contracts such as piece rates and profit sharing are designed to solve principal-agent problems when effort is not observable. There is little need to provide "incentive contracts" to secretaries given the presence of bosses in the workplace. In particular, it is very easy to monitor the secretaries' effort; they usually are within the boss's eyesight, and there are numerous opportunities to observe the quality of their work (e.g., letters for the boss's signature). Thus, there is no real separation between the "principal" (the boss) and the agent (the secretary); the secretary's "boss" knows when the secretary "messes up" and can fire him or her if performance is consistently low. In most instances, this provides secretaries with a stronger incentive to work hard than would paying them a fraction of the profits generated by the effort of all employees in the firm.

Paying secretaries piece rates would be an administrative nightmare; it would be extremely costly to keep track of all of the pages typed and tasks performed during the course of a week. Piece rates may also encourage secretaries to worry more about the quantity instead of the quality of the work done. All things considered, hourly wages are a reasonable way to compensate most secretaries—provided their bosses are given an incentive to monitor them.

Time Clocks and Spot Checks

Many firms use time clocks to assist managers in monitoring workers. Time clocks are generally not useful for avoiding the principal-agent problem. Time clocks essentially are designed to verify when an employee arrives at and departs from the job. They do not monitor effort; rather, they simply measure presence at the workplace at the beginning and end of the workday.

A more useful mechanism for monitoring workers is for a manager to engage in spot checks of the workplace. In this case, the manager enters the workplace from time to time to monitor workers. Spot checks allow the manager to verify not only that workers are physically present but also that worker effort and the quality of the work are satisfactory.

The advantage of spot checks is that they reduce the cost of monitoring workers. With spot checks, the manager needn't be in several places at the same time. Because workers do not know when the manager will show up, they will put forth more effort than they would otherwise, since getting caught "goofing off" may lead to dismissal or a reduction in pay. Thus, to be effective, spot checks need to be random; that is, workers should not be able to predict when the manager will be monitoring the workplace.

A disadvantage of spot checks is that they must occur frequently enough to induce workers not to risk getting caught shirking and that some penalty must be imposed on workers caught shirking. Spot checks work, in

Profit Sharing, Piece Rates, and Dismissals as Incentive Devices: How Do They Compare?

When managers design incentives for their workers, they must consider both positive and negative reward systems. The most commonly observed negative incentive used by firms is dismissal of an unproductive worker. Positive rewards include payments based on the number of units produced (piece rates), profit-sharing plans, and hourly wages.

From the viewpoint of a worker, an hourly wage rate is the least risky in that the worker is assured a given payment per hour. However, it usually has little effect on worker motivation; thus, workers paid an hourly wage require the most monitoring by supervisors. Because there is no downside risk to the hourly-wage earner, employers often use threats of dismissal to motivate employees.

Piece-rate systems are better motivators. A piece-rate pay system encourages employees to produce large quantities of the product. However, they fail to ensure quality. Thus, piece-rate systems usually need to be combined with a quality control mechanism, which necessitates employing quality control personnel, who bring on another level of incentive problems.

Profit sharing eliminates many of the problems associated with hourly wage rates and piece-rate pay schemes. When productivity and quality are high, so are profits—and when quality and productivity are low, profits are low as well. Therefore, profit sharing puts a lot of the burden on employees. Most workers, however, would prefer not to bear the cost of lower wages when there is a slowdown in the economy. Another problem with profit sharing is that when production is a team process, it is difficult to assess who should get what. This leaves monitoring to team members. Ultimately the question of which pay scheme to use must be determined by the manager. Fortunately, there is some scientific evidence on how different internal compensation arrangements affect productivity.

Kornelius Kraft conducted a study comparing the above pay mechanisms. Kraft estimated an industrywide regression that provides insights into the ways incentive schemes affect productivity. His results are based on the metal-working industry in Germany. One of Kraft's findings is that firing 1 percent of workers instead of none increased overall productivity by 4.26 percent. The increase in productivity was due to the fact that workers who were retained increased their effort due to the greater likelihood of being fired if they failed to perform.

Kraft's results also reveal that a manager can be too aggressive in firing workers. If a large fraction of the work force is dismissed, morale declines, which adversely affects productivity.

Kraft's study reveals that by increasing the fraction of labor payments based on profit sharing by 1 percent, total worker productivity increases by about 3 percent. Similarly, for every 1 percent reduction in the fraction of labor payments based on piece rates, a 9 percent increase in productivity occurs.

Because piece-rate incentive mechanisms have a negative effect on productivity, we would expect to see their use decline as managers become more aware of this shortcoming. Likewise, the positive effect profit-sharing mechanisms have on productivity should lead more firms to use such schemes. This change in incentive mechanisms is exactly what researchers have observed. The use of piece-rate schemes declined from 40 percent in 1984 to less than 30 percent in 1990, whereas the use of profit-sharing plans grew from 16 percent in 1980 to 27 percent in 1990.

Sources: Kornelius Kraft, "The Incentive Effects of Dismissals, Efficiency Wages, Piece-Rates, and Profit-Sharing," *Review of Economics and Statistics* 73 (August 1991), pp. 451–59; M. Cannell and P. Long, "What's Changed about Incentive Pay?" *Personnel Management* (October 1991), pp. 58–61.

effect, through threat. Performance bonuses, on the other hand, work through a promise of reward. These characteristics can have different psychological effects on workers.

Answering the Headline

The key to defending Eisner's contract is to point out that the incentives created by the contract—not the level of pay—is the important issue. The separation of ownership and control at Disney creates a principal-agent problem, and the best way to boost shareholder wealth is to provide Eisner with an incentive to make superior managerial decisions. In fact, this very point was made by Raymond Watson, one of the Disney directors who was involved with Eisner's compensation negotiations. According to Watson, the compensation package was designed to signal to Eisner that "If you make the shareholders wealthy, you're going to get wealthy."[2] Presumably, the reason Eisner earned a fortune is because his actions boosted Disney's earnings, stock price, and thus shareholder wealth.

Summary

In this chapter, we examined the optimal institutional choice for input procurement and the principal-agent problem as it relates to managerial compensation and worker incentives. The manager must decide which inputs will be purchased from other firms and which inputs the firm will manufacture itself. Spot exchange generally is the most desirable alternative when there are many buyers and sellers and low transaction costs. It becomes less attractive when substantial specialized investments generate opportunism, resulting in transaction costs associated with using a market.

When market transaction costs are high, the manager may wish to purchase inputs from a specific supplier using a contract or, alternatively, forgo the market entirely and have the firm set up a subsidiary to produce the required input internally. In a fairly simple contracting environment, a contract may be the most effective solution. But as the contracting environment becomes more complex and uncertain, internal production through vertical integration becomes an attractive managerial strategy.

The chapter also demonstrated a solution to the principal-agent problem: Rewards must be constructed so as to induce the activities desired of workers. For example, if all a manager wants from a worker is for the worker to show up at the workplace, an hourly wage rate and a time clock

---

[2]For a further discussion of these issues, see Joseph G. Haubrich, "Fear and Loathing in Executive Pay," *Economic Commentary*, November 1, 1994, and "Consultant: Disney Overpays Eisner," *Reuters News Service*, November 18, 1994.

form an excellent incentive scheme. If it is desirable to produce a high level of output with very little emphasis on quality, piece-rate pay schemes work well. However, if both quantity and quality of output are concerns, profit sharing is an excellent motivator.

Key Terms and Concepts

contracts
dedicated assets
human capital
incentive contracts
opportunism
physical-asset specificity
piece-rate system
principal-agent problem

profit sharing
relationship-specific exchange
revenue sharing
site specificity
specialized investments
spot exchange
transaction costs
vertical integration

Problems

1. Determine whether the following transactions involve spot exchange, contracts, or vertical integration.
   a. Texaco refines gasoline from crude oil produced by oil wells that it owns.
   b. Transcontinental, an interstate natural-gas pipeline, has a legal obligation to purchase a specified amount of gas per week from a well owned by Fred Smith in Enid, Oklahoma.
   c. A cabinetmaker purchases a dozen wood screws from the local hardware store.
   d. An electric utility purchases coal from an underground mine.

2. In general, automobile manufacturers produce their own engines but purchase tires from independent suppliers. Why?

3. Which of the following transactions are likely to result in relationship-specific exchange?
   a. Purchasing gasoline for the company car.
   b. Hiring an employee to operate a machine that only your company uses.
   c. Buying napkins for the company snack bar.
   d. Purchasing coal for the factory furnace.
   e. Buying electricity.

4. Explain how each of the following affect the optimal method of acquiring an input.

  a. A complex contracting environment.
  b. A specialized investment.
  c. Opportunism.
  d. Bargaining costs.
  e. The costs of bureaucracy.
  f. Gains from specializing.

5. Jiffyburger, a fast-food outlet, sells approximately 8,000 quarter-pound hamburgers in a given week. To meet that demand, Jiffyburger needs 2,000 pounds of ground beef delivered to its premises every Monday morning by 8:00 A.M. sharp. If you were the manager of a Jiffyburger franchise, how would you acquire the ground beef? Explain.

6. Explain why people in the following occupations are compensated as they are.
  a. Insurance agents.
  b. Football players.
  c. Authors.
  d. CEOs of major corporations.
  e. Food servers.

7. A manager derives satisfaction from income and leisure on the job (shirking).
  a. If the manager is paid a fixed salary of $100,000, how much leisure will he or she consume on the job during an eight-hour day? Explain.
  b. When the manager is given a salary of $100,000 plus 10 percent of the firm's profits, she or he chooses to spend six hours managing and two hours consuming leisure, and salary and bonus total $120,000. Does the manager necessarily prefer this situation to the situation in part *a*? Explain.

8. Is it necessarily in the best interest of shareholders for management to ensure that there is absolutely no shirking in the workplace? Explain carefully.

9. Discuss the benefits and costs of the following methods of monitoring worker performance.
  a. Hidden video cameras in the workplace.
  b. Time clocks.
  c. Paying workers based on the output they produce.

10. According to *Industry Week*, a shoe manufacturer recently had a production run that resulted in 100,000 pairs of defective shoes. Workers on the production line knew the shoes were defective as they were being produced, but did nothing to fix the problem. Do you think a profit sharing plan for workers would mitigate future problems? Explain.

11. College Retirement Equities Fund (CREF) is a pension fund that has billions of dollars invested in the stock market. Fund participants recently voted on a proposal that would have placed strict limits on the amount of compensation paid to CREF executives. Why do you think 75 percent of the participants voted against the proposal?

12. The study described in Inside Business 6–5 revealed that

$$W = \$690{,}000 + 634\pi + 11.05S.$$

   a. Provide a brief interpretation of this equation.

   b. Based on this equation, if a new manager increased the firm's profits by $10 million and increased sales by $7 million, how much would this improvement in performance increase this manager's compensation over the former manager's?

13. Suppose a principal knew with certainty the level of profits that would result if an agent put forth maximum effort.

   a. Would there be a principal-agent problem?

   b. Devise two incentive contracts that would induce the manager to put forth maximum effort in this instance.

14. Dallas-based Southwest Airlines recently announced a 10-year contract that gives pilots a greater opportunity to share in the profits of the airline. According to the terms of the contract, the pilots will receive options to buy 14 million shares of the firm's stock over ten years. What impact do you think this new contract will have on Southwest Air?

15. Art-R-Us makes hand-painted art reproductions. The owner-manager wishes to hire another artist, and is considering paying a fixed wage plus either (1) a share of the profits from each painting sold or (2) a fixed payment for each piece produced. Which plan would you choose if you were the owner? Explain.

Selected Readings

Alchian, Armen A. and Demsetz, Harold, "Production, Information Costs, and Economic Organization." *American Economic Review* 62, December 1972, pp. 777–95.

Antle, Rick and Smith, Abbie, "An Empirical Investigation of the Relative Performance Evaluation of Corporate Executives." *Journal of Accounting Research* 24(1), Spring 1986, pp. 1–39.

Coase, R. H., "The Nature of the Firm." *Economica*, November 1937, pp. 366–405.

Gibbons, Robert and Murphy, Kevin J., "Relative Performance Evaluation for Chief Executive Officers." *Industrial and Labor Relations Review* 43, February 1990, pp. 30–51.

Jensen, Michael C., "Takeovers: Their Causes and Consequences." *Journal of Economic Perspectives* 1, Winter 1988, pp. 21–48.

Jensen, Michael C. and Murphy, Kevin J., "Performance Pay and Top Management Incentives." *Journal of Political Economy* 98(2), April 1990, pp. 225–64.

Klein, Benjamin, Crawford, Robert G., and Alchian, Armen A., "Vertical Integration, Appropriable Rents, and the Competitive Contracting Process." *Journal of Law and Economics* 21(2), Oct. 1978, pp. 297–326.

Lewis, Tracy R. and Sappington, David E. M., "Incentives for Monitoring Quality." *Rand Journal of Economics* 22(3), Autumn 1991, pp. 370–84.

Williamson, Oliver E., "Markets and Hierarchies: Some Elementary Considerations." *American Economic Review* 63, May 1973, pp. 316–25.

Winn, Daryl N. and Shoenhair, John D., "Compensation Based (Dis)incentives for Revenue Maximizing Behavior: A Test of the "Revised" Baumol Hypothesis." *Review of Economics and Statistics* 70(1), February 1988, pp. 154–58.

Appendix
An Indifference Curve Approach to
Managerial Incentives

The essence of the problem with compensation payments that are not tied to performance is depicted graphically in Figure 6–6. The manager views both leisure and income to be goods. Moreover, the manager is willing to substitute between leisure on the job (shirking) and income. This is why his indifference curve has the usual shape in Figure 6–6, where we measure the quantity of leisure consumed at the workplace on the horizontal axis and income on the vertical axis. Note that while the manager enjoys shirking, the owner does not want the manager to shirk.

When the manager is offered a fixed salary of $50,000, his opportunity set becomes the shaded area in Figure 6–6. The reason is simple: Since the owner is not physically present at the workplace, the manager will receive the same $50,000 regardless of whether he works a full eight hours (and hence doesn't shirk) or spends the entire day at home (and shirks eight hours). If profits are low, the owner will not know whether this is due to poor managerial effort or simply bad luck. The manager can take advantage of the separation of ownership from control by pushing his indifference curve as far to the northeast as possible until he is in equilibrium at point A, where he shirks the entire day every day of the year but still collects the $50,000.

From the viewpoint of the firm's owner, the fixed salary has an adverse effect on profits because it does not provide the manager with an incentive to monitor other employees. To see this, suppose the profits of the firm are a simple linear function of the amount of shirking done by the manager during each eight-hour period. Such a relationship is graphed in Figure 6–7. The line through point C

FIGURE 6–6

Impact of a fixed salary on managerial behavior

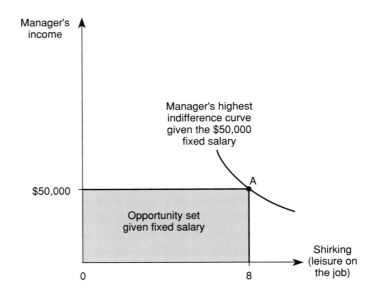

FIGURE 6–7

A profit-sharing incentive bonus

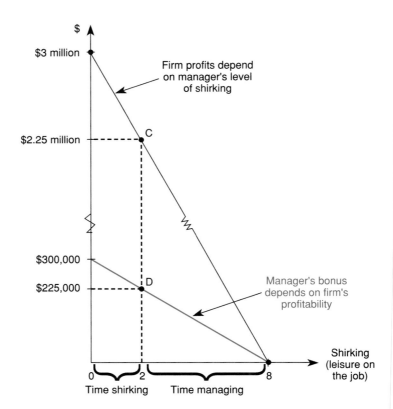

defines the level of firm profits, which depends on the manager's degree of shirking. For example, if the manager spends the entire day on the job monitoring other employees, shirking is zero and firm profits are $3 million. If the manager spends the entire day shirking, profits are zero. If the manager shirks two hours and thus works six hours, the profits of the firm are $2.25 million. Since the fixed salary of $50,000 provides the manager with an incentive to shirk eight hours, the profits of the firm will be zero if it uses that compensation plan.

How can the owner get the manager to spend time monitoring the production process? You might think that if she paid the manager a bigger salary the manager would work harder. But this is not correct; a larger salary would simply shift the vertical intercept of the opportunity set in Figure 6–6 above $50,000, but the equilibrium would still imply eight hours of shirking. In essence, the employment contract is such that there is absolutely no cost to the manager of shirking.

Suppose the owner offers the manager the following type of employment contract: a fixed salary of $50,000, plus a bonus of 10 percent of profits. In this instance, if the manager spends eight hours shirking, profits are zero and the manager gets only $50,000. If the manager does not shirk at all, the firm earns $3 million in profits and the manager gets a bonus equal to 10 percent of those profits. In this instance, the bonus is $300,000. The bonus to the manager, as a function of his level of shirking, is depicted in Figure 6–7 as the line through point D. Note that

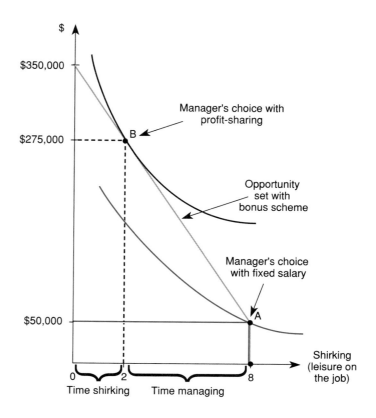

when the manager shirks for two hours each day, the firm earns $2.25 million in gross profits and the manager's bonus is $225,000.

The effect of a salary plus a bonus compensation plan on managerial behavior is illustrated in Figure 6–8. The manager's opportunity set is now given by the line through points A and B. For example, if the manager shirks eight hours, profits are zero and he receives no bonus; therefore, his income is $50,000. If the manager does not shirk at all, a bonus of $300,000 is added to his fixed salary; thus, the manager can earn $350,000 if he does not shirk.

Exactly what the manager does under the salary-plus-bonus plan depends on his preferences. But as we see in Figure 6–8, this manager can attain a higher indifference curve by shirking less and moving from point A to point B. At point B, the manager earns $275,000 in income—$225,000 in the form of a bonus payment and $50,000 as a fixed salary. The manager clearly prefers this compensation scheme. Note also that the manager still shirks two hours each day, but this is considerably less than under the fixed-salary/no-bonus plan.

What is the impact of the bonus on the owner of the firm? In Figure 6–7, we see that when the manager shirks two hours each day, the firm earns $2.25 million in gross profits. Thus, the salary plus bonus increases the owner's gross profits from zero (under the fixed salary) to $2.25 million. The bonus has increased the welfare not only of the manager but of the owner; profits, net of managerial compensation, are

$$\$2,250,000 - \$275,000 = \$1,975,000.$$

The Nature of Industry

Headline

Microsoft Puts Halt to Merger Plans

In April 1995 the nightly news and newspapers across the world reported that the U.S. Justice Department filed suit to block software giant Microsoft's planned acquisition of financial software maker, Intuit. Estimated reports placed Microsoft's share of the personal finance software market at about 20 percent, compared with Intuit's 70 percent share.

After spending over $4 million on merger plans, Microsoft announced in May 1995 that it had decided to call off the merger. In light of the dynamic nature of the software industry, Microsoft did not want to be tied up in a lengthy legal battle. In addition to the lost $4 million, Microsoft paid Intuit over $40 million for calling off the deal.

Given Microsoft's desire to avoid a lengthy legal battle, do you think it should have spent $4 million on merger plans in the first place? Explain.

Introduction

Managers of firms do not make decisions in a vacuum. Numerous factors affect decisions such as how much output to produce, what price to charge, how much to spend on research and development, advertising, and so on. Unfortunately, no single theory or methodology provides managers with the answers to these questions. The optimal pricing strategy for an automobile manufacturer generally will differ from that of a computer firm; the level of research and development will differ for food manufacturers and defense contractors. In this chapter we highlight important differences that exist among industries. In subsequent chapters, we will see why these differences arise and examine how they affect managerial decisions.

Much of the material in this chapter is factual and is intended to acquaint you with aspects of the "real world" that are relevant for managers. You will be exposed to statistics for numerous industries. Some of these statistics summarize how many firms exist in various industries; others indicate which firms and industries are the largest and which industries tend to charge the highest markups.

The numbers presented in this chapter will change over time; the largest firm today is unlikely to be the largest firm in 40 years. Consequently, the most important thing for you to grasp in this chapter is that industries differ substantially in nature; not all industries are created equal. Our task in the remaining chapters of this book is to determine what it is about firms and industries that gives rise to systematic differences in price-cost markups, advertising expenditures, and other managerial decision variables. This will be particularly valuable to you as a manager, since you do not know in which industry you will work during the next 40 years of your career. An effective manager is able to adapt to the nature of the industry in which his or her firm competes. As the nature of the industry changes, so will the manager's optimal decisions.

Market Structure

Market structure refers to factors such as the number of firms that compete in a market, the relative size of the firms (concentration), technological and cost conditions, demand conditions, and the ease with which firms can enter or exit the industry. Different industries have different structures, and these structures affect the decisions the prudent manager will make. The following subsections provide an overview of the major structural variables that affect managerial decisions.

Firm Size

It will come as no surprise to you that some firms are larger than others. Consider Table 7–1, which lists the sales of the largest firm in each of 26 U.S. industries. Notice that there are considerable differences in the size of the largest firm in each industry. General Motors is the largest firm in the motor vehicles and parts industry, with sales of over $133 billion. In contrast, the largest firm in the jewelry and silverware industry is Jostens, with sales of slightly over $.9 billion. One important lesson for future managers is that some industries naturally give rise to larger firms than do other industries. A goal of the remaining chapters in this book is to explain why.

TABLE 7–1   The Largest Firms in Selected U.S. Industries

Industry	Largest Company	Sales (millions of dollars)
Aerospace	Boeing	25,285
Apparel	Levi Strauss	5,892
Beverages	PepsiCo	25,021
Building materials	Corning	4,005
Chemicals	DuPont	32,621
Computers, office equipment	IBM	62,716
Electronics, electrical equipment	General Electric	60,823
Food	Philip Morris	50,621
Forest products	International Paper	13,685
Furniture	Interco	1,657
Industrial and farm equipment	Tenneco	13,255
Jewelry, silverware	Jostens	915
Metal products	Gillette	5,411
Metals	ALCOA	9,056
Mining, crude oil	Hanson Industries	8,111
Motor vehicles and parts	General Motors	133,622
Petroleum refining	Exxon	97,825
Pharmaceuticals	Johnson & Johnson	14,138
Publishing and printing	R. R. Donnelly	4,388
Rubber and plastics	Goodyear Tire	11,643
Scientific and photographic equipment	Eastman Kodak	20,059
Soaps, cosmetics	Procter & Gamble	30,433
Textiles	Shaw Industries	2,321
Tobacco	RJR Nabisco	15,104
Toys, sporting goods	Hasbro	2,747
Transportation equipment	Brunswick	2,354

Source: *Fortune*, April 18, 1994, pp. 257–276; and author's calculations.

Industry Concentration

The data in Table 7–1 reveal considerable variation in the size of the largest firm in various industries. Another factor that affects managerial decisions is the size distribution of firms within an industry; that is, are there many small firms within an industry or only a few large firms? This question is important because, as we will see in later chapters, the optimal decisions of a manager who faces little competition from other firms in the industry will differ from those of a manager who works in an industry in which there are many firms.

Some industries are dominated by a few large firms, while others are composed of many small firms. Before we consider the data that overview the concentration of various U.S. industries, we will examine two measures economists use to gauge the degree of concentration in an industry.

Measures of Industry Concentration

Concentration ratios measure how much of the total output in an industry is produced by the largest firms in that industry. The most common concentration ratio is the four-firm concentration ratio (C_4). The *four-firm concentration ratio* is the fraction of total industry sales produced by the four largest firms in the industry.

**four-firm
concentration ratio**
The fraction of total
industry sales
generated by the
four largest firms
in the industry.

Let S_1, S_2, S_3, and S_4 denote the sales of the four largest firms in an industry, and let S_T denote the total sales of all firms in the industry. The four-firm concentration ratio is given by

$$C_4 = \frac{S_1 + S_2 + S_3 + S_4}{S_T}.$$

Equivalently, the four-firm concentration ratio is the sum of the market shares of the top four firms:

$$C_4 = w_1 + w_2 + w_3 + w_4,$$

where $w_1 = S_1/S_T$, $w_2 = S_2/S_T$, $w_3 = S_3/S_T$, and $w_4 = S_4/S_T$.

When an industry is composed of a very large number of firms, each of which is very small, the four-firm concentration ratio is close to zero. When four or fewer firms produce all of an industry's output, the four-firm concentration ratio is 1. The closer the four-firm concentration ratio is to zero, the less concentrated is the industry; the closer the ratio is to 1, the more concentrated is the industry.

DEMONSTRATION PROBLEM 7–1

Suppose an industry is composed of six firms. Four firms have sales of $10 each, and two firms have sales of $5 each. What is the four-firm concentration ratio for this industry?

Answer

Total industry sales are $S_T = \$50$. The sales of the four largest firms are

$$S_1 + S_2 + S_3 + S_4 = \$40.$$

Therefore, the four-firm concentration ratio is

$$C_4 = \frac{40}{50} = .80.$$

This means that the four largest firms in the industry account for 80 percent of total industry output.

Concentration ratios provide a very crude measure of the size structure of an industry. Four-firm concentration ratios that are close to zero indicate markets in which there are many sellers, giving rise to much competition among producers for the right to sell to consumers. Industries with four-firm concentration ratios close to 1 indicate markets in which there is little competition among producers for sales to consumers.

Herfindahl-Hirshman index (HHI)
The sum of the squared market shares of firms in a given industry multiplied by 10,000.

Another measure of concentration is the Herfindahl-Hirshman index. The *Herfindahl-Hirshman index (HHI)* is the sum of the squared market shares of firms in a given industry, multiplied by 10,000 to eliminate the need for decimals. By squaring the market shares before adding them up, the index weights firms with high market shares more heavily.

Suppose firm i's share of the total market output is $w_i = S_i/S_T$, where S_i is firm i's sales and S_T is total sales in the industry. Then the Herfindahl-Hirshman index is

$$HHI = 10,000 \sum w_i^2$$

The value of the Herfindahl-Hirshman index lies between 0 and 10,000. A value of 10,000 exists when a single firm (with a market share of $w_1 = 1$) exists in the industry. A value of zero results when there are numerous infinitesimally small firms.

DEMONSTRATION PROBLEM 7–2

Suppose an industry consists of three firms. Two firms have sales of $10 each, and one firm has sales of $30. What is the Herfindahl-Hirshman index for this industry? What is the four-firm concentration ratio?

Answer

Since total industry sales are $S_T = \$50$, the largest firm has a market share of $w_1 = 30/50$ and the other two firms have a market share of 10/50 each. Thus, the Herfindahl-Hirshman index for this industry is

$$HHI = 10,000 \left[\left(\frac{30}{50} \right)^2 + \left(\frac{10}{50} \right)^2 + \left(\frac{10}{50} \right)^2 \right] = 4,400.$$

The four-firm concentration ratio is 1, since the top three firms account for all industry sales.

The Concentration of U.S. Industry

Now that you understand the algebra of industry concentration and Herfindahl-Hirshman indices, we may use these indices to examine the concentration of representative industries within the United States. Table 7–2 provides concentration ratios (in percentages) and Herfindahl-Hirshman indices for selected U.S. industries. Notice that there is considerable variation among industries in the degree of concentration. The top four producers of cereal breakfast foods account for 86 percent of the total output of breakfast cereals, suggesting considerable concentration. Similarly, the markets for motor vehicles and car bodies, household refrigerators and freezers, and chewing gum also have high four-firm concentration ratios. In contrast, the four-firm concentration ratios for ready-mix concrete, women's and misses' dresses, and fluid milk are lower, suggesting greater competition among producers. For example, the four largest producers of women's and misses' dresses account for only 6 percent of the total market.

On balance, the Herfindahl-Hirshman indices reported in Table 7–2 reveal a similar pattern: The industries with high four-firm concentration ratios tend to have higher Herfindahl-Hirshman indices. There are exceptions, however. Notice that according to the four-firm concentration ratio, the newspaper industry is more concentrated than the periodical industry. However, the Herfindahl-Hirshman index for the periodical industry is higher than that for the newspaper industry. Why do the conclusions drawn from these two indices differ?

First, the four-firm concentration indices are based on the market shares of only the four largest firms in an industry, while the Herfindahl-Hirshman indices are based on the market shares of all firms in an industry. In other words, the C_4 does not take into account how large the fifth largest firm is, whereas the Herfindahl-Hirshman index does. Second, the HHI is based on squared market shares, while the four-firm concentration ratio is not. Consequently, the Herfindahl-Hirshman index places a greater weight on firms with large market shares than does the four-firm concentration ratio. These two factors can lead to differences in the ranking of firms by the C_4 and the HHI.

Limitations of Concentration Measures

Statistics and other data should always be interpreted with caution, and the preceding measures of concentration are no exception. In concluding our discussion of the concentration of U.S. industries, it is important to point out three potential limitations of the numbers reported in Table 7–2.

Global Markets. The four-firm concentration and Herfindahl-Hirshman indices reported in Table 7–2 are based on a definition of the product market that excludes foreign imports. That is, in calculating C_4 and HHI, the Bureau of the Census does not take into account the penetration by foreign firms into U.S. markets. This tends to overstate the true level of concentration in industries in which a significant number of foreign producers serve the market.

For example, consider the four-firm concentration ratio for motor vehicles and car bodies. As noted earlier, the top four U.S. firms account for

TABLE 7-2   Four-Firm Concentration Ratios and Herfindahl-Hirshman Indices for Selected U.S. Industries

Industry	C_4	HHI
Bolts, nuts, rivets, and washers	13	102
Book publishing	17	190
Bottled and canned soft drinks	14	109
Breakfast cereal foods	86	N/A
Chewing and smoking tobacco	87	2,564
Chewing gum	95	N/A
Dog, cat, and other pet food	52	1,167
Electronic computing equipment	43	793
Fluid milk	16	151
Frozen fruits and vegetables	27	306
Household refrigerators and freezers	94	2,745
Luggage	41	669
Malt beverages	77	2,089
Meat-packing plants	29	325
Motor vehicles and car bodies	92	N/A
Newspapers	22	139
Periodicals	20	175
Ready-mix concrete	6	18
Soap and other detergents	60	1,306
Women's and misses' dresses	6	24

Source: *Concentration Ratios in Manufacturing*, U.S. Bureau of the Census, various years.

92 percent of this market. However, these numbers ignore the sales of foreign manufacturers. The four-firm concentration ratio based on both foreign and domestic sales would be considerably lower due to the presence of firms such as Honda, Nissan, Volkswagen, Mazda, and so forth.

National, Regional and Local Markets.   A second deficiency in the numbers reported in Table 7-2 is that they are based on figures for the entire United States. In many industries, the relevant markets are local and may be composed of only a few firms. When the relevant markets are local, the use of national data tends to understate the actual level of concentration in the local markets.

‚ For example, suppose that each of the 50 states had only one gasoline station. If all gasoline stations were the same size, each firm would have a market share of only 1/50. The four-firm concentration ratio, based on national data, would be 4/50, or 8 percent. This would suggest that the market for gasoline services is not very concentrated. However, it does a consumer in central Texas little good to have gas stations in 49 other states, since the relevant market for buying gasoline for this consumer is his or her local market. Thus, geographical differences among markets can lead to biases in concentration measures.

Now that you have a basic understanding of deficiencies in using national data to construct measures of market structure, let us reexamine Table 7–2. The top four newspapers account for 22 percent of total newspaper sales in the United States. This fact, coupled with a relatively low Herfindahl-Hirshman index, suggests that the newspaper industry is not very concentrated, at least when one looks at national data. Most cities, however, have only one or two local newspapers. Concentration ratios based on local or regional newspaper markets would be much higher than the numbers reported in Table 7–2.

In summary, indices of market structure based on national data tend to understate the degree of concentration when the relevant markets are local.

Industry Definitions and Product Classes.   We already emphasized that the geographic definition of the relevant market (local or national) can lead to a bias in concentration ratios. Similarly, the definition of product classes used to define an industry also affects indices.

Specifically, in constructing indices of market structure, there is considerable aggregation across product classes. Consider the four-firm concentration ratio for bottled and canned soft drinks, which is 14 percent in Table 7–2. This number may seem surprisingly low when one considers how Coca-Cola and Pepsi dominate the market for cola. However, the concentration ratio of 14 percent is based on a much more broadly defined notion of soft drinks. In fact, the product classes used by the Bureau of the Census to define the industry include many more types of bottled and canned drinks, including birch beer, root beer, fruit drinks, ginger ale, iced tea, lemonade, carbonated mineral water, and even pasteurized water.

How does one determine which products belong in which industry? As a general rule, products that are close substitutes (have large, positive cross-price elasticities) are considered to belong to a given industry class. Indeed, one would view the above-mentioned soft drinks to be close substitutes for cola drinks, thus justifying their inclusion into the industry before calculating concentration ratios.

Notice the similarity between this issue and the issue raised earlier concerning local versus national markets. If a newspaper published in New York City is a close substitute for one published in Los Angeles, it is reasonable to include both in the definition of the relevant market.

Technology

Industries also differ with regard to the technologies used to produce goods and services. Some industries are very labor intensive, requiring much labor to produce goods and services. Other industries are very capital intensive, requiring large investments in plant, equipment, and machines to be able to

Inside Business 7–1

Firm Size and Capital-Labor Substitution

Most people would agree that working for IBM is much different than working for Joe's Pizza. But why is there a difference? The late Nobel laureate George Stigler suggested that one reason is that larger firms face a greater cost in gathering information about their work forces than do smaller firms. After all, if you work for Joe's Pizza, Joe is likely to observe your on-the-job performance, but it is unlikely that the chair of the board would be your supervisor if you worked for IBM. To counter this increased labor cost, we would expect large firms to economize in their use of labor by using more capital and thus substituting capital for labor. In addition, large firms may try to hire more qualified workers, substituting quality for quantity. Similarly, they may offer more training to workers to increase worker productivity.

A recent study by three economists concluded that larger firms do indeed use more capital per worker. The study found that a 10 percent increase in the size of the firm resulted in a 1.2 percent increase in capital used per worker. In addition, it found that larger firms were more likely to offer training to their work forces, spend more resources per applicant in evaluating potential employees, and offer higher starting wages than did smaller firms. The necessity of observing the on-the-job performance of workers increases the cost of labor and thus induces firms to substitute toward more capital and higher-quality workers.

Sources: George J. Stigler, "Information in the Labor Market," *Journal of Political Economy* 70 (June 1962), pp. 95–105; John M. Barron, Dan A. Black, and Mark A. Loewenstein, "Employer Size: The Implications for Search, Training, Capital Investment, Starting Wages, and Wage Growth," *Journal of Labor Economics* 5 (January 1987), pp. 76–89.

produce. These differences in technology give rise to differences in production techniques across industries. In the petroleum-refining industry, for example, firms utilize approximately one employee for each $1 million in sales. In contrast, the beverage industry utilizes roughly 17 workers for each $1 million in sales.

Technology is also important within a given industry. In some industries, firms have access to identical technologies and therefore have similar cost structures. In other industries, one or two firms have access to a technology that is not available to other firms. In these instances, the firms with superior technology will have an advantage over other firms. When this technological advantage is significant, the technologically superior firm (or firms) will completely dominate the industry. In the remaining chapters, we will see how such differences in technologies affect managerial decisions.

Demand and Market Conditions

Industries also differ with regard to the underlying demand and market conditions. In industries with relatively low demand, the market may be able to sustain only a few firms. In industries in which demand is great, the market may require many firms to produce the quantity demanded. One of our tasks in the remaining chapters is to explain how the degree of market demand affects the decisions of managers.

The information accessible to consumers also tends to vary across markets. It is very easy for a consumer to find the lowest airfare on a flight from Washington to Los Angeles; all one has to do is call a travel agent (or call four or five airlines) and get price quotes. In contrast, it is much more difficult for consumers to obtain information about the best deal on a used car. The consumer not only has to bargain with potential sellers over the price but also must attempt to ascertain the quality of the used car. As we will learn in subsequent chapters, the optimal decisions of managers will vary depending on the amount of information available in the market.

Finally, the elasticity of demand for products tends to vary from industry to industry. Moreover, the elasticity of demand for an individual firm's product generally will differ from the market elasticity of demand for the product. In some industries, there is a large discrepancy between an individual firm's elasticity of demand and the market elasticity. The reason for this can be easily explained.

In Chapter 3 we learned that the demand for a specific product depends on the number of close substitutes available for the product. As a consequence, the demand for a particular brand of product (e.g., Seven Up) will be more elastic than the demand for the product group in general (soft drinks). In markets in which there are few close substitutes for a given firm's product, the elasticity of demand for that product will coincide with the market elasticity of demand for the product group (since there is only one product in the market). In industries in which many firms produce substitutes for a given firm's product, the demand for the individual firm's product will be more elastic than the overall industry demand.

Rothschild index
A measure of the sensitivity to price of a product group as a whole relative to the sensitivity of the quantity demanded of a single firm to a change in its price.

One measure of the elasticity of industry demand for a product relative to that of an individual firm is the Rothschild index. The *Rothschild index* provides a measure of the sensitivity to price of the product group as a whole relative to the sensitivity of the quantity demanded of a single firm to a change in its price.

The Rothschild index is given by

$$R = \frac{E_T}{E_F},$$

where E_T is the elasticity of demand for the total market and E_F is the elasticity of demand for the product of an individual firm.

The Rothschild index takes on a value between 0 and 1. When the index is 1, the individual firm faces a demand curve that has the same sensitivity to price as the market demand curve. In contrast, when the elasticity of

TABLE 7–3   **Market and Representative Firm Demand Elasticities and Corresponding Rothschild Indices for Selected U.S. Industries**

Industry	Own Price Elasticity of Market Demand	Own Price Elasticity of Demand for Representative Firm's Product	Rothschild Index
Food	−1.0	−3.8	0.26
Tobacco	−1.3	−1.3	1.00
Textiles	−1.5	−4.7	0.32
Apparel	−1.1	−4.1	0.27
Paper	−1.5	−1.7	0.88
Printing and publishing	−1.8	−3.2	0.56
Chemicals	−1.5	−1.5	1.00
Petroleum	−1.5	−1.7	0.88
Rubber	−1.8	−2.3	0.78
Leather	−1.2	−2.3	0.52

Source: Matthew D. Shapiro, "Measuring Market Power in U.S. Industry," National Bureau of Economic Research, Working Paper No. 2212, 1987.

demand for an individual firm's product is much greater (in absolute value) than the elasticity of the market demand, the Rothschild index is close to zero. In this instance, an individual firm's quantity demanded is more sensitive to a price increase than is the industry as a whole. In other words, when the Rothschild index is less than 1, a 10 percent increase in one firm's price will decrease that firm's quantity demanded by more than the total industry quantity would fall if all firms in the industry increased their prices by 10 percent. The Rothschild index therefore provides a measure of how price sensitive an individual firm's demand is relative to the entire market. When an industry is composed of many firms, each producing similar products, the Rothschild index will be close to zero.

Table 7–3 provides estimates of the firm and market elasticities of demand and the Rothschild indices for 10 U.S. industries. The table reveals that firms in some industries are more sensitive to price increases than firms in other industries. Notice that the Rothschild indices for tobacco and for chemicals are unity. This means that the representative firm in the industry faces a demand curve that has exactly the same elasticity of demand as the total industry demand. In contrast, the Rothschild index for food is .26, which means that the demand for an individual food producer's product is roughly four times more elastic than that of the industry as a whole. Firms in the food industry face a demand curve that is much more sensitive to price than the industry as a whole.

Inside Business 7–2

The Elasticity of Demand at the Firm and Market Levels

In general, the demand for an individual firm's product is more elastic than that for the industry as a whole. The exception is the case of monopoly (where a single firm comprises the market), in which case the demand for the individual firm's product is the same as the industry demand. How much more elastic is the demand for an individual firm's product compared to that for the market?

Table 7–4 provides an answer to this question. The second column gives the own price elasticity of the market demand for a given industry. This elasticity measures how responsive total industry quantity demanded is to an industrywide price increase. The third column provides the elasticity of demand for an individual firm's product. Thus, that column measures how responsive the quantity demanded of an individual firm's product is to a change in that firm's price.

Notice in Table 7–4 that the market elasticity of demand in the agriculture industry is -1.8. This means that a 1 percent increase in the industrywide price would lead to a 1.8 percent reduction in the total quantity demanded of agricultural products. In contrast, the elasticity of demand for a representative firm's product is -96.2. If an individual firm raised its price by 1 percent, the quantity demanded of the firm's product would fall by a whopping 96.2 percent. The demand for an individual agricultural firm's product is very elastic indeed, because there are numerous firms in the industry selling close substitutes. The more competition among producers in an industry, the more elastic will be the demand for an individual firm's product.

TABLE 7–4　Market and Representative Firm Demand Elasticities for Selected U.S. Industries

Industry	Own Price Elasticity of Market Demand	Own Price Elasticity of Demand for Representative Firm's Product
Agriculture	-1.8	-96.2
Construction	-1.0	-5.2
Durable manufacturing	-1.4	-3.5
Nondurable manufacturing	-1.3	-3.4
Transportation	-1.0	-1.9
Communication and utilities	-1.2	-1.8
Wholesale trade	-1.5	-1.6
Retail trade	-1.2	-1.8
Finance	-0.1	-5.5
Services	-1.2	-26.4

Source: Matthew D. Shapiro, "Measuring Market Power in U.S. Industry," National Bureau of Economic Research, Working Paper No. 2212, 1987.

DEMONSTRATION PROBLEM 7–3

The industry elasticity of demand for airline travel is -3, and the elasticity of demand for an individual carrier is -4. What is the Rothschild index for this industry?

Answer

The Rothschild index is

$$R = \frac{-3}{-4} = .75.$$

Potential for Entry

The final structural variable we discuss in this chapter is the potential for entry into an industry. In some industries, it is relatively easy for new firms to enter the market; in others, it is difficult for new firms to enter. The optimal decisions by firms in an industry will depend on the ease with which new firms can enter the market.

Numerous factors can create a *barrier to entry*, making it difficult for other firms to enter an industry. One potential barrier to entry is the explicit cost of entering an industry, such as capital requirements. Another is patents, which give owners of patents the exclusive right to sell their products for a specified period of time. In this instance, the patent serves as a barrier to entry; other firms cannot readily produce the product produced by the patent holder.

Economies of scale also can create a barrier to entry. In some markets, only one or two firms exist because of economies of scale. If additional firms attempted to enter, they would be unable to generate the volume necessary to enjoy the reduced average costs associated with economies of scale. As we will learn in subsequent chapters, barriers to entry have important implications for the long-run profits a firm will earn in a market.

Conduct

In addition to structural differences across industries, the *conduct*, or behavior, of firms also tends to differ across industries. Some industries charge higher markups than other industries. Some industries are more susceptible to mergers or takeovers than others. In addition, the amount spent on advertising and research and development tends to vary across industries. The following subsections describe important differences in conduct that exist across industries.

Pricing Behavior

Firms in some industries charge higher markups than firms in other industries. To illustrate this fact, we introduce what economists refer to as the *Lerner index*. The Lerner index is given by

Lerner index
A measure of the difference between price and marginal cost as a fraction of the product's price.

$$L = \frac{P - MC}{P},$$

where P is price and MC is marginal cost. Thus, the Lerner index measures the difference between price and marginal cost as a fraction of the price of the product.

When a firm sets its price equal to the marginal cost of production, the Lerner index is zero; consumers pay a price for the product that exactly equals the cost to the firm of producing another unit of the good. When a firm charges a price that is higher than marginal cost, the Lerner index takes on a value greater than zero, with the maximum possible value being unity. The Lerner index therefore provides a measure of how much firms in an industry mark up their prices over marginal cost. The higher the Lerner index, the greater the firm's markup. In industries in which firms rigorously compete for consumer sales by attempting to charge the lowest price in the market, the Lerner index is close to zero. When firms do not rigorously compete for consumers through price competition, the Lerner index is closer to 1.

The Lerner index is related to another measure of the markup charged by a firm. In particular, we can rearrange the formula for the Lerner index to obtain

$$P = \left(\frac{1}{1 - L}\right) MC.$$

In this equation, $1/(1 - L)$ is the markup factor. It defines the factor by which marginal cost is multiplied to obtain the price of the good. When the Lerner index is zero, the markup factor is 1, and thus the price is exactly equal to marginal cost. If the Lerner index is 1/2, the markup factor is 2. In this case, the price charged by a firm is two times the marginal cost of production.

Table 7–5 provides estimates of the Lerner index and markup factor for 10 U.S. industries. Notice that there are considerable differences in Lerner indices and markup factors across industries. The industry with the highest Lerner index and markup factor is the tobacco industry. In this industry, the Lerner index is 76 percent. This means that for each $1 paid to the firm by consumers, $.76 is markup. Alternatively, the price is 4.17 times the actual marginal cost of production.

TABLE 7–5   Lerner Indices and Markup Factors for Selected U.S. Industries

Industry	Lerner Index	Markup Factor
Food	0.26	1.35
Tobacco	0.76	4.17
Textiles	0.21	1.27
Apparel	0.24	1.32
Paper	0.58	2.38
Printing and publishing	0.31	1.45
Chemicals	0.67	3.03
Petroleum	0.59	2.44
Rubber	0.43	1.75
Leather	0.43	1.75

Sources: Michael R. Baye and Jae-Woo Lee, "Ranking Industries by Performance: A Synthesis," Texas A&M University, Working Paper No. 90-20, March 1990; Matthew D. Shapiro, "Measuring Market Power in U.S. Industry," National Bureau of Economic Research, Working Paper No. 2212, 1987.

In contrast, the Lerner index and markup factor for apparel are much lower. Based on the Lerner index for apparel, we see that for each $1 a clothing manufacturer receives, only $.24 is markup. Alternatively, the price of an apparel product is only 1.32 times the actual marginal cost of production. Again, the message for managers is that the markup charged for a product will vary depending on the nature of the market in which the product is sold. An important goal in the remaining chapters is to help managers determine the optimal markup for a product.

DEMONSTRATION PROBLEM 7–4

A firm in the airline industry has a marginal cost of $200 and charges a price of $300. What are the Lerner index and markup factor?

Answer

The Lerner index is

$$L = \frac{P - MC}{P} = \frac{300 - 200}{300} = \frac{1}{3}.$$

The markup factor is

$$\frac{1}{1-L} = \frac{1}{1-1/3} = 1.5.$$

Integration and Merger Activity

Integration and merger activity also differ across industries. *Integration* refers to the uniting of productive resources. Integration can occur through a merger, in which two or more existing firms "unite," or merge, into a single firm. Alternatively (and as discussed in Chapter 6), integration can occur during the formation of a firm. By its very nature, integration results in larger firms than would exist in the absence of integration.

Economists distinguish among three types of integration, or mergers: vertical, horizontal, and conglomerate.

Vertical Integration

Vertical integration refers to a situation where various stages in the production of a single product are carried out in a single firm. For instance, an automobile manufacturer that produces its own steel, uses the steel to make car bodies and engines, and finally sells an automobile is vertically integrated. This is in contrast to a firm that buys car bodies and engines from other firms and then assembles all the parts supplied by the different suppliers. A *vertical merger* is the integration of two or more firms that produce components for a single product. We learned in Chapter 6 that firms vertically integrate to reduce the transaction costs associated with acquiring inputs.

Horizontal Integration

Horizontal integration refers to the merging of the production of similar products into a single firm. For example, if two computer firms merged into a single firm, horizontal integration would occur. Horizontal integration involves the merging of two or more final products into a single firm, whereas vertical integration involves the merging of two or more phases of production into a single firm.

In contrast to vertical integration, which occurs because this strategy reduces transaction costs, the primary reasons firms engage in horizontal integration are (1) to enjoy the cost savings of economies of scale or scope and (2) to enhance their market power. In some instances, horizontal integration allows firms to enjoy economies of scale and scope, thus leading to cost savings in producing the good. As a general rule, these types of horizontal mergers are socially beneficial. On the other hand, a horizontal merger, by its very definition, reduces the number of firms that compete in the product market. This tends to increase both the four-firm concentration ratio and the Herfindahl-Hirshman index for the industry, which reflects an increase in the market power of firms in the industry. The social benefits of the reduced costs due to horizontal merger must be weighed against the social costs associated with a more concentrated industry.

When the benefits of cost reductions are small relative to the gain in market power enjoyed by the horizontally integrated firm, the government may choose to block the merger. Specifically, the U.S. Department of Justice can preclude firms from merging into a single firm. As a general rule, the Justice Department views industries with Herfindahl-Hirshman indices in excess of 1,800 to be "highly concentrated" and will attempt to block a merger if it will increase the Herfindahl-Hirshman index by more than 100. However, the Justice Department sometimes permits mergers in industries that have high Herfindahl-Hirshman indices when there is evidence of significant foreign competition, an emerging new technology, increased efficiency, or when one of the firms has financial problems.

Industries with Herfindahl-Hirshman indices below 1,000 after a merger generally are considered "unconcentrated" by the Justice Department, and mergers usually are allowed. If the Herfindahl-Hirshman index is between 1,000 and 1,800, the Justice Department relies more heavily on other factors, such as economies of scale and ease of entry into an industry, in determining whether to block a merger. In Chapter 13, we will discuss these and other government actions designed to reduce market power.

Conglomerate Mergers

Finally, a *conglomerate merger* involves the integration of different product lines into a single firm. For example, if a cigarette maker and a cookie manufacturer merged into a single firm, a conglomerate merger would result. A conglomerate merger is similar to a horizontal merger in that it involves the merging of final products into a single firm. It differs from a horizontal merger because the final products are not related.

Why do some firms find conglomerate merger advantageous? The cyclical nature of the demand for many products is such that there are times when demand is high and periods in which demand is low. Conglomerate mergers can improve firms' cash flows—revenues derived from one product line can be used to generate working capital when the demand for another product is low. This can reduce the variability of firm earnings and thus enhance a firm's ability to obtain funds in the capital market.

Trends in Mergers, Takeovers, and Acquisitions

Merger activity has varied considerably during the 20th century. As previously noted, mergers can result from an attempt by firms to reduce transaction costs, reap the benefits of economies of scale and scope, increase market power, or gain better access to capital markets. Some mergers are "friendly" in that both firms desire to merge into a single firm. Others are

The Language of Corporate Takeovers

Crown Jewel: The most valued asset held by an acquisition target; divestiture of this asset is frequently a sufficient defense to dissuade takeover.

Fair Price Amendment: Requires super majority approval of non-uniform, or two-tier, takeover bids not approved by the board of directors; can be avoided by a uniform bid for less than all outstanding shares (subject to prorationing under federal law if the offer is oversubscribed).

Going Private: The purchase of publicly owned stock of a company by the existing or another competing management group; the company is delisted and public trading in the stock ceases.

Golden Parachutes: The provisions in the employment contracts of top-level managers that provide for severance pay or other compensation should they lose their job as a result of a takeover.

Greenmail: The premium paid by a targeted company to a raider in exchange for his shares of the targeted company.

Leveraged Buyout: The purchase of publicly owned stock of a company by the existing management with a portion of the purchase price financed by outside investors; the company is delisted and public trading in the stock ceases.

Lockup Defense: Gives a friendly party (see White Knight) the right to purchase assets of firm, in particular the crown jewel, thus dissuading a takeover attempt.

Maiden: A term sometimes used to refer to the company at which the takeover is directed (target).

Poison Pill: Gives stockholders other than those involved in a hostile takeover the right to purchase securities at a very favorable price in the event of a takeover.

Proxy Contest: The solicitation of stockholder votes generally for the purpose of electing a slate of directors in competition with the current directors.

Raider: The person(s) or corporation attempting the takeover.

Shark Repellents: Antitakeover corporate charter amendments such as staggered terms for directors, super-majority requirement for approving merger, or mandate that bidders pay the same price for all shares in a buyout.

Standstill Agreement: A contract in which a raider or firm agrees to limit its holdings in the target firm and not attempt a takeover.

Stripper: A successful raider who, once the target is acquired, sells off some of the assets of the target company.

Target: The company at which the takeover attempt is directed.

Targeted Repurchase: A repurchase of common stock from an individual holder or a tender repurchase that excludes an individual holder; the former is the most frequent form of greenmail, while the latter is a common defensive tactic.

Tender Offer: An offer made directly to shareholders to buy some or all of their shares for a specified price during a specified time.

Two-Tier Offer: A takeover offer that provides a cash price for sufficient shares to obtain control of the corporation, then a lower non-cash (securities) price for the remaining shares.

White Knight: A merger partner solicited by management of a target who offers an alternative merger plan to that offered by the raider which protects the target company from the attempted takeover.

Source: Reprinted from Mack Ott and G. J. Santoni, "Mergers and Takeovers—The Value of Predators' Information," Federal Reserve Bank of St. Louis *Review*, December 1985, pp. 16–28.

"hostile," meaning that one of the firms does not desire the merger to take place.

In some instances, mergers or takeovers occur because it is perceived that the management of one of the firms is doing an inadequate job of managing the firm. In this instance, the benefit of the takeover is the increased profits that result from "cleaning house," that is, firing the incompetent managers. Many managers fear mergers and acquisitions because they are uncertain about the impact of a merger on their position.

The early 1980s saw significant merger activity. The oil and gas industry accounted for roughly 26 percent of all merger activity during the first half of the 1980s, and almost half of this activity occurred in 1984. Merger activity generally slowed during the late 1980s and early 1990s, but then accelerated toward the end of 1995. During the 1990s merger activity has been most prevalent in the banking and communication/entertainment sectors. Thus, we see that over the past 15 years there has been considerable variation in the level of merger activity, as well as variability in the industries engaged in that activity.

Research and Development

Earlier we noted that firms and industries differ with respect to the underlying technologies used to produce goods and services. One way firms gain a technological advantage is by engaging in research and development (R&D) and then obtaining a patent for the technology developed through the R&D. Table 7–6 provides R&D spending as a percentage of sales for

TABLE 7–6   R&D, Advertising, and Profits as a Percentage of Sales for Selected Firms

Company	Industry Group	R&D as a Percentage of Sales	Advertising as a Percentage of Sales	Profits as a Percentage of Sales
American Home Products	Health Care	8.0	6.0	24.0
AT&T	Telecommunications	5.1	1.2	9.3
Boeing	Aerospace	6.5	NA	7.2
Eastman Kodak	Leisure Products	8.0	3.1	5.2
General Motors	Automotive	4.4	1.2	1.9
Kellogg	Food	0.6	10.0	1.6
Microsoft	Software	12.5	NA	37.3
PepsiCo	Consumer Products	0.5	4.2	9.7
Procter and Gamble	Personal Care	3.1	7.9	1.1

Sources: *Advertising Age*, Sept. 28, 1994, pp. 3–11; *Business Week*, June 27, 1994, pp. 81–100; and author's calculations.

selected firms. In 1993 the average firm spent 3.8 percent of its sales on R&D activity. Importantly, there is considerable variation in R&D spending across industries. In the health-care industry, for example, 8 percent of sales revenue was reinvested in R&D by American Home Products Corp.; in the food industry, Kellogg reinvested less than 1 percent of sales revenue in R&D.

The message for managers is clear: The optimal amount to spend on R&D will depend on the characteristics of the industry in which the firm operates. One goal in the remaining chapters is to examine the major determinants of R&D spending.

Advertising

As Table 7–6 reveals, there is considerable variation across firms in the level of advertising utilized. Firms in the food industry, such as Kellogg, spend about 10 percent of their sales revenue on advertising. In contrast, firms in the automotive industry, such as General Motors, spend only between 1 and 2 percent of their sales revenue on advertising. Another goal of the remaining chapters is to examine why advertising intensities vary across firms in different industries. We will also see how firms determine the optimal amount and type of advertising to utilize.

Performance

Performance refers to the profits and social welfare that result in a given industry. It is important for future managers to recognize that profits and social welfare vary considerably across industries.

Profits

Table 7–6 highlights differences in profits across firms in different industries. General Motors generated more sales than any other firm on the list, yet its profits as a percentage of sales is among the lowest listed. One task in the next several chapters is to examine why "big" firms do not always earn big profits. As a manager, it would be a mistake to believe that just because your firm is large, it will automatically earn profits. In fact, nearly 25 percent of the nation's largest firms experienced losses in 1991.

Social Welfare

Another gauge of industry performance is the amount of consumer and producer surplus generated in a market. While this type of performance is difficult to measure, R. E. Dansby and R. D. Willig have proposed a useful

TABLE 7–7   **Dansby-Willig Performance Indices for Selected U.S. Industries**

Industry	Dansby-Willig Index
Food	0.51
Textiles	0.38
Apparel	0.47
Paper	0.63
Printing and publishing	0.56
Chemicals	0.67
Petroleum	0.63
Rubber	0.49
Leather	0.60

Source: Michael R. Baye and Jae-Woo Lee, "Ranking Industries by Performance: A Synthesis," Texas A&M Working Paper No. 90–20, March 1990.

Dansby-Willig performance index Ranks industries according to how much social welfare would improve if the output in an industry were increased by a small amount.

index. The *Dansby-Willig (DW) performance index* measures how much social welfare (defined as the sum of consumer and producer surplus) would improve if firms in an industry expanded output in a socially efficient manner. If the Dansby-Willig index for an industry is zero, there are no gains to be obtained by inducing firms in the industry to alter their outputs; consumer and producer surplus are maximized given industry demand and cost conditions. When the index is greater than zero, social welfare would improve if industry output was expanded.

The Dansby-Willig index thus allows one to rank industries according to how much social welfare would rise if the industry altered its output. Industries with large index values have poorer performance than industries with lower values. In Table 7–7, for instance, we see that the chemical industry has the highest DW index. This suggests that a slight change in output in the chemical industry would increase social welfare more than would a slight change in the output in any of the other industries. The textile industry has the lowest DW index, which reveals the best performance.

DEMONSTRATION PROBLEM 7–5

Suppose you are the manager of a firm in the textile industry. You have just learned that the government has placed the textile industry at the top of its list of industries it plans to regulate and intends to force the industry to expand output and lower the price of textile products. How should you respond?

Answer

You should point out to government's counsel that the textile industry has the lowest Lerner index out of the 10 major industries listed in Table 7–5, only \$.21 of each \$1 paid by consumers is markup. Furthermore, the Dansby-Willig index for the textile industry is the lowest of the nine industries listed in Table 7–7. The efficient way for government to improve social welfare is to alter output in the other industries first.

The Structure-Conduct-Performance Paradigm

You now have a broad overview of the structure, conduct, and performance of U.S. industry. The *structure* of an industry refers to factors such as technology, concentration, and market conditions. *Conduct* refers to how individual firms behave in the market; it involves pricing decisions, advertising decisions, and decisions to invest in research and development, among other factors. *Performance* refers to the resulting profits and social welfare that arise in the market. The *structure-conduct-performance paradigm* views these three aspects of industry as being integrally related.

The Causal View

The *causal view* of industry asserts that market structure "causes" firms to behave in a certain way. In turn, this behavior, or conduct, "causes" resources to be allocated in such and such a way, leading to either "good" or "poor" market performance. To better understand the causal view, consider a highly concentrated industry in which only a few firms compete for the right to sell products to consumers. According to the causal view, this structure gives firms market power, enabling them to charge high prices for their products. The behavior (charging high prices) is caused by market structure (the presence of few competitors). The high prices, in turn, "cause" high profits and poor performance (low social welfare). Thus, according to the causal view, a concentrated market "causes" high prices and poor performance.

The Feedback Critique

Today most economists recognize that the causal view provides, at best, an incomplete view of the relation among structure, conduct, and performance. According to the *feedback critique*, there is no one-way causal link among structure, conduct, and performance. The conduct of firms can affect market structure; market performance can affect conduct as well as market structure. To illustrate the feedback critique, let us apply it to the previous analysis, which stated that concentration causes high prices and poor performance.

According to the feedback critique, the conduct of firms in an industry may itself lead to a concentrated market. If the (few) existing firms are charging low prices and earning low economic profits, there will be no incentive for additional firms to enter the market. If this is the case, it could actually be low prices that "cause" the presence of few firms in the industry. In summary, then, it is a simplification of reality to assert that concentrated markets cause high prices. Indeed, the pricing behavior of firms can affect the number of firms. As we will see in subsequent chapters, low prices and good performance can occur even if only one or two firms are operating in an industry. A detailed explanation of this possibility will have to wait until we develop models for various market structures.

Overview of the Remainder of the Book

In the remaining chapters of this book, we examine the optimal managerial conduct under a variety of market structures. To have some terminology that will enable us to distinguish among various types of market structures, it is useful to introduce the four basic models we will use to accomplish this goal. Recognize, however, that our discussion of these four models provides only an overview; indeed, entire chapters will be devoted to making managerial decisions in each of these situations.

Perfect Competition

In *perfectly competitive* markets there are many firms, each of which is small relative to the entire market. The firms have access to the same technologies and produce similar products, so no firm has any real advantage over other firms in the industry. Firms in perfectly competitive markets do not have market power; that is, no individual firm has a perceptible impact on the market price, quantity, or quality of the product produced in the market. In perfectly competitive markets, both concentration ratios and Rothschild indices tend to be close to zero. We will study perfectly competitive markets in detail in the next chapter.

Monopoly

A *monopoly* is a firm that is the sole producer of a good or service in the relevant market. For instance, most local utility companies are the sole providers of electricity, natural gas, and local telephone services in a given city. Some towns have a single gasoline station or movie theater that serves the entire local market. All of these constitute local monopolies.

When there is a single provider of a good or service in a market, there is a tendency for the seller to capitalize on the monopoly position by restricting output and charging a price above marginal cost. Because there are no other firms in the market, consumers cannot switch to another producer in the face of higher prices. Consequently, consumers either buy some of the product at the higher price or go without it. In monopolistic markets, there is extreme concentration and the Rothschild index is unity.

Monopolistic Competition

In a *monopolistically competitive* market, there are many firms and consumers, just as in perfect competition. Thus, concentration measures are close to zero. Unlike in perfect competition, however, each firm produces a product that is slightly different from the products produced by other firms; Rothschild indices are greater than zero. Those who manage restaurants in a city containing numerous food establishments operate in a monopolistically competitive industry.

A firm in a monopolistically competitive market has some control over the price charged for the product. By raising the price, some consumers will remain loyal to the firm due to a preference for the particular characteristics of its product. But some consumers will switch to other brands. For this reason, firms in monopolistically competitive industries often spend considerable sums on advertising in an attempt to convince consumers that their brands are "better" than other brands. This reduces the number of customers who switch to other brands when a firm raises the price for its product.

Oligopoly

In an *oligopolistic* market, a few large firms tend to dominate the market. Firms in highly concentrated industries such as the airline, automobile, and aerospace industries operate in an oligopolistic market.

Inside Business 7–4

The Evolution of Market Structure in the Computer Industry

Industries can change dramatically over time. During the course of its evolution, a given industry may go through phases that include monopoly, oligopoly, monopolistic competition, and perfect competition. For this reason, it is important to understand how to make decisions in all four environments, even if you "know" you will work for a monopoly when you graduate. The following description of the evolution in the computer industry should convince you of this fact.

In the 1960s, a few large firms produced mainframe computers for universities, scientific

Inside Business 7–4 continued

Inside Business 7–4 concluded

think tanks, and large business applications. Each computer was designed almost exclusively for a specific user, and its cost often was over $100,000. Because each company kept its own standards, a customer whose computer needed repair was forced to go to the original manufacturer or write off the original purchase. This allowed the few companies that produced computers to act as virtual monopolists once they had a customer base. The early computer firms enjoyed high profit margins, some as high as 50 to 60 percent. These large profits induced several new firms to enter the computer market.

With entry came innovation in technology that reduced the size of mainframes, lowered the cost of production, and, because of increased competition, reduced the price to the customer. This influx of new competitors and products brought the market for computers into an oligopolistic-type structure. As a result, each firm became acutely aware of competitors and their actions. However, each firm held on to the specialized hardware and software for each user. Because of the specialized nature of the smaller machines, customers were still subject to their original purchases when it came to upgrades. However, since the price of the original machines was lower in the new environment, it was less costly to write off the original purchase and shift from one company to another than before. Of course, suppliers recognized this fact, which led to more vigorous competition. In the 1970s, the combination of lower prices and more competition decreased the returns in the market to 20 to 40 percent for the industry.

The 1980s brought the personal computer into many medium-size businesses that previously could not afford a computer. Along with the PC came workstations and minicomputers. Although profit margins had dropped in the 1970s, they were still high enough in the 1980s to entice new entry. The computer market of the 1980s resembled that of monopolistic competition, with a few large firms and many small firms, each producing slightly different styles of computers. Computers became affordable to many households and smaller businesses. As more firms entered the market, profit margins dropped drastically and copycat firms began opening the systems; thus, many parts became interchangeable among machines. Economic profits still were being earned, but profit margins had dropped to around 10 to 20 percent. Apple Computer was still earning a 30 to 40 percent return, but it was the only firm able to maintain these higher profit margins.

The lower prices of the 1980s and special firm incentives brought computers into almost every public school. Students received a formal education in the use of computers from an early age. By 1990, almost every high school graduate had had extensive hands-on experience with computers. This development brought on a new demand for computers and computer systems.

The mainstays of the industry had lost many of their customers and much of their market share to smaller firms in the 1980s. In an attempt to regain the profit margins enjoyed over the past 20 years, companies became more specialized. Software development became an industry in itself. The added competition in hardware that opened the systems made it possible for more firms to compete in upgrading machines. The open systems of the 1990s are leading to standardized technology at all levels in the computer industry. The early 1990s have been marked with extreme price reductions and low profits for almost all computer firms.

The increase in the number of firms and the standardization across machines has turned the "clone computer" industry into one resembling perfect competition. The rest of the 1990s should see a drastic change in the industry. Economic profits will no longer come to the industry as a whole. Instead, new innovators will see short-term profits quickly absorbed by increased competition. The computer industry thus provides an enlightening look at the dynamics of industry.

Source: Simon Forge, "Why the Computer Industry Is Restructuring Now," *Futures* 23 (November 1991), pp. 960–77.

When one firm in an oligopolistic market changes its price or marketing strategy, not only its own profits but the profits of the other firms in the industry are affected. Consequently, when one firm in an oligopoly changes its conduct, other firms in the industry have an incentive to react to the change by altering their own conduct. Thus, the distinguishing feature of an oligopolistic market is *mutual interdependence* among firms in the industry.

The interdependence of profits in an oligopoly gives rise to strategic interaction among firms. For example, suppose the manager of an oligopoly is considering increasing the price charged for the firm's product. To determine the impact of the price increase on profits, the manager must consider how rival firms in the industry will respond to the price increase. Thus, the strategic plans of one firm in an oligopoly depend on how that firm expects other firms in the industry to respond to the plans, if they are adopted. For this reason, it is very difficult to manage a firm that operates in an oligopoly. Because large rewards are paid to managers who know how to operate in oligopolistic markets, we will devote two chapters to an analysis of managerial decisions in such markets.

Answering the Headline

Given that Microsoft was unwilling to fight the battle in court, the safe strategy would have been not to spend $4 million on the merger plans in the first place. Since Microsoft's share of the financial software market was 20 percent and Intuit's was 70 percent, Microsoft should have realized that the only way the merger would be allowed is if it received special consideration from the Justice Department because of an emerging new technology or increased efficiency as a result of the merger. As we learned in this chapter, the Justice Department generally challenges mergers when the relevant Herfindahl-Hirshman index is greater than 1,800 and the resulting increase in the index as a result of the merger is more than 100. Based on the reported market shares of Microsoft and Intuit, the Herfindahl-Hirshman index for the personal finance software market was at least 5,300 before the proposed merger, and would have increased to at least 8,100 after the merger. Thus, it seems that Microsoft should have realized that the Justice Department would attempt to block the merger. Spending $4 million attempting to justify the merger on technological or efficiency grounds was a gamble that did not pay off for Microsoft.

Summary

This chapter reveals that different industries have different market structures and require different types of managerial decisions. The structure of an industry, and therefore the job of the manager, is dependent on the number of firms in the industry, the structure of demand and costs, the availability of information, and the behavior of other firms in the industry.

The four-firm concentration ratio is one measure of market structure. If the ratio equals one, the industry is a monopoly or oligopoly; if it is zero the industry is competitive. Another measure of market structure is the Herfindahl-Hirshman index (HHI), which can range from 10,000 for a monopoly to zero for a perfectly competitive industry. Of course, these indices must be used in conjunction with other information, including whether the market is local and whether the firm competes with foreign firms.

Other summary statistics include the Lerner index, the Rothschild index, and the Dansby-Willig index. These indices provide a manager information about industry cost and demand conditions. For instance, the greater the Lerner index in an industry, the greater the ability of a firm in the industry to charge a high markup on its product. The information needed to construct these indices can be obtained from sources listed in the resource list provided in the Appendix.

The data presented in this chapter reveal industry-wide differences in activities such as advertising and research and development. The remainder of the book will explain why these differences exist, and the optimal managerial decisions for alternative market structures. The next chapter begins with a study of managerial decisions under perfect competition, monopoly, and monopolistic competition.

Key Terms and Concepts

barriers to entry
conglomerate merger
Dansby-Willig index
feedback critique
four-firm concentration ratio
Herfindahl-Hirshman index
  (HHI)
horizontal merger
Lerner index

market structure
monopolistic competition
monopoly
oligopoly
perfect competition
Rothschild index
structure-conduct-performance
  paradigm
vertical merger

Problems

1. Firms like McDonald's and Wendy's sell hamburgers, salads, and other products that are differentiated in nature. While numerous fast-food restaurants exist in most locations, the differentiated nature of the firms' products permits them to charge prices that are in excess of marginal cost. Given these observations, is the fast-food industry most likely a perfectly competitive industry, a monopoly, monopolistically

competitive, or an oligopoly? Use the causal view of structure, conduct, and performance to explain the role of product differentiation in the industry, and explain how the feedback critique applies in this context.

2. An unemployed MBA has managerial expertise that is geared towards operating a firm with market power. Based on the numbers reported in Table 7–4, which industries represent the best match for the manager's expertise? What factors in the industries do you think give rise to the differences in market power?

3. During a sales meeting one of the regional managers of Toga Industries remarked that structural variables such as advertising and R&D activities by rival firms were likely to hamper the firm's sales over the next year. The manager received numerous stares after making the remark. Why?

4. Alpha Industries operates in a highly competitive market. While there are few other firms in the industry due to the high fixed costs of building plants, rival firms are very aggressive in their pricing strategies. Of the products sold in the industry, over 80 percent have 10 years of patent protection remaining. Does this industry meet an economist's definition of a perfectly competitive industry?

5. It is sometimes said that a manager of a monopoly can charge any price and customers will still have to buy the product. Do you agree or disagree? Why?

6. Omega Travel competes in the highly competitive market for travel. Consumers know that Omega has the best agents in the industry and offers superior service. Nonetheless, Omega earns zero economic profits because numerous competitors have entered the market over the last few years. Based on this information, does Omega operate in a perfectly competitive market? Why or why not?

7. "The law of comparative advantage suggests that managers should specialize in learning the tools needed to manage either a monopoly, oligopoly, monopolistically competitive, or perfectly competitive firm." Do you agree with this statement? Explain.

8. In Tuna, Texas, the retail gasoline market consists of six firms. Firm 1 has 35 percent of the market, Firm 2 has 25 percent, and the remaining firms have 10 percent each. What is the four-firm concentration ratio for this industry?

9. The widget industry is comprised of six firms of varying sizes. Firm 1 has 35 percent of the market, Firm 2 has 25 percent, and the remaining firms have 10 percent each. What is the Herfindahl-Hirshman index for the widget industry? Based on the U.S. Department of Justice merger guidelines described in the text, do you think the Justice Department would be likely to block a merger between firms 5 and 6?

10. The Beta Corporation operates in an industry that has a Herfindahl-Hirshman index of 800. Beta wants to merge with Alpha Enterprises, but Alpha has argued that the merger will be blocked by the Justice Department. Are there conditions under which the Justice Department would allow the merger? Explain.

11. Borris Industries operates in an industry that has a Rothschild index of 0.75. The firm gained access to a government report that revealed the own price elasticity of market demand within the industry to be -3. Use this information to obtain an estimate of the own price elasticity of demand for the product produced by Borris Industries.

12. Zelda Manufacturing has a rather unique product that sells for $15 per unit, and the marginal cost is $7.50. Determine the Lerner index for Zelda Manufacturing. Does this index indicate market power?

13. Based on the information in Table 7–4, which of the following industries resembles perfect competition? Why?
    a. Agriculture.
    b. Communications and utilities.
    c. Services.
    d. Finance.

14. Determine whether integration between the following types of firms would constitute a horizontal, vertical, or conglomerate merger.
    a. A food company and a drug company.
    b. A milk producer and a cheese producer.
    c. A computer chip manufacturer and a silicon producer.

15. Star Computer and a small telecommunications company are considering a merger. A socially minded member of Star Computer's board of directors is against the merger, however, because she is concerned that the merger might not benefit society as a whole. Provide the board member with an argument for why it may be socially beneficial for the merger to take place.

16. Do you think the Justice Department would block a merger between two firms in the breakfast cereal industry? Explain.

17. In a recent television interview, a consumer activist complained that for every dollar consumers spend on clothing, clothing manufacturers earn $.75 in profit. Is this complaint based on fact or fiction? Explain.

18. Based on what you have learned in this chapter, which industry do you believe has the most market power in the United States? The least market power? Defend your answer.

19. A host of best-selling books advance the thesis that increases in conglomerate mergers and concentration of U.S. industry are responsible for "obscene profits." Do you agree? Explain, using the Lerner index.

Selected Readings

Conant, John L., "The Role of Managerial Discretion in Union Mergers." *Journal of Economic Behavior and Organization* 20(1), January 1993, pp. 49–62.

Dansby, R. E. and Willig, R. D., "Industry Performance Gradient Indexes." *American Economic Review* 69, 1979, pp. 249–60.

Davis, Douglas D. and Holt, Charles A., "Market Power and Mergers in Laboratory Markets with Posted Prices." *Rand Journal of Economics* 25(3), Autumn 1994, pp. 467–87.

Golbe, Devra L. and White, Lawrence J., "Catch a Wave: The Time Series Behavior of Mergers." *Review of Economics and Statistics* 75(3), August 1993, pp. 493–99.

Johnson, Ronald N. and Parkman, Allen M., "Premerger Notification and the Incentive to Merge and Litigate." *Journal of Law, Economics and Organization* 7(1), Spring 1991, pp. 145–62.

Kim, E. Han and Singal, Vijay, "Mergers and Market Power: Evidence from the Airline Industry." *American Economic Review* 83(3), June 1993, pp. 549–69.

Lerner, A. P., "The Concept of Monopoly and the Measurement of Monopoly Power." *Review of Economic Studies*, October 1933, pp. 157–75.

O'Neill, Patrick B., "Concentration Trends and Profitability in U.S. Manufacturing: A Further Comment and Some New (and Improved) Evidence." *Applied Economics* 25(10), October 1993, pp. 1285–86.

Rothschild, K. W., "The Degree of Monopoly." *Economica* 9, 1942, pp. 24–39.

"Symposia: Horizontal Mergers and Antitrust." *Journal of Economic Perspectives* 1(2), Fall 1987.

APPENDIX
DATA SOURCES FOR MANAGERS

Information is one of a manager's most valuable assets. In this appendix, we provide a brief overview of data sources available to managers.

The Wall Street Journal

The Wall Street Journal is a business newspaper that is a highly useful information source for managers. It contains general information about trends in the economy, recent mergers and acquisitions, and government regulations. A section called "The Market Place" provides insights into strategies used by firms to enhance sales and market penetration.

Fortune and Forbes

Fortune and *Forbes* are business magazines that contain detailed information about individual firms in various industries. Numerous "special issues" are published that provide information about firms' profits and sales, changes in profits and sales by industry, and compensation paid to top executives at major U.S. firms.

Federal Reserve Publications

Regional Federal Reserve Banks publish reviews that provide insights into the economic outlook of the regional and national economies. For instance, the Federal Reserve Bank of Cleveland publishes *Economic Review*, the Federal Reserve Bank of St. Louis publishes *Review*, the Federal Reserve Bank of Dallas publishes *Economic Review*, and the Federal Reserve Bank of Philadelphia publishes *Business Review*.

World Wide Web

Numerous computer databases provide information for managers. America Online, Prodigy, and CompuServe provide a host of information ranging from stock quotes and profits of firms to flight information. Citibase provides detailed statistics about industries, including profits, sales, and employment. It also contains data on interest rates as well as data on the composition of the population and work force. The Dow Jones News Retrieval Service provides online access to articles carried by major wire services. My homepage on the Web (http://packrat.la.psu.edu/~mbaye/bayehom.htm) also contains information and links to other sites of interest.

Economic Journals

Numerous economic journals provide estimates of elasticities of demand for various goods and services. The *Review of Economics and Statistics* traditionally publishes regression results for problems of interest to managers, including demand and cost functions. Each issue contains estimates of elasticities of some underlying economic relationship. *Applied Economics* also publishes empirical studies of demand and costs. *The Journal of Human Resources* publishes studies of labor demand and supply. The *Journal of Economic Perspectives* publishes descriptive articles that provide managers with an overview of specific economic issues. For instance, a recent issue focused on the economics of horizontal mergers. The *Journal of Economics and Management Strategy* specializes in articles that are of particular interest to managers.

Statistical Abstracts of the United States

Statistical Abstracts of the United States provides voluminous data on wages, the composition of the population, prices, and other information.

The Economic Report of the President

The Economic Report of the President is published each February by the President's Council of Economic Advisers. The first part of the report contains a description of government policy objectives and an overview of the economy. The second part contains numerous statistics on the economy, including inflation, employment, interest rates, profits, and exports.

Managing in Competitive, Monopolistic, and Monopolistically Competitive Markets

---

Headline

No Profits, No Cake for Japanese VCR Makers

The 20th birthday of the VCR industry came and went in 1992 with no fanfare in Japan, where VCRs were first innovated. After seventeen years of growth in sales, Japanese producers have experienced three years of shrinking sales because of saturation in the market and increased foreign competition. In Japan over 80 percent of the households already own one or more VCRs. This has led to lagging sales in Japan's domestic market. The biggest market in the world for Japanese-made VCRs had been the United States, but consumers there have recently opted for cheaper versions produced in Southeast Asia and South Korea.

Why do you think profits of VCR makers like Matsushita, Toshiba, Hitachi, JVC, and Sanyo declined, and what strategies might they employ to bolster their profits?

Introduction

In the previous chapter, we examined the nature of industries and saw that industries differ with respect to their underlying structures, conduct, and performances. In this chapter, we characterize the optimal price and output decisions of managers operating in environments of (1) perfect competition, (2) monopoly, and (3) monopolistic competition. We will analyze oligopoly decisions in Chapters 9 and 10 and examine more sophisticated pricing strategies in Chapter 11. With an understanding of the concepts presented in these chapters, you will be prepared to manage a firm that operates in virtually any environment.

Because this is the beginning of our analysis of output decisions of managers operating in an industry, it is logical to start with the most simple case: a situation where managerial decisions have no perceptible impact on the market price. Thus, in the first section of this chapter we will analyze output decisions of managers operating in perfectly competitive markets. In subsequent sections, we will examine output decisions by firms that have market power: monopoly and monopolistic competition. The analysis in this chapter will serve as a building block for the analyses in the remainder of the book.

Perfect Competition

perfectly competitive market
A market in which (1) there are many buyers and sellers; (2) each firm produces a homogeneous product; (3) buyers and sellers have perfect information; (4) there are no transaction costs; and (5) there is free entry and exit.

We begin our analysis by analyzing the output decisions of managers operating in perfectly competitive markets. The key conditions for *perfect competition* are as follows:

1. There are many buyers and sellers in the market, each of which is "small" relative to the market.
2. Each firm in the market produces a homogeneous (identical) product.
3. Buyers and sellers have perfect information.
4. There are no transaction costs.
5. There is free entry into and exit from the market.

Taken together, the first four assumptions imply that no single firm can influence the price of the product. The fact that there are many small firms, each selling an identical product, means that consumers view the products of all firms in the market as perfect substitutes. Because there is perfect information, consumers know the quality and price of each firm's product. There are no transaction costs (such as the cost of traveling to a store); if one firm charged a slightly higher price than the other firms, consumers would not shop at that firm but instead would purchase from a firm charging a lower price. Thus, in a perfectly competitive market all firms charge the same price for the good, and this price is determined by the interaction of all buyers and sellers in the market.

The assumption of free entry and exit simply implies that additional firms can enter the market if economic profits are being earned, and firms are free to leave the market if they are sustaining losses. As we will show later in this chapter, this assumption implies that in the long run, firms operating in a perfectly competitive market earn zero economic profits.

One classic example of a perfectly competitive market is agriculture. There are many farmers and ranchers, and each is so small relative to the market that he or she has no perceptible impact on the prices of corn, wheat, pork, or beef. Agricultural products tend to be homogeneous; there is little difference between corn produced by farmer Jones and corn produced by farmer Smith. The retail mail-order market for computer software and computer memory chips also is close to perfect competition. A quick look at the back of a computer magazine reveals that there are hundreds of mail-order computer product retailers, each selling identical brands of software packages and memory chips and charging the same price for a given product. The reason there is so little price variation is that if one mail-order firm charged a higher price than a competitor, consumers would purchase from another retailer.

Demand at the Market and the Firm

No single firm operating in a perfectly competitive market exerts any influence on price; price is determined by the interaction of all buyers and sellers in the market. The firm manager must charge this "market price" or consumers will purchase from a firm charging a lower price. Before we characterize the profit-maximizing output decisions of managers operating in perfectly competitive markets, it is important to explain more precisely the relation between the market demand for a product and the demand for a product produced by an individual perfectly competitive firm.

In a competitive market, price is determined by the intersection of the market supply and demand curves. Because the market supply and demand curves depend on all buyers and sellers, the market price is outside the control of a single perfectly competitive firm. In other words, because the individual firm is "small" relative to the market, it has no perceptible influence on the market price.

firm demand curve
The demand curve for an individual firm's product; in a perfectly competitive market, is simply the market price.

Figure 8–1 illustrates the distinction between the market demand curve and the demand curve facing a perfectly competitive firm. The left-hand panel depicts the market, where the equilibrium price, P^e, is determined by the intersection of the market supply and demand curves. From the individual firm's point of view, the firm can sell as much as it wishes at a price of P^e; thus, the demand curve facing an individual perfectly competitive firm is given by the horizontal line in the right-hand panel, labeled D^f. The fact that the individual firm's demand curve is perfectly elastic reflects the fact that if the firm charged a price even slightly above the market price, it would sell nothing. Thus, in a perfectly competitive market, the demand curve for an individual firm's product is simply the market price.

Since the demand curve for an individual perfectly competitive firm's product is perfectly elastic, the pricing decision of the individual firm is trivial: Charge the price that every other firm in the industry charges. All that remains is to determine how much output should be produced to maximize profits.

FIGURE 8–1

Demand at the market and firm levels under perfect competition

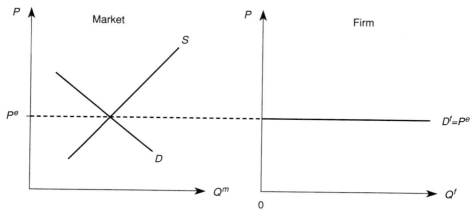

Short-Run Output Decisions

Recall that the short run is the period of time in which there are some fixed factors of production. For example, suppose a building is leased at a cost of $10,000 for a one-year period. In the short run (for one year) these costs are fixed, and they are paid regardless of whether the firm produces zero or 1 million units of output. In the long run (after the lease is up), this cost is variable; the firm can decide whether or not to renew the lease. To maximize profits in the short run, the manager must take as given the fixed inputs (and thus the fixed costs) and determine how much output to produce given the variable inputs that are within his or her control. The next subsection characterizes the profit-maximizing output decision of the manager of a perfectly competitive firm.

Maximizing Profits

marginal revenue
The change in revenue attributable to the last unit of output; for a competitive firm, MR is the market price.

Under perfect competition, the demand for an individual firm's product is the market price of output, which we denote P. If we let Q represent the output of the firm, the total revenue to the firm of producing Q units is $R = PQ$. Since each unit of output can be sold at the market price of P, each unit adds exactly P dollars to revenues. As Figure 8–2 illustrates, there is a linear relation between revenues and the output of a competitive firm. *Marginal revenue* is the change in revenue attributable to the last unit of output. Geometrically, it is the slope of the revenue curve. Expressed in economic terms, the marginal revenue for a competitive firm is the market price.

FIGURE 8–2

Revenue, costs, and profits for a perfectly competitive firm

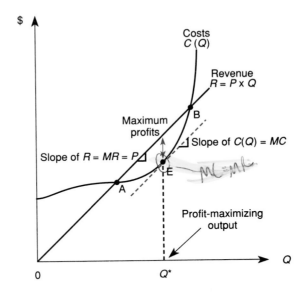

A Calculus Alternative

Marginal revenue is the derivative of the revenue function. If revenues are a function of output,

$$R = R(Q),$$

then

$$MR = \frac{dR}{dQ}.$$

Principle

Competitive Firm's Demand
The demand curve for a competitive firm's product is a horizontal line at the market price. This price is the competitive firm's marginal revenue:

$$D^f = P = MR.$$

A Calculus Alternative

Marginal revenue is the derivative of the revenue function. For a perfectly competitive firm, revenue is

$$R = PQ.$$

where P is the market equilibrium price. Thus,

$$MR = \frac{dR}{dQ} = \frac{d[PQ]}{dQ} = P.$$

The profits of a perfectly competitive firm are simply the difference between revenues and costs:

$$\pi = PQ - C(Q).$$

Geometrically, profits are given by the vertical distance between the cost function, labeled $C(Q)$ in Figure 8–2, and the revenue line. Note that for output levels to the left of A, the cost curve lies above the revenue line, which implies that the firm would make losses if it produced any output to the left of point A. The same is true of output levels to the right of point B.

For output levels between points A and B, the revenue line lies above the cost curve. This implies that these outputs generate positive levels of profit. The profit-maximizing level of output is the level at which the vertical distance between the revenue line and the cost line is greatest. This is given by the output level Q^* in Figure 8–2.

There is a very important geometric property of the profit-maximizing level of output. As we see in Figure 8–2, the slope of the cost curve at the profit-maximizing level of output (point E) exactly equals the slope of the total revenue line. Recall that the slope of the cost curve is marginal cost and the slope of the revenue line is marginal revenue. Therefore, the profit-maximizing output is the output at which marginal revenue equals marginal cost. Since marginal revenue is equal to the market price for a perfectly competitive firm, the manager must equate price with marginal cost to maximize profits.

An alternative way to express the competitive output rule is depicted in Figure 8–3, where standard average and marginal cost curves have been drawn. If the market price is given by P^e, this price intersects the marginal cost curve at an output of Q^*. Thus, Q^* represents the profit-maximizing level of output. For outputs below Q^*, price exceeds marginal cost. This implies that by expanding output, the firm can sell additional units at a price that exceeds the cost of producing the additional units. Thus, a profit-maximizing firm will not choose to produce output levels below Q^*. Similarly, output levels above Q^* correspond to the situation in which marginal cost exceeds price. In this instance, a reduction in output would reduce costs by more than it would reduce revenue. Thus, Q^* is the profit-maximizing level of output.

The shaded rectangle in Figure 8–3 represents the maximum profits of the firm. To see this, note that the area of the shaded rectangle is given by its base (Q^*) times the height $[P^e - ATC(Q^*)]$. Recall that $ATC(Q^*) = C(Q^*)/Q^*$; that is, average total cost is total cost divided by output. The area of the shaded rectangle is

$$Q^*\left[P^e - \frac{C(Q^*)}{Q^*}\right] = P^e Q^* - C(Q^*),$$

which is the definition of profits. Intuitively, $[P^e - ATC(Q^*)]$ represents the profits per unit produced. When this is multiplied by the profit-maximizing

FIGURE 8–3

Profit maximization under perfect competition

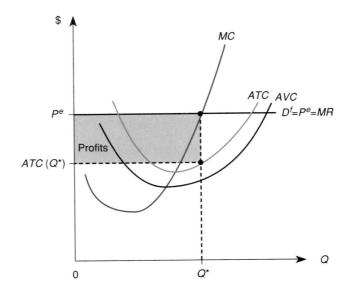

level of output (Q^*), the result is the amount of total profits earned by the firm.

Principle

Competitive Output Rule
To maximize profits, a perfectly competitive firm produces the output at which price equals marginal cost in the range over which marginal cost is increasing:

$$P = MC(Q).$$

A Calculus Alternative

The profits of a perfectly competitive firm are

$$\pi = PQ - C(Q).$$

The first-order condition for maximizing profits requires that the marginal profits be zero:

$$\frac{d\pi}{dQ} = P - \frac{dC(Q)}{dQ} = 0.$$

Thus, we obtain the profit-maximizing rule for a firm in perfect competition.

$$P = \frac{dC}{dQ},$$

or

$$P = MC.$$

DEMONSTRATION PROBLEM 8–1

The cost function for a firm is given by

$$C(Q) = 5 + Q^2.$$

If the firm sells output in a perfectly competitive market and other firms in the industry sell output at a price of $20, what price should the manager of this firm put on the product? What level of output should be produced to maximize profits? How much profits will be earned?
(Hint: Recall that for a cubic cost function,

$$C(Q) = f + aQ + bQ^2 + cQ^3,$$

the marginal cost function is

$$MC(Q) = a + 2bQ + 3cQ^2.$$

Since $a = 0$, $b = 1$, and $c = 0$ for the cost function in this problem, we see that the marginal cost function for the firm is $MC(Q) = 2Q$.)

Answer

Since the firm competes in a perfectly competitive market, it must charge the same price other firms charge; thus, the manager should price the product at $20. To find the profit-maximizing output, we must equate price with marginal cost. This firm's marginal costs are $MC = 2Q$. Equating this with price yields

$$20 = 2Q,$$

so the profit-maximizing level of output is 10 units. The maximum profits are thus

$$\pi = (20)(10) - (5 + 10^2) = 200 - 5 - 100 = \$95.$$

Minimizing Losses

In the previous section, we demonstrated the optimal level of output to maximize profits. In some instances, short-run losses are inevitable. Here we analyze procedures for minimizing losses in the short run. If losses are sustained in the long run, the best thing for the firm to do is exit the industry.

Short-Run Operating Losses.   Consider first a situation where there are some fixed costs of production. Suppose the market price, P^e, lies below the average total cost curve but above the average variable cost curve, as in Figure 8–4. In this instance, if the firm produces the output Q^*, where $P^e = MC$, a loss of the shaded area will result. However, since the price exceeds the average variable cost, each unit sold generates more revenue than the cost per unit of the variable inputs. Thus, the firm should continue to produce in the short run, even though it is incurring losses.

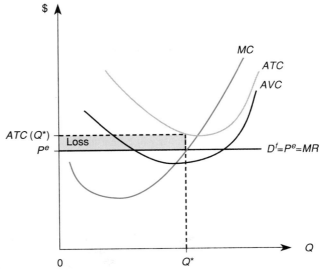

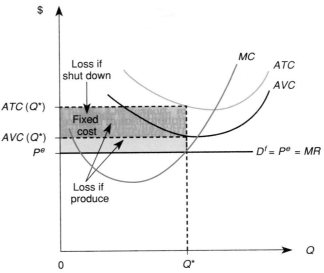

The Decision to Shut Down.   Now suppose the market price is so low that it lies below the average variable cost, as in Figure 8–5. If the firm produced Q^*, where $P^e = MC$ in the range of increasing marginal cost, it would incur a loss equal to the sum of the two shaded rectangles in Figure 8–5. In other words, for each unit sold, the firm would lose

$$ATC(Q^*) - P^e.$$

When this per-unit loss is multiplied by Q^*, negative profits result that correspond to the sum of the two shaded rectangles in Figure 8–5.

Now suppose that instead of producing Q^* units of output, this firm decided to shut down its operation. In this instance, its losses would equal its fixed costs, that is, those costs that must be paid even if no output is produced. Geometrically, fixed costs are represented by the top rectangle in Figure 8–5, since the area of this rectangle is

$$[ATC(Q^*) - AVC(Q^*)]Q^*,$$

which equals total fixed costs. Thus, when price is less than the average variable cost of production, the firm loses less by shutting down its operation (and producing zero) than it does by producing Q^* units. To summarize, we have demonstrated the following principle:

Principle

Short-Run Output Decision under Perfect Competition
To maximize short-run profits, a perfectly competitive firm should produce in the range of increasing marginal cost where $P = MC$, provided that $P \geq AVC$. If $P < AVC$, the firm should shut down its plant to minimize its losses.

DEMONSTRATION PROBLEM 8–2

Suppose the cost function for a firm is given by $C(Q) = 100 + Q^2$. If the firm sells output in a perfectly competitive market and other firms in the industry sell output at a price of $10, what level of output should the firm produce to maximize profits or minimize losses? What will be the level of profits or losses if the firm makes the optimal decision?

Answer

First, note that there are fixed costs of 100 and variable costs of Q^2, so the question deals with a short-run scenario. If the firm produces a positive level of output, it will produce where price equals marginal cost. The firm's marginal costs are $MC = 2Q$. Equating this with price yields $10 = 2Q$, or $Q = 5$ units. The average variable cost of producing 5 units of output is $AVC = 5^2/5 = 25/5 = 5$. Since $P \geq AVC$, the firm should produce 5 units in the short run. By producing 5 units of output, the firm incurs a loss of

$$\pi = (10)(5) - (100 + 5^2) = 50 - 100 - 25 = -\$75,$$

which is less than the loss of $100 (fixed costs) that would result if the firm shut down its plant in the short run.

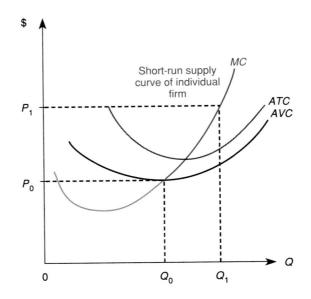

The Short-Run Firm and Industry Supply Curves

The Short-Run Firm and Industry Supply Curves

Now that you understand how perfectly competitive firms determine their output, we will examine how to derive firm and industry short-run supply curves.

Recall that the profit-maximizing perfectly competitive firm produces the output at which price equals marginal cost. For example, when the price is given by P_0 as in Figure 8–6, the firm produces Q_0 units of output (the point where $P = MC$ in the range of increasing marginal cost). When the price is P_1, the firm produces Q_1 units of output. For prices between P_0 and P_1, output is determined by the intersection of price and marginal cost.

When the price falls below the *AVC* curve, however, the firm produces zero units, because it does not cover the variable costs of production. Thus, to determine how much a perfectly competitive firm will produce at each price, we simply determine the output at which marginal cost equals that price. To ensure that the firm will produce a positive level of output, price must be above the average variable cost curve.

Principle

The Firm's Short-Run Supply Curve
The short-run supply curve for a perfectly competitive firm is its marginal cost curve above the minimum point on the *AVC* curve, as illustrated in Figure 8–6.

The market (or industry) supply curve is closely related to the supply curve of individual firms in a perfectly competitive industry. Recall that the

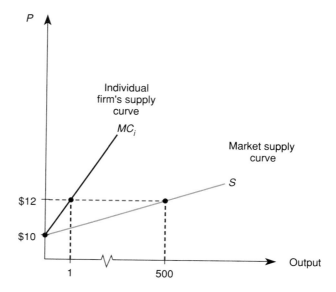

market supply curve reveals the total quantity that will be produced in the
market at each possible price. Since the amount an individual firm will produce at a given price is determined by its marginal cost curve, the horizontal
sum of the marginal costs of all firms determines how much total output will
be produced at each price. More specifically, since each firm's supply curve
is the firm's marginal cost curve above the minimum *AVC*, the market supply
curve for a perfectly competitive industry is the horizontal sum of the individual marginal costs above their respective *AVC* curves.

Figure 8–7 illustrates the relation between an individual firm's supply
function (MC_i) and the market supply function (S) for a perfectly competitive industry composed of 500 firms. When the price is $10, each firm pro-
duces zero units, and thus total industry output also is zero. When the price
is $12, each firm produces 1 unit, so the total output produced by all 500
firms is 500 units. Notice that the industry supply curve is flatter than the
supply curve of an individual firm and that the more firms in the industry,
the farther to the right is the market supply curve.

Long-Run Decisions

One important assumption underlying the theory of perfect competition is
that of free entry and exit. If firms earn short-run economic profits, in the
long run additional firms will enter the industry in an attempt to reap some
of those profits. As more firms enter the industry, the industry supply curve
shifts to the right. This is illustrated in Figure 8–8 as the shift from S^0 to
S^1, which lowers the equilibrium market price from P^0 to P^1. This shifts

FIGURE 8–8

Entry and exit: the market and firm's demand

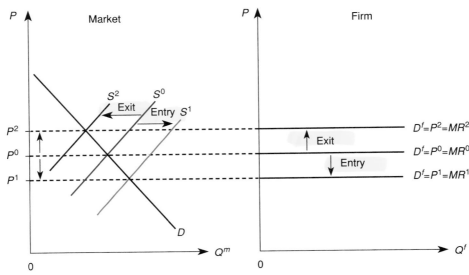

down the demand curve for an individual firm's product, which in turn lowers its profits.

If firms in a competitive industry sustain short-run losses, in the long run they will exit the industry since they are not covering their opportunity costs. As firms exit the industry, the market supply curve decreases from S^0 in Figure 8–8 to S^2, thus increasing the market price from P^0 to P^2. This, in turn, shifts up the demand curve for an individual firm's product, which increases the profits of the firms remaining in the industry.

The process just described continues until ultimately the market price is such that all firms in the market earn zero economic profits. This is the case in Figure 8–9. At the price of P^e, each firm receives just enough to cover the average costs of production (AC is used because in the long run there is no distinction between fixed and variable costs), and profits are zero. If profits were positive, entry would occur and the market price would fall until the demand curve for an individual firm's product was just tangent to the AC curve. If profits were negative, exit would occur, increasing the market price until the firm demand curve was tangent to the AC curve.

Principle

Long-Run Competitive Equilibrium
In the long run, perfectly competitive firms produce a level of output such that

1. $P = MC$.
2. $P = $ minimum of AC.

FIGURE 8–9

Long-run competitive equilibrium

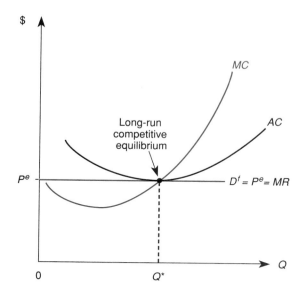

These long-run properties of perfectly competitive markets have two important welfare implications. First, note that the market price is equal to the marginal cost of production. The market price reflects the value to society of an additional unit of output. This valuation is based on the preferences of all consumers in the market. Marginal cost reflects the cost to society of producing another unit of output. These costs represent the resources that would have to be taken from some other sector of the economy to produce more output in this industry.

To see why it is important, from a social perspective, that price equal marginal cost, suppose price exceeded marginal cost in equilibrium. This would imply that society would value another unit of output more than it would cost to produce another unit of output. If the industry produced an output such that price exceeded marginal cost, it would thus be inefficient; social welfare would be improved by expanding output. Since in a competitive industry price equals marginal cost, the industry produces the socially efficient level of output.

The second thing to note about long-run competitive equilibrium is that price equals the minimum point on the average cost curve. This implies not only that firms are earning zero economic profits (that is, just covering their opportunity costs) but also that all economies of scale have been exhausted. There is no way to produce the output at a lower average cost of production.

It is important to remember the distinction we made in Chapter 5 between economic profits and accounting profits. The fact that a firm in a perfectly competitive industry earns zero economic profits in the long run does not mean that accounting profits are zero; rather, zero economic profits implies that accounting profits are just high enough to offset any implicit costs of production, which include the opportunity costs. The firm earns no

Inside Business 8–1

Competition in the Poultry Market

The years 1983–1991 showed continuous but falling profits in the poultry industry. Because of positive profits in the industry, the market capacity for producing broilers grew over that eight-year span. The expansion came from existing farms adding capacity and from new farms entering the industry.

Figure 8–10 shows representative market supply and demand curves and a potential cost structure for an individual farm. S^1 in Figure 8–10(a) is the market supply as it was in 1983 before expansion. With market supply of S^1, the equilibrium price is P_1 in panel a. In panel b, an individual firm chooses to produce q_1 units of output, resulting in profits of the area ABCD for each firm. The profits in the industry induce entry. The increased entry shifts the market supply curve to the right, as shown by the shift from S^1 to S^2 in Figure 8–10(a). This increase in supply reduces the equilibrium price to P_2. The new market equilibrium is at point Z in Figure 8–10(a) and results in more chicken being purchased at a lower price. When the price declines to P_2, each individual farm decreases its output to q_2 in Figure 8–10(b), where the new price equals marginal cost. The new price also results in lower profits, which are now area EFGH in panel b. However, enough farms enter the market that total market output actually increases, even though individual farm output declines.

The preceding description of the broiler industry using the perfectly competitive model reflects what happened in the broiler industry from 1990–1992. Prices in the broiler industry declined from $.55 per pound in 1990 to $.51 in 1991 to $.47 in 1992. At the same time prices were declining, so were profits. Profits per pound declined from $.08 in 1990 to $.03 in 1992. In fact, the profits per pound in 1992 were approximately a 7 percent return on investment. This was very close to zero economic profits, since the opportunity cost of investing elsewhere in 1992 was about 7 percent. Further entry is unlikely unless cost or demand conditions change.

Source: Jon F. Scheid, "Poultry Markets Slow from Competition," *Feedstuffs*, December 16, 1991, p. 6.

more, and no less, than it could earn by using the resources in some other capacity. This is why firms continue to produce in the long run even though their economic profits are zero.

Monopoly

In the previous section, we characterized the optimal output decisions of firms that are small relative to the total market. In this context, *small* means the firms have no control whatsoever over the prices they charge for the product. In this section, we will consider the opposite extreme: monopoly. *Monopoly* refers to a situation where a single firm serves an entire market for a good for which there are no close substitutes.

monopoly
A market structure in which a single firm serves an entire market for a good that has no close substitutes.

Monopoly Power

In determining whether a market is characterized by monopoly, it is important to specify the relevant market for the product. For example, utility com-

FIGURE 8–10

Entry shrinks profits

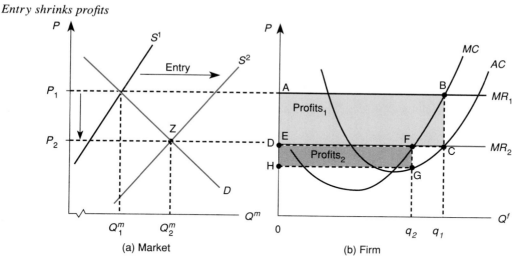

panies are local monopolies in that only one utility offers service to a given neighborhood. To be sure, there are almost as many utility companies as there are cities in the world, but the utilities do not directly compete against one another for customers. The substitutes for electric services in a given city are poor and, short of moving to a different city, consumers must pay the price for local utility services or go without electricity. It is in this sense that a utility company is a monopoly in the local market for utility services.

When one thinks of a monopoly, one usually envisions a very large firm. This needn't be the case, however; the relevant consideration is whether there are other firms selling close substitutes for the good in a given market. For example, a gas station located in a small town that is several hundred miles from another gas station is a monopolist in that town. In a large town there typically are many gas stations, and the market for gasoline is not characterized by monopoly.

The fact that a firm is the sole seller of a good in a market clearly gives that firm greater market power than it would have if it competed against other firms for consumers. A monopolist does not have unlimited power, however. Since there is only one producer in the market, the market demand curve is the demand curve for the monopolist's product. This is in contrast to the case of perfect competition, where the demand curve for an individual firm is perfectly elastic.

Figure 8–11 depicts the demand curve for a monopolist. Since all consumers in the market demand the good from the monopolist, the market demand curve, D^M, is the same as the demand for the firm's product, D^f. In the absence of legal restrictions, the monopolist is free to charge any price for the product. But this does not mean the firm can sell as much as it wants to at that price. Given the price set by the monopolist, consumers decide

FIGURE 8–11

*The monopolist's
demand*

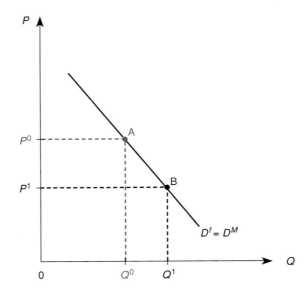

how much to purchase. For example, if the monopolist sets the relatively low price of P^1, the quantity demanded by consumers is Q^1. The monopolist can set a higher price of P^0, but there will be a lower quantity demanded of Q^0 at that price.

In summary, the monopolist is restricted by consumers to choose only those price-quantity combinations along the market demand curve. The monopolist can choose a price or a quantity, but not both. The monopolist can sell higher quantities only by lowering the price. If the price is too high, consumers may choose to buy nothing at all.

Sources of Monopoly Power

The next issue we will address is how a firm obtains monopoly power, that is, why a monopolist has no competitors. There are four primary sources of monopoly power. One or more of these sources create a barrier to entry that prevents other firms from entering the market to compete against the monopolist.

Economies of Scale

The first source of monopoly power we will discuss is technological in nature. First, however, it is useful to recall some important terminology. *Economies of scale* exist whenever average total costs decline as output increases. *Diseconomies of scale* exist whenever average total costs increase as output increases. For many technologies, there is a range over which economies of scale exist and a range over which diseconomies exist. For example in Figure 8–12 there are economies of scale for output levels below

economies of scale
Exist whenever
average total costs
decline as output
increases.

FIGURE 8–12

*Economies of scale
and minimum prices*

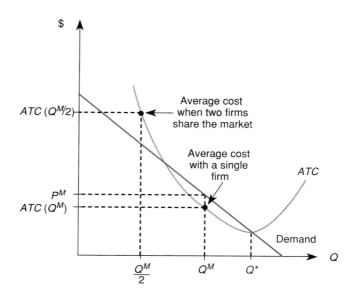

Average cost
when two firms
share the market

Average cost
with a single
firm

ATC

$ATC(Q^M/2)$

P^M
$ATC(Q^M)$

Demand

Q

$\dfrac{Q^M}{2}$ Q^M Q^*

**diseconomies of
scale**
Exist whenever
average total costs
increase as output
increases.

Q^* (since *ATC* is declining in this range) and diseconomies of scale for output levels above Q^* (since *ATC* is increasing this range).

Notice in Figure 8–12 that if the market were composed of a single firm
that produced Q^M units, consumers would be willing to pay a price of P^M
per unit for the Q^M units. Since $P^M > ATC(Q^M)$, the firm sells the goods at
a price that is higher than the average cost of production, and thus earns
positive profits. Now suppose another firm entered the market and the two
firms ended up sharing the market (each firm producing $Q^M/2$). The total
quantity produced would be the same, and thus the price would remain at
P^M. But with two firms, each producing only $Q^M/2$ units, each firm has an
average total cost of $ATC(Q^M/2)$—a higher average total cost than when a
single firm produced all of the output. Also notice in Figure 8–12 that each
firm's average cost is greater than P^M, which is the price consumers are
willing to pay for the total Q^M units produced in the market. Having two
firms in the industry leads to losses, but a single firm can earn positive
profits because it has higher volume and enjoys reduced average costs due
to economies of scale. Thus, we see that economies of scale can lead to a
situation where a single firm services the entire market for a good.

This analysis of economies of scale also reveals why it is so important
to define the relevant market when determining whether or not a firm is a
monopolist. As we noted earlier, a gas station may be a monopolist in a
small town located several hundred miles from another gas station, whereas
a gas station situated in a large city is unlikely to be a monopolist. In terms
of Figure 8–12, the demand for gasoline in a small town typically is low
relative to Q^*, which gives rise to economies of scale in the relevant range
(outputs below Q^*). In large cities the demand for gasoline is large relative

Inside Business 8–2

Minimum Efficient Scale and Monopoly Power

How large does a firm need to be to be able to fully exploit all economies of scale? The answer depends on the size of total industry demand in a country as well as on the nature of the underlying technology used to produce the product. One study estimated the number of individual plants needed to fully exploit economies of scale in various markets. Economies of scale are fully exploited when the average cost curve at a given plant is at its minimum. Table 8–1 provides the results of that study for twelve industries and six nations.

Consider the numbers reported for the storage battery industry. In the United States, the size of the market is large enough to permit 53.5 firms to operate in the market, with each plant fully exploiting all economies of scale. In contrast, in Sweden it takes only 1.4 firms to exploit all economies of scale. (Since there cannot be fractional parts of firms, the relevant number of firms is the closest integer.) The storage battery industry in Sweden is a natural monopoly; costs are minimized when only one firm is in the market.

Two aspects of the numbers reported in Table 8–1 bear pointing out. First, there is considerable variation across industries in the number of firms needed to fully exploit economies of scale. In some industries, the number of firms necessary to exploit economies of scale is small, giving rise

to monopoly or oligopoly. In others, such as the shoe industry, the cost structure is compatible with a more competitive market structure.

Second, note that there is also considerable variation across countries in the number of efficiently sized plants that can be accommodated. In Sweden, for instance, the market for cigarettes is not large enough to accommodate even one efficiently sized firm. A firm producing cigarettes in Sweden would have to charge a higher price than firms in all other countries, since the other countries can accommodate one or more efficiently sized firms. This puts producers of cigarettes in Sweden at a disadvantage when competing against firms that ship cigarettes to Sweden. In the presence of such a disadvantage, the Swedish government may impose tariffs or trade restrictions on imports of cigarettes to "protect" Swedish producers. This would benefit the producers, but smokers would end up paying higher prices for cigarettes than they would in the presence of free trade. The same phenomenon has occurred in the refrigerator industry in Canada.

Source: F. M. Scherer, A. Beckenstein, E. Kaufer, and R. D. Murphy, with the assistance of Francine Bougeon-Maassen, *The Economics of Multi-Plant Operation: An International Comparison Study* (Cambridge, Mass., and London: Harvard University Press, 1975).-

to Q^*, which makes it possible for several gas stations to coexist in the market.

Economies of Scope

Recall that *economies of scope* exist when the total cost of producing two outputs within the same firm is lower than when the outputs are produced by separate firms, that is, when it is cheaper to produce outputs Q_1 and Q_2 jointly.

TABLE 8–1   **Number of Efficient Plants Compatible with Domestic Consumption in Six Nations**

	Nation					
	U.S.	*Canada*	*U.K.*	*Sweden*	*France*	*Germany*
Brewing	29.0	2.9	10.9	0.7	4.5	16.1
Cigarettes	15.2	1.3	3.3	0.3	1.6	2.8
Fabrics	451.7	17.4	57.0	10.4	56.9	52.1
Paints	69.8	6.3	9.8	2.0	6.6	8.4
Petroleum refining	51.6	6.0	8.6	2.5	7.7	9.9
Shoes	532.0	59.2	164.5	23.0	128.2	196.9
Glass bottles	65.5	7.2	11.1	1.7	6.6	7.9
Cement	59.0	6.6	16.5	3.5	21.7	28.8
Steel	38.9	2.6	6.5	1.5	5.5	10.1
Bearings	72.0	5.9	22.8	3.3	17.0	n.a.
Refrigerators	7.1	0.7	1.2	0.5	1.7	2.8
Storage batteries	53.5	4.6	7.7	1.4	12.8	10.5

Source: F. M. Scherer, A. Beckenstein, E. Kaufer, and R. D. Murphy, with the assistance of Francine Bougeon-Maassen, *The Economics of Multi-Plant Operation: An International Comparison Study* (Cambridge, Mass., and London: Harvard University Press, 1975), p. 94. Reprinted by permission of the publishers. Copyright © 1975 by the President and Fellows of Harvard College.

In the presence of economies of scope, efficient production requires that a firm produce several products jointly. While multiproduct firms do not necessarily have more market power than firms producing a single product, economies of scope tend to encourage "larger" firms. In turn, this may provide greater access to capital markets, where working capital and funds for investment are obtained. To the extent that smaller firms have more difficulty obtaining funds than do larger firms, the higher cost of capital may serve as a barrier to entry. In extreme cases, the economies of scope can lead to monopoly power.

Cost Complementarity

Cost complementarities exist in a multiproduct cost function when the marginal cost of producing one output is reduced when the output of another product is increased, that is, when an increase in the output of product 2 decreases the marginal cost of producing output 1.

Multiproduct firms that enjoy cost complementarities tend to have lower marginal costs than firms producing a single product. This gives multiproduct firms a cost advantage over single-product firms. Thus, in the presence of cost complementarities, firms must produce several products to be able to compete against the firm with lower marginal costs. To the extent that greater capital requirements exist for multiproduct firms than for single-product firms, this requirement can limit the ability of small firms to enter the market. In extreme cases, monopoly power can result.

Patents and Other Legal Barriers

The sources of monopoly power just described are technological in nature. In some instances, government may grant an individual or a firm a monopoly right. For example, a city may prevent another utility company from competing against the local utility company. The most common example is the monopoly power generated by the patent system.

The patent system gives the inventor of a new product the exclusive right to sell the product for a given period of time (17 years in the United States). The rationale behind granting monopoly power to a new inventor is based on the following argument. Inventions take many years and considerable sums of money to develop. Once an invention becomes public information, in the absence of a patent system, other firms could produce the product and compete against the individual or firm that developed it. Since these firms do not have to expend resources developing the product, they would make higher profits than the original developer. In the absence of a patent system, there would be a reduced incentive on the part of firms to develop new technologies and products.

Maximizing Profits

Now that you know what monopoly power is and the factors that lead to monopoly power, we will see how the manager of a monopoly may exploit this power to maximize profits. In particular, in this section we presume that the manager is in charge of a firm that is a monopoly. Our goal is to characterize the price and output decisions that maximize the monopolist's profits.

Marginal Revenue

Suppose the monopolist faces a demand curve for its product such as the one in Figure 8–13(a). In Chapter 3, we learned that a linear demand curve is elastic at high prices and inelastic at low prices. If the monopolist produces zero units of output, its revenues are zero. As output is increased above zero, demand is elastic and the increase in output (which implies a lower price) leads to an increase in total revenue, as shown in Figure 8–13(b). This follows from the total revenue test. As output is increased beyond Q_0 into the inelastic region of demand, further increases in output actually decrease total revenue, until at point D the price is zero and revenues are again zero. This is depicted in Figure 8–13(b). Thus, total revenue is maximized at an output of Q^0 in Figure 8–13(b). This corresponds to the price of P^0 in Figure 8–13(a), where demand is unitary elastic.

The line labeled *MR* in Figure 8–13(a) is the marginal revenue schedule for the monopolist. Recall that marginal revenue is the change in total reve-

Factors That Affect Technological Progress

Many people view technological progress as the result of work by solitary scientists or inventors motivated solely by curiosity. Yet ample evidence suggests that economic factors influence innovation. Thomas Edison, after unsuccessfully trying to sell his first invention (an automatic vote counter), vowed that he would work only on ideas for things that people would buy. The size of the potential market determines the return on invention and therefore influences investment in applied research. Even in universities, the availability of funding influences the direction of basic research.

But invention is only the first step in technological progress. To raise economic growth, an idea must be translated into a marketable product or service, applied on a production line, or built into a new machine. Development, which brings the fruits of research to market, is expensive: two-thirds of U.S. research and development (R&D) expenditures in 1988 were devoted to development rather than to basic or applied research. The actual application of an innovation is an important step beyond development. Information about the technological advance must be disseminated, and workers must be trained to use it. In many cases, it is prohibitively expensive to modify the old capital stock to embody new technology. Therefore, the rate at which new technology actually augments productivity depends in part on the rate at which new capital goods are created, i.e., on the rate of investment. A recent study estimates that 20 percent of the contribution of technological change to growth in the United States between 1949 and 1983 came from advances that were embodied in capital.

Raising the rate of investment in the United States may increase the rate of technological progress in other ways, although the size of these effects is difficult to determine. Higher rates of investment shorten the lag between innovation and use, increasing the return on research efforts and spurring additional advances. Further, use of new capital equipment and facilities may trigger discoveries of new ways of doing business, new production processes, and new potential products.

The United States spent $127.7 billion on R&D in 1987. This level reflects dramatic growth, as real R&D spending grew more than fivefold since 1953 and doubled as a fraction of GNP. As shown in the accompanying table, the United States spends more on R&D than four other leading industrialized nations combined. The share of total world R&D performed by the United States has, however, fallen over the past 25 years as other countries have grown rapidly and have approached or reached the technological frontier.

To the extent that R&D produces knowledge with the same benefits regardless of the size of the economy, the absolute level of R&D spending is the critical measure of R&D investment. An alternative measure of national R&D spending is its intensity—the share of GNP devoted to R&D. The United States, West Germany, and Japan each currently spend about 2.8 percent of their GNP on R&D, with France and the United Kingdom spending only slightly smaller fractions of their GNP (see table). But a larger proportion of the R&D in the United States is defense-related. The $88.6 billion that the United States spent on nondefense R&D in 1987 was a smaller fraction of GNP than were nondefense R&D expenditures in West Germany and Japan.

Although investment in R&D is only part of the explanation for the rate of technological change, it is clearly important. Average private rates of return on R&D investment are extremely high: estimated rates exceed 20 percent a year.

Inside Business 8–3 continued

Inside Business 8–3 concluded

R&D Expenditures for Five Major Industrialized Countries, 1987

	France[1]	West Germany	Japan[2]	United Kingdom[2]	United States
R&D Expenditures (billions of dollars)	16.4	22.8	41.7	15.7	127.7
As a percent of GNP	2.4	2.8	2.8	2.4	2.8
Estimated Nondefense R&D Expenditures (billions of dollars)	13.1	21.6	41.4	11.7	88.6
As a percent of GNP	1.8	2.6	2.8	1.8	2.0

[1]Data for France are based on GDP; consequently, percentages may be slightly overstated compared to GNP.
[2]Data for Japan and the United Kingdom are for 1986.
Note: Foreign currency conversions to U.S. dollars are calculated based on Organization for Economic Cooperation and Development purchasing power parity exchange rates.
Source: National Science Foundation

Moreover, these returns do not reflect all of the returns to R&D, because it is difficult for an innovator to capture all of the benefits of an innovation. Some innovations cannot be patented; some patents are hard to defend; all patents eventually expire. An innovation may have spinoffs or ramifications that others bring to market. Users of the product, as well as the innovator, receive benefits. For these and other reasons, the returns to society of R&D investment are estimated to average twice those to the firm that makes the investment.

Source: Reprinted from *Economic Report of the President* (February 1990), pp. 112–13.

---

nue attributable to the last unit of output; geometrically, it is the slope of the total revenue curve. As Figure 8–13(a) shows, the marginal revenue schedule for a monopolist lies below the demand curve; in fact, for a linear demand curve, the marginal revenue schedule lies exactly halfway between the demand curve and the vertical axis. This means that for a monopolist, marginal revenue is less than the price charged for the good.

There are two ways to understand why the marginal revenue schedule lies below the monopolist's demand curve. Consider first a geometric explanation. Marginal revenue is the slope of the total revenue curve [$R(Q)$] in Figure 8–13(b). As output increases from zero to Q^0, the slope of the total revenue curve decreases until it becomes zero at Q^0. Over this range, marginal revenue decreases until it reaches zero when output is Q^0. As output expands beyond Q^0, the slope of the marginal revenue curve becomes negative and gets increasingly negative as output continues to expand. This means that marginal revenue is negative for outputs in excess of Q^0.

FIGURE 8–13

*Elasticity of demand
and total revenues*

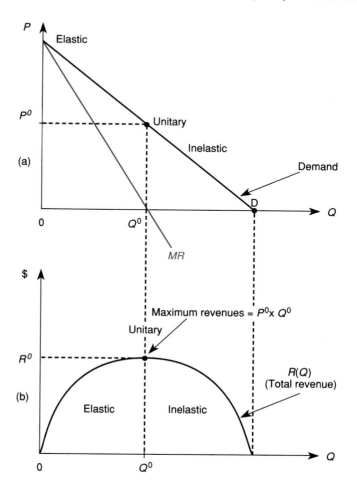

Formula: Monopolist's Marginal Revenue.   The marginal revenue of a monopolist is given by the following formula:

$$MR = P\left[\frac{1 + E}{E}\right],$$

where E is the elasticity of demand for the monopolist's product and P is the price charged for the product.

A Calculus Alternative

The monopolist's revenue is

$$R(Q) = P(Q)Q.$$

Taking the derivative with respect to Q yields

$$\frac{dR}{dQ} = \frac{dP}{dQ}Q + P$$

$$= P\left[\left(\frac{dP}{dQ}\right)\left(\frac{Q}{P}\right) + 1\right]$$

$$= P\left[\frac{1}{E} + 1\right]$$

$$= P\left[\frac{1 + E}{E}\right],$$

where E is the elasticity of demand. Since $dR/dQ = MR$, this means that

$$MR = P\left[\frac{1 + E}{E}\right].$$

DEMONSTRATION PROBLEM 8–3

Show that if demand is elastic (say, $E = -2$), marginal revenue is positive but less than price. Show that if demand is unitary elastic ($E = -1$), marginal revenue is zero. Finally, show that if demand is inelastic (say, $E = -0.5$), marginal revenue is negative.

Answer

Setting $E = -2$ in the marginal revenue formula yields

$$MR = P\left[\frac{1 - 2}{-2}\right] = \frac{-1}{-2}P,$$

so $MR = 0.5P$. Thus, when demand is elastic, marginal revenue is positive but less than price (in this example, marginal revenue is one-half of the price).

Setting $E = -1$ in the marginal revenue formula yields

$$MR = P\left[\frac{1 - 1}{-1}\right] = 0,$$

so $MR = 0$. Thus, when demand is unitary elastic, marginal revenue is zero.

Finally, setting $E = -0.5$ in the marginal revenue formula yields

$$MR = P\left[\frac{1 - .5}{-.5}\right] = P\left[\frac{.5}{-.5}\right] = -P,$$

so $MR = -P$. Thus, when demand is inelastic, marginal revenue is negative and less than price (in this example, marginal revenue is the negative of the price).

An alternative explanation for why marginal revenue is less than price for a monopolist is as follows. Suppose a monopolist sells one unit of output at a price of $4 per unit, for a total revenue of $4. What happens to revenue if the monopolist produces one more unit of output? Revenue increases by less than $4. To see why, note that the monopolist can sell one more unit of output only by lowering price, say, from $4 to $3 per unit. But the price reduction necessary to sell one more unit lowers the price received on the first unit from $4 to $3. The total revenue associated with two units of output thus is $6. The change in revenue due to producing one more unit thus is $2, which is less than the price charged for the product.

Since the price a monopolist can charge for the product depends on how much is produced, let $P(Q)$ represent the price per unit paid by consumers for Q units of output. This relation summarizes the same information as a demand curve, but because price is expressed as a function of quantity instead of the other way around, it is called an *inverse demand function*. The inverse demand function, denoted $P(Q)$, indicates the price per unit as a function of the firm's output. The most common inverse demand function is the linear inverse demand function. The *linear inverse demand function* is given by

$$P(Q) = a + bQ,$$

where a is a number greater than zero and b is a number less than zero.

In addition to the general formula for marginal revenue that is valid for all demand functions, it is useful to have the following formula for marginal revenue, which is valid for the special case of a linear inverse demand function.

Formula: MR for Linear Inverse Demand.   For the linear inverse demand function, $P(Q) = a + bQ$, marginal revenue is given by

$$MR = a + 2bQ.$$

A Calculus Alternative

With a linear inverse demand function, the revenue function is

$$R(Q) = (a + bQ)Q.$$

Marginal revenue is

$$MR = \frac{dR}{dQ} = a + 2bQ.$$

Demonstration Problem 8–4

$P = a + bQ$

$MR = c + 2bQ$

Suppose the inverse demand function for a monopolist's product is given by

$$P = 10 - 2Q.$$

What is the maximum price per unit a monopolist can charge to be able to sell 3 units? What is the marginal revenue associated with 3 units of output?

Answer

First, we set $Q = 3$ in the inverse demand function (here $a = 10$ and $b = -2$) to get

$$P = 10 - 2\,(3) = 4.$$

Thus, the maximum price per unit the monopolist can charge to be able to sell 3 units is \$4. To find marginal revenue when 3 units are produced, we set $Q = 3$ in the marginal revenue formula for linear inverse demand to get

$$MR = 10 - [(2)(2)(3)] = -2.$$

Thus, the third unit sold reduced revenue by \$2.

The Output Decision

Revenues are one determinant of profits; costs are the other. Since the revenue a monopolist receives from selling Q units is $R(Q) = Q[P(Q)]$, the profits of a monopolist with a cost function of $C(Q)$ are

$$\pi = R(Q) - C(Q).$$

Typical revenue and cost functions are graphed in Figure 8–14(a). The vertical distance between the revenue and cost functions in panel a reflects the profits to the monopolist of alternative levels of output. Output levels below point A and above point B imply losses, since the cost curve lies above the revenue function. For output levels between points A and B, the revenue function lies above the cost function, and profits are positive for those output levels.

Figure 8–14(b) depicts the profit function, which is the difference between R and C in panel a. As Figure 8–14(a) shows, profits are greatest at an output of Q^M, where the vertical distance between the revenue and cost functions is the greatest. This corresponds to the maximum profit point in panel b. A very important property of the profit-maximizing level of output

FIGURE 8–14

*Costs, revenues, and
profits under
monopoly*

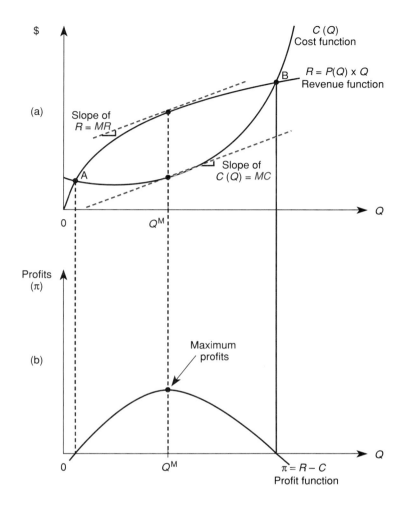

(Q^M) is that the slope of the revenue function in panel a equals the slope of
the cost function. In economic terms, marginal revenue equals marginal cost
at an output of Q^M.

Principle

Monopoly Output Rule
A profit-maximizing monopolist should produce the output, Q^M, such that marginal revenue
equals marginal cost:

$$MR(Q^M) = MC(Q^M).$$

FIGURE 8–15

Profit maximization under monopoly

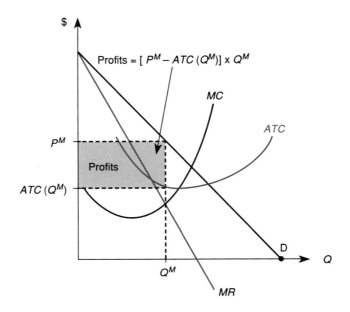

Profits = [P^M – $ATC(Q^M)$] x Q^M

A Calculus Alternative

The profits for a monopolist are

$$\pi = R(Q) - C(Q),$$

where $R(Q)$ is total revenue. To maximize profits, marginal profits must be zero:

$$\frac{d\pi}{dQ} = \frac{dR(Q)}{dQ} - \frac{dC(Q)}{dQ} = 0,$$

or

$$MR = MC.$$

The economic intuition behind this important rule is as follows. If marginal revenue were greater than marginal cost, an increase in output would increase revenues more than it would increase costs. Thus, a profit-maximizing manager of a monopoly should continue to expand output when $MR > MC$. On the other hand, if marginal cost exceeded marginal revenue, a reduction in output would reduce costs by more than it would reduce revenue. A profit-maximizing manager thus is motivated to produce where marginal revenue equals marginal cost.

An alternative characterization of the profit-maximizing output decision of a monopoly is presented in Figure 8–15. The marginal revenue curve intersects the marginal cost curve when Q^M units are produced, so the profit-maximizing level of output is Q^M. The maximum price per unit that consumers are willing to pay for Q^M units is P^M, so the profit-maximizing price is P^M. Monopoly profits are given by the shaded rectangle in the figure, which is the base (Q^M) times the height $[P^M - ATC(Q^M)]$.

Principle

Monopoly Pricing Rule
Given the level of output, Q^M, that maximizes profits, the monopoly price is the price on the demand curve corresponding to the Q^M units produced:

$$P^M = P(Q^M).$$

DEMONSTRATION PROBLEM 8–5

Suppose the inverse demand function for a monopolist's product is given by

$$P = 100 - 2Q$$

and the cost function is given by

$$C(Q) = 10 + 2Q.$$

Determine the profit-maximizing price and quantity and the maximum profits.

Answer

Using the marginal revenue formula for linear inverse demand and the formula for marginal cost, we see that

$$MR = 100 - (2)(2)(Q) = 100 - 4Q,$$

$$MC = 2.$$

Next, we set $MR = MC$ to find the profit-maximizing level of output:

$$100 - 4Q = 2,$$

or

$$4Q = 98.$$

Solving for Q yields the profit-maximizing output of $Q^M = 24.5$ units. We find the profit-maximizing price by setting $Q = Q^M$ in the inverse demand function:

$$P = 100 - 2(24.5) = 51.$$

Thus, the profit-maximizing price is $51 per unit. Finally, profits are given by the difference between revenues and costs:

$$\pi = P^M Q^M - C(Q^M)$$
$$= (51)(24.5) - [10 + 2(24.5)]$$
$$= \$1{,}190.50.$$

The Absence of a Supply Curve

Recall that a supply curve determines how much will be produced at a given price. Since perfectly competitive firms determine how much output to produce based on price ($P = MC$), supply curves exist in perfectly competitive markets. In contrast, a monopolist determines how much to produce based on marginal revenue, which is less than price ($P > MR = MC$). As a consequence, there is no supply curve in markets served by a monopolist.

Multiplant Decisions

Up until this point, we have assumed that the monopolist produces output at a single location. In many instances, however, a monopolist has different plants at different locations. An important issue for the manager of such a monopoly is the determination of how much output to produce at each plant.

Suppose the monopolist produces output at two plants. The cost of producing Q_1 units at plant 1 is $C_1(Q_1)$, and the cost of producing Q_2 units at plant 2 is $C_2(Q_2)$. Further, suppose the outputs produced at the two plants are identical, so the price per unit consumers are willing to pay for the total output produced at the two plants is $P(Q)$, where

$$Q = Q_1 + Q_2.$$

Profit maximization implies that the two-plant monopolist should produce output in each plant such that the marginal cost of producing in each plant equals the marginal revenue of total output.

Principle

Multiplant Output Rule

Let $MR(Q)$ be the marginal revenue of producing a total of $Q = Q_1 + Q_2$ units of output. Suppose the marginal cost of producing Q_1 units of output in plant 1 is $MC_1(Q_1)$ and that of producing Q_2 units in plant 2 is $MC_2(Q_2)$. The profit maximization rule for the two-plant monopolist is to allocate output among the two plants such that

$$MR(Q) = MC_1(Q_1)$$
$$MR(Q) = MC_2(Q_2).$$

**A Calculus
Alternative**

If profits are

$$\pi = R(Q_1 + Q_2) - C_1(Q_1) - C_2(Q_2),$$

the first-order conditions for maximizing profits are

$$\frac{d\pi}{dQ_1} = \frac{dR(Q_1 + Q_2)}{dQ_1} - \frac{dC_1(Q_1)}{dQ_1},$$

$$\frac{d\pi}{dQ_2} = \frac{dR(Q_1 + Q_2)}{dQ_2} - \frac{dC_2(Q_2)}{dQ_1}.$$

The economic intuition underlying the multiplant output rule is precisely the same as all of the profit maximization principles. If the marginal revenue of producing output in a plant exceeds the marginal cost, the firm will add more to revenue than to cost by expanding output in the plant. As output is expanded, marginal revenue declines until it ultimately equals the marginal cost of producing in the plant.

The conditions for maximizing profits in a multiplant setting imply that

$$MC_1(Q_1) = MC_2(Q_2).$$

This too has a simple economic explanation. If the marginal cost of producing in plant 1 is lower than that of producing in plant 2, the monopolist could reduce costs by producing more output in plant 1 and less in plant 2. As more output is produced in plant 1, the marginal cost of producing in the plant increases until it ultimately equals the marginal cost of producing in plant 2.

DEMONSTRATION PROBLEM 8–6

Suppose the inverse demand for a monopolist's product is given by

$$P(Q) = 70 - .5Q.$$

The monopolist can produce output in two plants. The marginal cost of producing in plant 1 is $MC_1 = 3Q_1$, and the marginal cost of producing in plant 2 is $MC_2 = Q_2$. How much output should be produced in each plant to maximize profits, and what price should be charged for the product?

Answer

To maximize profits, the firm should produce output in the two plants such that

$$MR(Q) = MC_1(Q_1)$$

$$MR(Q) = MC_2(Q_2).$$

In this instance, marginal revenue is given by

$$MR(Q) = 70 - Q,$$

where $Q = Q_1 + Q_2$. Substituting these values into the formula for the multiplant output rule, we get

$$70 - (Q_1 + Q_2) = 3Q_1,$$

$$70 - (Q_1 + Q_2) = Q_2.$$

Thus, we have two equations and two unknowns, and we must solve for the two unknowns. The first equation implies that

$$Q_2 = 70 - 4Q_1.$$

Substituting this into the second equation yields

$$70 - (Q_1 + 70 - 4Q_1) = 70 - 4Q_1.$$

Solving this equation, we find that $Q_1 = 10$. Next, we substitute this value of Q_1 into the first equation:

$$70 - (10 + Q_2) = 3(10).$$

Solving this equation, we find that $Q_2 = 30$. Thus, the firm should produce 10 units in plant 1 and 30 units in plant 2 for a total output of $Q = 40$ units.

To find the profit-maximizing price, we must find the maximum price per unit that consumers will pay for 40 units of output. To do this, we set $Q = 40$ in the inverse demand function:

$$P = 70 - .5(40) = 50.$$

Thus, the profit-maximizing price is $50.

Implications of Entry Barriers

Our analysis of monopoly reveals that a monopolist may earn positive economic profits. If a monopolist is earning positive economic profits, the presence of barriers to entry prevents other firms from entering the market to reap a portion of those profits. Thus, monopoly profits, if they exist, will continue over time so long as the firm maintains its monopoly power. It is important to note, however, that the presence of monopoly power does not imply positive profits; it depends solely on where the demand curve lies in relation to the average total cost curve. For example, the monopolist de-

FIGURE 8–16

A monopolist earning zero profits

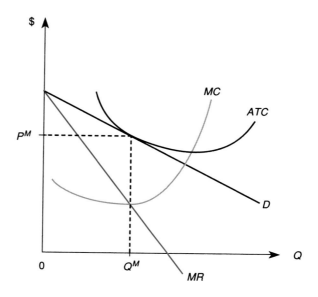

FIGURE 8–17

Deadweight loss of monopoly

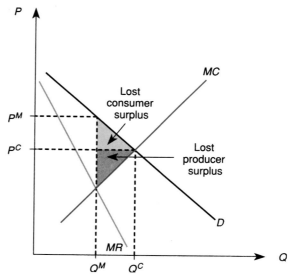

picted in Figure 8–16 earns zero economic profits, because the optimal price exactly equals the average total cost of production. Moreover, in the short run a monopolist may even experience losses.

The monopoly power a monopolist enjoys often implies some social costs to society. Consider, for example, the monopolist's demand, marginal revenue, and marginal cost curves graphed in Figure 8–17. For simplicity, these curves are graphed as linear functions of output, and the position of the average cost curve is suppressed for now. The profit-maximizing monopolist produces Q^M units of output and charges a price of P^M.

The first thing to notice about monopoly is that price exceeds the marginal cost of production: $P^M > MC$. The price in a market reflects the value to society of another unit of output. Marginal cost reflects the cost to society of the resources needed to produce an additional unit of output. Since price exceeds marginal cost, the monopolist produces less output than is socially desirable. In effect, society would be willing to pay more for one more unit of output than it would cost to produce the unit. Yet the monopolist refuses to do so because it would reduce the firm's profits. This is because marginal revenue for a monopolist lies below the demand curve.

deadweight loss of monopoly
The consumer and producer surplus that is lost due to the monopolist charging a price in excess of marginal cost.

In contrast, given the same demand and cost conditions, a firm in a perfectly competitive industry would continue to produce output up to the point where price equals marginal cost; this corresponds to an industry output and price of Q^C and P^C under perfect competition. Thus, the monopolist produces less output and charges a higher price than would a perfectly competitive industry. The shaded area in Figure 8–17 corresponds to the lost consumer and producer surplus that arises under monopoly. This *deadweight loss* reflects the welfare loss to society due to the monopolist producing output below the competitive level.

Monopolistic Competition

A market structure that lies between the extremes of monopoly and perfect competition is *monopolistic competition*. This market structure exhibits some characteristics present in perfect competition and others present under monopoly.

monopolistically competitive market
A market in which (1) there are many buyers and sellers; (2) each firm produces a differentiated product; and (3) there is free entry and exit.

Conditions for Monopolistic Competition

An industry is monopolistically competitive if

1. There are many buyers and sellers.
2. Each firm in the industry produces a differentiated product.
3. There is free entry into and exit from the industry.

There are numerous industries in which firms produce products that are close substitutes, and the market for hamburgers is a prime example. Many fast-food restaurants produce hamburgers, but the hamburgers produced by one firm differ from those produced by other firms. Moreover, it is relatively easy for new firms to enter the market for hamburgers.

The key difference between the models of monopolistic competition and perfect competition is that in a market with monopolistic competition, each firm produces a product that differs slightly from other firms' products. The products are close, but not perfect, substitutes. For example, other things being equal, some consumers prefer McDonald's hamburgers, whereas others prefer to eat at Wendy's, Burger King, or one of the many other restaurants that serve hamburgers. As the price of a McDonald's hamburger increases, some consumers will substitute toward hamburgers produced by another firm. But some consumers may continue to eat at McDonald's even if the price is higher than at other restaurants. The fact that the products are not perfect substitutes in a monopolistically competitive industry thus implies that each firm faces a downward-sloping demand curve for its product. To sell more of its product, the firm must lower the price. In this sense, the demand curve facing a monopolistically competitive firm looks more like the demand for a monopolist's product than like the demand for a competitive firm's product.

There are two important differences between a monopolistically competitive market and a market serviced by a monopolist. First, while a monopolistically competitive firm faces a downward-sloping demand for its product, there are other firms in the industry that sell similar products. Second, in a monopolistically competitive industry, there are no barriers to entry. As we will see later, this implies that firms will enter the market if existing firms earn positive economic profits.

Profit Maximization

The determination of the profit-maximizing price and output under monopolistic competition is precisely the same as for a firm operating under monopoly. To see this, consider the demand curve for a monopolistically competitive firm presented in Figure 8–18. Since the demand curve slopes

FIGURE 8–18

Profit maximization under monopolistic competition

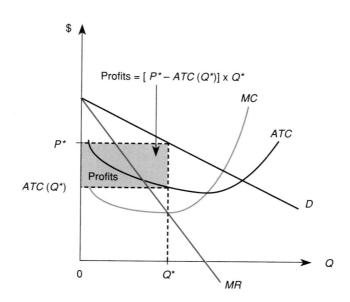

downward, the marginal revenue curve lies below it, just as under monopoly. To maximize profits, the monopolistically competitive firm produces where marginal revenue equals marginal cost. This output is given by Q^* in Figure 8–18. The profit-maximizing price is the maximum price consumers are willing to pay for Q^* units of the firm's output, namely P^*. The firm's profits are given by the shaded region.

Now that you understand that the basic principles of profit maximization are the same under monopolistic competition and monopoly, it is important to highlight one important difference in the interpretation of our analysis. The demand and marginal revenue curves used to determine the monopolistically competitive firm's profit-maximizing output and price are based not on the market demand for the product but on the demand for the individual firm's product. The demand curve facing a monopolist, in contrast, is the market demand curve.

In fact, because the firms in a monopolistically competitive industry produce differentiated products, the notion of an industry or market demand curve is not well defined. To find market demand, one must add up the total quantities purchased from all firms in the market at each price. But in monopolistically competitive markets, each firm produces a product that differs from other firms' products. Adding up these different products would be like adding up apples and oranges.

Principle

Profit Maximization Rule for Monopolistic Competition
To maximize profits, a monopolistically competitive firm produces where its marginal revenue equals marginal cost. The profit-maximizing price is the maximum price per unit that consumers are willing to pay for the profit-maximizing level of output. In other words, the profit-maximizing output, Q^*, is such that

$$MR(Q^*) = MC(Q^*),$$

and the profit-maximizing price is

$$P^* = P(Q^*).$$

DEMONSTRATION PROBLEM 8–7

Suppose the inverse demand function for a monopolistically competitive firm's product is given by

$$P = 100 - 2Q$$

and the cost function is given by

$$C(Q) = 5 + 2Q.$$

Determine the profit-maximizing price and quantity and the maximum profits.

Answer

Using the marginal revenue formula for linear inverse demand and the formula for marginal cost, we see that

$$MR = 100 - (2)(2)(Q) = 100 - 4Q,$$

$$MC = 2.$$

Next, we set $MR = MC$ to find the profit-maximizing level of output:

$$100 - 4Q = 2,$$

or

$$4Q = 98.$$

Solving for Q yields the profit-maximizing output of $Q^* = 24.5$ units. The profit-maximizing price is found by setting $Q = Q^*$ in the inverse demand function:

$$P = 100 - 2 \cdot 24.5 = 51.$$

Thus, the profit-maximizing price is $51 per unit. Finally, profits are given by the difference between revenues and costs:

$$\pi = P^*Q^* - C(Q^*)$$

$$= (51)(24.5) - 5 [5 + 2 (24.5)]$$

$$= \$1,195.50.$$

Long-Run Equilibrium

Because there is free entry into monopolistically competitive markets, if firms earn short-run profits in a monopolistically competitive industry, additional firms will enter the industry in the long run to capture some of those profits. Similarly, if existing firms incur losses, in the long run some firms will exit the industry.

To explain the impact of entry and exit in monopolistically competitive markets, suppose a monopolistically competitive firm is earning positive economic profits. The potential for profits induces other firms to enter the market and produce slight variations of the existing firm's product. As additional firms enter the market, some consumers who were buying the firm's product will begin to consume one of the new firms' products. Thus, one would expect the existing firms to lose a share of the market when new firms enter.

To make this notion more precise, suppose a monopolistically competitive firm that sells brand X faces an initial demand curve of D^0 in Figure 8–19. Since this demand curve lies above the *ATC* curve, the firm is earning positive economic profits. This, of course, lures more firms into the industry. As additional firms enter, the demand for this firm's product will decrease because some consumers will substitute toward the new products offered by the entering firms. Entry continues until the demand curve decreases to D^1, where it is just tangent to the firm's average cost curve. At this point, firms in the industry are earning zero economic profits, and there is no incentive for additional firms to enter the industry.

The story is similar if firms in the industry initially are incurring losses. However, in this instance firms will exit the industry, and the demand for the products offered by the firms that remain will increase. This process leads to increased profits (or, more accurately, reduced losses) for the remaining firms. Ultimately, firms stop leaving the industry when the remaining firms earn zero economic profits.

Thus, the long-run equilibrium in a monopolistically competitive industry is characterized by the situation in Figure 8–20. Each firm earns zero economic profits but charges a price that exceeds the marginal cost of producing the good.

Principle

The Long-Run and Monopolistic Competition

In the long run, monopolistically competitive firms produce a level of output such that

1. $P > MC$.
2. $P = ATC >$ minimum of average costs.

As in the case of monopoly, the fact that price exceeds marginal cost implies that monopolistically competitive firms produce less output than is socially desirable. In essence, consumers are willing to pay more for another unit than it would cost the firm to produce another unit; yet the firm will not produce more output because of its concern with profits.

Because price equals average costs, firms earn zero economic profits just as firms in perfectly competitive markets do. Even though the firms have some control over price, competition among them leads to a situation where no firm earns more than its opportunity cost of producing.

Finally, note that the price of output exceeds the minimum point on the average cost curve. This implies that firms do not take full advantage of economies of scale in production. In a sense there are too many firms in the industry to enable any individual firm to take full advantage of economies of scale in production. On the other hand, some argue that this is simply the cost to society of having product variety. If there were fewer firms, economies of scale could be fully exploited, but there would be less product variety in the market.

FIGURE 8–19

Effect of entry on a monopolistically competitive firm's demand

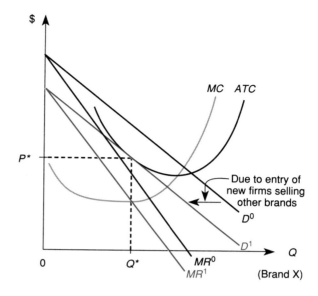

FIGURE 8–20

Long-run equilibrium under monopolistic competition

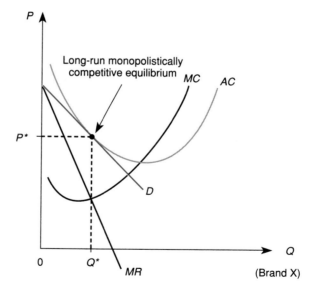

Implications of Product Differentiation

The key difference between perfect competition and monopolistic competition is the assumption that firms produce differentiated products. Since there are many products in a monopolistically competitive industry, the only reason firms have any control over their price is that consumers view the products as differentiated. The demand for a firm's product is less elastic when consumers view other firms' products as poor substitutes for it. The less elastic the demand for a firm's product, the greater the potential for earning profits.

For this reason, many firms in monopolistically competitive industries continually attempt to convince consumers that their products are better than those offered by other firms. A number of examples of such industries come readily to mind: fast-food restaurants, toothpaste, mouthwash, gasoline, aspirin, car wax—undoubtedly you can add other industries to the list. Each of these industries consists of many firms, and the different brands offered by firms in each industry are very close substitutes. In some instances, firms introduce several varieties of products; each soft-drink producer, for example, produces a variety of cola and noncola drinks.

Firms in monopolistically competitive industries employ two strategies to persuade consumers that their products are better than those offered by competitors. First, monopolistically competitive firms spend considerable amounts on advertising campaigns. Very typically, the advertisements are designed to differentiate a given firm's product from the products of other firms. Some would argue that from the viewpoint of social efficiency, such advertising is inefficient; in many instances, the products are virtually identical.

Second, firms in monopolistically competitive industries frequently introduce new products into the market to further differentiate their products from other firms'. These include not only "new, improved" products, such as an "improved" version of laundry detergent, but completely different product lines. An example of a new product line is the introduction of salads at a fast-food restaurant.

As the manager of a firm in a monopolistically competitive industry, it is important to remember that, in the long run, additional firms will enter the market if your firm earns short-run profits with its product. Thus, while you may make short-run profits by introducing a new product line, in the long run other firms will mimic your product and/or introduce new product lines, and your profits will decrease to zero.

Answering the Headline

The market for VCRs has many features of monopolistic competition. In a monopolistically competitive market, firms can earn short-run profits due to market power gained by selling differentiated products. But in the long run, new firms will penetrate the market and existing firms will see their profits fall. This is precisely what happened in the market for VCRs as a result of increased entry by non-Japanese firms. The problem was exacerbated by the fact that VCRs are now in 80 percent of Japanese homes, and existing owners there and in the United States mainly buy new ones every three to five years when their existing ones break down.

In monopolistically competitive markets, firms can earn profits by introducing new products more quickly than the competition. In fact, this is precisely the strategy that Japanese producers like Matsushita, Toshiba, Hitachi, JVC, and Sanyo are employing to turn profits back around. These firms are all introducing high end products that will play for up to 16 hours, make digital recordings, send a wireless signal, and pick up satellite signals. Their hope is that by introducing new products and more strongly differentiating their products from the competition, they can earn higher profits—at least in the short run.

Summary

In this chapter, we examined managerial decisions in three market environments: perfect competition, monopoly, and monopolistic competition. Each of these market structures provides a manager with a different set of variables that can influence the firm's profits. A manager may need to pay particularly close attention to different decision parameters because different market structures allow control of only certain variables. Managers who recognize which variables are relevant for a particular industry will make more profits for their firms.

Managers in perfectly competitive markets should concentrate on producing the proper quantity and keeping costs low. Because perfectly competitive markets contain a very large number of firms that produce perfect substitutes, a manager in this market has no control over price. A manager in a monopoly, in contrast, needs to recognize the relation between price and quantity. By setting a quantity at which marginal cost equals marginal revenue, the manager of a monopoly will maximize profits. This is also true for the manager of a firm in a monopolistically competitive market, who also must evaluate the firm's product periodically to ensure that it is differentiated from other products in the market. In many instances, the manager of a monopolistically competitive firm will find it advantageous to slightly change the product from time to time to enhance product differentiation.

Key Terms and Concepts

cost complementarities

dead weight loss of monopoly

diseconomies of scale

economies of scale

economies of scope

free entry

free exit

marginal revenue

monopolistic competition

monopoly

multiplant monopoly

patents

perfect information

perfectly competitive market

product differentiation

Problems

1. Pic Industries produces plastic toothpicks that it sells to distributors in the Southwest. During the early 1990s, the price of the plastic it uses to produce toothpicks fell by 46 percent, due to a local glut of recycled plastic containers. Assuming that the market for plastic toothpicks most closely resembles that of perfect competition and that other firms in the industry do not experience similar cost savings in the short run, what impact would this have on the profit-maximizing output, price, and profits of Pic Industries?

2. Beta Industries manufactures floppy disks that consumers perceive as identical to those produced by numerous other manufacturers. Recently, Beta hired an econometrician to estimate its cost function for producing boxes of one dozen floppy disks. The estimated cost function is:

$$C = 20 + 2Q^2.$$

   a. What are the firm's fixed costs?

   b. What is the firm's marginal cost?

   Now suppose other firms in the market sell the product at a price of $10.

   c. How much should this firm charge for the product?

   d. What is the optimal level of output to maximize profits?

   e. How much profit will be earned?

   f. In the long run, should this firm continue to operate or shut down? Why?

3. Keds—the traditional maker of white canvas tennis shoes—was near oblivion in the early 1980s because competitors like Nike, Reebok, Adidas, and Brooks took away many of its customers. If you were at the helm of Keds, what would you have done to turn the company around?

4. Manufacturers of laundry detergent and dishwashing soap reinvest a relatively large percentage of their sales revenues on advertising campaigns. Most of these advertisements that appear on television stress the fact that their product is "New and Improved." Why?

5. Suppose the cost function for your firm is: $C = 50 + 4Q + 2Q^2$.
   a. What is the average fixed cost of producing 5 units of output?
   b. What is the average variable cost of producing 5 units of output?
   c. What are the average total cost and marginal cost of producing 5 units of output?

6. U.S. Air experienced huge losses for several years in the 1990s, yet it continued to operate its fleets. Why didn't U.S. Air shut down its operations to avoid the losses?

7. In 1994 Pentium users around the world learned that their $4.00 pocket calculators could perform some operations more accurately than their $5,000 desktop computers. It took several months before Intel—the maker of the chip—agreed to offer its customers replacement chips. In contrast, Walmart guarantees satisfaction to all customers, with a "no questions asked" return policy on nearly all of the products it sells. Why do you think these firms employ such different consumer relations policies?

8. Suppose you are the manager of Alpha Enterprises— a firm that holds a patent that makes it the exclusive manufacturer of bubble memory chips. Based on estimates provided by a consultant, you know that the relevant demand and cost functions for bubble memory chips are:

$$Q = 25 - .5P$$

$$C = 50 + 2Q.$$

   a. What is the firm's inverse demand function?
   b. What is the firm's marginal revenue when producing 4 units of output?
   c. What are the levels of output and price when you are maximizing profits?
   d. What will be the level of your profits?

9. Suppose you are a monopolist operating two plants at different locations. Both plants produce the same product; Q_1 is the quantity produced at plant 1, and Q_2 is the quantity produced at plant 2. You face the following inverse demand function:

$$P = 500 - 2Q,$$

where $Q = Q_1 + Q_2$. The cost functions for the two plants are:

$$C_1 = 25 + 2Q_1^2$$

$$C_2 = 20 + Q_2^2$$

  a. What are your marginal revenue and marginal cost functions?
  b. To maximize profits, how much should you produce at plant 1? At plant 2?
  c. What is the price that maximizes profits?
  d. What are the maximum profits?

10. Why does the government grant patents to inventors? Why does the government give monopoly power to utility companies?

11. Would you expect an industry to be monopolistically competitive if consumers did not value variety in the market? Explain.

12. What is the primary facet of monopolistic competition that does not allow for the presence of long-run profits? If firms are making short-run profits in a monopolistically competitive industry, what will eventually occur that will cause long-run economic profits to be zero?

13. Regardless of the economic environment, every firm will maximize profits by operating at the minimum point of its average total cost curve. Is this statement true or false? Explain.

14. What market can you think of, besides that for VCRs, that has shown short-run profits but, over time, has seen profits disappear due to entry?

15. You are a manager in a perfectly competitive market. The price in your market is $35. Your total cost curve is:

$$C(Q) = 10 + 2Q + .5Q^2.$$

  a. What level of output should you produce in the short run?
  b. What price should you charge in the short run?
  c. Will you make any profits in the short run?
  d. What will happen in the long run?
  e. How would your answer change if your cost were:

$$C(Q) = 80 + 5Q + 30Q^2?$$

16. You are the manager of a firm that has an exclusive license to produce your product. The inverse market demand curve is:

$$P = 900 - 1.5Q.$$

Your cost function is:

$$C(Q) = 2Q + Q^2 + \frac{1}{3}Q^3.$$

Determine the output you should produce, the price you should charge, and your profits. Show your results graphically.

17. Monsanto, the maker of Nutrasweet, owned the patent to aspartame, the official name of the sweetener. In 1987 Monsanto's patent expired in Europe, allowing other firms to produce aspartame under other

brand names. What impact do you think this had on the market for aspartame and Monsanto's profits?

18. If a monopolist has an own price demand elasticity of $-.8$, is it maximizing profits? Explain.

19. You are a monopolist with the following cost and demand conditions:

$$P = 100 - 2Q \text{ and } C(Q) = 50 + Q^2.$$

   a. Determine the profit-maximizing output and price.
   b. Graph this solution.
   c. Show your profits and the deadweight loss to society in your graph.
   d. Determine the actual amount of deadweight loss.

20. You are the manager of a monopolistically competitive firm. The present demand curve you face is:

$$P = 100 - 4Q.$$

Your cost function is:

$$C(Q) = 50 + 8.5Q^2.$$

   a. What level of output should you choose to maximize profits?
   b. What price should you charge?
   c. What will happen in your market in the long run? Explain.

21. Would you expect the demand for a monopolistically competitive firm's product to be more or less elastic than that for a monopolist's product? Explain.

22. You are the manager of a monopolistically competitive firm. The inverse demand for your product is given by $P = 200 - 10Q$, and your marginal cost is $MC = 5 + Q$.
   a. What is the profit-maximizing level of output?
   b. What is the profit-maximizing price?
   c. What are the maximum profits?
   d. What do you expect to happen to the demand for your product in the long run? Explain.

23. Genentech owns a patent on tissue plasminogen activator (TPA), which is an enzyme that helps the body break down blood clots. TPA is particularly valuable to cardiac patients, since it often allows heart problems to be treated with medication rather than surgery. Recently, however, firms in the medical industry have come under fire by some members of Congress and the press for charging high prices and earning monopoly profits. Do you think cardiac patients would benefit if the government stripped Genentech and other pharmaceutical firms of their patents? Explain.

Selected Readings

Gal Or, Esther and Spiro, Michael H., "Regulatory Regimes in the Electric Power Industry: Implications for Capacity." *Journal of Regulatory Economics* 4(3), September 1992, pp. 263–78.

Gius, Mark Paul, "The Extent of the Market in the Liquor Industry: An Empirical Test of Localized Brand Rivalry, 1970–1988." *Review of Industrial Organization* 8(5), October 1993, pp. 599–608.

Lamdin, Douglas J., "The Welfare Effects of Monopoly versus Competition: A Clarification of Textbook Presentations." *Journal of Economic Education* 23(3), Summer 1992, pp. 247–53.

Nguyen, Dung, "Advertising, Random Sales Response, and Brand Competition: Some Theoretical and Econometric Implications." *Journal of Business* 60(2), April 1987, pp. 259–79.

Malueg, David A., "Monopoly Output and Welfare: The Role of Curvature of the Demand Function." *Journal of Economic Education* 25(3), Summer 1994, pp. 235–50.

Simon, Herbert, A., "Organizations and Markets." *Journal of Economic Perspectives* 5(2), Spring 1991, pp. 25–44.

Stegeman, Mark, "Advertising in Competitive Markets." *American Economic Review* 81(1), March 1991, pp. 210–23.

Zupan, Mark A., "On Cream Skimming, Coase, and the Sustainability of Natural Monopolies." *Applied Economics* 22(4), April 1990, pp. 487–92.

APPENDIX
THE CALCULUS OF PROFIT MAXIMIZATION

Perfect Competition

The profits of a perfectly competitive firm are

$$\pi = PQ - C(Q).$$

The first-order conditions for maximizing profits require that marginal profits be zero:

$$\frac{d\pi}{dQ} = P - \frac{dC(Q)}{dQ} = 0.$$

Thus, we obtain the profit-maximizing rule for a firm in perfect competition:

$$P = \frac{dC}{dQ},$$

or

$$P = MC.$$

The second-order condition for maximizing profits requires that

$$\frac{d^2\pi}{dQ^2} = -\frac{d^2C}{dQ^2} = -\frac{dMC}{dQ} < 0.$$

This means that $d(MC)/dQ > 0$, or that marginal cost must be increasing output.

Monopoly and Monopolistic Competition

MR = MC **Rule:** The profits for a firm with market power are

$$\pi = R(Q) - C(Q),$$

where $R(Q) = P(Q) Q$ is total revenue. To maximize profits, marginal profits must be zero:

$$\frac{d\pi}{dQ} = \frac{dR(Q)}{dQ} - \frac{dC(Q)}{dQ} = 0,$$

or

$$MR = MC.$$

The second-order condition requires that

$$\frac{d^2\pi}{dQ^2} = \frac{d^2R(Q)}{dQ^2} - \frac{d^2C(Q)}{dQ^2} < 0,$$

which means that

$$\frac{dMR}{dQ} < \frac{dC(Q)}{dQ}.$$

But this simply means that the slope of the marginal revenue curve must be less than the slope of the marginal cost curve.

APPENDIX
THE ALGEBRA OF PERFECTLY COMPETITIVE SUPPLY FUNCTIONS

This appendix shows how to obtain the short-run firm and industry supply functions from cost data. Suppose there are 500 firms in a perfectly competitive industry, with each firm having a cost function of

$$C(q_i) = 50 + 2q_i + 4q_i^2.$$

The corresponding average total cost *(ATC)*, average variable cost *(AVC)*, and marginal cost *(MC)* functions are

$$ATC_i = \frac{50}{q_i} + 2 + 4q_i$$

$$AVC_i = 2 + 4q_i$$

$$MC_i = 2 + 8q_i.$$

Recall that the supply curve for each firm is the firm's marginal cost curve above the minimum of average variable cost. Since *AVC* is at its minimum where it equals marginal cost, to find the quantity where average variable cost equals marginal cost we must set the two functions equal to each other and solve for q_i. When we do this for the above equations, we find that the quantity at which marginal cost equals average variable cost is $q_i = 0$.

Next, we recognize that an individual firm maximizes profits by equating $P = MC_i$, so

$$P = 2 + 8q_i.$$

Solving for q_i gives us the individual firm's supply function:

$$q_i = -\frac{2}{8} + \frac{1}{8}P.$$

To find the supply curve for the industry, we simply sum the above equation over all 500 firms in the market:

$$Q = \sum_{i=1}^{500} q_i = 500 \left(-\frac{2}{8} + \frac{1}{8}P \right) = -\frac{1{,}000}{8} + \frac{500}{8}P,$$

or

$$Q = -125 + 62.5\,P.$$

Basic Oligopoly Models

Headline

Crude Oil Prices Fall, but Consumers in Some Areas See No Relief at the Pump

The price of crude oil declined during the first half of the 1990s, from about $20 per barrel in 1990 to $16 per barrel in 1995. As a result of declining crude oil prices, consumers in most locations enjoyed lower gasoline prices.

Not all consumers reaped the benefits of lower crude oil prices, however. In a few isolated areas, consumers cried foul because gasoline retailers did not pass on the price reductions to those who pay at the pump. Consumer groups argued that this corroborates their claims that gasoline retailers in these areas are colluding in order to earn monopoly profits. For obvious reasons, the gasoline retailers involved deny the allegations.

Based on the evidence, do you think that gasoline stations in these areas were colluding in order to earn monopoly profits? Explain.

Introduction

Up until now, our analysis of markets has not considered the impact of strategic behavior on managerial decision making. At one extreme, we examined profit maximization in perfectly competitive and monopolistically competitive markets. In these types of markets, there are so many firms competing with one another that no individual firm has any effect on other firms in the market. At the other extreme, we examined profit maximization in a monopolistic market. In this instance there is only one firm in the market, and strategic interactions among firms thus are irrelevant.

This chapter is the first of two chapters in which we examine managerial decisions in oligopolistic markets. Here we focus on basic output and pricing decisions in four specific types of oligopolies: Sweezy, Cournot, Stackelberg, and Bertrand. In the next chapter, we will develop a more general framework for analyzing other decisions, such as advertising, research and development, entry into an industry, and so forth. First, let us briefly review what is meant by the term *oligopoly*.

Conditions for Oligopoly

oligopoly
A market structure in which there are only a few firms, each of which is large relative to the total industry.

Oligopoly refers to a situation where there are a relatively few large firms in an industry. No explicit number of firms is required for oligopoly, but the number usually is somewhere between two and ten. The products the firms offer may be either identical or differentiated. An oligopoly composed of only two firms is called a *duopoly*.

Oligopoly is perhaps the most interesting of all market structures; in fact, the next chapter is devoted entirely to the analysis of situations that arise under oligopoly. But from the viewpoint of the manager, a firm operating in an oligopoly setting is the most difficult to manage. The key reason is that there are few firms in an oligopolistic market and the manager must consider the likely impact of her or his decisions on the decisions of other firms in the industry. Moreover, the actions of other firms will have a profound impact on the manager's optimal decisions. It should be noted that due to the complexity of oligopoly, there is no single model that is relevant for all oligopolies.

The Role of Beliefs and Strategic Interaction

To gain an understanding of oligopoly interdependence, consider a situation where several firms selling differentiated products compete in an oligopoly. In determining what price and output to charge, the manager must consider the impact of his or her decisions on other firms in the industry. For example, if the price for the product is lowered, will other firms lower their prices or maintain their existing prices? If the price is increased, will other firms do likewise or maintain their current prices? The optimal decision of whether to raise or lower price will depend on how the manager believes other managers will respond. If other firms lower their prices when the firm lowers its price, it will not sell as much as it would if the other firms maintained their existing prices.

As a point of reference, suppose the firm initially is at point B in Figure 9–1, charging a price of P_0. Demand curve D_1 is based on the as-

FIGURE 9–1

A firm's demand depends on actions of rivals

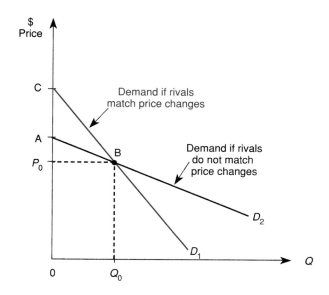

sumption that rivals will match any price change, while D_2 is based on the assumption that they will not match a price change. Note that demand is more inelastic when rivals match a price change than when they do not. The reason for this is simple. For a given price reduction, a firm will sell more if rivals do not cut their prices (D_2) than it will if they lower their prices (D_1). In effect, a price reduction increases quantity demanded only slightly when rivals respond by lowering their prices. Similarly, for a given price increase, a firm will sell more when rivals also raise their prices (D_1) than it will when they maintain their existing prices (D_2).

DEMONSTRATION PROBLEM 9–1

Suppose the manager is at point B in Figure 9–1, charging a price of P_0. If the manager believes rivals will not match price reductions but will match price increases, what does the demand for the firm's product look like?

Answer

If rivals do not match price reductions, prices below P_0 will induce quantities demanded along curve D_2. If rivals do match price increases, prices above P_0 will generate quantities demanded along D_1. Thus, if the manager believes rivals will not match price reductions but will match price increases, the demand curve for the firm's product is given by CBD_2.

DEMONSTRATION PROBLEM 9–2

Suppose the manager is at point B in Figure 9–1, charging a price of P_0. If the manager believes rivals will match price reductions but will not match price increases, what does the demand for the firm's product look like?

Answer

If rivals match price reductions, prices below P_0 will induce quantities demanded along curve D_1. If rivals do not match price increases, prices above P_0 will induce quantities demanded along D_2. Thus, if the manager believes rivals will match price reductions but will not match price increases, the demand curve for the firm's product is given by ABD_1.

The preceding analysis reveals that the demand for a firm's product in oligopoly depends critically on how rivals respond to the firm's pricing decisions. If rivals will match any price change, the demand curve for the firm's product is given by D_1. In this instance, the manager will maximize profits where the marginal revenue associated with demand curve D_1 equals marginal cost. If rivals will not match any price change, the demand curve for the firm's product is given by D_2. In this instance, the manager will maximize profits where the marginal revenue associated with demand curve D_2 equals marginal cost. In each case, the profit-maximizing rule is the same as that under monopoly; the only difficulty for the firm manager is determining whether or not rivals will match price changes.

Profit Maximization in Four Oligopoly Settings

In the following subsections, we will examine profit maximization based on alternative assumptions regarding how rivals will respond to price or output changes. Each of the four models has different implications for the manager's optimal decisions, and these differences arise because of differences in the way rivals respond to the firm's actions.

Sweezy Oligopoly

The Sweezy model is based on a very specific assumption regarding how other firms will respond to price increases and price cuts. An industry is characterized as a *Sweezy oligopoly* if:

1. There are few firms in the market serving many consumers.
2. The firms produce differentiated products.
3. Each firm believes rivals will cut their prices in response to a price reduction but will not raise their prices in response to a price increase.
4. Barriers to entry exist.

Sweezy oligopoly
An industry in which (1) there are few firms serving many consumers; (2) firms produce differentiated products; (3) each firm believes rivals will respond to a price reduction but will not follow a price increase; and (4) barriers to entry exist.

Because the manager of a firm competing in a Sweezy oligopoly believes other firms will match any price decrease but not match price increases, the demand curve for the firm's product is given by ABD_1 in Figure 9–2. For prices above P_0, the relevant demand curve is D_2; thus, marginal revenue corresponds to this demand curve. For prices below P_0, the relevant demand curve is D_1, and marginal revenue corresponds to D_1. Thus, the marginal revenue curve (MR) the firm faces is initially the marginal revenue curve associated with D_2; at Q_0, it jumps down to the marginal revenue curve corresponding to D_1. In other words, the Sweezy oligopolist's marginal revenue curve, denoted MR, is ACEF in Figure 9–2.

The profit-maximizing level of output occurs where marginal revenue equals marginal cost, and the profit-maximizing price is the maximum price consumers will pay for that level of output. For example, if marginal cost is

FIGURE 9–2

Sweezy oligopoly

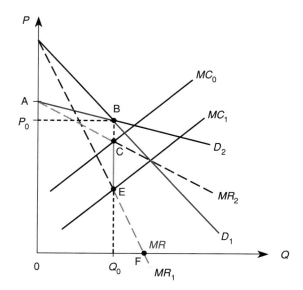

given by MC_0 in Figure 9–2, marginal revenue equals marginal cost at point C. In this case the profit-maximizing output is Q_0 and the optimal price is P_0.

An important implication of the Sweezy model of oligopoly is that there will be a range (CE) over which changes in marginal cost do not affect the profit-maximizing level of output. This is in contrast to competitive, monopolistically competitive, and monopolistic firms, all of which increase output when marginal costs decline.

To see why firms competing in a Sweezy oligopoly may not increase output when marginal cost declines, suppose marginal cost decreases from MC_0 to MC_1 in Figure 9–2. Marginal revenue now equals marginal cost at point E, but the output corresponding to this point is still Q_0. Thus the firm continues to maximize profits by producing Q_0 units at a price of P_0.

In a Sweezy oligopoly, firms have an incentive not to change their pricing behavior provided marginal costs remain in a given range. The reason for this stems purely from the assumption that rivals will match price cuts but not price increases. Firms in a Sweezy oligopoly do not want to change their prices because of the effect of price changes on the behavior of other firms in the market.

Cournot Oligopoly

In contrast to the Sweezy model, the Cournot model applies when the manager believes her or his output decisions do not affect the output decisions of rival firms. Unlike the Sweezy model, which is relevant only in situations where firms produce differentiated products, the Cournot model applies to situations where the products are either identical or differentiated.

An industry is characterized as a *Cournot oligopoly* if

Cournot oligopoly
An industry in which (1) there are few firms serving many consumers; (2) firms produce either differentiated or homogeneous products; (3) each firm believes rivals will hold their output constant if it changes its output; and (4) barriers to entry exist.

1. There are few firms in the market serving many consumers.
2. The firms produce either differentiated or homogeneous products.
3. Each firm believes rivals will hold their output constant if it changes its output.
4. Barriers to entry exist.

Reaction Functions and Equilibrium

To highlight the implications of Cournot oligopoly, suppose there are only two firms competing in a Cournot duopoly. Since this is a Cournot duopoly, firm 1 believes firm 2 will hold its output constant as it changes its own output. The profit-maximizing level of output for firm 1 depends on the output of firm 2. This information is summarized in the reaction function. A *reaction function* defines the profit-maximizing level of output for a firm for given output levels of the other firm. More formally, the profit-maximizing level of output for firm 1 given that firm 2 produces Q_2 units of

reaction function
A function that defines the profit-maximizing level of output for a firm for given output levels of another firm.

output is

$$Q_1 = r_1(Q_2).$$

Similarly, the profit-maximizing level of output for firm 2 given that firm 1 produces Q_1 units of output is given by

$$Q_2 = r_2(Q_1).$$

Cournot reaction functions for a duopoly are illustrated in Figure 9–3, where firm 1's output is measured on the horizontal axis and firm 2's output is measured on the vertical axis.

To understand why reaction functions are shaped as they are, let us highlight a few important points in the diagram. First, if firm 2 produced zero units of output, the profit-maximizing level of output for firm 1 would be Q_1^M, since this is the point on firm 1's reaction function (r_1) that corresponds to zero units of Q_2. This combination of outputs corresponds to the situation where only firm 1 is producing a positive level of output; thus, Q_1^M corresponds to the situation where firm 1 is a monopolist. If instead of producing zero units of output firm 2 produced Q_2^* units, the profit-maximizing level of output for firm 1 would be Q_1^*, since this is the point on r_1 that corresponds to an output of Q_2^* by firm 2.

The reason the profit-maximizing level of output for firm 1 decreases as firm 2's output increases is as follows. The demand for firm 1's product depends on the output produced by other firms in the market. When firm 2 increases its level of output, the demand and marginal revenue for firm 1 decline. The profit-maximizing response by firm 1 is to reduce its level of output.

FIGURE 9–3

Cournot reaction functions

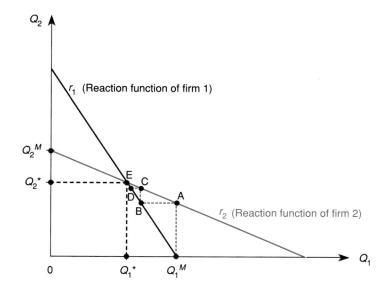

DEMONSTRATION PROBLEM 9–3

In Figure 9–3, what is the profit-maximizing level of output for firm 2 when firm 1 produces zero units of output? What is it when firm 1 produces Q_1^* units?

Answer

If firm 1 produces zero units of output, the profit-maximizing level of output for firm 2 will be Q_2^M, since this is the point on firm 2's reaction function that corresponds to zero units of Q_1. The output of Q_2^M corresponds to the situation where firm 2 is a monopolist. If firm 1 produces Q_1^* units, the profit-maximizing level of output for firm 2 will be Q_2^*, since this is the point on r_2 that corresponds to an output of Q_1^* by firm 1.

To examine equilibrium in a Cournot duopoly, suppose firm 1 produces Q_1^M units of output. Given this output, the profit-maximizing level of output for firm 2 will correspond to point A on r_2 in Figure 9–3. Given this positive level of output by firm 2, the profit-maximizing level of output for firm 1 will no longer be Q_1^M, but will correspond to point B on r_1. Given this reduced level of output by firm 1, point C will be the point on firm 2's reaction function that maximizes profits. Given this new output by firm 2, firm 1 will again reduce output to point D on its reaction function.

How long will these changes in output continue? Until point E in Figure 9–3 is reached. At point E, firm 1 produces Q_1^* and firm 2 produces Q_2^* units. Neither firm has an incentive to change its output given that it believes the other firm will hold its output constant at that level. Point E thus corresponds to the Cournot equilibrium. *Cournot equilibrium* is the situation where neither firm has an incentive to change its output given the output of the other firm. Graphically, this condition corresponds to the intersection of the reaction curves.

Cournot equilibrium
A situation in which neither firm has an incentive to change its output given the other firm's output.

Thus far, our analysis of Cournot oligopoly has been graphical rather than algebraic. However, given estimates of the demand and costs within a Cournot oligopoly, we can explicitly solve for the Cournot equilibrium. How do we do this? To maximize profits, a manager in a Cournot oligopoly produces where marginal revenue equals marginal cost. The calculation of marginal cost is straight forward; it is done just as in the other market structures we have analyzed. The calculation of marginal revenue is a little more subtle. Consider the following formula:

Formula: Marginal Revenue for Cournot Duopoly.   If the (inverse) demand in a homogeneous-product Cournot duopoly is

$$P = a - b(Q_1 + Q_2),$$

where a and b are positive constants, then the marginal revenues of firms 1 and 2 are

$$MR_1(Q_1, Q_2) = a - bQ_2 - 2bQ_1$$

$$MR_2(Q_1, Q_2) = a - bQ_1 - 2bQ_2.$$

A Calculus Alternative

Firm 1's revenues are

$$R_1 = PQ_1 = [a - b(Q_1 + Q_2)]Q_1.$$

Thus,

$$MR_1(Q_1, Q_2) = \frac{\partial R_1}{\partial Q_1} = a - bQ_2 - 2bQ_1.$$

A similar analysis yields the reaction function for firm 2.

Notice that the marginal revenue for each Cournot oligopolist depends not only on the firm's own output but also on the other firm's output. In particular, when firm 2 increases its output, firm 1's marginal revenue falls. This is because the increase in output by firm 2 lowers the market price, resulting in lower marginal revenue for firm 1.

Since each firm's marginal revenue depends on the other firm's output, the profit-maximizing output of each firm also depends on the other firm's output. This dependence is summarized in a firm's reaction function.

Formula: Reaction Functions for Cournot Duopoly. For the linear (inverse) demand function,

$$P = a - b(Q_1 + Q_2),$$

and cost functions,

$$C_1(Q_1) = c_1 Q_1$$

$$C_2(Q_2) = c_2 Q_2$$

the reaction functions are

$$Q_1 = r_1(Q_2) = \frac{a - c_1}{2b} - \frac{1}{2}Q_2$$

$$Q_2 = r_2(Q_1) = \frac{a - c_2}{2b} - \frac{1}{2}Q_1.$$

A Calculus Alternative

To maximize profits, firm 1 sets output such that

$$MR_1(Q_1, Q_2) = MC_1.$$

For the linear (inverse demand) and cost functions, this means that

$$a - bQ_2 - 2bQ_1 = c_1.$$

Solving this equation for Q_1 in terms of Q_2 yields

$$Q_1 = r_1(Q_2) = \frac{a - c_1}{2b} - \frac{1}{2}Q_2.$$

The case for firm 2 is computed similarly.

DEMONSTRATION PROBLEM 9–4

Suppose the inverse demand function for two Cournot duopolists is given by

$$P = 10 - (Q_1 + Q_2)$$

and their costs are zero.
(1) What is each firm's marginal revenue?
(2) What are the reaction functions for the two firms?
(3) What are the Cournot equilibrium outputs?
(4) What is the equilibrium price?

Answer

(1) Using the formula for marginal revenue under Cournot duopoly, we find that

$$MR_1(Q_1, Q_2) = 10 - Q_2 - 2Q_1$$

$$MR_2(Q_1, Q_2) = 10 - Q_1 - 2Q_2.$$

(2) Similarly, the reaction functions are

$$Q_1 = r_1(Q_2) = \frac{10}{2} - \frac{1}{2}Q_2$$

$$= 5 - \frac{1}{2}Q_2$$

$$Q_2 = r_2(Q_1) = \frac{10}{2} - \frac{1}{2}Q_1$$

$$= 5 - \frac{1}{2}Q_1.$$

(3) To find the Cournot equilibrium, we must solve the two reaction functions for the two unknowns:

$$Q_1^C = 5 - \frac{1}{2}Q_2^C$$

$$Q_2^C = 5 - \frac{1}{2}Q_1^C.$$

Inserting Q_2^C into the first reaction function yields

$$Q_1^C = 5 - \frac{1}{2}\left[5 - \frac{1}{2}Q_1^C\right].$$

Solving for Q_1^C yields

$$Q_1^C = \frac{10}{3}.$$

To find Q_2^C, we plug $Q_1^C = 10/3$ into firm 2's reaction function to get

$$Q_2^C = 5 - \frac{1}{2}\left(\frac{10}{3}\right)$$

$$= \frac{10}{3}.$$

(4) Total industry output is

$$Q = Q_1^C + Q_2^C = \frac{10}{3} + \frac{10}{3} = \frac{20}{3}.$$

The price in the market is determined by the (inverse) demand for this quantity

$$P = 10 - (Q_1 + Q_2)$$

$$= 10 - \frac{20}{3}$$

$$= \frac{10}{3}.$$

Isoprofit Curves

Now that you have a basic understanding of Cournot oligopoly, we will examine how to graphically determine the firm's profits. Recall that the profits of a firm in an oligopoly depend not only on the output it chooses to produce but also on the output produced by other firms in the oligopoly. In a duopoly, for instance, increases in firm 2's output will reduce the price of the output. This is due to the law of demand: As more output is sold in the market, the price consumers are willing and able to pay for the good declines. This will, of course, alter the profits of firm 1.

isoprofit curve
A function that defines the combinations of outputs produced by all firms that yield a given firm the same level of profits.

The basic tool used to summarize the profits of a firm in Cournot oligopoly is an *isoprofit curve*, which defines the combinations of outputs of all firms that yield a given firm the same level of profits.

Figure 9–4 presents the reaction function for firm 1 (r_1), along with three isoprofit curves (labeled π_0, π_1 and π_2). Four aspects of Figure 9–4 are important to understand:

1. Every point on a given isoprofit curve yields firm 1 the same level of profits. For instance, points F, A, and G all lie on the isoprofit curve labeled π_0; thus, each of these points yields profits of exactly π_0 for firm 1.

2. Isoprofit curves that lie closer to firm 1's monopoly output (Q_1^M) are associated with higher profits for that firm. For instance, isoprofit curve π_2 implies higher profits than does π_1, and π_1 is associated with higher profits than π_0. In other words, as we move down firm 1's reaction function from point A to point C, firm 1's profits increase.

3. The isoprofit curves for firm 1 reach their peak where they intersect firm 1's reaction function. For instance, isoprofit curve π_0

FIGURE 9–4

Isoprofit curves for firm 1

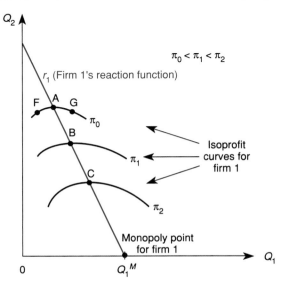

peaks at point A, where it intersects r_1; π_1 peaks at point B, where it intersects r_1, and so on.

4. The isoprofit curves do not intersect one another.

With an understanding of these four aspects of isoprofit curves, we now provide further insights into managerial decisions in a Cournot oligopoly. Recall that one assumption of Cournot oligopoly is that each firm takes as given the output decisions of rival firms and simply chooses its output to maximize profits given other firms' output. This is illustrated in Figure 9–5, where we assume firm 2's output is given by Q_2^*. Since firm 1 believes firm 2 will produce this output regardless of what firm 1 does, it chooses its output level to maximize profits when firm 2 produces Q_2^*. One possibility is for firm 1 to produce Q_1^A units of output, which would correspond to point A on isoprofit curve π_1^A. However, this decision does not maximize profits, because by expanding output to Q_1^B, firm 1 moves to a higher isoprofit curve (π_1^B, which corresponds to point B). Notice that profits can be further increased if firm 1 expands output to Q_1^C, which is associated with isoprofit curve π_1^C.

It is not profitable for firm 1 to increase output beyond Q_1^C, given that firm 2 produces Q_2^*. To see this, suppose firm 1 expanded output to, say, Q_1^D. This would result in a combination of outputs that corresponds to point D, which lies on an isoprofit curve that yields lower profits. We conclude that the profit-maximizing output for firm 1 is Q_1^C whenever firm 2 produces Q_2^* units. This should not surprise you: This is exactly the output that corresponds to firm 1's reaction function.

FIGURE 9–5

Firm 1's best response to firm 2's output

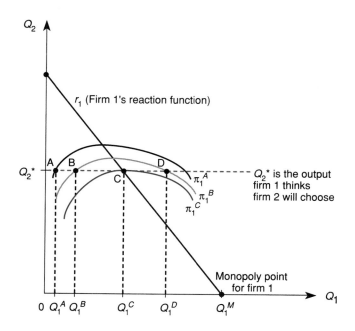

To maximize profits, firm 1 pushes its isoprofit curve as far down as possible (as close as possible to the monopoly point), until it is just tangent to the given output of firm 2. This tangency occurs at point C in Figure 9–5.

DEMONSTRATION PROBLEM 9–5

Graphically depict isoprofit curves for firm 2, and explain the relation between points on the isoprofit curves and firm 2's reaction function.

Answer

Isoprofit curves for firm 2 are the mirror image of those for firm 1. Representative isoprofit curves are depicted in Figure 9–6. Points G, A, and F lie on the same isoprofit curve and thus yield the same level of profits for firm 2. These profits are π_1, which are less than those of curves π_2 and π_3. As the isoprofit curves get closer to the monopoly point, the level of profits for firm 2 increases. The isoprofit curves begin to bend backward at the point where they intersect the reaction function.

FIGURE 9–6

Firm 2's reaction function and isoprofit curves

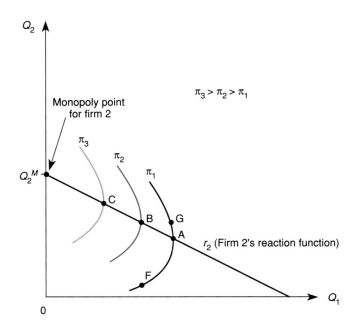

We can use isoprofit curves to illustrate the profits of each firm in a Cournot equilibrium. Recall that Cournot equilibrium is determined by the intersection of the two firms' reaction functions, such as point C in Figure 9–7. Firm 1's isoprofit curve through point C is given by π_1^C, and firm 2's isoprofit curve is given by π_2^C.

Changes in Marginal Costs

In a Cournot oligopoly, the effect of a change in marginal cost is very different than in a Sweezy oligopoly. To see why, suppose the firms initially are in equilibrium at point E in Figure 9–8, where firm 1 produces Q_1^* units and firm 2 produces Q_2^* units. Now suppose firm 2's marginal cost declines. At the given level of output, marginal revenue remains unchanged but marginal cost is reduced. This means that for firm 2, marginal revenue exceeds the lower marginal cost, and it is optimal to produce more output for any given level of Q_1. Graphically, this shifts firm 2's reaction function up from r_2 to r_2^{**}, leading to a new Cournot equilibrium at point F. Thus, the reduction in firm 2's marginal cost leads to an increase in firm 2's output, from Q_2^* to Q_2^{**}, and a decline in firm 1's output from Q_1^* to Q_1^{**}. Firm 2 enjoys a larger market share due to its improved cost situation.

The reason for the difference between the preceding analysis and the analysis of Sweezy oligopoly is the difference in the way a firm perceives how other firms will respond to a change in its decisions. These differences lead to differences in the way a manager should optimally respond to a

FIGURE 9–7

Cournot equilibrium

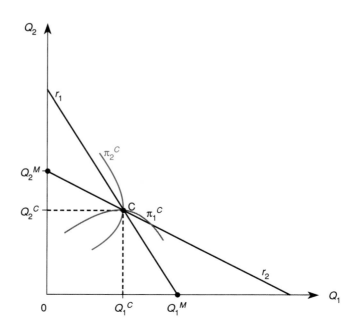

FIGURE 9–8

*Effect of decline in
firm 2's cost on
Cournot equilibrium*

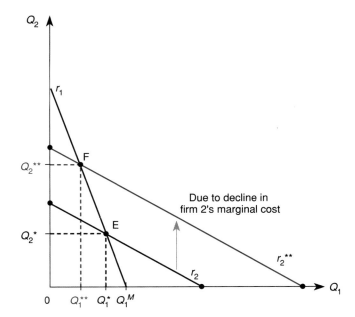

FIGURE 9–8

*Effect of decline in
firm 2's cost on
Cournot equilibrium*

reduction in the firm's marginal cost. If the manager believes other firms will follow price reductions but not price increases, the Sweezy model applies. In this instance, we learned that it may be optimal to continue to produce the same level of output even if marginal cost declines. If the manager believes other firms will maintain their existing output levels if the firm expands output, the Cournot model applies. In this case, it is optimal to expand output if marginal cost declines. The most important ingredient in making managerial decisions in markets characterized by interdependence is obtaining an accurate grasp of how other firms in the market will respond to the manager's decisions.

Collusion

Whenever a market is dominated by only a few firms, firms can benefit at the expense of consumers by "agreeing" to restrict output or, equivalently, charge higher prices. Such an act by firms is known as *collusion*. In the next chapter, we will devote considerable attention to collusion; for now, it is useful to use the model of Cournot oligopoly to show why such an incentive exists.

In Figure 9–9, point C corresponds to a Cournot equilibrium; it is the intersection of the reaction functions of the two firms in the market. The equilibrium profits of firm 1 are given by isoprofit curve π_1^C and those of firm 2 by π_2^C. Notice that the shaded lens-shaped area in Figure 9–9 contains output levels for the two firms that yield higher profits for both firms than

FIGURE 9–9

*The incentive to
collude in a Cournot
oligopoly*

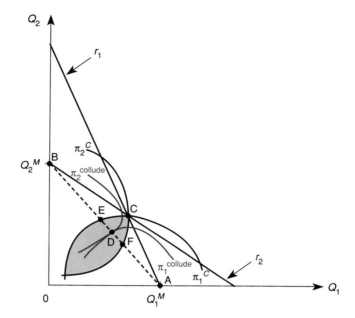

they earn in a Cournot equilibrium. For example, at point D each firm produces less output and enjoys greater profits, since each of the firm's isoprofit curves at point D is closer to the respective monopoly point. In effect, if each firm agreed to restrict output, the firms could charge higher prices and earn higher profits. The reason is easy to see. Firm 1's profits would be highest at point A, where it is a monopolist. Firm 2's profits would be highest at point B, where it is a monopolist. If each firm "agreed" to produce an output that in total equaled the monopoly output, the firms would end up somewhere on the line connecting points A and B. In other words, any combination of outputs along line AB would maximize total industry profits.

The outputs on the line segment connecting points E and F in Figure 9–9 thus maximize total industry profits, and since they are inside the lens-shaped area, they also yield both firms higher profits than would be earned if the firms produced at point C (the Cournot equilibrium). If the firms colluded by restricting output and splitting the monopoly profits, they would end up at a point like D, earning higher profits of π_1^{collude} and π_2^{collude}.

It is not easy for firms to reach such a collusive agreement, however. We will analyze this point in greater detail in the next chapter, but we can use our existing framework to see why collusion is sometimes difficult. Suppose firms agree to collude, with each firm producing the collusive output associated with point D in Figure 9–10 to earn collusive profits. Given that firm 2 produces $Q_2^{\text{collusive}}$, firm 1 has an incentive to "cheat" on the collusive agreement by expanding output to point G. At this point, firm 1 earns even

FIGURE 9–10

The incentive to renege on collusive agreements in Cournot oligopoly

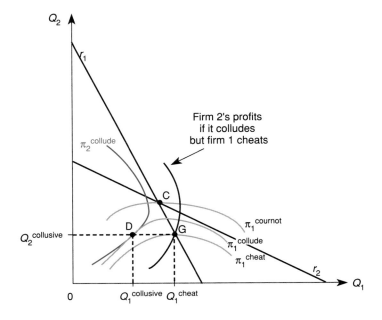

higher profits than it would by colluding, since $\pi_1^{\text{cheat}} > \pi_1^{\text{collude}}$. This suggests that a firm can gain by inducing other firms to restrict output and then expanding its own output to earn higher profits at the expense of its collusion partners. Because firms know this incentive exists, it is often difficult for them to reach collusive agreements in the first place. This problem is amplified by the fact that firm 2 in Figure 9–10 earns less at point G (where firm 1 cheats) than it would have earned at point C (the Cournot equilibrium).

Stackelberg oligopoly
An industry in which (1) there are few firms serving many consumers; (2) firms produce either differentiated or homogeneous products; (3) a single firm (the leader) chooses an output before rivals select their outputs; (4) all other firms (the followers) take the leader's output as given and select outputs that maximize profits given the leader's output; and (5) barriers to entry exist.

Stackelberg Oligopoly

Up until this point, we have analyzed oligopoly situations that are symmetric in that firm 2 is the "mirror image" of firm 1. In many oligopoly markets, however, firms differ from one another. In a *Stackelberg oligopoly*, firms differ with respect to when they make decisions. Specifically, one firm (the leader) is assumed to make an output decision before the other firms. Given knowledge of the leader's output, all other firms (the followers) take as given the leader's output and choose outputs that maximize profits. Thus, in a Stackelberg oligopoly, each follower behaves just like a Cournot oligopolist. However, firm 1 (the leader) does not act like a Cournot oligopolist. In fact, the leader does not take the followers' outputs as given but instead chooses an output that maximizes profits given that each follower will react to this output decision according to a Cournot reaction function.

FIGURE 9–11

Stackelberg equilibrium

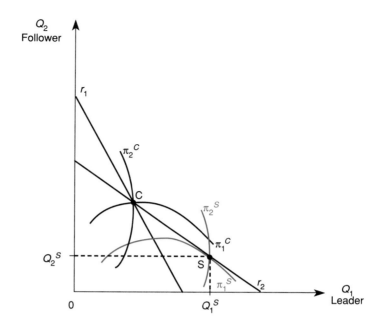

An industry is characterized as a Stackelberg oligopoly if:

1. There are few firms serving many consumers.
2. The firms produce either differentiated or homogeneous products.
3. A single firm (the leader) chooses an output before all other firms choose their outputs.
4. All other firms (the followers) take as given the output of the leader and choose outputs that maximize profits given the leader's output.
5. Barriers to entry exist.

To highlight a Stackelberg oligopoly, let us consider a situation where there are only two firms. Firm 1 is the *leader* and thus has a "first-mover" advantage; that is, firm 1 produces before firm 2. Firm 2 is the *follower* and maximizes profit given the output produced by the leader.

Because the follower produces after the leader, the follower's profit-maximizing level of output is determined by its reaction function. This is denoted by r_2 in Figure 9–11. However, the leader knows the follower will react according to r_2. Consequently, the leader must choose the level of output that will maximize its profits given that the follower reacts to whatever the leader does.

How does the leader choose the output level to produce? Since it knows the follower will produce along r_2, the leader simply chooses the point on the follower's reaction curve that corresponds to the highest level of its profits. Because the leader's profits increase as the isoprofit curves get closer to the monopoly output, the resulting choice by the leader will be at point S in Figure 9–11. This isoprofit curve, denoted π_1^S, yields the highest profits consistent with the follower's reaction function. It is tangent to firm 2's reaction function. Thus, the leader produces Q_1^S. The follower observes this output and produces Q_2^S, which is the profit-maximizing response to Q_1^S. The corresponding profits of the leader are given by π_1^S, and those of the follower by π_2^S. Notice that the leader's profits are higher than they would be in Cournot equilibrium (point C), and the follower's profits are lower than in Cournot equilibrium. By getting to move first, the leader earns higher profits than would otherwise be the case.

The algebraic solution for a Stackelberg oligopoly can also be obtained, provided firms have information about market demand and costs. In particular, recall that the follower's decision is identical to that of a Cournot model. For instance, with linear demand and constant marginal cost, the output of the follower is given by the reaction function

$$Q_2 = r_2(Q_1) = \frac{a - c_2}{2b} - \frac{1}{2} Q_1,$$

which is simply the follower's Cournot reaction function. However, the leader in the Stackelberg oligopoly takes into account this reaction function when it selects Q_1. With a linear inverse demand function and constant marginal costs, the leader's profits are

$$\Pi_1 = \left\{ a - b\left[Q_1 + \left(\frac{a - c_2}{2b} - \frac{1}{2} Q_1 \right) \right] \right\} Q_1 - c_1 Q_1.$$

The leader chooses Q_1 to maximize this profit expression. It turns out that the value of Q_1 that maximizes the leader's profits is

$$Q_1 = \frac{a + c_2 - 2c_1}{2b}.$$

Formula: Equilibrium Outputs in Stackelberg Oligopoly. For the linear (inverse) demand function

$$P = a - b(Q_1 + Q_2)$$

and cost functions

$$C_1(Q_1) = c_1 Q_1$$

$$C_2(Q_2) = c_2 Q_2,$$

the follower sets output according to the Cournot reaction function

$$Q_2 = r_2(Q_1) = \frac{a - c_2}{2b} - \frac{1}{2} Q_1.$$

The leader's output is

$$Q_1 = \frac{a + c_2 - 2c_1}{2b}.$$

A Calculus Alternative

To maximize profits, firm 1 sets output so as to maximize

$$\Pi_1 = \left\{ a - b \left[Q_1 + \left(\frac{a - c_2}{2b} - \frac{1}{2} Q_1 \right) \right] \right\} Q_1 - c_1 Q_1.$$

The first-order condition for maximizing profits is

$$\frac{d\pi_1}{dQ_1} = a - 2bQ_1 - \left(\frac{a - c_2}{2} \right) + bQ_1 - c_1 = 0.$$

Solving for Q_1 yields the profit-maximizing level of output for the leader:

$$Q_1 = \frac{a + c_2 - 2c_1}{2b}.$$

The formula for the follower's reaction function is derived in the same way as that for a Cournot oligopolist.

DEMONSTRATION PROBLEM 9–6

Suppose the inverse demand function for two firms in a homogeneous-product Stackelberg oligopoly is given by

$$P = 50 - (Q_1 + Q_2)$$

and cost functions for the two firms are

$$C_1 = 5 + 2Q_1$$
$$C_2 = 5 + 2Q_2.$$

Firm 1 is the leader, and firm 2 is the follower.
(1) What is firm 2's reaction function?
(2) What is firm 1's profit function?
(3) What is firm 1's output?
(4) What is firm 2's output?
(5) What is the market price?

Answer

(1) Using the formula for the follower's reaction function we find,

$$Q_2 = r_2(Q_1) = 24 - \frac{1}{2}Q_1.$$

(2) By plugging the answer to (1) into the profit function given for the Stackelberg leader, we find

$$\pi_1(Q_1) = \left\{ 50 - \left[Q_1 + \left(24 - \frac{1}{2}Q_1 \right) \right] \right\} Q_1 - (5 + 2Q_1).$$

(3) Using the formula given for the Stackelberg leader, we find

$$Q_1 = \frac{50 - 2}{2} = 24.$$

(4) By plugging the answer to (3) into the reaction function in (1), we find the follower's output to be

$$Q_2 = 24 - \frac{1}{2}(24) = 12.$$

(5) The market price can be found by adding the two firms' outputs together and plugging the answer into the inverse demand function:

$$P = 50 - (12 + 24) = 14.$$

Bertrand Oligopoly

Bertrand oligopoly
An industry in which
(1) there are few
firms serving many
consumers; (2) firms
produce identical
products at a
constant marginal
cost; (3) firms
compete in price and
react optimally to
competitors' prices;
(4) consumers have
perfect information
and there are no
transaction costs;
and (5) barriers to
entry exist.

To further highlight the fact that there is no single model of oligopoly a manager can use in all circumstances and illustrate that oligopoly power does not always imply firms will make positive profits, we will next examine Bertrand oligopoly. The treatment here assumes the firms sell identical products; the case where firms sell differentiated products is presented in the appendix. The next chapter also contains a more detailed analysis of Bertrand oligopoly.

An industry is characterized as a *Bertrand oligopoly* if

1. There are few firms in the market serving many consumers.
2. The firms produce identical products at a constant marginal cost.
3. Firms engage in price competition and react optimally to prices charged by competitors.
4. Consumers have perfect information and there are no transaction costs.
5. Barriers to entry exist.

From the viewpoint of the manager Bertrand oligopoly is undesirable, for it leads to zero profits even if there are only two firms in the market. From the viewpoint of consumers Bertrand oligopoly is desirable, for it leads to precisely the same outcome as a perfectly competitive market.

To explain more precisely the preceding assertions, consider a Bertrand duopoly. Because consumers have perfect information, have zero transaction costs, and the products are identical, all consumers will purchase from the firm charging the lowest price. For concreteness, suppose firm 1 charges the monopoly price. By slightly undercutting this price, firm 2 would capture the entire market and make positive profits, while firm 1 would sell nothing. Therefore, firm 1 would retaliate by undercutting firm 2's lower price, thus recapturing the entire market.

When would this "price war" end? When each firm charged a price that equaled marginal cost: $P_1 = P_2 = MC$. Given the price of the other firm, neither firm would choose to lower its price, for then its price would be below marginal cost and it would make a loss. Also no firm would want to raise its price, for then it would sell nothing. In short, Bertrand oligopoly and homogeneous products lead to a situation where each firm charges marginal cost and economic profits are zero.

Comparing Oligopoly Models

To see further how each form of oligopoly affects firms, it is useful to compare the models covered in this chapter in terms of individual firm outputs, prices in the market, and profits per firm. To accomplish this, we will use the same market demand and cost conditions for each firm when examining results for each model. The inverse market demand function we will use is

$$P = 1,000 - (Q_1 + Q_2).$$

The cost function of each firm is identical and given by

$$C_i(Q_i) = 4Q_i,$$

so the marginal cost of each firm is 4. We will now see how outputs, prices, and profits vary according to the type of oligopolistic interdependence that exists in the market.

Cournot

We will first examine Cournot equilibrium. The profit function for the individual Cournot firm given the preceding inverse demand and cost functions is

$$\pi_i = [1000 - (Q_1 + Q_2)]Q_i - 4Q_i.$$

The reaction functions of the Cournot oligopolists are

Inside Business 9–1

Stackelberg Oligopoly and International Trade

Many international markets are dominated by relatively few firms that possess not only market power but, in many instances, significant first-mover advantages. A recent article examines trade restrictions in duopolistic international markets in which one trading partner enjoys a first-mover advantage. The analysis shows that trade restrictions can enable foreign and domestic firms to earn higher economic profits. Moreover, when the home country enjoys a first-mover advantage, a quota placed below the existing level of imports generally reduces the output of both foreign and domestic firms.

To see why this is true, suppose the market for international trade is characterized by a Stackelberg duopoly in which both firms sell output only in the home country (say, the United States). The foreign firm observes the domestic firm's output and, based on this, determines how much of its product to deliver to the home country. Thus, the home firm (the leader) possesses a first-mover advantage and sets output, while the foreign firm (the follower) is a second mover; that is, the foreign firm perceives that the home-country firm will maintain the same output regardless of the foreign firm's export decision.

The foreign firm's reaction function—that is, the profit-maximizing response to any given output of the firm in the home country—is given by the line AC in Figure 9–12. Stackelberg equilibrium in the absence of trade restrictions is at point E, where the home country's isoprofit curve is tangent to the foreign firm's reaction function. The foreign firm ships Q_f units of output to the home country, and the domestic firm sells Q_h units; π_h and π_f represent the profits enjoyed by the home and foreign firms, respectively.

Now suppose an export restraint of X is imposed on the foreign producer, as in Figure 9–13. This may be either a quota imposed by the domestic government or an export restraint imposed by the foreign government that restricts how much its firms can export abroad. The export restraint makes it illegal for the firm in the foreign market to export more than X units to the home country.

Under an export restraint of X, the foreign firm's "effective" reaction function becomes XGC in Figure 9–13. Hence, the domestic firm's profits are maximized where its isoprofit curve is tangent to XGC, namely at point I. But this implies a lower output for the domestic firm (Q_h^*), greater output by the foreign firm (X), and higher profits for both firms ($\pi_h^* > \pi_h$ and $\pi_f^* > \pi_f$).

Thus, the export restraint increases the profits of foreign and domestic producers. While it is not surprising that it increases the domestic firm's profits, it may at first seem surprising that the foreign firm also benefits by facing an export restraint. The economic intuition, however, is simple. In the absence of controls on its foreign rival, the domestic firm knows that if it produces less than Q_h, the foreign firm will attempt to capitalize on the higher price by expanding its output. The export restraint restricts the amount by which the foreign firm can expand its output. If the export restraint is set at X, the foreign firm is unable to expand output beyond X in response to the output reduction by the domestic firm. At X, the domestic firm reduces its output because it knows the foreign firm cannot react to the higher price by expanding its output beyond X. As a consequence, both firms enjoy higher profits.

A foreign firm exporting to a market in which the home producer enjoys a first-mover advantage would be happy to have its government initiate and enforce a suitable export restraint. Indeed, this is precisely what occurred in Japan; the Japanese government has set export restraints limiting the number of cars that can be shipped to the United States.

Source: Michael R. Baye, "Export Restraints as Commitments in Stackelberg Trade Equilibrium," *Jahrbücher für Nationalökonomie und Statistik* 209 (1992), pp. 22–30.

FIGURE 9–12

Equilibrium before export restraint is at point E

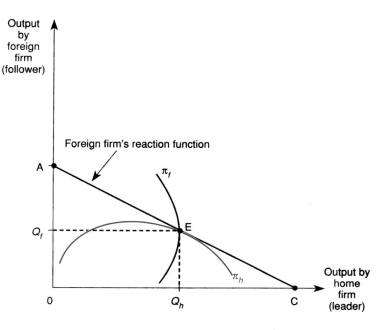

FIGURE 9–13

Equilibrium after export restraint moves from point E to point I

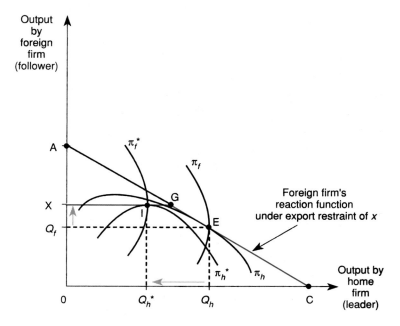

Managerial Compensation in Bertrand and Cournot Oligopoly

The issue of executive compensation has received considerable attention from academics and the popular press. Much of the work in this area attempts to estimate the relationship between firm performance and executive compensation. Classical microeconomic theory suggests that managers will be rewarded for maximizing firm profits. In 1959, William Baumol proposed that firms benefit from increases in sales. Since then, analysts have attempted to analyze the relationship among executive pay, profits, and sales.

More recently, Chaim Fershtman and Kenneth Judd developed a model of compensation contracting that incorporates aspects of oligopoly theory. These authors argue that managers of perfectly competitive firms will be rewarded only for profits; however, they find that managers of oligopolistic firms may be rewarded or penalized for increases in firm sales. The model suggests that by carefully choosing the terms of compensation contracts, firm owners are able to influence the decisions of both their own manager and managers of competing firms. Whether managers are rewarded or penalized for increases in firm sales depends on whether firms interact in a Cournot (quantity-setting) or Bertrand (price-setting) environment.

For example, assume two firms, Acme and Mustang, are quantity setters. If Mustang's manager is rewarded only for increases in profits while Acme's manager is rewarded for increases in both profits and sales, Acme's manager will become a more aggressive seller. As a result, Acme's sales will increase and the market price of the product will fall, which in turn will lead Mustang's manager to reduce output and sales. Acme will become the dominant firm. It can be shown that the best thing Mustang's owner can do, regardless of the contract written by Acme's owner,

is to also reward his or her manager for increases in sales. It is interesting to note that when both managers are rewarded for increases in sales, both firms' profits and product prices decrease as sales increase.

In contrast, if these firms are price setters, owners will penalize their managers for increases in sales. When Acme's manager is penalized for sales, this signals to Mustang's manager a willingness to price less aggressively. Mustang's manager, in turn, will increase the price of her or his product. It can be shown that when managers are price setters, compensation contracts that penalize them for increases in sales are optimal. In this case, output will be lower, and profits and prices greater than in the Bertrand pricing game without contracting.

In each scenario just outlined, performance can be thought of as a linear combination of profits and sales, with owners choosing α:

Performance $= \alpha$ *Profits* $+ (1 - \alpha)$ *Sales.*

In a Cournot oligopoly $\alpha < 1$, while in a Bertrand oligopoly $\alpha > 1$.

Marc Chopin adapted this model to empirically examine executive compensation in oligopolies. The empirical model includes an estimate of the salary payment and the degree to which measured performance affects compensation. The degree of dependence is represented as δ in the following equation:

Pay $= Salary + \delta[\alpha$ *Profits* $+ (1 - \alpha)$ *Sales*].

Using this model, Chopin estimated the terms of incentive contracts for 233 firms competing in 50 industries and found significant differences in the terms of compensation contracts across firms.

Inside Business 9–2 continued

Inside Business 9–2 concluded

As Table 9–1 shows, retail variety stores appear to have almost homogeneous measures of performance, with the majority of the weight placed on profits and a small but significant disincentive for sales. As suggested by the estimates of δ, the effect of performance on pay varies significantly across firms.

For example, these estimates indicate that the CEO of Dayton-Hudson will receive an additional $545.95 for each $1 million increase in profits (since 517 × 1.056 = 545), while cash compensation falls by $28.95 for each increase in sales of $1 million (since 517 × (1 − 1.056) = −28.95). When compared to Zayre's CEO, Dayton-Hudson's manager appears relatively insulated from performance. The CEO of Zayre earns additional cash compensation of $2,882.74 for each $1 million increase in profits; cash compensation decreases by $165.74 for each $1 million increase in sales.

TABLE 9–1   Estimates of Owners' Choices of α and the Degree of Dependence of Compensation on Measured Performance for Retail Variety Stores

Firm	δ (t-statistic in parentheses)	α (standard deviation in parentheses)
Dayton-Hudson	517 (3.57)	1.056 (0.009)
K Mart	170 (2.27)	1.035 (0.010)
Woolworth	847 (4.92)	1.048 (0.013)
Zayre	2,717 (2.08)	1.061 (0.007)

Sources: William J. Baumol, *Business Behavior, Value and Growth* (New York: Macmillan, 1959); Marc C. Chopin, "Market Structure, Compensation, and Incentives: An Empirical Analysis of CEO Compensation," Ph.D. dissertation, Texas A&M University, 1991; Chaim Fershtman and Kenneth L. Judd, "Equilibrium Incentives in Oligopoly," *American Economic Review* 5 (December 1987), pp. 927–40.

$$Q_1 = r_1(Q_2) = 498 - \frac{1}{2} Q_2$$

$$Q_2 = r_2(Q_1) = 498 - \frac{1}{2} Q_1.$$

Solving these two reaction functions for Q_1 and Q_2 yields the Cournot equilibrium outputs, which are $Q_1 = Q_2 = 332$. Total output in the market thus is 664, which leads to a price of $336. Plugging these values into the profit function reveals that each firm earns profits of $110,224.

Stackelberg

With these demand and cost functions, the output of the Stackelberg leader is

$$Q_1 = \frac{a + c_2 - 2c_1}{2b} = \frac{1,000 + 4 - 2(4)}{2} = 498.$$

The follower takes this level of output as given and produces according to its reaction function:

$$Q_2 = r_2(Q_1) = \frac{a - c}{2b} - \frac{1}{2} Q_1 = \frac{1,000 - 4}{2} - \frac{1}{2} (498) = 249.$$

Inside Business 9–3

Using Experiments to Understand Oligopoly Behavior

It often is difficult to find data that allow one to test theory in its purest form. Therefore, social scientists often use experimental methods to test their theories. In the case of economics, using the laboratory as a place to test and develop theory is relatively new. The first experiments were run by E. Chamberlain in 1948. The next attempt at running economic experiments came in 1963 and were conducted by Fouraker and Siegel. Since 1960, several economists have taken up the tool of experimental economics to help determine how different environments and informational situations affect behavior. Many experiments have been used to specifically address the different forms of oligopoly theories.

In experiments, subjects (usually students) are recruited to participate as economic agents. As such, they are participants in a decision-making process in which their decisions and the decisions of other people in the experiment determine the outcome of some market process. To induce the students to take the experiment seriously and to motivate behavior, their decisions are tied di-

rectly to monetary rewards. Each student is given a set of instructions for the market in which he or she is participating. In these instructions, students are told how their decisions map into monetary rewards. However, they are not instructed on *how* to act in the market. Any money a participant earns is paid in cash to the student at the end of the experiment.

The results of oligopoly experiments are decidedly mixed. Several experiments have allowed participants to take the role of producer in the same market. Some have given the participants quantity as their available choice, and some have given them price. The number of participants in the market makes a big difference in the results of these experiments.

When the number of participants in an experiment is two, collusion often results. Fouraker and Siegel, Dolbear et al., Holt, Phillips, Battalio, and Holcomb and Beil have all found generally the same results in two-person quantity-setting

Inside Business 9–3 continued

Total output in the market thus is 747 units. Given the inverse demand function, this output yields a price of $253. Total market output is higher in a Stackelberg oligopoly than in a Cournot oligopoly. This leads to a lower price in the Stackelberg oligopoly than in the Cournot oligopoly. The profits for the leader are $124,002, while the follower earns only $62,001 in profits. The leader does better in a Stackelberg oligopoly than in a Cournot oligopoly due to its first-mover advantage. However, the follower earns lower profits in a Stackelberg oligopoly than in a Cournot oligopoly.

Bertrand

The Bertrand equilibrium is simple to calculate. Recall that firms that engage in Bertrand competition end up setting price equal to marginal cost. Therefore, with the given inverse demand and cost functions, price equals marginal cost ($4) and profits are zero for each firm. Total market output is 996 units. Given symmetric firms, each firm gets half of the market.

experiments. Approximately 60 percent of the duopoly pairs are able to find and maintain a collusive action with nothing other than their output decisions to guide them. About 25 percent of the participants have market outcomes that are not statistically different from Cournot output levels. However, the Cournot result does not tend to be stable in the sense that participants produce the Cournot output level every time. Instead, output fluctuates around the Cournot level of output. It appears participants would like to move toward collusive outcomes but are unable to accomplish this. The remaining 15 percent of the participants are split equally between output levels that lie between Cournot and collusive and between Cournot and perfectly competitive solutions. When the number of participants in these experiments rises to three or more in each market, Cournot levels of output are almost always observed.

In addition to the quantity-setting experiments, several price-setting experiments have been conducted, including experiments by Four-

aker and Siegel; Phillips, Battalio, and Holcomb; and Harrison and McKee. As in the quantity-setting experiments, almost 60 percent of the markets with two participants produce a collusive level of output. However, when the number of participants in each market rises above two, Bertrand equilibrium is found to prevail approximately 90 percent of the time.

Sources: E. H. Chamberlain, "An Experimental Imperfect Market," *Journal of Political Economy* 56 (1948), pp. 95–108; L. E. Fouraker and S. Siegel, *Bargaining Behavior* (New York: McGraw-Hill, 1963); F. T. Dolbear, L. B. Lave, G. Bowman, A. Lieberman, E. Prescott, F. Rueter, and A. Sherman, "Collusion in Oligopoly: An Experiment on the Effect of Numbers and Information," *Quarterly Journal of Economics* 82 (May 1968), pp. 506–15; C. A. Holt, "An Experimental Test of the Consistent Conjectures Hypothesis," *American Economic Review* 76 (June 1985), pp. 314–25; G. W. Harrison and M. McKee, "Monopoly Behavior, Decentralized Regulation, and Contestable Markets: An Experimental Evaluation," *Rand Journal of Economics* 16 (Spring 1985), pp. 51–69; O. R. Phillips, R. C. Battalio, and J. H. Holcomb, "Duopoly Behavior with Market History," manuscript, University of Wyoming, 1990; R. O. Beil, "Collusive Behavior in Experimental Oligopoly Markets," Ph.D. dissertation, Texas A&M University, 1988.

Collusion

Finally, we will determine the collusive outcome, which results when the firms choose output to maximize total industry profits. When firms collude, total industry output is the monopoly level, based on the market inverse demand curve. Since the market inverse demand curve is

$$P = 1,000 - Q,$$

the associated marginal revenue is

$$MR = 1,000 - 2Q.$$

Notice that this marginal revenue function assumes the firms act as a single profit-maximizing firm, which is what collusion is all about. Setting marginal revenue equal to marginal cost (which is $4) yields

$$1,000 - 2Q = 4,$$

or $Q = 498$. Thus, total industry output under collusion is 498 units, with each firm producing half. The price under collusion is

$$P = 1,000 - 498 = \$502.$$

Each firm earns profits of $124,002.

Comparison of the outcomes in these different oligopoly situations reveals the following. The highest market output is produced in a Bertrand oligopoly, followed by Stackelberg, then Cournot, and finally collusion. Profits are highest for the Stackelberg leader and the colluding firms, followed by Cournot, then the Stackelberg follower. The Bertrand oligopolists earn the lowest level of profits. If you become a manager in an oligopolistic market, it is important to recognize that your optimal decisions and profits will vary depending on the type of oligopolistic interaction that exists in the market.

Contestable Markets

Thus far, we have emphasized strategic interaction among existing firms in an oligopoly. Strategic interaction can also exist between existing firms and potential entrants into a market. To illustrate the importance of this interaction and its similarity to Bertrand oligopoly, let us suppose a market is served by a single firm but there is another firm (a potential entrant) free to enter the market whenever it chooses.

Before we continue our analysis, let us make more precise what we mean by *free entry*. What we have in mind here is what economists refer to as a *contestable market*. A market is contestable if

contestable market
A market in which
(1) all firms have
access to the same
technology; (2)
consumers respond
quickly to price
changes; (3) existing
firms cannot respond
quickly to entry by
lowering their
prices; and (4) there
are no sunk costs.

1. All producers have access to the same technology.
2. Consumers respond quickly to price changes.
3. Existing firms cannot respond quickly to entry by lowering price.
4. There are no sunk costs.

If these four conditions hold, incumbent firms (existing firms in the market) have no market power over consumers. This is true even if there is only one existing firm in the market.

The reason for this result follows. If existing firms charged a price in excess of what they required to cover costs, a new firm could immediately enter the market with the same technology and charge a price slightly below the existing firms' prices. Since the incumbents cannot quickly respond by lowering their prices, the entrant would get all the incumbents' customers by charging the lower price. Because the incumbents know this, they have no alternative but to charge a low price equal to the cost of production to keep out the entrant. Thus, if a market is perfectly contestable, incumbents are disciplined by the threat of entry by new firms.

An important condition for a contestable market is the absence of sunk costs. In this context, *sunk costs* are defined as costs a new entrant must bear that cannot be recouped upon exiting the market. For example, if an entrant pays $100,000 for a truck to enter the market for moving services,

De Beers: The Stackelberg Leader or Cartel Ring Leader

The diamond industry is dominated by De Beers Corporation, which produces 80 percent of the world's mined diamonds. One-hundred-four-year-old De Beers mined most of the world's diamonds in its early years. Most of the stones De Beers owns were mined in South Africa. Today the firm owns mining interests in South Africa and in several other countries. The London branch of De Beers weighed, purchased, and stored an average of $15 million in diamonds per day in 1991. De Beers' diamond inventory has been valued at more than $2.5 billion. In the mid-1980s, Australia increased the world's new mining of diamonds by 50 percent, yet De Beers held on to its control of the market. How did it accomplish this feat?

De Beers' strong position in the market comes from two sources. First, because the firm owns 80 percent of the mined diamonds in the world, it could flood the market if other companies made a bid for lower prices. Consequently, most small producers of diamonds let De Beers move first in the market and follow along with the decisions made by De Beers. The size of De Beers' market share induces other firms to allow it to enjoy a first-mover advantage, which leads to larger profits for De Beers.

Second, De Beers has set itself up as a clearinghouse for almost all of the world's uncut diamonds. By acting as a clearinghouse, it effectively makes "cartellike" decisions for the diamond industry. This results in a relatively high, stable price of diamonds. This stability is very attractive to other mining concerns, since they are affected less by economic downturns than are other industries.

With its strong leadership position and its ability to act as a clearinghouse for diamonds, De Beers has little to fear from competition in the diamond market. Interestingly, De Beers is not allowed to operate in the United States because of U.S. antitrust laws. However, through its ad agency, N. W. Ayer of New York, De Beers spent approximately $52 million on advertising in 1991. Its biggest success came in the 1920s, however, when the firm set the standard for engagement rings; the ad stated that a young man should spend two months' salary on a ring.

Source: Richard S. Teitelbaum, "Hard Times for Diamonds," *Fortune*, April 22, 1991, pp. 167–78.

but receives $80,000 for the truck upon exiting the market, $20,000 represents the sunk costs of entering the market. Similarly, if a firm pays a non-refundable fee of $20,000 for the nontransferable right to lease a truck for a year to enter the market, this reflects a sunk cost associated with entry. Or if a small firm must incur a loss of $2,000 per month for six months while waiting for customers to "switch" to that company, it incurs $12,000 of sunk costs.

Sunk costs are important for the following reason. Suppose incumbent firms are charging high prices, and a new entrant calculates that it could earn $70,000 by entering the market and charging a lower price than the existing firms. This calculation is, of course, conditional upon the existing firms continuing to charge their present prices. Suppose that to enter, the firm must pay sunk costs of $20,000. If it enters the market and the incumbent firms keep charging the high price, entry is profitable; indeed, the firm will make $70,000. However, if the incumbents do not continue charging the high price but instead lower their prices, the entrant can be left with no customers. In this instance, the entrant loses the sunk cost of $20,000. In short, if a potential entrant must pay sunk costs to enter a market and has reason to believe incumbents will respond to entry by lowering their prices, it will find it unprofitable to enter even though prices are high. The end result is that with sunk costs, incumbents may not be disciplined by potential entry, and higher prices may prevail.

Answering the Headline

Although the price of oil fell in the early 1990s, in a few areas there were no declines in the price of gasoline. The headline asks whether this is evidence of collusion by gasoline stations in those areas. To answer this question, notice that oil is an input in producing gasoline. A reduction in the price of oil leads to a reduction in the marginal cost of producing gasoline—say, from MC_0 to MC_1. If gasoline firms were colluding, a reduction in marginal cost would lead the firms to lower the price of gasoline. To see this, recall that under collusion, both the industry output and the price are set at the monopoly level and price. Thus, if firms were colluding when marginal cost was MC_0, the output that would maximize collusive profits would occur where $MR = MC_0$ in Figure 9–14. Thus, Q^* and P^* in Figure 9–14 denote the collusive output and price when marginal cost is MC_0. A reduction in the marginal cost of producing gasoline would shift down the marginal cost curve to MC_1, leading to a greater collusive output (Q^{**}) and a lower price (P^{**}). Thus, collusion cannot explain why some gasoline firms failed to lower their prices. Had these firms been colluding, they would have found it profitable to lower gasoline prices when the price of oil fell.

Since collusion is not the reason gasoline prices in some areas did not fall when the marginal cost of gasoline declined, one may wonder what could explain the pricing behavior in these markets. One explanation is that these gasoline producers are Sweezy oligopolists. The Sweezy oligopolist operates on the assumption that if she raises her price, her competitors will ignore the change. However if she lowers her price, all will follow suit and lower their prices. Figure 9–15 reveals that Sweezy oligopolists will not decrease gasoline prices when marginal cost falls from MC_0 to MC_1. They know they cannot increase their profits or market share by lowering their price, because all of their competitors will lower prices if they do.

FIGURE 9–14

Reduction in marginal cost lowers the collusive price

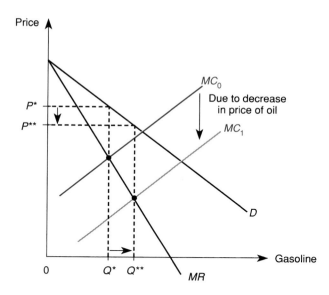

FIGURE 9–15

Price rigidity in Sweezy oligopoly

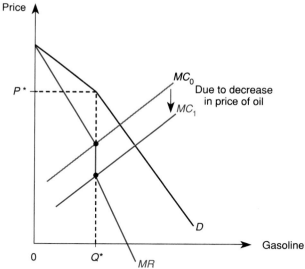

Summary

In this chapter, we examined several models of markets that consist of a small number of strategically interdependent firms. These models help explain several possible types of behavior when a market is characterized by oligopoly. You should now be familiar with the Sweezy, Cournot, Stackelberg, and Bertrand models.

In the Cournot model, a firm chooses quantity based on its competitors' given levels of output. Each firm earns some economic profits. Bertrand competitors, on the other hand, set prices given their rivals' prices. They end up charging a price equal to their marginal cost and earn zero economic profits. Sweezy oligopolists believe their competitors will follow price decreases but will ignore price increases, leading to extremely stable prices even when costs change in the industry. Finally, Stackelberg oligopolies have a follower and a leader. The leader knows how the follower will behave, and the follower simply maximizes profits given what the leader has chosen. This leads to profits for each firm but much higher profits for the leader than for the follower.

The next chapter will explain in more detail how managers go about reaching equilibrium in oligopoly. For now, it should be clear that your decisions will affect others in your market and their decisions will affect you as well.

Key Terms and Concepts

Bertrand oligopoly	leader
collusion	oligopoly
contestable markets	reaction function
Cournot equilibrium	Stackelberg equilibrium
Cournot oligopoly	Stackelberg oligopoly
follower	sunk costs
isoprofit curve	Sweezy oligopoly

Problems

1. In Gelate, Pennsylvania, the market for compact discs has evolved as follows. There are two firms that each use a marquee to post the price they charge for compact discs. Each firm buys CDs from the same supplier at a cost of $5.00 per disc. The market demand in their area is given by $P = 10 - 2Q$, where Q is the total output produced by the two firms.
   a. Solve for the Bertrand equilibrium price and market output.
   b. Would your answer differ if the products were not perfect substitutes? Explain.

2. Suppose you are the manager of a medium-sized firm that operates in an industry that has a four-firm concentration ratio of 100 percent. All firms in the industry are of equal size. In order to determine your firm's optimal output and price, you must obtain information about

how rivals would respond to changes in your decisions. If you were the manager, how would you obtain this information?

3. You are the manager of a firm operating in a differentiated-product oligopoly. Show graphically your optimal response to an increase in marginal cost if
   a. You believe rivals will follow price reductions but not price increases.
   b. You believe rivals will hold output constant if you decrease output.
   c. You believe rivals will follow price increases but not price decreases.

4. The (inverse) demand in a Cournot duopoly is

$$P = a - b(Q_1 + Q_2)$$

   and costs are

$$C_1(Q) = c_1 Q_1$$
$$C_2(Q) = c_2 Q_2.$$

   Show that the Cournot equilibrium levels of output are

$$Q_1^C = \frac{a + c_2 - 2c_1}{3b}$$

$$Q_2^C = \frac{a + c_1 - 2c_2}{3b}.$$

5. The market for widgets consists of two firms that produce identical products. Competition in the market is such that each of the firms independently produces a quantity of output, and these quantities are then sold in the market at a price that is determined by the total amount produced by the two firms. Firm 2 is known to have a cost advantage over firm 1. A recent study found that the (inverse) market demand curve faced by the two firms is

$$P = 280 - 2(Q_1 + Q_2)$$

   and costs are

$$C_1(Q_1) = 3Q_1$$
$$C_2(Q_2) = 2Q_2.$$

   a. Determine the marginal revenue for each firm.
   b. Determine the reaction function for each firm.
   c. How much output will each firm produce in equilibrium?
   d. What are the equilibrium profits for each firm?

6. When MCI announced a price discount plan designed to induce small firms to use its services, the price of its stock immediately declined.

Why do you think the stock market reacted negatively to MCI's plan to attract new customers?

7. The inverse demand curve for a Stackelberg duopoly is

$$P = 10{,}000 - 6Q.$$

The leader's cost structure is

$$C_L(Q_L) = 2{,}500 + 15Q_L.$$

The follower's cost structure is

$$C_F(Q_F) = 500 + 25Q_F.$$

   a. Determine the reaction function for the follower.
   b. Determine the equilibrium output levels for both the leader and the follower.
   c. What are the profits for the leader? For the follower?

8. What real-world evidence would lead you to believe that firms were acting as Cournot oligopolists? Stackelberg oligopolists? Bertrand oligopolists?

9. Zelda Industries is the only firm of its kind in the world. Due largely to historical accident, it began producing streganomas in 1985 in a vacant warehouse. Virtually anyone with a degree in college chemistry could easily replicate the firm's formula, which is not patent protected. Nonetheless, since 1985 Zelda has averaged accounting profits of 6 percent on investment. This rate is comparable to the average interest rate that large banks paid on deposits over the period. Do you think Zelda is earning monopoly profits? Why?

10. You are the manager of a firm in a new industry. You have gotten the jump on the only other producer in the market. You know what your competitor's cost function is, and it knows yours. Your products, although different to experts, are indistinguishable to the average consumer. Your marketing research team has provided you with the following market demand curve:

$$Q = 1{,}250 - .5P.$$

Your cost function is

$$C_A(Q_A) = 180 + 8Q_A.$$

Your competitor's cost function is

$$C_B(Q_B) = 350 + 6Q_B.$$

Your diligent effort will allow you to decide how much of your product to provide and allow you to place it on the market shortly before your competitor will be able to make its product available for sale. What output level will you choose, and what price will you charge? Explain.

11. In a recent company meeting, your boss expressed concern because the government was considering imposing restrictions that would limit your firm's ability to sell products to third-world countries. Your firm is the only firm in the industry that exports the goods to the third world, although the handful of firms in the third-world that sell there enjoy a significant first-mover advantage. Do you think the concerns of your boss are justified? Explain.

12. You are a potential entrant into a market that previously has had entry blocked by the government. Your market research has estimated that the market demand curve for this industry is

$$P = 22{,}500 - 75Q,$$

where

$$Q = \sum_{i=1}^{n} Q_i.$$

You estimate that if you enter the market, your own cost function will be

$$C_y(Q_y) = 50{,}000 + 3{,}000Q_y.$$

The government has invited your firm to enter the industry, but it will require you to pay a one-time license fee of $100,000. You do not know the cost functions of the firms presently in the market; however, the price is now $16,000. Last year 87 units were sold by existing firms. Would you choose to enter this market? Explain.

13. How would your answer in Problem 12 change if your estimated cost function were

$$C_y(Q_y) = 50{,}000 + 15{,}3000Q_y?$$

14. Compare and contrast the output levels and profits for the Cournot, Stackelberg, and Bertrand models. Use the following cost and demand conditions for your comparison, and suppose there are two firms:

$$P = 1{,}500 - 10Q.$$

Each firm has a marginal cost of 20 and fixed costs of zero.

15. Over the past 20 years, the 12 members of the Organization of Petroleum Exporting Countries have made repeated attempts to restrict output in order to maintain high crude oil prices. Between 1990 and 1995, however, crude oil prices have dropped by about 20 percent, due in part to increased production from the former Soviet Union, Latin America, Asia, and the North Sea. In light of these increases in oil

production from non-OPEC countries, what must OPEC do to maintain the price of oil at its desired level? Do you think this will be easy for OPEC to do? Explain.

16. In 1995, Chrysler announced a new incentive program on its minivans that included subsidized interest rates and cash allowances. Under the plan consumers could enjoy financing rates as low as 4.9 percent, as well as a $500 cash allowance toward the lease or purchase of a new minivan. What changes in sales would you anticipate if you were the manager of a Dodge/Plymouth franchise? Why?

Selected Readings

Alberts, William W., "Do Oligopolists Earn 'Noncompetitive' Rates of Return?." *American Economic Review* 74(4), September 1984, pp. 624–32.

Becker, Klaus G., "Natural Monopoly Equilibria: Nash and Von Stackelberg Solutions." *Journal of Economics and Business* 46(2), May 1994, pp. 135–39.

Brander, James A. and Lewis, Tracy R., "Oligopoly and Financial Structure: The Limited Liability Effect." *American Economic Review* 76(5), December 1986, pp. 956–70.

Caudill, Steven B. and Mixon, Franklin G., Jr., "Cartels and the Incentive to Cheat: Evidence from the Classroom." *Journal of Economic Education* 25(3), Summer 1994, pp. 267–69.

Friedman, J.W., *Oligopoly Theory*. Amsterdam: North Holland, 1983.

Gal-Or, E., "Excessive Retailing at the Bertrand Equilibria." *Canadian Journal of Economics* 23(2), May 1990, pp. 294–304.

Levy, David T. and Reitzes, James D., "Product Differentiation and the Ability to Collude: Where Being Different Can Be an Advantage." *Antitrust Bulletin* 38(2), Summer 1993, pp. 349–68.

Plott, C.R., "Industrial Organization Theory and Experimental Economics." *Journal of Economic Literature* 20, 1982, pp. 1485–1527.

Ross, Howard N., "Oligopoly Theory and Price Rigidity." *Antitrust Bulletin* 32(2), Summer 1987, pp. 451–69.

Showalter, Dean M., "Oligopoly and Financial Structure: Comment." *American Economic Review* 85(3), June 1995, pp. 647–53.

APPENDIX
DIFFERENTIATED-PRODUCT BERTRAND OLIGOPOLY

The model of Bertrand oligopoly presented in the text is based on Bertrand's classic treatment of the subject, which assumes oligopolists produce identical products. Because oligopolists that produce differentiated products may engage in price competition, this appendix presents a model of differentiated-product Bertrand oligopoly.

Suppose two oligopolists produce slightly differentiated products and compete by setting prices. In this case, one firm cannot capture all of its rival's customers by undercutting the rival's price; some consumers will have a preference for a firm's product even if the rival is charging a lower price. Thus, even if firm 2 were to "give its product away for free" (charge a zero price), firm 1 generally would find it profitable to charge a positive price. Moreover, as firm 2 raised its price, some of its customers would defect to firm 1, and thus the demand for firm 1's product would increase. This would raise firm 1's marginal revenue, making it profitable for the firm to increase its price.

In a differentiated-product price-setting oligopoly, the reaction function of firm 1 defines firm 1's profit-maximizing price given the price charged by firm 2. Based on the above reasoning, firm 1's reaction function is upward sloping, as illustrated in Figure 9–16. To see this, note that if firm 2 sets its price at zero, firm 1 will find it profitable to set price at $P_1^{min} > 0$, since some consumers will prefer its product to the rival's. Effectively, P_1^{min} is the price that maximizes firm 1's profits when it sells only to its brand-loyal customers (customers who do not want the other product, even for free). If the rival raises its price to, say, P_2^*, some of firm 2's customers will decide to switch to firm 1's product. Consequently, when firm 2 raises its price to P_2^*, firm 1 will raise its price to P_1^* to maximize profits given the higher demand. In fact, each point along firm 1's reaction function defines the profit-maximizing price charged by firm 1 for each price charged by firm 2. Notice that firm 1's reaction function is upward sloping, unlike in the case of Cournot oligopoly.

Firm 2's reaction function, which defines the profit-maximizing price for firm 2 given the price charged by firm 1, also is illustrated in Figure 9–16. It is upward sloping for the same reason firm 1's reaction function is upward sloping; in fact, firm 2's reaction function is the mirror image of firm 1's.

In a differentiated-product Bertrand oligopoly, equilibrium is determined by the intersection of the two firms' reaction functions, which corresponds to point A in

FIGURE 9–16

Reaction functions in a differentiated product Bertrand oligopoly

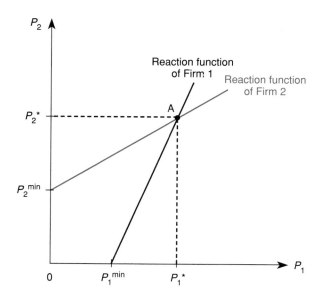

Figure 9–16. To see that point A is indeed an equilibrium, note that the profit-maximizing price for firm 1 when firm 2 sets price at P_2^* is P_1^*. Similarly, the profit-maximizing price for firm 2 when firm 1 sets price at P_1^* is P_2^*.

In a differentiated-product Bertrand oligopoly, firms charge prices that exceed marginal cost. The reason they are able to do so is that the products are not perfect substitutes. As a firm raises its price, it loses some customers to the rival firm, but not all of them. Thus, the demand function for an individual firm's product is downward sloping, similar to the case in monopolistic competition. But unlike in monopolistic competition, the existence of entry barriers prevents other firms from entering the market. This allows the firms in a differentiated-product Bertrand oligopoly to potentially earn positive economic profits in the long run.

Game Theory: Inside Oligopoly

Headline

Saudis Balk at Output Reduction; Analysts Predict Higher Oil Prices

During the early 1990s, OPEC had considerable difficulty maintaining high crude oil prices. While OPEC's overall plan was to restrict output to the collusive level, some member countries earned short-term windfalls by cheating on the cartel's output quotas. Venezuela has historically been one of the biggest defectors, but some analysts believe that it is now ready to cooperate with other OPEC members. Among the reasons cited: Venezuela needs funds to pay for the cost of fighting off a coup attempt.

Recently, Saudi Arabia—the usual leader in the cartel—vetoed an output reduction plan designed by Venezuela to boost crude oil prices. Nonetheless, some analysts predict that the Saudi's move marks a new beginning for OPEC that is likely to allow the cartel to enjoy higher future profits through collusion.

If Saudi Arabia refused to cooperate with Venezuela's output reduction plan, why are analysts saying that the cartel is likely to enjoy future profits through collusion?

Introduction

In this chapter we continue our analysis of strategic interaction. As we saw in the previous chapter, when only a few firms compete in a market, the actions of one firm will have a drastic impact on its rivals. For example, the pricing and output decisions of one firm in an oligopoly generally will affect the profits of other firms in the industry. Consequently, to maximize profits a manager must take into account the likely impact of his or her decisions on the behavior of other managers in the industry.

In this chapter we will delve more deeply into managerial decisions that arise in the presence of interdependence. We will develop general tools that will assist you in making a host of decisions in oligopolistic markets, including what prices to charge, how much advertising to use, whether to introduce new products, and whether to enter a new market. The basic tool we will use to examine these issues is *game theory*. Game theory is a very useful tool for managers. In fact, we will see that game theory can be used to analyze decisions within a firm, such as those related to monitoring and bargaining with workers.

Overview of Games and Strategic Thinking

Perhaps when you think of a game, a trivial game like tic-tac-toe, checkers, or Wheel of Fortune comes to mind. Game theory is actually a much more general framework to aid in decision making when your payoff depends on the actions taken by other players.

In a game, the players are individuals who make decisions. For example, in an oligopolistic market consisting of two firms, each of which must make a pricing decision, the firms (or, more precisely, the firms' managers) are the players. The planned decisions of the players are called *strategies*. The payoffs to the players are the profits or losses that result from the strategies. Due to interdependence, the payoff to a player depends not only on that player's strategy but also on the strategies employed by other players.

In the analysis of games, the order in which players make decisions is important. In a *simultaneous-move game,* each player makes decisions without knowledge of the other players' decisions. In a *sequential-move game,* one player makes a move after observing the other player's move. Tic-tac-toe, chess, and checkers are examples of sequential-move games (since players alternate moves), whereas matching pennies, dueling, and scissors-rock-paper are examples of simultaneous-move games. In the context of oligopoly games, if two firms must set prices without knowledge of each other's decisions, it is a simultaneous-move game; if one firm sets its price after observing its rival's price, it is a sequential-move game.

It is also important to distinguish between one-shot games and repeated games. In a *one-shot game,* the underlying game is played only once. In a *repeated game,* the underlying game is played more than once. For example, if you agree to play one, and only one, game of chess with a "rival," you are playing a one-shot game. If you agree to play chess two times with a rival, you are playing a repeated game.

Before we formally show how game theory can help managers solve business decisions, it is instructive to provide an example. Imagine that two gasoline stations are located side by side on the same block so that neither firm has a location advantage over the other. Consumers view the gasoline at each station as perfect substitutes and will purchase from the station that offers the lowest price. The first thing in the morning, the manager of a gas station must phone the attendant to tell him what price to put on the sign. Since she must do so without knowledge of the rival's price, this "pricing game" is a simultaneous-move game. This type of game often is called the *Bertrand duopoly game.*

Given the structure of the game, if the manager of station A calls in a higher price than the manager of station B, consumers will not buy any gas from station A. The manager of station A, therefore, is likely to reason, "I think I'll charge $1.50 per gallon. But if station B thinks I will charge $1.50, they will charge $1.49, so I'd better charge $1.48. But if manager B thinks I think she'll charge $1.49, she will try to 'trick' me by charging $1.47. So I'd better charge $1.46. But if she thinks I think she thinks . . ." Perhaps you have gone through a similar thought process in trying to decide what to study for an exam ("The professor won't test us on this, but if he thinks we think he won't, he'll ask it to get us . . .").

Game theory is a powerful tool for analyzing situations such as these. First, however, we must examine the foundations of game theory. We will begin with the study of simultaneous-move, one-shot games.

Simultaneous-Move, One-Shot Games

This section presents the basic tools used to analyze simultaneous-move, one-shot games. Recall that in a simultaneous-move game, players must make decisions without knowledge of the decisions made by other players. The fact that a game is "one-shot" simply means that the players will play the game only once.

Knowledge of simultaneous-move, one-shot games is important to managers making decisions in an environment of interdependence. For example, it can be used to analyze situations where the profits of a firm depend not only on the firm's action but the actions of rival firms as well. Before we look at specific applications of simultaneous-move, one-shot games, let us examine the general theory used to analyze such decisions.

strategy
In game theory, a decision rule that describes the actions a player will take at each decision point.

Theory

We begin with two key definitions. First, a *strategy* is a decision rule that describes the actions a player will take at each decision point. Second, the *normal-form* representation of a game indicates the players in the game, the

normal-form game
A representation of a
game indicating the
players, their
possible strategies,
and the payoffs
resulting from
alternative strategies.

possible strategies of the players, and the payoffs to the players that will result from alternative strategies.

Perhaps the best way to understand precisely what is meant by *strategy* and *normal-form game* is to examine a simple example. The normal form of a simultaneous-move game is presented in Table 10–1. There are two players, whom we will call A and B to emphasize that the theory is perfectly general; that is, the players can be any two entities that are engaged in a situation of strategic interaction. If you wish, you may think of the players as the managers of two firms competing in a duopoly.

Player A has two possible strategies: He can choose *up* or *down*. Similarly, the feasible strategies for player B are *left* or *right*. Again, by calling the strategies, *up, down,* and so on, we emphasize that these actions can represent virtually any decisions. For instance, *up* might represent raising the price and *down* lowering price, or *up* a high level of advertising and *down* a low level of advertising.

Finally, the payoffs to the two players are given by the entries in each cell of the matrix. The first entry refers to the payoff to player A, and the second entry denotes the payoff to player B. An important thing to notice about the description of the game is that the payoff to player A crucially depends on the strategy player B chooses. For example, if A chooses *up* and B chooses *left,* the resulting payoffs are 10 for A and 20 for B. Similarly, if player A's strategy is *up* while B's strategy is *right,* A's payoff is 15 while B's payoff is 8.

Since the game in Table 10–1 is a simultaneous-move, one-shot game, the players get to make one, and only one, decision and must make their decisions at the same time. For player A, the decision is simply *up* or *down*. Moreover, the players cannot make conditional decisions; for example, A can't choose *up* if B chooses *right* or *down* if B chooses *left*. The fact that the players make decisions at the same time precludes each player from basing his or her decisions on what the other player does.

What is the optimal strategy for a player in a simultaneous-move, one-shot game? As it turns out, this is a very complex question and depends on the nature of the game being played. There is one instance, however, in

TABLE 10–1

	Player B		
	Strategy	Left	Right
Player A	Up	10, 20	15, 8
	Down	−10, 7	10, 10

dominant strategy
A strategy that results in the highest payoff to a player regardless of the opponent's action.

which it is easy to characterize the optimal decision—a situation that involves a dominant strategy. A strategy is a *dominant strategy* if it results in the highest payoff regardless of the action of the opponent.

In Table 10–1, the dominant strategy for player A is *up*. To see this, note that if player B chooses *left*, the best choice by player A is *up* since 10 units of profits are better than the −10 he would earn by choosing *down*. If B chose *right*, the best choice by A would be *up* since 15 units of profits are better than the 10 he would earn by choosing *down*. In short, regardless of whether player B's strategy is *left* or *right*, the best choice by player A is *up*. *Up* therefore is a dominant strategy for player A.

In simultaneous-move, one-shot games where a player has a dominant strategy, the optimal decision is to choose the dominant strategy. By doing so, you will maximize your payoff regardless of what your opponent does. In some games a player may not have a dominant strategy, as illustrated in Demonstration Problem 10–1.

DEMONSTRATION PROBLEM 10–1

In the game presented in Table 10–1, does player B have a dominant strategy?

Answer

Player B does not have a dominant strategy. To see this, note that if player A chose *up*, the best choice by player B would be *left*, since 20 is better than the payoff of 8 she would earn by choosing *right*. But if A chose *down*, the best choice by B would be *right*, since 10 is better than the payoff of 7 she would realize by choosing *left*. Thus, there is no dominant strategy for player B; the best choice by B depends on what A does.

---

secure strategy
A strategy that guarantees the highest payoff given the worst possible scenario.

What should a player do in the absence of a dominant strategy? If a player is averse to risk, the player may decide to use a *secure strategy*—a strategy that guarantees the highest payoff given the worst possible scenario. By using a secure strategy, a player maximizes the payoff that would result in the "worst-case scenario." In other words, to find a secure strategy, a player examines the worst payoff that could arise for each of his or her actions and chooses the action that has the highest of these worst payoffs.

DEMONSTRATION PROBLEM 10–2

What is the secure strategy for player B in the game presented in Table 10–1?

Answer

The secure strategy for player B is *right*. By choosing *left* B can guarantee a payoff of only 7, but by choosing *right* she can guarantee a payoff of 8. Thus, the secure strategy by player B is *right*.

While useful, the notion of a secure strategy suffers from a shortcoming. In particular, suppose player B in Table 10–1 reasoned as follows: "Player A will surely choose *up*, since *up* is a dominant strategy. Therefore, I should not choose my secure strategy (*right*) but instead choose *left*." Assuming player A indeed chooses the dominant strategy (*up*) player B will earn 20 by choosing *left* but only 8 by choosing the secure strategy (*right*).

A very natural way of formalizing the "end result" of such a thought process is captured in the definition of Nash equilibrium. A set of strategies constitute a *Nash equilibrium* if, given the strategies of the other players, no player can improve her payoff by unilaterally changing her own strategy. The concept of Nash equilibrium is very important, because it represents a situation where every player is doing the best he or she can given what other players are doing.

Nash equilibrium
A condition describing a set of strategies in which no player can improve her payoff by unilaterally changing her own strategy, given the other players' strategies.

DEMONSTRATION PROBLEM 10–3

In the game presented in Table 10–1, what are the Nash equilibrium strategies for players A and B?

Answer

The Nash equilibrium strategy for player A is *up,* and that for player B is *left.* To see this, suppose A chooses *up* and B chooses *left.* Would either player have an incentive to change his or her strategy? No. Given that player A's strategy is *up,* the best player B can do is choose *left.* Given that B's strategy is *left,* the best A can do is choose *up.* Hence, given the strategies (*up, left),* each player is doing the best he or she can given the other player's decision.

Applications of One-Shot Games

Pricing Decisions

Let us now see how game theory can help formalize the optimal managerial decisions in a Bertrand duopoly. Consider the game presented in Table 10–2, where two firms face a situation where they must decide whether to charge low or high prices. The first number in each cell represents firm A's profits, and the second number represents firm B's profits. For example, if firm A charges a high price while firm B charges a low price, A loses 10 units of profits while B earns 50 units of profits.

While the numbers in Table 10–2 are arbitrary, their relative magnitude is consistent with the nature of Bertrand competition. In particular, note that the profits of both firms are higher when both charge high prices than when they both charge low prices, because in each instance consumers have no incentive to switch to the other firm. On the other hand, if one firm charges a high price and the other firm undercuts that price, the lower-priced firm will gain all of the other firm's customers and thus earn higher profits at the expense of the competitor.

We are considering a one-shot play of the game in Table 10–2, that is, a situation where the firms meet once, and only once, in the market. Moreover, the game is a simultaneous-move game in that each firm makes a pricing decision without knowledge of the decision made by the other firm. In a one-shot play of the game, the Nash equilibrium strategies are for each firm to charge the low price. The reason is simple. If firm B charges a high price, firm A's best choice is to charge a low price, since 50 units of profits are better than the 10 units it would earn if A charged the high price. Similarly, if firm B charges the low price, firm A's best choice is to charge the low price, since 0 units of profits are preferred to the 10 units of losses that would result if A charged the high price. Similar arguments hold from firm B's perspective. Firm A is always better off charging the low price regardless of what firm B does, and B is always better off charging the low price regardless of what A does. To summarize, in the one-shot version of the above game, each firm's best strategy is to charge a low price regardless of

TABLE 10–2

		Firm B	
	Strategy	Low price	High price
Firm A	Low price	0, 0	50, −10
	High price	−10, 50	10, 10

the other firm's action. The outcome of the game is that both firms charge low prices and earn profits of zero.

Clearly, profits are less than the firms would earn if they colluded and "agreed" to both charge high prices. For example, in Table 10–2 we see that each firm would earn profits of 10 units if both charged high prices. This is a classic result in economics and is called a *dilemma* because the Nash equilibrium outcome is inferior (from the viewpoint of the firms) to the situation where they both "agree" to charge high prices.

Why can't firms collude and agree to charge high prices? One answer is that collusion is illegal in the United States; firms are not allowed to meet and "conspire" to set high prices. There are other reasons, however. Suppose the firm managers did secretly meet and agree to charge high prices. Would they have an incentive to live up to their promises? Consider firm A's point of view. If it "cheated" on the collusive agreement by lowering its price, it would increase its profits from 10 to 50. Thus, firm A has an incentive to induce firm B to charge a high price so that it can "cheat" to earn higher profits. Of course, firm B recognizes this incentive, which precludes the agreement from being reached in the first place.

However, suppose the manager of firm A is "honest" and would never cheat on a promise to charge a high price. (She is "honest" enough to keep her word to the other manager, but not so honest as to obey the law against collusion.) What happens to firm A if the manager of firm B cheats on the collusive agreement? If B cheats, A experiences losses of $10. When firm A's stockholders ask the manager why they lost $10 when the rival firm earned profits of $50, how can the manager answer? She cannot admit she was cheated on in a collusive agreement, for doing so might send her to jail for having violated the law. Whatever her answer, she risks being fired or sent to prison.

Advertising and Quality Decisions

Our framework for analyzing simultaneous-move, one-shot games can also be used to analyze advertising and quality decisions. In oligopolistic markets, firms advertise and/or increase their product quality in an attempt to increase the demand for their products. While both quality and advertising can be used to increase the demand for a product, for our discussion we will use advertising as a placeholder for both quality and advertising.

An important issue in evaluating the consequences of advertising is to recognize where the increase in demand comes from. In most oligopolistic markets, advertising increases the demand for a firm's product by taking customers away from other firms in the industry. An increase in one firm's advertising increases its profits at the expense of other firms in the market; there is interdependence among the advertising decisions of firms.

A classic example of such a situation is the breakfast cereal industry, which has a four-firm concentration ratio of 86 percent; that is, four firms produce 86 percent of all breakfast cereals. By advertising its brand of cereal, a particular firm does not induce many consumers to eat cereal for lunch and dinner; instead, it induces customers to switch to its brand from another brand. This can lead to a situation where each firm advertises just to "cancel out" the effects of other firms' advertising, resulting in high levels of advertising, no change in industry or firm demand, and low profits.

DEMONSTRATION PROBLEM 10–4

Suppose your firm competes against another firm for customers. You and your rival know your products will be obsolete at the end of the year and must simultaneously determine whether or not to advertise. In your industry, advertising does not increase total industry demand but instead induces consumers to switch among the products of different firms. Thus, if both you and your rival advertise, the two advertising campaigns will simply offset each other, and you will each earn $4 million in profits. If neither of you advertises, you will each earn $10 million in profits. However, if one of you advertises and the other one does not, the firm that advertises will earn $20 million and the firm that does not advertise will earn $1 million in profits. Is your profit-maximizing choice to advertise or not to advertise? How much money do you expect to earn?

Answer

The description of the game corresponds to the matrix presented in Table 10–3. The game is a one-shot game. Note that the dominant strategy for each firm is to advertise, and thus the unique Nash equilibrium for the game is for each firm to advertise. Thus, the profit-maximizing choice by your firm is to advertise. You can expect to earn $4 million. Collusion would not work because this is a one-shot game; if you and your rival "agreed" not to advertise (in the hope of making $10 million each), each of you would have an incentive to cheat on the agreement.

TABLE 10–3

		Firm B	
	Strategy	Advertise	Don't advertise
Firm A	Advertise	4, 4	20, 1
	Don't advertise	1, 20	10, 10

Coordination Decisions

Thus far, our analysis of oligopoly has focused on situations where firms have competing objectives: One firm can gain only at the expense of other firms. Not all games have this structure, however.

Imagine a world where producers of electrical appliances have a choice of which type of electrical outlets to put on appliances: 90 volt, four-prong outlets or 120 volt, two-prong outlets. In an environment where different appliances require different outlets, a consumer who desires several appliances would have to spend a considerable sum wiring the house to accommodate all of the appliances. This would reduce the amount the consumer has available for buying appliances and therefore would adversely affect the profits of appliance manufacturers. In contrast, if the appliance manufacturers can "coordinate" their decisions (that is, produce appliances that require the same types of wiring), they will earn higher profits.

Table 10–4 presents a hypothetical example of what is called a *coordination game.* Two firms must decide whether to produce appliances requiring 120-volt or 90-volt outlets. If each firm produces appliances requiring 120-volt outlets, each firm will earn profits of $100. Similarly, if each firm produces appliances requiring 90-volt outlets, each firm will earn $100. However, if the two firms produce appliances requiring different types of outlets, each firm will earn zero profits due to the lower demand that will result from consumers' need to spend more money wiring their houses.

What would you do if you were the manager of firm A in this example? If you do not know what firm B is going to do, you have a very tough decision. All you can do is "guess" what B will do. If you think B will produce 120-volt appliances, you should produce 120-volt appliances as well. If you think B will produce 90-volt appliances, you should do likewise. You will thus maximize profits by doing what firm B does. Effectively, both you and firm B will do better by "coordinating" your decisions.

The game in Table 10–4 has two Nash equilibria. One Nash equilibrium is for each firm to produce 120-volt appliances; the other is for each firm to produce 90-volt appliances. The question is how the firms will get to one of these equilibria. If the firms could "talk" to each other, they could agree to produce 120-volt systems. Alternatively, the government could set a stan-

TABLE 10–4

		Firm B	
Firm A	Strategy	120-volt outlets	90-volt outlets
	120-volt outlets	$100, $100	$0, $0
	90-volt outlets	$0, $0	$100, $100

Inside Business 10–1

Coordinating Activities: How Hard Is It?

An interesting area of study has arisen out of the question "Can firms coordinate their activities?" Russell W. Cooper and his associates recently published the results of several experiments that address this topic. In the experiments, volunteers participated in market situations where they had a chance to earn substantial amounts of money. The choices made by each participant along with the other participants in their group determined their earnings. In these coordination experiments, two or more Nash equilibria existed. The experiments were designed to test whether people choose the dominant ("best") equilibrium—the Nash equilibrium that has the highest payoff.

Cooper et al. conducted experiments with a payoff matrix like the one in Table 10–5. There are two pairs of Nash equilibrium strategies in this game: (1, 1) and (2, 2). Participants generally would prefer to find themselves at equilibrium (2, 2), since it has the highest level of earnings of the two Nash equilibria. However, out of 110 opportunities participants chose the Nash equilibrium (1, 1) 83 times, the Nash equilibrium (2, 2) 26 times, and the nonequilibrium cell (1, 3) once. The reason the Nash equilibrium with the higher payoff was selected so infrequently is that participants apparently placed a high probability that their opponent would choose the "cooperative strategy" of 3, which would lead to a payoff of 1,000 if they chose 1.

TABLE 10–5

	Strategy	Player B 1	2	3
Player A	1	350, 350	350, 250	1000, 0
	2	250, 350	550, 550	0, 0
	3	0, 1000	0, 0	600, 600

Sources: Russell W. Cooper, Douglas V. DeJong, Robert Forsythe, and T. W. Ross, "Selection Criteria in Coordination Games: Some Experimental Results," *American Economic Review* 80 (March 1990), pp. 218–33.

dard that electrical outlets be required to operate on 120-volt, two-prong outlets. In effect, this would allow the firms to "coordinate" their decisions. Notice that once they agree to produce 120-volt appliances, there is no incentive to cheat on this agreement. The game in Table 10–4 is not analogous to the pricing or advertising games analyzed earlier; it is a game of coordination rather than a game of conflicting interests.

Monitoring Employees

Game theory can also be used to analyze interactions between workers and the manager. In Chapter 6, we discussed the principal-agent problem and argued that there can be conflicting goals between workers and managers. Managers desire workers to work hard, while workers enjoy leisure.

In our discussion of manager-worker principal-agent problems in Chapter 6, we noted that one way a manager can reduce workers' incentive to shirk is to engage in "random" spot checks of the workplace. Game theory provides a way of seeing why this can work. Consider a game between a worker and a manager. The manager has two possible actions: (1) monitor the worker or (2) don't monitor the worker. The worker has two choices: (1) work or (2) shirk. These possible actions and resulting payoffs are depicted in Table 10–6.

The interpretation of this normal-form game is as follows. If the manager monitors while the worker works, the worker "wins" and the manager "loses." The manager has spent time monitoring a worker who was already working. In this case, suppose the manager's payoff is −1 and the worker's payoff is 1. The payoffs are the same if the manager does not monitor the worker and the worker shirks; the worker wins because she gets away with shirking.

In contrast, if the manager monitors while the worker shirks, the manager wins 1 and the worker who gets caught loses 1. Similarly, if the worker works and the manager does not monitor, the manager wins 1 and the worker loses 1. The numbers in Table 10–6 are, of course, purely hypothetical, but they are consistent with the relative payoffs that arise in such situations.

Notice that the game in Table 10–6 does not have a Nash equilibrium, at least in the usual sense of the term. To see this, suppose the manager's strategy is to monitor the worker. Then the best choice of the worker is to work. But if the worker works, the manager does better by changing his strategy: choosing not to monitor. Thus, "monitoring" is not part of a Nash equilibrium strategy. The paradox, however, is that "not monitoring" isn't part of a Nash equilibrium either. To see why, suppose the manager's strategy is "don't monitor." Then the worker will maximize her payoff by shirking. Given that the worker shirks, the manager does better by changing the strategy to "monitor" to increase his payoff from −1 to 1. Thus, we see that "don't monitor" is not part of a Nash equilibrium strategy either.

The thing to notice in this example is that both the worker and the manager want to keep their actions "secret"; if the manager knew what the

TABLE 10–6

Manager	Worker		
	Strategy	Work	Shirk
	Monitor	−1, 1	1, −1
	Don't monitor	1, −1	−1, 1

worker was doing, it would be curtains for the worker, and vice versa. In such situations, players find it in their interest to engage in mixed, or randomized, strategies. What this means is that players "randomize" over their available strategies; for instance, the manager flips a coin to determine whether or not to monitor. By doing so, the worker cannot predict whether the manager will be present to monitor her and, consequently, cannot outguess the manager.

Those of you who have taken multiple-choice tests have had firsthand experience with randomized strategies. If your professor made *a* the correct answer more often than *b, c,* or *d,* you could gain by answering *a* in those instances when you did not know the correct answer. This would enable you to earn a higher grade than you deserved based on your knowledge of subject matter. To prevent this strategy from working for you, professors randomize which option is the correct answer so that you cannot systematically guess the correct answer on an exam.

Nash Bargaining

The final application of simultaneous-move, one-shot games we will consider is a simple bargaining game. In a *Nash bargaining* game, two players "bargain" over some object of value. In a simultaneous-move, one-shot bargaining game, the players have only one chance to reach an agreement, and the offers made in bargaining are made simultaneously.

To be concrete, suppose management and a labor union are bargaining over how much of a $100 surplus to give to the union. Suppose, for simplicity, that the $100 can be split only into $50 increments. The players have one shot to reach an agreement. The parties simultaneously write the amount they desire on a piece of paper (either 0, 50, or 100). If the sum of the amounts each party asks for does not exceed $100, the players get the specified amounts. But if the sum of the amounts requested exceeds $100, neither party receives anything; bargaining ends in a stalemate.

Table 10–7 presents the normal form of this hypothetical bargaining game. If you were management, what amount would you ask for? Suppose

---

TABLE 10–7

		Union		
	Strategy	0	50	100
	0	0, 0	0, 50	0, 100
Management	50	50, 0	50, 50	0, 0
	100	100, 0	0, 0	0, 0

you wrote down $100. Then the only way you would get any money is if the union asked for zero. Notice that if management asked for $100 and the union asked for $0, neither party would have an incentive to change its amounts; we would be in Nash equilibrium.

Before concluding that you should ask for $100, think again. Suppose the union wrote down $50. Management's best response to this move would be to ask for $50. And given that management asked for $50, the union would have no incentive to change its amount. Thus, a 50-50 split of the $100 also would be a Nash equilibrium.

Finally, suppose management asked for 0 and the union asked for the entire $100. This too would constitute a Nash equilibrium. Neither party could improve its payoff by changing its strategy given the strategy of the other.

What are we to make of all of this? First, notice that there are three Nash equilibrium outcomes to this bargaining game. One equilibrium splits the money evenly among the parties, while the other two give all the money to either the union or to management. Second, notice that six cells of the matrix in Table 10–7 yield payoffs that are less than the amount to be divided. Three of these payoffs (the bottom right portion of the matrix) yield zero to both parties because the parties ask for too much. For example, if each party asks for $100, each party gets nothing. Unfortunately, this is common in labor disputes. Both parties ask for more, in total, than there is to split, and the bargainers leave the bargaining table emptyhanded. In contrast, three cells in the matrix (the top left portion) contain payoffs that sum to less than $100. In each of these cases, one party could have asked for more and gotten it. For instance, if management asks for $50 and the union asks for nothing, a deal is struck, but the bargainers leave money on the table. The union could have asked for $50 and still had the deal; or management could have increased its demand to $100 and still made the deal.

In concluding, we leave you with some advice regarding how to play such a bargaining game and how not to. First, notice that asking for $0 is dominated by asking for either $50 or $100. You never do worse, and you sometimes benefit, by asking for more than $0. Thus, while asking for nothing is part of one Nash equilibrium, it is not an advisable strategy; it is dominated by asking for a positive amount. Second, note that if you ask for the entire $100, the only way you will receive anything is if the other party asks for nothing, which, as we just argued, is dominated by asking for a positive amount. Since it is not reasonable for you to expect the other party to choose a strategy that is dominated, this leaves the strategy of asking for $50. Asking for half of the money has two advantages, at least in this particular bargaining game. First, if you ask for $50, you have two ways of getting the payoff (if the other party asks for $0 or $50). Second, and perhaps more important, it is a natural "focal point" of the bargaining process. Experimental evidence suggests that most players perceive a 50-50 split to be "fair" and therefore tend to choose that strategy even though there are two other Nash equilibria. Clearly, if you expect the union to ask for $50, you, as management, should ask for $50—at least in this simultaneous-move, one-shot bargaining game.

DEMONSTRATION PROBLEM 10–5

Suppose a $1 bill is to be divided between two players according to a simultaneous-move, one-shot bargaining game. Is there a Nash equilibrium to the bargaining game if the smallest unit in which the money can be divided is $.01? Assume that if the players ask for more in total than is available, they go home emptyhanded.

Answer

Yes, in fact there are many Nash equilibria. Any amount the players ask for that sums to exactly 100 cents constitutes a Nash equilibrium. As examples, one player asks for $.01 and the other asks for $.99; one player asks for $.02 and the other asks for $.98 cents; and so on. In each case, neither party can gain by asking for more, given what the other player has asked for.

Infinitely Repeated Games

Based on our analysis of one-shot pricing and advertising games, one might be led to believe that collusion is impossible in an industry. This conclusion is erroneous, however, and stems from the fact that firms in some industries do not play a one-shot game. Instead, they compete week after week, year after year. In these instances, the appropriate mode of analysis is to consider a situation where a game is repeated over time. In this section, we analyze a situation where players perpetually interact.

infinitely repeated game
A game that is played over and over again forever and in which players receive payoffs during each play of the game.

An *infinitely repeated game* is a game that is played over and over again forever. Players receive payoffs during each repetition of the game.

Theory

When a game is played again and again, players receive payoffs during each repetition of the game. Due to the time value of money, a dollar earned during the first repetition of the game is worth more than a dollar earned in later repetitions; players must appropriately discount future payoffs when they make current decisions. For this reason, we will review the key aspects of present value analysis before we begin examining repeated games.

Review of Present Value

The value of a firm is the present value of all future profits earned by the firm. If the interest rate is i, π_0 represents profits today, π_1 profits one year from today, π_2 profits two years from today, and so on, the value of a firm that will be in business for T years is

$$PV_{Firm} = \pi_0 + \frac{\pi_1}{(1 + i)} + \frac{\pi_2}{(1 + i)^2} + \cdots + \frac{\pi_T}{(1 + i)^T} = \sum_{t = 0}^{T} \frac{\pi_t}{(1 + i)^t}.$$

If the profits earned by the firm are the same in each period ($\pi_t = \pi$ for each period, t) and the horizon is infinite ($T = \infty$), this formula simplifies to

$$PV_{Firm} = \left(\frac{1 + i}{i}\right)\pi.$$

As we will see, this formula is very useful in analyzing decisions in infinitely repeated games.

Supporting Collusion with Trigger Strategies

Now consider the simultaneous-move Bertrand pricing game presented in Table 10–8. The Nash equilibrium in a one-shot play of this game is for each firm to charge low prices and earn zero profits. Let us suppose the firms play the game in Table 10–8 day after day, week after week, for all eternity. Thus, we are considering an infinitely repeated Bertrand pricing game, not a one-shot game. In this section, we will examine the impact of repeated play on the equilibrium outcome of the game.

When firms repeatedly face a matrix such as that in Table 10–8, it is possible for them to "collude" without fear of being cheated on. They do this using trigger strategies. A *trigger strategy* is a strategy that is contingent on the past plays of players in a game. A player who adopts a trigger strategy continues to choose the same action until some other player takes an action that "triggers" a different action by the first player.

To see how trigger strategies can be used to support collusive outcomes, suppose firm A and firm B secretly meet, and agree to the following arrangement: "We will each charge the high price, provided neither of us has

TABLE 10–8

	Firm B		
	Price	Low	High
Firm A	Low	0, 0	50, −10
	High	−10, 50	10, 10

ever 'cheated' in the past (i.e., charged the low price in any previous period). If one of us cheats and charges the low price, the other player will 'punish' the deviator by charging the low price in every period thereafter." Thus, if firm A cheats, it pulls a "trigger" that leads firm B to charge the low price forever after, and vice versa. It turns out that if both firms adopt such a trigger strategy, there are conditions under which neither firm has an incentive to cheat on the collusive agreement. Before we show this formally, let us examine the basic intuition.

If neither firm in Table 10–8 cheats on the collusive agreement, each firm will earn $10 each period forever. But if one firm plays according to the agreement, the other firm could cheat and earn an immediate profit of $50 instead of $10. Thus, there is still the immediate benefit to a firm of cheating on the agreement. However, because the firms compete repeatedly over time, there is a future cost of cheating. According to the agreement, if a firm ever cheats, the other firm will charge a low price in all future periods. Thus, the best the firm that cheated can do is earn $0 in the periods after cheating instead of the $10 it would have earned had it not broken the agreement.

In short, the benefit of cheating today on the collusive agreement is earning $50 instead of $10 today. The cost of cheating today is earning $0 instead of $10 in each future period. If the present value of the costs of cheating exceeds the one-time benefit of cheating, it does not pay for a firm to cheat, and high prices can be sustained.

Now let us formalize this idea. Suppose the firms agree to the collusive plan just outlined, and firm A believes firm B will live up to the agreement. Does firm A have an incentive to cheat and charge a low price? If firm A cheats by charging a low price, its profits will be $50 today but $0 in all subsequent periods, since cheating today will lead firm B to charge a low price in all future periods. The best choice of firm A when firm B charges the low price in these future periods is to charge the low price to earn $0. Thus, if firm A cheats today, the present value of its profits are

$$PV_{Firm\ A}^{Cheat} = \$50 + 0 + 0 + 0 + 0 + \ldots$$

If firm A does not cheat, it earns $10 each period forever. Thus, the present value of the profits of firm A if it "cooperates" (does not cheat) are

$$PV_{Firm\ A}^{Coop} = 10 + \frac{10}{1 + i} + \frac{10}{(1 + i)^2} + \frac{10}{(1 + i)^3} + \cdots = \frac{10(1 + i)}{i},$$

where i is the interest rate. Firm A has no incentive to cheat if the present value of its earnings from cheating is less than the present value of its earnings from not cheating. For the numbers in this example, there is no incentive to cheat if

$$PV_{Firm\ A}^{Cheat} = 50 \leq \frac{10(1 + i)}{i} = PV_{Firm\ A}^{Coop},$$

which is true if $i \le 1/4$. In other words, if the interest rate is less than 25 percent, firm A will lose more (in present value) by cheating than it will gain. Since firm B's incentives are symmetric, the same is true for firm B. Thus, when oligopolistic firms compete repeatedly over time, it is possible for them to collude and charge high prices to earn \$10 each period. This benefits firms at the expense of consumers and also leads to a deadweight loss. This explains why there are laws against collusion.

More generally, we may state the following principle:

Sustaining Cooperative Outcomes with Trigger Strategies
Suppose a one-shot game is infinitely repeated and the interest rate is i. Further, suppose the "cooperative" one-shot payoff to a player is π^{Coop}, the maximum one-shot payoff if the player cheats on the collusive outcome is π^{Cheat}, the one-shot Nash equilibrium payoff is π^N, and

$$\frac{\pi^{Cheat} - \pi^{Coop}}{\pi^{Coop} - \pi^N} \le \frac{1}{i}.$$

Then the cooperative (collusive) outcome can be sustained in the infinitely repeated game with the following trigger strategy: "Cooperate provided no player has ever cheated in the past. If any player cheats, 'punish' the player by choosing the one-shot Nash equilibrium strategy forever after."

The condition written in the preceding principle above has a very intuitive interpretation. It can be rewritten as

$$\pi^{Cheat} - \pi^{Coop} \le \frac{1}{i}(\pi^{Coop} - \pi^N).$$

The left-hand side of this equation represents the one-time gain of breaking the collusive agreement today. The right-hand side represents the present value of what is given up in the future by cheating today. Provided the one-time gain is less than the present value of what would be given up by cheating, players find it in their interest to live up to the agreement.

DEMONSTRATION PROBLEM 10–6

Suppose firm A and firm B repeatedly face the situation presented in Table 10–8 on page 376, and the interest rate is 40 percent. The firms agree to charge a high price each period, provided neither firm cheated on this agreement in the past.
(1) What are firm A's profits if it cheats on the collusive agreement?
(2) What are firm A's profits if it does not cheat on the collusive agreement?
(3) Does an equilibrium result where the firms charge the high price each period?

Answer

(1) If firm B lives up to the collusive agreement but firm A cheats, firm A will earn $50 today and zero forever after.

(2) If firm B lives up to the collusive agreement and firm A does not cheat, the present value of firm A's profits are

$$10 + \frac{10}{1 + .4} + \frac{10}{(1 + .4)^2} + \frac{10}{(1 + .4)^3} + \cdots = \frac{10(1 + .4)}{.4} = 35.$$

(3) Since $50 > 35$, the present value of firm A's profits is higher if A cheats on the collusive agreement than if it does not cheat. Since the matrix is symmetric, each firm has an incentive to cheat on the collusive agreement, even if it believes the other firm will not cheat. In equilibrium, each firm will charge the low price each period to earn profits of $0 each period.

In summary, in a one-shot game there is no tomorrow; any gains must be had today or not at all. In an infinitely repeated game there is always a tomorrow, and firms must weigh the benefits of current actions against the future costs of those actions. The principal result of infinitely repeated games is that when the interest rate is low, firms may find it in their interest to collude and charge high prices, unlike in the case of a one-shot game. The basic reason for this important result is this: If a player deviates from the "collusive strategy," he or she is punished in future periods long enough to wipe out the gains from having deviated from the collusive outcome. The threat of punishment makes cooperation work in repeated games. In one-shot games there is no tomorrow, and threats have no bite.

Factors Affecting Collusion in Pricing Games

It is easier to sustain collusive arrangements via the punishment strategies outlined earlier when firms know (1) who their rivals are, so they know whom to punish should the need arise; (2) who their rivals' customers are, so that if punishment is necessary they can take away their customers by charging lower prices; and (3) when their rivals deviate from the collusive arrangement, so they know when to begin the punishments. Furthermore, they must (4) be able to successfully punish rivals for deviating from the collusive agreement, for otherwise the threat of punishment would not work. These factors are related to several variables reflected in the structure and conduct of the industry.

Number of Firms

Collusion is easier when there are few firms than when there are many. If there are n firms in the industry, the total amount of monitoring that must

Inside Business 10–2

Trigger Strategies in the Waste Industry

For trigger strategies to work, players must be able to monitor their rivals' actions, so that they know whether to take punitive actions. For punishments to deter cheating, players do not actually have to punish cheaters forever. As long as they punish cheaters long enough to take away the profits earned by cheating, no player will find it profitable to cheat. In this case, players can achieve collusive outcomes. Real-world firms recognize these points.

Firms that pick up trash in Dade County, Florida, devised a mechanism to use trigger strategies to enforce high prices in a Bertrand market. To ensure that competitors did not undercut their high prices, firms monitored one another quite closely.

One company hired several people to follow the trucks of rival firms to make sure they did not steal its customers by undercutting its price. What did the firm do if it found a competitor servicing one of its clients? It took away five or ten of the competitor's customers for every one that had been lost to punish the rival for stealing its customers. It accomplished this by offering these customers a more favorable price than the competitor offered. After awhile, its competitors learned that it did not pay to steal this firm's customers. In the end there was little cheating, and firms in the market charged collusive prices.

Before you decide to adopt similar methods, we should point out that we learned of this practice through court transcripts in the U.S. District Court of Southern Florida, where those involved in the conspiracy were tried. In situations with repeated interaction, trigger strategies can be used to enhance profits—but it is illegal to engage in such practices.

Source: Docket No. 84-6107-Cr-KING (MISHLER), March 17, 1986. U.S. District Court of Southern Florida, Miami Division.

go on to sustain the collusive arrangement is $n \times (n - 1)$. For example, let the firms be indexed by A, B, C, ... If there are only two firms in the industry, then to punish a firm for deviating, each firm must know whether its rival deviated and, if so, where its customers are so it can punish the rival by getting some of its customers. To do this, each must keep an eye on its rival. With two firms, this information may be obtained if A monitors B and B monitors A.

The total number of monitors needed in the market grows very rapidly as the number of firms increases. For example, if there are five firms, each firm must monitor four other firms, so the total number of monitors needed in the market is $5 \times 4 = 20$. The cost of monitoring rivals reduces the gains to colluding. If the number of firms is "large enough," the monitoring costs become so high relative to collusive profits that it does not pay to monitor the actions of other firms. Under these circumstances, the "threat" used to sustain the collusive outcome is not credible, and the collusion fails. This is one reason why it is easier for two firms to collude than it is for, say, four firms to do so.

Firm Size

Economies of scale exist in monitoring. Monitoring and policing costs constitute a much greater share of total costs for small firms than for larger firms. Thus, it may be easier for a large firm to monitor a small firm than for a small firm to monitor a large firm. For example, a large firm (with, say, 20 outlets) can monitor the prices charged by a small competitor (with 1 outlet) by simply checking prices at the one store. But to check the prices of its rival, the smaller firm must hire individuals to monitor 20 outlets.

History of the Market

One key issue not addressed thus far is how firms reach an understanding to collude. One way is for the firms to explicitly meet and verbally warn their rivals not to steal their customers, or else they will be punished. Alternatively, firms might not meet at all but instead gain an understanding over time of the way the game is played and thus achieve "tacit collusion." Tacit collusion occurs when the firms do not explicitly conspire to collude but accomplish collusion indirectly. For example, in many instances firms learn from experience how other firms will behave in a market. If a firm observes over time that it is "punished" each time it charges a low price or attempts to steal customers from a rival, it eventually will learn that it does not pay to charge low prices. In these instances, tacit collusion will be the likely outcome.

Alternately, if a firm learns over time that its opponents are unable to successfully punish it for undercutting prices, tacit collusion will be unlikely to result. If firms never carry out their threats, the history of the industry will be such that collusion by threat of reprisal is not an equilibrium. But if firms observe that rivals indeed carry out their threats, this "history" ultimately will result in collusion.

Punishment Mechanisms

The pricing mechanisms firms use also affect their ability to punish rivals that do not cooperate. For example, in a posted-price market, where a single price is posted and charged to all of a firm's customers, the cost of punishing an opponent is higher than in markets in which different customers are quoted different prices. The reason is as follows. If a single price is charged to all customers, a firm that wishes to punish a rival by stealing its customers not only has to charge a low price to the rival's customers but also must lower its price to its own customers. This is essentially what a retailer must do to get customers away from another retailer. In contrast, in an industry in which different prices are quoted to different customers, a firm can punish its rival by charging the rival's customers a low price while continuing to charge its own customers a higher price. This, of course, substantially reduces the cost of engaging in punishment.

An Application of Infinitely Repeated Games to Product Quality

The theory of infinitely repeated games can be used to analyze the desirability of firm policies such as warranties and guarantees. Effectively, a game occurs between consumers and firms: Consumers desire durable, high-quality products at a low price, while firms wish to maximize profits. In a one-shot game, any profits made by the firm must be made today; there is no prospect for repeat business. Thus, in a one-shot game, a firm may have an incentive to sell shoddy products. This is particularly true if consumers cannot determine the quality of the products prior to purchase.

To see this, consider the normal-form game in Table 10–9. Here the game is between a consumer and a firm. The consumer has two strategies: buy the product or don't buy it. The firm can produce a low-quality product or a high-quality product. In a one-shot play of the game, the Nash equilibrium strategy is for the firm to produce low-quality goods and for consumers to shun the product. To see this, note that if the consumer decided to buy the product, the firm would benefit by selling a low-quality product, since profits of 10 are better than the 1 it would earn by producing a high-quality product. Given a low-quality product, the consumer chooses not to buy, since 0 is better than losing 10 by purchasing a shoddy product. But since the consumer chooses not to buy, it does not pay for the firm to produce a high-quality product. In a one-shot game, the consumer chooses not to buy the product because he or she knows the firm will "take the money and run."

The story differs if the game is infinitely repeated. Suppose the consumer tells the firm, "I'll buy your product and will continue to buy it if it is of good quality. But if it turns out to be shoddy, I'll tell all my friends never to purchase anything from you again." Given this strategy by the consumer, what is the best thing for the firm to do? If the interest rate is not too high, the best alternative is to sell a high-quality product. The reason is simple. By selling a shoddy product, the firm earns 10 instead of 1 that period. This is, in effect, "the gain to cheating" (selling a poor-quality product). The cost of selling a shoddy product, however, is to earn zero forever after, as the firm's reputation is ruined by having sold such a product. When

TABLE 10–9

		Firm	
	Strategy	Low-quality product	High-quality product
Consumer	Don't buy	0, 0	0, −10
	Buy	−10, 10	1, 1

Inside Business 10–3

Experimental Research Results on Collusion

Recent experimental research has provided a number of examples where two firms are able to arrive at a stable, collusive outcome but three or more firms are unable to do so. Recently Richard Beil isolated an important factor that explains this phenomenon. In experimental duopoly markets, firms could send firm-specific punishments to their rivals for deviating, but in experimental quadopoly markets, firms could not inflict firm-specific punishments. Beil's experiments revealed the following interesting results. When monitoring was available but specific penalties were unavailable, 5 out of 11 duopoly pairs were able to reach a collusive solution, whereas none of the

20 quadopoly groups were able to do so. In contrast, when firm-specific penalties were allowed, 21 out of 45 quadopoly groups were able to achieve a tacit collusive solution.

In summary, recent experimental evidence suggests that when firms can monitor their rivals and punish specific firms for failing to collude, they are much more likely to achieve a tacit collusive agreement than when these types of punishment mechanisms are unavailable.

Source: Richard Beil, "Collusion and the Need of Punishments: An Experimental Examination," working paper, Auburn University, 1992.

the interest rate is low, the one-time gain will be more than offset by the lost future sales. It will not pay for the firm to "cheat" by selling shoddy merchandise.

The lesson to be drawn from this example is twofold. First, if your firm desires to be a "going concern," that is, infinitely lived, it does not pay to "cheat" customers if the one-time gain is more than offset by lost future sales. Notice that this is true even if your firm cannot be sued or if there are no government regulations against selling shoddy merchandise.

Second, you should recognize that any production process is likely to have "bad runs," in which some low-quality products are produced out of honest error. Notice in this example that even if the firm "tried" to produce high-quality merchandise but, due to an inadvertent error, one unit was defective, that error could ruin the firm. To guard against this, many firms offer guarantees that the product will be of high quality. That way, if an error occurs in production, the consumer can obtain a new item, be satisfied, and not "punish" the firm by spreading the news that it sells shoddy merchandise.

Finitely Repeated Games

So far we have considered two extremes: games that are played only once and games that are played infinitely many times. This section summarizes important implications of games that are repeated a finite number of times, that is, games that eventually end. We will consider two classes of finitely repeated games: (1) games in which players do not know when the game will end and (2) games in which players know when it will end.

Games with an Uncertain Final Period

Suppose two duopolists repeatedly play the pricing game in Table 10–10 until their products become obsolete, at which point the game ends. Thus, we are considering a finitely repeated game. Suppose the firms do not know the exact date at which their products will become obsolete. Thus, there is uncertainty regarding the final period in which the game will be played.

Suppose the probability that the game will end after a given play is Θ, where $0 < \Theta < 1$. Thus, when a firm makes today's pricing decision, there is a chance that the game will be played again tomorrow; if the game is played again tomorrow, there is a chance that it will be played again the next day; and so on. For example, if $\Theta = 1/2$ there is a 50-50 chance the game will end after one play, a 1/4 chance it will end after two plays, a 1/8 chance that it will end after three plays, or, more generally, a $(\frac{1}{2})^t$ chance that the game will end after t plays of the game. It is as if a coin is flipped at the end of every play of the game, and if the coin comes up heads, the game terminates. The game terminates after t plays if the first heads occurs after t consecutive tosses of the coin.

It turns out that when there is uncertainty regarding precisely when the game will end, the finitely repeated game in Table 10–10 exactly mirrors our analysis of infinitely repeated games. To see why, suppose the firms adopt trigger strategies, whereby each agrees to charge a high price provided the other did not charge a low price in any previous period. If a firm deviates by charging a low price, the other firm will "punish" it by charging a low price until the game ends. For simplicity, let us assume the interest rate is zero so that the firms do not discount future profits.

Given such trigger strategies, does firm A have an incentive to cheat by charging a low price? If A cheats by charging a low price when B charges a high price, A's profits are $50 today but are zero in all remaining periods of

---

TABLE 10–10

		Firm B	
	Price	Low	High
Firm A	Low	0, 0	50, −10
	High	−10, 50	10, 10

the game. This is because cheating today "triggers" firm B to charge a low price in all future periods, and the best A can do in these periods is to earn $0. Thus, if firm A cheats today, it earns

$$\Pi_{Firm\ A}^{Cheat} = \$50,$$

regardless of whether the game ends after one play, two plays, or whenever.

   If firm A does not cheat, it earns $10 today. In addition, there is a probability of $1 - \Theta$ that the game will be played again, in which case the firm will earn another $10. There is also a probability of $(1 - \Theta)^2$ that the game will not terminate after two plays, in which case A will earn yet another $10. Carrying out this reasoning for all possible dates at which the game terminates, we see that firm A can expect to earn

$$\Pi_{Firm\ A}^{Coop} = 10 + (1 - \Theta)10 + (1 - \Theta)^2 10 + (1 - \Theta)^3 10 + \cdots = \frac{10}{\Theta}$$

if it does not cheat today. In this equation, Θ is the probability the game will terminate after one play. Notice that when $\Theta = 1$, firm A is certain the game will end after one play; in this case, A's profits if it cooperates are $10. But if $\Theta < 1$, the probability the game will end after one play is less than 1 (there is a chance they will play again), and the profits of cooperating are greater than $10.

   The important thing to notice is that when the game is repeated a finite but uncertain number of times, the benefits of cooperating look exactly like the benefits of cooperating in an infinitely repeated game, which are

$$PV_{Firm\ A}^{Coop} = 10 + \frac{10}{1 + i} + \frac{10}{(1 + i)^2} + \frac{10}{(1 + i)^3} + \cdots = \frac{10(1 + i)}{i}$$

where i is the interest rate. In a repeated game with an uncertain end point, $1 - \Theta$ plays the role of $1/(1 + i)$; players discount the future not because of the interest rate but because they are not certain future plays will occur.

   In a finitely repeated game with an unknown endpoint, firm A has no incentive to cheat if it expects to earn less from cheating than from not cheating. For the numbers in our example, firm A has no incentive to cheat if

$$\Pi_{Firm\ A}^{Cheat} = 50 \leq \frac{10}{\Theta} = \Pi_{Firm\ A}^{Coop},$$

which is true if $\Theta \leq 1/5$. In other words, if after each play of the game the probability the game will end is less than 20 percent, firm A will lose more by cheating than it will gain. Since firm B's incentives are symmetric, the same is true for B. Thus, when oligopolistic firms compete a finite but uncertain number of times, it is possible for them to collude and charge high prices—to earn $10 each period—just as they can when they know the game will be played forever. The key is that there must be a sufficiently high probability that the game will be played in subsequent periods. In the extreme case where $\Theta = 1$, players are certain they will play the game only once. In this case, the profits of cheating ($50) are much greater than the profits of cooperating ($10), and collusion cannot work. This should come as no surprise to you; when $\Theta = 1$, the game is really a one-shot game, and the dominant strategy for each firm is to charge the low price.

DEMONSTRATION PROBLEM 10–7

Two cigarette manufacturers repeatedly play the following simultaneous-move billboard advertising game. If both advertise, each earns profits of $0 million. If neither advertises, each earns profits of $10 million. If one advertises and the other does not, the firm that advertises earns $20 million and the other firm loses $1 million. If there is a 10 percent chance that the government will ban cigarette sales in any given year, can the firms "collude" by agreeing not to advertise?

Answer

The normal form of the one-shot game that is to be repeated an uncertain number of times is presented in Table 10–11. Suppose the players have adopted a trigger strategy, whereby each agrees not to advertise provided the other firm did not advertise in any previous period. If a firm deviates by advertising, the other firm will "punish" the offender by advertising until the game ends. If firm A cheats on the agreement, its profits are $20 today but $0 in all subsequent periods until the game terminates. If firm A does not cheat, it can expect to earn

$$\Pi^{Coop}_{Firm\ A} = 10 + (.90)10 + (.90)^2 10 + (.90)^3 10 + \cdots = \frac{10}{.10} = 100$$

(this assumes the interest rate is 0). Since $20 < $100, firm A has no incentive to cheat. The incentives for firm B are symmetric. Thus, the firms can collude by using this type of trigger strategy.

TABLE 10–11

		Firm B	
	Strategy	Advertise	Don't advertise
Firm A	Advertise	0, 0	20, −1
	Don't advertise	−1, 20	10, 10

Repeated Games with a Known Final Period: The End-of-Period Problem

Now suppose a game is repeated some known finite number of times. For simplicity, we will suppose the game in Table 10–12 is repeated two times. However, the arguments that follow apply even when the game is repeated a larger number of times (e.g., 1,000 times), provided the players know precisely when the game will end.

The important thing about repeating the game in Table 10–12 two times is that in the second play of the game there is no tomorrow, and thus each firm has an incentive to use the same strategy during that period that it would use in a one-shot version of the game. Since there is no possibility of playing the game in the third period, the players cannot punish their rival for actions it takes in the second period. For this game, this implies that each player will charge a low price in period 2; even if firm B thought firm A would "cooperate" by charging a high price during the second period, A would maximize its profits by charging a low price during the last period. There is nothing B could do in the future to "punish" A for doing so. In fact, A would be very happy if B charged a high price in the second period; if it did, A could charge a low price and earn profits of $50.

Of course, firm B knows firm A has an incentive to charge a low price in period 2 (the last period) and will likewise want to charge a low price in this period. Since both players know their opponent will charge a low price in the second period, the first period is essentially the last period. There is a tomorrow, but it is the last period, and each player knows what the opponent will do the last period. Thus, in period 1, each player has an incentive to choose the same strategy as in a one-shot version of the game, namely, charge a low price. In short, the Nash equilibrium for the two-shot version of the game in Table 10–12 is to charge a low price each period. Each player earns zero profits during each of the two periods.

In fact, collusion cannot work even if the game is played for 3 periods, 4 periods, or even 1,000 periods, provided the firms know precisely when the game will end. The key reason firms cannot collude in a finitely repeated known endpoint version of the game in Table 10–12 is that eventually a point

TABLE 10–12

		Firm B	
	Price	Low	High
Firm A	Low	0, 0	50, −10
	High	−10, 50	10, 10

will come when both players are certain there is no tomorrow. At that point, any promises to "cooperate" made during previous periods will be broken, because there is no way a player can be punished tomorrow for having broken the promise. Effectively, then, a player has an incentive to break a promise in the second to the last period, since there is no effective punishment during the last period. Because all the players know this, there is effectively no tomorrow in the third period from the last. This type of "backward unraveling" continues until the players realize no effective punishment can be used during any period. The players charge low prices in every period, right up to the known last period.

DEMONSTRATION PROBLEM 10–8

You and a rival will play the game in Table 10–12 two times. Suppose your strategy is to charge a high price each period provided your opponent never charged a low price in any previous period. How much will you earn? Assume the interest rate is zero.

Answer

Given your strategy, your opponent's best strategy is to charge a high price the first period and a low price the second period. To see why, note that if she charges a high price each period, she will earn 10 the first period and 10 the second period, for a total of 20 units of profit. She does better by charging a high price the first period (earning 10 units) and a low price the second period (earning 50 units), for a total of 60 units of profit. You will earn 10 units the first period but lose 10 units the second period, for total profits of zero. Since each of you knows exactly when the game will end, trigger strategies will not enhance your profits.

Applications of the End-of-Period Problem

When players know precisely when a repeated game will end, what is known as the *end-of-period problem* arises. In the final period there is no tomorrow, and there is no way to "punish" a player for doing something "wrong" in the last period. Consequently, in the last period, players will behave just as they would in a one-shot game. In this section, we will examine some implications of the end-of-period problem for managerial decisions.

Resignations and Quits
As we discussed in Chapter 6, one reason workers find it in their interest to work hard is that they are implicitly threatened with the prospect of being fired if they get caught not working. As long as the benefits of shirking are

less than the cost to workers of getting fired, workers will find it in their interest to work hard.

When a worker announces that she or he plans to quit, say, tomorrow, the cost of shirking to the worker is considerably reduced. Specifically, since the worker does not plan to work tomorrow anyway, the benefits of shirking on the last day generally will exceed the expected costs. In other words, since the worker does not plan to show up tomorrow, the "threat" of being fired has no bite.

What can the manager do to overcome this problem? One possibility is to "fire" the worker as soon as he or she announces the plan to quit. While in some instances there are legal restrictions against this practice, there is a more fundamental reason why a firm should not adopt such a policy. If you, as a manager, adopt a strategy of firing workers as soon as they notify you they plan to quit, how will workers respond? The best strategy for a worker would be to wait and tell you at the end of the day he or she plans to quit! By keeping the plan to quit a secret, the worker gets to work longer than he or she would otherwise. Notice that the worker's incentive to shirk is just as strong as it would be if you did not adopt this policy. Consequently, you will not solve the end-of-period problem, but instead will be continually "surprised" by worker resignations, with no lead time to find new workers to replace them.

A better managerial strategy is to provide some rewards for good work that extend beyond the termination of employment with your firm. For instance, you can emphasize to workers that you are very well connected and will be pleased to write a letter of recommendation should a worker need one in the future. By doing this, you send a signal to workers that quitting is not really the end of the game. If a worker takes advantage of the end-of-period problem, you, being well connected, can "punish" the worker by informing other potential employers of this fact.

The "Snake-Oil" Salesman

In old TV westerns, "snake-oil" salesmen move from town to town, selling bottles of an elixir that is promised to cure every disease known to human-kind. Unfortunately, buyers of the "medicine" soon learn that it is worthless and that they have been had. Nonetheless, these salesmen made a livelihood selling the worthless substance because they moved from town to town. By moving about, they ensured that buyers could not "punish" them for selling worthless bottles of fluid. In contrast, if a local merchant sold worthless medicine, customers could have punished him or her by refusing to buy from the merchant in the future. As we saw earlier, this threat can be used to induce firms to sell products of good quality. But in the days of the snake oil salesman, no such threat was possible.

For punishments to work, there must be some way to link the past, present, and future as it relates to the seller. The inadequate communication networks of the Old West precluded consumers from spreading the word about the snake-oil salesman to future customers; thus, the loss of his "reputation" was not a threat to him. However, over time consumers learned from past experience not to trust such salesmen, and when a new salesman came to town, they would "run him out."

Perhaps you have learned from experience that "sidewalk vendors" sell inferior merchandise. The reason is, as you should now recognize, that consumers have no way of tracking such vendors down in the event the merchandise is inferior. These salespeople indeed take advantage of the end-of-period problem.

Multistage Games

An alternative class of games is called *multistage games.* Multistage games differ from the class of games examined earlier in that timing is very important.

Theory

extensive-form game
A representation of a game that summarizes the players, the information available to them at each stage, the strategies available to them, the sequence of moves, and the payoffs resulting from alternative strategies.

To understand how multistage games differ from one-shot and infinitely repeated games, it is useful to introduce the extensive form of a game. An *extensive-form game* summarizes who the players are, the information available to the players at each stage of the game, the strategies available to the players, the order of the moves of the game, and the payoffs that result from the alternative strategies.

Once again, the best way to understand the extensive-form representation of a game is by way of example. Figure 10–1 depicts the extensive form of a game. The circles are called *decision nodes,* and each circle indicates that at that stage of the game the particular player must choose a strategy. The single point (denoted A) at which all of the lines originate is the beginning of the game, and the numbers at the ends of the branches represent the payoffs at the end of the game. For example, in this game player A moves first. A's feasible strategies are *up* or *down.* Once player A moves, it is player B's turn. Player B must then decide whether to move *up* or *down.* If both players move *up,* player A receives a payoff of 10 and player B receives a payoff of 15. If player A moves *up* and player B moves *down,* both

FIGURE 10–1

A sequential-move game in extensive form

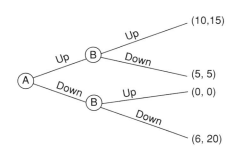

players receive a payoff of 5. Thus, the first number in parentheses reflects the payoff to player A (the first mover in the game), while the second number refers to the payoff of player B (the second mover).

As in simultaneous-move games, each player's payoff depends not only on his or her action but on the action of the other player as well. For example, if player A moves *down* and player B moves *up,* the resulting payoff to A is 0. But if player B moves *down* when player A moves *down,* A receives 6.

There is, however, an important difference between the sequential-move game depicted in Figure 10–1 and the simultaneous-move games examined in the previous sections. Since player A must make a decision before player B, A cannot make actions conditional on what B does. Thus, A can choose only *up* or *down.* In contrast, B gets to make a decision after A. Consequently, a strategy for player B will specify an action for both of his decision nodes. If player A chooses *up,* player B can choose either *up* or *down.* If A chooses *down,* B can choose either *up* or *down.* Thus, one example of a strategy for B is to choose *up* if A chooses *up,* and *down* if A chooses *down.* Notice that player B's strategy is allowed to depend on what player A has done, since this is a sequential-move game and B moves second. In contrast, there is no conditional "if" in player A's strategy.

To illustrate how strategies work in sequential-move games, suppose player B's strategy is: "Choose *down* if player A chooses *up,* and *down* if player A chooses *down.*" Given this strategy, what is the best choice by player A? If A chooses *up,* she earns 5, since B will choose *down.* If A chooses *down,* she earns 6, since B will choose *down.* Given a choice between earning 5 and 6, player A prefers 6 and therefore will choose *down.*

Given that player A chooses *down,* does player B have an incentive to change his strategy? B's strategy specifies that he choose *down* if A chooses *down.* By choosing *down* B earns 20, whereas he earns 0 by choosing *up.* We thus see that player B has no incentive to change his strategy given that player A chose *down.*

Since neither player has an incentive to change his or her strategies, we have found a Nash equilibrium to the game in Figure 10–1. These strategies are:

  Player A: *down*
  Player B: *down* if player A chooses *up,* and *down* if player A chooses *down.*

The payoffs that result in this equilibrium are 6 for player A and 20 for player B.

You should ask yourself whether this is a reasonable outcome for the game. In particular, notice that the highest payoff for player A results when A chooses *up* and B chooses *up* as well. Why didn't player A choose *up?* Because player B "threatened" to choose *down* if A chose *up.* Should player A believe this threat? If she chooses *up,* player B's best choice is *up,* since the payoff of 15 is better for B than the payoff of 5 that results from choosing *down*. But if B chooses *up,* A earns 10. This is higher than the payoff that resulted in the Nash equilibrium we examined earlier.

What do we make of all this? There is, in fact, another Nash equilibrium to this game. In particular, suppose player B's strategy is "Choose *up* if player A chooses *up,* choose *down* if player A chooses *down.*" Given this strategy by player B, player A earns 10 by choosing *up* and 6 by choosing *down*. Clearly the best response by A to this strategy by B is *up*. Given that player A chooses *up,* player B has no incentive to change his strategy, and thus we have another Nash equilibrium. In this Nash equilibrium, player A earns 10 and player B earns 15.

Which of these two Nash equilibrium outcomes is the more reasonable? The answer is the second one. The reason is as follows. In the first Nash equilibrium, player A chooses *down* because player B threatened to play *down* if A chooses *up*. But player A should recognize that this threat is really not credible. If this stage of the game (decision node) were in fact reached, player B would have an incentive to renege on his threat to choose *down*. Choosing *down* at this stage of the game would result in lower profits for B than he would earn by choosing *up*. Player B therefore has no incentive to do what he said he would do. In the jargon of game theory, the Nash equilibrium in which player A earns 6 and player B earns 20 is not a subgame perfect equilibrium. A set of strategies constitutes a *subgame perfect equilibrium* if (1) it is a Nash equilibrium and (2) at each stage of the game (decision node) neither player can improve her payoff by changing her own strategy. Thus, a subgame perfect equilibrium is a Nash equilibrium that involves only credible threats. For the game in Figure 10–1, the only subgame perfect equilibrium is for player A to choose *up,* and player B to follow this move with *up*.

The analysis in this section typically is difficult for students to grasp on the first or second reading, so I encourage you to review this section if you are not clear on the concepts presented. Before you do so, or move on to the next section, let me provide a fable that may help you understand the notion of a subgame perfect equilibrium.

A teenager is given the following instructions by her father: "If you're not home by midnight, I'll burn down the house and you will lose everything you own." If the teenager believes her father, it will certainly be in her best interest to return before midnight, since she does not want to lose everything she owns. And if the teenager returns before midnight, the father never has to burn down the house; there is no cost to the father of threatening to do so. The father's making such a threat and the daughter's returning before midnight are Nash equilibrium strategies. However, they are not subgame perfect equilibrium strategies. The father's threat to burn down the house, which is what led the teenager to choose to return before midnight, is not credible. The father will not find it in his interest to burn down his own house if his daughter returns late. If the daughter knows this, she knows that the threat is not credible and will not let it affect whether or not

subgame perfect equilibrium
A condition describing a set of strategies that constitutes a Nash equilibrium and allows no player to improve his own payoff at any stage of the game by changing strategies.

she returns home before midnight. Thus, since the Nash equilibrium is obtained by a threat that is not credible, it is not a subgame perfect equilibrium.

Applications of Multistage Games

The Entry Game
To illustrate the use of the theory of multistage games in a market setting, consider the extensive-form game presented in Figure 10–2. Here, firm B is an existing firm in the market and firm A is a potential entrant. Firm A must decide whether to enter the market *(in)* or stay out *(out)*. If A decides to stay out of the market, firm B continues its existing behavior and earns profits of $10 million, while A earns $0. But if A decides to enter the market, B must decide whether to engage in a price war *(hard)* or to simply share the market *(soft)*. By choosing *hard,* firm B ensures that firm A incurs a loss of $1 million, but B makes only $1 million in profits. On the other hand, if firm B chooses *soft* after A enters, A takes half of the market and each firm earns profits of $5 million.

   It turns out that there are two Nash equilibria for this game. The first occurs where firm B threatens to choose *hard* if A enters the market, and thus A stays *out* of the market. To see that these strategies indeed comprise a Nash equilibrium, note the following. Given that firm B's strategy is to choose *hard* if firm A enters, A's best choice is not to enter. Given that A doesn't enter, B may as well threaten to choose *hard* if A enters. Thus, neither firm has an incentive to change its strategy; firm A earns $0, and firm B earns profits of $10 million.

   However, this Nash equilibrium involves a threat that is not credible. The reason firm A chooses not to enter is that firm B threatens to choose *hard* if A enters. Does B have an incentive to carry through its threat of choosing *hard* if firm A enters? The answer is no. Given that firm A enters the market, firm B will earn $5 million by choosing *soft* but only $1 million by choosing *hard*. If firm A enters, it is not in firm B's best interest to play *hard.* Thus, the outcome in which firm A stays out of the market because firm B threatens to choose *hard* if it enters is a Nash equilibrium, but it is

FIGURE 10–2

An entry game

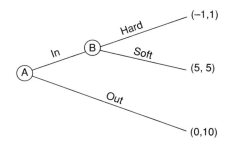

not a subgame perfect equilibrium. It involves a threat that is not credible, namely, the threat by firm B to engage in a price war if firm A enters.

The other Nash equilibrium for this game is for firm A to choose *in* and firm B to follow this move by playing *soft*. In particular, if firm A enters, firm B's best choice is to play *soft* (by playing *soft,* B earns 5 instead of the 1 it would earn by playing *hard*). Given that firm B plays *soft* if firm A enters, A's best choice is to enter (by choosing *in,* A earns 5 instead of the 0 it would earn by staying out). This is a subgame perfect equilibrium, because it is clearly in firm B's self-interest to play *soft* whenever A chooses to enter. Thus, while there are two Nash equilibria for the entry game, there is a unique subgame perfect equilibrium in which firm A chooses *in* and firm B plays *soft*.

Innovation

Our analysis of the entry game reveals an important lesson for future managers: It does not pay to heed threats made by rivals when the threats are not credible. We can also use the theory of sequential, or multistage, games to analyze innovation decisions, as the next problem illustrates.

DEMONSTRATION PROBLEM 10–9

Your firm must decide whether or not to introduce a new product. If you introduce the new product, your rival will have to decide whether or not to clone the new product. If you don't introduce the new product, you and your rival will earn $1 million each. If you introduce the new product and your rival clones it, you will lose $5 million and your rival will earn $20 million (you have spent a lot on research and development, and your rival doesn't have to make this investment to compete with its clone). If you introduce the new product and your rival does not clone, you will make $100 million and your rival will make $0.
(1) Set up the extensive form of this game.
(2) Should you introduce the new product?
(3) How would your answer change if your rival has "promised" not to clone your product?
(4) What would you do if patent law prevented your rival from cloning your product?

Answer

(1) The new-product game is depicted in Figure 10–3. Note that this is a multistage game in which your firm (A) moves first, followed by your rival (B).
(2) If you introduce the product, B's best choice is to clone, in which case your firm loses $5 million. If you don't introduce the product, you earn $1 million. Thus, your profit-maximizing decision is not to introduce the new product.
(3) If you believe your rival's "promise" not to clone, you will earn $100 million by introducing the new product and only $1 million if you do not introduce it.

FIGURE 10–3

An innovation game

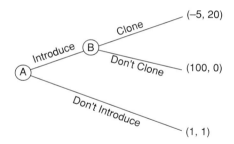

However, B's promise is not credible; B would love you to spend money developing the product so that it could clone it and earn profits of $20 million. In this case, you stand to lose $5 million. Since the promise is not credible, you had better think twice about letting it affect your behavior.

(4) If you can obtain a patent on your new product, B will be forced by law to refrain from cloning. In this case, you should introduce the product to earn $100 million. This illustrates that the ability to patent a new product often induces firms to introduce products that they would not introduce in the absence of a patent system.

Sequential Bargaining

The final application of multistage games that we will consider is a *sequential-move bargaining* game. Specifically, suppose a firm and a labor union are engaged in negotiations over how much of a $100 surplus will go to the union and how much will go to management. Suppose management (M) moves first by offering an amount to the union (U). Given the offer, the union gets to decide to accept or reject the offer. If the offer is rejected, neither party receives anything. If the offer is accepted, the union gets the amount specified and management gets the residual. To simplify matters, suppose management can offer the union one of three amounts: $1, $50, or $99.

The extensive form of this game is depicted in Figure 10–4. Notice that the union gets to make its decision after it learns of management's offer. For instance, if management offers the union $1 and the union accepts the offer, management gets $99 and the union gets $1. If the union rejects the offer, both parties get $0.

Suppose you are management and the union makes the following statement to you before you make an offer: "Give us $99 or else we will reject the offer." What should you do? If you believe the union, then if you offered it a lower amount, it would reject the offer and you would get nothing. Given the union's strategy, your best choice is to give the union $99, since that action gives you a payoff of $1 instead of $0. And given that you offer the union $99, its best choice is to accept the offer. Thus, one Nash

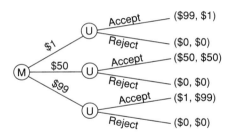

equilibrium outcome of this sequential bargaining process yields $1 for management and $99 for the union.

Does this mean that the optimal action for management is to give the union $99? The answer is no. Notice that this equilibrium is supported by a union threat that is not credible. According to the union, if management offered the union $1, the union would reject the offer. But by rejecting such an offer, the union would earn $0 instead of the $1 it could earn by accepting it. Thus, it is not in the union's best interest to reject the offer.

In fact, the unique subgame perfect equilibrium for this sequential bargaining game is for management to offer the union $1 and for the union to accept the offer. To see this, notice that if management offered the union $1, the union's best choice would be to accept, since $1 is preferred to the $0 it would earn by rejecting the offer. In this sequential-move bargaining game, the unique subgame perfect equilibrium is for management to get $99 and the union $1.

DEMONSTRATION PROBLEM 10–10

Consider the bargaining game just described, but suppose the order of play is reversed: The union gets to make an offer, and then management decides whether to accept or reject it. What is the subgame perfect equilibrium outcome of this bargaining process?

Answer

The profit-maximizing choice by management to any offer is to accept it if that yields more than the $0 management would earn by rejecting the offer. Therefore, the subgame perfect equilibrium is for the union to offer management $1 and keep $99 for itself. Given this offer, management's best choice is to accept it. Any threat by management to refuse an offer of $1 or $50 would not be credible.

This section has illustrated a remarkable feature of two-stage sequential bargaining games. Effectively, the first mover in the bargaining game makes a take-it-or-leave-it offer. The second mover can accept the offer or reject it and receive nothing. The player making the take-it-or-leave-it offer extracts virtually all of the amount bargained over. The following example illustrates this principle.

Suppose a consumer wishes to buy a car that the dealer values at $10,000. The consumer values the car at $12,000. Effectively, the bargaining game is over the $2,000 difference between the consumer's valuation and the dealer's cost. Suppose the consumer makes the following take-it-or-leave-it offer to the dealer: "I'll pay you $10,001 for the car. If you don't accept it, I will buy a car from the dealer down the road." If the dealer believes the consumer's threat to terminate the bargaining process if the offer is rejected, he will accept the offer; the dealer prefers earning $1 to earning $0 by not selling the car. The consumer buys the car at $1 over the dealer's cost.

In contrast, suppose the order of the bargaining process is reversed, and the dealer tells the consumer: "Another buyer wants the car. Pay me $11,999, or I'll sell it to the other customer." In this case, if the buyer believes the dealer's threat to sell to another buyer is credible, her best choice is to buy the car, since it costs $1 less than her valuation. In this case, the dealer makes a handsome profit.

In concluding this section, we note that several aspects of reality often complicate sequential-bargaining processes. First, the players do not always know the true payoffs to other players. For instance, if a car buyer does not know the dealer's cost of a car, he or she cannot make a take-it-or-leave-it offer and be assured of getting the car. Similarly, if a dealer does not know the maximum price a consumer will pay for a car, she or he cannot be assured of making a sale by making a take-it-or-leave-it offer. In bargaining processes, it is worthwhile to invest some time in learning about your opponent. This explains why there is a market for publications that specialize in providing information to consumers about the dealer cost of automobiles.

Second, an important assumption in the bargaining process analyzed in this section is that bargaining terminates as soon as the second player rejects or accepts an offer. If this were not the case, the person making the decision to accept or reject the offer might reason as follows: "If I reject the offer, perhaps the other party will make a new, more attractive offer." Effectively, this changes the game and can change the players' underlying decisions. On the other hand, a player who can credibly commit to making a take-it-or-leave-it offer will do very well in the bargaining game. But if the commitment is not credible, he or she may end up "eating crow" when the other party makes a counteroffer that the first player would prefer over walking away from the bargaining table.

Answering the Headline

Why are analysts predicting that OPEC is likely to achieve the collusive outcome in the future now that Saudi Arabia refused to go along with the low production levels suggested by Venezuela? Venezuela has cheated on almost every OPEC agreement it has entered, and it reaped large financial benefits at the expense of Saudi Arabia and other cooperating members of OPEC. In order to sustain collusive outcomes in an infinitely repeated setting, firms must punish those who fail to live up to cooperative agreements. While such punishments typically harm all the parties in the short run, in the long run they provide incentives for everyone to live up to their agreements. Thus, the analysts perceive that Saudi Arabia is disciplining Venezuela for having violated past agreements, in order to teach them that cheating does not pay. Saudi Arabia's failure to cut output now might ultimately lead to more collusion in the future, as Venezuela and other OPEC countries learn that Saudi Arabia will punish them if they attempt to cheat on future cartel agreements.

Summary

This chapter opened with the study of Nash equilibrium in one-shot, simultaneous-move games. We learned that the resulting payoffs are sometimes lower than would arise if players colluded. The reason higher payoffs cannot be achieved in one-shot games is that each participant has an incentive to cheat on a collusive agreement. In many games, what primarily motivates firms to cheat is the fact that cheating is a dominant strategy. Dominant strategies, when they exist, determine the optimal decision in a one-shot game.

We also examined solutions to games that are infinitely repeated. The use of trigger strategies in these games enables players to enter and enforce collusive agreements when the interest rate is low. By adopting strategies that punish cheaters over long periods of time, collusive agreements can be self-enforcing when the game is infinitely repeated. Other factors that affect collusion are the number of firms, the history in the market, the ability of firms to monitor one another's behavior, and the ability to punish cheaters. Similar features of repeated interaction also help consumers and businesses continue trading with each other and keep product quality high.

Finally, we covered finitely repeated games with both uncertain and known terminal periods, as well as sequential-move entry and bargaining games. When the interaction among parties is for a known time period, problems with cheating in the last period can unravel cooperative agreements that would have been supported by trigger strategies in infinitely repeated games or games with an uncertain endpoint. In sequential-move games, one must determine whether the threats used to induce a particular outcome in the game are credible.

Key Terms and Concepts

coordination game	normal-form game
dominant strategy	one-shot game
end-of-period problem	repeated game
extensive-form game	secure strategy
finitely repeated game	sequential bargaining
game theory	sequential-move game
infinitely repeated game	simultaneous-move game
mixed (randomized) strategy	strategy
multistage game	subgame perfect equilibrium
Nash equilibrium	trigger strategy
Nash bargaining	

Problems

1. In a one-shot game, if you advertise and your rival advertises, you will each earn $5 million in profits. If neither of you advertises, your rival will make $4 million and you will make $2 million. If you advertise and your rival does not, you will make $10 million and your rival will make $3 million. If your rival advertises and you do not, you will make $1 million and your rival will make $3 million.
   a. Write the above game in normal form.
   b. Do you have a dominant strategy?
   c. Does your rival have a dominant strategy?
   d. What is the Nash equilibrium for the one-shot game?
   e. How much would you be willing to bribe your rival not to advertise? Explain carefully.

2. You operate in a duopoly in which you and a rival must simultaneously decide what price to advertise in the weekly newspaper. If you each charge a low price, you each earn zero profits. If you each charge a high price, you each earn profits of $3. If you charge different prices, the one charging the higher price loses $5 and the one charging the lower price makes $5.
   a. Find the Nash equilibrium for a one-shot version of this game.
   b. Now suppose the game is infinitely repeated. If the interest rate is 10 percent, can you do better than you could in a one-shot play of the game? Explain.

c. Explain how "history" affects the ability of firms in this game to achieve an outcome superior to that of the one-shot version of the game.

3. You are considering entering a market serviced by a monopolist. You currently earn $0 economic profits, while the monopolist earns $5. If you enter the market and the monopolist engages in a price war, you will lose $5 and the monopolist will earn $1. If the monopolist doesn't engage in a price war, you will each earn profits of $2.

a. Write out the extensive form of the above game.

b. There are two Nash equilibria for the game. What are they?

c. Is there a subgame perfect equilibrium? Explain.

d. If you were the potential entrant, would you enter? Explain why or why not.

4. OPEC was an effective cartel for many years, but recently it has been unable to maintain a high price of oil. What factors do you think are contributing to the demise of OPEC?

5. The NCAA prohibits schools that are caught paying athletes from participating in bowl games, and sometimes even worse. Explain why schools don't break away from the NCAA and form a league in which athletes can legitimately be paid. (Hint: Use hypothetical payoffs to construct an illustrative normal-form game in which the strategies are "pay players" and "don't pay players." Then analyze the game in one-shot and infinitely repeated contexts.)

6. Based on your knowledge of one-shot and repeated games, would you expect tipping behavior to differ depending on whether a person is eating in a hometown diner or in a restaurant located in Timbuktu? Explain.

7. According to a spokesperson for cereal maker Kellogg, ". . . for the past several years, our individual company growth has come out of the other fellow's hide."[1]

a. What implications does this statement have for the level of advertising in the cereal industry?

b. Using the hypothetical data in Table 10–3, explain how a trigger strategy can be used to support the collusive level of advertising in an infinitely repeated game. For what values of the interest rate can collusion be sustained?

8. You are the manager of a firm that is "bargaining" with another firm over how much to pay for a key input your firm uses in production. Which type of bargaining would be "better" from your firm's point of view, simultaneous-move bargaining or take-it-or-leave-it bargaining? Explain carefully.

---

[1]See F. M. Scherer, "The Welfare Economics of Product Variety: An Application to the Ready-to-Eat Cereals Industry," *Journal of Industrial Economics* (December 1979).

9. You are the manager of the ABC novelty store, and your only competition is the XYZ novelty store. You are both trying to decide on which magic tricks and party favors to carry in stock. The product mixes available to both of you are low, medium, and high in variety. Your expected earnings in this market are shown in the following table.

		Firm XYZ		
	Strategy	Low	Medium	High
Firm ABC	Low	100, 100	150, 200	200, 300
	Medium	200, 75	125, 150	225, 195
	High	300, 200	100, 225	150, 250

   a. Find the Nash equilibrium (or equilibria) for a simultaneous-move, one-shot play of this game.
   b. What outcome would you expect in this one-shot game? Why?

10. You are the owner-operator of the Better Gas Station in a small southeastern town. Over the past 20 years, you and your rival have successfully kept prices at a very high level. You recently learned that your competitor is retiring and closing his station in two weeks. What should you do today? Why?

11. You are the manager of Copies Are Us. The only other copy store in town, the Carbon Copy, recently got bids on adding a color copier. You must decide whether to obtain a color copier, but you can base your decision on what your rival does. If your rival adds a color copier and you don't, you expect your profits to fall by $1,000 per week and its profits to rise by $1,500 per week. However, if you both do the same thing (add color copiers or not), you each expect profits to stay at their current level. Show the extensive form of this game, and find the Nash equilibrium (or equilibria). Is there a subgame perfect equilibrium?

12. You are the bargaining coordinator for Sun Car Manufacturers. At present you are renegotiating the labor contract with the union representative. You are bargaining over an expected 20 percent increase in earnings over the next three-year contract period. You are trying to decide whether to offer one-third, one-half, or all of the increase in earnings to the union. The union rules are such that all contracts must be voted on. The additional earnings are contingent on getting started on the new contract next week. If an agreement isn't

reached on the first round of negotiations the firm will go out of business. The union representative tells you that if you do not give the union all of the additional profits, the union members will not vote for the agreement.

    a. Show the extensive form of this game.

    b. What will you offer the union? Why?

13. Would collusion be more likely in the shoe industry or in the airline industry? Why?

14. According to various trade publications, over 200,000 changes are made in airfares each day. Why do you think this is the case?

15. Two executives were arrested by authorities for embezzling money from their firm. Short of a confession, the prosecutor only had enough evidence to put them away for 10 years. Given a confession, however, she was certain to put them behind bars for life without parole, since they killed a law enforcement officer who was investigating the case. The prosecutor put the two prisoners in separate rooms, and told them the following:

    "If you confess and your partner does not, I'll give you a year's probated sentence but put your partner in the slammer for life without parole. Of course, if your partner confesses and you don't, you'll get the life sentence without parole and he'll get one year's probation. I must warn you, however, that if you both confess I'll have enough evidence to put you both away for life without parole."

    a. Do you think the prosecutor's bargain will induce the two executives to confess? Explain.

    b. Would your answer change if the life sentence carried the possibility of parole? Explain.

16. In the early 1990s, there was considerable uncertainty in the computer industry about whether the dominant operating system for future personal computers would be IBM's OS/2 or Microsoft's Windows. Ultimately, Windows emerged as the dominant system despite the fact that several trade publications viewed OS/2 as the superior system. Why do you think this outcome prevailed?

Selected Readings

Bolton, Gary E., "A Comparative Model of Bargaining: Theory and Evidence." *American Economic Review* 81(5), December 1991, pp. 1096–136.

Friedman, James W., ed., *Problems of Coordination in Economic Activity.* Boston: Kluwer Academic, 1994.

Gardner, Roy; Ostrom, Elinor, "Rules and Games." *Public Choice* 70(2), May 1991, pp. 121–49.

Gilbert, Richard J., "The Role of Potential Competition in Industrial Organization." *Journal of Economic Perspectives* 3(3), Summer 1989, pp. 107–28.

Hansen, Robert G. and Samuelson, William F., "Evolution in Economic Games." *Journal of Economic Behavior and Organization* 10(3), October 1988, pp. 315–38.

Morrison, C. C. and Kamarei, H., "Some Experimental Testing of the Cournot-Nash Hypothesis in Small Group Rivalry Situations." *Journal of Economic Behavior and Organization* 13(2), March 1990, pp. 213–31.

Rasmusen, Eric, *Games and Information: An Introduction to Game Theory.* New York: Basis Blackwell, 1989.

Rosenthal, Robert W., "Rules of Thumb in Games." *Journal of Economic Behavior and Organization* 22(1), September 1993, pp. 1–13.

CHAPTER 11

Pricing Strategies for Firms with Market Power

Headline

Kids Ride Free at Disneyland?

In 1993 the Walt Disney Company shocked Wallstreet by issuing over 300 million dollars in bonds. The shock waves did not stem from the size of the issue, but from the fact that the Disney bonds do not mature until the year 2093. Virtually all other corporate bonds have maturities of 30 years or less—about one-third the length of these 100-year Disney bonds.

Some wag surmised that the lengthy maturity date on the Disney bonds stems from the peculiar pricing policy that the firm employs at Disneyland. There, Disney charges a fixed entrance fee and allows customers to take as many rides as they desire at no additional cost. Wouldn't the company earn higher profits and be able to pay off its debt quicker if Disneyland priced rides on a per-unit basis—say, $5 per ride?

Introduction

In this chapter, we deal with pricing decisions by firms that have some market power: firms in monopoly, monopolistic competition, and oligopoly. As we learned in Chapter 8, firms in perfect competition have no control over the prices they charge for their products; prices are determined by market forces. Therefore, the pricing decision in perfect competition is simple: Charge the same price other firms in the market charge for their products.

In contrast, firms with market power have some influence over the prices they charge. Therefore, it is important for you, as a manager, to learn some basic pricing strategies for maximizing a firm's profits. This chapter provides practical advice that you can use to implement such pricing strategies, typically using information that is readily available to managers. For instance, we will see how a manager can use publicly available information about demand elasticities to determine the profit-maximizing markup used to set product price.

The optimal pricing decisions will vary from firm to firm depending on the underlying market structure of the industry and the instruments (such as advertising) available. Thus, we will begin with basic pricing strategies used by firms in monopoly, monopolistic competition, and oligopoly to set the price that maximizes profits. Then we will develop more sophisticated pricing strategies that enable a firm to extract even greater profits. As you work through this chapter, remember that some of these more advanced pricing strategies will work in some situations but will not be viable in others. You should familiarize yourself not only with how to implement the strategies but also with the conditions under which each type of strategy is feasible.

Basic Pricing Strategies

In this section we will examine the most basic pricing strategy used by firms with market power: charging a single price to all customers such that marginal revenue equals marginal cost. We will begin with a review of the economic basis for such a pricing strategy and then discuss how it can be easily implemented in monopoly, monopolistic competition, and Cournot oligopoly.

Review of the Basic Rule of Profit Maximization

Firms with market power face a downward-sloping demand for their products. This means that by charging a higher price, the firm reduces the amount it will sell. Thus, there is a trade-off between selling many units at a low price and selling only a few units at a high price.

In Chapter 8 we learned how the manager of a firm with market power balances off these two forces: Output is set at the point where marginal revenue (MR) equals marginal cost (MC). The profit-maximizing price is the maximum price per unit that consumers will pay for this level of output. The following problem summarizes what we learned in Chapter 8 about the profit-maximizing pricing decision of a firm with market power.

DEMONSTRATION PROBLEM 11–1

Suppose the (inverse) demand for a firm's product is given by

$$P = 10 - 2Q$$

and the cost function is

$$C(Q) = 2Q.$$

What is the profit-maximizing level output and price for this firm?

Answer

For this (inverse) demand function, marginal revenue is

$$MR = 10 - 4Q$$

and marginal cost is

$$MC = 2.$$

Setting $MR = MC$ yields

$$10 - 4Q = 2.$$

Thus, the profit-maximizing level of output is $Q = 2$. Substituting this into the inverse demand function yields the profit-maximizing price:

$$P = 10 - 2(2) = \$6.$$

A Simple Pricing Rule for Monopoly and Monopolistic Competition

As we saw in the previous section, in instances where a manager has estimates of the demand and cost functions for the firm's product, calculation of the profit-maximizing price is straight forward. In some cases, a manager lacks access to an estimated form of demand or cost functions. This is particularly true of managers of small firms that do not have research departments or funds to hire economists to estimate demand and cost functions.

Fortunately, all is not lost in these instances. It turns out that given minimal information about demand and costs, a manager can do a reasonably good job of determining what price to charge for a product. Specifically, most retailers have a rough estimate of the marginal cost of each item sold. For instance, the manager of a clothing store knows how much the store pays the supplier for each pair of jeans and thus has crude information about the marginal cost of selling jeans. (This information is "crude" because the cost to the firm of buying jeans will slightly understate the true marginal cost of selling jeans, since it does not include the cost of the sales force, etc.)

Inside Business 11–1

Pricing Markups as Rules of Thumb

Many malls and flea markets sponsor shows to which home producers and do-it-yourselfers bring their products for fun and profit. Most of these small businesses are run by crafts people with little or no knowledge of economics, yet they often reap large profits. One might ask how these artisans find a price that maximizes their profits—or do they?

If you ask them, you will find that most artists who frequent these shows use a rule-of-thumb markup strategy. They take the price of the materials, and add an hourly wage rate for themselves, then charge from between 1.5 to 5 times their marginal cost. How do they determine the price to charge? Through trial and error and word of mouth from artisan to artisan.

Who has higher markups, and who has lower markups? Those products that are extremely unique and show a high degree of crafting skill have the high markup, whereas the products that almost anyone with some free time could make have the low markups. This is exactly what economic theory would predict. The more unique products will have fewer substitutes and therefore will have a more inelastic demand than those that are easily copied. This fact, in turn, implies a higher profit-maximizing markup.

The clothing store manager also has some crude information about the elasticity of demand for jeans at its store. Chapter 7 provided tables with estimates of the elasticity of demand for a "representative firm" in broadly defined industries. For instance, Table 7–3 presented a study that estimated the own price elasticity of demand for a representative apparel firm's product to be -4.1. In the absence of better information, the manager of a clothing store can use this estimate to approximate the elasticity of demand for jeans sold at his or her store.

Thus, even small firms can obtain some information about demand and costs from publicly available information. All that remains is to show how this information can be used to make pricing decisions. The key is to recall the relation between the elasticity of demand for a firm's product and marginal revenue, which we derived in Chapter 8. This relation is summarized in the following formula.

Formula: Marginal Revenue for a Firm with Market Power.   The marginal revenue for a firm with market power is given by

$$MR = P \left[\frac{1 + E_F}{E_F} \right],$$

where E_F is the own price elasticity of demand for the firm's product and P is the price charged.

Since the profit-maximizing level of output is where marginal revenue equals marginal cost, this formula implies that

$$P\left[\frac{1 + E_F}{E_F}\right] = MC$$

at the profit-maximizing level of output. If we solve this equation for P, we obtain the profit-maximizing price for a firm with market power:

$$P = \left[\frac{E_F}{1 + E_F}\right] MC.$$

In other words, the price that maximizes profits is a number K times marginal cost:

$$P = (K)MC.$$

where $K = E_F/(1 + E_F)$. The number K can be viewed as the profit-maximizing markup factor. For the case of the clothing store, the manager's best estimate of the elasticity of demand is -4.1, so $K = -4.1/(1 - 4.1) = 1.32$. In this instance, the profit-maximizing price is 1.32 times marginal cost:

$$P = (1.32)MC.$$

Principle

Profit-Maximizing Markup for Monopoly and Monopolistic Competition
The price that maximizes profit is given by

$$P = \left[\frac{E_F}{1 + E_F}\right] MC,$$

where E_F is the own price elasticity of demand for the firm's product and MC is the firm's marginal cost. The term in brackets is the optimal markup factor.

A manager should note two important things about this pricing rule. First, the more elastic the demand for the firm's product, the lower the profit-maximizing markup. Since demand is more elastic when there are many available substitutes for a product, managers that sell such products should have a relatively low markup. In the extreme case when the elasticity of demand is perfectly elastic ($E_F = -\infty$), this markup rule reveals that price should be set equal to marginal cost. This should come as no surprise, since we learned in Chapter 8 that a perfectly competitive firm that faces a perfectly elastic demand curve charges a price equal to marginal cost.

The second thing to notice is that the higher the marginal cost, the higher the profit-maximizing price. Firms with higher marginal costs will charge higher prices, other things being the same, than firms with lower marginal costs.

DEMONSTRATION PROBLEM 11–2

The manager of a convenience store competes in a monopolistically competitive market and buys cola from a supplier at a price of $1.25 per liter. The manager thinks that because there are several supermarkets nearby, the demand for cola sold at her store is slightly more elastic than the elasticity for the representative food store reported in Table 7–3 in Chapter 7 (which is -3.8). Based on this information, she perceives that the elasticity of demand for cola sold by her store is -4. What price should the manager charge for a liter of cola to maximize profits?

Answer

The marginal cost of cola to the firm is $1.25, or 5/4 per liter, and $K = 4/3$. Using the pricing rule for a monopolistically competitive firm, the profit-maximizing price is

$$P = \left[\frac{4}{3}\right]\left[\frac{5}{4}\right] = \frac{5}{3},$$

or about $1.67 per liter.

A Simple Pricing Rule for Cournot Oligopoly

Recall that in Cournot oligopoly, there are few firms in the market servicing many consumers. The firms produce either differentiated or homogeneous products, and each firm believes rivals will hold their output constant if it changes its own output.

In Chapter 9 we saw that to maximize profits, a manager of a firm in Cournot oligopoly produces where marginal revenue equals marginal cost. We also saw how to calculate the profit-maximizing price and quantity given information about demand and cost curves. Recall that this procedure requires full information about the demand and costs of all firms in the industry and is complicated by the fact that the marginal revenue of a Cournot oligopolist depends on the outputs produced by all firms in the market. Ultimately, the solution is based on the intersection of reaction functions.

Fortunately, we can also provide a simple pricing rule that can be used by managers in Cournot oligopoly. Suppose an industry consists of N Cournot oligopolists, each having identical cost structures and producing similar products. In this instance, the profit-maximizing price in Cournot equilibrium is given by a simple formula.

Profit-Maximizing Markup for Cournot Oligopoly
If there are N identical firms in a Cournot oligopoly, the profit-maximizing price for a firm in this market is

$$P = \left[\frac{NE_M}{1 + NE_M}\right] MC,$$

where N is the number of firms in the industry, E_M is the market elasticity of demand, and MC is marginal cost.

Instead of having to memorize this formula, we can simply substitute the relation between a Cournot oligopolist's own price elasticity of demand and that of the market into the formula for the markup rule for monopoly and monopolistic competition. In particular, for a homogeneous-product Cournot oligopoly with N firms, we will show that the elasticity of demand for an individual firm's product is N times that of the market elasticity of demand:

$$E_F = NE_M.$$

When we substitute this in for E_F in the pricing formula for monopoly and monopolistic competition, the result is the pricing formula for Cournot oligopoly.

To see that $E_F = NE_M$, we need a little calculus. Specifically, if

$$Q = \sum_{i=1}^{N} Q_i$$

is total industry output and industry demand is $Q = f(P)$, the own price elasticity of market demand is

$$E_M = \left(\frac{dQ}{dP}\right)\frac{P}{Q} = \left[\frac{df(P)}{dP}\right]\frac{P}{Q}.$$

The demand facing an individual firm (say, firm 1) is

$$Q_1 = f(P) - Q_2 - Q_3 - \cdots - Q_N.$$

Thus, since the firm views the output of other firms as fixed, the elasticity of demand for an individual firm is

$$E_F = \left(\frac{\partial Q_1}{\partial P}\right)\frac{P}{Q_1} = \left[\frac{df(P)}{dP}\right]\frac{P}{Q_1}.$$

But with identical firms $Q_1 = Q/N$, so

$$E_F = \left[\frac{df(P)}{dP}\right]\frac{PN}{Q} = NE_M,$$

which is what we needed to establish.

The pricing rule given for a firm in Cournot oligopoly has a very simple justification. When firms in a Cournot oligopoly sell identical products, the elasticity of demand for an individual firm's product is N times the market elasticity of demand:

$$E_F = NE_M.$$

If $N = 1$ (monopoly), there is only one firm in the industry, and the elasticity of demand for that firm's product is the same as the market elasticity of demand ($E_F = E_M$). When $N = 2$ (Cournot duopoly), there are two firms in the market, and each firm's elasticity of demand is twice as elastic as that for the market ($E_F = 2E_M$). Thus, the markup formula for Cournot oligopoly is really identical to that presented in the previous section, except that we are using the relation between elasticity of demand for an individual firm's product and that of the market.

Three aspects of this pricing rule for Cournot oligopoly are worth noting. First, the more elastic the market demand, the closer the profit-maximizing price is to marginal cost. In the extreme case where the absolute value of the market elasticity of demand is infinite, the profit-maximizing price is marginal cost, regardless of how many firms are in the industry. Second, notice that as the number of firms increases, the profit-maximizing price gets closer to marginal cost. Notice that in the limiting case where there are infinitely many firms ($N = \infty$), the profit-maximizing price is exactly equal to marginal cost. This is consistent with our analysis of perfect competition: When many firms produce a homogeneous product, price equals marginal cost. Thus, perfect competition can be viewed as the limiting case of Cournot oligopoly, as the number of firms approaches infinity. Finally, notice that the higher the marginal cost, the higher the profit-maximizing price in Cournot oligopoly.

DEMONSTRATION PROBLEM 11–3

Suppose three firms compete in a homogeneous-product Cournot industry. The market elasticity of demand for the product is -2, and each firm's marginal cost of production is $50. What is the profit-maximizing equilibrium price?

Answer

Simply set $N = 3$, $E_M = -2$, and $MC = \$50$ in the markup formula for Cournot oligopoly to obtain

$$P = \left[\frac{(3)(-2)}{1 + (3)(-2)} \right] \$50 = \$60.$$

Strategies That Yield Even Greater Profits

The analysis in the previous section demonstrated how a manager can implement the familiar $MR = MC$ rule for setting the profit-maximizing price. Given estimates of demand and cost functions, such a price can be computed directly. Alternatively, given publicly available estimates of demand elasticities, a manager can implement the rule by using the appropriate markup formula.

In some markets, managers can enhance profits above those they would earn by simply charging a single per-unit price to all consumers. As we will see in this section, several pricing strategies can be used to yield profits above those earned by simply charging a single price where marginal revenue equals marginal cost.

Extracting Surplus from Consumers

The first four strategies we will discuss—price discrimination, two-part pricing, block pricing, and commodity bundling—are strategies appropriate for firms with various cost structures and degrees of market interdependence. Thus, these strategies can enhance profits of firms in industries with monopolistic, monopolistically competitive, or oligopolistic structures. The pricing strategies discussed in this section enhance profits by enabling a firm to extract additional consumer's surplus from consumers.

Price Discrimination

Up until this point, our analysis of pricing decisions presumes the firm must charge the same price for each unit that consumers purchase in the market. Sometimes, however, firms can earn higher profits by charging different prices for the same product, a strategy referred to as *price discrimination*. The three basic types of price discrimination—first-, second-, and third-degree price discrimination—are examined next. As we will see, each type requires that the manager have different types of information about consumers.

price discrimination
The practice of charging different prices to consumers for the same good.

Ideally, a firm would like to engage in *first-degree price discrimination*—that is, charge each consumer the maximum price he or she would be willing to pay for each unit of the good purchased. By adopting this strategy, a firm extracts all surplus from consumers and thus earns the highest possible profits. Unfortunately for managers, first-degree price discrimination (also called perfect price discrimination) is extremely difficult to implement because it requires the firm to know precisely the maximum price each consumer is willing and able to pay for alternative quantities of the firm's product.

Nonetheless, some service-related businesses, including car dealers, mechanics, doctors, and lawyers, successfully practice a form of first-degree price discrimination. For instance, most car dealers post sticker prices on cars that are well above the dealer's actual marginal cost, but offer "discounts" to customers on a case-by-case basis. The best salespersons are able to size up customers to determine the minimum discount necessary to get them to drive away with the car. In this way they are able to charge different prices to different consumers depending on each consumer's willingness and ability to pay. This practice permits them to sell more cars and to earn higher profits than they would if they charged the same price to all consumers. Similarly, most professionals also charge rates for their services that vary, depending on their assessment of customers' willingness and ability to pay.

Panel (a) of Figure 11–1 shows how first-degree price discrimination works. Each point on the market demand curve reflects the maximum price that consumers would be willing to pay for each incremental unit of output. Consumers start out with 0 units of the good, and the firm can sell the first incremental unit for $10. Since the demand curve slopes downward, the maximum price the firm can charge for each additional unit declines, ultimately to $4 at an output of 5 units. The difference between each point on the demand curve and the firm's marginal cost represents the profits earned on each incremental unit sold. Thus, the shaded area between the demand curve and the firm's marginal cost curve reflects the firm's total profit when it charges each consumer the maximum price they will pay for small increments of output between 0 and 5 units. This strategy allows the firm to earn the maximum possible profits. Notice that consumers receive no consumer surplus on the 5 units they purchase: the firm extracts all surplus under first-degree price discrimination. As noted earlier, however, this favorable outcome (from the firm's perspective) can occur only if the manager has

FIGURE 11–1

First- and second-degree price discrimination

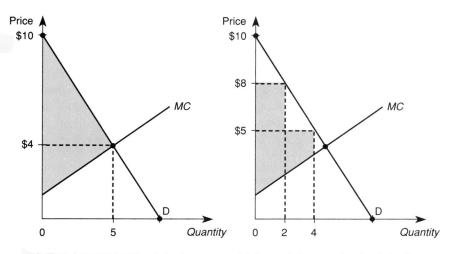

(a) First-degree price discrimination

(b) Second-degree price discrimination

perfect information about the prices that each consumer is willing and able to pay for each incremental unit of output.

In situations where the firm does not know the maximum price that each consumer will pay for a good, or when it is not practical to post a continuous schedule of prices for each incremental unit purchased, a firm might be able to employ second-degree price discrimination to extract part of the surplus from consumers. *Second-degree price discrimination* is the practice of posting a discrete schedule of declining prices for different ranges of quantities. This practice is very common in the electric utility industry, where firms typically charge a higher rate on the first hundred kilowatt hours of electricity used than on subsequent units. The primary advantage of this strategy is that the firm can extract some consumer surplus from consumers without needing to know beforehand the identity of the consumers who will choose to purchase small amounts (and thus are willing and able to pay a higher price per unit). Given the posted schedule of prices, consumers sort themselves according to their willingness to pay for alternative quantities of the good. Thus, the firm charges different prices to different consumers, but does not need to know the specific characteristics about individual consumers.

To illustrate how second-degree price discrimination works, suppose the Acme Floppy Disk Company charges consumers $8 per unit for the first two boxes of floppy disks purchased, and $5 per unit for boxes of disks purchased in excess of 2. The shaded region in panel (b) of Figure 11–1 shows the profits that Acme earns with this strategy. The first two units are sold at a price of $8, and the region between this price and the marginal cost curve reflects the firm's profits on the first two units. The second two units are priced at $5, so the region between that price and the marginal cost curve between 2 and 4 units of output reflects the firm's profits on the second two units sold. Notice that consumers end up with some consumer surplus, which means that second-degree price discrimination yields lower profits for the firm than it would have earned if it were able to perfectly price discriminate. Nonetheless, profits are still higher than they would have been if the firm had used the simple strategy of charging the same price for all units sold. In effect, consumers purchasing small quantities (or alternatively, those having higher marginal valuations) pay higher prices than those who purchase in bulk.

The final type of price discrimination is a commonly used practice by firms that recognize that the demand for their product differs systematically across consumers in different demographic groups. In these instances firms can profit by charging different groups of consumers different prices for the same product, a strategy referred to as *third-degree price discrimination*. For example, it is common for stores to offer "student discounts" and for hotels and restaurants to offer "senior citizen discounts." These practices effectively mean that students and senior citizens pay less for some goods than do other consumers. Similarly, telephone companies charge lower rates on weekends than during the day, meaning that businesses may pay a higher price for telephone services than households. One might think that these pricing strategies are instituted to benefit students, senior citizens, and households, but there is a more compelling reason: to increase the firm's profits.

To see why third-degree price discrimination enhances profits, suppose a firm with market power can charge two different prices to two groups of consumers and the marginal revenues of selling to group 1 and group 2 are MR_1 and MR_2, respectively. The basic profit-maximizing rule is to produce output such that marginal revenue is equal to marginal cost. This principle is still valid, but the presence of two marginal revenue functions introduces some ambiguity.

It turns out that to maximize profits, the firm should equate the marginal revenue from selling output to each group to marginal cost: $MR_1 = MC$ and $MR_2 = MC$. To see why, suppose $MR_1 > MC$. If the firm produced one more unit and sold it to group 1, it would increase revenue by more than costs would increase. As additional output is sold to group 1, marginal revenue declines until it ultimately equals marginal cost.

Since $MR_1 = MC$ and $MR_2 = MC$, it follows that the firm will allocate output between the two groups such that $MR_1 = MR_2$. To see why, suppose the marginal revenue for group 1 is 10 and the marginal revenue for group 2 is 5. If one less unit were sold to group 2, revenue from that group would fall by 5. If the extra unit of output were sold to group 1, revenue would increase by 10. Thus, it pays for the firm to allocate output to the group with the greater marginal revenue. As additional output is allocated to the group, its marginal revenue falls until, in equilibrium, the marginal revenues to the two groups are exactly equal.

To understand the basis for third-degree price discrimination, suppose two groups of consumers have elasticities of demand of E_1 and E_2, and the firm can charge group 1 a price of P_1 and group 2 a price of P_2. Using the formula for the marginal revenue of a firm with market power, it follows that the marginal revenue of selling the product to group 1 at a price of P_1 is

$$MR_1 = P_1 \left[\frac{1 + E_1}{E_1} \right],$$

while the marginal revenue of selling to group 2 at a price of P_2 is

$$MR_2 = P_2 \left[\frac{1 + E_2}{E_2} \right].$$

As mentioned, a profit-maximizing firm should equate the marginal revenue of each group to marginal cost, which implies that $MR_1 = MR_2$. Using the formula for marginal revenue, this condition may be rewritten as

$$P_1 \left[\frac{1 + E_1}{E_1} \right] = P_2 \left[\frac{1 + E_2}{E_2} \right].$$

If $E_1 = E_2$, the terms in brackets are equal, and thus the firm will maximize profits by charging each group the same price. If the demand by group 1 is more elastic than that by group 2, $E_1 < E_2 < 0$. In this instance, the firm should charge a lower price to group 1, since it has a more elastic demand than group 2.

Thus, a necessary condition for third-degree price discrimination to enhance profits is differences in the elasticity of demand of various consumers. In the examples cited earlier, there is reason to believe that senior citizens have a more elastic demand for a hotel room or a restaurant meal than other consumers. Most retired individuals are on fixed incomes and thus are much more sensitive to price than people who still work. The fact that they are charged lower prices for a hotel room is a simple implication of third-degree price discrimination, namely charging a lower price to people with more elastic demands.

Another condition that must exist for third-degree price discrimination to be effective is that the firm have some means of identifying the elasticity of demand by different groups of consumers; otherwise, the firm has no way of knowing to which group of consumers to charge the higher price. In practice, this is not difficult to do. Hotels require individuals seeking a senior citizens' discount to present evidence of their age, such as a driver's license. This effectively identifies an individual as likely to have a more elastic demand for a hotel room.

Finally, note that no type of price discrimination will work if the consumers purchasing at lower prices can resell their purchases to individuals being charged higher prices. In this instance, consumers who purchase the good at a low price could buy extra quantities and resell them to those who face the higher prices. The firm would sell nothing to the group being charged the higher price, because those consumers would save money by buying from consumers who purchased at the low price. In essence, the possibility of resale makes the goods purchased by the consumers charged the low price a perfect substitute for the firm's product. Those consumers can undercut the price the firm is charging the other group, thus reducing the firm's profits.

Formula: Third-Degree Price Discrimination Rule.   To maximize profits, a firm with market power produces the output at which the marginal revenue to each group equals marginal cost:

$$\underbrace{P_1 \left[\frac{1 + E_1}{E_1} \right]}_{MR_1} = MC$$

$$\underbrace{P_2 \left[\frac{1 + E_2}{E_2} \right]}_{MR_2} = MC.$$

DEMONSTRATION PROBLEM 11–4

You are the manager of a pizzeria that produces at a marginal cost of $6 per pizza. The pizzeria is a local monopoly near campus (there are no other restaurants or food stores within 500 miles). During the day, only students eat at your restaurant. In the evening, while students are studying, faculty members eat there. If students have an elasticity of demand for pizzas of -4 and the faculty has an elasticity of demand of -2, what should your pricing policy be to maximize profits?

Answer

Assuming faculty would be unwilling to purchase cold pizzas from students, the conditions for price discrimination to be effective hold. It will be profitable to charge one price—say, P_L—on the "lunch menu" (effectively a student price) and another price, such as P_D, on the "dinner menu" (effectively a faculty price). To determine precisely what price to put on each menu, note that the people buying pizza off the lunch menu have an elasticity of demand of -4, while those buying off the dinner menu have an elasticity of demand of -2. The conditions for profit maximization require that the marginal revenue of selling a pizza to each group equal marginal cost. Using the third-degree price discrimination rule, this means that

$$P_L \left[\frac{1 + E_L}{E_L} \right] = MC$$

and

$$P_D \left[\frac{1 + E_D}{E_D} \right] = MC.$$

Setting $E_D = -2$, $E_L = -4$, and $MC = 6$ yields

$$P_L \left[\frac{1 - 4}{-4} \right] = 6$$

$$P_D \left[\frac{1 - 2}{-2} \right] = 6,$$

which simplifies to

$$P_L \left[\frac{3}{4} \right] = 6$$

$$P_D \left[\frac{1}{2} \right] = 6.$$

Solving these two equations yields $P_L = \$8$ and $P_D = \$12$. Thus, to maximize profits, you should price a pizza on the lunch menu at $8 and a pizza on the dinner menu at $12. Since students have a more elastic demand for pizza than do faculty members, they should be charged a lower price to maximize profits.

Two-Part Pricing

Another strategy that firms with market power can use to enhance profits is two-part pricing. With *two-part pricing,* a firm charges a fixed fee for the right to purchase its goods, plus a per-unit charge for each unit purchased. This pricing strategy is commonly used by athletic clubs to enhance profits. Golf courses and health clubs, for instance, typically charge a fixed "initiation fee" plus a charge (either per month or per visit) to use the facilities. In this section, we will see how such a pricing strategy can enhance the profits of a firm.

Figure 11–2(a) provides a diagram of the demand, marginal revenue, and marginal cost for a firm with market power. Here the demand function is $Q = 10 - P$ and the cost function is $C(Q) = 2Q$. If the firm adopted a

FIGURE 11–2

Comparisons of standard monopoly pricing and two-part pricing

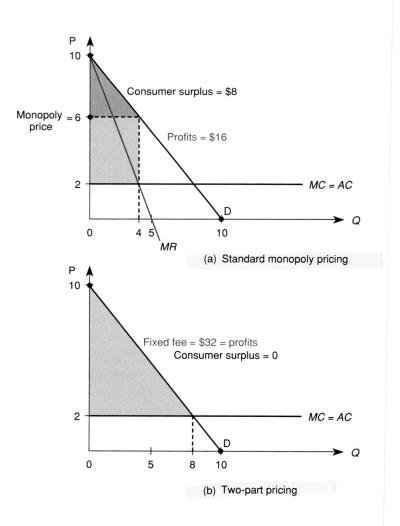

pricing strategy of simply charging a single price to all consumers, the profit-maximizing level of output would be $Q = 4$ and the profit-maximizing price would be $P = 6$. This price-quantity combination corresponds to the point where marginal revenue equals marginal cost. Notice that the firm's profits are given by the shaded rectangle, which is

$$(\$6 - \$2)4 = \$16.$$

Notice that the consumer surplus received by all consumers in the market—the value received but not paid for—corresponds to the upper triangle in Figure 11–2(a), which is

$$\frac{1}{2}[(10 - 6)4] = \$8.$$

In other words, all consumers together receive a value of $8 from the four units purchased that they do not have to pay for.

Like first-degree price discrimination, two-part pricing allows a firm to extract all consumer surplus from consumers. In particular, suppose the demand function in Figure 11–2(a) is that of a single individual and the firm uses the following pricing scheme: a fixed fee of $32 that gives the consumer the right to buy the product at a per-unit charge of $2. This situation is depicted in Figure 11–2(b) for the same demand and cost functions as in Figure 11–2(a). With a per-unit charge of $2, the consumer will purchase eight units and receive a consumer surplus of

$$\frac{1}{2}[(10 - 2)8] = \$32.$$

By charging a fixed fee of $32, the firm extracts all of this consumer's surplus. The firm sells each unit at its marginal cost of $2, and thus makes no profit on each unit sold at this price. But the firm also receives the fixed payment of $32, which is pure profit. The $32 in profits earned using the two-part pricing scheme is larger than the $16 the firm would earn by using a simple pricing strategy.

Principle

Two-Part Pricing
A firm can enhance profits by engaging in two-part pricing: charge a per-unit price that equals a marginal cost, plus a fixed fee equal to the consumer surplus each consumer receives at this per-unit price.

We mentioned that athletic clubs often engage in two-part pricing. They charge an initiation fee, plus a per-unit fee for each visit to the facility. Notice that if the marginal cost is low, the optimal per-unit fee will be low as well. In the extreme case where marginal cost is zero, the profit-maximizing two-part pricing strategy of an athletic facility will be to charge $0 for each visit but a fixed initiation fee equal to a consumer's surplus. With two-part pricing, all profits are derived from the fixed fee. Setting the per-unit fee equal to marginal cost ensures that the surplus is as large as possible, thus allowing the largest fixed fee consistent with maximizing profits.

There are numerous other examples of two-part pricing strategies. Buying clubs are an excellent example. By paying a membership fee in a buying club, members get to buy products at "cost." Notice that if the membership fee is set equal to each consumer's surplus, the owner of a buying club actually makes higher profits than would be earned by simply setting the monopoly price.

DEMONSTRATION PROBLEM 11–5

Suppose the total monthly demand for golf services is $Q = 20 - P$. The marginal cost to the firm of each visit is $1. If this demand function is based on the individual demands of 10 golfers, what is the optimal two-part pricing strategy for this golf services firm? How much profit will the firm earn?

Answer

The optimal per-unit charge is marginal cost. At this price, $20 - 1 = 19$ rounds of golf will be played each month. The total consumer surplus received by all 10 golfers at this price is thus

$$\frac{1}{2}[(20 - 1)19] = \$180.50.$$

Since this is the total consumer surplus enjoyed by all 10 consumers, the optimal fixed fee is the consumer surplus enjoyed by an individual golfer ($180.50/10 = $18.05 per month). Thus, the optimal two-part pricing strategy is for the firm to charge a monthly fee to each golfer of $18.05, plus greens fees of $1 per game. The total profits of the firm thus are $180.50 per month, minus the firm's fixed costs.

Two-part pricing allows a firm to earn higher profits than it would earn by simply charging a price for each unit sold. By charging a fixed fee, the firm is able to extract consumer surplus, thus enhancing its profits. Unlike price discrimination, two-part pricing does not require that consumers have different elasticities of demand for the firm's product. By charging a per-unit fee for each unit purchased, consumers can vary the amounts they purchase according to their individual demands for the product.

Block Pricing

Another way a firm with market power can enhance profits is to engage in *block pricing*. If you have purchased toilet paper in packages of three rolls or cans of soda in a six-pack, you have had firsthand experience with block pricing.

Let us see how block pricing can enhance a firm's profits. Suppose an individual consumer's demand function is $Q = 10 - P$ and the firm's costs are $C(Q) = 2Q$. Figure 11–3 graphs the relevant curves. We see that if a firm charges a price of $2 per unit, it will sell eight units to the consumer. Notice, however, that the consumer receives a surplus of the upper triangle, which is

$$\frac{1}{2}[(10 - 2)8] = \$32.$$

This consumer's surplus reflects the value the consumer receives over and above the cost of buying eight units. In fact, in this case the consumer pays $2 \times 8 = \$16$ to the firm for the eight units, but receives additional surplus of $32. The total value to the consumer of the eight units is $16 + \$32 = \$48$.

Block pricing provides a means by which the firm can get the consumer to pay the full value of the eight units. It works very simply. Suppose the

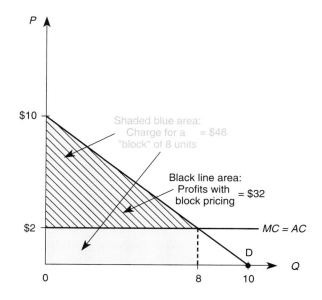

FIGURE 11–3

Block pricing

firm packaged eight units of its product and charged a price for the package. In this case, the consumer has to make an all-or-none decision between buying eight units and buying nothing. We just saw that the total value to the consumer of eight units is $48. Thus, so long as the price of the package of eight units is not greater than $48, this consumer will find it in her or his interest to buy the package.

Thus, the profit-maximizing price for the firm to charge for the package of eight units is $48. By charging this price for a package of eight instead of pricing each unit separately and letting the consumer choose how many units to buy, the firm earns $32 in profits—the value of the would-be consumer's surplus when the price is $2.

Principle

Block Pricing
By packaging units of a product and selling them as one package, the firm earns more than by posting a simple per-unit price. The profit-maximizing price on a package is the total value the consumer receives for the package, including consumer surplus.

DEMONSTRATION PROBLEM 11–6

Suppose a consumer's (inverse) demand function for gum produced by a firm with market power is given by $P = .2 - .04Q$ and the marginal cost is zero. What price should the firm charge for a package of five pieces of gum?

Answer

When $Q = 5$, $P = 0$; when $Q = 0$, $P = .2$. This linear demand is graphed in Figure 11–4. Thus, the total value to the consumer of five pieces of gum is

$$\frac{1}{2}[(.2 - 0)5] = \$.50,$$

which corresponds to the shaded area in Figure 11–4. The firm extracts all of this surplus by charging a price of $.50 for a package of five pieces of gum.

Block pricing enhances profits by forcing consumers to make an all-or-none decision to purchase units of a good. Unlike price discrimination, block pricing can enhance profits even in situations where consumers have identical demands for a firm's product.

FIGURE 11–4

Optimal block pricing with zero marginal cost

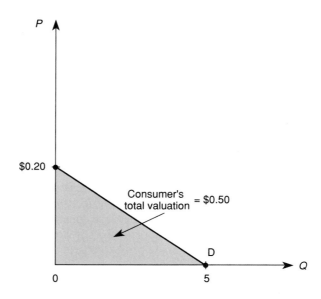

Commodity Bundling

commodity bundling
The practice of bundling several different products together and selling them at a single "bundle price."

Another strategy managers can use to enhance profits is commodity bundling. *Commodity bundling* refers to the practice of bundling two or more different products together and selling them at a single "bundle price." For instance, travel companies often sell "package deals" that include airfare, hotel, and meals at a bundled price instead of pricing each component of a vacation separately. Computer firms bundle computers, monitors, and software and sell them at a bundled price. Many car dealers bundle options such as air-conditioning, power steering, and automatic transmission and sell them at a "special package price." Let us see how these practices can enhance profits.

Suppose the manager of a computer firm knows there are two consumers who value its computers and monitors differently. Table 11–1 shows the maximum amount the two consumers would pay for a computer and monitor. The first consumer is willing to pay $2,000 for a computer and $200 for a monitor. The second consumer is willing to pay $1,500 for a computer and $300 for a monitor. However, the manager does not know the identity of each consumer; thus, she cannot price discriminate by charging each consumer a different price.

Suppose the manager priced each component separately: one price for a computer, P_C, and another price for a monitor, P_M. (To simplify profit computations, suppose the cost to the firm of computers and monitors is zero.) If the firm charged $2,000 for a computer, it would sell a computer only to consumer 1 and earn $2,000, because consumer 2 is willing to pay only $1,500 for a computer. If the firm charged $1,500 for a computer, both

TABLE 11–1

Consumer	Valuation of Computer	Valuation of Monitor
1	$2,000	$200
2	1,500	300

consumers would buy a computer, netting the firm $3,000. Clearly the profit-maximizing price to charge for a computer is $1,500.

Similarly, if the firm priced monitors at $300, only consumer 2 would purchase a monitor, because consumer 1 would pay only $200 for a monitor. By pricing monitors at $200, it would sell two monitors and earn $400. The profit-maximizing price to charge for a monitor thus is $200.

On the surface, it appears that the most the firm can earn is $3,400, by pricing computers at $1,500 and monitors at $200. In this case, the firm sells two computers and two monitors. However, the firm can earn higher profits by bundling computers and monitors and selling the bundle at a price of $1,800. To see why, notice that the total value to the first consumer of a computer and a monitor is $2,000 + $200 = $2,200, and the total value to the second consumer of a computer and a monitor is $1,500 + $300 = $1,800. By bundling a computer and a monitor and selling the bundle for $1,800, the firm will sell a bundle to both consumers and earn $3,600—a full $200 more than it would earn if it did not engage in commodity bundling.

This example illustrates that commodity bundling can enhance profits when consumers differ with respect to the amounts they are willing to pay for multiple products sold by a firm. It is important to emphasize that commodity bundling can enhance profits even when the manager cannot distinguish among the amounts different consumers are willing to pay for the firm's products. If the manager did know precisely how much each consumer was willing to pay for each product, the firm could earn even higher profits by engaging in price discrimination: charging higher prices to those consumers willing to pay more for its products.

DEMONSTRATION PROBLEM 11–7

Suppose three purchasers of a new car have the following valuations for options:

Consumer	Air-Conditioner	Power Brakes
1	$1,000	$500
2	$ 800	$300
3	$ 100	$800

The firm's costs are zero.

(1) If the manager knows the valuations and identity of each consumer, what is the optimal pricing strategy?

(2) Suppose the manager does not know the identities of the buyers. How much will the firm make if the manager sells brakes and air-conditioners for $800 each but offers a special options package (power brakes and an air-conditioner) for $1,100?

Answer

(1) If the manager knows the buyers' identities, he will maximize profits through price discrimination, since resale for these products is unlikely; charge consumer 1 $1,500 for an air-conditioner and power brakes; charge consumer 2 $1,100 for an air-conditioner and power brakes; and charge consumer 3 $900 for an air-conditioner and power brakes. The firm's profits will be $3,500. It makes no difference whether the manager charges the consumers a bundled price equal to their total valuation of an air-conditioner and power brakes or charges a separate price for each component that equals the consumers' valuation.

(2) The total value of a bundle containing an air-conditioner and power brakes is $1,500 for consumer 1, $1,100 for consumer 2, and $900 for consumer 3. Thus, consumers 1 and 2 will buy the option package, because a bundle with an air-conditioner and power brakes is worth at least $1,100 to each of them. The firm earns $2,200 on these consumers. Consumer 3 will not buy the bundle, because the total cost of the bundle is greater than the consumer's valuation ($900). However, Consumer 3 will buy power brakes at the price of $800. Thus, the firm earns $3,000 with this pricing strategy—$2,200 comes from consumers 1 and 2, who each purchase the special options package for $1,100, and $800 comes from consumer 3, who chooses to buy only power brakes.

Pricing Strategies for Special Cost and Demand Structures

The pricing strategies we will discuss in this section—peak-load pricing and cross subsidization—enhance profits for firms that have special cost and demand structures.

Peak-Load Pricing

Many markets have periods in which demand is high and periods in which demand is low. Toll roads tend to have more traffic during rush hour than at other times of the day; utility companies tend to have higher demand during the day than during the late-night hours; and airlines tend to have heavier traffic during the week than during weekends. When the demand during peak times is so high that the capacity of the firm cannot serve all customers at the same price, the profitable thing for the firm to do is engage in *peak-load pricing.*

Figure 11–5 illustrates a classic case of such a situation. Notice that marginal cost is constant up to Q_H, where it becomes vertical. At this point, the firm is operating at full capacity and cannot provide additional units at any price.

The two demand curves in Figure 11–5 correspond to peak and off-peak demand for the product: D_{Low} is the off-peak demand, which is lower than D_{High}, the peak demand. In general, when there are two types of demand, a firm will maximize profits by charging different prices to the different de-manders. As we learned in the section on price discrimination, by redistributing output among the groups until the marginal revenues associated with each group are equal, the firm can enhance profits. In the case of peak-load pricing, the "groups" refer to those who purchase at different times during the day.

Peak-load pricing is similar to price discrimination but, due to capacity limitations, the firm is unable to fully equate the marginal revenues of those who purchase at different times. In Figure 11–5, for instance, demand during low-peak times is such that marginal revenue equals marginal cost at point Q_L. Thus, the profit-maximizing price during low-peak times is P_L. In contrast, during high-peak times, marginal revenue equals marginal cost

FIGURE 11–5
Peak-load pricing

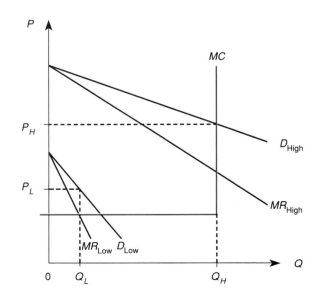

at point Q_H, which corresponds to the firm's full capacity. The profit-maximizing price during high-peak times is P_H. Thus, as is the case in price discrimination, the firm charges two different prices: a low price during low-peak demand and a high price during high-peak demand.

Notice in Figure 11–5 that if the firm charged a high price of P_H at all times of the day, no one would purchase during low-peak periods. By lowering the price during low-peak times but charging a high price during high-peak times, the firm increases its profits by selling to some consumers during low-peak times. Similarly, if the firm charged a low price during all times of the day, it would lose money during high-peak times, when consumers are willing to pay a higher price for services.

Principle

Peak-Load Pricing
When demand is higher at some times of the day than at other times, a firm may enhance profits by peak-load pricing: charge a higher price during peak times than is charged during off-peak times.

DEMONSTRATION PROBLEM 11–8

Airports typically charge a higher price for parking during holidays than they do during other times of the year. Why?

Answer

It pays for airports to engage in peak-load pricing. Since the demand for parking is much higher during holidays, when travelers spend extended periods with families, parking lots tend to fill up during that time. If airports charged a high price year round, they would have empty spaces most of the time. If they charged low prices year round, they would lose out on the additional amount consumers are willing to pay during holidays. Thus, with peak-load pricing, airports earn higher profits.

Cross-Subsidies

The second cost-based pricing strategy we will discuss—cross-subsidies—is relevant in situations where a firm has cost complementarities and the demand by consumers for a group of products is interdependent. A firm that engages in a strategy of *cross-subsidies* uses profits made with one product to subsidize sales of another product.

Consider a firm that sells two different types of computer software. One type is a disk operating system (DOS), and the other is an application that runs on the DOS (say, a word processor). Clearly there are economies of scope and cost complementarities in making the two products jointly; cost savings arise due to designing the software within the firm. Furthermore, the demand for the two products is likely to be interdependent; the word processor is valuable to a consumer only to the extent that it runs on his or her version of the DOS.

In such instances, a firm may find it profitable to sell one of the products at or below cost and charge a relatively high price for the other product. For instance, the firm may price the DOS below cost to induce numerous consumers to use it to run their computers. Once consumers commit to the firm's version of the DOS, the firm can charge a higher price for its applications software.

The advantage of cross-subsidization for the firm is twofold. First, it permits the firm to sell multiple products, which leads to cost savings in the presence of economies of scope. Second, if the two products have demands that are interdependent, the firm can induce consumers to buy more of each product than they would otherwise.

Principle

Cross-Subsidization
Whenever the demand for two products produced by a firm are interrelated through costs or demand, the firm may enhance profits by cross-subsidization: selling one product at or below cost and the other product above cost.

Transfer Pricing

Thus far our analysis of pricing decisions presumes that a single manager is in charge of pricing and output decisions. However, most large firms have upstream and downstream managers who must make price and output decisions for their own divisions. For example, automakers like General Motors have upstream managers who control the production of inputs (like car engines) produced in upstream divisions. These inputs are "transferred" to downstream divisions, where downstream managers operate plants that use the inputs to produce the final output (automobiles). An important issue in this setting is optimal *transfer pricing*—the internal price at which an upstream division should sell inputs to the firm's downstream division in order to maximize the overall profits of the firm.

Transfer pricing is important because most division managers are provided an incentive to maximize their own division's profits. As we will see, if the owners of a firm do not set optimal transfer prices, but instead let division managers set the prices of internally manufactured inputs so as to maximize their division's profits, the result might be lower overall profits for the firm.

To illustrate, suppose there is no outside market for the input produced by the upstream division, and that divisional managers are instructed to maximize the profits of their divisions. In this case the upstream division manager has market power, and maximizes the profits of the upstream division by producing where the marginal revenue derived from selling to the downstream division equals the upstream division's marginal cost of producing the input. Because of the monopoly power enjoyed by the upstream division, the input is sold to the downstream division at a price that exceeds the firm's actual marginal cost. Given this input price, the downstream manager would then maximize divisional profits by producing where the marginal revenue it earns in the final product market (MR_d) equals its marginal cost. This implies that it, too, prices above marginal cost. Moreover, because the price the downstream division pays the upstream division for the input is higher than the true marginal cost of the input, the downstream division ends up charging a price for the final product that is actually higher than the price that maximizes overall firm profits. In short, when both divisions mark up prices in excess of marginal cost, *double marginalization* occurs and the result is less than optimal overall firm profits.

To circumvent the problem of double marginalization, transfer prices must be set that maximize the overall value of the firm rather than the profits of the upstream division. To see how this can be accomplished, suppose the downstream division requires one unit of the input (one engine, say) to produce one unit of the final output (one car). Assume that the downstream division has a marginal cost of assembling the final output, denoted MC_d, that is in addition to cost of acquiring the input from the upstream division. In this case the overall profits of the firm are maximized when the upstream division produces engines such that its marginal cost, MC_u, equals the net marginal revenue to the downstream division (NMR_d):

$$NMR_d = MR_d - MC_d = MC_u.$$

To see why, notice that it costs the firm MC_u to produce another unit of the input. This input can be converted into another unit of output and sold to generate additional revenues of MR_d in the final product market only after the downstream division expends an additional MC_d to convert the input into the final output. Thus, the actual marginal benefit to the firm of producing another unit of the input is NMR_d. Setting this equal to the marginal cost of producing the input maximizes overall firm profits.

Now that we know the necessary conditions for maximizing overall firm profits, we show how a firm can institute an incentive system that induces the divisional managers to indeed maximize overall firm profits. Suppose higher authorities within the firm determine that the level of final output that maximizes overall firm profits is Q^*. They set the transfer price, P_T, equal to the upstream division's marginal cost of producing the amount of input required by the downstream division to produce Q^* units of final output. According to this internal pricing scheme, the downstream manager can now purchase as many units of the input as it desires from the upstream division at a fixed price of P_T per unit. The upstream and downstream managers are instructed to maximize divisional profits, taking as given the transfer price set by higher authorities within the firm.

Since the upstream division now must sell the input internally at a fixed price of P_T per unit, it behaves like a perfectly competitive firm and maximizes profits by producing where price equals marginal cost: $P_T = MC_u$. Since one unit of input is required for each unit of output, the downstream division's marginal cost of producing final output is now $MC = MC_d + P_T$. The downstream divisional manager maximizes divisional profits by producing where marginal revenue equals marginal cost: $MR_d = MC_d + P_T$. Since $P_T = MC_u$, we may rewrite this as $MR_d - MC_d = MC_u$, which is exactly our condition for maximizing overall firm profits. Thus, we see that by setting the transfer price at the upstream division's marginal cost of producing the firm's profit maximizing quantity of the input, the problem of double marginalization is avoided even though divisional managers operate independently to maximize their division's profits.

A concrete example will help illustrate how a firm can implement optimal transfer pricing. Suppose that the (inverse) demand for Aviation General's single-engine planes is given by $P = 15,000 - Q$. Its upstream division produces engines at a cost of $C_u(Q_e) = 2.5Q_e^2$, and the downstream division's cost of assembling planes is $C_d(Q) = 1,000\,Q$. Let us derive the optimal transfer price when there is no external market for engines.

The optimal transfer price is set where the firm's net marginal revenue from engine production equals the upstream division's marginal cost of producing the engines. Downstream marginal revenue and marginal cost is $MR_d = 15,000 - 2Q$ and $MC_d = 1,000$, respectively, while the upstream division's marginal cost of producing engines is $MC_u = 5Q_e$. Since it takes one engine to produce one plane ($Q = Q_e$), equating NMR_d and MC_u implies

$$NMR_d = 15,000 - 2Q_e - 1,000 = 5Q_e.$$

Solving for Q_e, we see that to maximize overall firm profits, the upstream division should produce 2,000 engines. Since $Q_e = Q$, the downstream division should produce 2,000 planes to maximize overall firm profits. The optimal transfer price is the upstream division's marginal cost of producing 2,000 engines, or $P_T = \$10,000$. Thus, the firm maximizes its overall profits when its accountants set the (internal) transfer price of engines at $10,000 per unit, and divisional managers are provided an incentive to maximize divisional profits given this price.

Pricing Strategies in Markets with Intense Price Competition

The final pricing strategies we will examine—price matching, inducing brand loyalty, and randomized pricing—are valuable for firms competing in Bertrand oligopoly. Recall that firms in Bertrand oligopoly compete in price and sell similar products. As we learned in Chapters 9 and 10, in these instances price wars will likely result, leading to prices that are close to marginal cost and profits that are near zero. While the pricing strategies discussed in this section can be used in situations other than Bertrand oligopoly, they are particularly useful for mitigating the price wars that frequently occur in such a market.

Price Matching

In Chapters 9 and 10, we showed that when two or more firms compete in a homogeneous-product Bertrand oligopoly, the Nash equilibrium is for each firm to charge marginal cost and earn zero profits. However, in Chapter 10 we showed that if the game is infinitely repeated, firms can maintain collusive outcomes by adopting trigger strategies, which punish rivals that deviate from the high price. In an infinitely repeated game, punishments are threatened in the future if a firm cheats on a collusive agreement, and this can lead to a situation where firms end up charging high prices. However, recall that this strategy can work only if the interest rate is low and firms can effectively monitor the behavior of other firms in the market.

In cases where trigger strategies do not work (because the game is not infinitely repeated or the firms cannot monitor other firms' behavior), there is another way firms can attain higher profits: by advertising a price-matching strategy. A firm that uses a *price-matching strategy* advertises a price and a promise to "match" any lower price offered by a competitor.

price matching
A strategy in which a firm advertises a price and a promise to match any lower price offered by a competitor.

To illustrate how such a strategy can enhance profits, suppose the firms in a market play a one-shot Bertrand pricing game. However, in addition to advertising a price, the firms advertise a commitment to match any lower price found in the market. Such an advertisement would look something like the following:

> Our price is *P.* If you find a better price in the market, we will match that price. We will not be undersold!

This sound like a good deal for consumers; indeed, simply announcing this strategy may induce some consumers to buy from the firm to be "assured" of a great deal.

It turns out, however, that if all firms in the market announce such a policy, they can set the price (*P*) to the high monopoly price and earn large profits instead of the zero profits they would earn in the usual one-shot Bertrand oligopoly. How does this work?

Suppose all firms advertised the high monopoly price but promised to match any lower price found by consumers. Since all firms are charging the same high price, consumers can't find a better price in the market. The result is that firms share the market, charge the monopoly price, and earn high profits. Furthermore, notice that no firm has an incentive to charge a lower price in an attempt to steal customers from rivals. If a firm lowered its price, the rivals would match that price and gain back their share of the market. By lowering its price, a firm effectively triggers a price war, which results in no greater share of the market and lower profits. Thus, if all firms adopt

Beat-or-Pay Strategies

Another strategy a firm uses is to promise to pay consumers some amount if it fails to provide the best price in the market. For instance, a recent advertisement by a car dealer promised to pay consumers $1,000 if they bought a car at a lower price than the dealer could offer. To collect the money, a consumer had to (1) give the dealer a chance to beat the offer and, if the dealer did not beat the offer, (2) bring proof that the car was indeed purchased at another dealer at that price.

Such a beat-or-pay strategy enhances profits in two ways. First, it is a great gimmick to get consumers into the store. Second, it gives rivals a disincentive to get into a price war with your firm. Let us see why.

For simplicity, suppose the marginal cost of a new car is zero and there are two dealers. Bertrand competition for consumers would lead to a situation where each firm charged a price of zero for a new car; each firm would earn zero profits. Suppose consumers are willing to pay $10,000 for a new car. Then in the absence of a competi-

tor, the profit-maximizing strategy would be to charge $10,000 for a car and earn profits of $10,000. Of course, such profits are not earned with simple Bertrand competition.

Now suppose both dealers set a price of $10,000 but one of them (the "beat" dealer) promises to pay consumers $1,000 if it does not provide the better deal. What will a consumer do? First, the consumer will go to the other dealer, get the quote of $10,000, and take it to the "beat" dealer. This dealer undercuts the price by, say, $1, since it is better off selling the car for $9,999 than paying the consumer $1,000 for failing to beat the price. The consumer could then return to the other dealer with this new price and ask the dealer to offer a better price. Would the first dealer have an incentive to offer a better deal? Suppose it did. Then the consumer would return to the "beat" dealer and ask it to undercut the price. This process would continue until the

Inside Business 11–2 continued

price-matching strategies, the result is that each firm charges the monopoly price and shares the market to earn high profits.

An important aspect of price-matching policies is that the firms need not monitor the prices charged by rivals. This is in contrast to trigger strategies, in which firms must monitor rivals' prices to know whether to punish a rival that has charged a low price. With a price-matching strategy, it is up to a consumer to show the firm that some rival is offering a better deal. At that point, the firm can match the price for that consumer. The consumers who have not found a better deal continue to pay the higher price. Thus, even if some other firm happened to charge a low price, a firm using a price-matching strategy would get to price discriminate between those consumers who found such a price and those who did not.

Before you choose to adopt a price-matching strategy, there are two things to consider. First, you must devise a mechanism that precludes consumers from claiming to have found a lower price when in fact they have not. Otherwise, consumers will have an incentive to tell you that another

---

Inside Business 11–2 concluded

consumer was quoted a price equal to the wholesale price of the car—in this case, zero—by the first dealer.

What happens when the consumer takes the wholesale price to the "beat" dealer? The dealer has two choices: pay the consumer $1 to take a car or pay the consumer $1,000 for its failure to offer a better deal than the rival. Clearly the best thing for the "beat" dealer to do is give the consumer the car and $1. At this point, when the consumer asks the other dealer to beat this deal, it says no; it has no incentive to sell a car below cost. The end of this process is that the "beat" dealer sells a car at $1 below cost.

Why, then, would the dealer run the ad if it will lose $1 by doing so? The answer lies in transaction costs. In the preceding analysis, we ignored the cost to the first dealer of continually making an offer when, in the end, it knows the car will be purchased from the "beat" dealer. Specifically, the first dealer knows what will happen at the end of this process. The "beat" dealer is willing to sell a car at $1,000 below cost, since otherwise it would lose $1,000 when it paid the

consumer for failing to undercut it. Thus, the first dealer knows that the only way it will be able to sell a car is to sell one at $1,000 below cost. In short, the dealer would spend considerable time making offers to the consumer, but it knows that in the end, the consumer will buy the car from the "beat" dealer. Given this knowledge, it is best for the first dealer not to deal with the consumer.

Now consider the profit-maximizing response of the first dealer when the consumer returns with the first offer of $9,999 from the "beat" dealer. The first dealer knows the rival will beat any offer, so it finds it in its best interest to tell the consumer, "Sorry, but we can't compete with that." It knows it does not pay to get into a price war with the other dealer. The dealer that ran the beat-or-pay advertisement makes a handsome profit: It sells a car for $9,999 above cost.

Source: Michael R. Baye and Dan Kovenock, "How to Sell a Pickup Truck: Beat-or-Pay Strategies as Facilitating Devices," *International Journal of Industrial Organization* 25 (1994), pp. 21–31.

---

firm is "giving goods away" and ask you to match this lower price. One way firms avoid such deception is by promising to match prices that are advertised in some widely circulated newspaper. In this case, the consumer must bring in the advertisement before the price will be matched.

Second, you can get into trouble with a price-matching strategy if a competitor has lower costs than your firm. For instance, if your competitor's marginal cost is $300 for a television set and yours is $400, the profit-maximizing (monopoly) price set by your firm will be higher than that set by the rival. In such an instance, the monopoly price set by your rival may be lower than your cost. In this case, if you have to match your rival's price, you will incur losses on each unit sold.

Inducing Brand Loyalty

Another strategy a firm can use to reduce the tension of Bertrand competition is to adopt strategies that induce *brand loyalty*. Brand-loyal customers will continue to buy a firm's product even if another firm offers a (slightly) better price. By inducing brand loyalty, a firm reduces the number of consumers who will "switch" to another firm if it undercuts its price.

Firms can use several methods to induce brand loyalty. One of the more common methods is to engage in advertising campaigns that promote a firm's product as being better than those of competitors. If advertisements make consumers believe that other products in the market are not perfect substitutes, higher profits can be earned by firms engaging in price competition. When a rival undercuts a firm's price, some customers will remain loyal to the firm, allowing it to charge a higher price and make positive profits.

Notice, however, that such an advertising strategy will not work if consumers believe products to be homogeneous. A self-service gasoline station would be hard-pressed to convince consumers that its product is really "different" from the identical brand sold across the street. In these instances, firms can resort to alternative strategies to promote brand loyalty.

Some gasoline stations now have "frequent-filler" programs, modeled after the frequent-flyer programs initiated by the airlines. Frequent-filler programs provide consumers with a cash rebate after a specified number of fill-ups. With this strategy, even though the products are identical, the consumer has an incentive to remain loyal to the same station to maximize the number of times he or she obtains a rebate. For example, suppose a station offers a $5 rebate after 10 fill-ups. If the consumer fills up at 10 different stations, he or she does not get the rebate, but if all 10 fill-ups are at the same station, the consumer gets $5. Thus, a frequent-filler strategy provides the consumer with an incentive to remain loyal to a particular station even though it offers products identical to its rivals'.

Randomized Pricing

The final strategy firms can use to enhance profits in markets with intense price competition is to engage in randomized-pricing strategies. With a *randomized-pricing strategy,* a firm varies its price from hour to hour or day to day. Such a strategy can benefit a firm for two reasons.

First, when firms adopt randomized pricing strategies, consumers cannot learn from experience which firm charges the lowest price in the market. On some days, one firm charges the lowest price; on another day, some other firm offers the best deal. By increasing the uncertainty about where the best deal exists, firms reduce consumers' incentive to shop for price information. Because one store offers the best deal today does not mean it will also offer the best deal tomorrow. To continually find the best price in the market, a consumer must constantly shop for a new deal. In effect, there is only a one-shot gain to a consumer of becoming informed; the information is worthless when new prices are set. This reduces consumers' incentive to invest in information about prices. As consumers have less information about the prices offered by competitors, firms are less vulnerable to rivals stealing customers by setting lower prices.

The second advantage of randomized prices is that it reduces the ability of rival firms to undercut a firm's price. Recall that in Bertrand oligopoly, a firm wishes to slightly undercut the rival's price. If another firm offers a slightly better deal, informed consumers will switch to that firm. Randomized pricing not only reduces the information available to consumers but it precludes rivals from knowing precisely what price to charge to undercut a given firm's price. Randomized-pricing strategies tend to reduce rivals' incentive to engage in price wars and thus can enhance profits.

We should point out that it is not always profitable to engage in randomized-pricing strategies. In many instances, other strategies, such as trigger or price-matching strategies, can be a more effective means of enhancing profits. Moreover, in some instances it may not be feasible to change prices as frequently as randomized-pricing strategies require. The cost of hiring personnel to continually change price tags can be prohibitive. Randomized pricing can work, however, when prices are entered in a computer and not directly on the products. It can also work when firms advertise "sales" in a weekly newspaper. In these instances, the prices advertised in the sales circular can be varied from week to week so the competition will not know what price to advertise to undercut the firm's price.

Answering the Headline

Why does Disneyland charge a cover fee for entering the park and then let everyone who enters ride for free? The answer lies in the ability to extract consumer surplus by engaging in two-part pricing. In particular, the marginal cost of an individual ride at an amusement park is close to zero, as in Figure 11–6. If the average consumer has a demand curve like the one in Figure 11–6, setting the monopoly price would result in a price of $5 per ride. Since each customer would go on three rides, the amusement park would net $15 per customer. (This ignores fixed costs, which must be paid regardless of the pricing strategy.) But this would leave the average consumer with $7.50 in consumer surplus. By charging an entry fee of $30 but pricing each ride at $0, each consumer rides an average of six rides and the park extracts all consumer surplus and earns higher profits.[1]

---

[1]Walter Oi, "A Disneyland Dilemma: Two-Part Tariffs for a Mickey Mouse Monopoly," *Quarterly Journal of Economics* 85 (February 1971), pp. 77–96.

FIGURE 11–6

The Disneyland dilemma

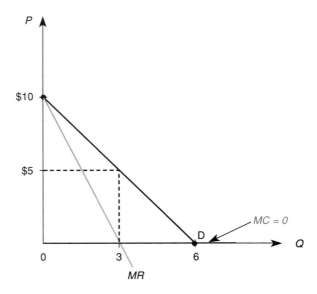

Summary

This chapter presented pricing strategies used by firms with some market power. Unlike firms in a perfectly competitive market, when there are a small number of firms and products are slightly differentiated, a manager can use pricing strategies that will foster positive economic profits. These strategies range from simple markup rules to more complex two-part pricing strategies that enable a firm to extract all consumer surplus.

This chapter showed how markup rules come into existence. If a firm is monopolistic or monopolistically competitive, the elasticity from the firm's demand function can be used to find the markup factor that will maximize the firm's profits. If a manager operates in a Cournot oligopoly, the firm's own price elasticity is simply the number of firms in the market times the market elasticity. Knowing this, a manager in this kind of market can easily calculate the appropriate markup rule for his or her pricing strategies.

In some markets, the manager can actually do better than the single monopoly price. This can be accomplished through price discrimination or two-part pricing. Other pricing strategies that enhance profits include peak-load pricing, block pricing, commodity bundling, cross-subsidization, and optimal transfer pricing. The chapter concluded with descriptions of strategies that can help managers in a Bertrand oligopoly avoid the tendency toward zero economic profits.

Randomized Pricing in the Airline Industry

There are over 215,396 changes in airfares each day. This translates into 150 changes per minute. Domestic airlines spend considerable sums of money in an attempt to monitor the prices of other firms. As noted by Marius Schwartz:

> Delta Airlines assigns 147 employees to track rivals' prices and select quick responses—on a typical day, comparing over 5,000 industry pricing changes against Delta's more than 70,000 fares. New fares filed the prior day with Air Tariff Publishing Co. are tracked by a Delta computer. "Secret" price changes that are deliberately withheld from the Air Traffic Publishing system for several days are tracked through local newspapers or calls to other airlines' reservation offices. Once Delta learns of a competitor's pricing move, it can put a matching fare into its reservation system within two hours.

Why do airlines take such drastic measures to learn the prices set by their rivals? The airlines compete in a Bertrand market. Firms need to know rivals' prices so that they can undercut them. Despite some brand loyalty created by frequent-flyer programs, a large number of airline customers choose a carrier based purely on price. To get these customers, an airline must succeed in charging the lowest price in the market. By continually monitoring rivals' prices, airlines are in a better position to set profit-maximizing prices.

Why do airfares change so frequently? Given the structure of the airline market, airlines find it profitable to "randomize" their prices so that rivals and consumers cannot learn from experience exactly what the price of a particular route is. By frequently changing its prices, an airline prevents rivals from learning the price they have to undercut to steal customers. With prices that vary randomly over time, an airline may be charging the highest price or lowest price in the market at a given instant. When it charges the lowest price, it sells tickets to both its price-conscious and loyal customers. When it charges high prices, it sells tickets only to its loyal customers, as the price-conscious flyers buy tickets from another airline.

Sources: Marius Schwartz, "The Nature and Scope of Contestability Theory," *Oxford Economic Papers,* supplement 3, 1986, pp. 46–49; Michael R. Baye and Casper G. de Vries, "Mixed Strategy Trade Equilibrium," *Canadian Journal of Economics* 25 (May 1992), pp. 281–93; *Travel and Leisure,* May 1992, p. 184.

Key Terms and Concepts

block pricing
brand loyalty
commodity bundling
cross-subsidies
double marginalization
downstream division
first-degree price
  discrimination
optimal transfer price
peak-load pricing
randomized pricing

second-degree price
  discrimination
simple pricing rule for Cournot
  oligopoly
simple pricing rule for monopoly
  and monopolistic
  competition
third-degree price
  discrimination
two-part pricing
upstream division

Problems

1. A local dentist read an article published by the American Dental Association estimating that the elasticity of demand for the representative dentist's services is -2.5. How much should the dentist mark up her price over marginal cost?

2. You are a truck farmer and bring produce to a farmer's market every Wednesday. You have found that on a typical day, five other farmers bring their produce to market. Years of experience have taught you that you make the most money by pricing your produce at 1.15 times your marginal cost. What is your elasticity for demand in this Cournot oligopoly? What is the market elasticity of demand?

3. You are the only pharmacist in a small town; the next closest drugstore is 50 miles away. The population in your town consists of young farmers and older retired families. You have noticed that the young farmers are less sensitive to price changes than the retired population. Specifically you have found that the working population has an own price elasticity of demand of -2 and the retired farmers have an own price elasticity of -4. How can you use this information to your advantage?

4. You have just been hired as manager of a new health spa in Retirement Village, Florida. The owner has commissioned a market study that estimates the average customer's monthly demand curve for visiting the health spa to be

$$Q^d = 50 - .25\,P.$$

The cost of operating is $C(Q) = 3Q$, where Q is the number of visits. The owner has been charging a $20 per-month membership fee and a $5 per-visit fee. Part of your salary is 10 percent of the monthly profits. Suggest a pricing strategy that will increase your salary.

5. Suppose a typical consumer's inverse demand function for bottled water at a resort area where one firm owns all the rights to a local spring is given by

$$P = 15 - 3\,Q.$$

The marginal cost for gathering and bottling the water is $3 per gallon. Find the optimal number of bottles to package together for sale and the profit-maximizing price to charge for the package. Show the solution graphically.

6. As manager of the only video store in town, you have noticed that on Thursday through Sunday the demand for renting your movies is much higher than it is on Monday through Wednesday. You therefore conducted a study that revealed two different market demand curves. On weekends, your market inverse demand curve is

$$P = 10 - .001\,Q;$$

on weekdays, it is

$$P = 5 - .01\ Q.$$

The marginal cost of renting a movie is $.50 cents. Your average customer never rents more than one movie at a time. What pricing strategy will maximize your profits?

7. During the early 1990s, several airlines were on the brink of bankruptcy. These same airlines were giving away millions of dollars in free airline travel through their frequent-flyer programs. Do you think it would be a good idea for these airlines to eliminate their frequent flyer programs in order to earn higher profits? Explain.

8. Many restaurants have found that it is advantageous to offer free appetizers with a two-drink minimum during a limited number of hours. Is this profit-maximizing behavior? Why or why not?

9. You run a golf course at a tourist resort. At your resort, there are two distinct groups of players. One group owns property at the resort and resides there most of the year. On average, each of these consumers has a monthly inverse demand for golf services of

$$P = 100 - .5Q.$$

The other group visits for one week at a time and has a total weekly demand curve of

$$P = 40 - .1Q.$$

What pricing strategy will maximize your profits?

10. An auto dealer in Chicago recently told his mother that he makes no money on the sales of his cars but the markup on accessories is 200 percent. Can this possibly be a profit-maximizing strategy? Explain.

11. In 1990 Chrysler offered rebates on almost all of its cars. In May it announced that the rebate program would end on June 30. It also announced that no further rebates would be offered in 1990. Chrysler guaranteed this by promising that if it did offer any rebates larger than those offered between May 1 and June 30, all customers who purchased cars before the new rebate would get the full rebate. How should this announcement have affected the pricing behavior of other car manufacturers for the remainder of 1990?

12. In most cities all lumber yards advertise that they have the lowest price in town. In addition, they often claim that they will match the prices of any other lumber yards. Is this Bertrand competition that brings about zero economic profits? Explain.

13. Grocery stores make most of their profits on soft drinks, beer, chips, and candy. A casual look at prices of these items reveals that these prices change extremely often and can vary as much as 50 percent. Is this because the wholesale price of these items fluctuates this dramatically, or is there some other possible explanation?

14. You are the owner of a mom-and-pop store that buys milk from a supplier at a cost of $1 per gallon. If you estimate the elasticity of demand for milk sold at your store to be -3.5, what are your profit-maximizing markup and price?

15. You are the manager of a gas station in a small town, and your goal is to maximize profits. Based on your experience, the elasticity of demand of Texans for a car wash is -2, while that of non-Texans is -1.5. Your marginal cost is $6.
    a. Are the conditions necessary for price discrimination to be an effective means of enhancing profits being met? Explain.
    b. What is the profit-maximizing price to charge a Texan for a car wash?
    c. What is the profit-maximizing price to charge a Californian for a car wash?

16. An industry produces 10,000 units of output at a price of $100. At the equilibrium price and quantity, the market elasticity of demand is -0.75. Does this industry consist of a profit-maximizing monopolist? Explain.

17. A monopolist is profit maximizing where the elasticity of demand is -2 and price is $4. What is the monopolist's marginal cost?

18. Most wholesalers post a "suggested retail price" on packages, which in turn are sold by retailers. Is there an economic basis for the suggested retail price? As the manager of a retailing outlet, what factors will determine whether you should charge the suggested retail price or some higher or lower price?

19. Table 7–3 in Chapter 7 provided estimates of elasticities of demand for representative firms in 10 industries. Based on those elasticities, compute the profit-maximizing markup factor for each industry.

20. Before the breakup of AT&T, the firm charged a price for local telephone services that was roughly one-half of its cost of providing the services. In contrast, it charged almost two times its cost for long distance services. Why do you think AT&T adopted this pricing strategy?

21. Three consumers who want to buy a new car have the following valuations for dealer options:

	Air-Conditioner	*Power Brakes*
Consumer One	$1,000	$500
Consumer Two	$ 800	$300
Consumer Three	$ 100	$800

Assuming costs are zero, how much would the dealer make if it priced power brakes at $800, priced air conditioners at $200, and sold the bundle for $1,300?

22. You are the CEO of Comchip, a firm that sells specialized computers. Each of the firm's computers contain a unique chip that is produced at Comchip's west coast plant at a cost of $C_w(Q_c) = Q_c^2$. Once produced, the chips are shipped exclusively to the firm's east coast plant. There, the computers are assembled, boxed, and shipped to the market at a cost of $C_e(Q) = 200Q$. An economic consultant recently estimated the demand for Comchip's computers and found it to be $P = 5,000 - Q$. Determine the Comchip's optimal output and price for computers, and explain how it can induce plant managers to produce the required number of chips and computers.

Selected Readings

Adams, William J. and Yellen, Janet I., "Commodity Bundling and the Burden of Monopoly." *Quarterly Journal of Economics* 90, August 1976, pp. 475–98.

Cain, Paul and Macdonald, James M., "Telephone Pricing Structures: The Effects on Universal Service." *Journal of Regulatory Economics* 3(4), December 1991, pp. 293–308.

Karni, Edi and Levin, Dan, "Social Attributes and Strategic Equilibrium: A Restaurant Pricing Game." *Journal of Political Economy* 102(4), August 1994, pp. 822–40.

Masson, Robert and Shaanan, Joseph, "Optimal Oligopoly Pricing and the Threat of Entry: Canadian Evidence." *International Journal of Industrial Organization* 5(3), September 1987, pp. 323–39.

McAfee, R. Preston, McMillan, John, and Whinston, Michael D., "Multiproduct Monopoly, Commodity Bundling, and Correlation of Values." *Quarterly Journal of Economics* 104(2), May 1989, pp. 371–83.

Oi, Walter Y., "A Disneyland Dilemma: Two-Part Tariffs for a Mickey Mouse Monopoly." *Quarterly Journal of Economics* 85, February 1971, pp. 77–96.

Romano, Richard E., "Double Moral Hazard and Resale Price Maintenance." *Rand Journal of Economics* 25(3), Autumn 1994, pp. 455–66.

Scitovsky, T., The Benefits of Asymmetric Markets." *Journal of Economics Perspectives* 4(1), Winter 1990, pp. 135–48.

CHAPTER

12

The Economics of Information

Headline

Firm Chickens-Out in the FCC Spectrum Auction

In 1993 the U.S. Congress passed legislation that required the FCC to abandon its "public hearing" format for awarding radio spectrum licenses. As a result of the legislation, the FCC now auctions off spectrum rights; the high bidder in the auction obtains exclusive rights to the spectrum for a period of 10 years. In its first auction the FCC auctioned off 10 licenses, netting the U.S. Treasury $600 million in revenues from the winning bidders.

To individual bidders like Bell South and McCaw, the auction format involved considerable uncertainty. While the value of a given license is virtually identical to all of the bidders, no single firm knew for sure what their profits would be if they won the auction. Each firm had its own private estimates of the value of a license, but these estimates differed across bidders.

One firm's private estimate of the value of a license was $85 million. This means that the firm estimated that it would earn $85 million over and above all costs (in present value terms) if it were awarded a license. Yet, this firm dropped out of the bidding when the auction price reached $80 million.

Why do you think the firm dropped out of the bidding when the price was below its private estimate of the value of a license?

Introduction

Throughout most of this book, we have assumed that participants in the market process—both consumers and firms—enjoy the benefits of perfect information. One need not look very hard at the real world to notice that this assumption is more fiction than fact. Nevertheless, our analyses in the preceding chapters can help us understand the market process. In fact, it is the basis for more complicated analysis that incorporates the effects of uncertainty and imperfect information.

More advanced courses in economics build in the foundations set forth in earlier chapters of this book by relaxing the assumption that people enjoy perfect information. While formal theoretical models of decision making in the presence of imperfect information are well beyond the scope and purpose of this book, it is useful to present an overview of some of the more important aspects of decision making under uncertainty. First, we will describe more formally what we mean by *uncertainty* and examine the impact of uncertainty on consumer behavior. Then we will briefly demonstrate means by which the manager can cope with risk. Finally, we will look at several important implications of uncertainty on the market process, including auction markets.

The Mean and the Variance

The easiest way to summarize information about uncertain outcomes is to use the statistical concepts of the mean and the variance of a random variable. More specifically, suppose there is some uncertainty regarding the value of some variable. The random variable, x, might represent profits, the price of output, or consumer income. Since x is a random variable, we cannot be sure what its actual value is. All we know is that with given probabilities, different values of the random variable will occur. For example, suppose someone promises to pay you (in dollars) whatever number comes up when a fair die is tossed. If x represents the payment to you, it is clear that you cannot be sure how much you will be paid. If you are lucky, you will roll a 6 and be paid $6. If you are unlucky, you will roll a 1 and receive $1. The probability that any number between 1 and 6 is rolled is 1/6, because there are six sides on the die. The expected value (or mean) of x is given by

$$Ex = \frac{1}{6}(\$1) + \frac{1}{6}(\$2) + \frac{1}{6}(\$3) + \frac{1}{6}(\$4) + \frac{1}{6}(\$5) + \frac{1}{6}(\$6) = \$3.50.$$

mean (expected value)
The sum of the probabilities that different outcomes will occur multiplied by the resulting payoffs.

In other words, even though you do not know for certain how much you will be paid when you roll the die, on average you will earn $3.50.

The *mean,* or *expected value,* of a random variable, x, is defined as the sum of the probabilities that different outcomes will occur times the resulting payoffs. Formally, if the possible outcomes of the random variable are $x_1, x_2, \ldots, x_n$ and the corresponding probabilities of the outcomes are $q_1, q_2, \ldots, q_n$, the expected value of x is given by

$$Ex = q_1x_1 + q_2x_2 + \ldots + q_nx_n,$$

where $q_1 + q_2 + \ldots + q_n = 1$.

The mean of a random variable thus collapses information about the likelihood of different outcomes into a single statistic. This is a very convenient way of economizing on the amount of information needed to make decisions.

DEMONSTRATION PROBLEM 12–1

The manager of XYZ Company is introducing a new product that will yield $1,000 in profits if the economy does not go into a recession. However, if a recession occurs, demand for the normal good will fall so sharply that the company will lose $4,000. If economists project that there is a 10 percent chance the economy will go into a recession, what are the expected profits to XYZ Company of introducing the new product?

Answer

If there is a 10 percent chance of a recession, there is a 90 percent chance that there will not be a recession. Using the formula for the expected value of a random variable, the expected profits of introducing the new product are found to be

$$Ex = q_1x_1 + q_2x_2 = .1(-\$4,000) + .9(\$1,000) = \$500.$$

Thus, the expected profits of introducing the new product are $500.

The mean provides information about the average value of a random variable but it yields no information about the degree of risk associated with the random variable. To illustrate the importance of considering risk in making decisions, consider the following two options:

Option 1: Flip a coin. If it comes up heads, you receive $1; if it comes up tails, you pay $1.

Option 2: Flip a coin. If it comes up heads, you receive $10; if it comes up tails, you pay $10.

Even though the stakes are much higher under option 2 than under option 1, each option has an expected value of zero. On average, you will neither make nor lose money with either option. To see this, note that there is a 50-50 chance the coin will land on heads. Thus, the expected value of option 1 is

$$E_{Option\ 1}[x] = \frac{1}{2}(\$1) + \frac{1}{2}(-\$1) = 0,$$

and the expected value of option 2 is

$$E_{Option\ 2}[x] = \frac{1}{2}(\$10) + \frac{1}{2}(-\$10) = 0.$$

The two options have the same expected value but are inherently different in nature. By summarizing information about the options using the mean, we have lost some information about the risk associated with the two options. Regardless of which option you choose, you will either gain money or lose money by flipping the coin. Under option 1, half the time you will make $1 more than the average and half the time you will make $1 less than the average. Under option 2, the deviation from the mean of the actual gain or loss is much greater: Half the time you will make $10 more than the average, and half the time you will lose $10 more than the average. Since these deviations from the mean are much larger under option 2 than under option 1, it is natural to think of option 2 as being more risky than option 1.

While the preceding discussion provides a rationale for calling option 2 more risky than option 1, it is often convenient for the manager to have a number that summarizes the risk associated with random outcomes. The most common measure of *risk* is the variance, which depends in a special way on the deviations of possible outcomes from the mean. The *variance* of a random variable is the sum of the probabilities that different outcomes will occur times the squared deviations from the mean of the random variable. Formally, if the possible outcomes of the random variable are x_1, $x_2, \ldots, x_n$, their corresponding probabilities are $q_1, q_2 \ldots, q_n$, and the expected value of x is given by Ex, the variance of x is given by

variance
The sum of the probabilities that different outcomes will occur multiplied by the squared deviations from the mean of the random variable.

$$\sigma^2 = q_1(x_1 - Ex)^2 + q_2(x_2 - Ex)^2 + \ldots + q_n(x_n - Ex)^2.$$

The *standard deviation* is simply the square root of the variance:

standard deviation
The square root of the variance.

$$\sigma = \sqrt{\sigma^2} = \sqrt{q_1(x_1 - Ex)^2 + q_2(x_2 - Ex)^2 + \ldots + q_n(x_n - Ex)^2}.$$

Let us apply these formulas to our coin tossing examples to see how the variance can be used to obtain a number that summarizes the risk associated with the options. In each case, only two possible outcomes occur with equal probabilities, so $q_1 = q_2 = 1/2$. The mean of each option is zero. Thus, the variance of option 1 is

$$\sigma^2_{Option\ 1} = \frac{1}{2}(1 - 0)^2 + \frac{1}{2}(-1 - 0)^2 = \frac{1}{2}(1) + \frac{1}{2}(1) = 1.$$

The variance of option 2 is

$$\sigma^2_{Option\ 2} = \frac{1}{2}(10 - 0)^2 + \frac{1}{2}(-10 - 0)^2 = \frac{1}{2}(100) + \frac{1}{2}(100) = 100.$$

Since

$$\sigma^2{}_{Option\ 1} = 1 < \sigma^2{}_{Option\ 1} = 100,$$

option 2 is more risky than option 1. Since the standard deviation is the square root of the variance, the standard deviation of option 1 is 1 and the standard deviation of option 2 is 10.

DEMONSTRATION PROBLEM 12–2

Consider again the manager of XYZ Company who is introducing a new product that will yield $1,000 in profits if the economy does not go into a recession. If a recession occurs, the company will lose $4,000. If economists project that there is a 10 percent change the economy will go into a recession, how risky is the introduction of the new product?

Answer

There is a 10 percent chance of a recession and a 90 percent chance of no recession. Thus, there is a 10 percent chance the firm will lose $4,000 and a 90 percent chance it will make $1,000. We already calculated the expected profits to be $500. Using variance as a measure of risk,

$$\begin{aligned}
\sigma^2 &= .1(-4,000 - 500)^2 + .9(1,000 - 500)^2 \\
&= .1(-4,500)^2 + .9(500)^2 \\
&= 2,025,000 + 225,000 \\
&= 2,250,000.
\end{aligned}$$

The standard deviation is

$$\sigma = \sqrt{2,250,000} = 1,500.$$

Uncertainty and Consumer Behavior

Now that you understand how to calculate the mean and variance of an uncertain outcome, we will see how the presence of *uncertainty* affects economic decisions of both consumers and managers.

Risk Aversion

In Chapter 4 we assumed consumers have preferences for bundles of goods, which were assumed to be known with certainty. We now will extend our analysis to preferences over uncertain outcomes.

Inside Business 12–1

The Likelihood of Business Failure

Many managers are tempted to quit their jobs and use their expertise to start their own business. Based on the numbers in Table 12–1, we see that during the early 1990s the probability of a new business failing averaged about 1 percent. This seems quite low and may entice you to one day break away from your company to start your own enterprise. Before you do so though, you may wish to reconsider. Why?

The numbers in Table 12–1 are based on data for large and small businesses alike. It turns out that small new businesses—those with liabilities under $100,000—are much more likely to fail than larger new businesses. In fact, in 1990 almost two-thirds of all business failures were small firms.

Why are small firms more likely to fail than larger firms? One reason is that small businesses are frequently funded with private capital. To start a small business, entrepreneurs simply must convince themselves to sink their own savings into the new business. In contrast, individuals who wish to open a large business will require capital from other sources, including banks and other investors. Consequently, entrepreneurs opening a large business must convince not only themselves of the worthiness of the project but also the bank and other investors. Investors and banks "filter out" the worst projects and fund the best. Consequently, larger firms are less likely to fail than smaller firms.

TABLE 12–1   Business Formation and Business Failures, 1960–1994

Year	New-Business Incorporations (number)	Business Failure Rate (per 10,000 listed enterprises)
1960	182,713	57.0
1961	181,535	64.4
1962	182,057	60.8
1963	186,404	56.3
1964	197,724	53.2
1965	203,897	53.3
1966	200,010	51.6
1967	206,569	49.0
1968	233,635	38.6
1969	274,267	37.3
1970	264,209	43.8
1971	287,577	41.7
1972	316,601	38.3
1973	329,358	36.4
1974	319,149	38.4
1975	326,345	42.6
1976	375,766	34.8
1977	436,170	28.4
1978	478,019	23.9
1979	524,565	27.8
1980	533,520	42.1
1981	581,242	61.3
1982	566,942	89.0
1983	600,400	110.0
1984	634,991	107.0
1985	662,047	115.0
1986	702,738	120.0
1987	685,572	102.0
1988	685,095	98.0
1989	676,565	65.0
1990	647,366	74.0
1991	628,604	107.0
1992	666,800	110.0
1993	706,537	109.0
1994	741,657	86.0

Source: *Economic Report of the President*, 1996, p. 385.

Let F and G represent two uncertain prospects. F might represent the prospects associated with buying 100 shares of stock in company F, and G the prospects associated with buying 100 shares of stock in company G. When you purchase a stock, you are uncertain what your actual profits or losses will be; all you know is that there is some mean and variance in return associated with each stock. Different people exhibit different preferences for the same set of prospects. You may prefer F to G, while a friend prefers G to F. It simply is a matter of taste for risky prospects.

Because attitudes toward risk will differ among consumers, we must introduce some additional terminology to differentiate among these attitudes. First, a *risk-averse* person prefers a sure amount of $M to a risky prospect with an expected value of $M. A *risk-loving* individual prefers a risky prospect with an expected value of $M to a sure amount of $M. Finally, a *risk-neutral* individual is indifferent between a risky prospect with an expected value of $M, and a sure amount of $M.

It is possible that for some prospects individuals will be risk loving, while for others they will be risk averse. For small gambles people typically are risk loving, whereas for larger gambles they are risk averse. You may be willing to bet a quarter that you can guess whether a flipped coin will come up heads or tails. The expected value of this gamble is zero. In this instance, you are behaving as a risk lover: You prefer the gamble with an expected payoff of zero to not playing (receiving zero for certain). If the stakes are raised to, say, $25,000, you will most likely choose not to bet. In this instance, you will prefer not betting (zero for certain) to the gamble with an expected value of zero.

risk averse
Preferring a sure amount of $M to a risky prospect with an expected value of $M.

risk loving
Preferring a risky prospect with an expected value of $M to a sure amount of $M.

risk neutral
Indifferent between a risky prospect with an expected value of $M and a sure amount of $M.

Managerial Decisions with Risk-Averse Consumers

For gambles with nontrivial outcomes, most individuals are risk averse. Here we will point out some implications of risk-averse consumers for optimal managerial decisions.

Product Quality.   The analysis of risk can be used to analyze situations where consumers are uncertain about product quality. For instance, suppose a consumer regularly purchases a particular brand of car wax and thus is relatively certain about the underlying quality and characteristics of the product. If the consumer is risk averse, when will she be willing to purchase a car wax newly introduced to the market?

A risk-averse consumer prefers a sure thing to an uncertain prospect of equal expected value. Thus, if the consumer expects the new car wax to work just as well as the one she regularly purchases, then, other things equal, she will not buy the new product. The reason is that there is risk associated with using a new product; the new wax may make a car look much better than the old wax, or it may damage the paint on the car. When the consumer weighs these possibilities and concludes that the new wax is expected to be just as good as the wax she now uses, she decides not to buy

---

Inside Business 12–2

Risk Aversion and the Value of Selling the Firm: The St. Petersburg Paradox

Corporations often are sold at a price that seems much lower than the expected value of future profits. Before you conclude the market is not rational, ask yourself how much you would be willing to pay for the right to toss a coin when

- You receive 2 cents if the first heads is on the first flip.
- You receive 4 cents if the first heads is on the second flip.
- You receive 8 cents if the first heads is on the third flip.
- More generally, you receive 2^n cents if the first heads is on the nth toss.

Since coin flips are independent events, the expected value of participating in this coin toss gamble is

$$Ex = \left(\frac{1}{2}\right)2 + \left(\frac{1}{2}\right)^2 2^2 + \left(\frac{1}{2}\right)^3 2^3 + \left(\frac{1}{2}\right)^4 2^4 + \ldots$$

$$= 1 + 1 + 1 + 1 + \ldots$$

$$= \infty \text{ cents.}$$

Thus, the expected value of this gamble is infinity: On average, you will make an infinite amount of money if you play this game. Of course, I know of no person willing to give up the world to play this particular game. I have found that in a class of 200 undergraduates the most students will pay is about $2, which is considerably lower than the infinite expected value of the gamble. This outcome is known as the *St. Petersburg paradox.*

The answer to this paradox is that it is the utility individuals receive from winning a gamble, not the money itself, that is important. The satisfaction you derive from winning your first $1 million is much greater than that derived from winning your second $1 million, and so on. This diminishing marginal utility of income gives rise to risk aversion, meaning that individuals are willing to pay less than the expected value. For the case of the coin flip above, the difference between the expected value and the amount an individual is willing to pay is substantial. The same can be true when corporations are up for sale.

---

the new product. The consumer prefers the sure thing (the current brand) to the risky prospect (the new product).

Firms use two primary tactics to induce risk-averse consumers to try a new product. First, the firm's manager may lower the price of the new product below that of the existing product to compensate the consumer for the risk associated with trying the new product. When firms send out free samples, they essentially use this technique because to the consumer the price of the new product is zero.

Alternatively, the manager can attempt to make the consumer think that the expected quality of the new product is higher than the certain quality of the old product. Typically firms do this using comparison advertising. For example, an advertisement might show 50 cars being waxed with a new wax and 50 cars being waxed with competitors' products; then the cars are repeatedly washed until only the 50 cars waxed with the new product still shine. If consumers are convinced by such an advertisement, they may go ahead and purchase the new product because its higher expected quality offsets the risk associated with trying a new product.

Chain Stores.   Risk aversion also explains why it may be in a firm's interest to become part of a chain store instead of remaining independent. For example, suppose a consumer drives through Smalltown, USA, and decides to eat lunch. There are two restaurants in the town: a local diner and a national hamburger chain. While the consumer knows nothing about this particular diner, his experience suggests that local diners typically are either very good or very bad. On the other hand, national hamburger chains have standardized menus and ingredients; the type and quality of product offered are relatively certain, albeit of average quality. Because the consumer is risk averse, he will choose to eat at the national chain, unless he expects the product of the local diner to be sufficiently better than the chain restaurant.

There is nothing special about the restaurant example; similar examples apply to retailing outlets, transmission shops, and other types of stores. While there are exceptions, out-of-town visitors typically prefer to make purchases at chain stores. Local customers are in a better position to know for certain the type and quality of products offered at stores in their town and may shop at the local store instead of the national chain. The key thing to notice is that even if the local store offers a better product than the national chain, the national chain can remain in business if the number of out-of-town customers is large enough.

Insurance.   The fact that consumers are risk averse implies that they are willing to pay to avoid risk. This is precisely why individuals choose to buy insurance on their homes and automobiles. By buying insurance, individuals give up a small (relative to potential losses) amount of money to eliminate the risk associated with a catastrophic loss. For example, if a $100,000 house burns down, an uninsured homeowner loses $100,000; if it does not burn down, the homeowner loses nothing. Most homeowners are willing to pay several hundred dollars to avoid this risk. If the house burns down, the insurance company reimburses the homeowner for the loss. Thus, to a consumer insurance represents a purchase of a "sure thing"—a house that is worth $100,000 regardless of whether or not it burns down.

Some firms give insurance to customers through "money-back guarantees." Other firms sell a form of insurance to customers. For example, many car manufacturers sell extended-warranty plans to customers whereby the company agrees to pay repair costs. This eliminates the risk associated with owning a car, thus making car ownership more attractive to risk-averse consumers.

Consumer Search

Up until now, we have assumed consumers know the prices of goods with certainty. The analysis is more complicated in situations where consumers do not know the prices charged by different firms for the same product.

Suppose consumers do not know the prices charged by different stores for some homogeneous commodity. Suppose there are numerous stores charging different prices for the same brand of watch. A consumer would like to purchase the product from the store charging the lowest price, but she does not know the prices being charged by individual stores. Let c denote the cost of obtaining information about the price charged by an individual store. For example, c might represent the cost of making a phone call, the cost of traveling to a store to find out what price it charges for a watch, or the cost of looking up a price in a catalog.

Suppose that three-quarters of the stores in the market charge $100 for a particular brand of watch and one-quarter charge $40. If the consumer locates a store that sells a watch for $40, she clearly should stop searching; no store charges a price below $40.

What should a risk-neutral consumer do if she visits a store that charges $100? For simplicity, suppose the consumer searches with *free recall* and with *replacement*. By free recall we mean that the consumer is free to return to the store at any time to purchase the watch for $100. The fact that a consumer searches with replacement means that the distribution of prices charged by other firms does not change just because the consumer has learned that the one store charges $100 for a watch. Under these assumptions, if the consumer searches again, one-quarter of the time she will find a price of $40 and thus will save $100 − $40 = $60. But three-quarters of the time the consumer will find a price of $100, and the gains from having searched will be zero. Thus, the expected benefit of an additional search is

$$EB = \frac{1}{4}(\$100 - \$40) + \frac{3}{4}(0) = \$15.$$

In other words, if the consumer searches for a price lower than $100, one-quarter of the time she will save $60, and three-quarters of the time she will save nothing. The expected benefit of searching for a lower price thus is $15.

The consumer should search for a lower price so long as the expected benefits are greater than the cost of an additional search. For example, if the cost of each search is $5, the consumer will find it in her interest to continue to search for a lower price. But if the cost of searching once more for a lower price is $20, it doesn't pay to continue searching for a better price.

This example reveals that the expected benefits of searching depend on the lowest price found during previous searches. If the lowest known price is p, the expected benefits *(EB)* from searching for a price lower than p slopes upward, as in Figure 12–1. Intuitively, as lower prices are found, the savings associated with finding even lower prices diminish.

FIGURE 12–1

The optimal search strategy

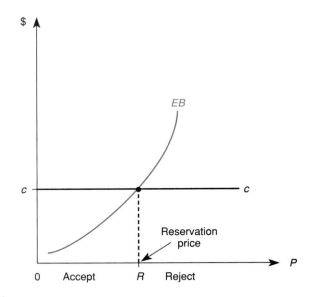

Figure 12–1 also illustrates the optimal search strategy for a consumer. The cost of each search is the horizontal line labeled *c*. If the consumer finds a price higher than *R*, the expected benefits of searching are greater than the cost, and the consumer should reject this price (continue to search for a lower price). On the other hand, if the consumer locates a price below *R*, it is best to accept this price (stop searching and purchase the product). This is because the expected benefits of searching for an even lower price are less than the cost of searching. If the consumer located a price of *R*, she would be indifferent between purchasing at that price and continuing to search for a lower price.

The *reservation price, R,* is the price at which the consumer is indifferent between purchasing at that price and searching for a lower price. Formally, if *EB(p)* is the expected benefit of searching for a price lower than *p*, and *c* represents the cost per search, the reservation price satisfies the condition

reservation price
The price at which a consumer is indifferent between purchasing at that price and searching for a lower price.

$$EB(R) = c.$$

Principle

The Consumer's Search Rule
The optimal search rule is such that the consumer rejects prices above the reservation price (*R*) and accepts prices below the reservation price. Stated differently, the optimal search strategy is to search for a better price when the price charged by a firm is above the reservation price and stop searching when a price below the reservation price is found.

FIGURE 12–2

*An increase in
search costs raises
the reservation price*

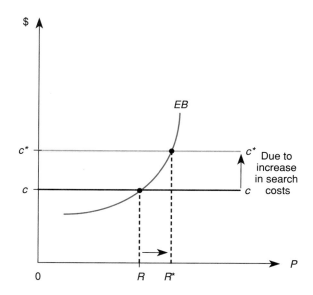

What happens if the cost of searching increases? As Figure 12–2 shows, an increase in search costs shifts up the horizontal line to c^*, resulting in a higher reservation price, R^*. This means the consumer will now find more prices acceptable and will search less intensively. Similarly, if the cost of searching for lower prices falls, the consumer will search more heavily for lower prices.

Our analysis of a consumer's decision to shop for lower prices can be used to aid managers in setting prices. In particular, when consumers have imperfect information about prices and search costs are low, the optimal prices set by a manager will be lower than when search costs are high. Moreover, managers must be careful not to price their products above consumers' reservation price; doing so will induce consumers to seek out lower prices at other firms. If you observe a large number of consumers "browsing" in your store but not making purchases, it may be a sign that your prices are set above their reservation price and that they have decided to continue to search for a lower price.

Uncertainty and the Firm

We have seen that the presence of uncertainty has a direct impact on consumer behavior and that the firm manager must take these effects into account to fully understand the nature of consumer demand. Uncertainty also affects the manager's input and output decisions. In this section, we will examine the implications of uncertainty for production and output decisions.

It is important to point out that all of our analysis of the impact of uncertainty on consumer behavior is directly applicable to the firm's manager. We will briefly discuss extensions of the analysis of uncertainty to highlight its direct influence on managerial decisions.

Risk Aversion

Just as consumers have preferences regarding risky prospects, so does the manager of the firm. A manager who is risk neutral is interested in maximizing expected profits; the variance of profits does not affect a risk-neutral manager's decisions. If the manager is risk averse, he or she may prefer a risky project with a lower expected value if it has lower risk than one with a higher expected value. Alternatively, if given a choice between a risky project with an expected return of $1 million and a certain return of $1 million, a risk-averse manager will prefer the sure thing. For the manager to be willing to undertake a risky project, the project must offer a higher expected return than a comparable "safe" project. Just how much higher depends on the manager's particular risk preferences.

Whenever a manager faces a decision to choose among risky projects, it is important to carefully evaluate the risks and expected returns of the projects and then to document this evaluation. The reason is simple. Risky prospects may result in bad outcomes. A manager is less likely to get fired over a bad outcome if she or he provides evidence that, based on the information available at the time the decision was made, the decision was sound. A convenient way to do this is to use mean-variance analysis, as the next demonstration problem illustrates.

DEMONSTRATION PROBLEM 12–3

A risk-averse manager is considering two projects. The first project involves expanding the market for bologna; the second involves expanding the market for caviar. There is a 10 percent chance of a recession and a 90 percent chance of an economic boom. During a boom, the bologna project will lose $10,000 whereas the caviar project will earn $20,000. During a recession, the bologna project will earn $12,000 and the caviar project will lose $8,000. If the alternative is earning $3,000 on a safe asset (say, a Treasury bill), what should the manager do. Why?

Answer

The first thing the manager should do is summarize the available information to document the relevant alternatives:

Project	Boom (90%)	Recession (10%)	Mean	Standard Deviation
Bologna	−$10,000	$12,000	−$ 7,800	6,600
Caviar	20,000	−8,000	17,200	8,400
Joint	10,000	4,000	9,400	1,800
T-bill	3,000	3,000	3,000	0

The "joint" option reflects what would happen if the manager adopted both the bologna and caviar projects. The entries under this option are obtained by vertically summing the payoffs of the individual options. For example, if the manager jointly adopted the caviar and bologna projects, during a boom the firm would lose $10,000 on the bologna project but make $20,000 on the caviar project. Thus, during a boom the joint project will result in a return of $10,000. Similar calculations reveal that the joint project will yield a return of $4,000 during a recession.

Based on the preceding table, what should a prudent manager do? The first thing to note is that the manager should not invest in a Treasury bill. The joint project will generate profits of $4,000 during a recession and $10,000 during a boom. Thus, regardless of what happens to the economy, the manager is assured of making at least $4,000 under the joint project, which is greater than the return of $3,000 on the Treasury bill.

The second thing to notice is that the expected (mean) profits of the bologna project are negative. A risk-averse manager would never choose this project (neither would a risk-neutral manager). Thus, the manager should adopt either the caviar project or the joint project. Precisely which choice the manager makes will depend on his or her preferences for risk.

The returns associated with the joint project in the preceding problem reveal the important notion of *diversification,* which is taught in basic business and finance courses. By investing in multiple projects, the manager may be able to reduce risk. This is merely a technical version of the old adage, "Don't put all of your eggs in one basket." As the example reveals, there are benefits to diversification, but whether it is optimal to diversify depends on a manager's risk preference and the incentives provided to the manager to avoid risk.

While many managers are risk averse, generally the owners of the firm (the stockholders) want the manager to behave in a risk-neutral manner. A manager who is risk neutral cares only about the expected value of a risky project, not the underlying risk. More specifically, a risk-neutral manager's objective is to take actions that maximize the expected present value of the firm, that is, actions that maximize expected profits. A risk-neutral manager would choose a risky action over a sure thing provided the expected profits of the risky prospect exceeded those of the sure thing.

Why would shareholders want managers to take actions that maximize expected profits even when doing so might involve considerable risk? Shareholders can pool and diversify risks by purchasing shares of many different firms to eliminate the systematic risk associated with the firm's operation. It therefore is inefficient for managers to spend time and money attempting to diversify against risk when doing so will reduce the firm's expected profits. Thus, while the owners of a firm may be risk averse, they prefer managers who make risk-neutral decisions.

A simple example will illustrate why shareholders desire managers to behave in a risk-neutral manner. Suppose a manager must decide which of two projects to undertake. The first project is risky, with a 50-50 chance of yielding profits of $2 million or zero profits. The second project will yield a certain return of $900,000. The expected profits earned by the risky project are $1 million, which is greater than those of the project yielding a certain return. But the variance of the risky project is greater than that of the certain one; half of the time profits will be zero, half of the time they will be $2 million. Why would shareholders want the manager to undertake the risky project even though it has greater risk? The answer is that shareholders can purchase shares of many firms in the economy. If the managers of each of these firms choose the risky project, the projects will not pay off for some firms but will pay off for others. If the profits earned by one firm are independent of those earned by other firms, then, on average, the unfavorable outcomes experienced by some firms will be more than offset by the favorable outcomes at other firms. This situation is similar to flipping a coin: Flip a coin once, and you cannot be sure it will turn up heads; flip a coin many times, and you can rest assured that half the flips will be heads. Similarly, when shareholders own shares of many different firms, each of which takes on risky projects, they can rest assured that half of the firms will earn $2 million.

For these reasons, as a manager you are likely to be given an incentive to maximize the expected profits of your firm. If you are provided with such incentives, you will behave in a risk-neutral manner even if you and the owners of the firm are risk averse.

Producer Search

Just as consumers search for stores charging low prices, producers search for low prices of inputs. When there is uncertainty regarding the prices of inputs, optimizing firms employ optimal search strategies. The search strategy for a risk-neutral manager will be precisely the same as that of a risk-neutral consumer. Rather than repeat the basic theory, it is more useful to illustrate these concepts with an example.

Inside Business 12–3

Searching for Workers

Managers spend considerable time searching for new employees. Thus, it is important for them to know when to continue searching for another employee and when to stop searching by hiring one who has already been interviewed. How many applicants does the average manager reject before finding an employee willing to work for an acceptable wage? How much time (a component of search costs) is spent engaging in these activities? A recent study provides answers to these questions.

The average manager searching for an employee sees about 3.7 applicants before finding a qualified worker willing to work at a wage below the firm's reservation price. The time cost of searching for workers is substantial; the average manager spends about 6.4 hours examining each applicant he or she sees. There is, however, considerable variation in these numbers for managers seeking different types of workers. For instance, managers tend to search more when hiring workers who require a lot of training. For each 10 percent increase in the amount of training required, firms spend about 1.8 percent more time per applicant. Firms also search more heavily when hiring a manager or a professional worker—about 33 percent more time per application—than when hiring a blue-collar worker. Firms also search more intensely for permanent workers than for temporary or seasonal workers; in fact, firms spend about 24 percent less time per applicant when hiring a temporary worker.

Larger firms also spend much more time searching than smaller firms: A firm with 500 employees spends about 80 percent more time per applicant than a firm with 100 employees. Thus, managers of large firms should expect to spend more time searching for workers than managers of smaller firms.

Source: John M. Barron, Dan A. Black, and Mark A. Loewenstein, "Job Matching and On-the-Job Training," *Journal of Labor Economics* 7 (January 1989), pp. 1–19.

DEMONSTRATION PROBLEM 12–4

A risk-neutral manager is attempting to hire a worker. All workers in the market are of identical quality but differ with respect to the wage at which they are willing to work. Suppose half of the workers in the labor market are willing to work for a salary of $40,000 and half will accept a salary of $38,000. The manager spends three hours interviewing a given worker and values this time at $300. The first worker the manager interviews says he will work only if paid $40,000. Should the firm manager make him an offer, or interview another worker?

Answer

This is an optimal search problem with a search cost of $300. If the manager searches for another worker, half of the time she will find one willing to work for $38,000 and thus will save $2,000. But half of the time the manager will find a worker just like the one she chose not to hire, and the effort will have been for nothing. Thus, the expected benefit of interviewing another worker is

$$EB = \frac{1}{2}(\$2,000) + \frac{1}{2}(0) = \$1,000.$$

Since this is greater than the cost of $300, the manager should not hire the worker but instead search for a worker willing to work for $38,000.

Profit Maximization

The basic principles of profit maximization can also be modified to deal with uncertainty. To illustrate how the basic principles of profit maximization are affected by the presence of uncertainty, let us suppose the manager is risk neutral and demand is uncertain. Recall that the goal of a risk-neutral manager is to maximize expected profits.

The risk-neutral manager must determine what output to produce before she is certain of the demand for the product. Because demand is uncertain, revenues are uncertain. This means that to maximize expected profits, the manager should equate expected marginal revenue with marginal cost in setting output:

$$EMR = MC.$$

The reason is simple. If expected marginal revenue exceeded marginal cost, the manager could increase expected profits by expanding output. The production of another unit of output would, on average, add more to revenue than it would to costs. Similarly, if expected marginal revenue were less than marginal cost, the manager should reduce output. This is because by reducing output, the firm would reduce costs by more than it would reduce expected revenue.

Thus we see that when the manager is risk neutral, profit maximization under uncertain demand is very similar to profit maximization under certainty. All that needs to be done is adjust the corresponding formula to represent what the manager expects marginal revenue to be.

DEMONSTRATION PROBLEM 12–5

Appleway Industries produces apple juice and sells it in a competitive market. The firm's manager must determine how much juice to produce before he knows what the market (competitive) price will be. Economists estimate that there is a 30 percent chance the market price will be $2 per gallon and a 70 percent chance it will be $1 when the juice hits the market. If the firm's cost function is $C = 200$

$+ .0005Q^2$, how much juice should be produced to maximize expected profits? What are the expected profits of Appleway Industries?

Answer

The profits of Appleway Industries are given by

$$\pi = pQ - 200 - .0005Q^2.$$

Since price is uncertain, the firm's revenues and profits are uncertain. For a competitive firm, $MR = p$; thus, marginal revenue also is uncertain. Marginal cost is given by $MC = .001Q$. To maximize expected profits, the manager equates expected price with marginal cost:

$$Ep = .001Q.$$

The expected price is given by

$$Ep = .3(2) + .7(1) = .60 + .70 = \$1.30.$$

Equating this with marginal cost, we obtain

$$1.30 = .001Q.$$

Solving for Q, we find that the output that maximizes expected profits is $Q = 1,300$ gallons. Expected profits for Appleway Industries are

$$E\pi = EpQ - 200 - .0005Q^2$$
$$= 1.30(1,300) - 200 - .0005(1,300)^2$$
$$= 1,690 - 200 - 845 = \$645.$$

Thus, Appleway Industries can expect to make \$645 in profits.

While our analysis of profit maximization under uncertainty is far from exhaustive, it points out that much of our previous analysis can be easily extended to deal with uncertainty. In fact, these extensions are important topics in more advanced courses in economics.

Uncertainty and the Market

The presence of uncertainty can have a profound impact on the ability of markets to efficiently allocate resources. In this section, we examine some problems created in markets when there is uncertainty.

Asymmetric Information

When some people in the market have better information than others, the people with the least information may choose not to participate in a market.

**asymmetric
information**
A situation that
exists when some
people have better
information than
others.

To see why this is so, suppose someone offers to sell you a box full of money. You do not know how much money is in the box, but she does. Should you choose to buy the box?

The answer is no. Since she knows how much money is in the box, she will never sell you the box unless you offer her more for the box than is in it. Suppose she knows the box contains $10. If you offered her $6 for the box, she would have no incentive to engage in the transaction. If you offered her $12, she would gladly sell you the box, and you would lose $2.

As the preceding example reveals, asymmetric information can result in a situation where people with the least information rationally refuse to participate in the market. If you think of the box in the example as being a company whose stock is traded on the New York Stock Exchange, it should be clear why there is so much concern over insider trading—the buying and selling of stocks by persons who have privileged information about a firm. If some people know for certain what a stock will sell for tomorrow (say, due to a takeover) and others do not, asymmetric information exists. The only time insiders will purchase stock is when they know it is selling at a price below what it is worth; the only time insiders will sell stock is when they know it is selling at a premium over what it is worth. If people know that insiders regularly trade in the stock market, people who are not insiders may rationally choose to stay out of the stock market to avoid paying too much for a stock or selling it for too little. In extreme cases, this situation can completely destroy the stock market, as no one is willing to buy or sell shares of firms' stock. For this reason, there are laws that restrict persons with privileged information about a firm from buying shares of that firm's stock.

Asymmetric information between consumers and the firm can affect firm profits. For example, suppose a firm invests in developing a new product that it knows to be superior to existing products in the market. Consumers, on the other hand, are unlikely to know whether the new product is truly superior to existing products or whether the firm is falsely claiming the product to be superior. If the degree of asymmetric information is severe enough, consumers may refuse to buy a new product even if it really is better than existing products. The reason is that they do not know the product is indeed superior.

Asymmetric information affects many other managerial decisions, including hiring workers and issuing credit to customers. In particular, job applicants have much better information about their own capabilities than does the person in charge of hiring new workers. A job applicant who claims to have excellent skills may be lying or telling the truth; the personnel manager has less information than the applicant. This is why firms spend considerable sums designing tests to evaluate job applicants, doing background checks, and the like. The basic reason for these types of expenditures is to provide the firm with better information about the capabilities of and tendencies of job applicants. Similarly, a consumer who wishes to make a purchase on credit has much better information about his own ability to pay off the debt than does the creditor. Of course, every consumer seeking to purchase on credit will claim that he or she will pay off the debt. Asymmetric information makes it difficult for the firm to know whether a person actually will pay off the debt. In fact, firms pay sizable sums to credit bureaus to obtain better information about their credit customers. These expenditures reduce asymmetric information and make it more difficult to customers to take advantage of it.

With this overview of some problems that can arise in the presence of asymmetric information, we turn now to two specific manifestations of asymmetric information: adverse selection and moral hazard. These two concepts are often difficult to distinguish, so it is useful first to distinguish between the types of asymmetric information that generally lead to adverse selection and moral hazard.

Adverse selection generally arises when an individual has *hidden characteristics*—characteristics that it knows, but that are unknown by the other party in an economic transaction. In our example of the job applicant, for instance, the worker knew his own abilities but the employer did not. The worker's ability thus reflects a hidden characteristic. In contrast, moral hazard generally occurs when one party takes *hidden actions*—actions that it knows another party cannot observe. For example, if the manager of a firm cannot monitor a worker's effort, then the worker's effort represents a hidden action. Just as it is often difficult to distinguish between ability (a characteristic) and effort (an action), it is sometimes difficult to distinguish between adverse selection and moral hazard.

Adverse Selection
Adverse selection refers to a situation where a selection process results in a pool of individuals with economically undesirable characteristics. A simple example highlights the basic issues involved in adverse selection.

Consider an industry in which all firms allow their employees five days of paid sick leave. Suppose one firm decides to increase the number of paid sick leave days from five to ten to attract more workers. If the workers have hidden characteristics—that is, if the firm cannot distinguish between healthy and unhealthy workers—the plan will probably lure many workers away from other firms. But what type of workers is the firm most likely to attract? Workers who know they are frequently ill, and thus who value sick leave the most. Workers who know they never get sick will have little incentive to leave their current employers, but those who are frequently sick will. From the firm's point of view, the policy attracts undesirable workers. In economic terms, the policy results in adverse selection.

Adverse selection explains why people with poor driving records find it difficult to buy automobile insurance. Suppose there are two types of people with bad driving records: (1) those who are poor drivers and frequently have accidents and (2) those who are good drivers but, due purely to bad luck, have been involved in numerous accidents in the past. Past accidents by bad drivers are a result of their driving habits and are good indicators of the number of expected future accidents. Past accidents by good drivers, on the other hand, are not a good indicator of the expected number of future accidents; they merely reflect an unusual string of bad luck.

An insurance company has asymmetric information; it does not know whether a person with a bad driving record is truly a poor driver or whether past accidents were unusual events due to bad luck. Assuming that those who have poor driving records know their own type, we have a situation where one side of the insurance market has hidden characteristics. Suppose an insurance company decides to insure drivers with poor driving records, but at a very high premium to cover the anticipated future claims due to bad driving. The insurance company must charge all drivers with bad records the same insurance rate, since it cannot distinguish between those who are good drivers and those who are bad drivers. By charging the same price to both types of drivers, adverse selection results. As the insurance company raises insurance rates to cover the losses of bad drivers, the only people who will be willing to pay the higher price are those drivers who know they are most likely to have accidents. The good drivers, who know that their past accidents were unusual events, will not be willing to pay the high rate. Thus, the insurance company will end up selling policies only to the drivers most likely to wreck their cars. Since insurance works only when there are some drivers who pay premiums and do not wreck their automobiles, insurance companies typically find it in their interest to charge lower prices for insurance and refuse to insure any driver with a bad driving record. Doing otherwise would lead to adverse selection within the pool of drivers with poor records.

Moral Hazard

Sometimes, one party agrees to insulate from economic loss the other party to a contract. If the contract induces the party that is insulated from loss to take a hidden action that harms the other party, we say that *moral hazard* exists.

Consider, for instance, the principal-agent problem we first examined in Chapter 6. In this setting the owner hires a manager to operate the firm, which earns profits that vary randomly with economic conditions. Unfortunately, profits also depend on the manager's effort, which is unobservable to the owner. Thus, the effort of the manager represents a hidden action. Notice that if the owner agrees to pay the manager a fixed salary of $50,000 (the contract), then the manager is completely insulated from any economic loss that might arise due to random fluctuations in the firm's profits. The manager now has an incentive to spend less time at the office (the hidden action), and the reduced effort of the manager results in lower firm profits (and thus harms the owner). In other words, the fixed salary contract, coupled with the hidden action of the manager, results in moral hazard. As we learned in Chapter 6, the owner can overcome this problem by either monitoring the manager (taking away the hidden action) or by making the manager's pay contingent on the firm's profits (taking away the manager's insurance against economic loss).

As you might suspect, the nature of insurance markets makes insurance companies particularly vulnerable to the moral hazard problem. As we discussed earlier in this chapter, the fact that individuals are risk averse provides an incentive for them to purchase insurance against large losses. Most people have insurance on their homes and automobiles, and some form of health insurance. Usually the probability of a loss depends on the hidden effort expended by the insured to avoid the loss. Thus, a moral hazard exists: When individuals are fully insured, they have a reduced incentive to put forth effort to avoid a loss.

For example, suppose a company rents cars and fully insures renters against damage to the cars. Obviously, the company cannot observe the effort put forth by renters to avoid damages to rented vehicles. Since renters are fully insured and can take hidden actions that affect damages to cars, they are indifferent between returning the car with a stolen radio and returning the car in perfect condition. If a radio is stolen, the replacement cost is paid for out of the company's pocket. Thus, when the car is fully insured, the driver has no incentive to take the time to lock the car or to avoid parking the car in areas where theft is likely. If the car were uninsured, the driver would have to replace stolen items with his or her own money and therefore would be much more careful with the car. Thus, if the company insures renters against damage, drivers will be less careful with cars than if they were not insured against damage. In economic terms, a moral hazard exists.

One way car insurance companies attempt to reduce moral hazard is by requiring a deductible on all insurance claims. If the deductible is $200, the first $200 in losses is paid by the insured. This effectively means that the person buying insurance must pay something in the event of a loss and thus has an incentive to take actions to reduce the likelihood of a loss.

Moral hazard is one factor that has contributed to rising medical costs during the past decade. When individuals have health insurance or belong to a health maintenance organization (HMO), they do not pay for the full marginal cost of medical services. As a consequence, individuals are more likely to visit a doctor when they have a minor illness (say, a cold) than they would if they had to pay the full marginal cost of going to a doctor.

The effect of this is twofold. First, the moral hazard results in an increase in the demand for medical services, leading to a higher equilibrium price of medical services. This is because individuals do not pay the full cost of a visit to a doctor and thus use physicians' services more frequently than they would if they were required to pay the full cost of each visit. Second, insurance companies must increase the rates they charge for medical insurance to cover the higher costs of insurance claims due to more frequent visits. This might lead those who know they are in good health to decide against insurance coverage, which means that the higher medical insurance premiums also lead to adverse selection. In this case the insurance company is left to insure a pool of less healthy individuals, which exacerbates the problem. Thus, moral hazard and adverse selection may be partially responsible for the recent increases in the cost of medical insurance.

Auctions

In an *auction,* potential buyers compete for the right to own a good, service, or, more generally, anything of value. Auctions are used to sell a variety of things, including art, Treasury bills, furniture, real estate, oil leases, and even corporations. When the auctioneer is a seller, as in an art auction, she or he wishes to obtain the highest possible price for the item. Buyers, on the other hand, seek to obtain the item at the lowest possible price. In some instances, the auctioneer is the person seeking bids from potential suppliers. For instance, a firm that needs new capital equipment may hold an auction in which potential suppliers bid prices that reflect what they would charge for the equipment. In auctions with multiple bidders, competition among bidders leads to more favorable terms for the auctioneer.

Auctions are important for managers to understand because in many instances, firms participate either as the auctioneer or as a bidder in the auction process. In other words, a firm may wish to sell a good in an auction or buy a good (or input) in an auction. For this reason it is important for managers to understand the implications of auctions for managerial decisions.

The Auctioneer and the Bidders

It is important to note that the bidders and the auctioneer have competing objectives. When the auctioneer is a seller, as we will assume throughout this section, the auctioneer wishes to fetch the highest possible price for the item. The bidders, on the other hand, wish to obtain the item at the lowest possible price.

It turns out that the risk preferences of the bidders can affect the revenue the auctioneer receives, as well as the optimal bids of auction participants. Thus, we will consider situations where bidders are risk neutral and where they are risk averse to point out differences that arise in auctions due to risk-averse bidders. First, we will consider four types of auctions.

Types of Auctions

There are four basic types of auction: English (ascending-bid); first-price, sealed-bid; second-price, sealed-bid; and Dutch (descending-bid) auctions. These auctions differ with respect to (1) the timing of bidder decisions (whether bids are made simultaneously or sequentially) and (2) the amount the winner is required to pay. Keep these two sources of differences in auctions in mind as we discuss each type of auction.

English Auction

English auction
An ascending sequential-bid auction in which bidders observe the bids of others and decide whether or not to increase the bid. The auction ends when a single bidder remains; this bidder obtains the item and pays the auctioneer the amount of the bid.

The auction you probably are most familiar with is the English auction. In an *English auction,* a single item is to be sold to the highest bidder. The auction begins with an opening bid. Given knowledge of the opening bid, the auctioneer asks if anyone is willing to pay a higher price. The bids continue to rise until no other participants wish to increase the bid. The highest bidder—the only bidder left—pays the auctioneer his or her bid and takes possession of the item.

Notice that in an English auction, the bidders continually obtain information about one another's bids. Given this information, if they think the item is worth more than the current high bid, they will increase their bids. The auction ends when no other bidder is willing to pay more for the item than the highest bid. For this reason, in an English auction the person who ends up with the item is the one who values the item the most.

To illustrate, suppose three firms are competing for the right to purchase a machine in an English auction at a bankruptcy sale. Firm A values the machine at $1 million, firm B values it at $2 million, and firm C values it at $1.5 million. Which firm will acquire the machine, and at what price?

All three firms will bid up to $1 million for the machine. Once the bid is slightly above this amount, firm A will drop out, since it values the machine at less than $1 million. When the bid reaches $1.5 million, firm C will drop out, which means firm B will acquire the machine for $1.5 million (or perhaps $1.5 million plus $.01). Effectively, the winner of the auction simply has to top the second highest valuation of the machine.

First-Price, Sealed-Bid Auction

first-price, sealed-bid auction
A simultaneous-move auction in which bidders simultaneously submit bids on pieces of paper. The auctioneer awards the item to the high bidder, who pays the amount bid.

In a *first-price, sealed-bid auction,* the bidders write their bids on pieces of paper without knowledge of bids made by other players. The auctioneer collects the bids and awards the item to the high bidder. The high bidder pays the auctioneer the amount he or she has written on the piece of paper.

Thus, in a first-price, sealed-bid auction, the highest bidder wins the item just as in an English auction. However, unlike in an English auction, the bidders do not know the bids of other players. As we will see, this characteristic can affect bidding behavior and, consequently, the price collected by the auctioneer.

Second-Price, Sealed-Bid Auction

A *second-price, sealed-bid auction* is similar to a first-price, sealed-bid auction in that bidders submit bids without knowledge of the bids submitted by others. The person submitting the highest bid wins, but has to pay only the amount bid by the second highest bidder. Consider, for instance, the situation where a machine is auctioned off to one of three firms in a

second-price, sealed-bid auction
A simultaneous-move auction in which bidders simultaneously submit bids. The auctioneer awards the item to the high bidder, who pays the amount bid by the second highest bidder.

Dutch auction
A descending sequential-bid auction in which the auctioneer begins with a high asking price and gradually reduces the asking price until one bidder announces a willingness to pay that price for the item.

second-price, sealed-bid auction. If Firm A bids $1 million, Firm B bids $2 million, and Firm C bids $1.5 million, then the high bidder—Firm B—wins the item. But it pays only the second highest bid, which is $1.5 million.

Dutch Auction

In a *Dutch auction,* the seller begins by asking for a very high price for the item (a price so high that she or he is certain no one will be willing to buy). The auctioneer gradually lowers the price until one buyer indicates a willingness to buy the item at that price. At this point, the auction is over: The bidder buys the item at the last announced price. Dutch auctions are used extensively in the Netherlands to auction flowers such as tulips. Car dealers sometimes use a Dutch auction to sell cars; a price for a particular car is posted each day on a marquee, and the price is lowered each day until someone purchases the car.

The information available to bidders in a Dutch auction is identical to that in a sealed-bid auction. In particular, no information is available about the bids of other players until the auction is over, that is, when the first bidder speaks up. Consequently, a Dutch auction is strategically equivalent to a first-price, sealed-bid auction. The reason is that in both types of auction, bidders do not know the bids of other players. Furthermore, in each case the bidder pays what he or she bid for the item. In terms of optimal bidding behavior and the profits earned by the auctioneer, the Dutch auction and the first-price, sealed-bid auctions are identical.

Principle

Strategic Equivalence of Dutch and First-Price Auctions
The Dutch and first-price, sealed-bid auctions are strategically equivalent; that is, the optimal bids by participants are identical for both types of auction.

Information Structures

The four basic types of auction differ with respect to the information bidders have about the bids of other players. In the English auction, players know the current bid and can choose to raise it if they so desire. In the other three types of auction, players make bids without knowledge of other players' bids; they cannot decide to increase their own bids based on bids made by others.

In analyzing an auction, it is also important to consider the information players have about the value of the item being auctioned. We will discuss this issue next.

Perfect Information

One possibility is that each bidder in an auction knows for certain what the item is worth to that bidder, and furthermore, all players know the valuations of other players in an auction. For example, if a $5 bill were being

---

FCC's Auction Procedures for Broadband PCS C Block

In 1995 the FCC detailed its auction procedures for the broadband Personal Communications Services (PCS) C block auction that it held on August 29, 1995. These licenses were awarded through a simultaneous multiple-round auction. Bids were accepted on all licenses in each round of the auction, and high bid amounts were posted after the end of the bid submission period in each round of bidding. In addition, information regarding all valid bids submitted and all bid withdrawals in each round was provided to the auction participants. Here is a synopsis of the rules for the auction that the FCC posted on its Web page prior to the auction:

"Each bidder may submit bids once in each round, for as many licenses as it is eligible, according to the limit of its deposited up front payment. Bidders will be able to place their bids electronically or by telephone. Each bidder will be required to log-in to the FCC auction computer system, using a log-in code and confidential password unique to that bidder, and in addition must provide its bidder identification number and FCC account number in order to place or withdraw a bid.

"A high bidder who wishes to withdraw one or more of its high bids during the bid withdrawal period may do so electronically or telephonically subject to the bid withdrawal penalty specified in the Commission's Rules. If a high bid is withdrawn, the license will be offered in the next round at the second highest bid price, which may be less than or equal to (in the case of tie bids) the amount of the withdrawn bid. The FCC will be identified as the high bidder on the license until a new valid bid is submitted on that license. In addition, to prevent a bidder from strategically delaying the close of the auction, the FCC retains the discretion to limit the number of times that a bidder may re-bid on a license from which it has withdrawn a high bid.

"There will be no minimum opening bid and no minimum bid increment for a license until the license has received an initial bid. Once a bid has been received on a license, the minimum bid increment for that license will be set initially at the greater of five (5) percent of the previous high bid or $0.02 per MHz-pop. The Commission retains the discretion to vary the minimum bid increments in each round of the auction for individual licenses or groups of licenses by announcement prior to each round.

"Each bid will be date- and time-stamped when it is entered into the computer system. In the event of tie bids, the Commission will identify the high bidder on the basis of the order in which bids are received by the Commission, starting with the earliest bid."

---

auctioned off, every bidder would know that the item is worth $5 to each bidder. This is the case of *perfect information*.

Common Values

Another possibility is that the item being auctioned is worth the same to each bidder but the bidders do not know precisely what this value is. For instance, if a bag of money were being auctioned off, but no bidder knew for sure how much was in the bag, this would represent a *common-values* auction. Each bidder has some belief about how much is in the bag, and these beliefs generally will differ among bidders. However, once the bag is auctioned and a player opens the bag, all individuals value the amount in the bag identically.

Private Values

In some auctions, the item being auctioned is worth a different amount to different bidders. Furthermore, the bidders do not know the valuations of other bidders. In an art auction, for instance, some participants will value a certain painting more than others. While each individual knows how much she or he values the painting, none know the value other participants place on it. This situation is the case of *private values*.

DEMONSTRATION PROBLEM 12–6

Determine whether the following auctions most likely have a perfect-information, common-values, or private-values information structure.
(1) A university in need of money decides to name a building on campus after the person willing to pay the most for the privilege.
(2) Three firms submit bids to the government for the rights to an offshore oil lease.
(3) Two firms have identical technologies and purchase labor and capital in competitive markets to produce janitorial services. A manager asks the two firms to bid for the right to clean the building.

Answer

(1) Presumably each bidder knows what it is worth to him or her to have the building named in her or his honor but does not know what it is worth to other bidders. Thus, this is a case of private values.
(2) The firms are most likely unsure of how much oil is in the ground, although each firm has its own estimate. However, whatever amount actually is in the ground, it is worth the same to all three firms. Thus, this is a common-values information structure.
(3) Since the inputs are purchased in competitive input markets, each firm pays the same (competitive equilibrium) price for inputs. Since they have the same technology, neither firm has a cost advantage over the other. But if both firms know this, they also know the value (profits) each firm will receive if it wins the bid. In this case, perfect information exists.

Expected Revenues with Alternative Auction Structures

Now that you have a basic understanding of auctions, we will examine the prices that result, on average, in each type of auction. In particular, suppose an auctioneer is interested in maximizing profits. Which type of auction will

TABLE 12–2   A Comparison of Expected Revenues in Auctions

Information Structure	Risk Preference of Bidders	Expected Revenues
Perfect information	Risk preference is irrelevant when there is perfect information	English = Second price = First price = Dutch
Independent private values	Risk neutral	English = Second price = First price = Dutch
	Risk averse	Dutch = First price > English = Second price
Common values	Risk neutral	English > Second price > Dutch = First price
	Risk averse	English > Second price ≥ Dutch = First price

generate the highest profits: English, second-price, first-price, or Dutch? As Table 12–2 shows, the "best" auction from the auctioneer's viewpoint depends on the information structure of the auction and the risk preferences of the bidders. Accordingly, in the following sections we will examine the results in this table to characterize the profit-maximizing auction under various information structures and levels of risk aversion. For simplicity, we will assume bidders are not constrained by the smallest unit of currency (cents) when making bids; a bidder can submit a bid that involves fractional cents, such as a bid of $10.000001.

Perfect Information

In the case of perfect information, each bidder knows how much he or she and the other bidders value the object. In this case, all four auction types generate precisely the same revenue to the auctioneer:

$$\text{Dutch} = \text{First price} = \text{English} = \text{Second price.}$$

This revenue, or the price at which the item is sold, equals the value that the bidder with the second highest valuation places on the object.

This result should not surprise you; indeed, with perfect information, each bidder knows precisely what must be bid to win. In an English auction, the player with the highest valuation continues to bid until the price is equal (or perhaps $.01 above) the second highest valuation, at which point that player wins the auction. In a first-price, sealed-bid auction, by bidding $.01 cent above the second highest valuation—which is known due to the perfect information—the bidder with the highest valuation is assured of winning the item. (For simplicity, we will henceforth ignore this one cent difference in bids, since the difference vanishes as money becomes increasingly divisible.) The same is true in a second-price, sealed-bid auction. In fact, the payment of the winner will equal the second highest valuation of all the bidders.

Risk-Neutral Bidders with Independent, Private Values

Next, we will examine the prices that arise in the case of independent, private-values auctions. Recall that with private valuations, each bidder knows her or his own valuation but is uncertain of the valuations of other bidders. The fact that valuations are independent simply means that each bidder's valuation of the item is not related to the valuation placed on the item by other participants.

It turns out that the revenues derived in various types of independent, private-values auctions depend on whether players are risk neutral or risk averse. This section examines the case of risk-neutral bidders.

When bidders are risk neutral, their goal is to maximize their expected profits in the auction. They are indifferent, for example, between receiving $1 for certain and a risky prospect with an expected payoff of $1. It turns out that with risk-neutral bidders and independent, private valuations, all four auction types yield the same expected revenue to the auctioneer. Expressed differently, the auctioneer can expect to obtain the same price in all four auctions:

$$\text{Dutch} = \text{First price} = \text{English} = \text{Second price.}$$

In fact, on average, the winning bid will equal the second-highest valuation of all the bidders. Let us examine the intuition for why this is the case.

In an English auction, the person with the highest private valuation clearly will win the object and pay the valuation of the bidder with the second highest valuation. Effectively, in an English auction players learn more and more about the valuations of other players as the auction progresses. In the end, the winner knows that she or he values the item more than all the other bidders, who have dropped out.

In contrast, in a first-price auction players must write their bids down secretly. Since they do not know the valuations of other bidders, players are uncertain whether they have the highest valuation even though they know what the item is worth to them. On the one hand, players have an incentive to bid slightly less than their valuation, since doing so gives them the possibility of greater profits. On the other hand, bidding lower reduces the likelihood that they will submit the high bid. When the bidders are risk neutral, these forces are balanced such that, on average, the auctioneer earns the same amount in an English auction as in a first-price, sealed-bid auction! The average winning bid is equal to the valuation of the participant with the second highest valuation, just as in the English auction. As noted earlier, the Dutch auction is strategically equivalent to the first-price auction, so the result is the same for the Dutch auction.

In a second-price auction with independent, private valuations, something remarkable happens: Each player has an incentive to bid precisely his or her own valuation of the item. Since each player bids her or his own valuation, the second highest bid equals the second highest valuation, just as in the English auction. Thus, all four auction types yield the same price on average.

Why do players have an incentive to bid their true valuations in an independent, private-values, second-price auction? The reason is quite simple. Since the winner pays the bid of the second highest bidder, not his or her own bid, it does not pay for players to bid more or less than their own valuations. To see this, suppose a player bid more than the item was worth to him to increase the likelihood of being the high bidder. If the second highest bid is less than his value, this strategy yields no additional returns; he could have won by bidding his true valuation. If the second bid is above his valuation, then by bidding more than his valuation he may indeed win. But if he does win, he pays the second highest bid, which we assumed is above his own valuation! In this case, he pays more for the item than the item is worth to him. Thus, it does not pay for a player to bid more than her or his valuation in a second-price auction. Will a player ever bid less than his valuation? No. A player who bids less merely reduces the chance of winning, since the player never pays his or her own bid! Thus, the dominant strategy for bidders in a second-price, sealed-bid auction is to bid their valuations.

Principle

Dominant Strategy in Second-Price, Sealed-Bid Auction
The dominant strategy in a second-price, sealed-bid auction is to bid one's own valuation regardless of the information structure or level of risk aversion.

Risk-Averse Bidders with Independent, Private Values

We have seen that in English and second-price auctions, the winner pays the price of the second highest bidder. Thus, the winner obtains the item at a price that generally is less than his or her own valuation and therefore earns some surplus. The same principle applies when the bidders are risk averse. In short, in English and second-price auctions, players do not have to "guess" what the second highest bid will be. In an English auction, players simply continue to up their bids until they win or drop out. We showed that in a second-price auction, the dominant strategy is for a player to bid her or his own valuation.

This is not the case for a first-price auction when bidders are risk averse. In particular, in a first-price auction, a bidder pays her own bid. By shaving down the bid, she increases her surplus if she wins, but she also reduces the likelihood that she will be the high bidder. Risk-averse bidders increase their bids (compared to risk-neutral bidders) to guard against the risk that some other player will outbid them. Consequently, the winning bid in a first-price auction will be greater, on average, than the winning bid in an English or second-price auction. A seller facing risk-averse buyers who have independent, private valuations will earn more by holding a first-price auction (or, equivalently, a Dutch auction) than the other auction types:

$$\text{Dutch} = \text{First price} > \text{English} = \text{Second price.}$$

Risk-Neutral Bidders with Common Values

Suppose 10 firms bid for the rights to an oil lease in a common-values auction. Thus, each bidder is uncertain about the true amount of oil in the ground, but nevertheless it is worth the same to each bidder. Before participating in the bidding process, each firm runs an independent test to obtain an estimate of the amount of oil in the ground. Naturally, these estimates vary randomly from firm to firm.

Given this scenario, the differences in estimates of oil in the ground are due purely to random variations in test procedures. Some firms think there is more oil in the ground than others, not because they are better informed but due purely to random chance. The firm that submits the winning bid will tend to be the firm with the most optimistic estimate of the amount of oil in the ground. This gives rise to what is known as the *winner's curse:* The winner in a common-values auction is the player who is the most optimistic about the true value of the item.

The winner's curse arises in our oil lease example because the winning firm thinks there is more oil in the ground than the other nine firms believe. Since we assumed the differences in valuations are due purely to random variation, the bidder with the highest estimate of value is no more likely to be correct than the others. In fact, if bidders could pool their information and average it, they would have a more precise estimate of the true amount of oil in the ground. But, as we will see, this does not happen.

Thus, the "curse" of the winner refers to the fact that if the winning bidder bases the bid on his or her private estimate of the true value, the person will, on average, have paid more than the item is worth! To avoid the winner's curse, the optimal thing for a bidder to do is revise the private estimate downward to avoid having regrets for submitting the winning bid.

Principle

Avoiding the Winner's Curse
In a common-values auction, the winner is the bidder who is the most optimistic about the true value of the item. To avoid the winner's curse, a bidder should revise downward his or her private estimate of the value of the item.

Because bidders in a common-values auction shrink their bids in order to avoid the winner's curse, the average revenue earned by the auctioneer is reduced. With risk-neutral bidders and common-values, the reduction in revenue is lower for the English auction than for the three simultaneous-move auctions. The reason is as follows.

In an English auction—the only auction type we examined in which bidders get to observe the bids of other players—bidders have information about other players' bids and can use this information to update their own estimates of the valuation. In our oil lease example, the firm with a low estimate of the value will observe that numerous other bidders continue to bid, implying that their tests indicate more oil is in the ground than their own tests revealed. In this case, the firm can adjust upward its estimate of the amount of oil in the ground by taking into account the information in the bids of other bidders. This in turn reduces the incentive firms have to shrink their bids to avoid the winner's curse. Thus, in an English auction, firms pool their information to some extent by observing the behavior of other bidders. Consequently, the average winning bid tends to be higher in an English auction than in a simultaneous-move auction. Moreover, when bidders are risk neutral, the second-price auction has the highest expected revenue of the three simultaneous-move auction types:

$$\text{English} > \text{Second price} > \text{Dutch} = \text{First price.}$$

Risk-Averse Bidders with Common Values

The case of risk-averse bidders is similar to that analyzed earlier, in that the English auction generates more revenue for the seller than the second-price auction does. However, there is no clear-cut relation between the revenues under second-price and first-price auctions; with risk-averse bidders and common-values, the expected revenue in a Dutch (or equivalently, a first-price) auction may be greater or less than that in a second-price auction:

$$\text{English} > \text{Second price} \gtreqless \text{Dutch} = \text{First price.}$$

DEMONSTRATION PROBLEM 12–7

Suppose your firm is in need of cash and plans to auction off a subsidiary to the highest bidder. Which type of auction will maximize your firm's revenues from the sale if (1) the bidders are risk neutral and each values your subsidiary differently or (2) the bidders are risk neutral and do not know the true value of the subsidiary?

Answer

(1) With either perfect information or independent private valuations, all four auction types will lead to identical expected revenues under these conditions.
(2) With common valuations and risk-neutral bidders, the English auction will yield the highest expected revenues.

Inside Business 12–5

Uncertainty and Real Estate Foreclosure Sales

Almost everyone has seen an advertisement in a magazine or on television pushing a scheme to get rich in real estate. A typical program encourages the consumer to pay a fee to gain information about how to buy and sell property that has gone into either bankruptcy, foreclosure, or receivership. The "bottom line" is that you can purchase these properties for 20 percent less than their "market value." It turns out that most homes in foreclosure do indeed sell for approximately 20 percent less than other homes in the area, but this does not mean they sell for 20 percent less than their "market value."

When a bankruptcy or foreclosure is in place, the seller is no longer the person who took out the loan on the property; the seller is the court system. This increases the level of uncertainty to the buyer regarding when and whether a deal will be consummated, because often there are multiple liens on the property that must first be cleared. This increase in risk reduces the price individuals are willing to pay for the property.

Second, properties sold in foreclosure auctions often represent properties that individuals were unable to sell in the usual real estate market.

Thus, due to adverse selection, the pool of properties sold in foreclosure auctions tend to have characteristics that prevent them from selling in the usual market. Consequently, many of the houses sold in foreclosure auctions have features that are of lower value to buyers than other homes. This also leads to lower prices for the pool of foreclosed houses.

Finally, many foreclosed properties are sold in sealed-bid auctions. In most instances, there is uncertainty about the "true" value of the house, and each potential bidder has his or her own private estimate of the value. In this instance, rational bidders will bid less than their true valuations of the house to avoid the winner's curse. This also tends to reduce the prices at which foreclosed properties sell.

For all of these reasons, homes that have reached bankruptcy usually are sold at about 20 percent below the prices of other houses in the area. These can be good deals for the person who finds a home in excellent condition. But the uncertainty is greater, which makes purchasing a foreclosed property a riskier prospect.

Answering the Headline

The opening headline asked why one of the firms in the FCC auction dropped out of the bidding before the price reached its private estimate of $85 million for a license. Since the spectrum rights auction was a common values auction, the firm that has the highest private estimate is the firm with the most optimistic estimate of the true value of the license. If firms as a whole form correct expectations of the value, this means that the winner's estimated value is likely to overestimate the true value of a license. In this case a firm that bids its private estimate would expect to lose money over the 10-year life of the license. To circumvent this winner's curse, the firm correctly dropped out of the bidding before the price reached its private estimate of $85 million.

Summary

In this chapter, we examined some of the problems uncertainty and asymmetric information add to managerial decision problems. It should be clear that in many instances, consumers and firms' managers have imperfect information about demand functions, costs, sources of products, and product quality. Decisions are harder to make, because the outcomes are uncertain. If your information is probabilistic in nature, you should take the time to find the mean, variance, and standard deviation of outcomes that will result from alternative actions. By doing this, you often can use marginal analysis to make optimal decisions.

Consumers and producers have different risk preferences. Some people like to go to the mountains to ski treacherous slopes, while others prefer to sit in the lodge and take in the scenery outside. Similarly, some individuals have a preference for risky prospects, while others are risk averse. If you or the firm you work for has a preference for not taking risks (i.e., is risk averse), you will accept projects with low expected returns, provided the corresponding risk is lower than projects with higher expected returns. However, if risk taking excites you, you will be willing to take on riskier projects.

Risk structures and the use of the mean, variance, and standard deviation also help identify how customers will respond to uncertain prospects. For example, those individuals who most actively seek insurance and are willing to pay the most for it frequently are bad risks. This results in adverse selection. Moreover, once individuals obtain insurance, they will tend to take fewer precautions to avoid losses than they would without it. This creates a moral hazard.

We also examined how consumers will react to uncertainty about prices or quality through search behavior. Consumers will change their search for quality and "good" prices based on both their perceptions of the probability of finding a better deal and the value of their time. Putting this information to work can help you keep more of your customers. When your customers have a low value of time, you know you will need to lower prices to keep them, because their opportunity cost of searching is low.

Finally, we examined auctions, which play a central role in capitalistic economies. We covered four types of auctions: the English auction, the Dutch auction, the first-price, sealed-bid auction, and the second-price, sealed-bid auction. Expected revenues (or costs) vary across auction types depending on whether bidders are risk averse and the item being auctioned has private or common values.

Key Terms and Concepts

adverse selection	private values
asymmetric information	replacement
common values	reservation price
Dutch auction	risk
English auction	second-price, sealed-bid
first-price, sealed-bid auction	auction
free recall	standard deviation
hidden actions	uncertainty
hidden characteristics	variance
mean (expected) value	winner's curse
moral hazard	

Problems

1. Joe's search costs are $7 per search. He wants to buy a VCR for his wife for Christmas, and the lowest price he's found so far is $200. Joe thinks one-third of the stores charge $300 for a VCR, one-third charge $200, and one-third charge $185. Should Joe continue to search or buy a VCR at a price of $200?

2. A risk-neutral price-taking firm must set output before it knows for sure the market price. There is a 50 percent chance the market demand curve will be $Q^d = 10 - 2P$ and a 50 percent chance it will be $Q^d = 20 - 2P$. The market supply curve is estimated to be $Q^S = 2 + P$.
   a. Calculate the expected (mean) market price.
   b. Calculate the variance of the market price.
   c. If the firm's marginal cost is given by $MC = .01 + .5Q$, what level of output maximizes expected profits?

3. Explain why a used car that is only six months old and has been driven only 5,000 miles typically sells for 20 percent less than a new car with the same options.

4. Why do life insurance policies have clauses stipulating that the company will not pay benefits for suicide within one year from the policy date?

5. A risk-averse manager is considering a project that will cost $100. There is a 10 percent chance the project will generate revenues of $100, an 80 percent chance it will yield revenues of $50, and a 10 percent chance it will yield revenues of $500. Should the manager adopt the project? Explain.

6. As the manager of We Do It Right Construction, you need to make a decision on how many homes to build in a new residential area. There

is a 20 percent chance of a recession, a 60 percent chance the economy will remain as it is, and a 20 percent chance there will be an economic upturn. If a recession hits, your inverse demand curve for new homes will be

$$P = 100,000 - 4Q.$$

If things remain as they are, your inverse demand curve will be

$$P = 115,000 - 3Q.$$

If economic growth occurs, your inverse demand curve will be

$$P = 130,000 - 2Q.$$

Your cost function in all three scenarios is

$$C(Q) = 70,000 + 2Q + .5Q^2.$$

If you are risk neutral, how many homes will you start?

7. You are the manager of a new computer company that manufactures PCs to order. Devise a plan that will convince potential customers your quality is the best in the business.

8. You are considering opening your own hamburger restaurant. List the information that will influence your decision about whether to start your own restaurant, or go with a franchise.

9. Will consumers spend more time searching when stores are located in a mall or when they are spread all over town? Explain.

10. As the personnel director of a major consulting firm, you have been asked to decide whether to hire new employees. Presently the economy is in a recession, and you have more people than you need to operate the business. Next year there is a 65 percent chance you will need more people and a 35 percent chance you will need fewer people. What additional information would you need when making this decision? Explain.

11. During the recession in the early 1990s, retailers observed that consumers were spending a lot more time searching for good bargains than ever before, which led the retailers to lower prices. Why?

12. "Guaranteed issue" is a controversial issue in the insurance market. It requires firms offering health coverage for one employee to offer the same coverage to all employees, regardless of their health risks. Why is this so controversial?

13. When Olympia and York was in the process of restructuring its loans to avoid bankruptcy, its lenders asked the firm to disclose full information about its revenues and costs. Olympia and York, on the other hand, was reluctant to share all its information with the lenders. Why?

14. The text describes four kinds of auctions. If you are risk neutral, which auction would you prefer given the following scenarios? Give both the seller's and the buyer's point of view.
    a. A common-value item.
    b. A private-value item.
    c. Perfect information.

15. How would your answer to Problem 14 change if you were risk averse?

16. What is the "winner's curse"? As a participant in an auction, how can you avoid the winner's curse?

17. Suppose five bidders compete for the right to purchase the following items. Determine whether the most likely structure is common values or private values.
    a. A painting.
    b. An offshore oil lease.
    c. A used car.

18. At Econ Tech, the average grade in a course that all students know to be a "blow-off" course is the same as the average grade in the toughest math course. Why?

19. A risk-averse manager is considering two projects. The first project is to introduce a new product; the second is to revamp the production facilities at the existing plant. There is a 20 percent chance a rival will enter the market and an 80 percent chance it will not. If the rival enters, the firm will lose $20,000 if it introduces the new product, whereas revamping the production facilities will earn it $50,000 in profits. If the rival does not enter, the firm will earn $15,000 if it introduces the new product, and revamping the production facilities will net profits of $60,000. What should the manager do? Why?

20. Your firm is planning to hold an auction to sell its mining facility. Your boss has asked you to determine the best type of auction to hold to maximize expected profits from selling the facility. Based on your knowledge of auctions, provide your boss with a suggestion.

21. During the 1980s S&L deposits were insured by the Federal Savings and Loan Corporation (today the FDIC insures deposits at S&Ls as well as at banks). In the early 1980s Congress passed legislation that allowed S&Ls to make a broader array of loans. The legislation was designed to provide relief to the ailing thrift industry, which was at a competitive disadvantage relative to banks. As a result of bad loans, however, the problems within the industry got even worse, and the government ultimately spent nearly $150 billion to bail out troubled thrifts. What do you think was the main cause of the S&L problem, and why do you think the FDIC now insures deposits at thrifts?

Selected Readings

Bikhchandani, Sushil, Hirshleifer, David, and Welch, Ivo, "A Theory of Fads, Fashion, Custom, and Cultural Change in Informational Cascades." *Journal of Political Economy* 100(5), October 1992, pp. 992–1026.

Cummins, J.David and Tennyson, Sharon, "Controlling Automobile Insurance Costs." *Journal of Economic Perspectives* 6(2), Spring 1992, pp. 95–115.

Hamilton, Jonathan H., "Resale Price Maintenance in a Model of Consumer Search." *Managerial and Decision Economics* 11(2), May 1990, pp. 87–98.

Kagel, John, Levine, Dan, and Battalio, Raymond, "First Price Common Value Auctions: Bidder Behavior and the 'Winner's Curse.'" *Economic Inquiry* 27, April 1989, pp. 241–58.

Lind, Barry and Plott, Charles, "The Winner's Curse: Experiments with Buyers and with Sellers." *American Economic Review* 81, March 1991, pp. 225–346.

Machina, Mark J., "Choice Under Uncertainty: Problems Solve and Unsolved." *Journal of Economic Perspectives* 1, Summer 1987, pp. 121–154.

McAfee, R. Preston and McMillan, John, "Auctions and Bidding." *Journal of Economic Literature* 25(2), June 1987, pp. 699–738.

McMillan, John, "Selling Spectrum Rights." *Journal of Economic Perspectives* 8(3), Summer 1994, pp. 145–62.

Milgrom, Paul, "Auctions and Bidding: A Primer." *Journal of Economic Perspectives* 3(3), Summer 1989, pp. 3–22.

Riley, John G., "Expected Revenues from Open and Sealed Bid Auctions." *Journal of Economic Perspectives* 3(3), Summer 1989, pp. 41–50.

Salop, Steven, "Evaluating Uncertain Evidence with Sir Thomas Bayes: A Note for Teachers." *Journal of Economics Perspectives* 1, Summary 1987, pp. 115–60.

Chapter 13

A Manager's Guide to Government in the Marketplace

Headline

Justice Department Settles Price-Fixing Case Involving Eight Major Airlines

In 1994 the U.S. Department of Justice (DOJ) settled a case against eight airlines that it had earlier charged with price-fixing. According to the DOJ, these airlines used the computer reservation system that stores the fare records of all major airlines to communicate collusive arrangements. (The DOJ claimed that over 50 collusive arrangements were made using the system.) In addition to helping the airlines communicate collusive prices on certain routes, the computer system also made it easy for the airlines to enforce their agreements since an airline could easily detect and respond to violations of the collusive agreement within a few hours.

As a result of the charges, the airlines involved reached a settlement with the DOJ that was approved by a federal court. Among other things, the settlement agreement forbids carriers from using the features of the computer system that facilitate price-fixing, and requires the airlines to compensate the passengers harmed by giving them vouchers good for reduced fares on a specified number of future flights.

Why do you think the airlines were willing to settle with the Justice Department, rather than fight their case in court?

Introduction

Throughout most of this book, we have treated the market as a place where firms and consumers come together to trade goods and services with no intervention from government. But as you are aware, rules and regulations that are passed and enforced by government enter into almost every decision firms and consumers make. As a manager, it is important not only to understand the regulations passed by government but to know why such regulations have been passed and how they affect optimal managerial decisions.

We will begin by examining four reasons why free markets may fail to provide the socially efficient quantities of goods: (1) market power, (2) externalities, (3) public goods, and (4) incomplete information. Our analysis includes an overview of government policies designed to alleviate these "market failures" and an explanation of how the policies affect managerial decisions. The power of politicians to institute policies that affect the allocation of resources in markets provides those adversely affected with an incentive to engage in lobbying activities. We will illustrate the underlying reasons for these types of rent-seeking activities. Finally, we will examine how these activities can lead politicians to impose restrictions such as quotas and tariffs in markets affected by international trade.

Market Failure

One of the main reasons for government involvement in the marketplace is that free markets do not always result in the socially efficient quantities of goods at socially efficient prices. In this section, we will consider why markets do not always lead to socially efficient outcomes and examine how government policies designed to correct "market failures" affect managerial decisions. We will begin by examining market failure due to the presence of market power.

Market Power

A firm has *market power* when it sells output at a price that exceeds its marginal cost of production. In such instances, the value to society of another unit of the good is greater than the cost of the resources needed to produce that unit; there would be a net gain to society if additional output were produced. In these instances, government may intervene in the market and regulate the actions of firms in an attempt to increase *social welfare*.

To see the potential benefits of government intervention in a market, consider a market serviced by a monopoly. Figure 13–1 shows the monopolist's demand, marginal cost, and marginal revenue curves. Assuming the monopolist must charge the same price to all consumers in the market, the profit-maximizing output is Q^M units, and these units are sold at the monopoly price of P^M. At this price, consumers pay more for the last unit of output than it cost the producer to manufacture and sell it. Total social welfare under monopoly is the sum of producer surplus and consumer surplus, which is the region labeled W in Figure 13–1.

Notice in Figure 13–1 that the area of triangle ABC is the *deadweight loss* of the monopoly—welfare that would have accrued to society if the

FIGURE 13–1

*Welfare and
deadweight loss
under monopoly*

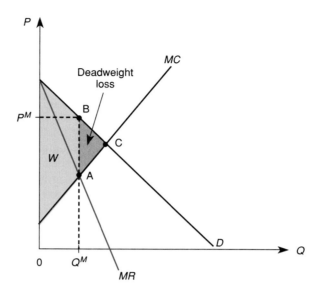

industry were perfectly competitive but is not realized because of the market power the monopolist enjoys. The failure of the market to fully maximize social welfare is due to market power; the deadweight loss triangle provides a measure of this welfare loss to society.

The government uses antitrust policy to enact and enforce laws that restrict the formation of monopolies. The rationale for these policies is that by preventing monopoly power from emerging, the deadweight loss of monopoly can be avoided. In some instances, however, the presence of economies of scale make it desirable to allow the formation of a monopoly. In these cases, government attempts to reduce the deadweight loss by regulating the price charged by the monopolist.

Antitrust Policy

Antitrust policy attempts to eliminate the deadweight loss of monopoly by making it illegal for managers to engage in activities that foster monopoly power, such as price-fixing agreements and other collusive practices. The cornerstone of U.S. antitrust policy is contained in Sections 1 and 2 of the *Sherman Antitrust Act* of 1890:

Sec. 1

Every contract, combination in the form of trust or otherwise, or conspiracy, in restraint of trade or commerce among the several states, or with foreign nations, is hereby declared to be illegal. Every person who shall make any such contract or engage in any such combination or conspiracy shall be deemed guilty of a felony, and, on conviction thereof, shall be punished by fine not exceeding five thousand dollars (one million dollars if a corporation, or, if any other person, one hundred thousand dollars) or by imprisonment not exceeding one (three) years, or by both said punishments, in the discretion of the court.

Sec. 2

Every person who shall monopolize, or attempt to monopolize, or combine or conspire with any person or persons, to monopolize any part of the trade or commerce among the several States, or with foreign nations, shall be deemed guilty of a felony, and, on conviction thereof, shall be punished by fine not exceeding five thousand dollars (one million dollars if a corporation, or, if any other person, one hundred thousand dollars) or by imprisonment not exceeding one (three) years, or by both said punishments, in the discretion of the court.[1]

Among other things, the Sherman Act makes it illegal for managers of U.S. firms to collude with other domestic or foreign firms. Thus, even though OPEC is not bound by U.S. law (it is composed of foreign nations), the manager of a U.S. oil company cannot legally participate in the OPEC oil cartel.

The interpretation of antitrust policy is largely shaped by the courts, which rule on ambiguities in the law and previous cases. For example, the first successful use of the Sherman Antitrust Act was in 1897, when the Supreme Court held that rate agreements are illegal in *United States v. Trans-Missouri Freight Association*. This ruling was again upheld in *United States v. Joint Traffic Association* (1898). The court extended its interpretation to include collusive bidding in *Addyston Pipe & Steel Company v. United States* (1899). The full power of the Sherman Antitrust Act was not realized until the conclusion of *United States v. Standard Oil of New Jersey* in 1911. The last case is interesting and provides useful caveats to future managers.

Standard Oil of New Jersey, along with Standard Oil of Ohio, was charged with attempting to fix the prices of petroleum products and the prices at which the products would be shipped. Standard Oil in particular was accused of numerous activities designed to enhance monopoly power: using physical threats to shippers and other producers, setting up bogus companies, using espionage by bribing employees of other companies, engaging in restraint of trade, and making several attempts to monopolize the oil industry. Managers, of course, should avoid all of these practices; as a result of these actions, the court dissolved Standard Oil into 33 subsidiaries, many of which survive today under the names Exxon, Mobil, Chevron, Amoco, and BP America. More important than breaking up the Standard Oil Trust, however, was the Supreme Court's new *Rule of Reason,* as defined in Justice White's majority opinion:

Thus not specifying, the indubitably contemplating and requiring a standard, it follows that it was intended that the standard of reason which had been applied at

---

[1]The penalties have been amended twice, in 1955 and in 1970. The penalties in parentheses represent the 1970 change.

the common law and in this country in dealing with subjects of the character embraced by the statute was intended to be the measure used for the purpose of determining whether, in a given case, a particular act had or had not brought about the wrong against which the statute provided.

The rule of reason has since become the code of decision making used by the court for determining antitrust cases. Effectively, the rule of reason stipulates that not all trade restraints are illegal; rather, only those that are "unreasonable" are prohibited. For example, in applying this rule, the courts determined that the size of a firm alone is not sufficient evidence to convict a firm under Section 2 of the Sherman Act:

> To hold to the contrary would require the conclusion either that every contract, act, or combination of any kind or nature, whether it operated in restraint of trade or not, was within the statute.

Effectively, this means that a firm must take an explicit action designed to lessen competition before it can be found guilty of violating Section 2 of the Sherman Act. For example, the rule of reason was used in the decision against American Tobacco, which was found guilty of monopolizing the U.S. cigarette market by engaging in predatory pricing—pricing explicitly designed to harm other firms and thus enhance the firm's own monopoly power.

The problem with the rule of reason is that it makes it difficult for managers to know in advance whether particular pricing strategies used to enhance profits are in fact violations of the law. Congress attempted to clarify its intent by more precisely defining illegal actions in the *Clayton Act* (1914) and its amendment, the *Robinson Patman Act* (1936). For example, Section 2(a) of the Robinson Patman Act amends Section 2 of the Clayton Act and makes price discrimination illegal if it is designed to lessen competition or create a monopoly:

> **Sec. 2(a)**   That it shall be unlawful for any person engaged in commerce, in the course of such commerce, either directly or indirectly, to discriminate in price between different purchasers of commodities of like grade and quality, . . . where such discrimination may be substantially to lessen competition or tend to create a monopoly in line of commerce, or to injure, destroy, or prevent competition.

Price discrimination that arises because of cost or quality differences is permitted under the act, as is price discrimination when it is necessary to meet a competitor's price in a market. Still, there is considerable ambiguity regarding whether a particular type of price discrimination is illegal under the law.

The Clayton Act contains more than 20 sections that, among other things, make it illegal for firms to (1) hide kickbacks as commissions or brokerage fees; (2) use rebates unless they are made available to all customers; (3) engage in exclusive dealings with a supplier unless the supplier adds to the furnishing of the buyer and/or offers to make like terms to all other potential suppliers; (4) fix prices or engage in exclusive contracts if such a practice will lead to lessening of competition or monopoly; and (5) acquire one or more other firms if such an acquisition will lead to a lessening of competition.

The *Cellar-Kefauver Act* (1950) strengthened Section 7 of the Clayton Act by making it more difficult for firms to engage in mergers and acquisitions without violating the law:

Sec. 7
That no corporation engaged in commerce shall acquire, directly or indirectly, the whole or any part of the stock or other share capital and no corporation subject to the jurisdiction of the Federal Trade Commission shall acquire the whole or any part of the assets of another corporation engaged also in commerce, where in any line of commerce in any section of the country, the effect of such acquisition may be substantially to lessen competition, or to tend to create a monopoly.

Merger policy changed, however, when new merger guidelines were written in 1982, amended in 1984, and revised in 1992. The guidelines are based on the *Herfindahl-Hirshman index (HHI),* which is the sum of the squared shares of the market for every firm in a particular market times 10,000:

$$HHI = 10,000 \sum_{i=1}^{N} w_i^2.$$

Under the *Merger Guidelines,* a merger can be challenged if (1) the HHI in an industry is greater than 1,800, or would be after merger, or (2) the HHI is between 1,000 and 1,800, in which case the merger is to be carefully examined. Mergers may not be blocked even if the HHI indices are large, provided there is significant foreign competition, an emerging new technology, increased efficiency, or one of the firms has financial problems.

The main theme of the *Merger Guidelines* is summarized as follows:

The primary benefit of mergers to the economy is their efficiency potential, which can increase the competitiveness of firms and result in lower prices to consumers. . . . In the majority of cases, the Guidelines will allow firms to achieve efficiencies through mergers without interference from the Department.[2]

The Antitrust Division of the Department of Justice (DOJ) and the Federal Trade Commission (FTC) are charged with the task of enforcing antitrust regulations. The FTC has limited judicial power; taking violators to court falls almost exclusively on the Antitrust Division of the DOJ. Instead, the FTC issues cease-and-desist orders based on information gathered in a specific case. If the cease-and-desist order is not followed, the FTC may levy a fine of up to $10,000 on the guilty party. If further noncompliance occurs, the FTC usually enjoins the DOJ for further prosecution.

---

[2]Department of Justice, *Merger Guidelines,* 1984, sec. 1.

This historical division of labor between the DOJ and FTC is likely to change as a result of the revised *Merger Guidelines* that were released in 1992. These guidelines were *jointly* issued by the DOJ and the FTC (previous guidelines were released solely by the DOJ). This means that, for the first time in U.S. history, the FTC and DOJ now use identical yardsticks to gauge the social benefits and costs of horizontal mergers. The FTC and DOJ are thus likely to work more closely in the future to block mergers that are deemed socially undesirable.

Price Regulation

In the presence of large economies of scale (as is often the case for utility companies), it may be desirable for a single firm to service a market. In these instances, government may allow a firm to exist as a monopoly but choose to regulate its price to reduce the deadweight loss. In this section, we will see how such regulation affects managerial decisions and social welfare.

Consider the situation depicted in Figure 13–2, where an unregulated monopolist produces Q^M units of output at a price of P^M. A competitive industry would produce Q^C units, where marginal cost intersects the demand curve. Suppose the government imposed and enforced a regulated price of P^C, which corresponds to the price a competitive industry would charge for the product given identical demand and cost conditions. How should the manager respond to maximize the firm's profits?

The monopolist cannot legally charge a price above P^C, so the maximum price it can charge for units less than Q^C is P^C. For units above Q^C, the maximum price it can charge is the price along the inverse demand curve, since the amount consumers are willing to pay is less than the ceiling.

FIGURE 13–2

Regulating a monopolist's price at the socially efficient level

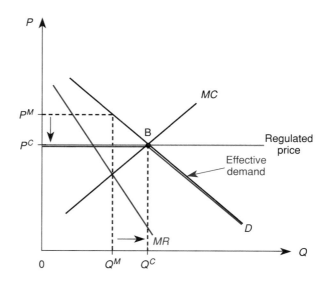

As a consequence, the effective inverse demand curve of the monopolist is given by $P^C BD$. Notice that for points to the left of B, the demand curve is horizontal, just as it is for a perfectly competitive firm. But if the monopolist wishes to sell more than Q^C units of output, it can do so only by lowering price below P^C.

Since the monopolist can sell each unit up to Q^C at a price of P^C, the marginal revenue for these units is simply P^C; each additional unit of output up to Q^C adds exactly P^C to the firm's revenue. In effect, the ceiling creates a situation where the demand curve the monopolist faces is just like that of a perfectly competitive firm for these output levels. To maximize profits, the regulated monopolist will produce where the marginal revenue of the effective demand curve (P^C) equals marginal cost, which is at point B. This corresponds to an output of Q^C. Thus, when the monopolist's price is regulated at P^C in Figure 13–2, the firm maximizes profits by producing Q^C units and selling them at the regulated price of P^C.

Notice that the impact of the price regulation is to induce the profit-maximizing monopolist to produce the perfectly competitive output at the perfectly competitive price. The result of the price regulation is to completely eliminate the deadweight loss of the monopoly. The government policy thus reduces monopoly profits but increases social welfare.

On the basis of Figure 13–2, one might be tempted to conclude that it is always beneficial to regulate the price charged by a monopolist. This is not the case, however. To see why, consider the monopoly situation in Figure 13–3. Suppose the government regulates the price at the level P^*. Given the regulated price, the effective demand curve for the monopolist is now P^*FD, and the corresponding marginal revenue curve for units produced below Q^*

FIGURE 13–3

Regulating a monopolist's price below the socially efficient level

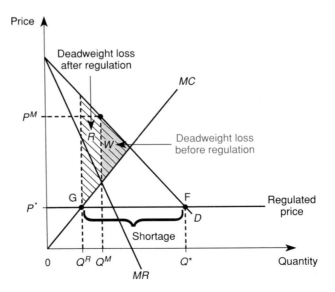

is given by line P^*F. To maximize profits, the regulated monopolist will produce where the marginal revenue of the effective demand curve (P^*) equals marginal cost, which is at point G. This corresponds to an output of Q^R, which is less than the output the monopolist would have produced in the absence of regulation. Moreover, the quantity demanded at a price of P^* is Q^*, so there is a shortage of $Q^* - Q^R$ units under the regulated price. Furthermore, the deadweight loss under this regulated price (regions $R + W$) is actually larger than the deadweight loss in the absence of regulation (region W). If the government lacks accurate information about demand and costs, or for some other reason regulates the price at too low a level, it can actually reduce social welfare and create a shortage of the good.

It is very important to note that the analysis in Figures 13–2 and 13–3 suppresses the position of the average total cost curve. To see why it is important to consider the position of the average total cost curve before reaching conclusions about the welfare loss arising from monopoly, consider the situation in Figure 13–4, where the monopolist is just breaking even at point A. In this instance, an unregulated monopolist would produce Q^M units and charge a price of P^M. Since price is equal to the average total cost of production, this monopolist earns zero economic profits in the absence of regulation.

Now suppose the price is regulated at P^C. In the long run, how much output will the firm produce? The answer is zero output. To see why, note that under the regulated price, average total cost lies above the regulated price, so the monopolist would experience a loss if it produced. Thus, in the long run the monopolist in Figure 13–4 would exit the market if the price were regulated at P^C, and everyone in the market would be made worse off

FIGURE 13–4

A case where price regulation drives the monopolist out of business

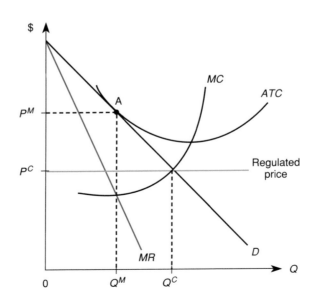

(there would be no product to consume). To keep this from happening, the government would have to subsidize the monopoly by agreeing to compensate it for any losses incurred. These funds would come from taxes, and thus consumers would indirectly be paying for the lower price through higher taxes. Moreover, the manager of a subsidized monopoly would have no incentive to keep costs low; any losses that resulted would be subsidized by the government. Consequently, the manager would have an incentive to spend enormous sums of money on plush offices, corporate jets, and the like, since losses would be reimbursed by the government.

The analysis in Figure 13–4 points out a very important caveat regarding comparisons of monopoly and perfect competition. One key source of monopoly power is the presence of economies of scale. These economies of scale may render it impossible for output to be produced in a competitive industry. For example, a competitive industry could not sustain an output of Q^C in Figure 13–4, because the intersection of the marginal cost and demand curves lies below the average total cost curve.

DEMONSTRATION PROBLEM 13–1

Many firms that sell in small markets are effectively monopolies; they are the sole provider of a good in their area. Yet most of these firms are allowed to operate as monopolies without regulation by government. Why?

Answer

In situations where economies of scale are large relative to market demand, only a single firm will be able to service the market. In these instances, it is not desirable to break the firm up into smaller firms using antitrust policy. There would, however, be a potential gain in social welfare if the firm's price were regulated at the socially efficient level. This gain must be weighed against the cost of setting up a regulatory body to administer the regulation. If the cost of setting up and running the regulative body exceeds the deadweight loss of monopoly—as it likely will in small markets—there will be a net loss in social welfare by regulation. In these instances, social welfare would be better served by leaving the firm alone even though it creates a deadweight loss. In effect, it would cost more to fix the problem than would be gained by eliminating the deadweight loss.

Externalities

Unfortunately, some production processes create costs for people who are not part of the production or consumption process for the good. These external costs are called *negative externalities*.

The most common example of a negative externality is pollution. When a firm creates wastes that either do not easily biodegrade or have harmful effects on other resources, it does not pay the full cost of production. For example, a firm that produces textiles usually creates waste products that contain dioxin, a cancer-causing chemical. When a textile manufacturer can dispose of this waste "for free" by dumping it into a nearby river, it has an incentive to dump more waste into the river than is socially optimal. While the firm benefits from dumping waste into the river, the waste reduces the oxygen content of the water, clogs normal waterway routes, and creates reproduction problems for birds, fish, reptiles, and aquatic animals. These results negatively affect people who are not involved in the production or consumption process.

To see why the market fails to provide the efficient level of output when there are externalities in production, consider Figure 13–5. If a firm emits pollutants into the water as a by-product of producing steel, a cost, or negative externality, is borne by members of society. Figure 13–5 shows the negative externality as the marginal cost of pollution to society. This cost represents the cost to society of dirtier water due to increases in steel production. The production of only a little steel results in only minor damage to water, but as increasing amounts of steel are produced, more and more pollutants collect in the water. The marginal cost of pollution to society thus increases as more steel is produced.

Assuming the market for steel is perfectly competitive, the market supply curve in *S* in Figure 13–5, which is the sum of the marginal costs of the firms producing in the industry. The supply curve is based on the costs paid by the steel firms; thus, if they are allowed to dump pollutants into the water

FIGURE 13–5

The socially efficient equilibrium in the presences of external costs

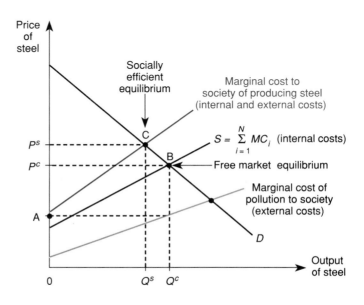

for free, the market equilibrium is at point B, where the market demand and supply curves intersect. The result is that Q^c units will be produced and purchased at a price of P^c per unit of steel.

However, at this quantity of output, society pays a marginal price of A, on top of the price of P^c paid to the steel firms. This amount is the additional cost to society of the pollution. In particular, since the firms are dumping pollutants into the water for free, the cost of pollution is not internalized by those who buy and sell steel; rather, society pays for the dumping of pollutants by having to endure polluted water. If the firms were to take into account the cost of pollution to society, the sum of their marginal cost curves would be the vertical sum of the supply curve and the marginal cost of pollution to society. This sum is shown as the marginal cost to society of producing steel in Figure 13–5. The socially efficient level of output, which takes into account all the costs and benefits of producing steel, is at point C, where the marginal cost to society of producing steel intersects the market demand curve. The socially efficient level of steel output is Q^s, which is less than the output produced in the perfectly competitive market. The socially efficient price of steel is P^s, which is greater than the perfectly competitive price of P^c. In other words, in the presence of external costs, the market equilibrium output is greater than the socially efficient level, and the market price is below the socially efficient level. In effect, consumers get to purchase too much output at too low a price.

The basic reason for the "market failure" is the absence of well-defined *property rights;* the steel firms believe they have the right to use the river to dump waste, and environmentalists believe they have the right to a clean river. This failure often can be solved when government defines itself to be the owner of the environment. It can then use its power to induce the socially efficient levels of output and pollution.

To induce the socially efficient level of output, government may force firms to internalize the costs of emitting pollutants by enacting policies that shift the internal cost of production up to where it actually equals the social cost of production. A prime example of a government policy designed to do this is the Clean Air Act.

The Clean Air Act
To solve the externality problem that exists in polluting air, Congress passed the *Clean Air Act* in 1970 and a sweeping amendment in 1990. The amended Clean Air Act covers 189 toxic air pollutants and was the most comprehensive antipollution act passed by any country as of 1992. The Clean Air Act now covers any industry that releases over 10 tons per year of any of the listed pollutants or 25 tons per year of any combination of those pollutants. Previous law covered only industries that released 100 tons per year of a much smaller list of pollutants, but the new act covers a much broader set of industries. The amended Clean Air Act is so voluminous that guidelines for compliance usually comprise several hundred pages. Due to

the comprehensive nature of the act, we will examine only one aspect of the new law that specifically uses the market as an enforcement mechanism.

A firm in an industry covered by the Clean Air Act is required to obtain a permit to be able to pollute. These permits are limited in availability and require the firm to pay for each unit of pollutants emitted. For an existing firm, these permits increase both the fixed and variable costs of producing goods. They are a variable cost because as output increases, the level of pollutants emitted rises, and a fee must be paid on each of these units of pollution. The fixed-cost component is the fee required to obtain a permit in the first place. Along with the permit, the Clean Air Act requires new entrants into an industry to match or improve on the most effective pollution removal system used in the industry. Existing firms must follow suit and upgrade within three years. Once purchased from the government, the permits may be bought from and sold to other firms.

Figure 13–6(a) illustrates the effects of the new policy on the cost structure of a firm that pollutes as a by-product of production. MC_1 and ATC_1 represent the marginal and average total cost of production before the regulation took effect. If the market price of the final product was P_0, the firm maximized profits by producing q_0 units of the final product and dumped pollution into the air or water for free. When the act took effect, the average total cost curve shifted up to ATC_2, as the firm now had to pay the fixed cost of obtaining a permit. The marginal cost curve also shifted up to MC_2, since the firm now had to pay for each unit of pollution resulting from the production process. The result of the Clean Air Act was that firms now internalize the cost of pollution and, as a result, reduce their output to q_1 to maximize profits. The profits of these firms fall due to their internalizing the pollution costs.

FIGURE 13–6

Impact of the Clean Air Act

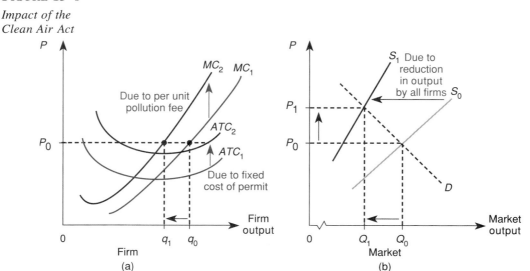

Notice in Figure 13–6(b) that as each firm's marginal cost curve shifts up, the market supply decreases: Less of the product is available in the market at any price. Consequently, the ultimate effect of the Clean Air Act is to decrease the market equilibrium quantity from Q_0 to Q_1 in Figure 13–6(b) and to raise the market price from P_0 to P_1. The change caused by the permits is exactly what is called for in Figure 13–5 to solve the negative externality of pollution: less output at a higher price.

An interesting aspect of this new legislation is the fact that permits can be sold by one firm to another both within and across industries. This aspect of the permits does two things that allow the market to reduce pollution. First, it allows new firms to enter an industry when demand increases. Second, it provides an incentive for existing firms to invest in new technology to create cleaner production methods.

To see this, suppose demand in a nonpolluting industry increases. As a result, the price increases, economic profits will be earned in the short run, and in the long run new firms will enter the market until economic profits return to zero. However, in a polluting industry that is not allowed to buy and sell permits to pollute, entry cannot occur; the fixed number of pollution permits are already allocated, and new entrants face a barrier to entry because of their inability to obtain a permit. In contrast, if the permits can be traded across industries, a potential entrant can purchase these rights from a firm in another industry or bring less polluting technology into the existing industry and buy some of the rights to pollute from existing firms. Thus, by making the pollution rights marketable, new firms can enter markets when consumer preferences indicate that more of the good is desired. Firms wishing to enter an industry that produces a highly valued product can purchase permits from firms that produce products that consumers do not value as highly.

The ability to sell the permits also provides an incentive for firms to develop and innovate new technologies that produce less pollution. In particular, a firm that develops a pollution-reducing technology can sell the pollution rights it no longer needs to firms in industries where the technology is not available. This allows the innovating firm to recover a portion of the cost of developing pollution-reducing technologies.

DEMONSTRATION PROBLEM 13–2

Suppose the external marginal cost of producing steel is

$$MC_{External} = 3Q$$

and the internal marginal cost is

$$MC_{Internal} = 6Q.$$

The inverse demand for steel is given by

$$P = 100 - Q.$$

(1) What is the socially efficient level of output?
(2) How much output would a competitive industry produce?
(3) How much output would a monopoly produce?

Answer

(1) The socially efficient level of output occurs where the marginal cost to society of producing another unit equals demand. The social marginal cost is

$$MC_{Social} = MC_{External} + MC_{Internal} = 3Q + 6Q = 9Q.$$

Equating this with price yields

$$9Q = 100 - Q,$$

or $Q = 10$ units.
(2) A competitive industry produces where the internal marginal cost equals price:

$$6Q = 100 - Q,$$

or about $Q = 14.3$ units. Thus, a competitive industry produces too much steel, because it ignores the cost society pays for the pollution.
(3) A monopolist produces where marginal revenue equals the internal marginal cost. Since $MR = 100 - 2Q$, we have

$$100 - 2Q = 6Q,$$

or $Q = 12.5$ units. Thus, given these demand and cost functions, a monopolist will produce more than the socially efficient level of steel with these cost conditions. Note, however, that since the monopolist has a tendency to restrict output, given these cost and demand functions it produces closer to the socially efficient level than does a competitive industry.

Public Goods

public good
A good that is nonrival and nonexclusionary in consumption.

nonrival consumption
A good is nonrival in consumption if the consumption of the good by one person does not preclude other people from also consuming the good.

Another source of market failure is the provision of *public goods*—goods that are nonrival and nonexclusionary in nature and therefore benefit persons other than those who buy the goods. Public goods differ from most goods you consume, which are rivalrous in nature. This simply means that when you consume the good, another person is unable to consume it as well. For example, when you buy and wear a pair of shoes to protect your feet, you prevent someone else from wearing the same pair; the consumption of shoes is rivalrous in nature.

Nonrival goods include radio signals, lighthouses, national defense, and protecting the environment. When you receive a radio signal in your car, you do not prevent other drivers from picking up the same station in their cars. This is in sharp contrast to your purchasing a pair of shoes.

nonexclusionary consumption
A good or service is nonexclusionary if, once provided, no one can be excluded from consuming it.

The second aspect of a public good is that it is *nonexclusionary:* Once a public good is made available, everyone gets it; no one can be excluded from enjoying the good. Most goods and services are by nature exclusionary. For example, when a car manufacturer produces a car, it can keep people from using the car by putting a lock on the door and giving the key only to the person who is willing to pay for the car.

Goods and services such as clean air, national defense, and radio waves are nonexclusionary goods. For example, when the air is clean, everyone gets to consume the clean air; it cannot be allocated to a single person.

What is it about public goods that leads the market to provide them in inefficient quantities? The answer is that since everyone gets to consume a public good once it is available, individuals have little incentive to purchase the good; rather, they prefer to let other people pay for it. Once it becomes available, they can "free ride" on the efforts of others to provide the good. But if everyone thinks this way, no one will buy the good and it will not be available. One person alone may be unable to afford to purchase the good.

DEMONSTRATION PROBLEM 13–3

Every time you go to your firm's lounge to get a cup of coffee, the pot is empty. Why?

Answer

There is a free-rider problem caused by the public-goods nature of making a pot of coffee. If you make a pot when it is empty, you benefit by getting a cup, but so do the next seven people who come into the lounge after you. Thus, people typically wait to let someone else make the coffee, which results in an empty coffee pot.

A concrete example will help you see why public goods are not provided in the socially efficient quantity. Suppose individuals value streetlights in their neighborhood because streetlights help prevent crime. Three people live in the neighborhood: A, B, and C. All three individuals have identical inverse demand functions for streetlights: $P_A = 30 - Q$, $P_B = 30 - Q$, and $P_C = 30 - Q$. The inverse demand curves reveal how much each person values another streetlight.

Because streetlights are nonexclusionary and nonrival in nature, everyone benefits once a streetlight is installed. For this reason, the total demand for a public good such as streetlights is the vertical sum of the individual inverse demand curves; it reveals the value of each additional streetlight to everyone in the neighborhood. Given A's, B's, and C's individual demands, the total demand for streetlights is given by

$$P_A + P_B + P_C = 90 - 3Q.$$

The individual and total demand curves are graphed in Figure 13–7. Notice that the total demand curve is the vertical sum of all three individual demand curves, and thus every point on it is three times higher than each point on the individual demand curves.

The socially efficient level of streetlights is at point A in Figure 13–7, where the marginal cost of producing streetlights exactly equals the total demand for streetlights. Algebraically, if the marginal cost of providing streetlights is $54 per light, the socially efficient quantity of streetlights is the quantity that equates

$$54 = 90 - 3Q,$$

which is 12 lights.

Since the marginal cost of each streetlight is $54 and lies above each individual's demand curve for streetlights in Figure 13–7, none of them will be willing to pay for even one streetlight on their own. However, if each person paid $18 per light, together they would pay $54 per light and could afford to purchase the socially efficient quantity of lights. The only way the people in this neighborhood can achieve the socially efficient quantity of lights is to pool their resources. If they accomplish this and each pays $18 per light, each will enjoy a consumer surplus of the shaded region in Figure 13–7, which is $72.

The problem, however, is that each individual would be better off by letting the other two install the streetlights. In particular, it is strategically

FIGURE 13–7

The demand for a public good

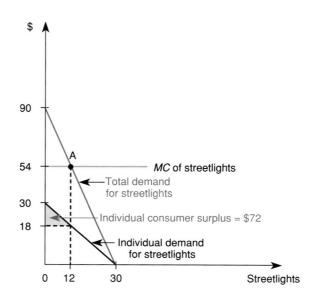

advantageous for each person to misrepresent his or her true personal demand function (valuation of the public good). If A claimed she did not want streetlights, and let the others pay for them, she would get to enjoy the lights for free (due to the nonrival and nonexclusionary nature of the good). This is similar to "cheating" on a cooperative agreement and is called *free riding.*

To illustrate this idea, suppose that instead of revealing her true demand for streetlights, A stated that she does not value streetlights at all. If A is the only one who did this, the revealed demand function would be the vertical sum of B's and C's inverse demand functions, which is shown in Figure 13–8(a). Since this demand curve intersects the $54 marginal cost at three streetlights, B and C would each pay $27 per light and purchase three lights. A, on the other hand, would get to enjoy the three streetlights for free, because she misrepresented her true demand for streetlights. By consuming three streetlights for free, she would enjoy a consumer surplus of $85.50, which corresponds to the shaded region in Figure 13–8(b). In contrast, if she had truthfully revealed her demand for streetlights, her consumer surplus would be only $72—the shaded region in Figure 13–7. A thus is better off by misrepresenting her true preferences for streetlights and letting B and C buy them.

Of course, the same is true of the other two individuals: If they think the others will contribute to buying streetlights, they are better off claiming not to want them. And if they think no one else will pay for streetlights, they will not pay for even one, since the cost is greater than their own individual demand. In the end, no streetlights are provided; the market failed to provide the public good.

Government solves the public-goods problem by forcing everyone to pay taxes regardless of whether or not a given taxpayer claims to want

FIGURE 13–8

The free-rider problem

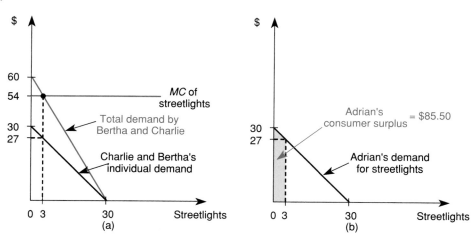

government services. Government then uses this revenue to fund public projects such as streetlights and national defense, which would not be provided in the absence of government intervention in the marketplace. Thus, while few of us enjoy paying taxes, it does provide a means for obtaining funds for public goods.

It is important to note that government may not provide the socially efficient quantity of public goods; it may in fact provide too much of them. The reason is that when a government official asks a citizen how much of a public good she or he desires, the person may misrepresent the quantity desired. Since most people believe their tax bill is an extremely small percentage of the total funds used to provide public goods, they perceive that the personal cost of the goods is zero and report to the official how many units of the public good they would desire if it were free. In our streetlight example, this means that all three people would tell the official they wanted 30 streetlights—more than twice the socially efficient quantity.

DEMONSTRATION PROBLEM 13–4

A firm has 20 employees, each of whom desires a more pleasant work environment. Accordingly, they are considering planting shrubs near the firm's parking lot. Each employee has an inverse demand for shrubs of $P = 10 - Q$, where Q is the number of shrubs. The marginal cost of planting shrubs is $20 each.
(1) What is the socially efficient quantity of shrubs to plant?
(2) How much would each person have to pay per shrub to achieve the efficient quantity?
(3) How many shrubs are likely to be planted? Why?

Answer

(1) The total demand for shrubs (a public good) is

$$P = 200 - 20Q.$$

Equating this with the marginal cost of planting shrubs yields the socially efficient quantity of shrubs:

$$200 - 20Q = \$20,$$

or $Q = 9$ shrubs.
(2) If each person paid his or her marginal valuation of another shrub, which is

$$P = 10 - 9 = \$1,$$

the 20 employees together would pay $20 for each shrub.
(3) Since there is a free-rider problem, no shrubs are likely to be planted unless the boss exerts "moral suasion" and collects $9 from each employee to plant nine shrubs.

We conclude by pointing out that it may be advantageous for a firm to contribute to public goods in its market area. Doing things such as cleaning up a local park or giving money to public television creates goodwill toward the firm and as a result may create brand loyalty or increase the demand for the firm's product. Since public goods are nonrival and nonexclusionary, $1 spent on cleaning up a park or subsidizing public TV is $1 spent on everyone who finds a clean park or public TV appealing. This makes the provision of public goods an inexpensive way for a firm to "benefit" numerous consumers and thus may be a useful advertising strategy in some situations. Another advantage is that it may put the firm on more favorable terms with politicians, who have considerable latitude in affecting the environment in which the firm operates. Unfortunately, there is no easy way to explicitly calculate the optimal amount that a firm should voluntarily contribute to public goods. But ultimately, if the firm's goal is to maximize profits, the last dollar spent on contributions to public projects should bring in one additional dollar in revenue.

Incomplete Information

For markets to function efficiently, participants must have reasonably good information about things such as prices, quality, available technologies, and the risks associated with working in certain jobs or consuming certain products. When participants in the market have *incomplete information* about such things, the result will be inefficiencies in input usage and in firms' output.

Consider the consumption of cigarettes. If individuals did not know that cigarettes are hazardous, some people who currently do not smoke because of the known health risks would smoke out of ignorance of the dangers of smoking. The decision to smoke would be based on incomplete information about the dangers of smoking. For reasons such as these, government serves as a provider of information in many markets, dispensing information to consumers about the ingredients of certain foods, the dangers of certain products and drugs, and the like. Firms print some of this information on the labels of their products due to regulations imposed by government. Government even regulates the work environment by ensuring that workers are aware of the dangers of chemicals such as asbestos and the benefits of precautions such as wearing hard hats in construction jobs. In these instances, the regulations are carried out by the Occupational Safety and Health Administration (OSHA).

One of the more severe causes of market failure is asymmetric information, a situation where some market participants have better information than others. As we saw in Chapter 12, the presence of asymmetric information can lead buyers to refuse to purchase from sellers out of fear that the seller is willing to get rid of the product because it is worth less than they are willing to pay. In the extreme case, the market can collapse altogether. For this reason, several government policies are designed to alleviate the problems caused by asymmetric information. A few of the policies that affect managers are discussed next.

Rules Against Insider Trading

One example of a government regulation designed to alleviate market failures due to asymmetric information is the law against *insider trading* in the stock market. The purpose of the law is to ensure that asymmetric information (better information by insiders) does not destroy the market by inducing outsiders to stay out of it.

For example, suppose Jane CEO has just learned that her research staff has made a discovery that will revolutionize the industry. If Jane can keep the discovery quiet for a short time while she purchases some of her company's stock at its present price, she will make a bundle. When the announcement of the discovery is made public and the market price of the stock increases dramatically, she can resell the stock and make a large profit. Unfortunately, if potential investors believe CEOs and other insiders buy and sell stock based on inside information, they will stay out of the market. The only time the insiders will sell is when they know the price will fall, and they will buy only when the price will rise. There is no way for outsiders to earn money in a market dominated by insiders, and they will refuse to buy or sell stock. This reduces the marketability of assets in markets dominated by insiders, which decreases the welfare of all potential market participants.

To prevent insider trading from destroying the market for financial assets, the government has enacted rules against insider trading. The regulations on insider trading come from Section 16 of the *Securities and Exchange Act* (1934). They were amended in 1990 and took effect May 1, 1991.

Certification

Another policy government uses to disseminate information and reduce asymmetric information is the certification of skills and/or authenticity. The purpose of *certification* is to centralize the cost of gathering information. All licensing done by the government falls under certification; this includes all nonprofit organizations, such as charities. Certification can also be a set of minimum standards, such as those for schools and physicians. The purpose is to assure consumers that the products or services have been certified as meeting a certain set of minimum standards. Without a central authority to fulfill this information-gathering role, each individual would have to pay the cost of gaining knowledge about the quality of a product or service. This would lead to inefficiencies due to duplication of information-gathering efforts.

Schools are an example of a potential asymmetric information problem. Without the government certifying a school as satisfying some minimum

Inside Business 13–1

Rules on Insider Trading

The 1990 changes in the Securities and Exchange Act (1934) has had sweeping effects on compensation packages of officers of firms. The basic rationale for the changes was to minimize the interpretive inconsistency in Section 16 of the act, thus decreasing court costs because almost all decisions were made on a case-by-case basis.

"The new rules completely alter the focus of the short-swing trading rules as they apply to so-called derivative securities, such as stock options, certain stock appreciation rights (SARs), warrants, convertible securities, put options, and call options. Other changes narrow the definition of the term *officer,* modify the forms used by insiders for reporting their holdings and transactions in company securities, and impose new reporting requirements. Certain provisions remain unchanged."

Prior to the changes, officers of a firm were not allowed to take advantage of several employee stock plans. These plans allowed employees to receive benefits in the form of stock compensation once or twice a year. Previously, if an officer received compensation in this manner,

he or she was precluded from selling the stock while employed by the firm because of short-term swings. Since 1990, if the stockholders agree, this form of compensation can be used for officers as long as they hold the stock for at least six months. Formerly any profits earned from selling the stock reverted to the company. The negative side of the new rule is that options given to officers in this matter are no longer tax deferred.

The new legislation also has changed the definition of *officer.* Previously an officer was anyone with the title of vice president or higher. Now the regulations cover only employees who regularly perform "significant policymaking functions." The courts still must determine what constitutes a significant policymaking function.

Source: Brent M. Longnecker and Steven L. Cross, "Amendments to Section 16 Insider Trading Rule," *Journal of Compensation and Benefits* (July/August 1991), pp. 18–22. Reprinted with permission from *Journal of Compensation and Benefits* 7, no. 1, copyright © 1991 by Warren Gorham Lamont, a division of Research Institute of America, Inc., 210 South Street, Boston, MA 02111. 1-800-950-1211. All rights reserved.

standard, anyone could open a school. Parents who wanted to educate their children would choose a school based on appearance, cost, proximity to their home, advertising, and reputation. When the school first opens, it may look like a very good deal. But to save money, the school might choose to use unsafe equipment, hire undereducated teachers, and crowd classrooms far beyond a size that is conducive to learning. In the long run, the market would correct these problems; their reputation for poor quality would drive bad schools out of business. In the short run, however, parents who had enrolled their children would lose their investment in education, and the students would have wasted potentially valuable time.

Physician certification is another example of the short-run benefits of government certification. In the absence of physician certification, some less than reputable person could hang a sign stating "Medical Service Here." If improperly trained, this person might prescribe a medicine that could make a patient worse, cause a drug addiction, or even lead to death. In the presence of a government-enforced set of standards, however, this short-run scenario is much less likely.

Truth in Lending

A set of legislation over the years has made gathering information for borrowing purposes less difficult. Confusion caused by the *Truth in Lending Act* (1969) led Congress to pass the *Truth in Lending Simplification Act (TLSA)* in 1980. TLSA is enforced by the Federal Reserve Board (FRB). In 1980, the FRB passed *Regulation Z* to provide guidelines for enforcement; it amended Regulation Z in 1982.

Regulation Z and TLSA require that all creditors comply with the act. A creditor is defined as anyone who loans money subject to a finance charge, where the money is to be paid back in four or more installments. A creditor must also be the person to whom the original obligation is payable. There are some exemptions regarding the types of loans covered under TLSA, the most notable being business, agricultural, and commercial loans.

TLSA requires the following information to be disclosed to the debtor in writing before consummation of the loan: (1) the creditor's identity, (2) the amount being financed, (3) itemization of the amount financed, (4) itemization of all finance charges, (5) the annual interest rate charged, (6) any variable rates available for the specific loan, (7) the repayment schedule, (8) the total amount of all payments, (9) any demand feature, (10) the total purchase price, including any down payment, (11) any rebates or prepayment penalties, (12) the amount of any late payments and the date on which a payment becomes late, (13) all security tied to the loan, (14) any insurance tied to the loan, (15) all filing fees, (16) any policies allowing a loan to be assumed by another party, and (17) any required deposit on the loan. The purpose of this law is to ensure that all debtors are given an opportunity to understand all aspects of borrowing money from a specific creditor, thus creating more symmetric information between borrowers and lenders.

The Truth in Lending Act affects both the supply of and the demand for credit. Potential borrowers now have more complete information about what a loan involves. This increased knowledge reduces the risk involved in repayment for the borrower. The reduced risk shifts the demand curve for loans to the right. The suppliers of loans (creditors) are affected mainly by the increased cost of complying with the government regulations (the long list presented above). This shifts the creditors' supply curve to the left. Since the demand curve for loans shifts to the right and the supply curve shifts to the left, the effect of this law is to increase the price of loans (the interest rate).

Truth in Advertising

Often firms have better information about their products than do consumers. This advantage may give firms an incentive to make false claims about the merits of their products to capitalize on consumers' lack of information.

In some instances, such practices can lead consumers to switch from one firm's product to a competitor's product. In extreme cases, the asymmetric information can induce consumers to ignore advertising messages altogether, out of fear that the messages are false. Government often can alleviate these market failures by regulating the advertising practices of firms.

Advertising regulation usually is enforced by civil suits. Under Section 43 of the *Lanham Act,* false and misleading advertising is prohibited. Technically the FTC can bring suit against any false advertising using the Lanham Act, although most cases are filed in civil court by those harmed by deceptive advertising rather than by the FTC.

The Lanham Act, in concert with the Clayton Act, allows someone who is harmed by false or misleading advertising to stop the deceptive practice and receive treble damages. If a firm finds that a competitor's deceptive advertising reduces the demand for its product, it may sue under the Lanham Act. The plaintiff must first prove that the advertisement is either false or misleads consumers. The plaintiff must also prove that the misleading or false advertising harmed it.

In Figure 13–9(a), a false advertisement increases the demand for the advertiser's product from D_1 to D_2. The cost of placing the advertisement increases the average total cost of production from AC_1 to AC_2 but leaves the marginal cost function unchanged. The false advertisement is advantageous only if the price increase, along with the change in quantity sold, increases total revenues more than costs. The more a false advertisement can shift a demand curve, the stronger is the incentive to place a false advertisement.

FIGURE 13–9

The impact of false advertisements

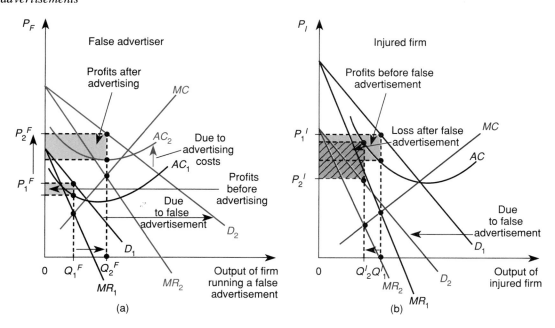

(a)

(b)

Some false advertisements have a negative impact on other firms in the market, particularly advertisements that falsely claim that one firm's product is better than another firm's. Figure 13–9(b) shows what happens when a false advertisement draws customers away from a rival firm. As a result of the false advertising, the demand curve shifts to the left from D_1 to D_2, resulting in lower profits for the rival. The damages caused by the false advertisement are the difference between the profits before and after the false advertisement.

When government regulates advertising, the injured party can seek legal action and possibly receive treble damages for the harm caused by the rival's false advertisement. In particular, if the injured party can prove that the advertising is either strictly false or misleads consumers through innuendo, it can bring civil suit under the Lanham Act. If the suit is successful, the defendant usually must cease running the advertisement, recall any units of the product that have the false or misleading claim on their label, and pay three times the damages caused by the advertisement to the plaintiff.

Enforcing Contracts

Another way government solves the problems of asymmetric information is through *contract enforcement.* In Chapters 6 and 10, we learned that contracts are written to keep the parties from behaving opportunistically in the final period of a game. For example, suppose your boss "promised" you payment for labor services at the end of the month. After you have worked for a month, your boss refuses to pay you—in effect gaining a month's worth of your labor for free. In Chapters 6 and 10 we saw that these types of problems do not arise when reputation is important or when there is the potential for repeated interaction among the parties. In these instances, the one-time gain to behaving opportunistically will be more than offset by future losses.

In short-term relationships, however, one or more parties may take advantage of the "end period" by behaving opportunistically. If you knew your boss would not pay you at the end of the month, you would refuse to work. The problem, however, is that you do not know what your boss will do at the end of the month—only she does. In effect, you are uncertain whether your boss is "honest" (will keep a promise) or dishonest (will break a promise). This asymmetric information can destroy the ability of individuals to use contracts to solve the problem of opportunism; even if a contract is written, a boss may not honor it. Because of this, you may refuse to work for your boss even is she is honest, because you do not *know* whether she is honest.

One solution to this problem is for government to enforce contracts. By enforcing contracts, government effectively solves the "end-of-period" problem by requiring dishonest people to honor the terms of contracts. In this case, even if you do not know whether your boss is honest, you will be

---

False Advertisements

Perhaps the movie *Crazy People* had the right idea when it showed truthful advertising as a boon to the business. Lawsuits in the late 1980s and early 1990s showed that firms must tell the truth in their advertising or be sued. In 1990 alone, more than a dozen court decisions forced firms to change advertisements due to untruthful information.

Coors was sued because it claimed the water used in its product came from a mountain spring. Quaker Oats lost a suit over its claim that eating its cereal would reduce the risk of heart attacks. The maker of Mazola was required to remove its statement that eating its margarine would reduce one's cholesterol level. Sara Lee was forced to remove the word *light* from its whipped desserts.

Sterling Drug was fined over $100,000 for being unable to substantiate its claims about the performance of Midol. RJ Reynolds had to cease claiming that tobacco products aren't as hazardous as people think.

How will this trend change advertising? Ron Jackson, the CEO of the Jackson/Ridey & Company Advertising Agency of Cincinnati, thinks it will move advertising toward no words at all. An example is Nike's "Just Do It" commercials, which use almost no other words. Perhaps the company has learned that "if you can't tell the truth, don't say anything at all."

Source: Howard Schlossberg, "The Simple Truth: Ads Will Have to Be Truthful," *Marketing News* 24 (December 24, 1990), p. 6.

---

willing to work under contract. If she turns out to be dishonest, the government will force her to pay you. Thus, government enforcement of contracts can solve market failures caused by the end-of-period problem.

Rent Seeking

The preceding analysis shows how government policies can improve the allocation of resources in the economy by alleviating the problems associated with market power, externalities, public goods, and incomplete information. It is important to note, however, that government policies generally benefit some parties at the expense of others. For this reason, lobbyists spend considerable sums in attempts to influence government policies. This process is known as *rent seeking*.

To illustrate rent seeking and its consequences, suppose a politician has the power to regulate the monopoly in Figure 13–10. The monopoly currently charges a price of P^M, produces Q^M units of output, and earns profits described by the shaded region A. At the monopoly price and output, consumer surplus is given by triangle C.

FIGURE 13–10

The incentives to engage in rent-seeking activities

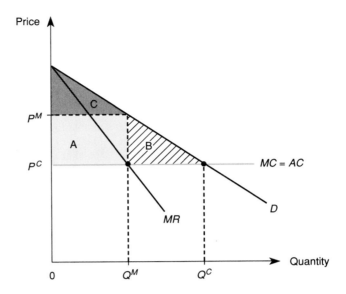

If consumers could persuade the politician to regulate the monopolist's price at the competitive level (P^C), the result would be an output of Q^C. If this happened, the monopoly would lose all of its profits (rectangle A). Consumers, on the other hand, would end up with total consumer surplus of regions A, B, and C.

Since the monopolist stands to lose rectangle A if the regulation is imposed, it has an incentive to lobby very hard to prevent the regulation from being imposed. In fact, the monopolist is willing to spend up to the amount A to avoid the regulation. These expenditures may be in the form of legal activities, such as campaign contributions or wining and dining the politician, or illegal activities such as bribes.

Notice that the consumers in Figure 13–10 also would be willing to spend money to persuade the politician to regulate the monopoly. In fact, as a group they would be willing to spend up to A + B to impose the competitive solution, since this is the additional consumer surplus enjoyed when the price is P^C. Of course, each individual consumer stands to gain much less than the group (regulation is a public good in that it benefits all consumers). Consequently, each consumer has an incentive to "free ride," and in the end the amount the consumers spend as a group will be very low. The monopolist, on the other hand, is a single entity. Avoiding regulation is not a public good to the monopolist; the monopolist will receive private gains if it can avoid the legislation. As a result, the monopolist generally will spend much more on lobbying activities than the consumers and thus will often avoid legislation by engaging in rent-seeking activities.

DEMONSTRATION PROBLEM 13–5

You are the manager of a monopoly that faces an inverse demand curve of $P = 10 - Q$ and has a cost function of $C(Q) = 2Q$. The government is considering legislation that would regulate your price at the competitive level. What is the maximum amount you would be willing to spend on legal lobbying activities designed to stop the regulation?

Answer

If the regulation passes, your firm's price will be regulated at marginal cost (\$2) and the firm will earn zero profits. If not, the firm can continue to produce the monopoly output and charge the monopoly price. The monopoly output is determined by the point where $MR = MC$:

$$10 - 2Q = 2.$$

Solving for Q yields the monopoly output of $Q^M = 4$ units. The monopoly price is obtained by inserting this quantity into the demand function to obtain

$$P^M = 10 - (4) = 6.$$

Thus, your firm stands to lose monopoly profits of $P^M Q^M - C(Q^M) = \$16$ if the regulation is imposed. The most you would be willing to spend on legal lobbying activities thus is \$16.

Government Policy and International Markets

Sometimes rent seeking manifests itself in the form of government involvement in international markets. Such policies usually take the form of tariffs or quotas that are designed to benefit specific firms and workers at the expense of others. In this section, we will examine how government tariff and quota policies affect managerial decisions.

Quotas

Quotas in Perfectly Competitive Markets

The purpose of a *quota* is to limit the number of units of a product that foreign competitors can bring into the country. For example, a quota on Japanese automobile imports limits the number of cars Japanese automakers can sell in the United States. This reduces competition in the domestic automobile market, which results in higher car prices, higher profits for domestic firms, and lower consumer surplus for domestic consumers. Domestic

FIGURE 13–11

*The impact of
a foreign import
quota on the
domestic market*

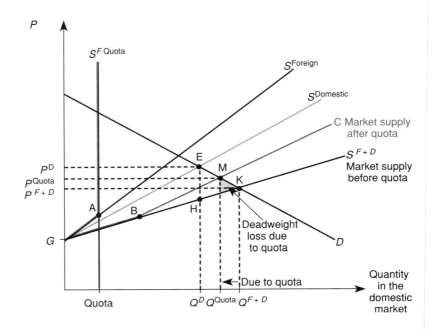

producers thus benefit at the expense of domestic consumers and foreign producers.

To see why these results occur, consider Figure 13–11, which shows the domestic market for a product. Before the imposition of a quota, the domestic demand curve is D, the supply curve for foreign producers is $S^{Foreign}$, the supply curve for domestic producers is $S^{Domestic}$, and the market supply curve—the horizontal summation of the foreign and domestic supply curves—is S^{F+D}. Equilibrium in the absence of a quota is at point K, where the equilibrium price is P^{F+D} and the equilibrium quantity is Q^{F+D}.

Now suppose a quota is imposed on foreign producers that restricts them from selling more than the quota in the domestic market. Under the quota, foreign supply is $GAS^{F\,Quota}$, while the supply by domestic firms remains at $S^{Domestic}$. Thus, market supply in the domestic market after the quota is GBC, resulting in an equilibrium at point M. The quota increases the price received by domestic producers to P^{Quota}, and domestic firms now earn higher profits. The shaded triangle in Figure 13–11 represents the deadweight loss due to the quota. Total welfare declines as a result of the quota even though domestic producers earn higher profits. The reason for the decline in total welfare is that domestic consumers and foreign producers are harmed more than domestic producers gain from the quota. Domestic producers therefore have a strong incentive to lobby for quotas on foreign imports into their market.

DEMONSTRATION PROBLEM 13–6

Suppose domestic producers in Figure 13–11 successfully persuaded politicians to completely ban sales by foreign manufacturers in the domestic market. What would be the resulting price and deadweight loss?

Answer

In the absence of foreign supply, the supply curve in the domestic market in Figure 13–11 is $S^{Domestic}$ and equilibrium is at point E. The resulting price is P^D. The deadweight loss of the ban on foreign producers is given by the triangle HEK.

DEMONSTRATION PROBLEM 13–7

Suppose the supply of a good by domestic firms is $Q^{SD} = 10 + 2P$ and the supply by foreign firms is $Q^{SE} = 10 + P$. The domestic demand for the product is given by $Q^d = 30 - P$.
(1) In the absence of a quota, what is the total supply of the good?
(2) What are the equilibrium price and quantity of the good?
(3) Suppose a quota of 10 units is imposed. What is the total supply of the product?
(4) Determine the equilibrium price in the domestic market under the quota of 10 units.

Answer

(1) The total supply is the sum of foreign and domestic supply, which is

$$Q^T = Q^{SD} + Q^{SF} = (10 + 2P) + (10 + P) = 20 + 3P.$$

(2) Equilibrium is determined by equating total demand and supply:

$$30 - P = 20 + 3P$$

Solving for P yields the equilibrium price of $P = \$2.50$. Given this price, domestic firms produce

$$Q^{SD} = 10 + 2(2.5) = 15 \text{ units}$$

and foreign firms produce

$$Q^{SF} = 10 + 2.5 = 12.5 \text{ units,}$$

for a total equilibrium output of $Q^T = 27.5$ units.
(3) With a quota of 10 units, foreign firms will sell only 10 units in the domestic market. Thus, total supply is

$$Q^T = Q^{SD} + Q^{SF} = (10 + 2P) + 10 = 20 + 2P.$$

(4) Equilibrium is determined by equating total demand and supply:

$$30 - P = 20 + 2P.$$

Solving for P yields the equilibrium price of $P = \$3.33$. The quota increases the price of the good in the domestic market due to the reduction in foreign competition.

Quotas When Firms Have Market Power

The analysis of quotas is similar when domestic firms have market power. To see this, suppose the demand for a firm's product before the imposition of a quota is given by D^1 in Figure 13–12 so that its marginal revenue curve (MR^1) lies below the demand curve. In the absence of a quota, the firm produces q^1 units of output and charges a price of P^1.

A quota on foreign imports limits available substitutes for a domestic firm's product and hence shifts the demand for the domestic firm's product to the right to D^2. The firm in this case increases price to P^2, and the quantity sold increases to q^2. Notice that domestic consumers now pay a higher price for the domestic firm's product; profits of the domestic firm therefore rise.

Tariffs

Tariffs, like quotas, are designed to limit foreign competition in the domestic market to benefit domestic producers. The benefits to domestic producers accrue at the expense of domestic consumers and foreign producers.

We will address two types of tariffs: lump-sum tariffs and excise or per-unit tariffs. A *lump-sum tariff* is a fixed fee that foreign firms must pay the

FIGURE 13–12

The impact of a foreign import quota on a domestic firm that enjoys market power

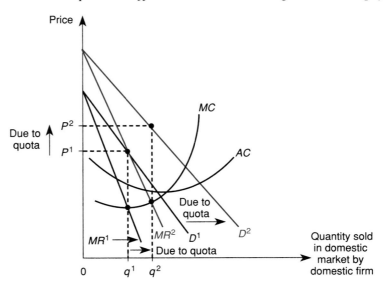

domestic government to be able to sell in the domestic market. In contrast, a *per-unit* or *excise tariff* requires the importing firms to pay the domestic government a fee on each unit they bring into the country.

Lump-Sum Tariffs

Figure 13–13 shows the marginal and average cost curves for an individual foreign firm before and after the imposition of a lump-sum tariff. The first thing to notice about the lump-sum tariff is that it does not affect the marginal cost curve. This is because the importer must pay the same amount of tariff regardless of how much of the product it brings into the country. Since the lump-sum tariff raises average costs from AC^1 to AC^2, an importer is unwilling to pay the tariff to enter the domestic market unless the price in the domestic market is at least P^2.

Figure 13–14 shows the effect of a lump-sum tariff on the market. Before the tariff is imposed, the supply curve for foreign competitors is ES^F, that for domestic producers is ES^D, and the market supply curve—the summation of domestic and foreign supply—is ES^{D+F}. After the lump-sum tariff is imposed, the foreign supply curve becomes AS^F, because importers will not pay the lump-sum tariff to enter the domestic market unless the price is above P^2. Thus, the market supply curve in the presence of a lump-sum tariff is given by $EBCS^{D+F}$. The overall effect of this policy is to remove foreign competitors from the domestic market if the demand curve crosses the domestic supply curve at a price below P^2. A lump-sum tariff increases

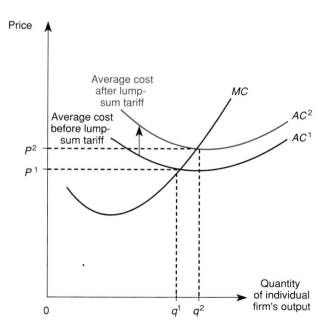

FIGURE 13–13

Impact of a lump-sum tariff on a firm

FIGURE 13–14

Impact of a lump-sum tariff on market supply

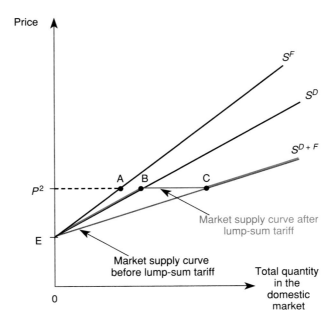

the profits of domestic producers if demand is low but has no effect on their profits if demand is high.

Excise Tariffs

If an excise tariff is imposed on foreign producers instead of a lump-sum tariff, domestic producers benefit at all levels of demand. To see this, consider Figure 13–15, which shows the effect of an excise tariff. S^F is the supply curve for the foreign producers before the tariff, S^D is the supply curve for the domestic producers, and ABS^{D+F} is the market supply curve before the tariff. Equilibrium in the absence of a tariff is at point H.

When a tariff of T is imposed on each unit of the product, the marginal cost curve for foreign firms shifts up by the amount of the tariff, which in turn decreases the supply of all foreign firms to S^{F+T} in Figure 13–15. The market supply under a per-unit tariff is now ACS^{D+F+T}, and the resulting equilibrium is at point E. The tariff raises the price domestic consumers must pay for the product, which raises the profits of domestic firms at the expense of domestic consumers and foreign producers.

Answering the Headline

Why did the airlines agree to settle their price-fixing case rather than fight the case in court? For one thing the Sherman Act makes price-fixing a felony offense, with penalties that can include both fines and imprisonment, at

FIGURE 13–15

Impact of an excise tariff on market supply

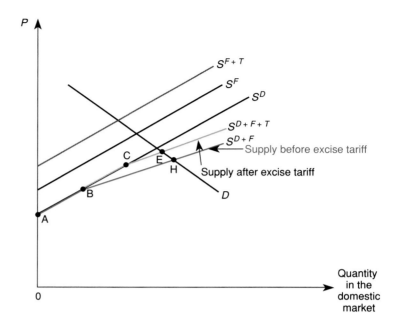

Inside Business 13–3

Motorcycle Tariffs

Harley-Davidson was the king of the road when it came to big motorcycles. From its beginnings in 1907, Harley-Davidson made the largest, fastest bike in the world. Its success came from a "diehard" group of bikers who knew that a Harley was indestructible. However, in the early 1960s Harley got lax; quality started to slide, and Japanese imports started making inroads into its market. By 1979, Harley had only 5 percent of the overall motorcycle market and was down to 21 percent of the market for large bikes. By 1983, its share of the market had slipped to 9 percent.

The Japanese had come to compete in the market. Harley still had only two engine blocks, and they were extremely heavy. On top of that, quality had slipped to the point where once devoted fans of Harley-Davidson said they would never buy another Harley. Instead, customers

were going to Japanese makers of large bikes like Kawasaki, Honda, Yamaha, and Suzuki. Harley's competition had 14 different models to chose from; also, they were lighter, faster, and higher in quality.

In 1981 Vaughn Beals, a vice president of Harley, organized a leveraged buyout and purchased Harley-Davidson. The first thing Beals noticed was that labor was extremely lax; the second was that the manufacturing equipment was old and worn-out. So Beals launched a pep-squad-style management team and put quality control in the hands of line workers. Then he borrowed and invested $160 million in retooling and redesigning the Harley.

The boldest thing Beals did was ask the International Trade Commission for an excise tariff of

Inside Business 13–3 continued

49.4 percent on Japanese imports of bikes with 700cc and larger engines. Despite President Reagan's then recent pledge to open up markets and do away with tariffs and quotas, the ITC and the president got behind Harley's proposal. What was it about the proposal that brought the Reagan administration around?

Beals explained to the ITC that Harley's problem was a short-term one and the firm would need the tariffs for only five years to become competitive again. He proposed that the tariff decline from 49.4 percent in 1983 to 29.4 percent in 1988 and then be removed completely. This was a chance for American business to show it could be competitive in world markets when times were getting tough. So the Reagan administration backed the plan completely.

Did the tariff work? Japanese sales of motorcycles larger than 750cc dropped from 88,000 in the first half of 1983 to under 21,000 in the first half of 1984. Of course, this had the Japanese producers calling foul, but it gave Harley some time to reorganize. Sales of Harley bikes rose, and so did their prices. But the tariffs alone would not save Harley-Davidson. With retooling in progress, along with 12 new models and quality control that was even tighter than that of the Japanese manufacturers, Harley-Davidson was able to rebound.

In an effort to break the tariffs, the Japanese responded by producing a 699cc machine that was recarburetted so that it performed better than their earlier 750cc models. They also moved a large number of their plants to the United States to avoid the tariff. But this plan took a couple of years to implement and proved to be too little too late. By 1987 Harley was back in the black. Its market share had increased to 46.5 percent of the large-bike market in the United States and was gaining ground in Europe and Japan.

The success of the temporary reprieve and reorganization was so swift that Harley asked for the tariff to be removed in 1987. The Reagan administration obliged. At the beginning of 1992, Harley-Davidson couldn't produce enough motorcycles to keep up with demand. However, Vaughn Beals knows that for Harley to stay on top, quality will have to stay high, the design department will have to produce a large selection of new models, and Harley will have to continue competing with Japanese manufacturers.

Sources: Michael Kolbenschlag, "Harley-Davidson Takes Lessons from Arch-Rivals' Handbook," *International Management* (February 1985), pp. 46–48; Vineeta Anand, "Japanese Management Style Puts Harley-Davidson on the Road Again," *Global Trade Executive* (May 1986), pp. 66–68; Peter C. Reid, *Well Made in America: Lessons from Harley-Davidson on Being the Best* (New York: McGraw-Hill, 1990).

---

the discretion of the court. Second, the very thing that allowed the airlines to successfully collude in the first place—the computer records—contained evidence that increased the Justice Department's prospects for winning the case in court. This is because the high-tech form of collusion practiced by the airlines is easier to document in court than the more traditional case that involves the managers of several firms fixing prices verbally behind closed doors. Finally, while the settlement did require the airlines to pay damages to passengers who were harmed by price-fixing, most of the damages were actually paid in the form of vouchers rather than in cash. These vouchers permit some of the passengers who were harmed to purchase a specific number of future tickets at a discount of about 10 percent. Thus, the settlement actually permits the airlines to engage in a form of price discrimination—a practice that might actually enhance their overall revenues and profits.

Summary

In this chapter, we focused on government's activity in the market to correct market failures caused by market power, externalities, public goods, and incomplete information. The government's ability to regulate markets gives market participants an incentive to engage in rent-seeking activities, such as lobbying, to affect public policy. These activities may extend to international markets, where government imposes tariffs or quotas on foreign imports to increase the profits of special interests.

In the United States, the government influences markets through devices such as antitrust legislation, price regulation, insider-trading restrictions, and truth-in-advertising/truth-in-lending regulations, as well as policies designed to alleviate market failure due to externalities or public-goods problems. The rules that affect the decisions of future managers are spelled out in documents such as the Sherman Antitrust Act, the Clayton Act, the Robinson Patman Act, the Cellar-Kefauver Act, the Lanham Act, the Securities and Exchange Act, Regulation Z, and the Clean Air Act.

Key Terms and Concepts

Antitrust Division of the
  Department of Justice
  (DOJ)
antitrust policy
Cellar-Kefauver Act (1950)
Clayton Act (1914)
Clean Air Act (1990)
deadweight loss
Federal Trade Commission
  (FTC)
Herfindahl-Hirshman index
  (HHI)
incomplete information
insider trading
Lanham Act
lump-sum tariffs
market power
Merger Guidelines
  (1984, 1992)

negative externalities
nonrival consumption
per-unit (excise) tariffs
property rights
public goods
quotas
Regulation Z
rent seeking
Robinson Patman Act (1936)
rule of reason
Securities and Exchange Act
  (1934)
Sherman Antitrust Act
  (1890)
social welfare
Truth in Advertising
Truth in Lending Act (1969)
Truth in Lending Simplification Act
  (1980)

Problems

1. In 1992 the Mobil Oil Corporation acquired the rights to increase their pollution by 900 pounds of sulfur-dioxide per day at their Torrance, California refinery. These rights were purchased from South Gate, California, at a price of $3 million after the latter acquired them from General Motors. As a result of this change, Mobil increased its output of noxious vapors in Torrance, California by 900 pounds per day. Do you think the environment was harmed as a result of the sale of these pollution rights? Explain.

2. In 1992 Japan reduced its exports of automobiles to the United States by 28 percent. If you were the manager of a Buick dealership, how would this change affect your pricing strategy? Explain.

3. Suppose a firm has 10 employees, all of whom desire a more pleasant work environment. Accordingly, they are considering removing litter from the grounds of the plant. Each employee has an inverse demand for "clean grounds" of $P = 100 - 2Q$, where Q is the number of empty beer cans removed from the premises. The marginal cost of removing beer cans is $1 per can.
   a. What is the socially efficient quantity of cans to remove?
   b. How much would each person have to pay per can to remove the socially efficient quantity?

4. Three years ago the CEO of a large firm instituted a plan that encourages division managers to share information obtained about the demographic characteristics of those who purchase the firm's final product. Since the plan was implemented, however, the CEO has noticed that less information is available than ever. Why do you think the CEO's plan backfired?

5. XYZ Labs—the sole producer of Diamatine—charges a price for its drug that is significantly above the firm's marginal cost. It takes XYZ Labs 10 years of research and development before products like Diamatine are finally sold in the market. Do you think government regulators would be wise to impose price ceilings on Diamatine in order to bring the price in line with marginal cost? Explain.

6. You are the manager of a monopoly that faces an inverse demand curve

$$P = 100 - 10Q,$$

and has constant average and marginal costs of $20 per unit. The government is considering legislation that would regulate your firm's price at $20 per unit. What is the maximum amount your firm should be willing to spend to lobby against the regulation?

7. Acme Water is a privately owned company that is the sole supplier of water to a rural town in Pennsylvania. The owner of the firm has

provided the manager of the company an incentive to maximize the firm's profits, and the manager is currently selling 100,000 gallons of water per week at a price of $.05 per gallon. The marginal cost of water is zero, but the firm's average cost of this level of output is $.01 per gallon.

   a. Determine Acme Water's profits.

   b. Now suppose the local government imposes a price ceiling on water at a price of $.01 per gallon. Will the firm earn economic profits of zero as a result of this price ceiling? Explain.

   c. Does the price ceiling of $.01 per gallon result in a shortage of water in Acme's service area?

8. The gadget industry is comprised of ten firms, each with a 10 percent market share. What is the Herfindahl-Hirshman index for the industry? Based on the U.S. Department of Justice Merger Guidelines described in the text, do you think the Justice Department would be likely to block a merger between two of the firms?

9. We learned in this chapter that there are laws against price discrimination. Yet, many firms openly engage in such practices. For instance, most hotel chains offer discounts to senior citizens that translate into prices that are about 10 percent lower than prices charged to other hotel guests. Why are such firms allowed to engage in such practices?

10. The manager of a paper mill is preparing for her most important test yet. On Tuesday morning, she must testify before a Senate Committee to "justify" the firm's high price. One Senator is particularly angry with the firm because its price is twice the firm's marginal cost. On Tuesday afternoon, the manager is scheduled to appear before the House Subcommittee on the Environment to explain why the firm should not be slapped with a per-unit tax on the firm's output to compensate for the pollution it discharges into a major river. What do you think will be the manager's game plan?

11. We learned in the text that Section 16(a) of the Security Exchange Act of 1934, as amended in 1990, requires that the officers, directors, and principal shareholders of companies disclose the extent of their ownership of equity securities of the company and any changes in the ownership. Section 16(b) permits companies to recover trading profits realized by such people arising from short-swing transactions in company securities. Do you think that, as a result of these laws, the government will be forced to spend more money on its auditing and enforcement efforts? Explain.

12. The manager of Roy's Video noticed a newspaper advertisement by a rival store that erroneously claimed, "We are the only firm in town that does not sell pornographic videos." He initially dismissed the deceptive advertisement but decided to reconsider his course of action

when the rival refused to stop running the advertisement. In the interim numerous churches and other organizations boycotted Roy's Video, resulting in an estimated loss of $25,000. Do you think it would be advisable for Roy to seek legal counsel? Explain.

13. You are the CEO of a firm with an industry HHI equal to 1,000. Your firm presently controls 20 percent of the market. The board of trustees wants you to consider merging with a firm that controls 10 percent of the market. Should you be concerned about antitrust proceedings? Explain.

14. Suppose the external marginal cost of pollution is

$$MC_{External} = 5Q$$

and the internal marginal cost is

$$MC_{Internal} = 10Q.$$

Further, assume the inverse demand for the product, Q, is given by

$$P = 90 - Q.$$

a. What is the socially efficient level of output?
b. How much output would a competitive industry produce?
c. How much output would a monopoly produce?
d. Discuss three ways government can induce firms to produce the socially efficient level of output.

15. Suppose the supply of wine by domestic firms is

$$Q^{SD} = 5 + P$$

and the supply of wine by foreign firms is

$$Q^{SF} = 5 + P.$$

The domestic demand for wine is given by

$$Q^d = 40 - P.$$

a. In the absence of a quota, what is the total supply of wine?
b. What are the equilibrium price and quantity of wine?
c. Suppose a quota of 5 units is imposed. What is the total supply of wine?
d. Determine the equilibrium price and quantity of wine in the domestic market under the quota of 5 units.
e. What is the loss in consumer surplus caused by the quota?

Selected Readings

Economides, Nicholas and White, Lawrence J., "Networks and Compatibility: Implications for Antitrust." *European Economic Review* 38(34), April 1994, pp. 651–62.

Elzinga, Kenneth and Breit, William, *The Antitrust Penalties A Study in Law and Economics.* New Haven: Yale University Press, 1976.

Formby, John P., Keeler, James P., and Thistle, Paul D., "X efficiency, Rent Seeking and Social Costs." *Public Choice* 57(2), May 1988, pp. 115–26.

Gradstein, Mark, Nitzan, Shmuel, and Slutsky, Steven, "Private Provision of Public Goods under Price Uncertainty." *Social Choice and Welfare* 10(4), 1993, pp. 371–82.

Inman, Robert P., "New Research in Local Public Finance: Introduction." *Regional Science and Urban Economics* 19(3), August 1989, pp. 347–52.

McCall, Charles W., "Rule of Reason versus Mechanical Tests in the Adjudication of Price Predation." *Review of Industrial Organization* 3(3), Spring 1988, pp. 15–44.

Rivlin, A. M., "Distinguished Lecture on Economics in Government: Strengthening the Economy by Rethinking the Role of Federal and State Governments." *Journal of Economic Perspectives* 5(2), Spring 1991, pp. 3–14.

Sreiner, R. L. "Intrabrand Competition—Stepchild of Antitrust." *Antitrust Bulletin,* 36(1), Spring 1991, pp. 155–200.

Answers to Selected End-of-Chapter Problems

Chapter 1

3. *a.* Option A has the highest first-year profits but the lowest second- and third-year profits. Option B earns less in the first year than A but more in years 2 and 3. Option C has the lowest first-year profits, but the greatest profits in years 2 and 3. Option A might represent a low current advertising budget; it doesn't cost much today (and thus current profits are relatively high). However, a low current advertising budget does not increase future profits as much as a moderate (option B) or intensive (option C) level of current advertising budget.

   b. Option A.

4. *a.* 200,000.

   b. 235,000.

   c. Revenues of $200,000.01 are needed to earn positive accounting profits.

6. Initially the number of people who major in HTCC will increase as they attempt to learn the skills required to earn the high salaries in the field. After 10 years, it is likely that enough people will have entered the field to decrease the salaries to the opportunity cost of entering this field of study.

8. *a.* $Q = 150$.

   b. $600.

   c. $MC = 600$.

   d. $224,900.

   e. Profits.

10. The present value of the cost of paying your dues annually is the present value of $125.00 today, $112.50 next year, and $101.25 the year after, which amounts to about $324.00. Since a three-year membership costs $300, you would save $24 by purchasing a three-year membership.

12. *a.* $Q = 25$.
    b. $Q = 0$.
    c. $Q = 24.5$.

Chapter 2

2. Originally P_1^E and Q_1^E were the equilibrium quantity and price of caviar in Figure A–1(a). The original equilibrium price and quantity of champagne were P_1^C and Q_1^C in Figure A–1(b). The increased pollution shifted the supply of caviar to the left from S to S^1 in Figure A–1(a), which caused the price to rise to P_2^E and the equilibrium quantity to decrease to Q_2^E. The increase in the price of caviar decreases demand for champagne (a complement), which is shown by the shift from

FIGURE A–1

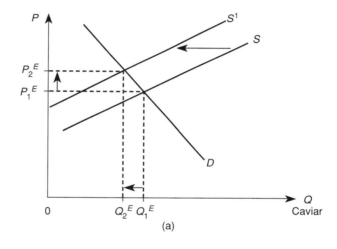

(a)

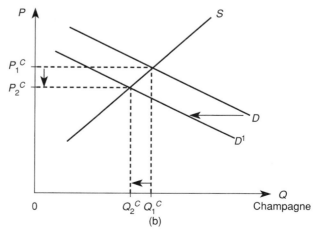

(b)

D to D^1 in Figure A–1(b). This decreases the equilibrium price of champagne to P_2^C and decreases the equilibrium quantity to Q_2^C.

5. *a.* The equilibrium price of oranges increases and the equilibrium quantity of oranges exchanged decreases due to the decrease in the supply of oranges.

    b. The equilibrium price of apples increases and the equilibrium quantity of apples exchanged increases due to an increase in demand for apples. The increased demand for apples is caused by the increase in the price of oranges (a substitute).

7. The supply curve shifts upward by $1, which results in a decreased equilibrium quantity and higher price of shoes. However, the price of shoes rises by less than $1.

16. The legislature is incorrect.

18. *a.* Z is a substitute for X; Y is a complement of X.

    b. Inferior.

    c. 3,860 units.

    d. The demand curve is labeled D in Figure A–2.

    e. It shifts to the right by 500 units as shown in the shift from D to D^1 in Figure A–2.

19. *b.* $P_X = 55 + (\frac{1}{4})Q_x^s.$

Chapter 3

3. *a.* 2.

    b. −4.

5. Disagree. Demand is inelastic and downward sloping.

FIGURE A–2

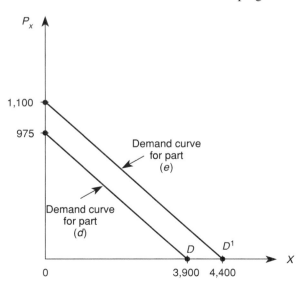

6. The quantity demanded of textbooks will decrease by 35 percent.

9. To expect a 37.5 percent decline in business.

12. Own price elasticity equals -1. The income elasticity equals 1.

14. The quantity sold will decrease by 5.6 percent while the price will increase by 8 percent. Therefore, total revenues will increase.

17. Since Art Deco furniture is an inferior good, it should reduce its orders of PVC pipe.

18. *a.* A 15 percent increase in demand for sunscreen.
    b. A 30 percent increase in the demand for sunscreen.
    c. Beach umbrellas.

Chapter 4

5. *a.* No; they are not transitive.

7. *a.* In Figure A–3, a representative consumer is at equilibrium at point A, where income is M_1, which results in S_1 units of shelter and F_1 units of food being consumed. If income declined to M_2, more than S_1 units of shelter would be consumed, which means the new equilibrium would be somewhere on segment BC of the new budget line. But everywhere along segment BC, the consumption of food is lower—say, at F_2. Therefore, food must be a normal good if shelter is an inferior good.

10. As shown in Figure A–4, the market rate of substitution is $-\frac{1}{2}$.

FIGURE A–3

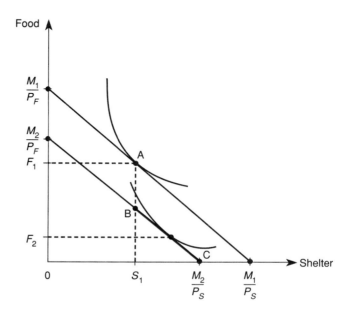

FIGURE A–4

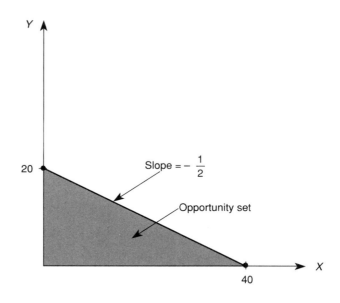

11. *a.* When both goods are normal, the consumption of both goods will decline. When one good is inferior, consumption of the inferior good will increase and consumption of the normal good will decrease.

    b. When both goods are normal, consumption of both will increase. When one good is inferior, consumption of the normal good will increase and consumption of the inferior good will decrease.

    c. Nothing will happen to the consumption of either good.

14. No. It means that a Saturn *and* $4,000 in additional goods are preferred to a Honda.

20. *a.* Earnings = $24 × Hours worked.

21. No.

Chapter 5

3. *c.* $K = 0, L = 5$.

7. *a.* They are both flat and equal to each other.

10. *a.* L is fixed, K is variable.

    f. Between 0 and 3 units of K.

13. Because Japanese wage rates are higher than those of American workers, the ratio of input prices between labor and capital is higher than that in the United States. Therefore, it is more cost effective to be more capital intensive in Japan than in the United States.

18. *a.* $34,000 is paid the first month regardless of how much output is produced.
    b. $34,000; to get the deposit back, $144,000 in rent must be paid.

Chapter 6

1. *a.* Vertical integration.
   b. Contract.
   c. Spot exchange.
   d. Spot exchange or contract.
5. By contract; this eliminates opportunism and allows for specialization in production.
7. *a.* 8 hours.
   b. Yes.
8. No. The manager should reduce shirking to the point where the marginal benefit from reducing shirking equals the marginal cost of reducing shirking.

Chapter 7

3. Market structure refers to factors such as firm size, the number of firms, concentration, number of close substitutes, technology, and potential for entry.
5. No. Once the monopoly has chosen the price, the customers will only buy a level of output stipulated by the demand curve. Consumers will not buy whatever the monopoly puts to the market once the price is fixed.
7. No. As industries mature and demand conditions change, industry structures often change.
8. Four-firm concentration ratio $= 0.8$.
10. The HHI ignores the geographical market and foreign competition. If these resulting biases are deemed significant, the merger might be allowed. It might also be allowed if one of the firms is in financial trouble, or if significant economies of scale exist in the industry.
16. The cereal industry has a C_4 ratio equal to .86. The corresponding HHI is probably higher than 1800. Hence the Justice Department would be likely to block such a merger, or at least look at it closely.

Chapter 8

2. *a.* 20.
   b. $4Q$.
   c. $10.

    d. 2.5.

    e. −7.5.

    f. Shut down because of negative profits.

5. *a.* 10.

    b. 14.

    c. 24.

8. *a.* $P = 50 - 2Q$.

    b. 34.

    d. \$238.

16. Use the quadratic formula to find

$$Q = \frac{-5 + \sqrt{5^2 + (4)(898)}}{2} = 27.57; P = \$858.66.$$

20. *a.* 4.

    b. 84.

    c. Firms will enter the industry because you are making positive economic profits.

21. More elastic, since there are available substitutes for a monopolistically competitive firm's product.

Chapter 9

1. *a.* $P = 5, Q = 2.5$.

    b. If the products were not perfect substitutes one firm could not steal all of the other firm's customers by lowering its price. Therefore, Bertrand competition with differentiated products would not result in marginal cost pricing.

5. *a.* $MR_1 = 280 - 2Q_2 - 4Q_1$; $MR_2 = 280 - 2Q_1 - 4Q_2$.

    b. $r_1(Q_2) = 69.25 - .5Q_2$; $r_2(Q_1) = 69.5 - .5Q_1$.

    c. $Q_1 = 46, Q_2 = 46.5$.

14. Cournot: $Q_1 = Q_2 = 43\frac{1}{3}$, $\pi_1 = \pi_2 = 24,270$.

    Stackelberg: $Q_{Leader} = 74$, $Q_{Follower} = 37$, $\pi_{Leader} = 27,380$, $\pi_{Follower} = 13,690$.

    Bertrand: $Q_1 = 74, Q_2 = 74, \pi_1 = 0, \pi_2 = 0$.

Chapter 10

1. *a.*

		Your Rival	
	Strategy	Advertise	Don't advertise
You	Advertise	\$5, \$5	\$10, \$3
	Don't advertise	\$1, \$3	\$2, \$4

     b. Yes, to advertise.

     c. No.

     d. Both advertise.

     e. At most, $.01 less than $5 million.

3. *a.* See Figure A–5.

     b. You enter and the monopolist does not engage in a price war; you do not enter.

     c. You enter and no price war occurs. Once you have entered the market, it is not in the interest of the monopolist to engage in a price war.

6. Eating at the local diner is a repeated game; there is a high probability that the waiter at the local diner will serve you again and thus can "punish" you next time (by providing less service) if you don't tip today. In contrast, in Timbuktu, you play a one-shot game and have a reduced incentive to tip.

7. *b.* $i \le 60\%$.

9. *a.* ABC picks medium and XYZ picks high.

Chapter 11

1. $P = \frac{5}{3}MC$.

4. Increase the membership fee to $4,851.12 per month, and reduce the cost per visit to $3.

6. Charge $5.25 per movie on weekends and $2.75 per movie on weekdays.

12. No.

14. Mark up by 1.4 times the marginal cost, which leads to a price of $1.40 per gallon.

17. $MC = \$2$.

Chapter 12

1. The expected benefit of searching further is $5. The cost of searching further is $7. Joe should not continue to search.

FIGURE A–5

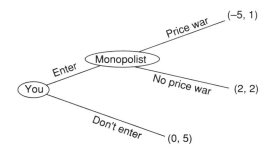

4. Moral hazard and adverse selection.
5. The expected revenues are $100. The expected costs are $100. Therefore, a risk-averse manager would not undertake the project.
6. $E(MR) = 115,000 - 6Q$, so you produce about 16,428 homes.
17. *a.* Private values.
    b. Common values.
    c. Private values.

Chapter 13

1. Mobil will be polluting the air far less than General Motors did when they had the rights. The sale of pollution rights, as allowed under the Clean Air Act as amended in 1990, allows firms to reduce pollution in the cost-minimizing way.
7. *a.* Acme's profits are ($.05 − $.01)100,000 = $4,000 per week.
    c. No shortage results.
14. *a.* 5.625 units.
    b. About 8.18 units.
    c. 7.5 units
15. *a.* $Q^{SD + SF} = 10 + 2P.$
    b. $P = \$10$, $Q = 30$; 15 units are produced by domestic firms and 15 units by foreign firms.
    c. $Q^S = 10 + P.$

Additional Readings and References

Chapter 1

Arnold, R. Douglas, "Political Control of Administrative Officials." *Journal of Law, Economics and Organization* 3(2), Fall 1987, pp. 279–86.

Balachandran, Kashi R. and Srinidhi, Bin, "A Stochastic Planning Model for Manufacturing Environments." *Atlantic Economic Journal* 20(1), March 1992, pp. 48–56.

Beck, Paul J. and Zorn, Thomas S., "Managerial Incentives in a Stock Market Economy." *Journal of Finance* 37(5), December 1982, pp. 1151–67.

Bryan, William R., Gruca, Thomas, and Linke, Charles M., "The Present Value of Future Earnings: Contemporaneous Differentials and the Performance of Dedicated Portfolios." *The Journal of Risk and Insurance* 57, September 1990, pp. 530–39.

Cannings, Kathleen and Lazonick, William, "Equal Employment Opportunity and the 'Managerial Woman' in Japan." *Industrial Relations* 33(1), January 1994, pp. 44–69.

Chan, Anthony and Chen, Carl R., "How Well Do Asset Allocation Mutual Fund Managers Allocate Assets?" *Journal of Portfolio Management* 18(3), Spring 1992, pp. 81–91.

Episcopos, Athanasios, "Investment under Uncertainty and the Value of the Firm." *Economics Letters* 45(3), July 1994, pp. 319–22.

Gaughan, Patrick, Lerman, Paul, and Manley, Donald, "Measuring Damages Resulting from Lost Functionality of Systems." *Journal of Legal Economics* 3(2), July 1993, pp. 11–24.

Gegax, Douglas, Gerking, Shelby, and Schulze, William, "Perceived Risk and the Marginal Value of Safety." *Review of Economics and Statistics* 73(4), November 1991, pp. 589–96.

Giordano, James N., "A Trucker's Dilemma: Managerial Behavior under an Operating Ratio Standard." *Managerial and Decision Economics* 10(3), September 1989, pp. 241–51.

Lange, Mark, Luksetich, William, and Jacobs, Philip, "Managerial Objectives of Symphony Orchestras." *Managerial and Decision Economics* 7(4), December 1986, pp. 273–78.

Ling, David C., "Optimal Refunding Strategies, Transaction Costs, and the Market Value of Corporate Debt." *Financial Review* 26, November 1991, pp. 479–500.

Marcus, Richard D., Swidler, Steve, and Zivney, Terry L., "An Explanation of Why Shareholders' Losses Are So Large after Drug Recalls." *Managerial and Decision Economics* 8(4), December 1987, pp. 295–300.

Prasnikar, Janez and Svejnar, Jan, "Workers' Participation in Management vs. Social Ownership and Government Policies: Yugoslav Lessons for Transforming Socialist Economics." *Comparative Economic Studies* 33(4), Winter 1991, pp. 27–45.

Ravenscraft, David J. and Wagner, Curtis L., III, "The Role of the FTC's Line of Business Data in Testing and Expanding the Theory of the Firm." *Journal of Law and Economics* 34(2), Part 2, October 1992, pp. 703–39.

Saltzman, Cynthia, Duggal, Vijaya G., and Williams, Mary L., "Income and the Recycling Effort: A Maximization Problem." *Energy Economics* 15(1), January 1993, pp. 33–38.

Sanghvi, Arun P. and Dash, Gordon H., Jr., "Core Securities: Widening the Decision Dimensions." *Journal of Portfolio Management* 4(3), Spring 1978, pp. 20–24.

Strong, John S. and Meyer, John R., "An Analysis of Shareholder Rights Plans." *Managerial and Decision Economics* 11(2), May 1990, pp. 73–86.

Tuckman, Howard P. and Chang, Cyril F., "Cost Convergence between for Profit and Not for Profit Nursing Homes: Does Competition Matter?" *Quarterly Review of Economics and Business* 28(4), Winter 1988, pp. 50–65.

Chapter 2

Barzel, Yoram. "Rationing by Waiting." *Journal of Law and Economics,* April 1974, pp. 73–96.

Bell, Frederick W. and Leeworthy, Vernon R., "Recreational Demand by Tourists for Saltwater Beach Days." *Journal of Environmental Economics and Management* 18(3), May 1990, pp. 189–205.

Bohanon, Cecil E., Lynch, Gerald J., and Van Cott, T. Norman, "A Supply and Demand Exposition of the Operation of a Gold Standard in a Closed Economy." *Journal of Economic Education* 16(1), Winter 1985, pp. 16–26.

Burrows, Thomas M., "Pesticide Demand and Integrated Pest Management: A Limited Dependent Variable Analysis." *American Journal of Agricultural Economics* 65(4), November 1983, pp. 806–10.

Chaloupka, Frank J. and Saffer, Henry, "Clean Indoor Air Laws and the Demand for Cigarettes." *Contemporary Policy Issues* 10(2), April 1992, pp. 72–83.

Crafton, Steven M., Hoffer, George E., and Reilly, Robert J., "Testing the Impact of Recalls on the Demand for Automobiles." *Economic Inquiry* 19(4), October 1981, pp. 694–703.

Craig, Ben and Batina, Raymond G., "The Effects of Social Security on a Life Cycle Family Labor Supply Simulation Model." *Journal of Public Economics* 46(2), November 1991, pp. 199–226.

Duncan, Kevin C., Prus, Mark J., and Sandy, Jonathan G., "Marital Status, Children and Women's Labor Market Choices." *Journal of Socio Economics* 22(3), Fall 1993, pp. 277–88.

Englander, Valerie and Englander, Fred, "The Demand for General Assistance in New Jersey: A New Look at the Deterrence Effect." *Journal of Behavioral Economics* 13(2), Winter 1984, pp. 53–65.

Gillespie, Robert W., "Measuring the Demand for Court Services: A Critique of the Federal District Courts Case Weights." *Journal of the American Statistical Association* 69(345), March 1974, pp. 38–43.

Gulley, O. David and Scott, Frank A., Jr., "The Demand for Wagering on State Operated Lotto Games." *National Tax Journal* 46(1), March 1993, pp. 13–22.

Kasulis, Jack J., Huettner, David A., and Dikeman, Neil J., "The Feasibility of Changing Electricity Consumption Patterns." *Journal of Consumer Research* 8(3), December 1981, pp. 279–90.

Knowles, Glenn, Sherony, Keith, and Haupert, Mike, "The Demand for Major League Baseball: A Test of the Uncertainty of Outcome Hypothesis." *American Economist* 36(2), Fall 1992, pp. 72–80.

Kridel, Donald J., Lehman, Dale E., and Weisman, Dennis L., "Option Value, Telecommunications Demand, and Policy." *Information Economics and Policy* 5(2), July 1993, pp. 125–44.

Martin, Randolph C. and Wilder, Ronald P., "Residential Demand for Water and the Pricing of Municipal Water Services." *Public Finance Quarterly* 20(1), January 1992, pp. 93–102.

Max, Wendy and Lehman, Dale E., "A Behavioral Model of Timber Supply." *Journal of Environmental Economics and Management* 15(1), March 1988, pp. 71–86.

Millner, Edward L. and Hoffer, George E., "A Re-examination of the Impact of Automotive Styling on Demand." *Applied Economics* 25(1), January 1993, pp. 101–10.

Munley, Vincent G., Taylor, Larry W., and Formby, John P., "Electricity Demand in Multi-family, Renter-Occupied Residences." *Southern Economic Journal* 57(1), July 1990, pp. 178–94.

Nickerson, Peter H., "Demand for the Regulation of Recreation: The Case of Elk and Deer Hunting in Washington State." *Land Economics* 66(4), November 1990, pp. 437–47.

O'Neill, June, Brien, Michael, and Cunningham, James, "Effects of Comparable Worth Policy: Evidence from Washington State." *American Economic Review* 79(2), May 1989, pp. 305–9.

Parker, Darrell F. and Rhine, Sherrie L. W., "Turnover Costs and the Wage Fringe Mix." *Applied Economics* 23(4A), Part A, April 1991, pp. 617–22.

Ramagopal, K. and Ramaswamy, Sunder, "Measuring the Efficiency Cost of Wage Taxation with Uncertain Labor Productivity." *Economics Letters* 42(1), 1993, pp. 77–80.

Saffer, Henry, "Alcohol Advertising Bans and Alcohol Abuse: An International Perspective." *Journal of Health Economics* 10(1), May 1991, pp. 65–79.

Scahill, Edward, "The Determinants of Average Salaries of Professional Football." *Atlantic Economic Journal* 13(1), March 1985, pp. 103–104.

Siegfried, John J. and Scott, Charles E., "Recent Trends in Undergraduate Economics Degrees." *Journal of Economic Education* 25(3), Summer 1994, pp. 281–86.

Vedder, Richard K. and Gallaway, Lowell, "Racial Differences in Unemployment in the United States, 1890-1990." *Journal of Economic History* 52(3), September 1992, pp. 696–702.

Watkins, Thomas G., "The Shortage of Math and Science Teachers: Are Financial Aid Incentives Enough?" *Journal of Economics (MVEA)* 18(0), 1992, pp. 29–34.

Wilson, John Sullivan, "The U.S. 1982–93 Performance in Advanced Technology Trade." *Challenge* 37(1), January–February 1994, pp. 11–16.

Wu, Mickey T. C. and Monahan, Dennis, "An Experimental Study of Consumer Demand Using Rats." *Journal of Behavioral Economics* 12(1), Summer 1983, pp. 121–38.

Zuber, Richard A. and Gandar, John M., "Lifting the Television Blackout on No Shows at Football Games." *Atlantic Economic Journal* 16(2), June 1988, pp. 63–73.

Yen, Steven T., "Cross Section Estimation of U.S. Demand for Alcoholic Beverage." *Applied Economics* 26(4), April 1994, pp. 381–92.

Chapter 3

Brooking, Carl G. and Taylor, Patrick A., "The Effect of Stochastic Variables on Estimating the Value of Lost Earnings." *Journal of Risk and Insurance* 58(4), December 1991, pp. 647–56.

Chressanthis, George A., "The Impacts of Tuition Rate Changes on College Undergraduate Headcounts and Credit Hours over Time. A Case Study." *Economics of Education Review* 5(2), 1986, pp. 205–17.

Combs, J. Paul and Elledge, Barry W., "Effects of a Room Tax on Resort Hotel/ Motels." *National Tax Journal* 32(2), June 1979, pp. 201–07.

Dubin, Jeffrey A. and Henson, Steven E., "An Engineering/Econometric Analysis of Seasonal Energy Demand and Conservation in the Pacific Northwest." *Journal of Business and Economic Statistics* 6(1), January 1988, pp. 121–34.

Dumas, Edward B. and Sengupta, Jati K., "Fundamentals and Fads in Asset Pricing: An Empirical Investigation." *Applied Financial Economics* 4(3), June 1994, pp. 175–80.

Fox, William F. and Campbell, Charles, "Stability of the State Sales Tax Income Elasticity." *National Tax Journal* 37(2), June 1984, pp. 201–12.

Heinen, D, "The Structure of Food Demand: Interrelatedness and Duality." *American Journal of Agricultural Economics* 64(2), May 1982, pp. 213–221.

Hsing, Yu, "Estimation of Residential Demand for Electricity with the Cross sectionally Correlated and Time Wise Autoregressive Model." *Resource and Energy Economics* 16(3), August 1994, pp. 255–63.

Jones, Clifton T., "A Single Equation Study of U.S. Petroleum Consumption: The Role of Model Specification." *Southern Economic Journal* 59(4), April 1993, pp. 687–700.

Lange, Mark D. and Luksetich, William A., "Demand Elasticities for Symphony Orchestras." *Journal of Cultural Economics* 8(1), June 1984, pp. 29–47.

Lee, Joe W. and Kidane, Amdetsion, "Tobacco Consumption Pattern: A Demographic Analysis." *Atlantic Economic Journal* 16(4), December 1988, pp. 92–94.

Lee, Tong Hun and Kong, Chang Min, "Elasticities of Housing Demand." *Southern Economic Journal* 44(2), October 1977, pp. 298–305.

Lin, An loh, Botsas, Eleftherios N., and Monroe, Scott A., "State Gasoline Consumption in the USA: An Econometric Analysis." *Energy Economics* 7(1), January 1985, pp. 29–36.

Loeb, Peter D., "Automobile Safety Inspection: Further Econometric Evidence." *Applied Economics* 22(12), December 1990, pp. 1697–1704.

Matulich, Scott C., Workman, William G., and Jubenville, Alan, "Recreation Economics: Taking Stock: Problems and Solutions in Estimating the Demand for and Value of Rural Outdoor Recreation." *Land Economics* 63(3), August 1987, pp. 310–16.

Newman, Robert J. and Sullivan, Dennis H., "Econometric Analysis of Business Tax Impacts on Industrial Location: What Do We Know, and How Do We Know It?" *Journal of Urban Economics* 23(2), March 1988, pp. 215–34.

Nguyen, Hong V., "Energy Elasticities under Divisia and Btu Aggregation." *Energy Economics* 9(4), October 1987, pp. 210–14.

Raffiee, Kambiz and Wendel, Jeanne, "Interactions between Hospital Admissions, Cost per Day and Average Length of Stay." *Applied Economics* 23(1), Part B, January 1991, pp. 237–46.

Ramin, Taghi, "A Regression Analysis of Migration to Urban Areas of a Less Developed Country: The Case of Iran." *American Economist* 32(2), Fall 1988, pp. 26–34.

Raymond, Richard D., Sesnowitz, Michael L., and Williams, Donald R., "The Contribution of Regression Analysis to the Elimination of Gender Based Wage Discrimination in Academia: A Simulation." *Economics of Education Review* 9(3), 1990, pp. 197–207.

Reaume, David M., "Migration and the Dynamic Stability of Regional Econometric Models." *Economic Inquiry* 21(2), April 1983, pp. 281–93.

Stine, William F., "Estimating the Responsiveness of Local Revenue to Intergovernmental Aid." *National Tax Journal* 38(2), June 1985, pp. 227–34.

Tashman, Leonard J. and Leach, Michael L., "Automatic Forecasting Software: A Survey and Evaluation." *International Journal of Forecasting* 7(2), August 1991, pp. 209–30.

Taube, Paul M., Huth, William L., and MacDonald, Don N., "An Analysis of Consumer Expectation Effects on Demand in a Dynamic Almost Ideal Demand System." *Journal of Economics and Business* 42(3), August 1990, pp. 225–36.

White, Michael D.; Luksetich, William A., "Heroin: Price Elasticity and Enforcement Strategies." *Economic Inquiry* 21(4), October 1983, pp. 557–64.

Wilder, Ronald P., Johnson, Joseph E., and Rhyne, R. Glenn, "Income Elasticity of the Residential Demand for Electricity." *Journal of Energy and Development* 16(1), Autumn 1990, pp. 1–13.

Chapter 4

Colburn, Christopher B., "Work Requirements and Income Transfers." *Public Finance Quarterly* 21(2), April 1993, pp.141–62.

Danziger, Sheldon and Taussig, Michael K., "The Income Unit and the Anatomy of Income Distribution." *Review of Income and Wealth* 25(4), December 1979, pp. 365–75.

Giertz, J. Fred and Sullivan, Dennis H., "On the Political Economy of Food Stamps." *Public Choice* 33(3), 1978, pp. 113–17.

Goodfellow, Gordon P., Jr. and Sweeney, Vernon E., "Vertically Parallel Indifference Curves with a Non-Constant Marginal Utility of Money." *American Economist* 13(2), Fall 1969, pp. 81–86.

Goodman, Allen C., "Estimation of Offset and Income Effects on the Demand for Mental Health Treatment." *Inquiry* 26(2), Summer 1989, pp. 235–48.

Johnston, Richard S.; Larson, Douglas M., "Focusing the Search for Giffen Behavior." *Economic Inquiry* 32(1), January 1994, pp. 168–74.

Kaun, David E., "Writers Die Young: The Impact of Work and Leisure on Longevity." *Journal of Economic Psychology* 12(2), June 1991, pp. 381–99.

Klingaman, David, "A Note on a Cyclical Majority Problem." *Public Choice* 6(0), Spring 1969, pp. 99–101.

Senauer, Ben and Young, Nathan, "The Impact of Food Stamps on Food Expenditures: Rejection of the Traditional Model." *American Journal of Agricultural Economics* 68(1), February 1986, pp. 37–43.

Chapter 5

Caves, Douglas W., Herriges, Joseph A., and Windle, Robert J., "The Cost of Electric Power Interruptions in the Industrial Sector: Estimates Derived from Interruptible Service Programs." *Land Economics* 68(1), February 1992, pp. 49–61.

Corman, Hope, Joyce, Theodore J., and Grossman, Michael, "Birth Outcome Production Function in the United States." *Journal of Human Resources* 22(3), Summer 1987, pp. 339–60.

Dobitz, Clifford P., "Energy Substitution in Irrigation." *Regional Science Perspectives* 14(1), 1984, pp. 25–29.

Duchatelet, Martine, "A Note on Increasing Returns to Scale and Learning by Doing." *Journal of Economic Theory* 27(1), June 1982, pp. 210–18.

Eckard. E. Woodrow, "Cost Competition: New Evidence on an Old Issue." *Applied Economics* 24(11), November 1992, pp. 1241–50.

Griffin, Peter, "The Substitutability of Occupational Groups Using Firm Level Data." *Economics Letters* 39(3), July 1992, pp. 279–82.

Grosskopf, Shawna and Yaisawarng, Suthathip, "Economies of Scope in the Provision of Local Public Services." *National Tax Journal* 43(1), March 1990, pp. 61–74.

Maxwell, W. D., "Production Theory and Cost Curves." *Applied Economics* 1(3), August 1969, pp. 221–224.

McDonald, J. R. Scott, Rayner, Tony J., and Bates, John M., "Productivity Growth and the UK Food System 1954–84." *Journal of Agricultural Economics* 43(2), May 1992, pp. 191–204.

Mullen, John K. and Williams, Martin, "Convergence, Scale and the Relative Productivity Performance of Canadian U.S. Manufacturing Industries." *Applied Economics* 26(7), July 1994, pp. 739–50.

Niroomand, Farhang and Sawyer, W. Charles, "The Extent of Scale Economies in U. S. Foreign Trade." *Journal of World Trade* 23(6), December 1989, pp. 137–46.

Okunade, Albert Ade, "Production Cost Structure of U.S. Hospital Pharmacies: Time Series, Cross Sectional Bed Size Evidence." *Journal of Applied Econometrics* 8(3), July–Sept. 1993, pp. 277–94.

Olson, Dennis O. and Jonish, James, "The Robustness of Translog Elasticity of Substitution Estimates and the Capital Energy Complementarity Controversy." *Quarterly Journal of Business and Economics* 24(1), Winter 1985, pp. 21–35.

Robison, H. David and Silver, Stephen J., "The Impact of Changing Oil Prices on Interfuel Substitution: Ethanol's Prospects in the United States to 1995." *Journal of Policy Modeling* 8(2), Summer 1986, pp. 241–53.

Sengupta, Jati K. and Okamura, Kumiko, "Scale Economies in Manufacturing: Problems of Robust Estimation." *Empirical Economics* 18(3), 1993, pp. 469–80.

Sexton, Robert L., Graves, Philip E., and Lee, Dwight R., "The Short and Long Run Marginal Cost Curve: A Pedagogical Note." *Journal of Economic Education* 24(1), Winter 1993, pp. 34–37.

Harris, R. Scott, "Planning, Flexibility, and Joint Specificity of Inputs: The Use of First Refusal Rights." *Zeitschrift fur die gesamte Staatswissenschaft (JITE)* 141(4), December 1985, pp. 576–85.

Hayashi, Paul M. and Ziegler, Lawrence F., "Separability and Substitutability of Inputs in the Production of Police Services and Their Implications for Budgeting." *Journal of Economics (MVEA)* 19(1), Spring 1993, pp. 23–30.

Holcomb, James H. and Evans, Dorla A., "The Effect of Sunk Costs on Uncertain Decisions in Experimental Markets." *Journal of Behavioral Economics* 16(3), Fall 1987, pp. 59–66.

Huckins, Larry E., "Capital Labor Substitution in Municipal Government." *Public Finance Quarterly* 17(4), October 1989, pp. 357–74.

Huettner, David A. and Landon, John H., "Electric Utilities: Scale Economies and Diseconomies." *Southern Economic Journal* 44(4), April 1978, pp. 883–912.

Johnson, Dennis A., "Opportunity Cost: A Pedagogical Note." *Southern Economic Journal* 50(3), January 1984, pp. 866–70.

Kim, H. Youn and Clark, Robert M., "Economies of Scale and Scope in Water Supply." *Regional Science and Urban Economics* 18(4), November 1988, pp. 479–502.

Coates, Daniel E. and Mulligan, James G., "Scale Economies and Capacity Utilization: The Importance of Relative Fuel Prices." *Energy Economics* 10(2), April 1988, pp. 140–46.

Koshal, Rajindar K. and Koshal, Manjulika, "Economies of Scale of State Road Transport Industry in India." *International Journal of Transport Economics* 16(2), June 1989, pp. 165–73.

Lichtenberg, Frank R. and Siegel, Donald, "The Impact of R&D Investment on Productivity New Evidence Using Linked R&D LRD Data." *Economic Inquiry* 29(2), April 1991, pp. 203–29.

MacDonald, James M., "R and D and the Directions of Diversification." *Review of Economics and Statistics* 67(4), November 1985, pp. 583–90.

Thomas, Janet M. and Callan, Scott J., "An Analysis of Production Cost Inefficiency." *Review of Industrial Organization* 7(2), 1992, pp. 203–25.

Toda, Yasushi, "Estimation of a Cost Function When the Cost Is Not Minimum: The Case of Soviet Manufacturing Industries, 1958-1971." *Review of Economics and Statistics* 58(3), Aug. 1976, pp. 259–68.

Wen, Guanzhong James, "Total Factor Productivity Change in China's Farming Sector: 1952–1989." *Economic Development and Cultural Change* 42(1), October 1993, pp. 1–41.

Williams, Martin and Moomaw, Ronald L., "Capital and Labour Efficiencies: A Regional Analysis." *Urban Studies* 26(6), December 1989, pp. 573–85.

Chapter 6

Allen, Bruce T., "Merger Statistics and Merger Policy." *Review of Industrial Organization* 1(2), Summer 1984, pp. 78–92.

Arnold, Michael A., "The Principal Agent Relationship in Real Estate Brokerage Services." *American Real Estate and Urban Economics Association Journal* 20(1), Spring 1992, pp. 89–106.

Aron, Debra J. and Olivella, Pau, "Bonus and Penalty Schemes as Equilibrium Incentive Devices, with Application to Manufacturing Systems." *Journal of Law, Economics and Organization* 10(1), April 1994, pp. 1–34.

Atkinson, Scott E., Stanley, Linda R., and Tschirhart, John, "Revenue Sharing as an Incentive in an Agency Problem: An Example from the National Football League." *Rand Journal of Economics* 19(1), Spring 1988, pp. 27–43.

Bull, Clive, Schotter, Andrew, and Weigelt, Keith, "Tournaments and Piece Rates: An Experimental Study." *Journal of Political Economy* 95(1), February 1987, pp. 1–33.

Byrd, John W. and Hickman, Kent A., "Do Outside Directors Monitor Managers? Evidence from Tender Offer Bids." *Journal of Financial Economics* 32(2), October 1992, pp. 195–221.

Cardell, Nicholas Scott and Hopkins, Mark Myron, "Education, Income, and Ability: A Comment." *Journal of Political Economy* 85(1), February 1977, pp. 211–15.

Cordell, Lawrence R., MacDonald, Gregor D., and Wohar, Mark E., "Corporate Ownership and the Thrift Crisis." *Journal of Law and Economics* 36(2), October 1993, pp. 719–56.

Cornwell, Christopher, Dorsey, Stuart, and Mehrzad, Nasser, "Opportunistic Behavior by Firms in Implicit Pension Contracts." *Journal of Human Resources* 26(4), Fall 1991, pp. 704–25.

Dearden, James, Ickes, Barry W., and Samuelson, Larry, "To Innovate or Not to Innovate: Incentives and Innovation in Hierarchies." *American Economic Review* 80(5), December 1990, pp. 1105–24.

Erekson, O. Homer and Sullivan, Dennis H., "A Cross Section Analysis of IRS Auditing." *National Tax Journal* 41(2), June 1988, pp. 175–89.

Hansen, Robert S. and Torregrosa, Paul, "Underwriter Compensation and Corporate Monitoring." *Journal of Finance* 47(4), September 1992, pp. 1537–55.

Hirao, Yukiko, "Task Assignment and Agency Structures." *Journal of Economics and Management Strategy* 2(2), Summer 1993, pp. 299–323.

Honig Haftel, Sandra and Martin, Linda R., "The Effectiveness of Reward Systems on Innovative Output: An Empirical Analysis." *Small Business Economics* 5(4), December 1993, pp. 261–69.

Ingberman, Daniel E., "Privatization as Institutional Choice: Comment." *Journal of Policy Analysis and Management* 6(4), Summer 1987, pp. 607–11.

Janjigian, Vahan and Bolster, Paul J., "The Elimination of Director Liability and Stockholder Returns: An Empirical Investigation." *Journal of Financial Research* 13(1), Spring 1990, pp. 53–60.

Kalt, Joseph P., Zupan, Mark A., "The Apparent Ideological Behavior of Legislators: Testing for Principal Agent Slack in Political Institutions." *Journal of Law and Economics* 33(1), April 1990, pp. 103–31.

Karpoff, Jonathan M. and Rice, Edward M., "Organizational Form, Share Transferability, and Firm Performance: Evidence from the AN CSA Corporations." *Journal of Financial Economics* 24(1), September 1989, pp. 69–105.

Louie, Kenneth K. T., Fizel, John L., and Mentzer, Marc S., "CEO Tenure and Firm Performance." *Journal of Economics (MVEA)* 19(1), Spring 1993, pp. 51–56.

Lyon, Thomas P. and Hackett, Steven C., "Bottlenecks and Governance Structures: Open Access and Long Term Contracting in Natural Gas." *Journal of Law, Economics and Organization* 9(2), October 1993, pp. 380–98.

Majumdar, Sumit K. and Ramaswamy, Venkatram, "Explaining Downstream Integration." *Managerial and Decision Economics* 15(2), March/April 1994, pp. 119–29.

Mulherin, J. Harold, Netter, Jeffry M., and Overdahl, James A., "Prices Are Property: The Organization of Financial Exchanges from a Transaction Cost Perspective." *Journal of Law and Economics* 34(2), Part 2, October 1992, pp. 591–644.

Nantz, Kathryn and Sparks, Roger, "The Labor Managed Firm under Imperfect Monitoring: Employment and Work Effort Responses." *Journal of Comparative Economics* 14(1), March 1990, pp. 33–50.

Shogren, Jason F. and Kask, Susan B., "Exploring the Boundaries of the Coase Theorem: Efficiency and Rationality Given Imperfect Contract Enforcement." *Economics Letters* 39(2), June 1992, pp. 155–61.

Singh, Nirvikar and Thomas, Ravi, "User Charges as a Delegation Mechanism." *National Tax Journal* 39(1), March 1986, pp. 109–13.

Zorn, Thomas S. and Larsen, James E., "The Incentive Effects of Flat Fee and Percentage Commissions for Real Estate Brokers." *American Real Estate and Urban Economics Association Journal* 14(1), Spring 1986, pp. 24–47.

Chapter 7

Adrangi, Bahram, Chow, Garland, and Gritta, Richard, "Market Structure, Market Share, and Profits in the Airline Industry." *Atlantic Economic Journal* 19(1), March 1991, pp. 98–99.

Amato, Louis and Wilder, Ronald P., "Market Concentration, Efficiency, and Antitrust Policy: Demsetz Revisited." *Quarterly Journal of Business and Economics* 27(4), Autumn 1988, pp. 3–19.

Bradley, James W. and Korn, Donald H., "Bargains in Valuation Disparities: Corporate Acquirer versus Passive Investor." *Sloan Management Review* 20(2), Winter 1979, pp. 51–64.

Carroll, Sidney L. and Scott, Loren C., "The Modification of Industry Performance through the Use of Government Monopsony Power." *Industrial Organization Review* 3(1), 1975, pp. 28–36.

Carter, John R., "Concentration Change and the Structure Performance Debate: An Interpretive Essay." *Managerial and Decision Economics* 5(4), December 1984, pp. 204–12.

Chang, Winston W. and Chen, Fang Yueh, "Vertically Related Markets: Export Rivalry between DC and LDC Firms." *Review of International Economics* 2(2), June 1994, pp. 131–42.

Crane, Steven E. and Welch, Patrick J., "The Problem of Geographic Market Definition: Geographic Proximity vs. Economic Significance." *Atlantic Economic Journal* 19(2), June 1991, pp. 12–20.

Deily, Mary E. and Gray, Wayne B., "Enforcement of Pollution Regulations in a Declining Industry." *Journal of Environmental Economics and Management* 21(3), November 1991, pp. 260–74.

Diamond, Charles A. and Simon, Curtis J., "Industrial Specialization and the Returns to Labor." *Journal of Labor Economics* 8(2), April 1990, pp. 175–201.

Dranove, David, Shanley, Mark, and White, William D., "Price and Concentration in Hospital Markets: The Switch from Patient Driven to Payer Driven Competition." *Journal of Law and Economics* 36(1), Part 1 April 1993, pp. 179–204.

Evans, William N. and Kessides, Ioannis, "Structure, Conduct, and Performance in the Deregulated Airline Industry." *Southern Economic Journal* 59(3), January 1993, pp. 450–67.

Hannan, Timothy H. and McDowell, John M., "The Impact of Technology Adoption on Market Structure." *Review of Economics and Statistics* 72(1), February 1990, pp. 164–68.

Hartley, Keith and Corcoran, William J., "Short-run Employment Functions and Defence Contracts in the UK Aircraft Industry." *Applied Economics* 7(4), Dec. 1975, pp. 223–33.

Haworth, Charles T. and Reuther, Carol Jean, "Industrial Concentration and Interindustry Wage Determination." *Review of Economics and Statistics* 6(1), Feb. 1978, pp. 85–95.

Hiebert, L. Dean, "Cost Flexibility and Price Dispersion." *Journal of Industrial Economics* 38(1), September 1989, pp. 103–9.

Jarrell, Stephen, "Research and Development and Firm Size in the Pharmaceutical Industry." *Business Economics* 18(4), September 1983, pp. 26–39.

Kyle, Reuben, Strickland, Thomas H., and Fayissa, Bichaka, "Capital Markets' Assessment of Airline Restructuring Following Deregulation." *Applied Economics* 24(10), October 1992, pp. 1097–1102.

Lane, Sylvai and Papathanasis, Anastasios, "Certification and Industry Concentration Ratios." *Antitrust Bulletin* 28(2), Summer 1983, pp. 381–95.

Levin, Sharon G., Levin, Stanford L., and Meisel, John B., "Market Structure, Uncertainty, and Intrafirm Diffusion: The Case of Optical Scanners in Grocery Stores." *Review of Economics and Statistics* 74(2), May 1992, pp. 345–50.

Mallela, Parthasaradhi and Nahata, Babu, "Effects of Horizontal Merger on Price, Profits, and Market Power in a Dominant Firm Oligopoly." *International Economic Journal* 3(1), Spring 1989, pp. 55–62.

Norton, Seth W., "Vertical Integration and Systematic Risk: Oil Refining Revisited." *Journal of Institutional and Theoretical Economics* 149(4), December 1993, pp. 656–69.

Peoples, James, Hekmat, Ali, and Moini, A. H., "Corporate Mergers and Union Wage Premiums." *Journal of Economics and Finance* 17(2), Summer 1993, pp. 65–75.

Salinger, Michael, "The Concentration Margins Relationship Reconsidered." *Brookings Papers on Economic Activity*, Special Issue, 1990, pp. 287–321.

Sandler, Ralph D., "Market Share Instability in Commercial Airline Markets and the Impact of Deregulation." *Journal of Industrial Economics* 36(3), March 1988, pp. 327–35.

Walsh, Carl E., "Taxation of Interest Income, Deregulation and the Banking Industry." *Journal of Finance* 38(5), December 1983, pp. 1529–42.

Yandle, Bruce and Hite, Arnold, "Branded Competition and Concentration Measures." *Southern Economic Journal* 43(4), April 1977, pp. 5176–81.

Chapter 8

Benson, Bruce L. and Faminow, M. D., "The Impact of Experience on Prices and Profits in Experimental Duopoly Markets." *Journal of Economic Behavior and Organization* 9(4), June 1988, pp. 345–65.

Besanko, David and Perry, Martin K., "Exclusive Dealing in a Spatial Model of Retail Competition." *International Journal of Industrial Organization* 12(3), 1994, pp. 297–329.

Brastow, Raymond and Rystrom, David, "Wealth Effects of the Drug Price Competition and Patent Term Restoration Act of 1984." *American Economist* 32(2), Fall 1988, pp. 59–65.

Brown, John Howard, "Airline Fleet Composition and Deregulation." *Review of Industrial Organization* 8(4), August 1993, pp. 435–49.

Chen, Yu Min and Jain, Dipak C., "Dynamic Monopoly Pricing under a Poisson-Type Uncertain Demand." *Journal of Business* 65(4), October 1992, pp. 593–614.

Cheng, Doris and Shieh, Yeung Nan, "Bilateral Monopoly and Industrial Location: A Cooperative Outcome." *Regional Science and Urban Economics* 22(2), June 1992, pp. 187–95.

De Bondt, Raymond, Slaets, Patrick, and Cassiman, Bruno, "The Degree of Spillovers and the Number of Rivals for Maximum Effective R & D." *International Journal of Industrial Organization* 10(1), 1992, pp. 35–54.

Feinberg, Robert M. and Shaanan, Joseph, "The Relative Price Discipline of Domestic versus Foreign Entry." *Review of Industrial Organization* 9(2), April 1994, pp. 211–20.

Gegax, Douglas and Nowotny, Kenneth, "Competition and the Electric Utility Industry: An Evaluation." *Yale Journal on Regulation* 10(1), Winter 1993, pp. 63–87.

Gupta, Barnali, Kats, Amoz, and Pal, Debashis, "Upstream Monopoly, Downstream Competition and Spatial Price Discrimination." *Regional Science and Urban Economics* 24(5), October 1994, pp. 529–42.

Holahan, William L. and Schuler, Richard E., "Competitive Entry in a Spatial Economy: Market Equilibrium and Welfare Implications." *Journal of Regional Science* 21(3), Aug. 1981, pp. 341–57.

Kats, Amoz, "Monopolistic Trading Economies: A Case of Governmental Control." *Public Choice* 20, Winter 1974, pp. 17–32.

Kripalani, G. K., "Monopoly Supply." *Atlantic Economic Journal* 18(4), December 1990, pp. 32–37.

Lau, Lawrence J. and Ma, Barry K., "The Short-Run Aggregate Profit Function and the Capacity Distribution." *Scandinavian Journal of Economics* 96(2), 1994, pp. 201–18.

Levy, David T. and Gerlowski, Daniel A., "Competition, Advertising and Meeting Competition Clauses." *Economics Letters* 37(3), November 1991, pp. 217–21.

Magas, Istvan, "Dynamics of Export Competition in High Technology Trade: USA, Japan, and Germany 1973–1987." *International Trade Journal* 6(4), Summer 1992, pp. 471–513.

Mirman, L. J., Tauman, I., and Zang, Y., "Cooperative Behavior in a Competitive Market." *Mathematical Social Science* 54(3), October 1991, pp. 227–49.

Oster, Clinton V., Jr. and Strong, John S., "The Worldwide Aviation Safety Record." *Logistics and Transportation Review* 28(1), March 1992, pp. 23–48.

Peck, J. and Shell, K., "Liquid Markets and Competition," *Games and Economic Behavior* 2(4), December 1990, pp. 362–77.

Phillips, Owen R. and Schutte, David P., "Identifying Profitable Self Service Markets: A Test in Gasoline Retailing." *Applied Economics* 20(2), February 1988, pp. 263–72.

Rock, Steven M. and Hall, W. Clayton, "Advertising and Monopoly Power: The Case of the Electric Utility Industry. Comment." *Atlantic Economic Journal* 15(1), March 1987, pp. 67–70.

Sattler, Edward L. and Scott, Robert C., "Price and Output Adjustments in the Two Plant Firm." *Southern Economic Journal* 48(4), April 1982, pp. 1042–48.

Schroeter, John R., Smith, Scott L., and Cox, Steven R., "Advertising and Competition in Routine Legal Service Markets: An Empirical Investigation." *Journal of Industrial Economics* 36(1), September 1987, pp. 49–60.

Seldon, Barry J. and Doroodian, Khosrow, "Does Purely Predatory Advertising Exist?" *Review of Industrial Organization* 5(3), Fall 1990, pp. 45–70.

Suslow, Valerie Y., "Estimating Monopoly Behavior with Competitive Recycling: An Application to Alcoa." *Rand Journal of Economics* 17(3), Autumn 1986, pp. 389–403.

Zietz, Joachim and Fayissa, Bichaka, "R&D Expenditures and Import Competition: Some Evidence for the U.S." *Weltwirtschaftliches Archiv* 128(1), 1992, pp. 52–66.

Chapter 9

Benson, Bruce L. and Hartigan, James C., "An Explanation of Intra-industry Trade in Identical Commodities." *International Journal of Industrial Organization* 2(2), June 1984, pp. 85–97.

Buschena, David E. and Perloff, Jeffrey M., "The Creation of Dominant Firm Market Power in the Coconut Oil Export Market." *American Journal of Agricultural Economics* 73(4), November 1991, pp. 1000–1008.

Cremer, Helmuth and Cremer, Jacques, "Duopoly with Employee Controlled and Profit Maximizing Firms: Bertrand vs Cournot Competition." *Journal of Comparative Economics* 16(2), June 1992, pp. 241–58.

Darrat, A. F., Gilley, O. W., and Meyer, D. J., "Petroleum Demand, Income Feedback Effects, and OPEC's Pricing Behavior: Some Theoretical and Empirical Results." *International Review of Economics and Finance* 1(3), 1992, pp. 247–59.

Friedman, Daniel, "Producers' Markets: A Model of Oligopoly with Sales Costs." *Journal of Economic Behavior and Organization* 11(3), May 1989, pp. 381–98.

Fuess, Scott M., Jr. and Loewenstein, Mark A., "On Strategic Cost Increases in a Duopoly." *International Journal of Industrial Organization* 9(3), 1991, pp. 389–95.

Hamilton, James L., "Joint Oligopsony Oligopoly in the U.S. Leaf Tobacco Market, 1924–39." *Review of Industrial Organization* 9(1), February 1994, pp. 25–39.

Hartigan, James C., Kamma, Sreenivas, and Perry, Philip R., "The Injury Determination Category and the Value of Relief from Dumping." *Review of Economics and Statistics* 71(1), February 1989, pp. 183–86.

Hwang, Hae Shin and Schulman, Craig T., "Strategic Non intervention and the Choice of Trade Policy for International Oligopoly." *Journal of International Economics* 34(12), February 1993, pp. 73–93.

Karikari, John A., "Tariffs versus Ratio Quotas under Oligopoly." *International Economic Journal* 6(3), Autumn 1992, pp. 43–48.

Katz, Barbara G. and Nelson, Julianne, "Product Availability as a Strategic Variable: The Implications of Regulating Retailer Stockouts." *Journal of Regulatory Economics* 2(4), December 1990, pp. 379–95.

Mai, Chao cheng, Yeh, Chiou nan, and Suwanakul, Sontachai, "Price Uncertainty and Production Location Decisions under Free Entry Oligopoly." *Journal of Regional Science* 33(4), November 1993, pp. 531–45.

Roufagalas, John, "Price Rigidity: An Exploration of the Demand Side." *Managerial and Decision Economics* 15(1), Jan./Feb. 1994, pp. 87–94.

Chapter 10

Ahlseen, Mark J., "The Impact of Unionization on Labor's Share of Income." *Journal of Labor Research* 11(3), Summer 1990, pages 337–46.

Basu, K., "Duopoly Equilibria When Firms Can Change Their Decisions Once." *Economic Letters* 32(3), March 1990, pp. 273–75.

Blair, Douglas H. and Crawford, David L., "Labor Union Objectives and Collective Bargaining." *Quarterly Journal of Economics* 99(3), August 1984, pp. 547–66.

Bowman, Gary W. and Blackstone, Erwin A., "Low Price Conspiracy: Trade Regulation and the Case of Japanese Electronics." *Atlantic Economic Journal* 18(4), December 1990, pp. 59–67.

Burgess, Paul L. and Marburger, Daniel R., "Do Negotiated and Arbitrated Salaries Differ under Final Offer Arbitration?" *Industrial and Labor Relations Review* 46(3), April 1993, pp. 548–59.

Cheung, Francis K. and Davidson, Carl, "Bargaining Structure and Strike Activity." *Canadian Journal of Economics* 24(2), May 1991, pp. 345–71.

Conrad, Cecilia and Duchatelet, Martine, "New Technology Adoption: Incumbent versus Entrant." *International Journal of Industrial Organization* 5(3), September 1987, pp. 315–21.

Hackett, Steven, Schlager, Edella, and Walker, James, "The Role of Communication in Resolving Commons Dilemmas: Experimental Evidence with Heterogeneous Appropriators." *Journal of Environmental Economics and Management* 27(2), September 1994, pp. 99–126.

Holcomb, James H. and Nelson, Paul S., "Cartel Failure: A Mistake or Do They Do It to Each Other on Purpose?" *Journal of Socio Economics* 20(3), Fall 1991, pp. 235–49.

Horowitz, I., "On the Effects of Cournot Rivalry Between Entrepreneurial and Cooperative Firms." *Journal of Comparative Economics* 15(1), March 1991, pp. 115–121.

Koeller, C. Timothy, "Union Activity and the Decline in American Trade Union Membership." *Journal of Labor Research* 15(1), Winter 1994, pp. 19–32.

Chapter 11

Beard, T. Randolph and Sweeney, George H., "Random Pricing by Monopolists." *Journal of Industrial Economics* 42(2), June 1994, pp. 183–92.

Benson, B. L., Greenhut, M. L., and Norman, G., "On the Basing Point System." *American Economic Review* 80(3), June 1990, pp. 584–88.

Blair, Roger D. and Fesmire, James M., "The Resale Price Maintenance Policy Dilemma." *Southern Economic Journal* 60(4), April 1994, pp. 1043–47.

Bosch, Jean Claude and Eckard, E. Woodrow, Jr., "The Profitability of Price Fixing: Evidence from Stock Market Reaction to Federal Indictments." *Review of Economics and Statistics* 73(2), May 1991, pp. 309–17.

Braid, Ralph M., "Uniform versus Peak Load Pricing of a Bottleneck with Elastic Demand." *Journal of Urban Economics* 26(3), November 1989, pp. 320–27.

DeSerpa, Allan C., "A Note on Second-Degree Price Discrimination and Its Implications." *Review of Industrial Organization* 2(4), 1986, pp. 368–75.

Greenhut, John G. and Smith, Dean H., "An Operational Model for Spatial Price Theory." *Review of Regional Studies* 23(2), Fall 1993, pp. 115–28.

Halperin, Robert and Srinidhi, Bin, "The Effects of the U.S. Income Tax Regulations' Transfer Pricing Rules on Allocative Efficiency." *Accounting Review* 62(4), October 1987, pp. 686–706.

Horsky, Dan and Nelson, Paul, "New Brand Positioning and Pricing in an Oligopolistic Market." *Marketing Science* 11(2), Spring 1992, pp. 133–53.

Koller, Roland H., II, "When is Pricing Predatory?" *Antitrust Bulletin* 24(2), Sum. 1979, pp. 283–306.

Malko, J. Robert, Lindsay, Malcolm A., and Everett, Carol T., "Towards Implementation of Peak Load Pricing of Electricity: A Challenge for Applied Economics." *Journal of Energy and Development* 3(1), Autumn 1977, pp. 82–102.

Nahata, Babu, Ostaszewski, Krzysztof, and Sahoo, P. K., "Direction of Price Changes in Third-Degree Price Discrimination." *American Economic Review* 80(5), December 1990, pp. 1254–58.

Ormiston, Michael B. and Phillips, Owen R., "Nonlinear Price Schedules and Tied Products." *Economica* 55(218), May 1988, pp. 219–33.

Page, Frank H. and Sanders, Anthony B., "On the Pricing of Shared Appreciation Mortgages." *Housing Finance Review* 5(1), Summer 1986, pp. 49–57.

Sass, Tim R. and Saurman, David S., "Mandated Exclusive Territories and Economic Efficiency: An Empirical Analysis of the Malt Beverage Industry." *Journal of Law and Economics* 36(1), Part 1 April 1993, pp. 153–77.

Shaanan, Joseph, "A Method for the Estimation of Limit Prices without Entry Data." *Managerial and Decision Economics* 11(1), February 1990, pp. 21–29.

Taylor, Thomas N. and Schwarz, Peter M., "The Long-run Effects of a Time of Use Demand Charge." *Rand Journal of Economics* 21(3), Autumn 1990, pp. 431–45.

Wirl, F., "Dynamic Demand and Noncompetitive Pricing Strategies." *Journal of Economics* 54(3), 1991, pp. 105–21.

Young, A. R. "Transactions Cost, Two-Part Tariffs, and Collusion." *Economic Inquiry* 29(3), July 1991, pp. 581–90.

Chapter 12

Albrecht, James W. and Vroman, Susan B., "Dual Labor Markets, Efficiency Wages, and Search." *Journal of Labor Economics* 10(4), October 1992, pp. 438–61.

Ballantine, John W., Cleveland, Frederick W., and Koeller, C. Timothy, "Profitability, Uncertainty, and Firm Size." *Small Business Economics* 5(2), June 1993, pp. 87–100.

Balvers, Ronald J. and Miller, Norman C., "Factor Demand under Conditions of Product Demand and Supply Uncertainty." *Economic Inquiry* 30(3), July 1992, pp. 544–55.

Biglaiser, Gary, "Middlemen as Experts." *Rand Journal of Economics* 24(2), Summer 1993, pp. 212–23.

Bodvarsson, Orn B., "Educational Screening with Output Variability and Costly Monitoring." *Atlantic Economic Journal* 17(1), March 1989, pp. 16–23.

Butler, Richard J. and Worrall, John D., "Claims Reporting and Risk Bearing Moral Hazard in Workers' Compensation." *Journal of Risk and Insurance* 58(2), June 1991, pp. 191–204.

Cabe, Richard and Herriges, Joseph A., "The Regulation of Non-Point Source Pollution under Imperfect and Asymmetric Information." *Journal of Environmental Economics and Management* 22(2), March 1992, pp. 134–46.

Camerer, Colin and Weigelt, Keith, "Information Mirages in Experimental Asset Markets." *Journal of Business* 64(4), October 1991, pp. 463–93.

Charles Joni S. James, "Information Externalities: Information Dissemination as a Policy Tool to Achieve Efficient Investment Decisions in a Two-Firm Oil Drilling Industry." *Studi Economici* 44(39), 1989, pp. 29–49.

Copeland, Thomas E. and Friedman, Daniel, "The Market Value of Information: Some Experimental Results." *Journal of Business* 65(2), April 1992, pp. 241–66.

Cotter, Kevin D. and Jensen, Gail A., "Choice of Purchasing Arrangements in Insurance Markets." *Journal of Risk and Uncertainty* 2(4), December 1989, pp. 405–14.

Dionne, Georges and Doherty, Neil A., "Adverse Selection, Commitment, and Renegotiation: Extension to and Evidence from Insurance Markets." *Journal of Political Economy* 102(2), April 1994, pp. 209–35.

Eaker, Mark, Grant, Dwight, and Woodard, Nelson, "International Diversification and Hedging: A Japanese and U.S. Perspective." *Journal of Economics and Business* 43(4), November 1991, pp. 363–74.

Engelbrecht Wiggins, Richard and Kahn, Charles M., "Protecting the Winner: Second Price versus Oral Auctions." *Economics Letters* 35(3), March 1991, pp. 243–48.

Fu, Jiarong, "Increased Risk Aversion and Risky Investment." *Journal of Risk and Insurance* 60(3), September 1993, pp. 494–501.

Giliberto, S. Michael and Varaiya, Nikhil P., "The Winner's Curse and Bidder Competition in Acquisitions: Evidence from Failed Bank Auctions." *Journal of Finance* 44(1), March 1989, pp. 59–75.

Hausch, Donald B. and Li, Lode, "A Common Value Auction Model with Endogenous Entry and Information Acquisition." *Economic Theory* 3(2), 1993, pp. 315–34.

Hayes, James A., Cole, Joseph B., and Meiselman, David I., "Health Insurance Derivatives: The Newest Application of Modern Financial Risk Management." *Business Economics* 28(2), April 1993, pp. 36–40.

Hoffer, George E., Pruitt, Stephen W., and Reilly, Robert J., "Market Responses to Publicly Provided Information: The Case of Automotive Safety." *Applied Economics* 24(7), July 1992, pp. 661–67.

Holt, Charles A., Jr. and Sherman, Roger, "Waiting Line Auctions." *Journal of Political Economy* 90(2), April 1982, pp. 280–94.

Horowitz, John K. and Lichtenberg, Erik, "Insurance, Moral Hazard, and Chemical Use in Agriculture." *American Journal of Agricultural Economics* 75(4), November 1993, pp. 926–35.

Kamma, Sreenivas, Kanatas, George, and Raymar, Steven, "Dutch Auction versus Fixed Price Self Tender Offers for Common Stock." *Journal of Financial Intermediation* 2(3), September 1992, pp. 277–307.

Kogut, Carl A., "Recall in Consumer Search." *Journal of Economic Behavior and Organization* 17(1), January 1992, pp. 141–51.

McCabe, Kevin, Rassenti, Stephen, and Smith, Vernon, "Auction Institutional Design: Theory and Behavior of Simultaneous Multiple Unit Generalizations of the Dutch and English Auctions." *American Economic Review* 80, December 1990, pp. 1276–1283.

Meador, Joseph W., Madden, Gerald P., and Johnston, David J., "On the Probability of Acquisition of Non-life Insurers." *Journal of Risk and Insurance* 53(4), December 1986, pp. 621–43.

Meurer, Michael J. and Stahl, Dale O., II, "Informative Advertising and Product Match." *International Journal of Industrial Organization* 12(1), 1994, pp. 1–19.

Rosenman, Robert E. and Wilson, Wesley W., "Quality Differentials and Prices: Are Cherries Lemons?" *Journal of Industrial Economics* 39(6), December 1991, pp. 649–58.

Schlarbaum, Gary C. and Racette, George A., "Measuring Risk: Some Theoretical and Empirical Issues." *Journal of Business Research* 2(3), July 1974, pp. 349–68.

St. Louis, Robert D., Burgess, Paul L., and Kingston, Jerry L., "Reported vs. Actual Job Search by Unemployment Insurance Claimants." *Journal of Human Resources* 21(1), Winter 1986, pp. 92–117.

Swaim, Paul and Podgursky, Michael, "Female Labor Supply Following Displacement: A Split Population Model of Labor Force Participation and Job Search." *Journal of Labor Economics* 12(4), October 1994, pp. 640–56.

Tenorio, Rafael, "Revenue Equivalence and Bidding Behavior in a Multiunit Auction Market: An Empirical Analysis." *Review of Economics and Statistics* 75(2), May 1993, pp. 302–14.

Vanderporten, Bruce, "Strategic Behavior in Pooled Condominium Auctions." *Journal of Urban Economics* 31(1), January 1992, pp. 123–37.

Wiggins, Steven N. and Lane, W. J., "Quality Uncertainty, Search, and Advertising." *American Economic Review* 73(5), December 1983, pp. 881–94.

Woodland, Bill M. and Woodland, Linda M., "The Effects of Risk Aversion on Wagering: Point Spread versus Odds." *Journal of Political Economy* 99(3), June 1991, pp. 638–53.

Zorn, Thomas S. and Sackley, William H., "Buyers' and Sellers' Markets: A Simple Rational Expectations Search Model of the Housing Market." *Journal of Real Estate Finance and Economics* 4(3), September 1991, pp. 315–25.

Chapter 13

Anthony, Peter Dean, "Regulation and Supply Externalities." *Atlantic Economic Journal* 13(2), July 1985, pp. 86–87.

Banaian, King and Luksetich, William A., "Campaign Spending in Congressional Elections." *Economic Inquiry* 29(1), January 1991, pp. 92–100.

Bender, Bruce and Shwiff, Steven, "The Appropriation of Rents by Boomtown Governments." *Economic Inquiry* 20(1), Jan. 1982, pp. 84–103.

Blackstone, Erwin A. and Bowman, Gary W., "Antitrust Damages: The Loss from Delay." *Antitrust Bulletin* 32(1), Spring 1987, pp. 93–100.

Butler, Richard V. and Maher, Michael D., "The Control of Externalities in a Growing Urban Economy." *Economic Inquiry* 20(1), Jan. 1982, pp. 155–63.

Dearden, James A. and Husted, Thomas A., "Do Governors Get What They Want?: An Alternative Examination of the Line Item Veto." *Public Choice* 77(4), December 1993, pp. 707–23.

Falkinger, J. "On Optimal Public Good Provision with Tax Evasion." *Journal of Public Economics* 45(1), June 1991, pp. 127–33.

Fon, Vincy, "Free Riding versus Paying under Uncertainty." *Public Finance Quarterly* 16(4), October 1988, pp. 464–81.

Formby, John P., Smith, W. James, and Thistle, Paul D., "Economic Efficiency, Antitrust and Rate of Return." *Review of Industrial Organization* 5(2), Summer 1990, pp. 59–73.

Gallo, Joseph C., Craycraft, Joseph L., and Bush, Steven C., "Guess Who Came to Dinner? An Empirical Study of Federal Antitrust Enforcement for the Period 1963–1984." *Review of Industrial Organization* 2(2), 1985, pp. 106–31.

Greenway, D. and Milner, C., "Fiscal Dependence on Trade Taxes and Trade Policy Reform." *Journal of Development Economics* 27(3), April 1991, pp. 95–132.

Hanemann, W. M., "Willingness to Pay and Willingness to Accept: How Much Can They Differ?" *American Economic Review*, 81(3), June 1991, pp. 635–47.

Huang, Peter H. and Wu, Ho Mou, "Emotional Responses in Litigation." *International Review of Law and Economics* 12(1), March 1992, pp. 31–44.

Hwang, H. and Mai, C.-C., "Optimum Discriminatory Tariffs under Oligopolistic Competition." *Canadian Economic Journal* 24(3), Aug. 1991, pp. 693–702.

Jianakoplos, Nancy Ammon and Irvine, F. Owen, "Did Financial Deregulation Help Consumers? Access to Market Yield Instruments." *Applied Economics* 24(8), August 1992, pp. 813–32.

Laband, David N. and Sophocleus, John P., "An Estimate of Resource Expenditures on Transfer Activity in the United States." *Quarterly Journal of Economics* 107(3), August 1992, pp. 959–83.

Lee, Eric Youngkoo and Szenberg, Michael, "The Price, Quantity and Welfare Effects of U.S. Trade Protection: The Case of Footwear." *International Economic Journal* 2(4), Winter 1988, pp. 95–110.

Lott, John R., Jr. and Bronars, Stephen G., "Time Series Evidence on Shirking in the U.S. House of Representatives." *Public Choice* 76(12), June 1993, pp. 125–49.

Lozada, Gabriel A., "The Conservationist's Dilemma." *International Economic Review* 34(3), August 1993, pp. 647–62.

Marshall, L., "New Evidence on Fiscal Illusion: the 1986 Tax 'Windfalls.'" *American Economic Review* 81(5), Dec. 1991, pp. 1336–44.

Mayshar, J., "On Measuring the Marginal Cost of Funds Analytically." *American Economic Review* 81(5), Dec. 1991, pp. 1329–35.

Millner, Edward L. and Pratt, Michael D., "Risk Aversion and Rent Seeking: An Extension and Some Experimental Evidence." *Public Choice* 69(1), February 1991, pp. 81–92.

Murthy, N. R. Vasudeva, "Bureaucracy and the Divisibility of Local Public Output: Further Econometric Evidence." *Public Choice* 55(3), October 1987, pp. 265–72.

Nollen, Stanley D. and Iglarsh, Harvey J., "Explanations of Protectionism in International Trade Votes." *Public Choice* 66(2), August 1990, pp. 137–53.

Pratt, Michael D. and Hoffer, George E., "The Efficacy of State-Mandated Minimum Quality Certification: The Case of Used Vehicles." *Economic Inquiry* 24(2), April 1986, pp. 313–18.

Rittennoure, R. Lynn and Pluta, Joseph E., "Theory of Intergovernmental Grants and Local Government." *Growth and Change* 8(3), July 1977, pp. 31–37.

Romer, Thomas, Rosenthal, Howard, and Munley, Vincent G., "Economic Incentives and Political Institutions: Spending and Voting in School Budget Referenda." *Journal of Public Economics* 49(1), October 1992, pp. 1–33.

Stanton, Timothy J., "Regional Conflict and the Clean Air Act." *Review of Regional Studies* 19(3), Fall 1989, pp. 24–30.

Thistle, Paul D., "United States versus United Shoe Machinery Corporation: On the Merits." *Journal of Law and Economics* 36(1), Part 1 April 1993, pp. 33–70.

Name Index

General Index